D0788100

3000 YEARS OF URBAN GROWTH

STUDIES IN POPULATION

Under The Editorship of: H. H. WINSBOROUGH

Department of Sociology
University of Wisconsin
Madison, Wisconsin

Samuel H. Preston, Nathan Keyfitz, and Robert Schoen. **Causes of Death:** *Life Tables for National Populations.*

Otis Dudley Duncan, David L. Featherman, and Beverly Duncan. **Socioeconomic Background and Achievement.**

James A. Sweet. **Women in the Labor Force.**

Tertius Chandler and Gerald Fox. **3000 Years of Urban Growth.**

3000 YEARS
OF URBAN GROWTH

TERTIUS CHANDLER
Middletown, Connecticut

GERALD FOX
San Francisco, California

With a Foreword by Lewis Mumford

ACADEMIC PRESS New York and London
A Subsidiary of Harcourt Brace Jovanovich, Publishers

ACADEMIC PRESS, INC.
111 Fifth Avenue, New York, New York 10003

United Kingdom Edition published by
ACADEMIC PRESS, INC. (LONDON) LTD.
24/28 Oval Road, London NW1

LIBRARY OF CONGRESS CATALOG CARD NUMBER: 72-84378

PRINTED IN THE UNITED STATES OF AMERICA

CONTENTS

FOREWORD

For reasons difficult to fathom, the study of cities was never seriously cultivated until the nineteenth century; and so-called histories of cities are too often only accounts of politics, war, trade, within the bounds of a particular urban area—while the city itself remains a shadow. Even the deluge of urban studies that has descended during the last quarter century has, with a few outstanding exceptions, done little to illuminate the forces that have given the city its specific form and character. One of the most serious defects of historical urban studies is the lack of specific statistical information about the area, the density, and the population of cities. This lack points to the belated development of statistics itself: a discipline that hardly dates back in the West before the seventeenth century. Small wonder, then, that Adna Ferrin Weber's pioneer work, "The Growth of Cities in the Nineteenth Century" has, for all its inevitable limitations, remained a classic for more than seventy years.

There are, of course, good reasons for this lack of population studies of even a single city, and still more for a comparative estimate of many cities: namely, the scarcity of accurate data, and in many cases the absence of anything worthy to be called a quantitative datum, whether accurate or not. Even to make a first survey of this no-man's land required a special kind of hardihood: for it not merely demanded a lifetime's dedication, but gave no assurance in advance that the effort would bring a sufficient reward. Anyone looking for a prosperous academic career would hesitate before giving himself to such a dubious exploration; yet until someone ventured into this area no one could be sure if there were any pay-dirt—though even a negative result, if arrived at after due effort, would at least relieve other sociologists of a guilty sense of possibly having overlooked a mine of important information.

Happily in Tertius Chandler the indispensable qualifications for this tedious, difficult, and doubtfully rewarding job were united in a single person. A passion for figures, a dogged persistence in exploring sources, an almost fanatic faith that something would come of his effort enabled him to devote himself to this task for more than thirty years. As far back as 1940—or was it earlier?—he began sending me his mimeographed tabulations of the populations of cities, covering the urbanization of the planet, so far as any figures on city populations could be discovered or deduced. Since until I wrote "The City in History" I had no special need for this kind of information, I duly filed these reports; moreover, I confess, I was a little chary of using Chandler's figures, for at no point until now did he explain his methods, list his sources, or critically review his results. Knowing, as Chandler did, the paucity and slipperiness of population figures, one can only marvel at his hardihood in working so long without even the encouragement of partial publication. Happily, on Chandler's return to Berkeley, where he had studied geography under Carl Sauer, he received substantial encouragement from Professor Fox and from Professor Kingsley Davis, a leading authority on social statistics; and with the critical assistance of Fox he was finally ready to publish the present volume.

To assess these tables properly, one must remember that it is the first work of its kind in existence; and even if its results were far more questionable than they are, they would still be valuable, as leading to more exhaustive studies by native scholars whose documents are not accessible to outsiders or to those unfamiliar with their language. Though Chandler first began with tables for the largest cities of the world going back only to A.D. 1400, he progressively pushed his dates back to 1360 B.C. In presenting these results he has put a quietus on the parochial notion that urbanization, urban overgrowth, and therewith urban congestion and disorganization, are distinctly novel phenomena, confined to recent industrial civilization in the West. This in itself is a salutary correction of current urban thinking, and it complements the work done by Max Weber, Werner Sombart, Patrick Geddes, Gideon Sjoberg, and a few others in putting modern urban development in historical perspective. Thus Chandler's bare figures tell us something of qualitative significance about the city.

As the base figure for his statistical definition of the city Chandler, up to 1800, takes 40,000 for

Asia, 20,000 for other continents: and after 1850, 40,000 for the whole planet. What he shows is a remarkably wide range of urban populations, not entirely accounted for by the fact that his definition of the city takes in areas lying outside strict municipal boundaries. I have not had the opportunity to analyze these accumulated figures, and relate them to their historic periods and cultures, or to the transformations effected by political conquest, war, colonization, food resources, and diseases: but I am sure that a careful study would reveal important new facts, again of a qualitative nature. Even where the statistical data may be vague and meager, the relative population figures may be reasonably trustworthy: and they would be even more interesting if the size and number of cities could be related to the total population of the area from which the urban inhabitants were drawn. This would indicate with even greater clarity the overall differences in urban population patterns, as disclosed by the number, size, and distribution of cities, grading down from the biggest to the smallest.

At this point however one must issue a *caveat*. Chandler for excellent reasons confined his survey to cities of a definite minimal size. But we must remember that for the larger part of history, as the geographer Max Sorre observed, small cities, country towns, and villages hugely outnumbered in total population the few large centers; that the city which took form in Mesopotamia or Greece had fewer than 5000 inhabitants; and that in Western Europe through the Middle Ages, the small city predominated, and that before 1700 only a few commercial and industrial cities like Milan, Venice, and Paris, had populations of over 100,000. London had only 45,000 inhabitants in the fifteenth century, and in spite of its royal and commercial concentration had not yet reached a million at the beginning of the nineteenth century.

The tendency even among urban sociologists to overemphasize the bigger units and to concentrate on the forces making for urban growth unfortunately gives a false picture of the natural history of urbanization, and in turn, gives an equally false image of the city itself, as if size and density of population alone sufficed to define a city and establish its rank by numerical measure alone. Biologically speaking, this would be like counting only adults as human, and disregarding infants, children, adolescents, and old people. Anyone who confined himself to Chandler's statistics alone would have an inadequate conception of the factors that make for stability, continuity, arrest, and disintegration. The failure to study the anatomy and physiology of the city in its successive stages of growth is one of the major oversights of contemporary urban sociology. It leads to the mischievous conception that only big overgrown cities are real cities—which is like saying that only giants are men.

Let me clinch this point. Anyone who confined himself to these statistics would never guess that the Roman New Towns like Piacenza, originally planned for 50,000 inhabitants still exhibit their original outlines and street patterns. Despite radical economic, political and technological changes over two millennia, Piacenza had but 43,048 in 1936; even now it has only 87,930 inhabitants. Yet in current discussions of New Towns, the very notion of setting any upper limit to population is often dismissed out of hand as impossible, even were it desirable. Since the dominant forces in urban life today favor constant quantitative growth as the key to pecuniary aggrandizement and power, it has become important to take into account the stabilizing and growth-limiting factors that have operated in the past. This may offer a clue to developing the "steady state economy" that many other thinkers besides Ezra Mishan now regard as essential, if we are to overcome the hyperdynamic forces of disintegration.

In short, there is still a lot of unsurveyed ground to be covered before we have an adequate statistical picture of characteristic urban population patterns. This is not a reflection on Tertius Chandler's path-breaking presentation: it shows rather how he has opened up for urgent further investigation the relation of population growth to changing geographic, economic, and political conditions. In current terms of megalopolitan expansion, size is often treated as an index of urban efficiency, and unlimited size is regarded as both a necessary feature of the urban megamachine, or even more, as its ideal terminus. This erroneous conception reaches a theoretical limit of absurdity in C. A. Doxiadis's projection of a planetary non-city to which he has affixed the name of Ecumenopolis.

Not the least valuable result of Chandler's study is that he has demonstrated how much valuable information of a statistical nature can be fathered, not from a direct count of population, but from a careful analysis of quite different material: the number of public baths or the area opened by the extension of walls, the number of soldiers who could be mustered, or the number of doctors available. Apart from this, his figures show reason to doubt the popular notion of urban "progress"; that cities have constantly grown bigger, and that there are no limits to this growth; for their decline and fall, their shrinkage or disappearance is statistically visible, not only in the fate of a few great centers like Rome but in many minor urban areas.

William Cobbett showed the way to this more realistic kind of interpretation when, passing through a deserted English countryside, he noted the number of well-built churches, and asked what had happened to the prosperous population that once built them and attended them. Though I have not myself any professional qualifications in statistics, I cannot examine a page of Chandler's figures without finding suggestions of interesting problems or possible answers. He himself would be the first to admit that, despite his thirty years of assiduous application, he has only made a beginning. But what a beginning it is! Any scholar who would criticize this work should first earn the right by familiarizing himself with the baffling territory it explores.

Lewis Mumford

PURPOSE AND SCOPE OF THE STUDY

Until recently, most population figures for cities have been markedly inexact. Censuses were rare. Such figures as there were have been mainly random estimates by a miscellany of casual observers, mostly travelers. Such makeshift data are scarcely adequate for the understanding of the past. Any study of important events or trends demands more accurate information, to appreciate how many people were involved.

Accurate population for all cities is simply not to be had. For nearly all cities however, some data, scant and incomplete as they may be, exist. But these data, even when weighed and posted, reveal only broken population histories. To fill in the gaps as far as possible, we have sought first to gather whatever plausible population figures and demographically related data are available for the major cities of the world, and second, to develop methods for estimating populations from scanty data.

This project began when Chandler presented to Fox tables compiled for the largest cities of the world back to 1400 A.D. Professor Kingsley Davis of I.P.U.R. arranged financing, and Chandler entered the stacks of the University of California for more data. This book can be accurately described as "compiled by Tertius Chandler, and inspected by Gerald Fox." Except for late insertions, every figure has been worked over and discussed by both authors and has been agreed to by both, often after considerable discussion and sometimes further library research by both Chandler and Fox. The period to be covered was first set at 1200-1800 and then expanded to 800-1850. The cities included are those which at anytime from 800 to 1800 reached a population of 40,000 for Asia, or 20,000 for the other continents. At 1850 the mark is set at 40,000 for all continents. Within this frame we have attempted to provide estimated century end population figures for the cities. These are accompanied by maps. A further expansion, done by Chandler alone, carries the coverage back to 1360 B.C., the time of Moses. Next come lists of the 75 largest cities of the world at the same dates, and also at some intermediate dates. After that comes a listing of the six largest on each continent.

The word "city," it should be understood, is used here in the sense of urban area, to include suburbs lying outside the municipal area. It amounts to a house-to-house unity. Only in the 1968 list, prepared by Forstall, is a somewhat wider definition applied, to take in more scattered, commuting suburbs, appropriate to the automobile era.

Finally, a short chapter traces the rivalry for largest city in the world from early antiquity down to the present.

SOURCES

We have collected population data from as wide a selection of sources as were readily available. No special attempt has been made to inspect the census documents for early nineteenth century Europe, and some small errors may have occurred in consequence. Materials that were used ranged the gamut from authoritative scholarly reports to travelers' diaries. Encyclopedias have been used as a first line of reference.

Much of our additional information came from exchanges with urban scholars and individual city librarians and archivists. These instances are so extensive that to thank individuals is impossible, but these scholars have been most generous in replies to questions and have made each his or her essential contribution to the volume. The materials from city libraries are virtually unobtainable elsewhere. While cooperation varied greatly, ranging down to refusal to supply any information at all in a couple of rare instances, in general the librarians from over the world were most helpful and resourceful in obtaining data.

1

Sundry other sources were used. Among the secondary ones, gazatteers and travel guides frequently contain references to the size of cities. Religious histories of cities or dioceses have been helpful, by giving the foundation date of the various churches, especially parish churches.

The figures at 1968 and 1970 are taken with permission from the very accurate Richard Forstall of Rand McNally and Company.

Our study does not—cannot—claim to completeness, and specialists may well know of additional material for individual cities, for which, incidentally the authors would be most grateful.

METHODS

Population-size estimating is actually an exercise in puzzle construction and solution. To determine an urban unit's population it is necessary to know two significant figures: a relevant figure for a demographic factor such as individuals, houses, parishes, etc., and a relevant multiplier. The ideal is a complete census of individuals, with, therefore, a demographic multiplier of one. This formula, a demographic factor with an accompanying appropriate multiplier, has been the methodological foundation of the estimates prepared for this study.

Occasionally, it is possible to improve accuracy by cross checking with several different demographic factors. A quick example will explain this procedure. Amsterdam in 1514 had 2,507 houses, 2,907 hearths or family units, and 9,000 Christian communicants. All these factors point to a population around 14,000, so we use that as our deduced figure. Another example is Bagdad in 932. At that date, data exist for the number of doctors, the number of public baths, the area, and even the number of houses. All these figures are compatible with each other, and from them a reasonable figure of the population can be derived.

Two special problems which emerged are the disparity between different sorts of data, and the preparation of estimates from what can be considered a data void.

As an example of conflicting data from different demographic factors, the problem of the relative size of Bangkok and Hanoi can serve. Round about 1830 Bangkok was said to be only half Saigon's size, yet its population was given as 77,000, whereas, the earliest figure for Saigon is only 50,000. The resolution of this particular problem has proved, so far, impossible.

Other examples show this problem in terms of one city. The factual information for Cordova shows evidence of an internal consistency of growth and eventual decline, yet contemporary estimates by the chroniclers always overstate the population of the city.

An example in contrast to Cordova is Hyderabad, whose population just before the first census was estimated by outsiders to be greatly lower than it actually was; the error in this case was a surprising 200,000.

A demographic void seemed at first the case for Anhilvada. Back of 1197, it did not have any figures whatever, except one for distance around and another for the number of marketplaces. Reluctantly we concluded we did not have a good ratio for marketplaces. That left the area and the spotty data at 1197, when 15,000 were slain and 20,000 were captured. Those slain would be presumably militia, and the captured, women. So 15,000 X the usual 6 for militia = 90,000. That does for 1197, but Anhilvada's height of glory was earlier. What of then? To then we could assign her area. This in turn could be compared to the area covered by Ahmedabad, a nearby city, when at its peak in the 1600s. And Anhilvada's peak was known to have been in the reign which went from 1094 to 1143. So we were able to assign a population of 125,000 in 1100 and, as the country was near its full size by 996, a further figure of 100,000 in 1000.

In situations where we wished to interpolate populations for a century-end figure, we have occasionally used estimated probable growth or decline rates based on consistency through a long period of years. Such a case is early Kyoto. Interpolations or estimates of this type are always indicated, with historical notes to back them up. These estimates over long periods are infrequent however and are used only in cases where prolonged stability or a steady rate of growth was very likely.

TOTAL SIZE ESTIMATES

Census figures, clearly the most desirable data for city populations, are available in only limited instances for the period covered in this study. If these censuses are accurate they are an ideal form of data, yet their accuracy, even in modern times, is frequently questionable. The most general error is simply one of undercounting the population. This error exists for two principle reasons: (1) the census was usually conducted by the local officials, whose efficiency varied, and (2) the purposes behind conducting a census were frequently ones which raised the populace's suspicions and therefore uncooperativeness— namely to prepare lists for drafting into military service, and to locate all taxpayers.

Nevertheless, in most cases the early censuses were quite accurate. Yet, persons living outside the city limits were seldom included, even though they were part of the greater city or urban area.

Another serious type of error in total population counts is the exclusion of one or more groups within the population from the count. No consistent pattern was used to select or include specific groups, and not all censuses indicate those groups excluded from the total figures. Even the assiduous Beloch, while giving very accurate counts for the major cities of Italy, sometimes fails to mention that certain groups are excluded. In many other cases censuses indicate that certain groups were in fact excluded from the count, but no information is available to even approximate the number of people excluded. Madrid (1757) excluded clergy and the garrison; Toulouse (1695 to 1790) excluded orphans and students; Troyes (1433) excluded the poor, certainly a substantial number; and Pernambuco (1845) excluded slaves. Ouro Preto (1735) astoundingly omitted non-slaves! The commonest omission was the Jews.

Contrasting with this exclusion is the contrary situation where rural populations are included in census figures, being within the municipal limits. This is habitually the case in southern Italy and Sicily, Messina being a classic example with census figures 1/3 too high for the truly urban population. The early censuses offer no information on what percentage of the people were rural; that has to be determined by a look at more recent censuses, which do have such a breakdown of the population, and sometimes by a look at maps.

Other instances of inflated figures are caused by the timing of the count. Travelers' estimates were apt to be made during large festivals. The Papal habit of holding a jubilee year at the end of each century from 1600 onward gave a special lift to figures for century's end at Rome. The Roman figures have been retained intact for this study however, as the city remained booming for much of the year, and the whole purpose of century-end dating is to compare actual present populations at one precise date. Rome just happens to get a statistical advantage from the popular penchant for using rounded dates for tables.

Another consideration is over the Chinese units called *hsien* and *fu*. *Fu* is used in two meanings, as a rather large administrative district, and as the capital city of such a district.

In the case of a national capital, the *fu* coincides with the city, surrounded by a wall. Some provincial capitals are the same way, and are even known as *fu,* as in the case of Tali-*fu.* A *hsien* is a smaller administrative district, but even so usually much more than a city. On the other hand a number of cities have expanded to the point where the city coincides with the *hsien,* or even with several *hsiens.* When that point was reached in any given case is extremely hard to know. Chinese city and provincial histories may tell, for they are very large; however, they have no index.

A difficulty in travelers' estimates is the lack of facilities for making an accurate guess; even contemporary policemen and trained demographic experts have difficulty in estimating large crowds. What frequently appears to be an enormous number of people is in fact likely to be only a few thousand, not several hundred thousand as often quoted. Even so, casual travelers are most frequently reliable, as they have no specific purpose other than curiosity in estimating the population, and they often asked for their information from well-informed townspeople or even local officials.

Several notorious examples exist, however, which illustrate population estimates with a specific purpose. In 1300 the city officials of Ghent were asked to estimate the population to aid the pope in determining the number of clergy to be assigned to the city. The burghers' estimate was specifically designed to allow the city more clergy, and was so totally out of proportion with the existing population that the estimate was laughable.

There is too the question of contemporary versus historical perspective in population estimating. Thus, Laborde, writing in 1798, was accurate on Spanish cities in his own time, using the recent census of 1797, but he was far too high in his reports of the traditionally stated size of Cordova back in 1236 or of Toledo back around 1000. Again, França's data for Lisbon from 1639 onward are excellent, but for earlier periods he found only estimates which as he himself admits are unreliable.

An instance of a reliable contemporary figure way back at 1326 is "over 30,000" claimed by the officials of Metz. That figure checks with the area at that time, and with the loss from the plague reported later on in the century.

Yaqut's figure 444,000 for Herat in 1217, though often repeated for the city, must be a district figure. Comparison with other cities in that area, cities of greater distinction, makes this certain. Elimination of figures like this from serious consideration is one of the aims of this book.

Acceptable however is Manrique's 660,000 plus foreigners for Agra around 1630. Agra's importance as the capital of the Mogul empire and its huge area make such a population reasonable. The main reason for accepting it, however, is the accuracy of Manrique's figures for other cities, especially Arakan, where a count of surviving stone houses proved him a reliable reporter.

A particularly useful traveler for our purposes was Leo Africanus. Leo wandered across most of Moslem Africa, notably south of the Sahara to and beyond Timbuktu. High-born and well-educated, he furnishes trustworthy population figures for many places for which no other demographic data of any kind are available for centuries before and after his time. Thanks to him, Africa at 1500 stands as one of the best-prepared lists in this book.

AREA

Area is a very useful tool for determining population. Sometimes a city's area is stated in the sources; much more often it has to be calculated from the circumference or perimeter, which is usually that of the city walls. Occasionally suburbs outside the walls are included, but generally not. Fortunately for the statistician, the large growth of suburbs had not begun before 1850 except in the newly rising industrial conurbations of Britain. The circuit of city walls varied in shape. For a wall that is square, the area is easily found by squaring the length of one side. For a circle, the area comes out 1/4 larger. For a rectangle with proportions of 4 to 1, the area comes out 1/3 less than the same length of city wall in a square. Once the area has been determined, the population can be estimated by using the population density of other cities in the same region, even at a much later date. This is possible, because the way of life remained unchanged for centuries. There is an abundance of evidence to prove that this constancy of life-style was real. The inventions that have transformed modern life were only just beginning to take effect in 1850. Except in Britain and America, cities then were generally surrounded by a wall, with all or nearly all the urban population living within it.

There is a problem, however, in that city walls cannot be readily moved to accommodate a growing population. Occasionally a small expansion was built to jut out beyond part of one side of a wall. More often however, the wall stayed as it had first been erected, while the population inside it grew somewhat crowded. Finally, a new wall would be constructed, beyond the limits of the old one. Hence, the density ratio for an old wall should be substantially higher than for a new one. This observation has been termed by Chandler as Fox's Law: that new walls should represent a lower density than usual, and that older walls should have the norm for the district, and a wall just before the building of a new wall must have a considerably higher density within it than the regional average. In a number of instances perimeter figures, from which areas can be calculated, are available for the old and the new wall, thus providing a ratio of the amount of expansion. We have become accustomed to standard ratios of 100 people per hectare (1/100 sq. km. or 1/259 of a sq. mile) in the Orient and much of Europe, of around 75 per ha. for new walls, of up to 200 per ha. just before a new wall is built, and of even higher densities in special geographic circumstances. Thus, Genoa in the later Middle Ages was the densest in Europe, with over 600 per ha. Edinburgh was nearly as dense by 1750. Both these cities are boxed in by mountains, which accounts for their unusually high density, resulting in old buildings up to 14 stories high.

INSTITUTIONAL FACTORS

The units of institutional life most serviceable for population estimates are: families, households and homes (these three vary very slightly, as a household may contain servants, and a home occasionally contains several families), and militia. In many cases in Europe very accurate figures are accessible for one or several of these units. Just as the consistent pattern of urban life made for the use of the same densities over our whole thousand-year period, so it makes too for steady multiplying factors for families, homes, etc. down the centuries. So the multiplier for families or housing is found by taking the ratio at some date when one of these, and also the population, are known. In a few cases such full information is on hand for a given city at several dates in our period, showing the extent to which the ratio has changed. The change turns out to be very little indeed, but of course we use the differences when we find them.

The following chart gives ratios of persons per institutional unit in specific cases:

		per household	per family	per house	per taxpayer				per household	per house
Florence	1401	4				Cork	1800			8
Genoa	1460			15		Prague	1605			30
Milan	1492	5				Warsaw	1609			12
Córdova	1000			4.5		Astrakhan	1767			8
Madrid	1597			11	10	Kiev	1766	8	
"	1787			11		Moscow	1725	8	
Oporto	1810			4.6		Santiago	1657			10
Coimbra	1732	3.7							
Dijon	1700	8							
Rouen	1250		6.25						
"	1700	5							
Tours	1598			15					
"	1698	5							
Antwerp	1645			5					
Brussels	1783			7					
Liège	1650			6-7					
Haarlem	1632			6.1					
Hague	1732			5.5					
Leiden	1659			5					

It should be obvious that some of the above figures given in the sources as for "houses" should be actually for families or households. The figures ranging from 10 to 30 should be for whole buildings.

The count of militia or arms-bearing males is frequently given and makes a very good basis for estimating population. The militia usually took 1 in 5 of the population in a crisis, or 1 in 6 otherwise. These high ratios hold good despite the fact that such elements as the clergy and usually Jews and aliens were excluded from military service. When a city was wholly unexposed to danger, its militia ratio might be too low to use in estimating the population, but such safety was all too rare. On the other hand, a garrison imposed on a city from outside merely reflected strategic importance and thus for another reason is usually valueless for the urban demographer. The militia, however, chosen by the citizenry from their own ranks, is a sound basis, available wherever cities had their freedom. The following are examples:

		militia	population	ratio
Cremona	1160		20000	
"	1259	5000	(30,000)	6
"	1304	6400		
"	1502		40000	
Lyon	1546	18000		6.7
"	1549		120000	
Paris	1313	50000		5.5
"	1328		c.274000	
Cologne	1359	1500		26
"	1400		40000	
Hamburg	1600	6600	40000	6
"	1680	10260	60000	6
Novgorod	1471	10000	60000	6
Hangchow	1273		432000	
"	1350	72000		6

So a demographic multiplier of 6 for militia is just about right, on the basis of the above data.

Probably for military purposes, otherwise for taxation, all the adult males in a city were often enumerated. Thus, Venice (1336) listed males 20-60 years old, York (1377) those over 14, and Pisa (1228) those of citizen status aged 15-70. Breslau (1403) likewise listed the male citizens, and Vienna, Frankfurt, and London enumerated voters—who were presumably the same as the male citizens.

The Catholic Church kept track of communicants of both sexes. At Tours (1672) it listed all over 7 years. At Lisbon (1758) the age was also set at 7.

The number of Christian clergy varies too much to be a satisfactory factor.

Such groups as merchants and skilled craftsmen provide little more than cross-checking possibilities. There might be an exception for bakers, as nearly everyone in most parts of Europe ate bread, but as it happened, where there were good data on the number of bakers, there were also superior demographic data of other sorts.

Religious institutions such as parishes, churches, mosques, and monasteries are also, somewhat surprisingly, usable as demographic factors. The ratio of 3000 persons per parish fits much of Christendom, while 9,000 per "main" or "Friday" mosque has proven passably acceptable for much of Islam. Northeast France has a much lower parish ratio, as at Reims and Metz, where 1250 fits the other data. Total churches or mosques are less reliable as factors, because of the tendency of rich men to build each his own family place of worship. We were able, however, to derive a multiplying ratio of 1250 for churches and 800 for mosques, and we have accepted Gen. Cunningham's 5 persons per Buddhist monk for early medieval India. The latter checks well with area in the case of Kanauj.

City quarters seem to have been derived from parishes, at least in France, where the same ratio of 3,000 fits well for such cities as Orléans. 5,000 however, lived in one of Caen's quarters as early as 1060.

For Ahmedabad we were fortunate enough to get a ratio for city wards at 1866, which made it possible to derive figures for the city at the time of its heyday around 1700.

Market-places proved a disappointment. There are data for several cities (Ahmednagar, Anhilvada, Adrianople, etc.), but some of them were not consistent with others, and we failed to derive a usable multiplier. We sincerely hope our successors, with fuller information, will be able to crack this problem, at least for some areas. Three thousand per market-place may be applicable for western India.

There are several items from which we failed to agree on any multiplier at all, such as the number of horses in Africa. The cities involved were Ikoso and Gbara. In the case of Troki in Europe, however, a multiplier of 5 was derived by comparisons with another city in the area for which both horse counts and other data happened to be available.

VOLUME OF LOCAL ACTIVITY

In a couple of cases (Karakorum, Vienna) there are data on the number of wagon-loads needed to provision a city daily. We didn't happen to need them, as Karakorum fell too swiftly to make any of our lists, but eventually this function may yet yield a demographic multiplier.

Inns have proved useless in estimating population, partly because the tales of their abundance seem to have grown in the telling.

A comparison of the number of notarized papers at Genoa and Pisa was of some help in fixing the population of Pisa at 1200.

Bread consumption is a good index in lands such as Italy. The recorded fact that

Florence ate 3/7 as much bread as Milan in 1280 helped us to fix the former's population in 1300.

The number of public baths has proven useful for Moslem cities, especially Bagdad, where it confirmed other data pointing to a highly important figure: the second urban population ever to top 1,000,000.

A marked shift in local activity occurs when a city becomes or ceases to be a capital. The departure of a royal court means an assured loss of several thousand people, usually followed by a further general decline; whereas, acquiring a court means a comparable measure of prosperity.

Business trends can be helpful. The quantity of tea trade and wine trade was indispensible in deriving estimates for Canton and Xérez, respectively, at 1700.

DISASTERS

A grim but demographically helpful category of information is the statistics of loss of life reported at disasters: plague, fire, earthquake, or flood. The losses reported in these "Acts of God" often provide a check which suggests that figures held to be accurate should be reevaluated.

Total destruction of a city, whether by nature or by the warfare of man, is particularly helpful to the demographer, as the total population is frequently given. In actuality a besieged city is apt to have a population swollen by refugees and by an enlarged garrison. Even so, those telling the tale are apt to repeat merely the standard population for the city at the last count before the war began.

A special case was the 20,000 maidens taken off into captivity from Cambay. We had considerable demographic discussion on this deplorable happenstance before arriving at the conclusion—partly supported by other evidence—that the amount of the females who would be considered worth the trouble of carrying off would be about half and that the total population of the city previous to the siege would therefore be 80,000.

Information about military reverses may often help in forming the century's end estimates of population. This is true not only when a place was wholly destroyed, such as Ayutia or Angkor, but also when it is only severely shaken. A well-known instance of severe economic decline brought on by violence is Antwerp after the Spanish sack of 1576.

COMPARATIVE RANK

A risky but sometimes usable criterion is the reported comparative rank of cities. Thus our figure for Alexandria at 1500 is based on a traveler's comparison of it with Cologne. The figure for Kano at 1600 is based on the chance that it was so close to Gao in size that a special house-count had to be made to see which was ahead. Loango toward 1700 was stated to be nearly as large in area as Rouen but with much smaller houses; from this evidence, plus a comparison with other West African cities, we managed to derive a figure.

Again let us warn that the figures presented here are by no means all susceptible to accurate assessment. The need for educated estimates has predisposed both the authors to try to derive figures where possible from almost any scrap of information. Indeed we were tempted at times to go much further even than we have done, in assuming constant population for over a century for cities untouched by war. We fairly well resisted that temptation. We hope we have not yielded to too many others. We believe our conclusions to be soundly enough based to make them viable for practical purposes of historical or sociological interpretation. This caveat does not however cover the data in the appendix, where a few special tables covering dates not included in the main text have been set; these were compiled rather hastily (comparatively speaking) and were worked on only by Chandler, without the benefit of inspection by Fox and resultant further research. They could do with some revising.

Corrections for any part of this book are welcome. Indeed we are eager to get them!

top 50

FRANKS			ITALIAN STATES	
Verona	30 000		Rome	50 000
Metz	25		Naples	30
Paris	25		Benevento	
Milan	25		Amalfi	
Tours	20		DENMARK–pagan	
Reims	20		Lejre	
Pavia			SLAV STATES–pagan	
Ratisbon			Prague	
Cologne	15		Krakow	
Trier	15		KHAZARS–Jewish	
Padua			Itil	
Lyon	12		Theodosia	
Orléans			Kiev	
Arles			BULGARIA–pagan	
Toulouse			Pliska	34 000
Poitiers	10		Madara	
ENGLAND			BYZANTIUM	
London			Constantinople	300 000
SPAIN–Moslem			Thessalonica	
Cordova	160 000		Corinth	
Seville			Syracuse	
Mérida	40		Malamocco	
Toledo	25		Athens	
Cartagena			Sofia	
Elvira	15		Plovdiv	
Lisbon	15		Adrianople	10
Barcelona				
Valencia				
Almería				
Zaragoza				
Murcia				

top 100

FRENCH STATES		GERMANY–ITALY	
Laon	25 000	Ratisbon	40 000
Paris	20	Amalfi	35
Rouen	20	Rome	35
Arles		Pavia	30
Orléans		Mainz	30
Reims		Naples	30
Angers	15	Milan	30
Toulouse		Cologne	21
Lyon		Verona	20
Rennes		Trier	20
Poitiers	12	Worms	
Tours		Salerno	
Bourges		Magdeburg	
Narbonne		Genoa	15
Soissons		Cremona	15
Caen		Metz	14
Marseille		Erfurt	
ENGLAND		Bergamo	13
London	25 000	Liège	12
Winchester	15	Ferrara	12
York	12	Mantua	12
Lincoln	8	Piacenza	
DENMARK		Bari	
Roskilde		Ragusa	
FLANDERS		Bologna	
Bruges	12 000	Padua	10
Ghent		Pisa	9
SPAIN–Moslem indented		Spires	
Cordova	450 000	Brescia	
Seville	90	Asti	
Almería	35	HUNGARY	
Cartagena	33	Esztergom	
Toledo	31	Székesfehérvár	
Elvira	22	POLAND	
Palma	20	Poznan	
Xérez	19	Gnieszno	
Murcia	19	Krakow	
León		RUSSIA AND GREAT BOLGARY	
Burgos		Kiev	45 000
Badajoz	16	Bolgary	25
Baeza		Novgorod	18
Lisbon	15	Chernigov	
Zaragoza		Smolensk	
Valencia		Polotsk	
Málaga		BULGARIA	
Barcelona		Ochrida	
Tortosa		Preslav	30 000
Denia		Plovdiv	20
SICILY		Corinth	
Palermo	75 000	Trnovo	
Messina		Belgrade	
Catania		BYZANTIUM	
BOHEMIA		Constantinople	450 000
Prague		Venice	45
		Thessalonica	40
		Adrianople	
		Candia	

Cities of Europe, 1200

top 100

FRANCE			BOHEMIA	
Paris	110 000		Prague	
Orléans	27		ENGLAND	
Ghent	25		London	40 000
Bruges	25		Rouen	40
Troyes	20		Angers	30
Provins	20		Poitiers	21
Laon			Tours	20
Ypres			Toulouse	20
Blois			Caen	20
Avignon	13		Dublin	17
Reims	12		Bordeaux	15
Arras	12		Winchester	15
PROVENCE			Bourges	
Marseille	25 000		Norway	
Arles	20		Bergen	
Béziers	20		DENMARK	
Narbonne			Roskilde	
ITALY			GERMANY	
Palermo	150 000		Cologne	50 000
Venice	70		Spires	30
Milan	60		Worms	25
Bologna	35		Mainz	25
Rome	35		Trier	25
Verona	33		Metz	23
Messina	30		Lyon	22
Genoa	30		Brunswick	21
Pisa	30		Erfurt	21
Naples	30		Liège	20
Ferrara	27		Ratisbon	
Cremona	25		Wiener-Neustadt	15
Pavia	25		Soest	15
Alessandria	20		Vienna	12
Lucca	20		HUNGARY	
Padua	20		Esztergom	18 000
Siena	15		Székesfehérvár	
Asti	15		POLAND	
Florence	15		Krakow	
Bergamo			Poznan	
Brescia			Halicz	
SPAIN—Moslem indented			RUSSIA—Moslem indented	
Seville	150 000		Kiev	40 000
Cordova	60		Smolensk	40
Granada	60		Novgorod	30
León	40		Bolgary	
Toledo	35		Vladimir	18
Palma	30		Polotsk	
Valencia	26		SERBIA	
Zaragoza	21		Prizren	
Badajoz	20		BULGARIA	
Barcelona			Trnovo	35 000
Málaga			BYZANTIUM	
Burgos	18		Constantinople	250 000
Almería			Thessalonica	30
Xérez	15		Plovdiv	20
Baeza			Adrianople	
PORTUGAL			Belgrade	
Coimbra	20 000			
Lisbon	15			

top 100

FRANCE		ENGLAND	
Paris	228 000	London	40 000
Rouen	50	Bordeaux	30
Bruges	50	Norwich	25
Marseille	40	Dublin	25
Orléans	36	NORWAY	
Toulouse	35	Bergen	15 000
Lyon	35	SWEDEN	
Angers	33	Visby	15 000
Provins	30	DENMARK	
Narbonne	30	Roskilde	22 000
Ypres	30	GERMANY	
Tours	25	Cologne	54 000
Troyes	25	Ghent	42
Reims	24	Metz	32
Caen	20	Liège	30
Arras	20	Erfurt	30
St. Omer	20	Spires	25
Poitiers		Lübeck	24
Arles	17	Mainz	24
ITALY		Vienna	21
Venice	110 000	Aachen	21
Milan	100	Worms	20
Genoa	100	Utrecht	20
Florence	60	Trier	
Palermo	40	Ratisbon	
Naples	40	Brunswick	18
Caffa	40	Valenciennes	
Bologna	40	Strassburg	
Padua	40	BOHEMIA-POLAND	
Cremona	39	Prague	40 000
Ferrara	38	HUNGARY	
Verona	36	Buda	15 000
Rome	35	LUTHUANIA	
Pavia	30	Troki	
Messina	25	RUSSIA—Moslem indented	
Pisa	25	Sarai	100 000
Brescia	24	Bolgary	50
Siena	21	Novgorod	40
Mantua		Vladimir	31
Lucca	18	Sudak	30
SPAIN—Moslem indented		Tver	27
Granada	150 000	Smolensk	25
Seville	90	Pskov	
Valencia	44	Crim	
Toledo	42	BULGARIA, SERBIA, WALLACHIA	
Cordova	40	Trnovo	35 000
Málaga	35	Plovdiv	
Montpellier	35	Skoplje	20
Barcelona	30	Campulung	
Almería	25	BYZANTIUM	
Murcia	25	Constantinople	150 000
León	25	Thessalonica	50
Burgos	21	Adrianople	
Zaragoza	21	ATHENS—CYPRUS	
Jaén		Athens	25 000
Palma		Nicosia	
PORTUGAL			
Lisbon	35 000		

top 100

FRANCE		PORTUGAL	
Paris	275 000	Lisbon	55 000
Bruges	125	Oporto	18
Genoa	100	ENGLAND	
Ghent	70	London	45 000
Rouen	70	Bordeaux	30
Lyon	35	Dublin	
Orléans	30	DENMARK	
Avignon	30	Roskilde	33 000
Brussels	26	GERMANY	
Angers	25	Prague	95 000
Tours	25	Cologne	40
Toulouse	23	Lübeck	30
Valenciennes	23	Liège	30
Marseille	21	Metz	25
Troyes	20	Vienna	24
Ypres	20	Erfurt	24
Dijon	19	Hamburg	22
Bourges		Breslau	20
Caen	18	Spires	21
Louvain	18	Magdeburg	20
Montpellier	17	Ulm	20
ITALY		Soest	18
Milan	125 000	Nuremberg	18
Venice	110	Utrecht	
Caffa	85	Frankfurt	17
Florence	61	Ratisbon	
Bologna	43	Aachen	
Naples	40	Brunswick	16
Ferrara	30	CYPRUS	
Verona	35	Nicosia	18 000
Cremona	35	POLAND-LITHUANIA	
Padua	34	Troki	50 000
Rome	33	Smolensk	25
Soldaia	30	Krakow	18
Brescia	27	HUNGARY	
Palermo	27	Buda	18 000
Mantua	25	RUSSIA	
Piacenza	25	Novgorod	50 000
Lucca	23	Pskov	35
Pavia	20	Moscow	30
Vicenza		Tver	20
Parma	17	WALLACHIA	
Siena	16	Tirgovishtea	25 000
Messina	16	Curtea de Arges	
SPAIN—Moslem indented		BYZANTIUM and GREEK STATES	
Granada	100 000	Constantinople	75 000
Seville	70	Athens	50
Valencia	48	TURKEY	
Toledo	45	Salonica	42 000
Málaga	42	Adrianople	28
Cordova	40	Üsküb	22
Barcelona	37	Sofia	20
Almería	30	Gallipoli	
Burgos	27	Plovdiv	18
Zaragoza	20		
Medina del Campo			
Palma			
Murcia			

top 100

FRANCE	
Paris	225 000
Milan	104
Lyon	80
Rouen	75
Genoa	62
Tours	60
Marseille	45
Toulouse	40
Bourges	32
Orléans	28
Angers	25
Caen	35
Piacenza	25
Dijon	24
Troyes	23
Dieppe	20
Bordeaux	20
Montpellier	20
Amiens	20
ENGLAND	
London	50 000
SCOTLAND	
Edinburgh	18 000
ITALY	
Naples	125 000
Venice	115
Florence	70
Brescia	61
Bologna	55
Palermo	48
Ferrara	42
Cremona	40
Verona	39
Rome	38
Lucca	30
Padua	29
Mantua	26
Vicenza	24
Siena	22
Messina	21
SPAIN	
Granada	70 000
Valencia	50
Seville	50
Valladolid	48
Toledo	47
Cordova	35
Medina del Campo	35
Barcelona	29
Jaén	25
Murcia	25
Segovia	22
Xérez	21
Zaragoza	20
Úbeda	20
Salamanca	18
Baeza	18

PORTUGAL	
Lisbon	70 000
Évora	18
GERMANY	
Bruges	90 000
Ghent	80
Nuremberg	52
Cologne	45
Vienna	45
Metz	40
Antwerp	37
Lübeck	32
Magdeburg	32
Brussels	31
Liège	25
Lille	25
Strassburg	24
Hamburg	22
Valenciennes	21
Frankfurt	20
Augsburg	20
Brunswick	20
s'Hertogenbosch	19
Erfurt	18
Bremen	18
DENMARK	
Roskilde	25 000
BOHEMIA-HUNGARY	
Prague	70 000
Belgrade	25
Breslau	21
Buda	20
POLAND	
Smolensk	50 000
Poznan	32
Danzig	30
Vilna	25
Krakow	22
MOLDAVIA	
Suceava	33 000
RUSSIA	
Pskov	52 000
Novgorod	42
Moscow	36
TATARS	
Caffa	50 000
Bakhchiserai	25
TURKEY	
Constantinople	200 000
Adrianople	125
Tirgovishtea	50
Üsküb	50
Salonica	40
Athens	40
Sofia	22
Nish	20

top 100

FRANCE			SPAIN	
Paris	250 000		Naples	275 000
Lyon	90		Seville	144
Rouen	70		Milan	119
Tours	65		Lisbon	110
Marseille	55		Granada	110
Toulouse	40		Palermo	105
Orléans	35		Valencia	86
Bordeaux	30		Toledo	80
Caen	25		Madrid	79
Angers	25		Barcelona	64
La Rochelle	25		Messina	61
Dijon	24		Valladolid	56
Avignon	23		Antwerp	55
ENGLAND and SCOTLAND			Brussels	50
London	187 000		Cordova	50
Edinburgh	30		Segovia	42
Dublin	26		Cremona	37
HOLLAND			Salamanca	36
Amsterdam	48 000		Xérez	33
Leiden	25		Jaén	31
Haarlem	25		Ghent	31
DENMARK			Lecce	30
Copenhagen	40 000		Murcia	27
GERMANY			Málaga	26
Prague	100 000		Bruges	26
Augsburg	48		Ocaña	25
Nuremberg	45		Baeza	24
Hamburg	40		Zaragoza	24
Cologne	37		Palma	23
Magdeburg	37		Palencia	22
Breslau	33		POLAND	
Lille	32		Danzig	49 000
Lübeck	31		Vilna	40
Vienna	30		Warsaw	35
Liège	30		Poznan	30
Strassburg	27		Krakow	26
Aachen	22		RUSSIA	
ITALIAN STATES			Moscow	80 000
Venice	151 000		Smolensk	64
Rome	109		WALLACHIA	
Genoa	70		Bucharest	60 000
Florence	65		Tirgovishtea	45
Bologna	62		TURKEY	
Verona	54		Constantinople	700 000
Brescia	42		Adrianople	160
Padua	34		Belgrade	55
Vicenza	34		Üsküb	55
Parma	33		Salonica	50
Ferrara	33		Serajevo	45
Mantua	31		Caffa	40
Piacenza	31		Athens	35
Lucca	24		Sofia	30
Turin	23		Bakhchiserai	30
Bergamo	23		Plovdiv	28
			Buda	25

top 100

FRANCE			SPAIN	
Paris	530 000		Naples	207 000
Marseille	88		Milan	124
Lyon	71		Palermo	113
Rouen	68		Madrid	110
Lille	55		Seville	80
Turin	43		Barcelona	73
Bordeaux	42		Brussels	70
Nantes	42		Granada	70
Orléans	41		Antwerp	67
Toulouse	40		Ghent	49
Caen	37		Valencia	45
Angers	35		Messina	43
Amiens	35		Bruges	37
Dijon	34		Cordova	34
Tours	33		Cádiz	33
Metz	30		Málaga	32
Strasbourg	28		Xérez	30
Aix	27		Zaragoza	29
Avignon	26		Murcia	25
Valenciennes	26		Toledo	25
Toulon	25		**DENMARK and SWEDEN**	
St.-Malo	25		Copenhagen	62 000
Montpellier	25		Stockholm	48
BRITAIN			**GERMAN STATES**	
London	550 000		Hamburg	70 000
Dublin	80		Cologne	39
Edinburgh	35		Liège	36
Norwich	29		Frankfurt	35
Bristol	25		Nuremberg	35
Newcastle	25		Königsberg	32
HOLLAND			Augsburg	26
Amsterdam	172 000		Munich	24
Leiden	62		Aachen	24
Rotterdam	51		Berlin	24
Haarlem	48		**AUSTRIA**	
the Hague	29		Vienna	105 000
Delft	26		Prague	48
Middelburg	25		Breslau	40
ITALIAN STATES			**POLAND**	
Rome	149 000		Danzig	50 000
Venice	144		Vilna	40
Florence	69		Krakow	30
Genoa	67		**RUSSIA**	
Bologna	63		Moscow	130 000
Verona	50		Nizhny-Novgorod	24
Padua	37		**TURKEY**	
Brescia	37		Constantinople	700 000
Parma	35		Adrianople	93
Piacenza	31		Belgrade	50
Bergamo	30		Bucharest	50
Ferrara	27		Salonica	40
Vicenza	25		Sofia	40
Valletta	24		Caffa	36
PORTUGAL			Plovdiv	25
Lisbon	188 000		Bakhchiserai	24

top 100

FRANCE		SPAIN	
Paris	560 000	Madrid	123 000
Lyon	115	Granada	70
Marseille	88	Barcelona	70
Rouen	88	Seville	68
Bordeaux	64	Valencia	60
Lille	54	Cádiz	60
Strasbourg	49	Málaga	36
Toulouse	48	Zaragoza	35
Nantes	41	Cordova	34
Orléans	36	Murcia	32
Caen	34	Xérez	30
Amiens	33	PORTUGAL	
Montpellier	33	Lisbon	213 000
Metz	31	Oporto	30
Nimes	31	DENMARK and SWEDEN	
Dijon	31	Copenhagen	79 000
Grenoble	30	Stockholm	60
Nancy	29	GERMANY (PRUSSIA indented)	
Toulon	27	Berlin	113 000
Rennes	26	Hamburg	90
Avignon	26	Dresden	60
BRITAIN		Breslau	52
London	676 000	Königsberg	52
Dublin	125	Cologne	44
Edinburgh	55	Frankfurt	38
Cork	53	Liège	37
Bristol	45	Augsburg	41
Norwich	35	Munich	30
Newcastle	29	Leipzig	30
HOLLAND		Nuremberg	30
Amsterdam	219 000	AUSTRIA	
Leiden	49	Vienna	169 000
Rotterdam	46	Milan	123
Haarlem	40	Florence	74
the Hague	40	Prague	58
ITALY		Brussels	55
Naples	324 000	Antwerp	43
Venice	158	Ghent	38
Rome	157	Leghorn	31
Palermo	124	Bruges	27
Genoa	72	RUSSIA	
Bologna	66	Moscow	161 000
Turin	60	St. Petersburg	138
Verona	49	Kazan	37
Padua	40	Tula	30
Brescia	37	Kaluga	27
Parma	34	TURKEY	
Bergamo	33	Constantinople	666 000
Piacenza	30	Adrianople	96
Ferrara	30	Salonica	45
Messina	28	Caffa	44
Mantua	27	Belgrade	40
Valletta	27	Plovdiv	30
Catania	26		
POLAND			
Danzig	47 000		
Warsaw	28		

top 100

FRANCE		SPAIN	
Paris	547 000	Madrid	169 000
Lyon	111	Barcelona	120
Marseille	110	Seville	96
Bordeaux	97	Cádiz	87
Rouen	85	Valencia	82
Nantes	72	Granada	70
Brussels	66	Zaragoza	55
Turin	66	Málaga	49
Lille	55	Murcia	44
Ghent	54	Cordova	35
Antwerp	53	Xérez	33
Toulouse	50	Cartagena	33
Strasbourg	49	**PORTUGAL**	
Cologne	41	Lisbon	237 000
Amiens	40	Oporto	67
Liège	40	**HOLLAND (BATAVIAN REP.)**	
Nimes	39	Amsterdam	201 000
Metz	37	Rotterdam	58
Orléans	36	the Hague	41
Montpellier	33	Utrecht	32
Angers	32	**SCANDINAVIA**	
BRITAIN		Copenhagen	100 000
London	861 000	Stockholm	75
Dublin	165	**GERMANY (PRUSSIA indented)**	
Glasgow	85	Berlin	172 000
Edinburgh	82	Hamburg	130
Manchester	81	Warsaw	75
Liverpool	76	Breslau	64
Birmingham	72	Dresden	61
Bristol	66	Königsberg	53
Cork	63	Munich	48
Leeds	52	Frankfurt	42
Sheffield	45	Danzig	41
Portsmouth	43	Magdeburg	34
Plymouth	42	Augsburg	32
Newcastle	36	Leipzig	32
Norwich	36	Bremen	31
Valletta	35	Brunswick	31
Bath	31	**AUSTRIA**	
ITALY		Vienna	231 000
Naples	430 000	Prague	77
Rome	153	Buda-Pesth	54
Venice	146	Lemberg	42
Palermo	146	**RUSSIA**	
Milan	134	Moscow	238 000
Genoa	90	St. Petersburg	220
Florence	79	Tula	46
Bologna	66	**TURKEY**	
Verona	55	Constantinople	570 000
Leghorn	52	Adrianople	200
Catania	48	Salonica	62
Padua	45	Sofia	46
Brescia	41	Bucharest	34
Messina	36		
Parma	33		
Alessandria	31		

top 100—with suburbs

FRANCE		BELGIUM	
Paris	1 314 000	Brussels	208 000
Lyon	254	Ghent	108
Marseille	193	Antwerp	99
Bordeaux	142	Liège	92
Rouen	104	HOLLAND	
Nantes	96	Amsterdam	225 000
Lille	96	Rotterdam	111
Toulouse	93	the Hague	65
Strasbourg	75	SCANDINAVIA	
Brest	71	Copenhagen	135 000
Roubaix	70	Stockholm	93
Toulon	68	ITALIAN STATES	
BRITAIN		Naples	416 000
London	2 320 000	Palermo	182
Liverpool	422	Rome	170
Manchester	404	Turin	138
Glasgow	346	Florence	107
Birmingham	294	Genoa	103
Dublin	263	Leghorn	84
Edinburgh	193	Bologna	71
Leeds	184	Messina	64
Bristol	150	Catania	63
Sheffield	141	GERMANY (PRUSSIA indented)	
Wolverhampton	112	Berlin	446 000
Newcastle	111	Hamburg	193
Plymouth	100	Munich	125
Bradford	100	Breslau	114
Belfast	99	Dresden	97
Nottingham	93	Cologne	95
Cork	89	Königsberg	76
Hull	83	Barmen-Elberfeld	75
Stoke	82	Frankfurt	72
Portsmouth	77	Danzig	65
Dundee	77	Leipzig	63
Aberdeen	71	AUSTRIA	
Oldham	71	Vienna	426 000
Preston	70	Milan	193
Norwich	67	Budapest	156
Sunderland	66	Venice	141
Brighton	63	Prague	117
Merthyr-Tydfil	61	Lemberg	71
Bolton	60	Triest	63
Valletta	60	RUSSIA	
Leicester	59	St. Petersburg	502 000
Stockport	58	Moscow	373
SPAIN		Warsaw	163
Madrid	263 000	Odessa	71
Barcelona	167	Riga	61
Valencia	110	Saratov	59
Seville	106	TURKEY	
Cádiz	87	Constantinople	785 000
Málaga	75	Bucharest	104
Granada	67	Adrianople	76
PORTUGAL		Salonica	75
Lisbon	259 000		
Oporto	99		

below the top 100

1600

Prizren	22
Utrecht	21
Bremen	21
Ulm	21
Polotsk	20
Frankfurt	20
Ávila	20
Medina del Campo	20
Middelburg	20
Munich	20
Úbeda	20

1700

Silistria	24
Oporto	24
Utrecht	24
Arles	24
Gouda	23
Kazan	23
Cremona	23
Lübeck	23
Lucca	23
Rustchuk	23
Prizren	22
Reims	22
Bremen	22
Pavia	22
Dresden	22
Leipzig	21
Dordrecht	21
Troyes	21
Warsaw	21
Mantua	21
Mainz	20
Valenciennes	20
Ratisbon	20
Lemberg	20
Poitiers	20
Tirgovishtea	20

1750

Vicenza	26
Rustchuk	26
Brunswick	25
Palma	25
Tver	25
Lemberg	25
Mainz	25
Utrecht	25
Nizhny-Novgorod	25
Valladolid	25
Voronezh	25
Smolensk	24
Tours	24
Graz	24
Aachen	24
Bakhchiserai	24
Pavia	24
Cremona	24
Pressburg	24
Budapest	24
Angers	23
Birmingham	23
Salerno	23
Aix	23
Bremen	23
Siena	23
Reims	23
Grenoble	23
Middelburg	23
Kiev	23
Silistria	22
Arles	22
Toledo	22
Jaén	22
Magdeburg	22
Besançon	22
Delft	22
Geneva	21
Alessandria	21
Vilna	21
Prizren	21
Lübeck	21
St.-Étienne	21
Glasgow	21
Lucca	20
Bourges	20
Troyes	20
Brest	20
Debrecen	20
Liverpool	20
Dordrecht	20
Clermont	20
Ratisbon	20
Astrakhan	20
Shumla	20
Iasi	20
Écija	20

1800

Leiden	31
Bruges	31
Limerick	30
Caen	30
Yannina	30
Ismail	30
Plovdiv	30
Ferrara	30
Valladolid	30
Besançon	30
Rustchuk	30
Nancy	30
Riga	29
Palma	29
Hull	28
Graz	28
Vicenza	28
Piacenza	28
Nottingham	28
Écija	28
Maria Theresiopel	28
Debrecen	27
Bergamo	27
Brest	27
Jaén	27
Potsdam	27
Aberdeen	26
Geneva	26
Rennes	26
Belgrade	26
Dundee	25
Krakow	25
Versailles	25
Vilna	25
Nuremberg	25
Kazan	25
Vidin	25
Orel	25
Shumla	25
Szegedin	25
Clermont	24
Mainz	24
Lübeck	24
Trapani	24
Paisley	24
Troyes	24
Saratov	24
Groningen	24
Pavia	23
Salerno	23
Nizhny-Novgorod	23
Kaluga	23
Aachen	23
Aix	23
Grenoble	23
Valenciennes	23
Pressburg	23
Ratisbon	23
Kursk	23
Stoke	22
Brünn	22
Triest	22
Tours	22
Yaroslavl	22
Mantua	22
Belfast	22
Voronezh	22
Schemnitz	22
Würzburg	22
Stuttgart	21
Sistova	21
Avignon	21
Haarlem	21
Tournai	21
Dunkerque	21
Cremona	21
Dijon	21
Toulon	21
Asti	21
Limoges	20
Kiev	20
Reims	20
St. Omer	20
Chatham	20
Dieppe	20
Prizren	20
Mondovi	20
Silistria	20
Iasi	20

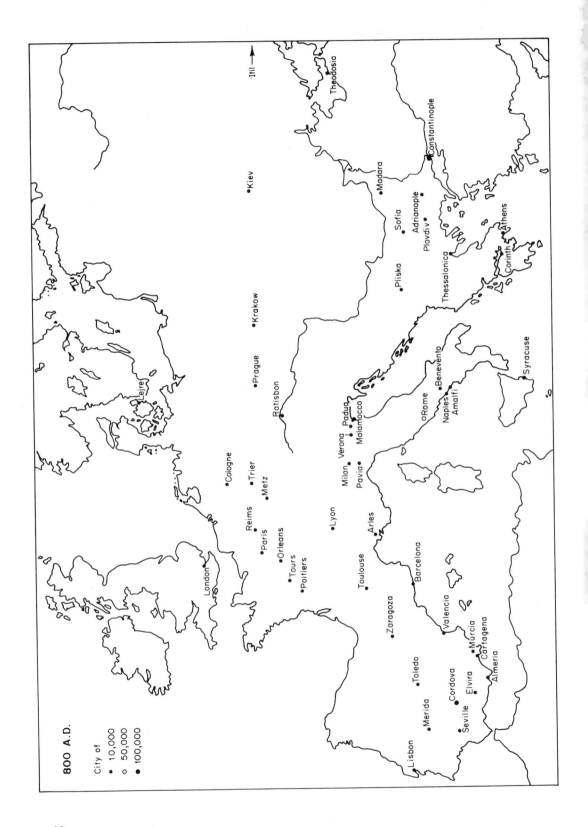

800 A.D.

City of
- • 10,000
- ◦ 50,000
- ● 100,000

Theodosia

Constantinople

Kiev

Madara

Adrianople
Sofia
Plovdiv

Pliska

Thessalonica

Corinth Athens

Krakow

Syracuse

Prague

Benevento

Ratisbon

oRome
Naples Amalfi

Padua
Verona
Malamocco

Lejre

Milan
Pavia

Cologne
Trier
Metz

Reims
Paris
Orleans

Lyon

Arles

Tours
Poitiers

Toulouse

Barcelona

London

Valencia

Zaragoza

Murcia
Cartagena

Toledo

Almeria

Cordova
Elvira

Merida

Seville

Lisbon

Itil

22

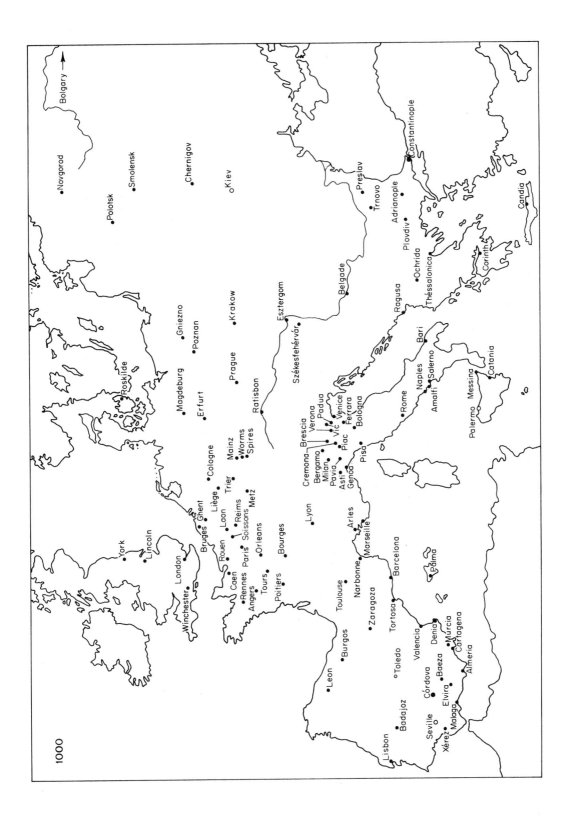

1000

Bolgary →

Novgorod
Polotsk
Smolensk
Chernigov
Kiev

Roskilde

Gniezno
Poznan
Magdeburg
Erfurt
Prague
Krakow
Esztergom
Ratisbon

Preslav
Trnovo
Adrianople
Plovdiv
Ochrida
Thessalonica
Corinth
Candia
Constantinople

Belgade
Ragusa

Székesfehérvár

York
Lincoln
Winchester
London
Bruges
Ghent
Liège
Laon
Cologne
Trier
Mainz
Worms
Spires

Rouen
Caen
Rennes
Paris
Soissons
Reims
Metz
Orleans
Bourges

Angers
Tours
Poitiers

Lyon
Arles
Marseille
Narbonne
Barcelona
Toulouse
Zaragoza
Tortosa
Palma

Cremona
Brescia
Verona
Padua
Venice
Ferrara
Vic
Piac
Bologna
Bergamo
Milan
Pavia
Asti
Genoa
Pisa

Rome
Naples
Amalfi
Salerno
Bari

Palermo
Messina
Catania

Burgos
Leon
Valencia
Denia
Murcia
Cartagena
Almeria
Toledo
Córdova
Baeza
Elvira
Malaga
Xérez
Seville
Badajoz
Lisbon

23

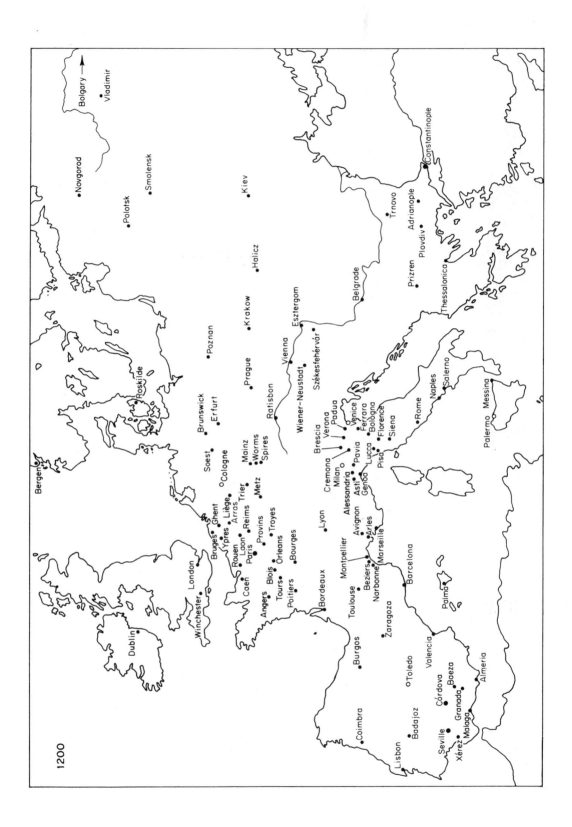

1200

Bergen

Dublin

London
Winchester

Roskilde

Bruges Ghent
Ypres Liège
Rouen Arras Trier
Caen Paris Reims Metz
Angers Blois Laon Troyes
Tours Orleans Provins
Poitiers Bourges

Bordeaux
Lyon
Toulouse Montpellier
Beziers Avignon
Narbonne Arles
Marseille

Soest
Cologne
Mainz
Worms
Spires

Brunswick
Erfurt

Ratisbon

Wiener-Neustadt

Poznan

Prague

Krakow

Vienna

Esztergom

Székesfehérvár

Belgrade

Halicz

Kiev

Smolensk

Polotsk

Novgorod

Bolgary →

Vladimir

Brescia
Verona
Padua
Cremona Venice
Milan Ferrara
Alessandria Pavia Bologna
Asti Lucca Florence
Genoa Pisa Siena

Rome

Naples
Salerno

Palermo Messina

Prizren
Plovdiv

Trnovo
Adrianople

Thessalonica

Constantinople

Barcelona

Palma

Zaragoza

Valencia

Burgos

Toledo

Boeza
Córdova
Granada
Seville
Xérez Malaga

Almeria

Coimbra

Lisbon

Badajoz

24

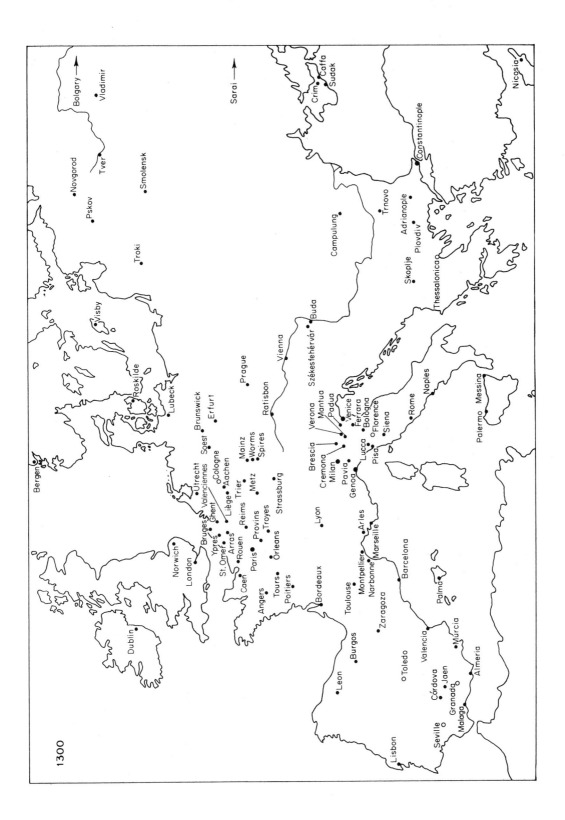

1300

Bolgary →
Vladimir
Novgorod
Pskov
Tver
Smolensk
Troki
Visby
Roskilde
Lübeck
Bergen
Dublin
Norwich
London
Ypres
Bruges
St. Omer
Ghent
Valenciennes
Arras
Rouen
Caen
Paris
Angers
Tours
Poitiers
Bordeaux
Léon
Burgos
Toulouse
Zaragoza
Toledo
Lisbon
Seville
Córdova
Jaen
Granada
Malaga
Murcia
Almeria
Valencia
Palma
Barcelona
Narbonne
Montpellier
Marseille
Arles
Lyon
Strassburg
Troyes
Provins
Orleans
Reims
Liège
Trier
Metz
Aachen
Cologne
Utrecht
Soest
Brunswick
Erfurt
Mainz
Worms
Spires
Ratisbon
Prague
Vienna
Buda
Székesfehérvár
Brescia
Cremona
Milan
Pavia
Genoa
Lucca
Pisa
Verona
Mantua
Padua
Venice
Ferrara
Bologna
Florence
Siena
Rome
Naples
Palermo
Messina
Campulung
Trnovo
Skoplje
Plovdiv
Adrianople
Thessalonica
Constantinople
Crim
Caffa
Sudak
Nicosia
Sarai →

25

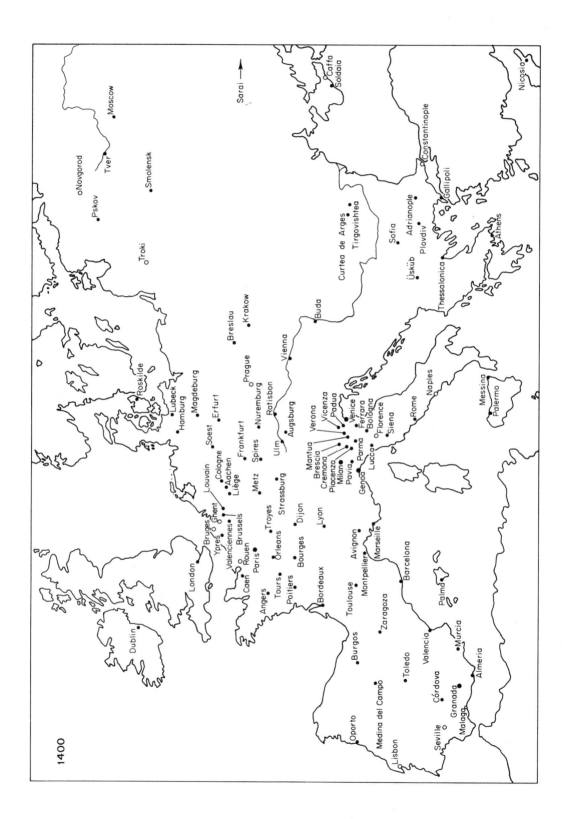

1400

Nicosia

Caffa
Soldaia

Moscow

Constantinople

Sarai →

Tver

Gallipoli

oNovgorod

Smolensk

Adrianople

Pskov

Curtea de Arges

Sofia

Athens

Tirgovishtea

Üsküb Plovdiv

Troki

Thessalonica

Breslau

Krakow

Buda

Vienna

Roskilde

Naples

Messina

Lubeck

Magdeburg

Rome Palermo

Hamburg

Erfurt

Soest

Prague

Ratisbon

Verona

Vicenza

Venice

Louvain

Cologne

Frankfurt

Nuremburg

Padua

Ferrara

Aachen

Spires

Ulm

Augsburg

Mantua

Brescia

Cremona

Piacenza

Milan

Pavia

Parma

Bologna

Florence

Lucca

Genoa

Siena

Liège

Metz

Bruges

Ypres Ghent

Strassburg

Dijon

Lyon

Valenciennes

Brussels

Troyes

London

Caen Rouen

Orleans

Bourges

Paris

Avignon

Marseille

Angers

Tours

Poitiers

Montpellier

Barcelona

Bordeaux

Toulouse

Palma

Dublin

Zaragoza

Murcia

Burgos

Valencia

Almeria

Medina del Campo

Toledo

Córdova

Oporto

Granada

Lisbon

Seville Malaga

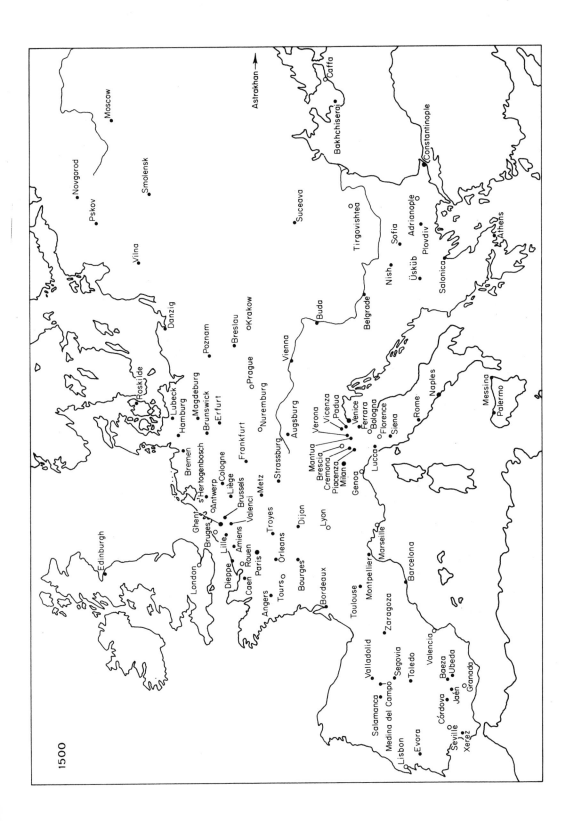

1500

27

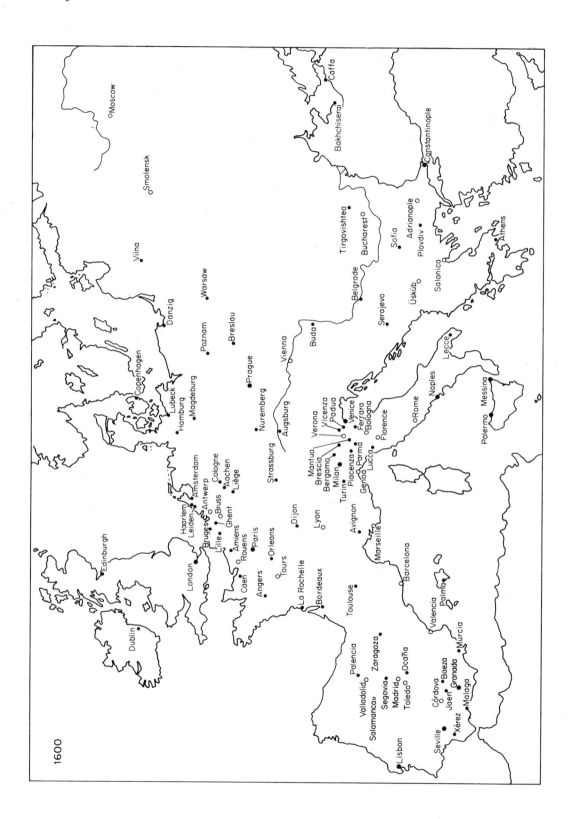

1600

Moscow

Caffa

Bakhchiserai

Constantinople

Smolensk

Tirgovishtea
Bucharest

Adrianople
Sofia
Plovdiv

Athens

Vilna

Warsaw

Breslau

Belgrade

Serajevo

Üsküb

Salonica

Danzig

Poznam

Copenhagen

Prague

Vienna

Buda

Lubeck
Hamburg
Magdeburg

Nuremberg

Augsburg

Verona
Vicenza
Padua
Venice
Ferrara
Bologna

Naples

Lecce

Messina

Palermo

Strasburg

Mantua
Brescia
Bergamo
Milan
Turin
Genoa
Parma
Piacenza
Lucca
Florence

Rome

Amsterdam
Cologne
Aachen
Liège

Haarlem
Leiden
Antwerp
Bruges
Ghent
Lille

Dijon
Lyon

Avignon

London

Amiens
Rouens
Paris
Orleans
Tours

Marseille

Barcelona

Edinburgh

Caen
Angers

La Rochelle
Bordeaux

Toulouse

Valencia
Palma

Murcia

Dublin

Palencia
Zaragoza

Valladolid
Segovia
Madrid
Salamanca
Toledo
Ocaña

Córdova
Baeza
Jaen Granada
Malaga

Seville
Xérez

Lisbon

28

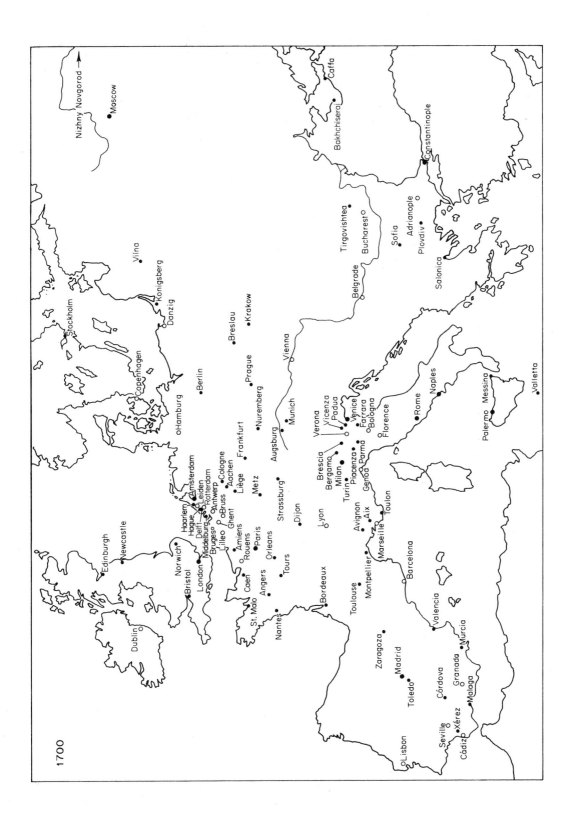

1700

Nizhny Novgorod →
Moscow

Caffa

Bakhchiserai

Constantinople

Vilna
Königsberg
Danzig

Tirgovishtea
Bucharest
Sofia Adrianople
Plovdiv

Salonica

Belgrade

Stockholm
Copenhagen
Breslau
Krakow
Berlin
Hamburg
Prague
Nuremberg
Vienna
Munich
Augsburg

Naples
Verona
Vicenza
Padua
Venice
Ferrara
Bologna
Rome
Palermo Messina
Florence
Valletta

Edinburgh
Newcastle

Haarlem Amsterdam
Hague Leiden
Delft Rotterdam
Middelburg Antwerp
Brugeso Ghent
Lilleo Cologne
Aachen
Liège
Frankfurt
Metz
Strassburg
Dijon
Lyon
Brescia
Bergamo
Milan Piacenza
Turin Parma
Genoa
Avignon
Aix
Marseille Toulon
Barcelona

Norwich
Bristol
London
Caen
St. Malo
Angers
Tours
Amiens
Rouens
Paris
Orleans
Bordeaux
Toulouse
Montpellier
Valencia
Murcia

Dublin

Nantes

Zaragoza
Madrid
Toledo
Córdova Granada
Málaga
Seville Xérez
Cádiz
Lisbon

29

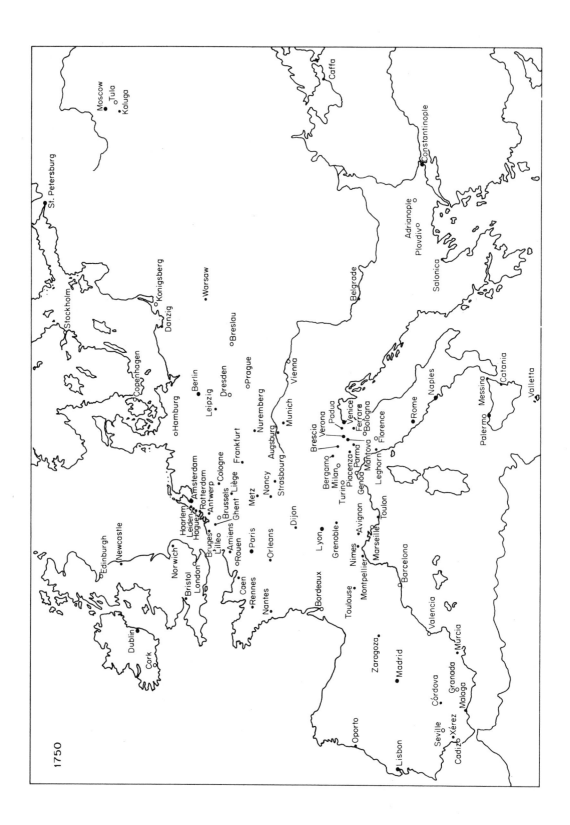

1750

30

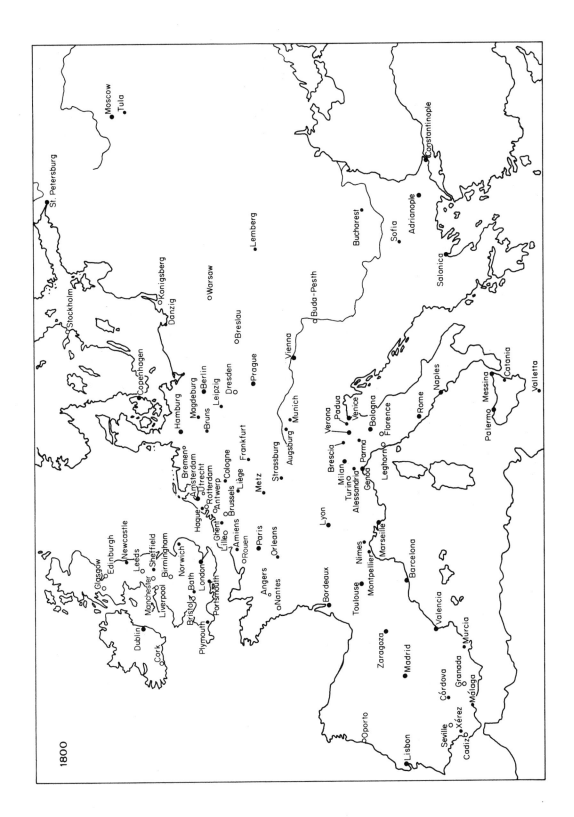

1800

Moscow
Tula
St. Petersburg
Constantinople
Adrianople
Bucharest
Sofia
Salonica
Stockholm
Königsberg
Warsaw
Danzig
Lemberg
Breslau
Buda-Pesth
Copenhagen
Vienna
Hamburg
Magdeburg
Berlin
Leipzig
Dresden
Prague
Bruns
Munich
Augsburg
Verona
Padua
Venice
Bologna
Florence
Rome
Naples
Palermo
Messina
Catania
Valletta
Bremen
Amsterdam
Utrecht
Rotterdam
Antwerp
Cologne
Liège
Frankfurt
Strassburg
Metz
Brescia
Milan
Turino
Alessandria
Genoa
Parma
Leghorn
Hague
Ghent
Brussels
Lilleo
Amiens
Lyon
Edinburgh
Newcastle
Glasgow
Leeds
Sheffield
Manchester
Birmingham
Liverpool
Norwich
Bath
London
Bristol
Portsmouth
Plymouth
Dublin
Cork
Paris
Orleans
Rouen
Angers
Nantes
Bordeaux
Toulouse
Nimes
Montpellier
Marseille
Barcelona
Valencia
Murcia
Granada
Málaga
Córdova
Xérez
Cadiz
Seville
Madrid
Zaragoza
Lisbon
Oporto

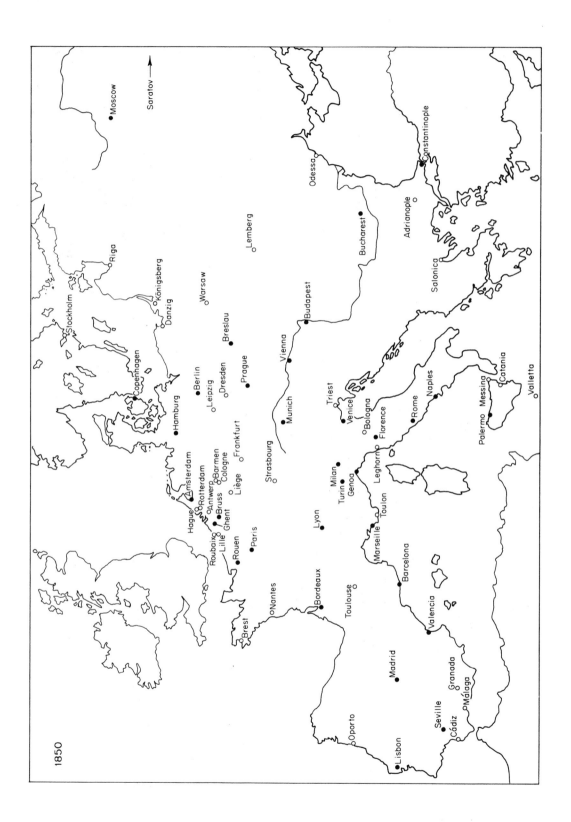

1850

Moscow
Saratov

Stockholm
Riga
Königsberg
Danzig
Warsaw
Lemberg
Copenhagen
Berlin
Leipzig
Dresden
Breslau
Prague
Hamburg
Budapest
Vienna
Munich
Triest
Venice
Bologna
Florence
Naples
Palermo Messina
Catania
Valletta
Amsterdam
Hague
Rotterdam
Barmen
Antwerp
Cologne
Bruss
Liège
Frankfurt
Ghent
Strasbourg
Roubaix
Lille
Rouen
Paris
Lyon
Milan
Turin
Genoa
Leghorn
Rome
Marseille Toulon
Nantes
Brest
Bordeaux
Toulouse
Barcelona
Valencia
Madrid
Granada
Málaga
Oporto
Seville
Cádiz
Lisbon
Odessa
Constantinople
Adrianople
Bucharest
Salonica

32

1850

800

1000

MIXTECS
Tilantongo

MIXTECS
Tilantongo

TOLTECS
Tula
Xochicalco
Cholula
Calixtlahuaca

TOLTECS
Tula
Cholula
Xochicalco
Azcapotzalco

ZAPOTECS
Monte Albán

MAYAS
Chichén-Itzá
Uxmal

MAYAS
Copán
Tikal   49 000
Dzibalchaltun
Piedras Negras
Chichén-Itzá

QUITO
Quito

PERUVIAN STATES
Tiahuanaco
Chincha
Vilcashuaman

PERU
Tiahuanaco   20 000
Vilcashuaman
Viñaque
Túmbez

1300

NORTHERN
Cahokia
Etowah

1200

NORTHERN
Etowah

CHICHIMECS
Cholula
Texcoco
Azcapotzalco

CHICHIMECS
Cholula
Azcapotzalco

CAPOTECS
Mitla

MAYAS
Chichén-Itzá
Mayapán
Uxmal

MAYAS
Chichén-Itzá
Mayapán
Uxmal

QUITO
Quito

QUITO
Quito

TÚMBEZ
Túmbez

TÚMBEZ
Túmbez

CHIMOR
Chanchán

CHIMOR
Chanchán
Moche

CUISMANCU
Cajamarquilla

CUISMANCU
Cajamarquilla

CHINCHA
Chincha

CHINCHA
Chincha

INCAS
Cuzco

INCAS
Cuzco

1400

NORTHERN
Cahokia
CHICHIMECS
  Texcoco   70 000
  Cholula
  Tenochtitlán
  Azcapotzalco
TARASCANS
  Tzintzuntzán
  Pátzcuaro
ZAPOTECS
  Zaachila
QUICHES
  Utatlán
MAYAS
  Mayapán   25 000
  Ticoh
  Mani
  Chakanputun
QUITO
  Riobamba
TÚMBEZ
  Túmbez
CHIMOR
  Chanchán   40 000
CUISMANCU
  Cajamarquilla   40 000
  Rimac
CHUQUIMANCU
  Chuquimancu
CHINCHA
  Chincha
INCAS
  Cuzco
  Pachacamac

1500

NORTHERN
Chillicothe
AZTECS
  Tenochtitlán   80 000
    (Mexico City)
  Texcoco   60
  Tlaxcala   40
  Cholula   36
TARASCANS
  Tzintzuntzán   40 000
  Pátzcuaro
ZAPOTECS
  Zaachila (Oaxaca)
CAKCHIQUELS
  Utatlán   60 000
  Iximché   24
MAYAS
  Ticoh   25 000
  Mani   22
  Chakanputun   20
CHIBCHAS
  Bogotá
INCAS
  Cuzco   45 000
  Chanchán   40
  Quito   30
  Huánuco   25
  Pachacamac   25
  Cajamarquilla
  Huarcu
  Túmbez

1600

SPANISH
  Potosí   148 000
  Mexico City   75
  Cuzco   30
  Puebla   25
  Guatemala City   25
  Tlaxcala   20
  Huancavelica   20

1700

SPANISH
  Mexico City   100 000
  Potosí   95
  Oruro   72
  Puebla   63
  Lima   37
  Cuzco   35
  Zacatecas   30
  Quito   30
  Guatemala City   30
  Havana   25
  Huamanga   25
  Mérida   20
PORTUGUESE
  Pernambuco   24 000
  Bahia   24
  Rio de Janeiro   20

	1750		1800

1750			1800		
BRITISH			**UNITED STATES**		
Boston	20 000		Philadelphia	68 000	
Philadelphia	20		New York	63	
SPANISH			Boston	35	
Mexico City	110 000		Baltimore	26	
Puebla	53		**SPANISH**		
Zacatecas	40		Mexico City	128 000	
Cuzco	40		Guanajuato	65	
Lima	40		Puebla	65	
Potosí	39		Havana	60	
Oruro	35		Lima	54	
Guatemala City	34		Buenos Aires	40	
Havana	34		Cuzco	34	
Quito	30		Zacatecas	33	
Guanajuato	30		Guadalajara	31	
Arequipa	26		Carácas	30	
Huamanga	26		Mérida	30	
Mérida	24		Arequipa	26	
Oaxaca	20		Oaxaca	25	
Guayaquil	20		Guatemala City	25	
Guadalajara	20		Huamanga	25	
Cochabamba	20		Cochabamba	22	
PORTUGUESE			La Paz	22	
Ouro Preto	60 000		Bogotá	21	
Bahia	53		Santiago	21	
Mariana	36		**PORTUGUESE**		
Pernambuco	35		Bahia	75 000	
Rio de Janeiro	29		Rio de Janeiro	44	
			Pernambuco	40	
			Ouro Preto	23	
			ENGLISH		
			Kingston	27 000	

1850
over 40 000—with suburbs

CANADA			Guadalajara	63
Montreal	48 000		Guanajuato	48
Quebec	40		Mérida	45
UNITED STATES			Querétaro	43
New York	682 000		San Luis Potosí	40
Philadelphia	426		**GUATEMALA**	
Boston	202		Guatemala City	50 000
Baltimore	169		**SPANISH**	
New Orleans	132		Havana	199 000
Cincinnati	130		**SOUTH AMERICA**	
St. Louis	77		Rio de Janeiro	166 000
Pittsburgh	69		Bahia	112
Troy	60		Pernambuco	106
Albany	55		Buenos Aires	74
Providence	49		Santiago	70
Louisville	45		Lima	70
Charleston	42		Valparaíso	45
Buffalo	42		Asunción	44
Washington	40		La Paz	44
MEXICO			Carácas	43
Mexico City	170 000		Cuzco	41
Puebla	71		Bogotá	40

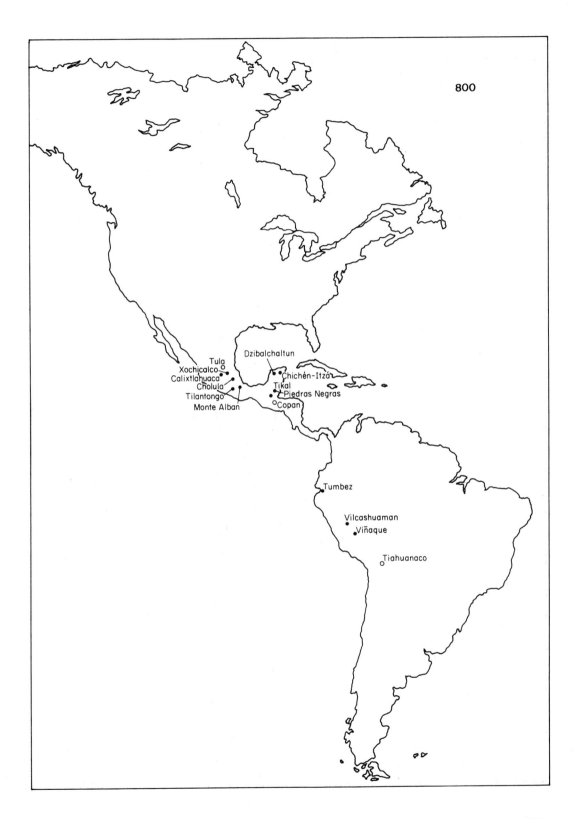

800

Tula
Xochicalco
Calixtlahuaca
Cholula
Tilantongo
Monte Alban

Dzibalchaltun
Chichén-Itzá
Tikal
Piedras Negras
Copan

Tumbez

Vilcashuaman
Viñaque

Tiahuanaco

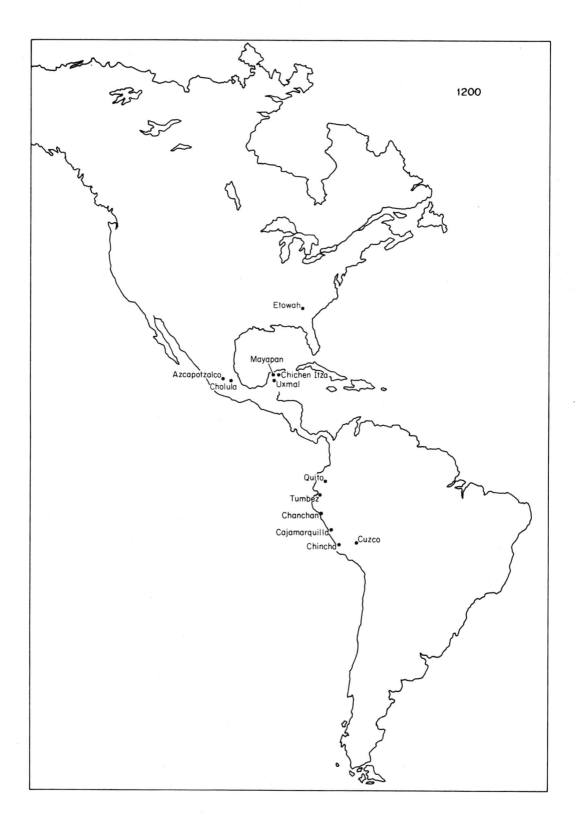

1200

Etowah

Mayapan
Azcapotzalco
Cholula
Chichen Itza
Uxmal

Quito
Tumbez
Chanchan
Cajamarquilla
Chincha
Cuzco

1500

Chillicothe●

Nanih Waiya●

Texcoco
Ticoh●
Tenochtitlán● ○Tlaxcala
Tzintzuntzan● ○Cholula Mani●
Patzcuaro●
Zaachila● Utatlan
Iximche○

Bogota●

Quito●

Tumbez●

Chanchan● Huanuco●
Cajamarquilla● Huarcu●
Pachacamac● ●Cuzco

1600

Zacatecas

Tlaxcala
Mexico City○ ●Puebla

Guatemala City●

Huancavelica● ●Cuzco

●Potosí

1800

Boston
New York
Philadelphia

Zacatecas
Guanajuato
Guadalajara
Puebla
Mexico City
Merida
Havana

Caracas

Pernambuco
Lima
Cuzco
Bahia

Rio de Janeiro

Buenos Aires

1850

Quebec
Montreal
Albany Troy
Buffalo NY Boston
Pittsburgh Providence
Cincinnati Philadelphia
Baltimore
St. Louis Louisville Washington
Charleston
New Orleans

San Luis Potosi
Guanajuato Queretaro
Guadalajara Havana
Mexico City Puebla Merida
Guatemala City

Caracas
Bogota
Quito
Pernambuco
Lima Bahia
La Paz
Rio de Janeiro
Asuncion
Valparaiso Buenos Aires
Santiago

over 20 000

800	
ARABIAN	
Alexandria	200 000
Fostat	100
Kairwan	80
Coptos	
Damietta	
Tunis	
Tinnis	
MOROCCO	
Meknes	
Fez	20 000
Sijilmessa	
DONGOLA	
Dongola	
ETHIOPIA	
Axum	
AWDAGHOST	
Awdaghost	
SHEBANS	
Zimbabwe	
Mapungubwe	

1000	
FATIMIDS	
Cairo	150 000
Tinnis	83
Kairwan	65
Coptos	
Tunis	
Mahdia	
Damietta	
Tlemcen	
Constantine	
SPANISH AFRICA (Moslem)	
Fez	75 000
Meknes	
Sijilmessa	
Salé	
DONGOLA	
Dongola	
GHANA	
Ghana	
BORNU	
Njimiye	
SONGHAI	
Gao	
SHEBANS	
Zimbabwe	
Mapungubwe	

1200	
EGYPT	
Cairo	200 000
Damietta	100
Alexandria	
Qus	
Rosetta	
MOROCCO	
Fez	250 000
Marrakesh	150
Rabat	
Mahdia	
Meknes	
Bougie	
Tunis	
Tlemcen	
Constantine	
Sijilmessa	
Kairwan	
Ceuta	
Tripoli	
Oran	
DONGOLA	
Dongola	30 000
Soba	
ETHIOPIA	
Axum	
Lalibala	
SOUTH MOSLEMS	
Njimiye	
Gao	
Kilwa	
Walata	
Ghana	
GUINEA	
Ife	
Kano	
Bussa	
Zagha	
BANTUS	
Zimbabwe	

1300	
EGYPT	
Cairo	400 000
Damietta	90
Qus	
Alexandria	
Rosetta	
Mansura	
MAGHREB	
Fez	200 000
Marrakesh	100
Tunis	75
Tlemcen	
Meknes	
Bougie	
Rabat	
Mahdia	
Ceuta	
Constantine	
Kairwan	
Tripoli	
Oran	
Biskra	
DONGOLA and ALOA	
Dongola	
Soba	
ETHIOPIA	
Tegulat	
Axum	
SOUTH MOSLEMS	
Njimiye	
Mali	
Kilwa	
Gao	
Walata	
Gober	
GUINEA	
Oyo	
Kano	
Ife	
Ikoso	
Krenik	
Nupé	
Bussa	
BANTUS	
Zimbabwe	

1400	
EGYPT	
Cairo	450 000
Damietta	80
Qus	
Alexandria	40
Asyut	
Mansura	
MAGHREB	
Fez	150 000
Tlemcen	70
Tunis	70
Marrakesh	
Meknes	
Bougie	
Constantine	
Mahdia	
Oran	
Ceuta	
Rabat	
Biskra	
Kairwan	
Tripoli	
Azammur	
DONGOLA and ALOA	
Dongola	
Soba	
ETHIOPIA	
Axum	30 000
SOUTH MOSLEMS	
Mali	50 000
Gao	
Kilwa	
Gober	
Timbuktu	20
GUINEA	
Oyo	
Kano	
Nupé	
Krenik	
Ife	
Benin	
Ouagadougou	
BANTUS	
Zimbabwe	
Congo	
KAFFA	
Chonga	

1500

EGYPT
Cairo	450 000
Fuwa	
Damietta	40
Asyut	
Alexandria	35
Qus	

MAGHREB
Fez	125 000
Tunis	75
Marrakesh	50
Tlemcen	40
Bougie	40
Constantine	40
Tagust	40
Oran	36
Meknes	35
Mahdia	
Tripoli	
Azammur	25
Taza	25
Kairwan	
Algiers	20
Tedsi	20

DONGOLA
Dongola	

ETHIOPIA
Axum	33 000

SOUTH MOSLEMS
Gao	60 000
Kano	50
Kazargamu	
Agades	45
Mali	35
Kilwa	
Gober	28
Timbuktu	25
Sennar	
Ngala	

GUINEA
Oyo	
Nupé	
Ife	
Benin	
Ouagadougou	
Ijebu	
Zaria	

BANTUS
São Salvador, Congo	
Zimbabwe	

1600

TURKISH
Cairo	400 000
Algiers	75
Tunis	
Tlemcen	
Asyut	
Tripoli	
Damietta	
Constantine	
Qus	

MOROCCO
Marrakesh	125 000
Fez	100
Tagust	30
Timbuktu	25
Meknes	

KAFFA
Bonga	

SOUTH MOSLEMS
Kazargamu	60 000
Zaria	50
Kano	40
Sennar	
Suramé	
Gober	
Agades	
Masenya	

GUINEA
Oyo	
Benin	65 000
Gbara	
Ife	

BANTUS
Dongo	30 000
Zimbabwe	
Loango	

	1700			1750
TURKISH			**TURKISH**	
Cairo	350 000		Cairo	300 000
Tripoli	50		Damietta	23
Damietta			**MAGHREB**	
Asyut			Tunis	100 000
MAGHREB			Algiers	75
Meknes	200 000		Meknes	
Algiers	85		Fez	
Fez			Rabat	
Tunis	75		Marrakesh	30
Salé-Rabat			Tripoli	
Constantine			Constantine	
Marrakesh			Tarudant	
Tarodant			**ETHIOPIA**	
Timbuktu			Gondar	70 000
ETHIOPIA			**BAMBARA**	
Gondar	80 000		Segu	
Emfras			**KAFFA**	
KAFFA			Bonga	
Bonga			**SOUTH MOSLEMS**	
BAMBARA			Katsina	75 000
Segu			Kazargamu	50
SOUTH MOSLEMS			Zaria	50
Kazargamu	50 000		Gober	
Zaria	50		Sennar	30
Katsina			Masenya	
Masenya			Kano	
Gober			Agades	
Kano			Zamfara	
Sennar	30		**GUINEA**	
Zamfara			Oyo	
Agades			Ife	
Kebbi			Benin	
GUINEA			Rabba	
Oyo			Iseyin	
Benin			Ogbomosho	
Allada	25 000		Abomey	24 000
Puje			Puje	
Ife			Oshogbo	
Jima			Kumasi	
Ogbomosho			**BANTUS**	
BANTUS			Chungo	
Dongo	30 000		Mengo	
Loango	30			
Mengo				
PORTUGUESE				
Loanda	20 000			

1800 over 20 000		1850 over 40 000	
TURKISH		**EGYPT**	
Cairo	263 000	Cairo	256 000
Damietta	25	Alexandria	138
Asyut	25	**MAGHREB**	
MAGHREB		Tunis	90 000
Tunis	120 000	Fez	85
Meknes	110	Meknes	56
Algiers	72	Rabat	55
Fez	60	Algiers	54
Marrakesh	50	Marrakesh	50
Rabat	43	**SOUTH MOSLEMS**	
Tarudant	25	Ilorin	65 000
ETHIOPIA		Zanzibar	60
Gondar	40 000	Kuka	50
BAMBARA		Zaria	50
Segu	30 000	Yakoba	40
SOUTH MOSLEMS		Kano	40
Katsina		Alkalawa	
Kazargamu		Ilade	
Zaria	40 000	**GUINEA**	
Masenya		Abeokuta	65 000
Alkalawa		Ibadan	55
Kano	30	Ijaye	50
Zamfara		Ogbomosho	
Kebbi		Ife	
Constantine	20	**BANTUS**	
Tripoli	20	Kasongo	
GUINEA		Mengo	
Oyo	85 000	**KAFFA**	
Ife		Bonga	
Kumasi	40	**MAURITIUS**	
Iseyin		Port Louis	49 000
Ogbomosho			
Gbara			
Abomey	25		
Ede			
Puje			
BANTUS			
Mengo			
KAFFA			
Bonga			

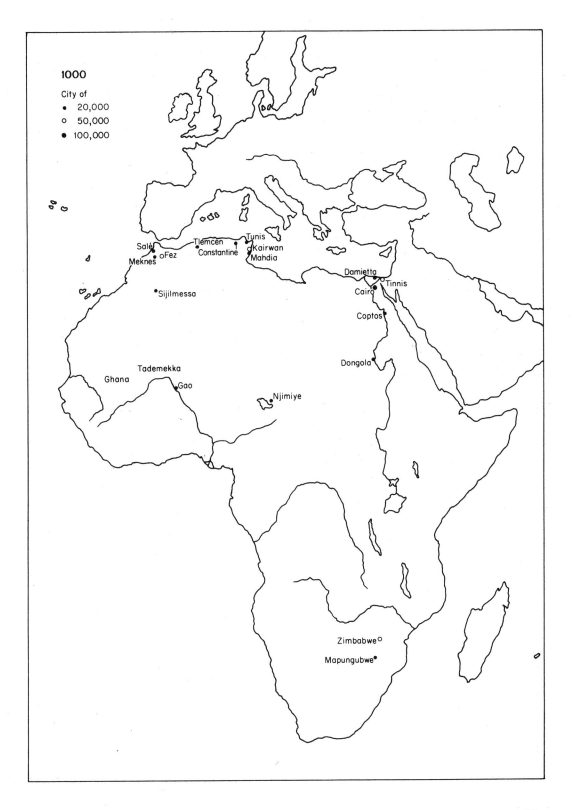

1000

City of
- 20,000
o 50,000
- 100,000

Salé
Meknes
oFez
Tlemcen
Constantine
Tunis
Kairwan
Mahdia
Damietta
Tinnis
Cairo
Coptos
Sijilmessa
Dongola
Tademekka
Ghana
Gao
Njimiye
Zimbabweo
Mapungubwe

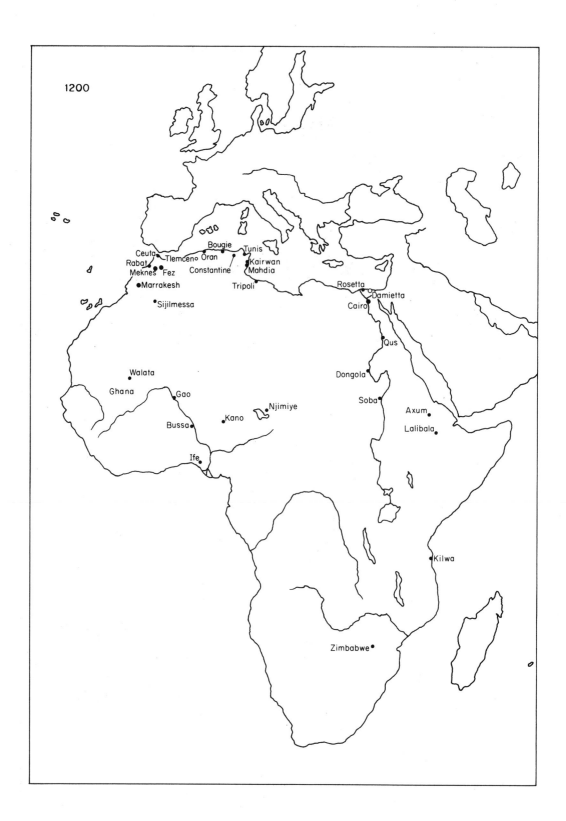

1200

Ceuta
Rabat
Meknes Fez
Tlemcen Oran
Bougie
Tunis
Constantine
Kairwan
Mahdia
Marrakesh
Tripoli
Rosetta
Damietta
Sijilmessa
Cairo
Qus
Walata
Dongola
Ghana
Gao
Soba
Njimiye
Axum
Kano
Lalibala
Bussa
Ife
Kilwa
Zimbabwe

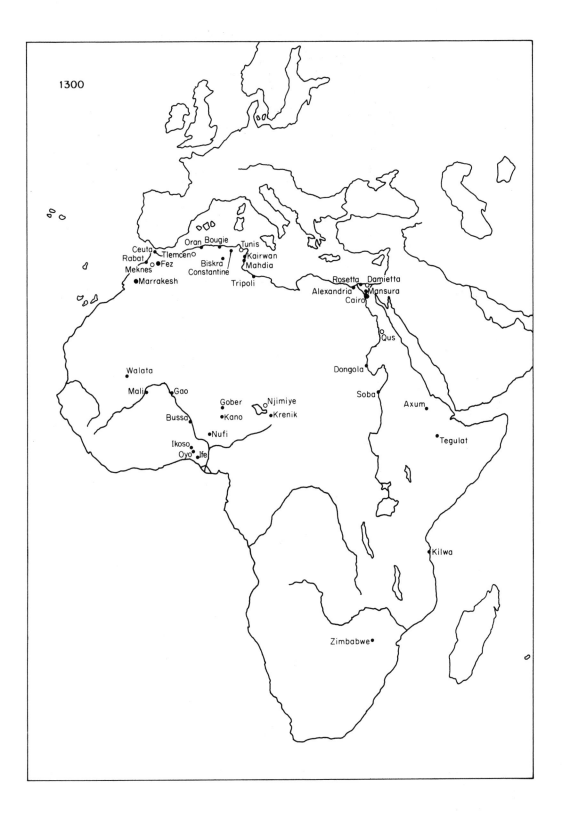

1300

Ceuta
Rabat
Meknes
Marrakesh
Oran Bougie
Tlemcen
Fez
Biskra
Constantine
Tunis
Kairwan
Mahdia
Tripoli
Rosetta
Damietta
Alexandria
Mansura
Cairo
Qus
Walata
Mali
Gao
Dongola
Soba
Axum
Gober
Njimiye
Kano
Krenik
Bussa
Nufi
Tegulat
Ikoso
Oyo
Ife
Kilwa
Zimbabwe

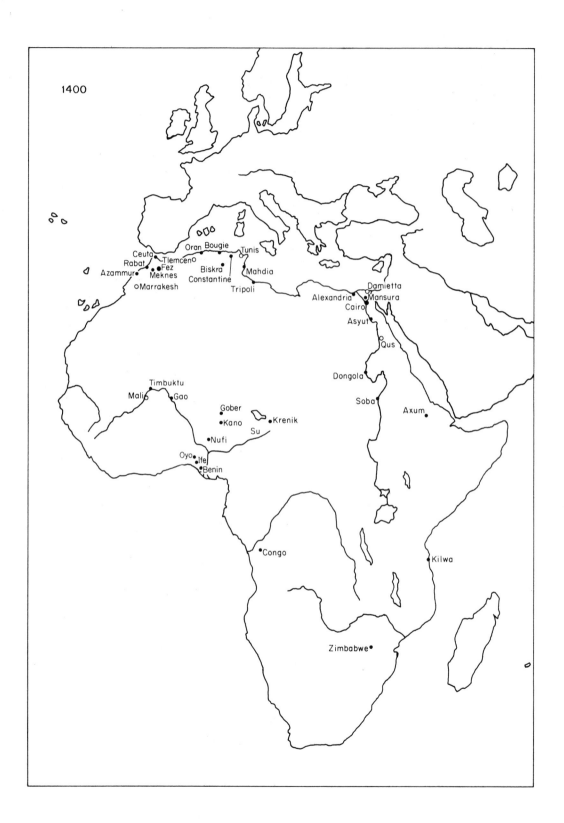

1400

Ceuta
Rabat
Tlemcen
Oran Bougie
Tunis
Fez
Azammur
Meknes
Biskra
Mahdia
Marrakesh
Constantine
Tripoli
Damietta
Alexandria
Mansura
Cairo
Asyut
Qus
Dongola
Timbuktu
Mali
Gao
Soba
Gober
Axum
Kano
Krenik
Su
Nufi
Oyo
Ife
Benin
Congo
Kilwa
Zimbabwe

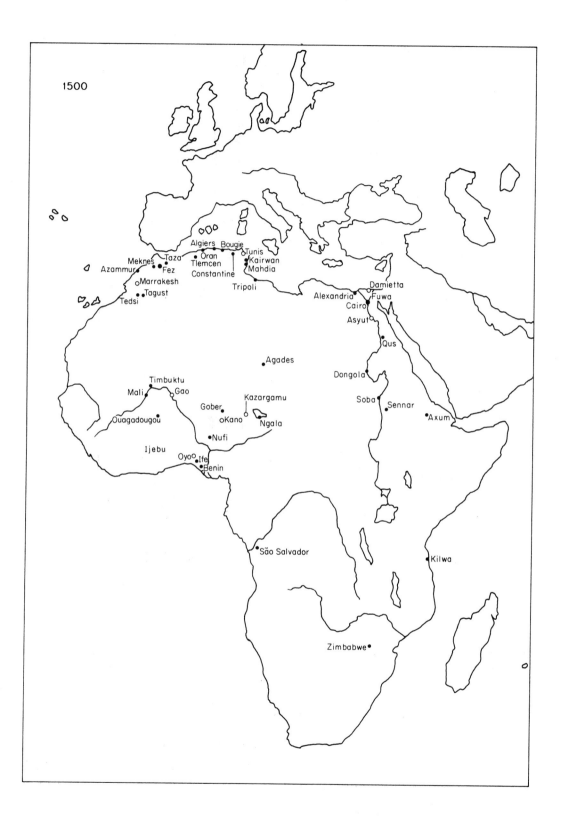

1500

Meknes
Azammur
Taza
Algiers Bougie
Oran Tunis
Tlemcen Kairwan
Constantine Mahdia
Fez
Marrakesh
Tagust
Tedsi
Tripoli

Alexandria Damietta
Fuwa
Cairo
Asyut
Qus

Agades

Dongola

Timbuktu
Mali Gao
Ouagadougou Gober
oKano
Kazargamu
Ngala
Soba Sennar
Axum

Nufi

Ijebu
Oyoo Ife
Benin

São Salvador
Kilwa

Zimbabwe

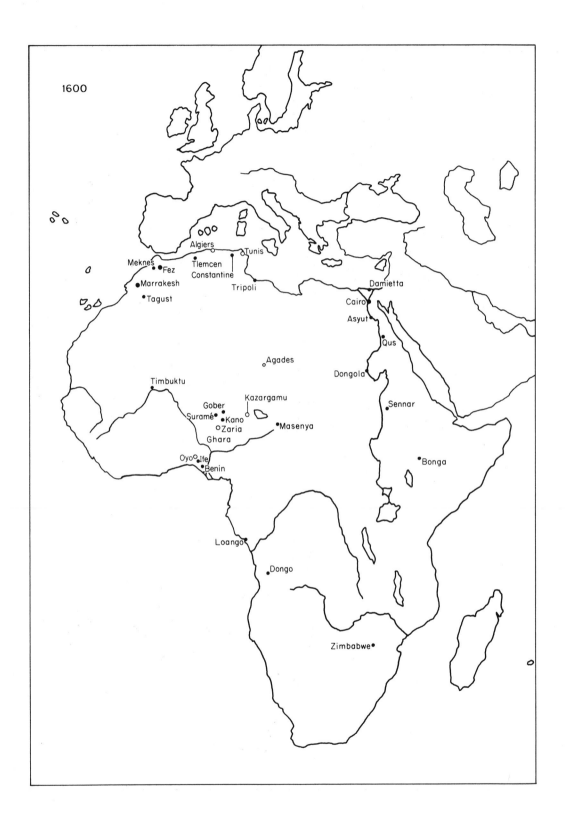

1600

Algiers
Tunis
Meknes
Fez
Tlemcen
Constantine
Marrakesh
Tripoli
Damietta
Tagust
Cairo
Asyut
Qus
Agades
Dongola
Timbuktu
Sennar
Kazargamu
Gober
Suramé
Kano
Zaria
Masenya
Ghara
Oyo
Ife
Benin
Bonga
Loango
Dongo
Zimbabwe

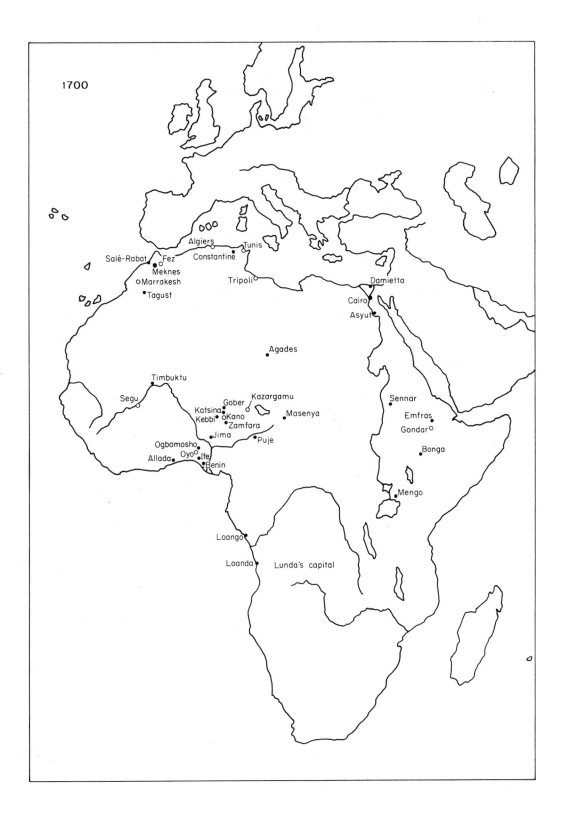

1700

Salé-Rabat
Fez
Meknes
Marrakesh
Tagust

Algiers
Constantine
Tunis
Tripoli
Damietta
Cairo
Asyut

Agades

Timbuktu

Segu

Gober
Kazargamu
Katsina
Kebbi
Kano
Zamfara
Jima
Puje
Masenya

Sennar
Emfras
Gondar
Bonga

Ogbomosho
Oyo
Ife
Allada
Benin

Mengo

Loango

Loanda
Lunda's capital

55

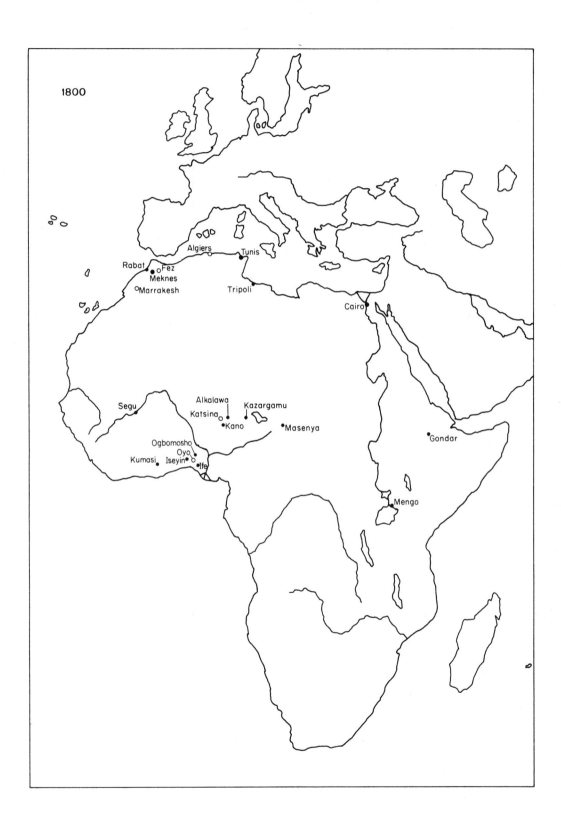

1800

Rabat
Fez
Meknes
Marrakesh
Algiers
Tunis
Tripoli
Cairo

Segu
Alkalawa
Katsina
Kano
Kazargamu
Masenya
Gondar

Ogbomosho
Oyo
Kumasi
Iseyin
Ife

Mengo

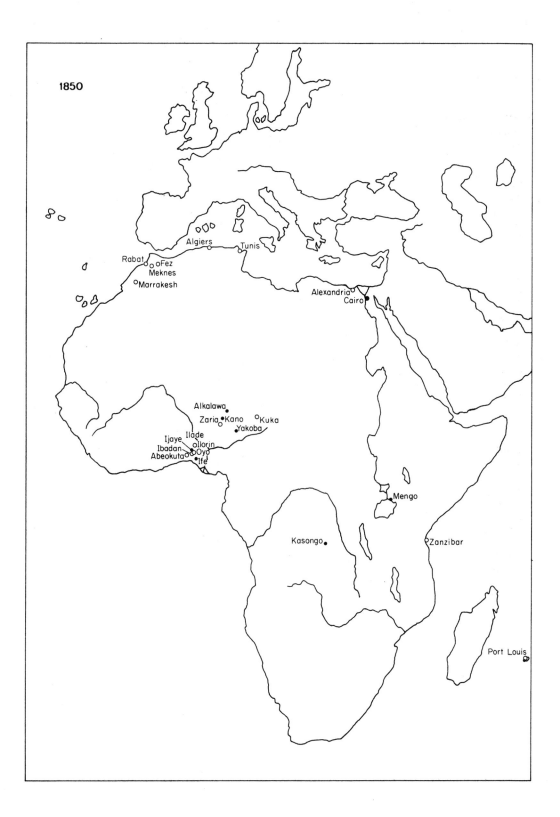

1850

Algiers
Tunis
Rabat o oFez
Meknes
oMarrakesh
Alexandria
Cairo

Alkalawa
Zaria Kano Kuka
Yakoba
Ijaye Ilade
Ibadan OIlorin
Abeokuta Oyo
Ife

Mengo

Kasongo
Zanzibar

Port Louis

Cities of Asia, 800

over 40 000

BYZANTINE		**BURMA**	
Caesarea		Pegu	
Sivas		Pagan	
ARAB CALIPHATE		**CHAMPA**	
Bagdad	700 000	Indrapura	
Basra		**CAMBODIA**	
Damascus		Indrapura	
Kufa		**MALAYS**	
Mecca	100	Palembang	
Rayy		**NANCHAO**	
Edessa		Tali	
Hamadan		**UIGHURS**	
Mansura		Balasaghun	
Jerusalem		**TIBET**	
Samarkand		Lhasa	
Merv		**KOREA**	
Qum		Kyongju	
Aleppo		Pyongyang	
Antioch		**CHINA**	
Siraf		Changan	800 000
Anbar		Loyang	
Nishapur		Hangchow	200
Gundishapur		Yangchow	100
INDIAN STATES		Chengtu	88
Ellora	90 000	Wuchang	84
Kanauj	80	Nanking	
Chunar		Soochow	75
Anhilvada		Kaifeng	75
Kanchi		Chüanchow	
Vengi		Canton	
Thaneswar		Nanchang	
Tanjore		Tsinan	
Cambay		Peking	
Ayodhya		**JAPAN**	
Tamralipti		Kyoto	200 000
Patna		Nara	
Mau-Sahanya		Osaka	
Benares			
Jayapuram			
Vatapi			

ARMENIA		BURMA	
Ani	75 000	Pagan	
BYZANTINE		CAMBODIA	
Caesarea		Angkor	
Sivas		CHAMPA	
Antioch		Binhdinh	
EGYPT		JAVA	
Edessa		Prambanan	
Aleppo	75 000	NANCHAO	
Damascus		Tali	
Jerusalem	60	TIBET	
Mecca		Lhasa	
OTHER ARAB STATES		UIGHURS	
Hasa	150 000	Nishapur	125 000
PERSIAN STATES		Bokhara	100
Bagdad	125 000	Samarkand	80
Rayy	100	Balasaghun	
Isfahan	92	Kashgar	
Hamadan		TANGUT	
Shiraz	52	Ninghsia	
Siraf	50	KHITANS	
Basra	50	Peking	80 000
INDIAN STATES		KOREA	
Khajuraho	100 000	Songdo	
Anhilvada	100	Pyongyang	
Chunar		Kyongju	
Tanjore		CHINA	
Vengi		Kaifeng	400 000
Manyakheta		Sian	300
Cambay		Loyang	150
Kanauj	60	Hangchow	
Benares		Chengtu	
Quilon		Canton	100
Tamralipti		Soochow	87
Mansura		Yangchow	
Somnath	54	Nanking	
Kanchi		Nanchang	
Thaneswar		Chüanchow	
Monghyr		Wuchang	
Ujjain		Siangyang	
Kayal		JAPAN	
		Kyoto	200 000

over 40 000

SELJUKIDS		**CRUSADERS**	
Konia	100 000	Acre	75 000
Kayseri		Antioch	
Sivas		**GEORGIA**	
Erzurum		Tiflis	80 000
EGYPT		**BURMA**	
Damascus	90 000	Pagan	180 000
Mecca		Pegu	
Aleppo		**CAMBODIA**	
Mosul	50	Angkor	150 000
Basra		Sukotai	
PERSIAN STATES		**CHAMPA**	
Bagdad	100 000	Binhdinh	
Hormuz		**ANNAM**	
Tabriz		Hanoi	
Shiraz		**NANCHAO**	
KHWARIZM		Tali	100 000
Nishapur	80 000	**KARA-KHITAI**	
Rayy	80	Samarkand	60 000
Gurganj		Bokhara	
Isfahan	70	Balasaghun	47
Merv	70	Kashgar	
Hamadan		**KINS and TANGUT**	
GHOR		Peking	150 000
Ghazni		Sian	150
Nadiya		Kaifeng	150
Gaur		Loyang	
Ghor		Ninghsia	
Delhi	60 000	Liaoyang	60
Lahore		Taitong	42
Herat		Siangyang	
INDIAN STATES		**KOREA**	
Cuttack	150 000	Songdo	
Kalinjar	100	Pyongyang	
Cambay		**CHINA**	
Quilon		Hangchow	255 000
Gangaikondapuram		Canton	200
Dhar		Nanking	180
Chitor		Yangchow	100
Tanjore		Chengtu	
Kalyan		Soochow	90
Warangal		Chüanchow	
Kanchi		Wuchang	
Ujjain		Nanchang	
Calicut		Taichow	
Kayal		Fuchow	
Goa		**JAPAN**	
CEYLON		Kamakura	175 000
Polonnaruwa	140 000	Kyoto	
HARIPUNJAI		Hyogo	
Haripunjai			

over 40 000

BYZANTINE	
Nicaea	
TREBIZOND	
Trebizond	60 000
SELJUKIDS	
Konia	
EGYPT	
Mecca	
Mosul	55 000
MONGOL PERSIA	
Tabriz	150 000
Isfahan	70
Maragheh	
Hamadan	
Shiraz	50
Hormuz	50
Bagdad	40
INDIAN STATES	
Cuttack	125 000
Delhi	100
Gaur	100
Quilon	100
Warangal	100
Dhar	90
Gangaikondapuram	
Chitor	60
Anhilvada	
Calicut	
Goa	50
Benares	
Thana	
Kanauj	
Kanchi	
Kayal	
Sonargaon	
Dorasamudra	40
SIAM	
Sukotai	

CAMBODIA	
Angkor	125 000
CHAMPA	
Virapura	
ANNAM	
Hanoi	
INDONESIA	
Majapahit	
MONGOL TURKESTAN	
Aksu	
MONGOL CHINA	
Hangchow	432 000
Peking	401
Canton	300
Nanking	300
Soochow	160
Sian	150
Chengtu	110
Chüanchow	100
Kaifeng	
Yangchow	
Songdo	
Tali	
Wuchang	
Fuchow	70
Siangyang	
Pyongyang	
Loyang	
Hsüchow	
Chinkiang	42
Nanchang	
Ninghsia	
Ningpo	
JAPAN	
Kamakura	200 000
Kyoto	
Sakai	

over 40 000

TREBIZOND		SIAM		
Trebizond		Ayutia		
KNIGHTS OF ST. JOHN		Chiengmai		
Smyrna		LAOS		
TURKEY		Luang Prabang		
Bursa		CAMBODIA		
Konia		Angkor	100 000	
EGYPT		CHAMPA		
Damascus	100 000	Virapura		
Aleppo	75	ANNAM		
Mecca		Hanoi		
TIMURIDS		MALAY PENINSULA		
Tabriz	200 000	Malacca		
Samarkand	100	INDONESIA		
Shiraz	100	Majapahit	50 000	
Bokhara		Gresik		
Hormuz	50	KOREA		
Sultaniya		Seoul	100 000	
JELAIRIDS		Pyongyang		
Bagdad	90 000	CHINA		
INDIAN STATES		Nanking	473 000	
Vijayanagar	350 000	Hangchow	325	
Pandua	150	Peking	320	
Cambay	125	Canton	300	
Gaur	100	Soochow	175	
Quilon	90	Sian	150	
Gulbarga		Chüanchow		
Cuttack		Chengtu	88	
Penukonda	75	Kaifeng		
Kamatapur		Yangchow		
Jaunpur		Fuchow	81	
Chitor	60	Wuchang	72	
Kanchi		Ningpo		
Anhilvada		Hsüchow	60	
Benares		Taiyüan	51	
Calicut	60	Kingtehchen		
Goa	50	Ninghsia		
Burhanpur	48	Tsinan		
Sonargaon		Changchow		
Daulatabad		Loyang		
Dhar		Siangyang		
Bihar		Chinkiang		
Warangal	42	Nanchang		
Tatta		Kiukiang	40	
Thana		JAPAN		
NEPAL		Kyoto	200 000	
Katmandu		Kamakura		
BURMA		Yoshino		
Pegu	60 000			
Ava	50			

over 40 000

TURKEY		ARAKAN	
Smyrna		Chittagong	50 000
Trebizond	40 000	Arakan	
EGYPT		SIAM	
Damascus	70 000	Ayutia	150 000
Aleppo	67	Chiengmai	
Mecca	60	LAOS	
PERSIAN STATES		Luang Prabang	50 000
Tabriz	250 000	ANNAM	
Qum		Hanoi	
Kerman	50	MALAYS	
Shiraz	50	Brunei	50 000
Isfahan	40	Demak	
TURKESTAN		Malacca	
Samarkand		KOREA	
Bokhara		Seoul	150 000
Kashgar		Pyongyang	
Herat	40 000	CHINA	
INDIAN STATES		Peking	672 000
Vijayanagar	500 000	Hangchow	375
Gaur	200	Nanking	285
Mandu	150	Canton	250
Cambay	125	Soochow	200
Delhi	100	Sian	150
Chitor	90	Chengtu	112
Penukonda	90	Kaifeng	
Gwalior	90	Fuchow	83
Bidar	80	Wuchang	
Ahmedabad	80	Yangchow	
Quilon	75	Ningpo	
Burhanpur	75	Chüanchow	
Chanderi	70	Kingtehchen	
Bijapur		Taiyüan	61
Calicut	60	Hsüchow	
Srinagar		Tientsin	
Kamatapur		Loyang	
Bihar	50	Changchow	
Jaunpur	50	Ninghsia	
Benares		Changsha	
Tatta		Yünnanfu	
Chandragiri		Nanchang	
Goa	42	Kiukiang	
Ahmednagar		JAPAN	
BURMA		Hakata	50 000
Ava		Sakai	
Toungoo		Yamaguchi	
Martaban			

Cities of Asia, 1600

over 40 000

TURKEY	
Tabriz	100 000
Smyrna	80
Bursa	70
Aleppo	61
Damascus	60
Mecca	60
Ankara	50
Medina	40
PERSIA	
Qazvin	150 000
Isfahan	124
Hamadan	
Herat	
Kerman	
MOGULS	
Agra	500 000
Lahore	350
Ahmedabad	225
Rajmahal	100
Jodhpur	
Surat	75
Patna	
Srinagar	
Ujjain	
Cambay	70
Benares	60
Gwalior	
Amber	
Bihar	50
Tatta	50
Allahabad	
Monghyr	
Delhi	
PORTUGUESE	
Hugli	70 000
Goa	63
Diu	50
REST OF INDIA	
Bijapur	200 000
Hyderabad	80
Chandragiri	
Ahmednagar	75
Burhanpur	
Golconda	
Udaipur	72
Bidar	
Penukonda	
Madurai	
Cochin	45
Calicut	42
Gargaon	40

ARAKAN	
Arakan	125 000
Chittagong	50
BURMA	
Toungoo	
SIAM	
Ayutia	100 000
ANNAM	
Hué	
MALAYS	
Bantam	50 000
Surabaja	50
UZBEKS	
Bokhara	
Samarkand	
Kashgar	
MONGOLIA	
Kuku Khoto	
KOREA	
Seoul	
CHINA	
Peking	706 000
Canton	350
Hangchow	350
Nanking	317
Soochow	175
Sian	160
Chengtu	130
Wuchang	
Kaifeng	
Tientsin	
Taiyüan	79
Fuchow	76
Yangchow	75
Kingtehchen	
Ningpo	
Hsüchow	
Yünnanfu	
Chüanchow	56
Fatshan	50
Changsha	50
Nanchang	45
Paoting	
JAPAN	
Osaka	400 000
Yedo	350
Kyoto	350
Nagoya	65
Kanazawa	50

over 40 000

TURKEY		DUTCH	
Smyrna	135 000	Batavia	52 000
Aleppo	72	PORTUGESE	
Damascus	70	Macao	75 000
Bursa	60	SIAM	
Mecca	60	Ayutia	150 000
Medina	45	TIBET	
Ankara		Lhasa	
PERSIA		TURKESTAN	
Isfahan	600 000	Bokhara	
Tabriz	150	KOREA	
Qazvin	70	Seoul	170 000
Kerman	60	Songdo	
Herat		Pyongyang	
Kandahar		CHINA	
Qum	45	Peking	
Kashan	40	Canton	300 000
MOGULS		Nanking	300
Delhi	500 000	Hangchow	292
Ahmedabad	380	Soochow	245
Dacca	200	Sian	167
Surat	200	Wuchang	150
Hyderabad	200	Mukden	
Patna	170	Tientsin	92
Srinagar	150	Fatshan	90
Aurangabad	100	Ninghsia	90
Jodhpur		Fuchow	
Lahore		Ningpo	88
Agra		Kingtehchen	
Benares		Chengtu	
Bijapur		Amoy	
Kasimbazar		Chinkiang	68
Ujjain		Kuku Khoto	
Rajmahal		Hwaian	65
Allahabad		Siangyang	
Cambay	50	Yangchow	60
Lucknow		Kaifeng	60
Multan		Kashgar	
Bihar	40	Hsüchow	
ENGLISH		Tsinan	55
Masulipatam		Changsha	
REST OF INDIA		Siangtan	
Seringapatam		Shanghai	45
Tanjore	50 000	Kweilin	
Calicut	50	JAPAN	
Broach	50	Yedo	500 000
Chanda	50	Osaka	370
BURMA, ARAKAN, and ANNAM		Kyoto	350
Arakan	100 000	Nagoya	69
Hanoi		Sendai	61
Ava		Nagasaki	59
Hué		Hiroshima	55
Pegu		Kagoshima	51
MALAYS			
Achin	45 000		
Kertasura			
Mataram			
Brunei	40		

top 100

TURKEY	
Smyrna	130 000
Damascus	80
Aleppo	80
Bagdad	
Bursa	65
Erzurum	
Basra	50
Mecca	50
PERSIA	
Meshhed	200 000
Qazvin	65
Isfahan	60
Tabriz	
Kerman	60
Shiraz	
AFGHANISTAN	
Lahore	
Kandahar	
TURKESTAN	
Bokhara	60 000
MOGULS	
Patna	200 000
Murshidabad	200
Dacca	135
Srinagar	100
Agra	
Benares	
Delhi	75
MARATHAS	
Surat	165 000
Ahmedabad	120
Ujjain	
Satara	
Tanjore	
Broach	50
BRITISH	
Calcutta	110 000
Bombay	77
Madras	55
FRENCH	
Chandernagore	95 000
Pondichéry	65
REST OF INDIA	
Hyderabad	225 000
Jodhpur	150
Lucknow	100
Jaipur	100
Fyzabad	90
Aurangabad	85
Rampur	
Bednur	
Seringapatam	60
Sira	60
Bareilly	50
Farrukhabad	50
Arcot	
DUTCH	
Batavia	94 000

SPANISH	
Manila	50 000
PORTUGUESE	
Macao	60 000
SIAM	
Ayutia	150 000
BURMA	
Ava	
ANNAM, ARAKAN, and ACHIN	
Hué	
Hanoi	
Arakan	
Achin	45 000
KOREA	
Seoul	183 000
Pyongyang	
Songdo	
CHINA	
Peking	900 000
Canton	500
Hangchow	350
Soochow	302
Nanking	285
Sian	195
Wuchang	165
Mukden	
Ningpo	144
Fatshan	130
Lanchow	130
Kingtehchen	120
Fuchow	
Chengtu	
Ninghsia	90
Chinkiang	90
Tientsin	80
Kaifeng	78
Amoy	
Yangchow	
Hwaian	
Kuku Khoto	
Lhasa	65
Nanchang	
Changsha	
Hsüchow	
Siangtan	
Siangyang	
Shanghai	60
Tsinan	
Yünnanfu	
Kweilin	
Kalgan	
JAPAN	
Yedo	509 000
Osaka	403
Kyoto	362
Nagoya	96
Kanazawa	78
Sendai	66
Kagoshima	57
Hiroshima	52

top 100

TURKEY		DUTCH	
Smyrna	125 000	Batavia	92 000
Damascus	90	SPANISH	
Erzurum	80	Manila	77 000
Bagdad	80	MALAYS	
Aleppo	70	Surakarta	105 000
Bursa	70	Jogjakarta	90
Basra	60	ANNAM	
Hama	50	Hué	
PERSIA		Hanoi	
Qazvin	60 000	KOREA	
Isfahan	50	Seoul	190 000
Meshhed	50	Pyongyang	
TURKESTAN		CHINA	
Bokhara		Peking	1 100 000
AFGHANISTAN		Canton	800
Srinagar	125 000	Hangchow	500
Kabul	80	Soochow	392
Peshawar	90	Sian	224
Kandahar		Nanking	220
MARATHAS		Ningpo	200
Delhi	125 000	Wuchang	
Poona	100	Mukden	
Ujjain	100	Fatshan	175
Ahmedabad	89	Fuchow	
Nagpur	80	Tientsin	
Baroda	80	Lanchow	150
Amritsar	80	Kingtehchen	138
Banda		Chungking	
Agra	60	Chengtu	110
Maheshwar		Chinkiang	106
OTHER INDIAN STATES		Shanghai	100
Lucknow	300 000	Nanchang	
Hyderabad	200	Changsha	
Jodhpur	80	Amoy	
Bharatpur	75	Kaifeng	80
Jaipur	72	Ninghsia	
Aurangabad	70	Wanhsien	
Rampur		Hwaian	
Farrukhabad	66	Yangchow	
Bareilly	65	Jehol	68
Bangalore	60	Tsinan	
Fyzabad	60	Siangtan	
BRITISH		Siangyang	
Patna	235 000	Lhasa	60
Calcutta	200	Kashgar	60
Murshidabad	185	Kweilin	
Benares	179	Liaoyang	
Bombay	174	Shaohing	
Surat	130	Kanchow	
Madras	125	Hsüchow	
Dacca	110	JAPAN	
Trichinopoly	80	Yedo	492 000
Muttra		Kyoto	377
Arcot		Osaka	373
Burdwan	52	Nagoya	97
BURMA		Kanazawa	97
Amarapura	175 000	Kagoshima	66
		Sendai	62

Cities of Asia, 1850

top 100

TURKEY	
Smyrna	150 000
Damascus	108
Bursa	100
Aleppo	95
Bagdad	80

OMAN	
Muscat	60 000

PERSIA	
Tabriz	125 000
Tehran	80
Isfahan	60

TURKESTAN	
Bokhara	70 000
Tashkent	65
Kokand	60

AFGHANISTAN	
Kabul	60 000

INDIA—practically all BRITISH	
Bombay	575 000
Calcutta	413
Madras	310
Lucknow	300
Patna	263
Hyderabad	200
Benares	185
Delhi	156
Bangalore	131
Nagpur	111
Amritsar	110
Cawnpore	108
Agra	108
Baroda	106
Bareilly	101
Jaipur	100
Surat	99
Ahmedabad	96
Murshidabad	96
Lahore	94
Multan	80
Rampur	80
Mirzapur	77
Trichinopoly	76
Gwalior	74
Poona	73
Amroha	72
Allahabad	70
Bharatpur	69
Farrukhabad	68
Muttra	65
Shahjahanpur	62
Dacca	60
Jhansi	60
Indore	60

BURMA	
Amarapura	

DUTCH	
Surakarta	100 000
Batavia	71
Surabaja	60

SPANISH	
Manila	114 000

SIAM	
Bangkok	160 000

ANNAM	
Hanoi	75 000
Hué	60

KOREA	
Seoul	194 000
Pyongyang	80

CHINA	
Peking	1 648 000
Canton	800
Hangchow	700
Soochow	550
Sian	275
Fuchow	250
Shanghai	250
Chengtu	240
Wuchang	
Ningpo	230
Nanking	200
Tientsin	200
Chungking	200
Mukden	180
Fatshan	175
Lanchow	170
Kingtehchen	144
Chinkiang	130
Siangtan	
Changsha	
Nanchang	
Kaifeng	95
Amoy	85
Liaoyang	80
Hwaian	
Wanhsien	
Siangyang	
Shaohing	
Tsinan	70
Jehol	70
Yarkand	70
Kalgan	70
Yangchow	
Hsüchow	60
Taiwan	60
Kulja	60

JAPAN	
Yedo	567 000
Kyoto	323
Osaka	300
Kanazawa	116
Nagoya	100
Kagoshima	72
Matsmaye	66

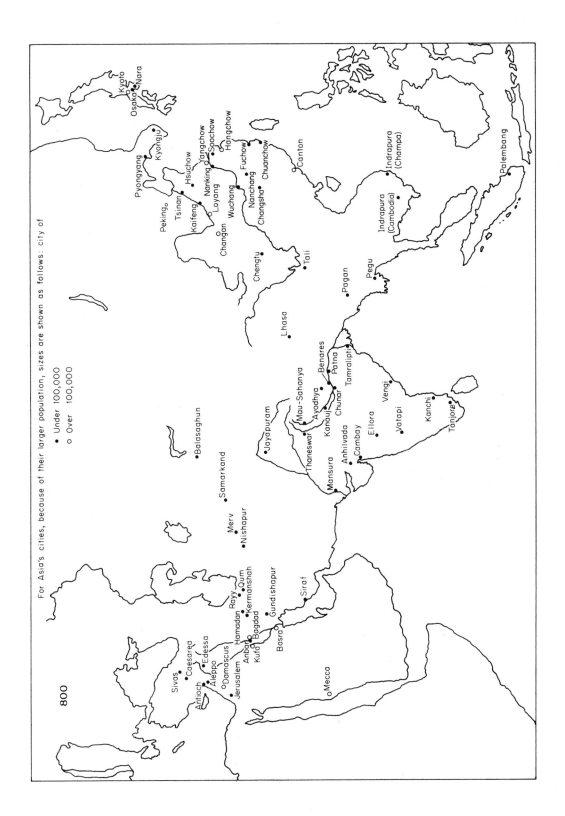

For Asia's cities, because of their larger population, sizes are shown as follows: city of

● Under 100,000
○ Over 100,000

800

Kyoto
Osaka ● Nara
Kyongju
Pyongyang
Peking
Tsinan
Kaifeng
Hsuchow
Nanking ● Yangchow
Loyang ○ Soochow
Changan
Wuchang Hangchow
Fuchow
Nanchang
Chengtu
Changsha Chuanchow
Canton
Tali
Pagan
Indrapura (Champa)
Palembang
Indrapura (Cambodia)
Pegu
Lhasa
Balasaghun
Samarkand
Jayapuram
Benares
Mau-Sohanya
Ayodhya Patna
Kanauj Chunar Tamralipti
Thaneswar Vengi
Anhilvada Ellora Vatapi
Merv Mansura Cambay Kanchi
Nishapur Tanjore
Ray ● Qum
Hamadan ● Kermanshah
Anbar Gundishapur
Kufa Bagdad Siraf
Basra
Sivas Caesarea
Edessa
Antioch Aleppo
Jerusalem ○ Damascus
○ Mecca

69

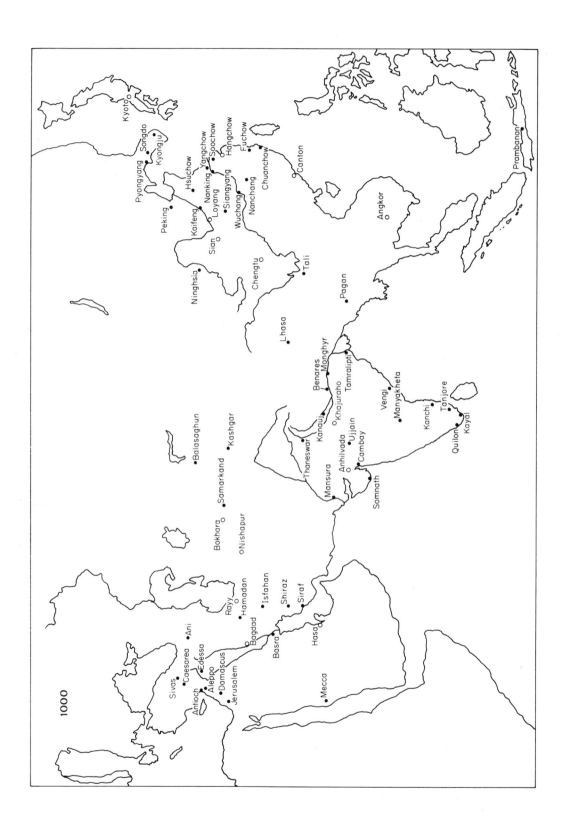

1000

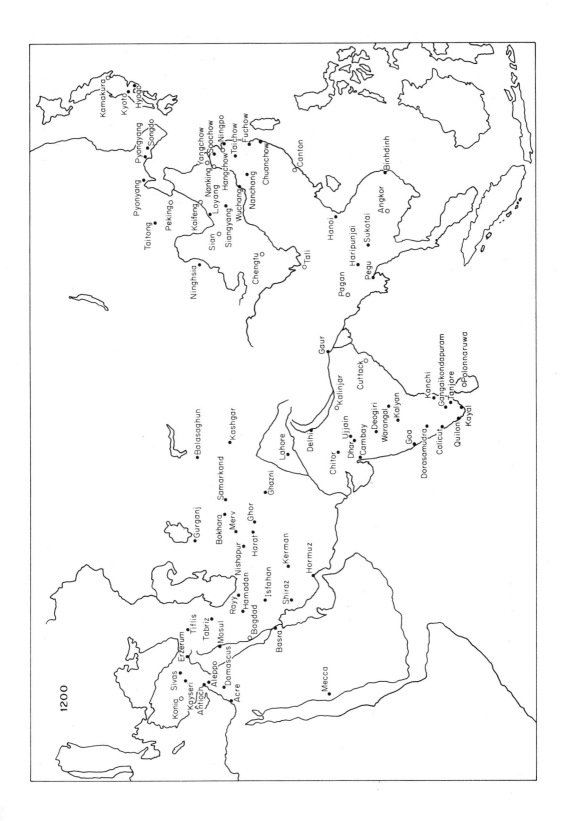

1200

Kamakura
Kyoto
Hyogo
Pyongyang
Songdo
Pyonyang
Pekingo
Taitong
Kaifeng
Nanking
Yangchow
Soochow
Loyang
Hangchow
Ningpo
Taichow
Fuchow
Chuanchow
Canton
Binhdinh
Sian
Siangyang
Wuchang
Nanchang
Angkor
Sukotai
Hanoi
Ninghsia
Chengtu
Tali
Haripunjai
Pegu
Pagan
Gaur
Cuttack
Kalinjar
Gangaikondapuram
Kanchi
Tanjore
Polonnaruwa
Balasaghun
Kashgar
Lahore
Delhi
Ujjain
Deogiri
Warangal
Kalyan
Kayal
Samarkand
Chitor
Dhar
Cambay
Goa
Dorasamudra
Calicut
Quilon
Gurganj
Bokhara
Merv
Ghor
Ghazni
Harat
Kerman
Nishapur
Hormuz
Rayy
Hamadan
Isfahan
Shiraz
Bagdad
Basra
Tiflis
Tabriz
Mosul
Erzerum
Sivas
Konia
Kayseri
Aleppo
Antioch
Damascus
Acre
Mecca

71

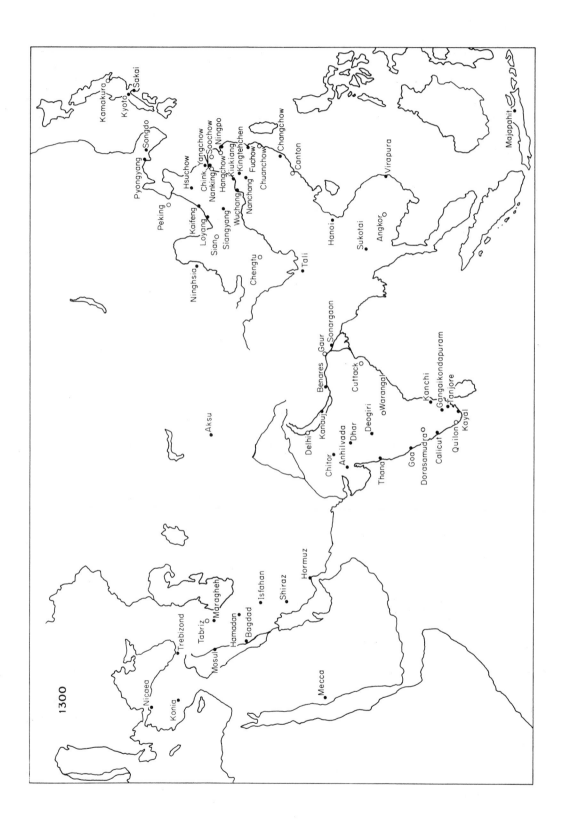

Kamakura
Kyoto
Sakai
Songdo
Pyongyang
Peking
Ninghsia
Kaifeng
Loyang
Sian
Hsuchow
Yangchow
Chink
Nanking
Siangyang
Wuchang
Chengtu
Tali
Soochow
Ningpo
Hangchow
Kingtehchen
Kiukiang
Nanchang
Fuchow
Chuanchow
Changchow
Canton
Hanoi
Sukotai
Angkor
Virapura
Majapahit

Aksu

Benares
Gaur
Sonargaon
Kanauj
Delhi
Cuttack
Warangal
Kanchi
Gangaikondapuram
Tanjore
Chitor
Anhilvada
Dhar
Deogiri
Kayal
Thana
Goa
Dorasamudra
Calicut
Quilon

Hormuz
Isfahan
Shiraz
Trebizond
Tabriz
Maragheh
Hamadan
Mosul
Bagdad
Mecca
Nicaea
Konia

1300

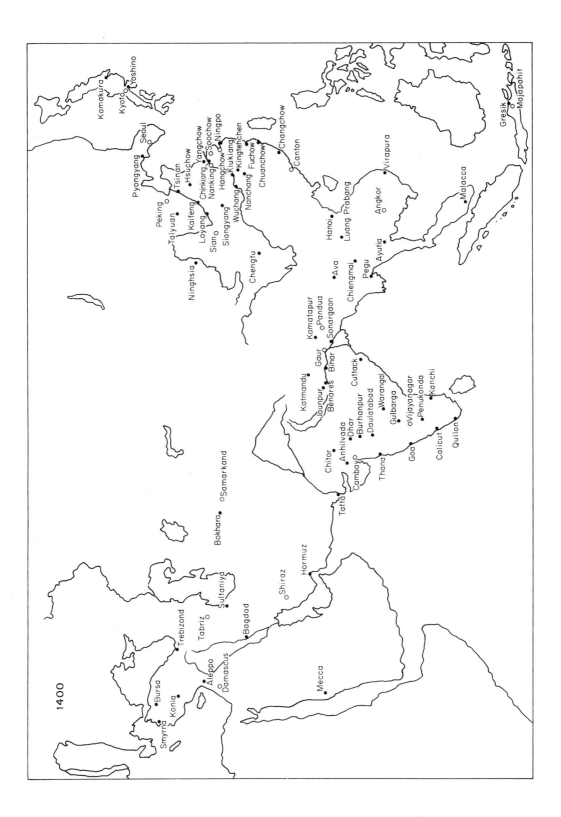

1400

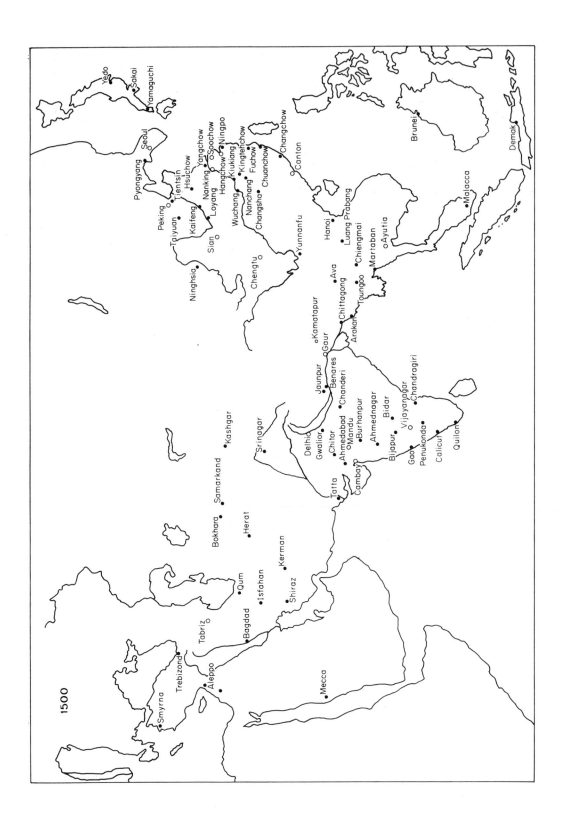

1500

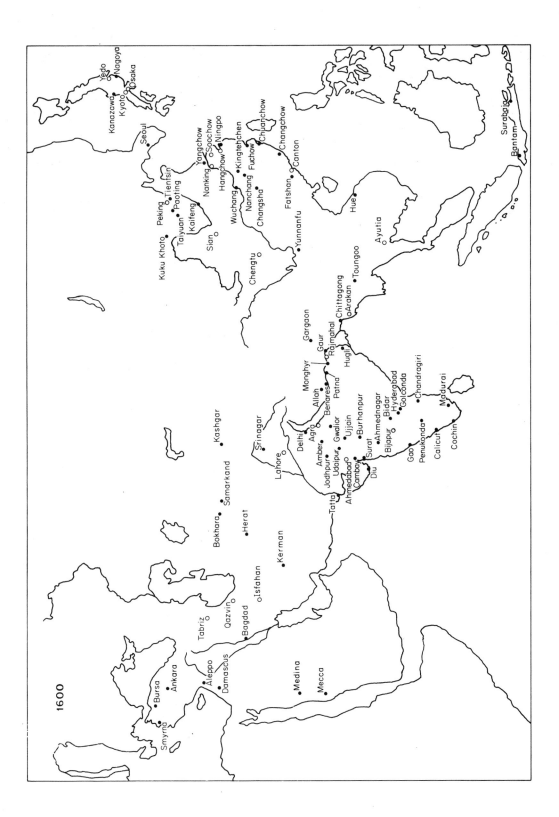

1600

Yedo
Nagoya
Kanazawa
Kyoto
Osaka
Seoul
Kuku Khoto
Peking
Tientsin
Paoting
Taiyuan
Kaifeng
Sian
Nanking
Yangchow
Soochow
Hangchow
Kingtehchen
Ningpo
Chuanchow
Changchow
Fuchow
Wuchang
Nanchang
Changsha
Fatshan
Canton
Chengtu
Yunnanfu
Hue
Ayutia
Bantam
Surabaja
Toungoo
Chittagong
Arakan
Gargaon
Gaur
Rajmahal
Hugli
Monghyr
Allah
Benares
Patna
Chandragiri
Madurai
Hyderabad
Bidar
Golconda
Agra
Delhi
Amber
Udaipur
Jodhpur
Gwalior
Ujjain
Burhanpur
Ahmednagar
Penukonda
Srinagar
Lahore
Surat
Bijapur
Goa
Calicut
Cochin
Ahmedabad
Cambay
Diu
Tatta
Kashgar
Samarkand
Bokhara
Herat
Kerman
Isfahan
Qazvin
Bagdad
Tabriz
Aleppo
Damascus
Medina
Mecca
Bursa
Ankara
Smyrna

75

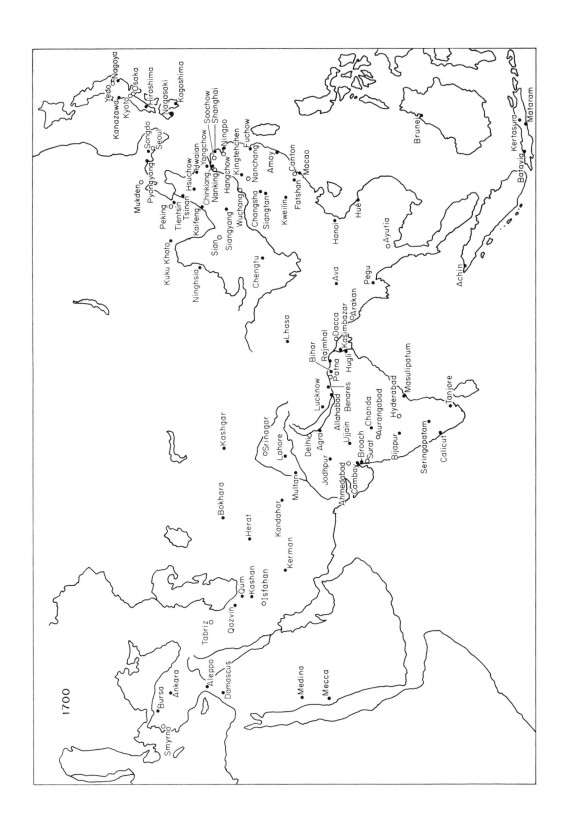

1700

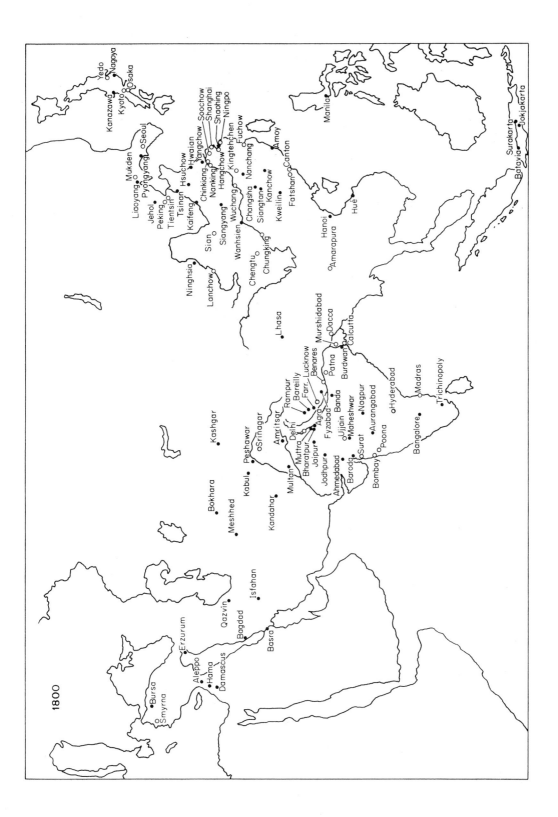

1800

Yedo
Nagoya
Kanazawa
Kyoto
Osaka
Seoul
Mukden
Pyongyang
Liaoyang
Jehol
Peking
Tientsin
Tsinan
Hsuchow
Kaifeng
Sian
Siangyang
Wuchang
Wanhsien
Chengtu
Chungking
Ninghsia
Lanchow
Chinkiang
Yangchow
Nanking
Hangchow
Kingtehchen
Soochow
Shanghai
Shaohing
Ningpo
Hwaian
Fuchow
Changsha
Nanchang
Siangtan
Kanchow
Kweilin
Fatshan
Canton
Amoy
Manila
Hanoi
Amarapura
Hue
Surakarta
Batavia
Jokjakarta

Lhasa
Murshidabad
Dacca
Calcutta
Patna
Burdwan
Benares
Lucknow
Farr.
Rampur
Bareilly
Trichinopoly
Madras
Kashgar
Peshawar
Srinagar
Amritsar
Delhi
Agra
Fyzabad
Banda
Ujjain
Maheshwar
Nagpur
Hyderabad
Bangalore
Muttra
Bharatpur
Jaipur
Aurangabad
Multan
Jodhpur
Surat
Poona
Ahmedabad
Baroda
Bombay
Kabul
Bokhara
Meshhed
Kandahar

Isfahan
Qazvin
Bagdad
Basra
Erzurum
Aleppo
Hama
Damascus
Bursa
Smyrna

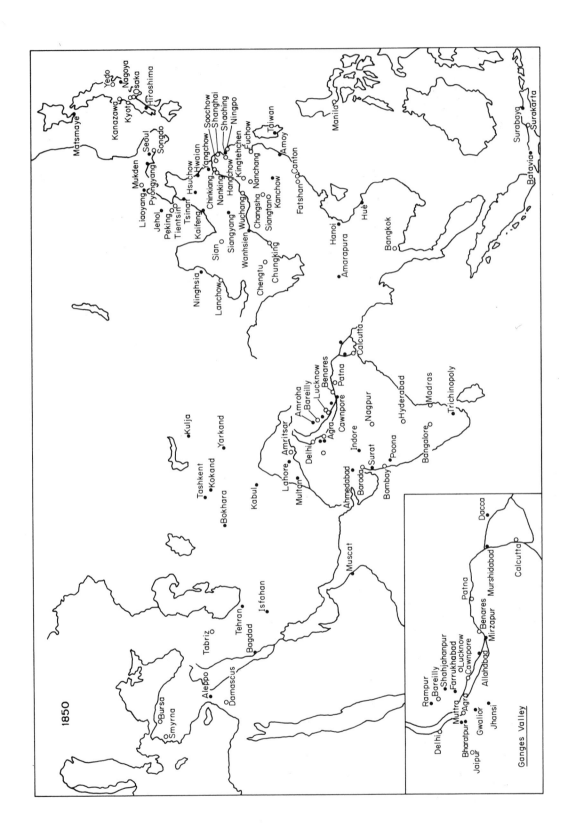

1850

Matsmaye
Yedo
Kanazawa
Kyoto
Nagoya
Osaka
Hiroshima
Kanazawa
Seoul
Songdo
Pyŏngyang
Mukden
Jehol
Peking
Liaoyang
Tientsin
Tsinan
Kaifeng
Hsuchow
Hwaian
Chinkiang
Nanking
Yangchow
Soochow
Shanghai
Shaohing
Ningpo
Hangchow
Kingtehchen
Fuchow
Nanchang
Changsha
Siangtano
Kanchow
Fatshan
Canton
Amoy
Taiwan
Manila
Sian
Siangyang
Wuchang
Wanhsien
Chengtu
Chungking
Hanoi
Hué
Bangkok
Amarapura
Ninghsia
Lanchow
Kulja
Yarkand
Kokand
Tashkent
Bokhara
Kabul
Multan
Lahore
Amritsar
Delhi
Agra
Amroha
Bareilly
Lucknow
Benares
Patna
Cawnpore
Indore
Nagpur
Hyderabad
Madras
Trichinopoly
Bangalore
Ahmedabad
Baroda
Surat
Bombay
Poona
Muscat
Isfahan
Tehran
Bagdad
Tabriz
Aleppo
Damascus
Bursa
Smyrna
Calcutta
Surabaya
Surakarta
Batavia

Ganges Valley

Delhi
Jaipur
Bharatpur
Muttra
Agra
Gwalior
Jhansi
Rampur
Bareilly
Shahjahanpur
Farrukhabad
Lucknow
Cawnpore
Allahabad
Benares
Mirzapur
Murshidabad
Patna
Dacca
Calcutta

78

1360 B.C.

Thebes	Largest in Egypt, where Memphis had 10,000 priests in 2100 B.C.	Kees, p. 158
Knossos	3/4 of Sparta's peak size	Strabo, 2:196
Khattushas	3.5 miles around (200 hectares in area: times 200 for population)	Bittel, map at p. 26, p. 50
Mycenae	Little if any over 30,000	Alsop, p. 99
Amarna (Akhetaton)	30,000	Griffith, p. 304
Mohenjo-daro	1 sq. mi.	Chambers, 1967

1200 B.C.

Thebes	100 gates (cf. Kazan, 1552, and Constantinople's 360 according to Schiltberger, p. 101)	Homer, "Iliad," 9:383-4
Khattushas	As at 1360 B.C.	
Athens	40,000 in Attica (c. 1/3 rural)	Plato, "Critias" 112 A-D
Mycenae	As at 1360 B.C.	

650 B.C.

Nineveh	120,000	Jonah 4:11 in Bible
Loyang	Wall 13.8 km. (8.5 miles, enclosing 1,170 ha.) through much or all the period 723-464 B.C.	Hsu, p. 134
Yenhsiatu	23 km. around (3,000 ha.) by end of the period 723-464 B.C.	Hsu, p. 135
Marib	Wall 6 Roman miles (the country was at its peak, and Marib Dam recently completed)	Pliny, 6:32:160
Miletus	Decidedly the largest Greek city (cf. Athens for size)	Ency. Brit, 1910
Athens	40,000 in Attica (c. 1/3 rural)	Plato, "Critias," 112 A-D

430 B.C.

Babylon	889 hectares (times 300, assuming a rather high density)	Kahrstedt
"	Many 3-4 storey houses	Kinneir, p. 270
Ecbatana	Area 2/3 of Babylon and larger than Athens	Diodorus in Beloch, 1886, p. 482
Athens	155,000	Gomme, p. 47
Sravasti	57,000 families c.500 B.C. (likely declined by 430)	Buddhaghosha in Puri, p. 106
Champa	Capital of India's main kingdom roughly 490-450 B.C.	Dey
Loyang	Wall still enclosed 1,170 hectares in 464 B.C. (times 125 for old-wall Chinese density; cf. Sian, 700 A.D.)	Hsu, p. 134
Syracuse	Over 100,000	Beloch, 1886, p. 478
Memphis	100,000	" " p. 477
Rome	150,000 in 500s B.C. (then probably declined)	Ency. Brit., 1853, XIX, p. 362n
Chicheng	210,000 in 221 B.C. when destroyed	Hsu, p. 137
Soochow	Wall 8 miles around	Crow, p. 104
Corinth	70,000	Beloch, 1886, p. 478
Marib	Wall 6 Roman miles	Pliny, 6:32:160

Benares	10,000 monks (times 5) in 440 B.C.	"Bihar," p. 335
Jerusalem	49,942 in 445 B.C.	Nehemiah 7:66 in Bible
Vaisali	7,707 heads of families	Roy, p. 200
Sparta	40,000	Beloch, 1886, p. 483
Argos	40,000	" " p. 478
Tarentum	40,000	" " "
Agrigentum (Acragas)	40,000	" " "
Megalopolis	40,000	" " "
Sidon	40,000 in 346 B.C.	Ency. Brit., 1910, "Phoenicia"
Tyre	Under 40,000; over 10,000 burghers	Beloch, 1886, p. 479
Cyrene	Under 40,000; over 10,000 burghers	" " p. 478
Corcyra	Under 40,000; over 10,000 burghers	" " "

200 B.C.

Patna	21 miles around; 350,000 at least at peak	Basham, p. 201; Brockhaus 1864
Alexandria	300,000 free citizens (c. 400,000 total) at c. 60 B.C.	Diodorus, 17:52:6
Seleucia	About Alexandria's size c. 1 A.D. (Likely at 200 B.C. too)	Beloch, 1886, p. 479
Carthage	Hardly over 200,000	" " p. 467
Rome	Rising fast. 322,000 in 147 B.C.	Ency. Brit., 1853, XIX, p. 362n
Antioch	120,000 in 145 B.C.	1 Maccabees in Douai Bible
Jerusalem	120,000	Aristaeus in Jewish Ency.
Anuradhapura	200,000 (Seems improbably high; likely based on some traveler's "over 100,000")	Pliny, 6:24:86
	15 km. around (1300 ha., at 100 per ha. amounts to 130,000)	Madrolle, 1916
Balkh	6.5 miles around	Ency. Brit., 1910
Rhodes	21,000 citizens over 18, and 10,000 metics	Livi, p. 29
Capua	181 ha. by 220 B.C.	Kahrstedt
	Taken by Rome and treated severely	Ency. Brit., 1910
London	70,000 slain in London, Colchester, and Verulamium in 61 A.D. (presumably over half in London)	Tacitus, 14:33

100 A.D.

Rome	Aurelian's wall, made in 271-80, enclosed 1,305 hectares (at 500 p. ha., a high density, this equals 650,000 population). Augustus's wall had been slightly larger	Ency. Brit., 1853, XIX, p. 362n
Alexandria	400,000	Diodorus, 17:52:6
Seleucia	600,000 about 50 A.D. (seems high)	Pliny, 6:30:122
	300-400,000 in 165 A.D. (presumably with Ctesiphon)	Downey, 1961, p. 583
	Its sister-city Ctesiphon founded 129 B.C. and grew at Seleucia's expense. 100,000 carried off from Seleucia in 165 A.D.	Ency. Brit., 1853
Ephesus	200,000	Beloch, 1886, p. 480
Antioch	200,000 about 125 A.D. (seems slightly high; cf. area in 380)	Chrysostom in Downey, 1961, p. 583
Anuradhapura	See in 200 B.C.	
Apamea	117,000 free citizens under Augustus	Chambers, 1967
Pergamum	120,000 probable, 180,000 possible	Beloch 1886, p. 480
Cádiz	100,000	Kahrstedt
Corinth	100,000	American Cycl.
Sardis	100,000	Harvard Graduate School Newsletter, March 31, 1969, p. 3
Carthage	80/184 as large as the former city, which had c. 200,000	Livy (epitome, 51); Beloch, 1886, p. 485
Taxila	6 sq. miles	Belfour
Teotihuacán	45,000 in 150 A.D.	Bernal, p. 30
Milan	133 ha.; 30-40,000	Beloch, 1886, p. 486
Autun	Under Rome eventually reached 250 hectares in area	Zocca, p. 111
London	Had recovered likely at least its importance as in 200 B.C.	

361

Constantinople	Capital from 330. In 447 it covered 960 built-up hectares.	Stein in Russell, 1958, p. 66
Rome	Declining as Constantinople rose	
Ctesiphon	See 100 A.D. Country thriving, but Romans had wholly destroyed Seleucia across the river	
Alexandria	Half its old peak size of 640 ha.	Durant, "Caesar and Christ," 1950 p. 666; Bury, II, p. 272
Antioch	150,000 in 363 6 miles around	Libanius in Downey, 1961, p. 583 Downey, 1962, p. 23
Ayodhya	Probably Gupta capital 325-75; twice its size of 70,000 in 1870	Balfour, "Faizabad"
Teotihuacán	90,000 in 350	Bernal, p. 30
Nishapur	15,000-pace wall built in 300s (9 miles, enclosing c. 1,300 ha.; times 40–as at 1000 A.D.)	Bosworth, p. 159
Trier	60,000	Ewig, p. 123
Jerusalem	Rebuilt, about half its former size, c. 135 A.D.	Ency. of Islam, 1897, "Kuds"
	Walls strengthened and 2 churches built c. 326	Ency. Brit., 1910
Thessalonica	Its 7,000 men slain in 390 (militia, times 6)	" " " "Salonica"

622

Constantinople	960 ha. built up by 447	Stein in Russell, p. 66
Loyang	109,000 households in 520s; partly laid waste by 547; in 622 co-capital	Ho, pp. 66, 95
Alexandria	32,000 dinars head-tax on adult males in 645 after Arab conquest 640-1 (times 6 for population)	Lane-Poole, p. 15n
Teotihuacán	125,000 probable	Millon, p. 1080
	100,000 in capital abandoned c.660 according to Nahua tradition	Howe, p. 163
Kanauj	9 miles around (peaked under Harsha, who moved N Indian capital there and ruled 606-47)	Playfair, V, p. 420
Kanchi	10,000 Buddhist monks, 80 Hindu temples	Hsüan Dsang, II, pp. 228-9
Antioch	Much declined since the earthquake of 526	Downey, 1961, p. 583
Aleppo	12,000 militia in 637	Baurain, p. 22
Isanapura	Capital of Cambodia c. 610-637, with eventually 20,000 families	Briggs, pp. 49, 51
Mecca	70,000 "angels"	Wüstenfeld, IV, p. 1
Malakuta	7 miles around (40 *li*)	Hsüan Dsang, II, p. 230
Benares	3,000 Buddhist monks, 10,000 Hindu monks (times 5); 8 miles around	" " "
Canton	Foreign port formally established c. 700; road north opened 705.	Berncastle, II, p. 111
Nishapur	Had same role as in 361, under same dynasty	
Hangchow	12-mile wall, half length of the one built in 893. (Density there seems to have been always low)	Crow, p. 94
Rome	50,000	Enci. Italiana
Jerusalem	92,000, all killed or removed in 614; 62,000 about 630	Cambridge Medieval History, II, p. 290; Margoliouth, p. 195
Kausambi	5 miles around	Hsüan Dsang, I, p. 235
Valabhi	5 miles around; 6,000 Buddhist monks (and probably some Hindus)	" " II, p. 266
Stakhr	40,000 in 649	Ency. of Islam, 1897
Kamarupa	5 miles around	Hsüan Dsang, II, p. 195
Pundravardhana	5 miles around	" " " p. 194

Italy

All underscored figures are our own estimates.

Alessandria

1174	15,000	Founding population	Haulleville, II, p. 194
1200	20,000		
1542	8,800	With 1,387 hearths	Beloch, 1937, III, p. 229
c.1600	13,900		" " " "
1734	11,619		" " " "
1741	22,084		Enci. Italiana
1750	21,000		
1774	18,581		Beloch, 1937, III, p. 229
1800	31,000		
1802	32,225		Morse, II, p. 390
1839	39,374		Enci. Italiana
1848	43,892	18,955 plus suburbs (20,898) and garrison (4,039)	Harper
1850	44,000		

Amalfi

975		Larger than Naples, and 1st in mainland Italy	Ibn Hawqal in Enci. Italiana
peak		70,000 (some probably outside city)	Ency. Brit., 1910
1000	35,000	See Naples, Rome	
1039-1100		Generally unfree	Enci. Italiana
1135, 1137		Smashed by Pisa	
1320	10-15,000	Including suburbs	Beloch, 1886, I, pp. 243, 272

Asti

1190	15,000	12 churches	Molina, pp. 71-72
1200	15,000		
1571	8,339		Beloch, 1937, III, p. 279
1734	13,269		" " " "
1774	14,365		" " " "
c.1800	21,225		Morse, II, p. 390
1839	24,283		Hoffmann

Bari

885-1071		Capital of Byzantine South Italy	
1278	10,000	2,000 hearths	Beloch, 1937, I, p. 256
1532	7,000	1,557 hearths	" " " "
1669	11,000	2,345 hearths	" " " "
1800	18,000		Enci. Italiana
1861	34,000		" "

Bergamo

1000	13,000	11 churches within walls	Belotti, p. 237
1548	17,707		Beloch, 1937, III, p. 145
1596	23,393		" " " "
1600	23,000		
1700	30,000		
1702	30,000		" " " "
1750	33,000		
1785	35,880		" " " "
1800	27,000		
1805	24,459		Morse, II, p. 394
1843	31,771		Cantù, I, p. 237
1850	33,000		
1857	35,733		" " "

Bologna

1100s		Considerable growth	Hessel, pp. 437-8
1200	35,000		
c.1200-1238		4 new parishes, and then some	" pp. 438-40
1249	55,000	Over 50,000; 16,000 families in its county (11,000 in 1371)	" p. 271n
1300	40,000	After loss of freedom 1280	Beloch, 1937, II, p. 98
1371	40,000		
1496	55,000		"　　"　　"　　"
1500	55,000		
1569	61,731		"　　"　　"　　"
1588	72,395	Not including 19,255 in extra-mural "suburbi," some of which may be urban (same for later dates)	"　　"　　" p. 101
1600	62,844		"　　"　　"　　"
1680	65,002		"　　"　　"　　"
1700	63,000		
1701	63,346		"　　"　　"　　"
1741	64,429		"　　"　　"　　"
1750	66,000		
1759	68,882		"　　"　　"　　"
1800	66,948		"　　"　　"　　"
1844	75,000		Ency. Brit., 1853
1850	71,500		Harper

Brescia

1249	21,000	7 parishes and (1258) 4,000 militia	Treccani, I, pp. 673, 680
1388	26,000	22 religious parts, i.e., churches	Lonati, p. 31
1400	27,000		
1440	30,000		Beloch, 1937, II, p. 121
1493	56,060		"　　"　　" p. 122
1500	61,000		
1505	65,000		"　　"　　" p. 124
1598	42,000		"　　"　　"　　"
1600	42,000		
c.1630	43,235		"　　"　　" pp. 124-5
1700	37,000		
1730	35,000		"　　"　　" p. 126
1750	37,000		
1764	38,889		"　　"　　"　　"
1785	38,291		"　　"　　"　　"
1800	41,000		
1805	41,972		Morse I, p. 394
1850	34,995		Harper
1862	40,499		Lippincott, 1868

Catania

1169	15,000	All died from volcanic eruption	Burigny, I, p. 490
1194		Sacked	
1277	10,000	Estimated from taxes	Beloch, 1937, I, p. 144
1501	10,000	14,216 less c. 1/4 in rural hamlets	"　　"　　" p. 145
1595	18,000	25,024 less c. 1/4 in rural hamlets	"　　"　　"　　"
1616	21,000	27,788 less c. 1/4 in rural hamlets	"　　"　　"　　"
1681	14,000	18,914 less c. 1/4 in rural hamlets	"　　"　　"　　"
1693		Volcano killed 9,000	"　　"　　" p. 146
1713	16,222		"　　"　　" p. 145
1747	25,715		"　　"　　"　　"

1750	26,000		
1798	48,000	45,081 plus cloistered clergy	Beloch, 1937, I, p. 146
1800	48,000		
1831	52,433		Hoffmann
1850	63,000		
1861	68,810		. Enci. Italiana

Cremona

c.1098-1322		A free commune	
1160	20,000		Haulleville, II, p. 161
1200	25,000		
1259	30,000	5,000 militia	Cavitelli, p. 92
1300	38,000		
1304	38,000	6,400 militia	'' p. 103
1360		5,000 cavalry	'' p. 134
1400	35,000		
1500	40,000		
1502	40,000		Beloch, 1937, III, p. 202
1599	37,184		'' '' '' p. 203
1600	37,000		
1686	23,000		'' '' '' p. 205
1700	23,000		
1750	24,110		'' '' '' ''
1800	21,111		Ungewitter, I, p. 741
1850	28,000		
1851	28,328		'' '' ''

Ferrara

768	9,000	3 churches	Mari and Savonuzzi, p. 2
1000	12,000	About 6 parishes	Scalabrini, pp. 63, 67, 232, 298, 354, 590
1200	27,000	18 parishes (ratio declining as Ferrara became a staunch pro-Papal center)	'' as above and pp. 2, 32, 64, 67, 73, 75, 130, 314, 336, 341, 358, 369
1300	36,000	23 parishes	'' and pp. 72, 163, 259, 300, 362
1310		3,470 citizens took an oath	Istoja, p. 2
1400	40,000	25 parishes	Scalabrini, as above, and pp. 64, 161
1500		25 parishes	
c.1500	42,000	Wall 4.6 miles in circuit (c. 340 hectares in area)	Correspondence from Ferrara city library
1577	46,000	41,710 plus c. 2800 clergy and c. 1500 Jews	Beloch, 1937, II, p. 112
1599	34,600	32,000 plus suburbs (2,621 in 1601)	'' '' '' p. 111
1600	33,000		
1601	32,860		'' '' '' p. 112
1676	28,000		'' '' '' ''
1700	27,000		
1701	27,326		'' '' '' ''
1740	30,291		Beloch, 1937, II, p. 112
1750	30,000		
1797	30,117		'' '' '' ''
1800	30,000		
1816	31,500		Enci. Italiana
1850	38,000		
1853	39,367		'' ''

Florence (Firenze)

1172-c.1200		New wall enclosed 105 hectares, triple the earlier area	Beloch, 1937, II, p. 128
1198	15,000	Very rough estimate	" " " pp. 129, 179
1200	15,000		
1200-1300		Grew 5-fold	Dante in Lestocquoy, p. 176
1280		Ate 3/7 as much bread as Milan	Renouard, pp. 278, 491
c.1300	60,000	New wall enclosed 512 hectares	Beloch, 1937, II, p. 128
1338		Ate 15% less bread than in 1280	Renouard, p. 491
1347	55,000		Beloch, 1937, II, p. 148
1380	61,500		" " " "
1400	61,000		
"		Pestilence killed 11,492	" " " "
1401	50,000	12,662 heads of families	" " " "
1470	54,000		" " " "
1500	70,000	Peak of Florence's glory	
1520	70,000		" " " "
1562	59,216		" " " "
1600	65,000		
1629	70,000		" " " p. 143
1688	66,000	64,428 plus omissions	" " " p. 146
1700	69,000		
1738	77,835		" " " p. 148
1750	74,000		
1751	73,951		" " " "
1794	80,560		" " " "
1800	79,000		
1806	78,093		" " " "
			line 6
1847	102,154		Enci. Italiana
1850	107,000		
1852	110,714		Ency. Brit. 1853

Genoa

1000	15,000	5 (parish) churches	Catholic Ency.
1200	30,000	10 (parish) churches	" "
1265-1291		Notarized papers increased 40%	Renouard, p. 159
1300	100,000		Ency. Brit. 1970
1380		Peak: lost its fleet to Venice	
1400	100,000		
1460	120,000	In 7,800 houses (5,600 within walls) with up to 6 hearths per house; population probably exaggerated (see next entry)	Heers, pp. 44-45
1500	62,000	60,000. Based on 6,298 houses, 2 hearths per house (1681/82 data), and 5 persons per hearth; plus c. 2,000 in suburbs (Beloch's arithmetic is faulty)	Beloch, 1937, III, p. 288
1600	70,000		" " " p. 295
1681	65,000		" " " pp. 295, 360
1700	67,000		
1750	72,000		
1788	77,563		" " " p. 294
1799	90,835		" " " "
1800	90,000	Before siege of that year	
1802	86,063		" " " "
1848	100,382		English Cyclopaedia
1850	103,000		
1855	112,000	Including garrison	Ency. Brit., 1853-(60)

Lecce

1532	17,000	20,400; 3,711 hearths (less 13%; cf. 1921)	Enci. Italiana; Beloch, I, p. 258
1595	31,000	36,000; 6,529 hearths (less 13%; cf. 1921)	Enci. Italiana; Beloch 1939, I, p. 258, III, p. 357
1600	30,000		
1648	22,000	25,400 (less 13%)	Enci. Italiana
1669	15,000	18,000 (less 13%)	" "
c.1800	13,000	15,500 (less 13%)	Beloch, 1937, I, p. 258
1861	18,000	21,300 (less 13%)	Enci. Italiana
1921		39,290, 87% urban	" "

Leghorn (Livorno)

1563	563		Beloch, 1937, II, p. 177
1601	3,958		" " " p. 178
1700	15,000	13,532 plus Jews and garrison	" " " "
1738	28,273	Including Jews	" " " "
1750	31,000		
1766	36,500	32,753 plus Jews	" " " "
1800	52,611		" " III, p. 361
1845	80,195		Hoffmann
1850	84,000		
1851	84,907		"

Lucca

c.1200	10,000	New wall begun, enclosing 75 hectares	Beloch, 1937, II, p. 165
1331	18-20,000		" " " pp. 165-6, 179
1400	23,000		
1500	30,000		Ency. Brit. 1910
1583	24,000		Beloch, 1937, II, p. 166
1600	24,000		
1645	25,000		" " " "
1700	23,000		" " " "
1744	20,770		" " " "
1750	20,000		
1800	17,000		
1806	17,160		Hassel, 1819, VI, p. 531

Mantua

1000	12,000	4 parish churches	Enci. Italiana, "Mantova"
1400	25,000		
1463	26,407	May exclude suburbs	Beloch, 1937, II, p. 287
1491	23,185	May exclude suburbs	" " " "
1500	26,000		
1511	30,000	Including suburbs	" " " p. 288
1592	31,422		" " " p. 290
1600	31,000		
1624	30,991		" " " "
1676	21,238		" " " p. 292
1700	21,000		
1714-1727	c.21,000	Estimated from births	Beloch, 1937, II, p. 292
1750	27,000		
1751	27,000	23,668 plus suburbs	" " " pp. 293-294
1789	24,000	21,787 plus Jews	" " " "
1800	22,000		
1802	21,902		" " " p. 293
1850	28,000		
1857	29,884		Brockhaus

Messina

1000s		Village, became a bishopric 1096	Trasselli, p. 12
1100s		Grew very fast, from the crusades	D. Smith, pp. 31, 55
1200	30,000		
1200-50		Kept stable and peaceful by Federick II	" p. 56
1277	30,000	Taxed 2/3 as much as Palermo	Beloch, I, pp. 136, 152
1300	25,000	After the "Sicilian Vespers"	
1501	21,000	31,385 less c. 1/3 in rural hamlets	" " p. 139
1595	50,000		" " p. 136
1600	61,000		
1606	72,000	100,774 less c.1/3 rural, plus clergy	" " p. 137
1653	47,000	71,426 less c.1/3 rural	" " p. 142
1713	43,000	40,393 plus clergy	" " p. 140, cf. p. 142
1747	28,000	26,699 plus clergy	" " p. 141, cf. p. 142
1798	35,000	49,504 less c. 1/3 in rural hamlets, plus cloistered clergy	" " " "
1831	57,000	86,772 less c. 1/3 in rural hamlets	" " p. 143
1850	64,000	97,074 less c. 1/3 in rural hamlets	Ency. Brit. 1853

Milan

800	25,000		
c.875	30,000	Wall rebuilt	Enci. Italiana
975		Smaller than Amalfi (cf. Amalfi)	
1000	30,000		
1045-57		Town meetings for whole population	" "
c.1170	58,000	234 hectares in area	Beloch, III, p. 175
1200	60,000		
1274		13,000 houses, some with several families	Bonvesin in Renouard, pp. 478
1288		60,000; 12,500 hearths; population estimate too low (cf. Florence)	Beloch, 1937, III, p. 190
1295		150,000	Calco in Renouard, p. 491
1300	100,000		
1400	125,000	Peak of its power	
1492	90,000	18,300 hearths	Beloch, 1937, III, p. 190
1500	104,000		
1503	110,000	Based on mortality	" " " "
1576	110,000		" " " pp. 182-183
1600	119,000		
1628	130,000		" " " p. 190
1688	125,829		" " " '
1700	124,000		
1715	123,595		" " " "
1750	123,618		" " " "
1800	134,528		" " " "
1850	193,000	30,000 for Corpi Santi	
1851	194,792	With Corpi Santi	English Cyclopaedia

Mondovi

1559-71		Savoyard ducal residence	
1571	20,000	25,999 in commune (cf. 1871)	Beloch, 1937, III, p. 279
1600	11,000		
1612	8,000	10,903 in commune (cf. 1871)	" " " "
1734	5,000	6,975 in commune (cf. 1871)	" " " "
1774	12,000	17,614 in commune (cf. 1871)	" " " "
1800	15,000		
1809	16,000	21,577 in commune (cf. 1871)	Morse, II, p. 390
1850	13,000		
1871	11,958	16,543, 11,958 urban	Enci. Italiana

Naples

763-1300	30-35,000	Over the entire period	Enci. Italiana
800	30,000		
1000	30,000		
1200	30,000		
1278	30-36,000	Estimated from the tax	Beloch, 1937, I, p. 170
1300	40,000		
1340	60,000		Enci. Italiana
1399	40,000		" "
1400	40,000		
1435	60,000		" "
1500	125,000	Faster growth in 16th century; cf. Palermo, Rome, Valencia	
1547	245,000		Beloch, 1937, I, p. 177
1599	275,000		" " " "
1600	275,000		
1606	280,746		" " " p. 176
1656		Pestilence killed 160,000	" " " p. 180
1688	186,769		" " " p. 185
1700	207,000		
1707	220,000	215,588 plus cloistered clergy	" " " p. 181
1742	305,021		" " " "
1750	324,000		
1797	438,000		Enci. Italiana
1800	430,000		
1801	426,339		Beloch, 1937, I, p. 183
1850	416,000		
1851	416,475		English Cyclopaedia

Padua

601		2 churches	Foligno, p. 10
1000	10,000		
1000s	10,000	Could scarcely be over this size	Beloch, 1937, III, p. 65
1195		76 hectares in area since Roman times	" " " "
1174	17,500	2,614 houses, or 3/4 the city, were burned	" " " "
1200	20,000		
c.1250		11,000 killed, the pro-Papal half of the population	A. Allen, p. 79
1281	39,000		Torres, p. 58
1300	39,000		
1320	30,000	Estimate of 25-30,000 (after unfree interval 1311-18)	Beloch, 1937, III, p. 74
1397	34,200		" " " "
1400	34,000		
1500	29,000	27,000 plus "termini"	" " " " cf. p. 69
1586	30,600		" " " p. 70
1600	34,000		
1605	36,054		" " " "
1648	32,714		" " " p. 74
1700	37,000		
1730	40,000		Beloch, 1937, III, p. 74
1750	40,000		
1766	40,795		" " " "
1785	41,753		" " " "
1800	45,000		
1802	45,475		" " " "
1837	35,225		Hoffmann
1850	47,000		
1857	53,584		"

Palermo

831		3,000 (adult males?)	Diehl, p. 56
972		5 quarters; 300 mosques—only Cordova had more	Ibn Hawqal in Waern, pp. 14, 16
1000	75,000		
1061		100,000 at most	Enci. Italiana
1061	90,000	Defended by 15,000 (times 6)	Amari, III, p. 75n
1127-97		Capital of Norman South Italy	
1200	150,000		
1277	50,000	Estimated from tax	Beloch, 1937, I, p. 152
1300	40,000	On historical grounds (Sicilian vespers)	
1374	26,000	4,082 hearths within wall (times 6; cf. 1606), plus clergy and Jews	" " " p. 135
1400	27,000		
1479	33,000	5,109 hearths within wall (times 6), plus clergy and small children	" " " p. 120
1500	48,000		
1501	48,000	8,000 hearths within wall, times 6 (Beloch estimates 25,000 population)	" " " "
1515	66,000		" " " p. 135
1591	99,631		" " " pp. 127-129
1600	105,000		
1606	110,000	104,983 with 18,518 hearths, plus total clergy	" " " p. 127
1625	135,000	128,417 with 19,246 hearths, plus total clergy	" " " p. 130
1700	113,000		
1737	107,000	102,106 plus total clergy	" " " p. 132
1747	123,000	117,600 plus total clergy	" " " "
1750	124,000		
1798	145,000	140,540 plus cloistered clergy	" " " p. 133
1800	146,000		
1815	158,000	152,294 plus cloistered clergy	" " " p. 134
1831	173,478		Hoffmann
1850	182,000		
1858	186,170		"

Parma

1261		26 guilds	Butler, p. 192
1395	20,000		Beloch, 1937, II, p. 243
1400	17,000		
1404	15,000		" " " "
1500	18,000		
1509	19,034		" " " "
1600	33,000	Estimated from baptisms	" " " "
1700	35,000		" " " "
1750	34,000		
1799	33,608	Omits Jews (212 in 1901)	" " " "
			Univ. Jewish Ency.
1800	33,000		
1820	32,640		" " "
1850	40,000		
1851	40,536		Brockhaus, 1851

Pavia

774-1024		Capital, where kings were crowned	
by 911	22,000	88 hectares in area (times 250; cf. Naples)	Beloch, 1937, III, p. 212
964		Second in Italy, behind Rome	Liutprand in Butler, p. 57

1000	30,000		
c.1200		Lost second place in Lombardy to Cremona	Butler, p. 22
1200	25,000		
1250	30,000		Beloch, 1937, III, p. 213
1300	30,000	Free republic until 1359	
1400	20,000		
1480	17,000		" " " pp. 213, 217
1542	16,000		" " " p. 217
1576	17,000	11,900 communicants	" " " pp. 215, 217
1600	18,000		
1700	22,000		
1750	24,432		" " " p. 217
1800	23,772		" " " "
1850	29,000		
1861	30,480		Enci. Italiana

Piacenza

1400	25,000		
1447	25,000		Beloch, 1937, II, p. 252
1500	25,000		
1546	26,760		" " " "
1579	30,000		" " " "
1600	31,000		
1618	33,038		" " " "
1700	31,000		
1750	30,000		
1758	30,590		" " " "
1800	28,000		
1820	27,920		" " " "
1850	36,000		
1861	39,318		Brockhaus 1864

Pisa

1000	9,000	3 churches at least	Catholic Ency.
1100	20-25,000		Miss Rossi in Renouard, p. 36
1152		Wall enclosed 114 hectares	Beloch, 1937, II, p. 161
1100s		1 new (parish) church	Catholic Ency.
1200	30,000		
1200s		Notarized papers as much as Genoa	Renouard, pp. 99, 159
1228	42,000	4,240 citizens (males, aged 15-70) took an oath (times 10; cf. Ferrara, 1300)	Beloch, 1937, II, p. 161
1284	36,000	30,000 in fleet (city's share 1/5; cf. 1551. Thus, 6,000 militia times 6)	Ency. Brit., 1910
"		5,000 slain, 11,000 lost into captivity; few ever returned	" "
1300	25,000		
1551	9,940		Beloch, 1937, II, p. 162
1642	12,902		" " " "
1745	14,015		" " " "
c.1800	17,000		Hassel, 1819, VI, p. 568
1850	30,000		
1861	33,676	In the urban center	Brockhaus, 1864

Rome

600-800	50,000		Enci. Italiana
800	50,000		" "
900	40,000		

970	35,000		Enci. Italiana
1000	35,000		
1198	35,000	Census	" "
1200	35,000		
1300	30,000	Pope left, 1304	
1377	17,000	As the Pope returned	Beloch, 1937, II, p. 1
1400	33,000		
1458	33,500	6,700 hearths	" " " p. 5
1500	38,000		
1513	40,000	Census	Enci. Italiana
1600	109,729	20,019 families	Beloch, 1937, II, p. 13
1700	149,447	30,782 families	" " " "
1750	157,882		Corridore, p. 56
1800	153,004		Beloch, 1937, II, p. 16
1850	170,824		Annuario Stat. Roma, p. 16

Salerno

1075-1127		Capital of Norman South Italy	
"	50,000	16 parish churches, 17 parishes	Mazza, pp. 62-63
1194		All killed or removed	Burigny, II, p. 3
1320	c.10,000	Taxed c. 1/3 Naples and c. 2/3 Amalfi	Beloch, 1937, I, p. 272
1455	3,500	697 hearths	" " " p. 244
1595	11,000	2,233 hearths	" " " "
1788	9,181		

Siena

1200	15,000	In a growing area, cf. Florence	
1250	20,000		Lestocquoy, p. 176
1300	21,000		
1347	22,000	20,000 plus clergy and Jews	Beloch, 1937, II, p. 160
1380	14,500	12,500 plus clergy and Jews	" " " "
1500	22,000		
1500s		Small addition to wall increased area to 101 ha.	" " " p. 150
1540	25,000	23,000 plus clergy and Jews	" " " p. 160
1579	18,779		" " " "
1612	18,659		" " " "
1717	15,963		" " " "
1784	16,173		" " " "
1843	20,333		Enci. Italiana
1850	21,000		
1861	22,560		" "

Turin

1377	3,500	700 hearths	Beloch, 1937, III, p. 276
1571	15,000	14,244 plus children under 2	" " " "
1600	23,000		
1612	27,000	24,410 plus children under 2, Jews, clergy, etc.	" " II, "
1631	40,000		" " " "
1700	43,000		
1702	43,866		" " " p. 277
1750	60,998		" " " "
1800	66,220		" " " "
1849	136,849		Hoffmann
1850	138,000		
1852	143,157		Ency. Brit., 1853

Venice

Year	Population	Notes	Source
809		Became capital	
906	35-40,000		Hazlitt, I, p. 71n
1000	45,000		
1170	64,000		" " "
1200	70,000		
1300	110,000	Early peak of power by 1261	
1339		40,100 males aged 20-60 (Beloch claims only 30,000)	" " p. 556, II, p. 741
1347	110,000	100,000, plus suburbs of Murano, Burano, and Malamocco, just before the plague	Beloch, 1937, III, p. 3
1379		100,000 in city again	" " " pp. 3-4
1400	110,000	Including suburbs	
1500	115,000		
1509	115,000	105,000 plus suburbs	" " " p. 17, cf. p. 7
1563	182,000	168,626 plus Jews, poor, and suburbs	" " " " "
1593	150,000	139,459 plus suburbs	" " " pp. 17, 26
1600	151,000		
1624	156,000	142,804 plus Jews, poor, and suburbs	" " " p. 17; cf. pp. 9-10
1696	143,000	132,637 plus suburbs	" " " " " "
1700	144,000		
1750	158,000		
1761	161,000	149,476 plus suburbs	" " " pp. 17, 26
1790	148,000	136,803 plus suburbs	" " " p. 17
1800	146,000		
1802	146,000	134,398 plus suburbs	
1850	141,000	126,768 plus suburbs and Austrian garrison	Harper

Verona

Year	Population	Notes	Source
800	30,000	Nearly 30 churches	A. Allen, p. 3
1000	20,000		
1100s		At least 4 new churches	Enci. Italiana
1200	33,000		
1234		8,000 taxpayers in and near city	Moscardo, p. 161
1238	34,000	34 churches	" p. 182
1270		1 new church	Enci. Italiana
1387	40,000	As it lost its independence	" "
1400	35,000		
1473	30,000	Based on census of 27,378	Beloch, 1937, III, p. 101
1491	38,500		" " " p. 102
1500	39,000		
1502	40,000		" " " p. 102, cf. p. 117
1577	53,280		" " " p. 117
1600	54,000		
1604	55,176		" " " "
1700	50,000		
1738	48,013		" " " "
1750	49,000		
1785	52,978		" " " "
1800	55,000		
1805	55,887		Morse, II, p. 398
1837	51,091		Hoffman
1850	56,000		
1857	59,169		

Vicenza

1500	24,000	
1539	28,400	Beloch, 1937, III, p. 357
1548	30,948	" " " pp. 87-88
1598	36,000	" " " p. 91
1600	34,000	
1602	32,000	Beloch, 1937, III, p. 91
1656	25,000	" " " p. 94
1700	25,000	
1710	25,802	" " " p. 97
1750	26,000	
1766	28,289	" " " p. 94
1800	28,000	
1802	28,995	" " " p. 97
1850	32,000	
1857	33,306	Brockhaus

Valletta (Valetta)

1632	21,075	Including garrison	Beloch, 1937, I, p. 166
1700	24,000		
1750	27,000		
1782	28,500	Including suburbs	Hassel, 1819, VII, p. 583
1798	39,000	23,680 in city	Morse, II, p. 409
1798-1800		Severe siege	Ency. Brit. 1875
1800		Garrison of 6,000	" "
"	35,000		
1807	41,222	Including 16,676 in Cospicua, Vittoriosa, and Senglea	Martin, 1839, p. 575
c.1850	60,000		Harper

Almería

831		Founded	Ency. of Islam, 1897
c.1000	35,000	118 hectares in area (times 300; Russell generally used c. 260 and Torres c. 350)	Russell, 1958, p. 92
1147		3,800 weavers; city sacked	Maqqari, p. 51
1147-72		Seat of a kingdom	Ency. of Islam, 1897
c.1200-c.1235		Again seat of a kingdom	" " "
1288		Annexed by Granada	" " "
1300	25,000	Presumably stable under Granadan rule to 1487	
1400	25,000		
1487-9		Surely grew, as Granada's only port (cf. Málaga)	
1489	30,000	5,000 houses	Münzer, p. 30
"		Fell to Spain and was treated harshly	
1594	7,000	966 taxpayers	González, p. 92
c.1800	7,200		Hassel, 1819, IX, p. 280
1850	20,000		
1857	23,018		Census of Spain, 1857, p. 863

Avila

1530	12,000	1,523 taxpayers	González, p. 61
1587	25,000	8 parishes; 3,155 1/2 taxpayers (1/2 = a widow)	" p. 183
1594	22,000	2,826 taxpayers	" p. 57
1600	20,000		
1646	5,000	1,123 male citizens	" p. 61
1694	4,000	965 male citizens	" "
1857	6,419		Census of Spain, 1857, p. 863

Badajoz

875-890		A free capital	
982		Supplanted Mérida as main city of Lusitania	
c.1000	16,000	81 hectares in area (times 200—lower than Almería because inland)	Russell, 1958, p. 92
1022-1094		A free capital again	
c.1250	15,000	5 parishes	Meyer, 1874
1850	22,000		
1857	22,195		Census of Spain, 1857, p. 863

Baeza

1227		Fell to Christians	
1227		From it and Úbeda 4,000 families fled	Büsching, 1769, p. 47
1407	9,000	1,785 male citizens	González, p. 92
1500	18,000		
1530	21,000	2,635 taxpayers	" "
1594	25,000	5,172 male citizens	" "
1600	24,000		
c.1625	17,000	3,496 male citizens	Ximenes, pp. 226-7
c.1850	10,800		Hoffmann

Barcelona

985		Destroyed by al-Mansur	
1300	30,000	c. 100 hectares in area (times 300; cf. Almería, 1000)	Jürgens, p. 28
1359	38,000	7,651 hearths	Bofarull, p. 1
1378	38,000	7,645 hearths	Usher, p. 345
1400	37,000		

1463	35,000		Tasis, p. 162
1492	28,500		" "
1497	28,500		Vicens, p. 179
1500	29,000		
1516	31,860	6,372 hearths	Tasis, p. 162
1600	64,000		
1600-1650		Birthrate constant	Nadal, p. 53
1647	64,000		Usher, p. 345
1700	73,000		" "
1716	32,791	After a hard siege	Vilar, II, p. 47
1750	70,000		
1755-1799		Births rose 50%	" " p. 53
1770	71,783		" " p. 56
1786	94,880		" " " cf. p. 36n
1789	111,410	Plus 9-10,000 garrison	Laborde, I, p. 29
1796	115,000	Census	Perpiña, IV, p. 278
1800	110,000		Vilar, p. 60n
"	120,000	With garrison	
1849	164,040	Including suburbs of Barceloneta, Gracia, and San Bertrán	Enci. Ilustrada
1850	167,000		
1857	195,772	Including 17,147 in Gracia	Census of Spain, 1857, pp. 96, 863

Bobastro

900	36,000	It had 6,000 cavalry (times 6)	Dozy, p. 376

Burgos

884	9,000	3 churches (presumably parish ones)	Torres, p. 39
1163	18,000	6 churches (presumably parish ones)	" "
1200s		1 new parish church	Enci. Universal
1300	21,000		
1300s		2 new parish churches	" "
1400	27,000		
1408		1 new parish church	" "
1400s		80,000 (clearly too high)	Ency. Brit., 1875
"	35-40,000	Plus foreigners	Laborde, III, p. 20
1530	7,000	1,500 male citizens	González, p. 7
1596	10,000	2,040 male citizens	López M., p. 283
1694	9,000	1,881 male citizens	González, p. 7
c.1800	10,000		Morse, II, p. 159
1850	23,000		
1857	24,329		Census of Spain, 1857, p. 863

Cádiz

1594	13,000	612 taxpayers, plus 1,069 more in Puerto de Santa Maria	González, p. 84
1694	31,000	5,191 male citizens, plus Puerto de Santa Maria (cf. 1712)	" "
1700	33,000		
1712	38,000	4,043 taxpaying families, plus at least 733 more in Puerto de Santa Maria	Uztariz, pp. 75-76
1750	60,000		
1787	97,000	65,987 plus Puerto de Santa Maria (16,000) and San Fernando (i.e., Isla de León, c. 15,000, reduced from Hassel's alleged 40,000, cf., 1849)	Hassel, 1819, IX, pp. 248, 251
1800	87,000		
1802		57,387 in city alone	Morse, II, p. 357

1849	85,470	53,920 plus Puerto de Santa Maria (17,930), San Fernando (9,729), and Puerto Real (3,981)	Lippincott, 1868
1850	89,000		
1857	115,773	63,513 plus 52,260 in the suburbs	Census of Spain, 1857, pp. 180, 863

Cartagena

c.1000	33,000	110 hectares in area (times 300; cf. Almería, 1000)	Russell, 1958, p. 92
1530	4,000	505 taxpayers	González, p. 75
1594	8,000	1,034 taxpayers	" "
1694	12,000	2,447 male citizens	" "
1744-82		Arsenal and docks built	Enci. Universal
c.1800	33,222		Nadal, p. 108
1845	27,727		English Cyclopaedia
1850	33,000		
1860	54,000		Enci. Universal

Cordova (Córdoba)

c.800	160,000	Based on 23,000 who had fled a tyrant and who had occupied less than 1/8 of the city	Madoz, VI, p. 652
822-976		Chief mosque doubled in size	Ency. Brit., 1910
c.1000		Peak; 200,000 houses, 600 mosques, 900 baths (all these figures seem much too large and may include area outside of the city)	" "
976-1002		Chief mosque doubled in size again	" "
c.1000		500,000 with 113,000 houses	Dozy, II, p. 174
1000	450,000		
1000		471 mosques	Bekri in Lévi-P., 1932, III, p. 362
1009		Circumference of walls was 12,420 meters, but urban area 10% longer around (thus, c. 1,170 hectares in area)	Sánchez-Albornoz, I, p. 315
1103	60,000	Moorish garrison 3/7 of Seville's	Lafuente, I, p. 273
1200	60,000	S. Spain stable 1100-1200 under Morocco	
1236		5 monasteries built as Christians took it	Ramírez, I, p. 349
1300	40,000	Monasteries times 6,700 (cf. Roskilde), plus Jews	
1400	40,000		
1408	36,000	12 parishes; pestilence killed 70,000 (Too high)	Enci. Univ.
1500	35,000		Vicens, p. 243
1530	46,000	5,845 taxpayers	González, p. 85
1594	50,000	6,257 taxpayers	" p. 84
1600	50,000		
1646	40,000	8,000 male citizens	" p. 85
1694	34,000	6,911 male citizens	" "
1700	34,000		
1750	34,000		
c.1800	35,000		Laborde, II, p. 119
1842	43,692		Madoz, VI, p. 612
1850	39,000		
1857	36,501		Census of Spain, 1857, p. 863

Écija

1587	28,000	23,076 souls (plus 1/4; cf. Úbeda, 1787, 1793), 5,379 houses, 6,958 taxpayers	González, p. 335
1594	16,000	5,078 taxpayers (cf. 1587)	" p. 83

1600	16,000		
1694	12,000	2,465 male citizens	González, p. 86
1750	20,000		
c.1800	28,176		Morse, II, p. 159
c.1849	28,370		Harper
1850	28,000		

Elvira

1000	22,000	See Granada	Gallego, pp. 68-69
1019		Whole population moved to Granada, the new local capital	'' p. 70

Granada

1000	22,000	75 hectares in area (times 300; cf. Almería)	Torres, III, pp. 55-6
1030-55		Rapid growth	Ency. of Islam, 1897
1103	60,000	Moorish garrison 3/7 as big as Seville's	Lafuente, I, p. 273
1200	60,000	S. Spain stable under Morocco 1100-1200	
c.1300	150,000	Larger than Damascus	Abulfeda, II, pt. 1, p. 253
1311		200,000 (seems high; cf. 1360, 1400)	Letter cited in Durant, 1950, p. 300
c.1360		130 mills	Lafuente, p. 55n
1400	100,000	15,000 militia	Qalqashandi in Bosque, p. 79
1476	200,000	33,000 militia, 30,000 taxpayers	Marmol in Bosque, p. 79
1491	200,000	Estimate by prominent citizen urging surrender of city	Abu'l-Kasim in Irving, p. 318
1492		Over 20,000 armed men paraded in protest of the surrender	Irving, p. 323
''		300,000 Moors out of 700,000 fled Castile; 5/7 of all Moors had lived in Granada kingdom	'' ''
1494	70,000	40,000 Moors, 20,000 Jews, 10,000 Christians	Münzer, p. 44
1500	70,000		
1594	110,000	13,757 taxpayers	González, p. 86
1600	110,000		
1700	70,000	After general decline in Spain in 17th century	
1750	70,000		
1764	70,000		Büsching, 1769, p. 47
1784	52,345	Probably intended for Census-year, 1787	Hassel, 1819, IX, p. 274
1797	70,026		Bosque, p. 94
1800	70,000		
1845	70,025		Ency. Brit., 1853
1850	67,000		
1857	63,113		Census of Spain, 1857, p. 863

Jaén

1500	25,000		
1530	26,000	4,253 taxpayers, 11 parishes	González, p. 86
1594	44,000	5,595 taxpayers	'' p. 85
1595	33,000	26,856 souls (plus 1/4; cf. Úbeda, 1787, 1793)	Bleiberg, XI, p. 205
1600	31,000		
1646	18,000	3,787 male citizens	González, p. 86
1750	22,000		
1792		17,849 souls (plus 1/4)	Bleiberg, XI, p. 206
c.1800	27,500		Morse
1850	20,000		
1857	19,738		Census of Spain, 1857, p. 863

Jérez—see Xérez

León

c.900-983		Capital of part or all of Castile	
1002-1230		Capital again; 13 parishes at peak	Laborde, II, p. 475
1200	40,000		
1752		1,116 houses	Bleiberg, XI, p. 457
c.1800	6,170		Townsend in Hassel, 1819, IX, p. 178
1860	9,866		Census of Spain, 1877, p. xvi-xvii

Madrid

1530	6,000	748 taxpayers	González, p. 70
1570	14,000		Vicens, p. 439
1597	75,000	59,285 in 11,857 families and 7,016 houses, plus clergy and garrison (cf. 1646); 7,500 taxpayers (1594)	González, pp. 69, 96
1600	79,000		
1617	108,000		Vicens, p. 439
1646	94,000	Including 20,000 untaxed	González, p. 96n
1699		150,000 (Exaggerated estimate)	Louville, p. 72
1700	110,000		
1750	123,000		
1757	125,000	101,037 plus clergy and garrison	Büsching, 1784, VII, p. 271
1787	156,672	In 14,100 houses	González, p. 389
1797	167,607		Census of Spain, 1797, p. 1
c.1800		133 churches	Ency. Edinensis
1800	169,000		
1826	181,400		Gazetteer of World
1849	260,714		Blackie, "Spain"
1850	263,000		
1857	281,170		Census of Spain, 1857, p. 863

Málaga

1100	11,000	37 hectares in ares (times 300, cf. Almería)	Torres, pp. 55-56
1100s		Area expanded	" p. 56
1234-1487		Stable, being the port of Granada	
1234-1487		Peak 80,000 (probably exaggerated)	Laborde, IV, p. 11
1300	40,000		
1360		Rivaled Salé	Ency. of Islam, 1897
1400	40,000		
1485-7		Farmers crowded into city for safety	Fitton, p. 58-9
1487	42,000	7,000 houses	Münzer, p. 57
1487	42,000	14 parts (almost certainly like parishes); population fell by over half	Guillén, pp. 308, 348
1594	26,000	3,357 taxpayers	González, p. 88
1600	26,000		
1700	32,000		
c.1750	36,000	In the period 1746-59	Büsching, "Magazin" 1769, II, p. 107
1764	42,000	8,000 families plus 2,000 clergy	" " " " "
1787	41,592		Hassel, 1819, IX, p. 276
1800	49,000		
1805	52,376		" " " "
1847	68,577		Ency. Brit., 1853
1850	75,000		
1857	92,611		Census of Spain, 1857, p. 863

Medina Del Campo

1500	35,000		
1530	31,000	3,872 taxpayers	González, p. 22
1594	22,000	2,760 taxpayers	'' p. 20
1600	20,000		
1646	3,000	650 male citizens	'' p. 22
1692	4,000	942 male citizens	'' ''
c.1850	2,700		Gazetteer of World

Mérida

25 B.C.-(928)		Throve as capital of Lusitania	Ency. Brit., 1910
800	30,000	Before its rise to semi-independence	
c. 900s	40,000	At peak	Laborde, IV, p. 11
928		Second only to Córdova (in regional power); revolted and was crushed	Maqqari, p. 61

Murcia

c.1000	19,000	65 hectares in area (times 300; cf. Almería, 1000)	Russell, 1958, p. 92
1500	25,000	Rough guess (perhaps high)	Vicens, p. 243
1530	20,000	2,595 taxpayers	González, p. 75
1594	27,000	3,370 taxpayers	'' ''
1600	27,000		
1646	19,000	3,960 male citizens	'' ''
1694	25,000	5,154 male citizens	'' ''
1700	25,000		
1750	32,000		
1787	38,000		Playfair, I, p. 114
1800	44,000		
1801	44,000		Morse, I, p. 358
1844	55,053		Ency. Brit., 1853
1850	41,000		
1857	26,888		Census of Spain, 1857, p. 863

Ocaña

1530	9,000	1,124 taxpayers	González, p. 74
1594	25,000	3,150 taxpayers	'' ''
1600	25,000		
c.1850	5,000		Gazetteer of World

Palencia

1530	11,000	1,364 taxpayers	González, p. 48
1594	24,000	3,063 taxpayers	'' p. 43
1600	22,000		
1646	4,000	800 male citizens	'' p. 48

Palma

1009		An independent capital	
1100	27,000	90 ha. in area (times 300; cf. Almería)	Torres, 1955, pp. 55-56
1200	30,000		
1229		30,000 fled; 20,000 stayed and were slain (looks exaggerated)	Montaner and Simon
1591	23,161		García P.
1600	23,000		
1650		Majorca's population 44% as large as in 1787	J. Vargas, p. 78
1715		Over 10,000	Damento, p. 74
1787	29,529		J. Vargas, p. 159
1800	29,000	No decline till wars after 1800	

1834	27,500		Hoffmann
1850	37,000		
1857	42,910		Census of Spain, 1857, p. 863

Salamanca

medieval	14,000		Mier, lxix
1530	19,000	2,459 taxpayers	González, p. 57
1594	39,000	4,953 taxpayers	" p. 49
1600	36,000		
1646	14,000	2,965 male citizens	" p. 57
1694	12,000	2,416 male citizens	" "
c.1800	9,500		Hassel, 1819, IX, p. 201
1857	15,203		Census of Spain, 1857, p. 863

Segovia

1500	22,000		
1530	22,000	2,850 taxpayers	González, p. 66
1594	44,000	5,548 taxpayers	" p. 61
1600	42,000		
1694	8,000	1,625 male citizens	" p. 66
c.1800	9,500		Hassel, 1819, IX, p. 166
1857	10,339		Census of Spain, 1857, p. 640

Seville

889	35,000	20,000—the majority—massacred	Dozy, pp. 337-8, 348
c. 915	50,000	6.5-km. wall built (c.250 ha.; times 200, a low ratio for Spain, because wall was new)	Lévi-Provencal, 1953, p. 338, map
c. 970		Its tax exceeded Córdova's	Maqqari, pp. 56 and 213
c.1000	90,000	300 ha. in area (times 300; cf. Almería)	Jürgens, p. 59
1200	150,000	Based on next two entries	Ballesteros, p. 135
1248		15 Friday mosques (times 9,000—cf. Constantinople, plus maybe 15,000 Christians)	
"		Moorish wall 5.5 miles (c. 490 hectares)	Laborde, II, p. 45
"		300,000 Moors fled (probably an area-wide estimate)	" " "
"	65,000	20 parishes after Christian conquest	Hazañas, p. 55
"		3 mosques converted to synagogues	Univ. Jewish Ency.
1300	90,000	cf. 1530	
c.1390		6,000-7,000 Jewish families (probably exaggerated); all expelled in 1391	Crescas in Univ. Jewish Ency.
1400	70,000		
c.1450		13,000 craftsmen	Grande Ency.
1500	50,000		
1520		45,395 souls (over 7?)	Bleiberg, XV, p. 642
1530	53,000	6,634 taxpayers; 32 parishes left over	González, p. 84 and n
1588		121,990 souls (over 7?)	Bleiberg, XV, p. 642
1594	144,000	18,000 taxpayers	González, p. 83
1600	144,000		
1644	120,000	24,000 male citizens	Méndez in Bennassar, p. 199
1646		18,000 male citizens (may just repeat 1594 figure—looks low)	González, p. 83
1649		60,000 died in epidemic	Vicens, p. 437
1694	80,000	16,081 male citizens	González, p. 83
1700	80,000		
1712	81,844		Uztariz, p. 73
1746	67,000	65,545 plus more than 1,419 clergy	Matute, II, p. 65

1787	80,268		Hassel, 1819, IX, p. 243
1797	96,000		" " " "
1800	96,000		
c.1844	100,498		Madoz, XIV, p. 288
1850	106,000		
1857	112,139		Census of Spain, 1857, p. 863

Toledo

711-1085		5 (parish) churches (times 3,000)	Enci. Universal
800	25,000	Christians revolted often, hence were majority	" "
900s		2 new mosques	
1000	31,000	See 1100	
1085-	27,000	11 parishes created around former mosques (times 2,500; cf. 1500)	Compiled from Enci. Universal
1100		106 hectares in area (reflects peak c. 1000)	Torres, 1955, p. 55
1200	35,000	14 parishes (times 2,500; cf. 1500)	Compiled from Enci. Universal
1300	42,000	17 parish churches	" " " "
1400	45,000	18 parish churches	" " " "
1500	47,000	19 parish churches	" " " "
1530	47,000	5,898 taxpayers	González, p. 71
1571		27 parishes	" pp. 345-346
1594	87,000	10,933 taxpayers	" p. 70
1600	80,000		
1646	25,000	5,000 male citizens	" p. 71
1694	25,000	5,000 male citizens	" "
1700	25,000		
1750	22,000		
1787	21,000	4,263 families	Laborde, III, p. 249
c.1800	18,000		Playfair, I, p. 128
c.1849	13,580		Blackie, "Spain"

Úbeda

1500	20,000		Vicens, p. 243
1530	20,000	2,605 taxpayers, 11 parishes	González, p. 86
1594		4,672 taxpayers	" p. 85
1597	20,000	15,441 souls (plus 1/3; cf. 1787 and 1793)	Bleiberg, XVI, p. 419
1600	20,000		
c.1625	19,000	3,860 male citizens	Ximenes, pp. 233-4
1646	14,000	2,923 male citizens	González, p. 86
1694	12,000	2,400 male citizens	" "
1787	16,000		Laborde, I, p. 115
1793		11,992 souls (over 7?)	Bleiberg, XVI, p. 419
c.1850	13,089		Gazetteer of World

Valencia

1100	13,000	44 hectares in area (times 300; cf. Almería, 1000)	Torres, pp. 55-56
1200	26,000		
1238	31,000	3,970 houses (times 8; cf. 1609)	Russell, 1958, p. 104
"		50,000 (Probably an exaggeration)	Boix, I, p. 145
1300	44,000	Prospered as new capital of Aragon	
c.1350	48,000	New wall enclosed 160 hectares	Jürgens, p. 41
1400	48,000		
1500	50,000		
1510-1609		Region gained 75%	González, p. 390
1600	86,000	(Growth stopped c. 1600)	

1609	86,000	12,327 houses (times 7; cf. 1820); 2/5 of region's population expelled	'' '' ; Riera p. 902; Miñano
1700	45,000		
1718	43,000	Regional pop. c. half its amount in 1600	Miñano
1750	60,000		
1787	82,000	100,654 minus 18,000 non-urban	Cavanilles, p. 403
1800	82,000		
c.1820	65,840	In 9,610 houses (7 p. house)	Miñano
1849	110,960		Harper
1850	110,000		
1857	106,435		Census of Spain, 1857, p. 863

Valladolid

1074	6,000	2 parishes	Enci. Universal
1100	9,000	3 parishes; 2,200 paces (2 miles) around	'' ''
1406-1561		Main Castilian capital	
1500	48,000		
1530	54,000	6,750 taxpayers	González, p. 22
1591	64,000	8,112 taxpayers	'' p. 20; Bennassar, pp. 165-6 for date
1600	56,000		
1646	15,000	3,000 male citizens	González, p. 22
1694	18,000	3,637 male citizens	'' ''
1700	18,000		
c.1750	25,000	5,000 hearths	Ensenada in Bennassar p. 199
c.1800	30,000		Hassel, 1819, IX, p. 190
1850	40,000		
1857	41,913		Census of Spain, 1857, p. 863

Xérez (Jérez)

c.1000	19,000	96 hectares in area (times 200—less than Almería because inland)	Russell, 1958, p. 92
1200	15,000	5 mosques of later parishes	Enci. Universal
1300	9,000	3 parishes (times 3,000)	'' ''
1400	15,000	5 parishes	'' ''
1500	21,000	7 parishes	'' ''
''		35,000 (an implausible estimate)	Vicens, p. 243
1500s		5 of its 12 monasteries built	Madoz
1587	27,000	6,154 taxpayers, 4,564 houses, 21,721 souls (plus 1/4; cf. Úbeda, 1787, 1793)	González, p. 337
1594	33,000	6,816 taxpayers	'' p. 83
1600	33,000		
1643		Sherry export virtually same as in 1795	Bleiberg
1700	30,000		
c.1750	30,513		Góngora, p. 21
1800	33,000		Morse, II, p. 159
1850	34,988		Gumprecht
1852	34,988		

Zaragoza (Saragossa)

1118	20,000	Including suburbs	Lacarra in Bleiberg, XVIII, p. 570
''		City alone 47 hectares in area	Torres, pp. 55-6
1200	21,000	5 parishes (times 3,000, plus 6,000 for suburbs; cf. 1118)	Asso, p. 200
1300	21,000		
1311	21,000	7 parishes	'' ''

1400	20,000		
1495	19,840	3,968 male citizens	Asso, p. 186
1500	20,000		
1548	26,000	25,000 in 4,451 houses, plus monks and the	" p. 201
1600	24,000		
1626	24,000		Anon. in Asso, p. 186
1650	28,000	5,588 male citizens	" " " p. 187
1700	29,000		
1725	30,000		Díaz de Arce in Asso, p. 201
1750	35,000		
1787	42,600		Laborde, II, p. 254
1797	55,000		Hassel, 1819, IX, p. 296
1800	55,000		
1845	40,482		English Cyclopaedia
1848	45,220		Madoz, XVI, p. 527
1850	48,000		
1857	58,978		Census of Spain, 1857, p. 863

Coimbra

1147-1256		Capital	
1200	20,000	See Lisbon, 1256	
c.1280-c.1380		Royal residence	
1527	1,329	First census (probably incomplete)	Grande Enci. Portuguesa, XV, p. 77
1537-1911		Seat of Portugal's main university	
1732	11,871	3,063 hearths; 9 parishes (perhaps left over from earlier time)	Büshing, 1784, pp. 87-88
1766	24,000		Gorani, p. 273
c.1795	15,000	In 3,003 houses	Hassel, 1819, IX, p. 458
1865	18,147		Meyer, 1874

Évora

1448-1578		Capital	
c.1500	18,000		Macbride, p. 8
1550-1759		Seat of a university	
1732	11,903	3,162 hearths; 5 parishes	Büsching, 1784, pp. 136-137
1758	15,000	12,500 plus children under 7	Pereira, p. 254
c.1800	14,200		Morse, II, p. 377
1868	11,965		Meyer, 1874

Lisbon

700	15,000		Enci. Italiana
800	15,000		
1000	15,000		
1147	15,000		Grande Enci. Portuguesa, XV, p. 196
1200	15,000		
1256-1448		Capital; quickly grew to 30,000	Ency. Brit., 1970
1300	35,000		
1375		New wall enclosed 101 hectares	França, p. 16
1400		60,000 but considered unreliable	" p. 17
"	55,000		
1430	64,000		Vivien
1500		80,000 but considered unreliable	França, p. 17
"	70,000		
1532	78,000		Vivien
1550		100,000 but considered unreliable	França, p. 17
1578		Became capital again	
1600	110,000		
1620	113,265		" "
1626	126,000		Grande Enci. Portuguesa, XV, p. 197
1639	165,000		França, p. 17
1700	188,000		
1729	200,000		" "
1750	213,000		
1755		10,000 died in earthquake	Pereira, p. 652
1758	208,000	156,359 plus children under 7, plus 3 unreported districts of city (c. 10% of population in 1911)	" pp. 923-925
1800	237,000		Grande Enci. Portuguesa, XV, p. 197
1841	241,500		Brockhaus, 1864
1850	259,000		
1858	275,286		Statesman's Yearbook, 1865

Oporto

-1147		Capital	
1383	c.18,000	Wall built, 3,000 paces around (2 3/4 miles, thus enclosing c. 125 ha.)	Vivien
1622	14,581		Rebello, p. 45
1732	20,737	In 7 parishes	" " ; Büsching, 1767, I, p. 265
1750	30,000		
1766	40,000	36,000 plus garrison	Gorani, p. 277
1787	63,505		Rebello, p. 46
1800	67,000		
1810	70,505	In 15,138 houses	Morse, II, p. 376
1850	99,690	Including suburbs of Villa Nova de Gaia, São João da Foz, etc.	Harper

Aix

794-814		Capital, but very small; only one church	Sullivan, pp. 40 and 60
1200s		15,000 estimated from peculiar hearth count of 48 1/2, times 300 per hearth	Fabre, III, p. 61
1263	9,000	1,176 ordinary hearths (times 8; cf. Arles)	Février, p. 121
1320-1345	12,000	1,500-1,600 ordinary hearths (times 8)	'' ''
1700	27,000	See 1760	
1720	24,000	After many years of war	Fabre, IV, p. 252n
1750	23,000		
1760		Births 83.1% as many as in 1700	Howlett, p. 135
1775	23,548	From births (1771-1780)	Messance, p. 51
1787	25,400		Levasseur, I, p. 227
1800	23,000		
1801	23,686		'' II, p. 346
1850	27,000		
1851	27,255		Ungewitter, I, p. 917

Amiens

1260		Wall length increased to 3,800 meters (c. 2.3 miles; thus c. 85 ha. in area)	Correspondence from François Vasselle
1471		Wall length increased to 5,660 meters (c. 3.5 mi.; thus 200 ha. in area)	'' '' '' ''
1500	20,000	Based on area	
1594		3,000 in militia, reduced to 1,500 following pestilence in 1597	'' '' '' ''
1698	35,000	Including suburbs	Deyon, p. 7
1700	35,000		
1745	32,648		Orry in Mols, II, p. 514
1750	33,000		
1768	35,000		Enci. Italiana
1787	37,935		Levasseur, I, p. 227
1800	40,000		
1801	40,289		'' II, p. 345
1850	53,000		
1851	53,619		Ungewitter, I, p. 884

Angers

1000	15,000	5 parishes	Rangeard, pp. 449-458
1200	30,000	10 parishes	'' ''
1300	33,000	11 parishes	'' ''
1300s		Only 1 new monastery (7 in 1400s, 10 in 1500s)	Anon. in "l'Anjou Historique" 1908, p. 577
1400	25,000		
1500	25,000		
1529	24,000	8 parishes	Bourdigné, p. 119
1583		8 parishes	Joubert, p. 88
1589-1599		Pestilence	'' p. 73
1600	25,000		
peak	51,000	17 parishes	'' p. 88
1670	50,000		Boulainvilliers, VI, p. 79
1698	36,000		'' '' ''
1700	35,000		
1726	30,000		Saugrain in Mols, II, p. 514
1745	22,607		Orry in Mols, II, p. 514
1750	23,000		

1775	29,457	From births (1771-1780)	Messance, p. 50
1787	28,188		Levasseur, I, p. 227
1800	32,000		
1801	33,000		″ II, p. 345
1850	46,000		
1851	46,599		Ungewitter, I, p. 900

Arles

		Former capital of Roman Gaul	
879-1150		Capital of Burgundy, including Provence	
1200	20,000		
1220		6,000 or more	Englemann, p. 66
1200s		60,000 estimated from peculiar hearth count of 200, times 300 as at Aix	Fabre, III, p. 61-62
1271	17,000	14 parishes (times 1,250; cf. Metz) and 2,181 ordinary hearths	Février, p. 150
c.1450	6,000	752 ordinary hearths (times 8; cf. 1271)	″ ″
1700	24,000		
1720	23,178		Fabre, IV, p. 252n
1750	22,000		
1765	21,562		Masson, p. 28
1787	16,281		Levasseur, I, p. 227
1801	17,187		″ II, p. 346
1850	23,000		
1851	23,208		Ungewitter, I, p. 917

Arras

1194		1,000 militia	Luchaire, p. 180
1200s		Grew incredibly	Lestocquoy, p. 177
1300	20,000		″ ″
1400	9,500		″ ″
1506	12,000	Similar in size to Amsterdam	Venetian envoy in Russell, 1958, p. 47
c.1700	17,000		Lestocquoy, p. 177
1787	21,492		Levasseur, I, p. 227
1801	19,364		″ II, p. 346
1846	24,321		Ency. Brit., 1853
1850	25,000		
1851	25,271		Ungewitter, I, p. 885

Avignon

1200	13,000	42-45 hectares in area (cf. 1370)	Lot, I, pp. 157-158
1309-1377		Seat of papacy	
1361		Plague killed 17,000	Okey, p. 161
1370	45,000	151 hectares; 2nd city of France	Lot, I, pp. 158-159
once	50,000		Okey, p. 288
1379-1402		Seat of Anti-Popes	″ p. 188-204
1400	30,000	See Rome	
1539	15,340		Lot, I, p. 159
1600	23,000		
1616	26,000		Ploetz, II, p. 34
1700	26,000		
1750	26,000		
1759	26,823		Okey, p. 161
1800	21,000		
1801	21,412		Levasseur, II, p. 345
1850	35,000		
1851	35,899		Ungewitter, I, p. 919

Besançon

1687	14,209		Fohlen, II, p. 85
1709	16,929		" " "
1745	12,480		Orry in Mols, II, p. 514
1771	38,720	Probably with garrison	Fohlen, p. 156 and n
1775	25,004	From births (1771-1780)	Messance, p. 50
1787	28,350		Levasseur, I, p. 227
1800	30,000		
1801	30,000		" II, p. 345
1850	41,000		
1851	41,295		Ungewitter, I, p. 896

Béziers

1200	20,000		
1209	20,000	All killed	Ency. Brit., 1910
1304	14,476		Lot, I, p. 159
1418	4,280		" " "
1698	18,000	3,639 families	Boulainvilliers, VIII, p. 475
1787	13,149		Levasseur, I, p. 227
1801	13,915	(Correction of obvious typographical error)	" II, p. 345
1851	17,376		Ency. Brit., 1853

Blois

865-1498		Seat of a countship; peak c. 1000-c.1200	
1685	18,000	But fell to 15,000	Guilbert, II, p. 697
1787	12,286		Levasseur, I, p. 227
1851	16,104		Ency. Brit., 1853

Bordeaux

1200	15,000		
1200-1300		Grew fast	Higounet, II, p. 84
1300	30,000		" " p. 224-225
1399-1453		Grew in commerce	Grande Enci.
1400	30,000		
1500	20,000	On historical grounds	
1500s		Regained its former splendor	" "
1550	30,000	3,767 houses (times 8; cf. 1747)	Higounet, IV, p. 153
c.1570	26,000	3,332 houses (times 8)	Archives de la Gironde XLVI, pp. 99-100
1585		Plague killed 14,000	Grande Enci.
1600	30,000		
1600s		Stagnated; only slowly grew to 40,000	Ploetz, II, p. 34
1628	36,000	4,700 houses; 6,000 men able to bear arms (times 6)	Archives Municipales de Bordeaux IX, p. 270
1698	42,000		Higounet, IV, p. 522
1700	42,000		
1715	55,000		" V, p. 325
1747	66,554		"
"		About 8 per house	Mols, II, p. 161
1750	64,000	Estimate from chart	Higounet, V, p. 327
1775	79,692	From births (1771-1780)	Messance, p. 51
1790	104,499		Higounet, V, p. 327
1800	97,000		
1801	95,957		" " p. 327
1850	142,000		
1851	143,827	130,927 plus 12,900 in Bègles, Bastide, Bouscat, and Cauderan	Ungewitter, I, p. 908; Forstall

Bourges

1100	over 10,000	Estimated from area (100 ha.)	Amman, p. 144
1360-1422		A Valois prince's home	Ency. Brit., 1910, "Berry"
1422-36		Capital of France	" " "Charles VII"
1487	32,350	Estimate	Lot, II, pp. 73-74
1500	32,000		
1697	14,800		Boulainvilliers, VI, p. 238
1750	20,000		
1775	24,543	From births (1771-1780)	Messance, p. 50
1787	20,574		Levasseur, I, p. 227
1801	15,340		" II, p. 345
1850	24,000		
1851	25,037		Ungewitter, I, p. 898

Brest

1660		Small	Bernard, p. 15
1710	16,000		" p. 14
1750	20,000	Including suburb of Recouvrance	" p. 15
1789	33,852		Gazetteer of World
1800	27,000		
1801	27,000		Levasseur, II, p. 345
1850	71,000		
1851	72,191	61,160 plus 11,031 in Lambázellec	Ungewitter, I, p. 902
			Lippincott 1868

Caen

c.1060	20,000	5,000 in one of its four quarters	Prentout, pp. 12, 31
1200	20,000	Said to rival Paris	Boulainvilliers, V, p. 55
1300	20,000		
1346		Considered larger than any English city except London; 3,000 in militia	Prentout, pp. 20, 28
1400	18,000		
1436		University founded	Ency. Brit., 1910
1500	25,000		
1542		6,000 militia	Delarue, II, p. 365
1584		10,000 died in epidemic	" p. 391
1589-94		Seat of parliament	" p. 393
1600	30,000		
1697	35-40,000		Boulainvilliers, V, p. 76
1700	37,000		
1726	36,000		Saugrain in Mols, II, p. 514
1745	34,784		Orry in Mols, II, p. 514
1750	34,000		
1775	31,374	From births (1771-1780)	Messance, p. 49
1787	31,266		Levasseur, I, p. 227
1800	30,000		
1801	30,900		" II, p. 345
1850	45,000		
1851	45,280		Ungewitter, I, p. 883

Clermont

1646	9,000	3 parishes	Planche in Leclerc, p. 30
1750	20,000		Dickinson, p. 296
1775	23,548	From births (1771-1780)	Messance, p. 51
1787	21,357		Levasseur, I, p. 227
1800	24,000		
1801	24,478		" II, p. 345

1850	33,000		
1851	33,516		Ungewitter, I, pp. 808-809

Dieppe

1282		Its 2nd and last parish founded	Desmarquets, p. 84
1400		3 quarters	Guilbert, V, p. 511
1500	20,000		
1550		60,000 (looks high, given next entry)	" p. 513
peak		10-12 priests in each of its 2 parishes	Desmarquets, p. 138
1562-1568		Decimated by religious wars	Guilbert, V, p. 522
1600		8 churches	Desmarquets, pp. 80-87
1778		28-30,000, official estimate (looks high)	Dainville, p. 468
1775	16,686	From births (1771-1780)	Messance, p. 49
1787	18,954		Levasseur, I. p. 227
1800	20,000		
1801	20,000		" II, p. 346
1851	16,216		Ency. Brit., 1853

Dijon

903		3 parishes	Ganshof, p. 49
1200		5 parishes	" "
1200s-1477		Capital of Burgundy	
1376	18,000	2,353 hearths (times 8; cf. 1550-1745)	Levasseur, I, p. 185n
1470	21,000	2,614 hearths (times 8)	" " "
1500	24,000		
1550	30,000		Courtpé in Roupnel, p. 108
1572	25,000	3,198 hearths (times 8)	Roupnel, p. 108
1600	24,000		
1602	24,000	3,029 hearths (times 8)	" "
1698	34,000	4,331 hearths (times 8)	" "
1700	34,000		
1745	34,000		Courtpé in Roupnel, p. 108
1750	31,000		
1753	30,302		Roupnel, p. 108
1787	20,925		Levasseur, I, p. 227
1800	21,000		
1801	21,000		" II, p. 345
1850	32,000		
1851	32,253		Ungewitter, II, p. 895

Dunkerque (Dunkirk)

1698	13,200		Boulainvilliers, IV, p. 527
1726	8,190		Saugrain in Mols, II, p. 514
1745	3,504		Orry in Mols, II, p. 514
1775	26,000	From births (1771-1780)	Messance, p. 49
1787	25,243		Levasseur, I, p. 227
1801	16,259		" II, p. 345
1850	28,000		
1851	29,080		Ungewitter, I, p. 887

Grenoble

1475	8-10,000	2,170 families	Lot, I, p. 62
1643	14,000		" " p. 63
1698	18,900		Boulainvilliers, VII, p. 234
1726	22,622		Lot, I, p. 63
1750	23,000		

1775	23,856	From births (1771-1780)	Messance, p. 51
1800	23,000		
1801	23,500		Levasseur, II, p. 345
1850	31,000		
1851	31,340		Ungewitter, I, p. 915

(le) Havre

1516		Founded	
1700	10,000		Dardel, p. 8
1775		Under 20,000; from births (1771-1780)	Messance, p. 49
1787	22,059		Levasseur, I, p. 227
1801	16,000		" II, p. 345
1846	43,778	Including 12,453 in Ingouville	Forstall
1850	43,000		
1851	43,332	Including 14,378 in Ingouville	"

Laon

898-991	28,000	French capital; had 23 parishes (times 1,250; cf. Metz)	Lemaitre, p. 2
1000	25,000		
1112		10 churches burned	LeLong, p. 210
1112-1331		Strong commune	
1769	10,000		Guilbert, II, p. 176
1791	7,034		Vercauteren, p. 360n

La Rochelle

1598		Became sole fortified French Protestant city	
1600	25,000		
1628	27,000	Before siege, 5,000 after	Guilbert, III, p. 587
1787	17,253		Levasseur, I, p. 227
1801	18,000		" II, p. 346
1856	14,157		Ency. Brit., 1853-(60)

Lille

1030		Founded	
1144	8,000	4 parishes (cf. 1300)	Brosse, V, b, p. 73
1300		7 parishes	" " " "
1300s	c.15,000		Mols, II, p. 520
1415-1470		Averaged 55 new burghers per year, compared to 56 for Frankfurt; quite close to rate in 14th century	Marquant, p. 23
1500	25,000		
1566		40,000 in 4,000 houses (multiplier of 10 probably too high)	St. Léger, p. 163
1600	32,000		
1617	32,604		St. Léger, p. 238
1669		Deaths averaging 2,400 per year	" p. 351
1698	55,000		Boulainvilliers, IV, p. 563
1700	55,000		
1726	50,780		Saugrain in Mols, II, p. 514
1740	54,028	Census	Dainville, p. 469
"		Deaths averaging 2,500 per year	St. Léger, p. 351
1745	52,740		Orry in Mols, II, p. 514
1750	54,000		

1775	65,644	From births (1771-1780)	Messance, p. 49
1787	65,907		Levasseur, I, p. 227
1800	<u>55,000</u>		
1801	54,756		" II, p. 345
1846	93,122	75,430 plus 17,692 in Fives, Moulins, and Wazemmes	Forstall
1850	<u>96,000</u>		
1851	97,374	75,795 plus 21,579 in above suburbs	"

Limoges

1698	14,000		Boulainvilliers, V, p. 509
1775	21,627	From births (1771-1780)	Messance, p. 50
1787	24,003		Levasseur, I, p. 227
1800	<u>20,000</u>		
1801	20,550		" II, p. 345
1850	<u>41,000</u>		
1851	41,630		Ungewitter, I, p. 905

Lyon

800	<u>12,000</u>	4 (parish) churches	Brosse, II, a, p. 85
1090-1173	<u>21,000</u>	3 parishes added	" " " p. 86
1200	<u>22,000</u>		
1193-1226		Substantial growth	Steyert, II, pp. 367, 389
c.1230		6 hospitals	" " p. 392
c.1250	<u>30,000</u>	10 parish churches, c. 80 city blocks	" " p. 393
1300	<u>35,000</u>	Time of peace and growth	
1400	35,000		" " p. 517
1450	60,000		" " p. 104
1500	<u>80,000</u>		
1546		18,000 in militia	" " "
1549	120,000	Nearly	" " "
1564		Pestilence killed 40,800	" " p. 253
1600	<u>90,000</u>	On historical grounds	
c.1667	117,000		" " p. 344
1697	69,000		" " "
1700	<u>71,000</u>		
1726	95,000		Saugrain in Mols, II, p. 514
1745	108,000		Orry in Mols, II, p. 514
1750	<u>115,000</u>		
1775	151,786	From births (1771-1780)	Messance, p. 50
1787	135,207		Levasseur, I, p. 227
1800	<u>111,000</u>		
1801	109,500		" II, p. 345
1850	<u>254,000</u>		
1851	258,494	177,190 plus 81,304 in Croix Rousse, Guillotière, and Vaise	Ungewitter, I, p. 907

Marseille

972	<u>6,000</u>	City had 2 parts, the upper town having 600 heads of families	Fabre, I, p. 261
1200	<u>25,000</u>		
1200s		Bit larger than Arles, according to all accounts	" III, p. 62
"		Grew rich on commerce	Rambert, II
1252		Decline began	" " p. 315

1263-1302		Grain supply fell 1/3	Rambert, p. 314
1294		3 parts (presumably parishes) within walls, 5 parish churches outside	Lesage, maps pp. 32, 34
1300	40,000	Churches times 3,000	
1263-1423		Grain supply fell 4/5	Rambert, II, p. 315
1400	21,000	See last 2 items	
1423-1500	45,000	Prospered, especially	" " p. 319, 334
1524	48,000	Formed municipal guard of 8,000-9,000, including all of an age to bear arms	Fabre, II, p. 46; Busquet, p. 165
"		30,000 (probably too low)	Baratier, p. 233
1600	55,000		
1630	60,000	More than 50,000 fled a pestilence, 9,000 died, and 1,000 remained	Méry, VI, p. ix
1665	65,000		Ploetz, III, p. 34
1694	87,700		Guilbert, I, p. 615
1700	88,000		
1721	90,000	Of whom 39,107 died in an epidemic	Fabre, IV, p. 252n
1745	88,420		Orry in Mols, II, p. 514
1750	88,000		
1770	90,056		Guilbert, I, p. 615
1790	106,585		Masson, p. 28
1800	110,000		
1801	111,130		Levasseur, II, p. 345
1850	193,000		
1851	195,257		Ungewitter, I, p. 917

Metz

800	25,000	20 parishes (times 1,250; cf. 1300)	Dollinger-Leonard, p. 199
900s	14,000	71 ha. in area (density as in 1300)	J. Schneider, p. 28
1100	21,000	17 parishes (times 1,250; cf. 1300)	Bégin, p. 51
1200	23,000	19 parishes	" p. 51, 129
1300	32,000	26 parishes; 159 hectares in area	J. Schneider, pp. 28, 55
1326		Over 30,000 claimed by city officials	" p. 60
1390		Plague killed 7,000	Guilbert, IV, p. 465
1400	25,000	After plague killed 6,000	" " "
"		155 hectares within walled area	Planitz, p. 204
1405	30,000	20 parishes (assuming a rising parish multiplier, cf. 1698-1700)	Guilbert, IV, p. 466
1500	40,000		
1552-1553		60,000 (probably exaggerated)	Ency. Brit., 1910
1570	24,000	Baptisms averaged 869 per year (crude birth rate assumed to be 35 per 1,000)	Mols, III, p. 83
1600	19,000	Baptisms averaged 673 per year (cf. 1570)	" " "
1610	19,432		Zeller, p. 60n
1675-1680	30,000	Baptisms averaged 1,056 per year (cf. 1570)	Mols, III, p. 83
1698		16 parishes	Boulainvilliers, III, p. 360
1700	30,000		
1715		A bit below 30,000	Mols, II, p. 516
1726	23,000		Saugrain in Mols, II, p. 514
1750	31,000		
1775	39,256	From births (1771-1780)	Messance, p. 49
1787	45,090		Levasseur, I, p. 227
1800	37,000		
1804	34,659		Hocquard, p. 28
1850	57,000		
1851	57,713		Ungewitter, I, p. 891

Montpellier

1090	c.1,000	Based on new wall enclosing 10 hectares	Russell, 1962, p. 358
late 1100s	5-6,000	Based on new wall enclosing 40 hectares	" " p. 356-357
1200	12-15,000		" " p. 358
c.1300		Larger than Bordeaux by a little	Higounet, III, p. 224
1300	35,000		
1347	40,000		Russell, 1962, p. 352
1349		c. 7,000 hearths	Grande Enci.
1367	22,000	4,520 households	Tilley, p. 208
1390		800 households	" "
1396	17,200		Russell, 1962, p. 349
1477-1480	13,560		" " "
1508	6,000		" " "
1550	12,000	4 churches, presumably parish ones	Platter, p. 34
c.1630		Made local capital by Louis XIII (1610-1643)	
1700	25,000		
1715	20-30,000		Mols, II, p. 516
1745			Orry in Mols, II, p. 514
1750	33,000		
1775	31,388	From births (1771-1780)	Messance, p. 51
1787	28,836		Levasseur, I, p. 227
1800	33,000		
1801	33,913		" II, p. 345
1850	45,000		
1851	45,811		Ungewitter, I, p. 913

Nancy

1698	8,000	1,745 families	Boulainvilliers, III, p. 398
1726	7,970		Saugrain in Mols, II, p. 514
1745	28,676		Orry in Mols, II, p. 514
1750	29,000		
1775	33,376	From births (1771-1780)	Messance, p. 49
1787	35,397		Levasseur, I, p. 227
1800	30,000		
1801	29,740		" II, p. 345
1850	44,000		
1851	45,129		Ungewitter, I, p. 889

Nantes

1212-1491		Capital of Brittany	
1500	12,000	2,000 (presumably male) inhabitants dined with visiting queen Anne	Guépin, p. 201
1557	14,000	2,300 militia	" p. 224
1700	42,309		Guilloux, cited in correspondence from Nantes Municipal Library
1745	38,728		Orry in Mols, II, p. 514
1750	41,000		
1775	56,927		Messance, p. 50
1787	51,057		Levasseur, I, p. 227
1800	72,000		
1801	73,879		" II, p. 345
1846	94,194		Forstall
1850	96,000		
1851	96,362		"

Narbonne

1200s	31,000	6,229 households	Tilley, p. 208
1300	30,000		
1378	1,250	250 households	" "
1698	8,000	1,626 families	Boulainvilliers, VIII, p. 472
1801	9,086		Levasseur, II, p. 346

Nimes

1399	1,000	200 homes	Maucomble, p. 49
1592	10,000		Ploetz, II, p. 34
1682		3,000 men paraded	Aillaud, p. 60
1700		10,590 families (probably much too high)	Boulainvilliers, VIII, p. 486
1722	18,141	Decline due to civil war	Maucomble, p. 158n
1734	20,225		" "
1750	31,000		
1775	49,056	From births (1771-1780)	Messance, p. 51
1787	43,146		Levasseur, I, p. 227
1800	39,000		
1801	38,800		" II, p. 345
1850	53,000		
1851	53,619		Ungewitter, I, p. 914

Orléans

999		Mostly destroyed by fire	Buzonnière, p. 37
1200	27,000	Based on early wall (cf. 1300)	
1300	36,000	Walled area expanded by 1/3 and divided in 36 quarters (presumably like parishes)	Illiers, p. 51
1400	30,000	France declining 1300-1400	
1428	30,000		Gower, p. 45
1484	26-28,000		Buzonnière, p. 132
1500	28,000		
1500s		150 hectares in area	Ganshof, p. 59
1600	35,000	See Paris for growth-rate to 1685	
1685	54,000		Guilbert, II, p. 599
"		10,000 Protestants emigrated	" " "
1700	41,000		
1738	35,811		Crozet, p. 257
1745	36,830		Orry in Mols, II, p. 514
1750	36,000		
1762	35,764		Crozet, p. 257
1787	41,040		Levasseur, I, p. 227
1800	36,000		
1801	36,165		" II, p. 345
1850	47,000		
1851	47,393		Ungewitter, I, p. 899

Paris

741-768		Capital	
c.800	25,000	20 churches	Poète, pp. 101-6
987-		Capital again	
c.1000	20,000	17 churches still in use	" pp. 147-9
1200	110,000		
1211		New wall enclosed 252 hectares	Géraud, pp. 470-1
1220	120,000		Maquet, p. 203

1292	216,000	At 4.5 per hearth	Levasseur, I, p. 170
1300	228,000		
1313		50,000 Parisians capable of bearing arms	Géraud, p. 467
1328	274,000	At 4.5 per hearth (Levasseur thought these estimates were slightly high, since the rural areas had 4 per hearth; Paris, however, had more persons, such as monks and soldiers, not covered by hearth-count)	Levasseur, I, p. 170
1367		439 hectares in area	Géraud, p. 469
1382	275,000	Based on 55,000 men who could bear arms	Froissart in Géraud, p. 469
1383		Its fine for revolting was 10 times Ypres'	" III, pp. 380, 413
1400	275,000		
1438		50,000 died of hunger	Dulaure, p. 261
1500	225,000	Rising after long war with England	
1553	260,000		Debrozy & Bachelet
1590	220,000		Voltaire in Levasseur II, p. 357
1600	250,000		
1637	412,000		Levasseur, II, p. 357
1675	540,000		" " "
1694		720,000 from a census, but probably an exaggeration since the expulsion of Protestants (1685) and war (from 1689) drained the population	" I, p. 203
1700	530,000		
1718	509,640	From births	Debrozy & Bachelet
1750	560,000		
1760	576,630	From births	" " "
1775	600,600		Messance, p. 47, 218
1787	600,000		" " "
1800	547,000	On historical grounds	
1801	547,756		" II, "
1846	1,270,000	Estimate slightly reduced to conform better to definition of urban area	Forstall
1850	1,314,000		
1851	1,325,000	Slightly reduced again	"

Poitiers

-741	5-9,000	Including suburbs	Claude, p. 64
741-840		Grew larger	" p. 150
800	10,000		
1000	12,000		
1083	15,000	5 parishes	" pp. 122-3
1100	over 20,000	Estimated from area (200 ha.)	Amman, p. 144
1200	21,000	7 parishes	Claude, pp. 122-3
1698		5 collegial churches (Rheims had 6) and 22 parish churches, mostly very small	Boulainvilliers, V, p. 360
1700	20,000		
1801	18,223		Levasseur, II, p. 345
1850	25,000		
1851	25,308		Ungewitter, I, p. 903

Provins

c.1150-1324		Co-capital (with Troyes) of Champagne	Vivien
1200	20,000		
1201-53		3,200 drapers and 1,700 cutlers	Bourquelot, I, pp. 252-3

1247	21,000	Ordered to divide the upper-town parish into 4 parishes, while the lower town had 3	Bourquelot, I, pp. 190-3
peak	25-30,000	Over 20 churches	" " p. 358
"		60,000 (apparently too high)	Guilbert, III, p. 94
1300	30,000		
1856	6,198		Ency. Brit., 1853

Reims (Rheims)

800	20,000		
800s	21,000	17 churches	Vercauteren, p. 65
1200	12,000	Hardly over 10-12,000	Boussinesq, I, p. 356
1200s		Medieval wall 6.5 km. (enclosing c. 250 ha.)	Ganshof, pp. 44, 46
1300	24,000		
1325	24,000	8 parishes	Desportes, p. 472
1360	15-20,000		Handwörterbuch, II, p. 680
1416	10,000		Desportes, p. 495
1482	12,000		" p. 467
1594	14,000		" p. 495
1615	21,000	4,335 taxpayers	Jadart, p. 151
1700	22,000		
1720		5,000 families	Vercauteran, p. 360n
1726	22,300		Saugrain in Mols, II, p. 514
1745	22,810		Orry in Mols, II, p. 514
1750	23,000		
1773	27,554		" " " " p. 361n
1800	20,000		
1801	20,295		Levasseur, II, p. 345
1850	45,000		
1851	45,754		Ungewitter, I, p. 888

Rennes

872-1212		Capital of Brittany	
1568		1,456 in militia, with suburbs	Ogée, II, p. 532
1726	18,600		Saugrain in Mols, II, p. 514
1750	26,000		
1775	34,832	From births (1771-80)	Messance, p. 50
1787	33,021		Levasseur, I, p. 227
1800	26,000		
1801	25,904		" II, p. 345
1850	41,000		
1851	41,295		Ungewitter, I, p. 901

Roubaix-Tourcoing

1804	8,703	In Roubaix; not yet adjoined to Tourcoing (11,889)	Blanchard, p. 441
1846	66,609	57,873 plus 8,736 in Wattrelos	Hoffmann
1850	70,000		
1851	71,745	62,313 plus 9,432 in Wattrelos	Brockhaus, 1864; Lippincott, 1868

Rouen

1000	20,000	Already Norman capital	
1100	over 20,000	Based on area of 200 hectares	Amman, p. 144

c.1100		3 new quarters which nearly equaled the old part	Guilbert, V, p. 421
1200	40,000	Based on 33 parishes within wall, times 1,250 (cf. 1246-1250)	
1246		38 parishes, probably by this date; new wall begun, taking in 5 new parishes	" pp. 419, 431-2
c.1250	50,000	Based on 8,000 families	Grande Enci.
1275	50,000	Estimate of archbishop, based on Pouillé (register of territorial possessions of diocese)	Guilbert, V. p. 431
1300	50,000		Levainville, p. 37
1364		10,000 in militia	Guilbert, V, p. 448
1400	70,000		
1412	75-80,000	15,000-16,000 in militia	" p. 452
1500	75,000	Larger than Nuremberg	Duby & Mandrou, I, p. 224
1525		2nd to Paris	Francis I in Grande Enci.
"		100,000 (probably exaggerated)	Grande Enci.
1600	70,000	On historical grounds	
1685	80,000		Levainville, p. 374
1694	60,000		" "
1700	68,000	Based on births (1690-1700) and 13,316 hearths	Messance in Levainville, p. 374
1726	80,690		Saugrain in Mols, II, p. 514
1745	92,480		Orry in Mols, II, p. 514
1750	88,000		
1775	70,644	From births (1771-80)	Messance, p. 49
1787	68,040		Levasseur, I, p. 227
1800	85,000		
1801	87,000		" II, p. 345
1846		99,295 in city alone	Forstall
1850	104,000		
1851	104,142	100,265 plus 3,877 in Sotteville	" Harper

St. Étienne

1726	16,000		Saugrain in Mols, II, p. 514
1750	21,000		
1775	27,496	From births (1771-80)	Messance, p. 51
1789	28,392		Gazetteer of World, "Étienne"
1801	16,259		Levasseur, II, p. 345
1850	55,000		
1851	56,030		Ungewitter, I, p. 907

St.-Malo

1601-10	14,600	Estimated from marriages	Delumeau, p. 16
1700	25,000		
1701-10	25,100	Estimated from marriages	
1751-1760	11,700	Estimated from marriages	" "
1787	16,767		Levasseur, I, p. 227
1792		St.-Servan became a separate town	Vivien

St.-Omer

1200s	20,000		Lestocquoy, p. 177
1300	20,000		
1313-5		Monopolized the wool trade	Werveke, 1944, p. 34
1320-5		" " " "	" " "

1787	16,254		Levasseur, I, p. 227
1800	20,000		
1801	20,100		″ II, p. 346
1850	22,000		
1851	22,054		Ungewitter, I, p. 885

Soissons

1000s		21 churches and chapels; retained its Roman area (12 ha.), but two new centers grew outside the wall	Vercauteren, pp. 129-30
-1306		Still an important countship	Larousse
1720	8,654		Guilbert, II, p. 176

Strasbourg (Strassburg)

1100		15 hectares within walled area	Plaintz, p. 201
1150	10,000		Schmoller, p. 82
1202-20	10,000	Wall enclosed 71 hectares	Ganshof, p. 58
1300	15,000	Wall enclosed 99 hectares	″ ″
1477	20,722	With 5,476 rural in addition	Keyser, 1941, p. 265
1500	24,000		
1537	30,000	May include some rural population	Schmoller, p. 82
1600	27,000		
1650	25,000		Ford, p. 2
1697	26,481		″ p. 115
1700	28,000		
1709	32,500		″ p. 134
1726	42,780		Saugrain in Mols, II, p. 514
1745	76,425	Inflated by military until 1748	Orry in Mols, II, p. 514
1750	49,870		Schmoller, p. 82
1787	49,705		Levasseur, I, p. 218
1800	49,000		
1802	49,056		Morse, II, p. 269
1850	75,000		
1851	75,565		Ungewitter, 1858-9, I, p. 891

Toulon

1314	3,500	700 families	Février, p. 121
1409	1,800	374 families	″ ″
1600	18,000		Lenthéric, p. 215
1700	25,000		
1720	26,277		Fabre, IV, p. 252n
1750	27,000		
1775	27,469	From births (1771-80)	Messance, p. 51
1787	27,540		Levasseur, I, p. 227
1800	21,000		
1801	20,500		″ II, p. 345
1850	68,000		
1851	69,474		Ungewitter, I, p. 918

Toulouse

1100	10-12,000		Correspondence from Coppolani
1200		12,000 (probably too low)	Sicard in Coppolani, p. 21
″	20,000	Seems reasonable	Correspondence from Coppolani
1300	35,000		
1335	over 30,000	On 140 hectares	Wolff, p. 72
1385	25,964		Dickinson in Russell, 1958, p. 110

1385		5,700 taxpayers; undoubtedly smaller than in 1273	Russell, 1962, p. 356
1400	23,000		
1405	22,136		Dickinson in Russell, 1958, p. 110
1500	40,000		
1550	50,000		Coppolani, p. 21
1600	40,000	Reduced by religious wars	
1640	43,000		〃 〃
1698	38,237		〃 p. 23
1700	40,000		
1750	48,000		〃 pp. 23-4
1790	59,000		p. 24
1800	50,000		
1801	50,171		Levasseur, II, p. 345
1846			Gazetteer of World
1850	93,000		
1851	94,195		Ungewitter, I, p. 912

Tours

Roman	20,000		Julian, p. 22
700	17,000	14 churches	Giraudet, I, p. 51
800	20,000		
850		21 churches in and nearby	Leveel, p. 29
853-903		Sacked 4 times	Vivier, p. 26
906-18		New wall built, smaller than the Roman city	〃 〃
997		28 churches burned in nearly total fire	Brosse, III, d, p. 160
1073-1300		5 new parishes	Giraudet, I, pp. 115-8
1100s		3 new parishes	Brosse, III, d, pp. 164-6
1200	20,000		
1300	25,000		
1354	25,000	c. 4,500-meter wall begun (c. 2.8 miles, enclosing c. 130 ha.), excluding 2 suburbs	Leveel, p. 43
〃	25,000	7 companies of militia; a company was 600 men in 1482	Chalmel, II, p. 134; Grande Ency. XX, p. 156
1400	25,000		
1420-1599		Often royal residence	Leveel, pp. 60-93
1500	60,000	20 parishes	Giraudet, p. 284
1598	67,000	55,331 communicants plus 128 Protestant families; 4,500 houses	〃 II, p. 97
1600	65,000		
1672	73,000	60,000 communicants (plus Protestants)	Boulainvilliers, VI, p. 27
1698	33,000	6,678 hearths	〃 〃 〃
1700	33,000		
1726	26,600		Saugrain in Mols, II, p. 514
1750	24,000		
1775	21,195	From births (1771-80)	Messance, p. 50
1787	28,161		Levasseur, I, p. 227
1800	22,000		
1801	22,000		〃 II, p. 345
1850	33,000		
1851	33,530		Ungewitter, I, pp. 899-900

Troyes

1125		59 hectares in area (but 43 ha. in suburbs)	Ganshof, p. 45
1125-1324		Co-capital (with Provins) of Champagne	
1200	20,000		
peak		50-60,000 (probably too high, cf. Provins; could be fair-time population)	Boulainvilliers, III, p. 548
1300	25,000		
medieval		99 hectares in area	Ganshof, p. 59
1400	20,000	Prior to Anglo-Burgundian invasion	
1433	18,000	15,309 plus 3,000 poor	Desportes, p. 467n
1500	23,000		Grande Enci.
1698	19,000		Boulainvilliers, III, p. 548
1726	13,500		Saugrain in Mols, II, p. 514
1745	18,400		Orry in Mols, II, p. 514
1750	20,000		
1775	31,914	From births (1771-80)	Messance, p. 49
1787	29,682		Levasseur, I, p. 227
1800	24,000		
1801	23,880		'' II, p. 345
1850	27,000		
1851	27,376		Ungewitter, I, p. 887

Valenciennes

1367		Tax 1/5 that of Hainaut, which had 23,467 families in 1406	Arnould, pp. 68n, 101n, 107
1400	23,000	See 1367	
1477	24,000	8 parishes	Paillard, p. 13
1500	21,000		
1569	15,000	3,000 hearths (families)	Arnould, p. 305
1600	15,000		
1700	20,288	Or 26,000 (seems high)	Loridan, p. 15
1726	22,550		Saugrain in Mols, II, p. 514
1745	16,440		Orry in Mols, II, p. 514
1775	19,124	From births (1771-80)	Messance, p. 49
1793	18,078		Loridan, p. 15
1801	17,180		Levasseur, II, p. 346
1850	23,000		
1851	23,263		Ungewitter, I, p. 887

Versailles

1744	5,000		Decaux, p. 160
1787	37,530		Levasseur, I, p. 227
1800	25,000		
1801	25,000		II, p. 345
1850	35,000		
1851	35,367		Ungewitter, I, p. 880

Geneva

1000	1,300-1,400		Blondel, I, p. 71
1200	3,300		" " "
1404	8,000		" " "
1475	11,000		" " "
1537	10,300		" " p. 227
1589	13,000		" " "
1698	16,934		Handwörterbuch, II, p. 678
1711	18,500		Blondel, I, p. 228
1750	21,000		
1755	21,816		Handwörterbuch, II, p. 678
1800	26,000		
1802	26,394	23,309 plus 3,085 in Carouge	Morse, II, p. 342
1850	42,123	31,238 plus 10,885 in Carouge, Eaux-Vives, Plainpalais, and Petit-Saconex	Blondel, II, pp. 92, 97; Hoffmann

Antwerp

1200		Only 31 hectares in area	Ganshof, pp. 45, 52
1374		C. 1,500 taxpayers (2,000 less than those in 13 smaller places)	Cuvelier, 1912, p. 11; cf. pp. 462-70
1437	19,000	3,440 houses (times 5.5; cf. 1526, 1645)	" " pp. 462-3
1496	36,000	6,586 houses (times 5.5)	" " "
1500	37,000		
1526	46,000	8,479 houses (times 5.5); hardly more than 50,000 people	" " " cccxxviii
1568	104,984	Including 14,981 aliens	Werveke, 1944, p. 61
1585	85,000	All Protestants expelled	Baedeker, 1901, p. 151
1589	55,000		" " "
1600	55,000		
1645	56,948	In 10,485 houses	Cuvelier, 1912, p. xxxn
1699	67,132	Within walls	Blockmans, 1952, p. 396
1700	67,000		
1750	43,000	Between wars	
1755	43,215	42,375 plus 840 in Markgravelei and Berchemse	" " pp. 375-6
1800	53,906		Heins, p. 11
1850	99,073	93,118 plus 5,955 in Borgerhout	Hoffmann

Bruges

961	12,000	4 parish churches	Duclos, 1918, p. 102
c.1000	12,000		Dickinson, 1951, p. 363n
1006		12,000 died from plague, but this number probably exaggerated	Duclos, p. 102
1089		Wall enclosed 70 hectares	Ganshof, pp. 45, 52
1100	15,000	8-10,000 in city alone in 3 parishes, but 5 total parishes	Duclos, p. 102
1200	25,000		
1200s	36,000	8 suburban parishes, plus 4 within the city (1247)	" pp. 102-3
1292	c.50,000	9,300 burghers	Häpke, p. 175
1300	50,000		
1309		Share of tax paid was more than 15%, compared to Ghent's 13% and Ypres' 10%	Duclos, p. 103
1340		35,000 (seems low; perhaps omits suburbs)	Smet, pp. 631-6
1340		6,250 hearths (also seems low)	Cited in Russell, 1958, p. 47
1340		6,253 in militia, plus 981 porters (militia count may be low due to heavy Flemish losses at battle of Sluys in 1330)	Verbruggen, p. 80
1400	125,000		
peak	150,000	According to chroniclers; Duclos regards this figure as possible	Duclos, p. 103
1417-		Depopulation, especially after 1440 and again after 1496	" "
1494		4-5,000 vacant houses	" p. 104
1500	90,000		
1537	70,000	In 14,683 houses	" "
1550	60,000	38,000 communicants, plus clergy, students,	Duclos, 1918, p. 104
1579		Less than 8,000 houses vacant	" "
1584	29,000		" "
1600	26,000		
1699	35,156		Wijffels, pp. 1,243-76
1700	35,000		
1738	27,821		" "
1750	27,000		

1768	26,000		Duclos, p. 105
1796	31,319		Wijffels, pp. 1,243-76
1800	31,000		
1804	30,826		" p. 106
1850	50,698		" "

Brussels

1357-79		New wall enclosed 450 hectares	Cuvelier, 1912, p. cxxiv
1374		At least 1/5 larger than Louvain	" " "
"		4,875 taxpayers	" " p. 15
"	18-22,000	C. 3,300-4,100 houses (derived from next two entries), times 5.5; cf. 1464	
1374-1437		Rate of growth of houses (non-poor only) between 56 and 95%	" " p. cxvi
1400	26,000		
1437	35,000	6,376 total houses (times 5.5)	" " pp. 446-7
1464		7,165 total houses (times 5.5); maximum of 40,000 in 15th century	" " " cccxxvii
1496	31,000	5,750 total houses (times 5.5)	" " p. 446-7
1500	31,000		
1526	32,000	5,953 total houses (times 5.5)	" " p. cclxxxiii
1600	55,000		
c.1650	70,000	Very roughly	Henne & Wauters, 1845, II, p. 53
1686	80,000	Nearly	Verniers, p. 337
1700	70,000		
1750	55,000		
1755	54,280		Mols, III, p. 198
1780		10,669 houses	Henne & Wauters, 1845, II, p. 297
1783	74,427		" " " " "
1800	66,297		" " " " "
1850	208,000		
1851	214,000	Including Anderlecht, Ixelles, Laeken Molenbeek, St. Gilles, Schaerbeek, and Uccle	Brockhaus, 1851

Charleroi

1850	41,210	7,937 plus 33,273 in Chatelet, Gilly, Gosselies, Jumet, Marchienne, and Roux	Hoffmann

Ghent

1100	12,000	4 parishes; 80 hectares in area	Werveke, 1946, pp. 19-20
c.1150		Main town of Flanders	Edrisi in Fris, 1913, p. 23
1191		Became capital of Flanders, succeeding Arras	
1200	25,000	See Arras	
1300		644 hectares in area	Werveke, 1946, p. 46
"	42,000		
1309	42,000	See Bruges, 1309	
c.1350	57,000	Based on men able to bear arms	Correspondence from Ghent Archive
1358		12,142 in militia; close to 60,000 population	Werveke, 1946, p. 64
1359	59,000	10,780 houses, times 5.5; cf. Antwerp (Russell's population figure unduly low)	Russell, 1958, p. 47

c.1380	60-70,000		Fris, p. vii
1382		Fell under French rule, disrupting wool trade with England	
1397		Wall measured 13 kilometers (c. 8 miles) in circuit	" 1913, p. vii
1400	70,000		
1467		c. 20,000 hearths (may be exaggerated) cf. next three entries	Schaschek in Fris, p. vii
1500	80,000		American Cyclopaedia
1539		Revolted, lost, and declined	Mols, II, p. 522
c.1550	50,000		
1566		55 churches still standing	Guicciardini in Fris, 1913, p. 186
1584		Fell to Spain; 1/3 fled	American Cyclopaedia
1600	31,000		
1610	31,000	Estimated from births and marriages	Werveke, 1946, p. 9
1690	52,000	Estimated from births and marriages	" " "
1700	49,000		
1740	38,000	Estimated from births and marriages	" " "
1750	38,000		
1800	54,000		
1802	55,161		Morse, II, p. 245
1850	108,256		Hoffmann

Liège

978	5,000	2 parishes (cf. 1015)	Kurth, 1910, I, p. 71
1000	12,000		
1015	17,000	14 churches, including 7 parish ones	" 1905, p. 376
-1100		Largest town in low countries	" " p. 169
1200-1800		24 parishes over whole period	" 1910, I, p. 171
1200	20,000		
1300	30,000	In fastest growing area of Europe	
1343		32 guilds	Blok, 1898, I, p. 292
1400	30,000		
1407		23,000 killed for revolting	Meyer, 1839, XXVI, p. 1168
1467		Raised 5,000 soldiers; crowd of 10,000 turned out to see a distinguished prisoner	Kurth, 1910, III, pp. 304, 305, 310
1468		Again destroyed for revolting	Larousse
1500	25,000		Harsin, II, p. 119
1600	30,000		
c.1650	30-36,000	Estimated from houses	Hélin, pp. 31, 35
1700	36,000		
1750	37,000		
1798	39,208		" p. 23
1800	40,000		
1850	92,164	79,901 plus 12,263 in Ans et Glain, Angleur, Chenée, and Flemalle	Hoffmann

Louvain

1100		60 hectares in area	Werveke, 1946, p. 21
1106-1383		Capital of Brabant	
1200	7,000		Cuvelier, 1935, p. 148
1252		4 parishes	" " pp. 148-9
1300	14,000		" " p. 148
c.1350	20,000	At maximum; largest town in Brabant	" " "
			" 1912, p. cxxiii
1357-63		New wall enclosed 410 hectares	Ganshof, pp, 52, 59
1374		3,850 taxpayers	Cuvelier, 1912, p. 15

1374	13-17,000	C. 2,500-3,150 houses (derived from next two entries), times 5.5; cf. 1526	
1374-1437		Rate of growth of houses (non-poor only) between 14 and 43%	Cuvelier, 1912, p. cxvi
1437	19,000	3,579 total houses (times 5.5)	" " pp. 432-3
1496	16,000	3,069 total houses (times 5.5)	" " "
1526	18-19,000	3,299 total houses (times 5.5)	" " "
			cclxvin
1597	9,000	1,658 total houses (times 5.5)	" 1935, p. 176
1631	9,000	1,796 households	" " "
1745	13,000	2,497 total houses (times 5.5)	" " "
1850	29,747		Hoffmann

Tournai

1365		3,991 men, plus apprentices	Mols, II, p. 7n
1800	21,000		
1802	21,349		Morse, II, p. 245
1850	30,000		
c.1855	30,225		Ungewitter, I, p. 691

Ypres

1258		40,000 including people outside the wall (probably an exaggeration)	Papal Bull in Demey, pp. 1034, 1048
1300	30,000		
1300s		112 hectares in area	Dickinson, 1951, p. 366
1309		See Bruges, 1309	
1311	30,000		Demey, p. 1040
1316		Pestilence killed 3,012	" p. 1036
1345		6,000 textile workers	" p. 1038
1365		7,000 died in pestilence	" p. 1037
1383		Fined 1/10 as much as Paris	Froissart, III, pp. 380, 413
1400	20,000		
1408		3,000-4,000 weavers	Demey, p. 1031
"	20,000		Werveke in Demey, p. 1042
1412	10,736		Demey, p. 1035
1491	7,390		" "
1506	9,563		" "
1600	5,000		Hymans, p. 80
1699	11,900		Demey, p. 1047
1786	11,860		Handwörterbuch, II, p. 681
c.1850	16,800		Brockhaus, 1864

(Netherlands—minus Belgium)

Amsterdam

1300	1,000		Blok, 1882, I, p. 67n
1494		1,919 houses	Brugmans, 1911, p. 48
1514		2,507 houses; 9,000 communicants	" " "
"	14,000	2,907 hearths	Brugmans & Peters, II, p. 466
1556	40,000	More than twice as many houses as in 1514	Brugmans, 1911, p. 48
1600	48,000	During wartime	Schraa, p. 10; cf. p. 17
1622	104,932		Stat. Amsterdam, p. 32
1630	115,249		" " "
1632		15,562 houses	Brugmans, 1911, p. 107
1685	158,000	Estimated from marriages	Schraa, p. 10, cf. p. 7
1700	172,000		
1750	219,000		" " " "
1795	217,024		Stat. Amsterdam, p. 32
1796	200,560		" " "
1800	201,000		
1809	201,747		" " "
1849	224,035		" " "
1850	225,000		" " "

Delft

1514	13,000	2,616 hearths	Brugmans & Peters, II, p. 467
1700	26,000		
1732	26,000	4,870 houses (times 5.5)	Büsching, 1767-71, V, p. 406
1750	22,000		
1796	13,737		
c.1850	17,500		Ency. Brit., 1853

Dordrecht

early		Capital of Holland countship	
1514	7,000	C. 1,500 hearths	Brugsmans & Peters, II, pp. 467-8
c.1660	17,000	3,274 houses, times 5.4	Oudenhouven, pp. 136-7; Mols, II, p. 160
1700	21,000	Peak of Dutch prosperity	
1732	21,000	3,950 houses (times 5.4)	Büsching, 1767, V, p. 405
1750	20,000		
1796	18,014		Morse, II, p. 236
1850	20,878		Ency. Brit., 1853, "Dort"

Gouda

1382	4,000	820 houses (times 5.5; cf. Amsterdam, 1494)	Brugmans & Peters, III, p. 121
1492	9,000	1,608 houses	" " II, p. 468
1700	23,000		
1732	23,000	3,974 houses; times 5.9	Büsching, 1767, V, p. 411; Mols, II, p. 160
1796	11,715		Morse, II, p. 237
1850	13,791		Ency.,Brit., 1853

Groningen

1796	23,770		Morse, II, p. 236
1800	24,000		
1840	30,260		Gazetteer of World
1850	33,000		
1863	36,762		Lippincott, 1868

Haarlem

1427		Paid much the highest Dutch tax	Orlers, p. 51
1514	13,000	2,714 hearths	Brugmans & Peters, II, p. 469
1572	18,000		Nieuwenhuis, 1946, p. 37
1600	25,000	See Amsterdam, Rotterdam	
1622	39,455		'' '' ''
1632		6,490 houses	'' '' ''
1700	48,000	Peak of Dutch prosperity	
1732	48,000	7,963 houses (times 6.1; cf. 1622-1632)	'' '' ''
1750	40,000		
1798	21,227		'' '' ''
1800	21,000		
1850	25,778		Ency. Brit., 1853

The Hague (s'Gravenhage)

1514	6,000		Enci. Italiana, "L'Aia"
1622	17,430		Ency. Brit., 1875
1680	26,000		Stat. Yearbook of Kingdom, 1956, p. 10
1700	29,000		
1732	34,000		Ency. Brit., 1875
1732		6,164 houses	Büshing, 1767, V, p. 416
1750	40,000		
1755	41,500	Including Scheveningen for first time	Stat. Yearbook of Kingdom, 1956, p. 10
1796	41,266		Ency. Brit., 1875
1800	41,000		
1811	42,350		Stat. Yearbook of Kingdom, 1956, p. 10
1837	59,000	54,000 plus Scheveningen	English Cyclopaedia
1850	65,000		
1854	69,600	64,000 plus 5,600 in Scheveningen	'' '' ; Ency. Brit. 1853

s'Hertogenbosch (Bois-le-duc)

1374		3,647 taxpayers	Cuvelier, 1912, p. 15
''	13-16,000	2,400-3,100 houses (derived from next 2 entries) times 5.5 as in Belgian cities	
1374-1437		Rate of growth of houses (non-poor only) between −6 and +19%	'' '' p. 15, p. cxvii
1437	15,000	2,883 total houses (times 5.5)	'' '' '' p. 476-7
1496	19,000	3,456 total houses	'' '' '' ''
1526	21,000	3,841 total houses	'' '' p. cclxxxiv
1796	12,627		Morse, II, p. 237
c.1850	21,000		Ency. Brit., 1853, "Bois-le-Duc"

Leiden (Leyden)

1502	6,000	976 taxable hearths, plus c. 35% more for hearths of the poor (cf. Rotterdam)	Brugsmans & Peters, II, p. 469
1550	15,000		Blok, 1882, III, p. 1
1600	25,000	See Amsterdam, Rotterdam	
1622	44,745		'' '' '' p. 6
1659	70,000	In 13,000 houses	'' '' '' '' ; Leewen, 1672, p. 72
1700	62,000		

1732	57,000	54,000 at 5 per house (multiplier raised to 5.3, the ratio at 1622-1632 and 1659)	Blok, 1882, III, p. 7; Mols, II, p. 160
1750	49,000		
1798	30,967	Census	Blok, 1882, IV, p. 1
1800	31,000		
1805	31,000		" " " p. 2
1850	36,000		" " " "

Middelburg

1600	20,000	See Amsterdam, Rotterdam	
1630s	26,000	Estimated from births	Mols, I, p. 288
1650s	30,000	Estimated from births	" " "
1700	25,000		
1700s	25,000	Estimated from births	" " "
1750	23,000		
c.1790	22,000	Estimated from births	" " "
1796	17,687	Census	Morse, II, p. 236
1855	16,253		Ency. Brit., 1853

Rotterdam

1496	5,000	972 houses, 303 of which poor (times 5.5; cf. Amsterdam, Hague)	Hazewinkel, p. 127
1514	6,000	1,137 houses (times 5.5); 3,500 communicants	Brugmans & Peters, II, p. 469
1553	6,000	1,200 houses (times 5.5)	Hazewinkel, p. 127
1622	19,780	Including Cool (at this and all later dates)	Van de Woude & Mentink, p. 1173
1632	30,000	5,048 houses (times 6; cf. Amsterdam)	Correspondence from Municipal Library of Rotterdam
1650	55,000		Enci. Italiana
1690	53,000	51-55,000	Van de Woude & Mentink, p. 1175
1700	51,000		
1732	39,000	6,621 houses	Büsching, 1767, V, p. 412
1745	45,000		Van de Woude & Mentink, p. 1175
1750	46,000		
1795	57,510		" " " p. 1173
1800	58,000		
1809	59,118		" " " "
1850	111,957	88,812, plus 23,145 in Delftshavn, Schiedam, and Vlaardingen	Harper; Blackie (Suppl.)

Utrecht

1100	3,000	1 parish	Ganshof, p. 48
1200	12,000	4 churches, i.e., parishes	Allan, pp. 63-75
1300-1600		7 churches (parishes)	" "
1300	20,000		
1480		2,000 in militia	Correspondence from Utrecht Archive
1557		c. 35,000 (seems exaggerated)	Mols, II, p. 522
1600	21,000		
1650	22,000		Correspondence from Utrecht Archive
1700	24,000	8 churches (parishes)	Allan, pp. 63-75

1748	25,244	Census in Utrecht Archive	Correspondence from Utrecht Archive
1750	25,000		
1796	32,294	Census in Utrecht Archive	" " " "
1800	32,000	9 churches, 1 synagogue	Allan, pp. 63-75
1848	48,246		" p. 48n
1850	48,000		
1853	49,176		" "

Aberdeen

1396	2,977		Groome, 1901
1581	5,833		" "
1643	8,750		" "
1708	5,556		" "
1755	15,730		" "
1800	26,000		
1801	26,992		" "
1841	63,288		" "
1850	71,000		
1851	71,973		" "

Bath

1700		Births 1/14 as many as in 1800	Warner, pp. 266-72
1800	31,000		
1801	32,150	Including suburbs	Capper
1841	52,346		Hoffmann
1850	54,000		
1851	54,240		English Cyclopaedia

Belfast

1757	8,549		Ency. Brit., 1910
1791	18,320		Benn in O'Brien, p. 297
1800	22,000		
1813	27,832		" " " "
1841	75,308		English Cyclopaedia
1850	99,000		
1851	102,103		Ency. Brit., 1853

Birmingham

1700	15,000		Ency. Brit., 1910
1750	23,688		Law, p. 93
1800	72,000		
1801	73,670		Capper
1841	235,207	182,922 plus 52,285 in Handsworth, Harborne, Smethwick, Wednesbury, and West Bromwich	Harper; Gazetteer of World; Hoffmann
1850	294,000		
1851	300,826	232,841 plus 67,985 in above suburbs	English Cyclopaedia; Blackie (Suppl.)

Blackburn

1801	11,980		Capper
1841	36,629		Hoffmann
1850	45,000		
1851	46,536		English Cyclopaedia

Bolton

1801	17,416		Capper
1841	49,763		English Cyclopaedia
1850	60,000		
1851	61,171		" "

Bradford

1801	7,302		Capper
1841	66,718		Gazetteer of World
1850	100,000		
1851	103,778		Ency. Brit., 1853

Brighton

1801	7,339		Capper
1841	46,601		English Cyclopaedia
1850	63,000		
1851	65,569		Ency. Brit., 1853

Bristol

1568	6,000		Brown Harris, p. 74
1607	12,000	10,549 plus suburbs	Latimer, 1900, p. 2
1700	25,000		" 1893, p. 6
1750	45,000		
1753	46,692		Brown Harris, p. 123
1800	66,000		
1801	66,933	Including Bedminster for 1st time	Capper
1841	140,158	Including Clifton	Hoffmann
1850	150,000		
1851	151,528	Including 14,200 in Clifton	Ency. Brit., 1853

Chatham

1801	20,285	10,505 plus 9,780 in Gillingham and Rochester	Capper
1841	35,905	17,903 plus 18,002 in Gillingham and Rochester	Gazetteer of World
1850	49,000		
1851	51,314	28,424 plus 22,890 in Gillingham and Rochester	Ency. Brit., 1853

Cork

c.1280		12 hectares in area	Russell, 1966, p. 506
1462		11 parish churches in and near	C. Smith, I, p. 371
1659	4,826		O'Sullivan, p. 85
1710-50		Tripled	" p. 224
1732	44,000	7,967 families at 7 per family (times 4/5; data for county; cf. 1831)	C. Smith, I, p. 389 [cf. Harper; Ency. Brit., 1853]
1749	53,000	7,366 houses, times 9 (cf. 1788-1791); reduced by 1/5 (cf. 1732)	C. Smith, I, p. 389
1750	53,000		
1788		8,073 houses in county	O'Sullivan, p. 255
1791	58,000	73,000 in county (reduced by 1/5)	Beaufort in O'Sullivan, p. 255
1800	63,000		
1831	84,000	In city and suburbs; 107,000 in county	Lewis
1841	80,723		Ency. Brit., 1853
1850	89,000		
1851	90,022	Including those in the poorhouse	English Cyclopaedia

Derby

1801	10,382		Capper
1841	36,395		Hoffmann
1850	40,000		
1851	40,609		English Cyclopaedia

Dublin

c.1050	4-5,000	47 hectares in area (population estimate may be too low, cf. 1280)	Russell, 1966, p. 505
1200	17,000	C. 20 churches in vicinity	Chart, p. 24

1246	20,000		Hollingsworth, p. 269
1280	25,000	Criticizing Russell's estimate of 10,000; 112 hectares in area	" " Russell, 1962, pp. 505-6
1300	25,000		
1300-99		In decline	Chart, p. 32
1600	26,000		
1610	26,000		Speed in Maxwell, pp. 46, 48
1682	64,483		Lewis
1700	80,000		
1750	125,000		
1753	128,570		"
1777	138,208		"
1800	165,000		
1802	167,899		Morse, II, p. 133
1804	172,370	Including 4,148 in Blackrock, Harold's Cross, and Sandy Mount	Ency. Edinensis
1841	238,819	232,726 plus 6,093 in Blackrock, Harold's Cross, and Ranelagh	Ency. Brit., 1853; Gazetteer of World
1850	263,000		
1851	265,896	258,361 plus 7,535 in Blackrock, Harold's Cross, Ranelagh, and Rathmines	English Cyclopaedia; Blackie (Suppl.)

Dundee

1746	5,302		Hoffmann
1800	25,000		
1801	26,084		Capper
1841	63,732		Groome
1850	77,000		
1851	78,931		"

Edinburgh

1385	2,000	Barely exceeded this size	J. Grant, I, p. 26
1450		New wall built, c. 1 mile in circuit, plus c. 1/2 mile boundary on lake (thus, area of c. 35 hectares).	" " p. 38
1500	18,000	Area over half that in 1600	
1500s		New wall built, 1 mile, 3 furlongs in circuit (thus, area of c. 65 ha.)	" " "
c.1600		Very densely populated; houses up to 15 stories	Smeaton, p. 74; Watkeys, pp. 101, 124, 188
"	30,000	Including Leith at this and all later dates	
1645		2,421 in Leith (1/2 the population) died of plague	Royal Comm. on Ancient Monuments, p. lvii
1678	35,500		Morse, II, p. 102
1700	35,000		
1705	35,692		Gazetteer of World
1750	55,000		
1755	57,195		Ency. Brit., 1853
1791	85,486		Gazetteer of World
1800	82,000		
1801	82,560		Morse, II, p. 103
1841	167,144	164,363 plus 2,781 in Portobello	Gazetteer of World; Hoffmann
1850	194,000		
1851	197,427	193,930 plus 3,497 in Portobello	Groome; Blackie (Suppl,); Hoffmann

Glasgow

1300	1,500		Groome, p. 727
1450	2,000		" "
1600	7,000		" "
1660	14,678		" "
1708	12,766		" "
1750	21,000		
1757	23,546		" "
1775	43,000		Capper
1800	85,000		
1801	86,630	77,385 plus suburbs and adjoining places	"
1841	274,366	255,650 plus 18,716 in Govan, Pollock-shaws, and Rutherglen	Groome, p. 727; Gazetteer of World; Hoffmann
1850	346,000		
1851	353,981	329,096 plus 24,885 in above suburbs and Coatbridge	Groome, p. 727; Blackie, (Suppl.)

Hull

1792	22,286		Law, p. 93
1800	28,000		
1801	29,516		Morse, II, p. 66
1841	67,308		Hoffmann
1850	83,000		
1851	84,690		English Cyclopaedia

Leeds

1771	16,380		Law, p. 93
1800	52,000		
1801	53,162		Capper
1841	165,400	152,054 plus 13,346 in Holbeck	Gazetteer of World
1850	184,000		
1851	186,422	172,270 plus 14,152 in Holbeck	Ency. Brit., 1853; Blackie, (Suppl.)

Leicester

1801	16,953		Capper
1841	50,365		Hoffmann
1850	59,000		
1851	60,584		English Cyclopaedia

Limerick

1659	3,105		Begley, p. 348
1760	16,000	25,000 in county (reduced by 1/3; cf., 1831)	O'Brien, p. 372
1775	20,000	30,000 in county (reduced by 1/3; cf., 1831)	" "
1800	30,000		
1821	39,000	59,045 in county (reduced by 1/3; cf., 1831)	Lewis
1831	44,100	In city and suburbs; 66,554 in county	"
1841	48,391		Gazetteer of World
1850	54,000		
1851	55,268	48,961 in city alone	Hoffmann; Ency. Brit., 1853

Lincoln

1000	8,000		

1066	8,000	1,140 houses	J. Hill, p. 54
1086	6,600	900 houses (thus, 7 1/3 per house)	" "
1377	5,354		Russell, 1958, p. 61
1801	7,197		Gazetteer of World
1851	17,536		" " "

Liverpool

1700		Tiny	Morse, II, p. 60
1750	20,000		
1760	25,787		" " "
1800	76,000		
1801	77,653		" " "
1841	297,587	286,487 plus 11,100 in Birkenhead and Liscard and Seacombe	Ency. Brit., 1853; Gazetteer of World; Hoffman
1850	422,000		
1851	440,323	376,065 plus 64,258 in above suburbs and West Derby	Ency. Brit., 1853; Blackie, (Suppl.)

London

1000	25,000		
1066	30,000	Before rise under Normans	
c.1199	40,000		Peter of Blois in Ency. Brit., 1910
1200	40,000		
1300	40,000		
1348-1349		Plague said to kill 40,000	Ency. Brit., 1910
1377	34,971	Poll count 23,314 plus 1/2 for children	Russell, 1948, p. 142
1189-1509	40-50,000	All the way, on the average	Creighton in Ency. Brit., 1910
1400	45,000		
1407		Plague said to kill 30,000	Capper
"	50,000		"
1532-5		Plague said to kill 20,000	
1593-5	62,000		Creighton in Ency. Brit., 1910
"	152,000		" " " " "
1600	187,000		
1605	224,000		" " " " "
1690	527,000		G. King, p. 18
1700	550,000		Ency. Brit., 1910, (based on King)
1750	676,000		" " " " " "
1800	861,000		
1801	864,845		Morse, II, p. 59
1851	1,948,417		Hoffmann
1850	2,320,000		
1851	2,362,236		English Cyclopaedia

Manchester

1588	10,000		Ency. Brit., 1875
1708	8,000		Morse, II, p. 62
1758	19,839	Including Salford	Law, p. 91
1773	29,151	Including Salford	" "
1800	81,000		
1801	84,020	70,409 plus 13,611 in Salford	Capper
1841	312,965	240,367 plus 72, 598 in Barton, Droylsden, Pendlebury, Salford, and Stretford	English Cyclopaedia; Hoffman; Gazetteer of World
1850	404,000		
1851	414,870	303,382 plus 111,488 in above suburbs	English Cyclopaedia; Blackie, (Suppl.)

Merthyr-Tydfil

1841	42,917		Gazetteer of World
1850	61,000		
1851	63,080		U.K. Census, 1851 report on religious worship

Newcastle

1400	4,000		Middlebrook, p. 321
1560	10,000		" "
1636		5,027 died of plague; 515 more died in Gateshead	Howell, p. 7
1665		2,513 households, but 5,187 hearths (without Gateshead)	" p. 351
1690-1700		7,000 people in Gateshead	Brand, I, p. 485
1700	25,000	18,000 plus Gateshead	Middlebrook, p. 321
1740	28,000	21,000 plus Gateshead	" "
1750	29,000		
1770	31,000	24,000 plus Gateshead	" "
1800	36,000		
1801	36,891	28,294 plus 8,597 in Gateshead	Capper
1841	90,009	70,504 plus 19,505 in Gateshead	Middlebrook, p. 321; Gazetteer of World
1850	111,000		
1851	113,352	87,784 plus 25,568 in Gateshead	Middlebrook, p. 321; English Cyclopaedia

Norwich

1086	5,000		Domesday Book in Chamber's Ency., 1907
1300	25,000		
1311	25,000	In 4,808 houses	Hollingsworth, p. 364
1377	7,000	3,952 paid poll tax (times 1.75 – Russell uses 1.5)	Russell, 1948, p. 51
1579	16,000		Ency. Brit., 1970
1693	28,881		Gazetteer of World
1700	29,000		
1750	36,000		
1752	36,169		Law, p. 92
1800	36,000		
1801	36,832		
1841	62,294		Gazetteer of World
1850	67,000		
1851	68,195		English Cyclopaedia

Nottingham

1739	10,720		Law, p. 92
1779	17,711		" "
1800	28,000		
1801	28,862		Capper
1841	84,142	Including Basford, Lenton, Radford, and Sneinton	Church, p. 8
1850	93,000		
1851	94,976	Including above places	" "

Oldham

1801	12,024		Gazetteer of World
1841	60,451		Hoffmann
1850	71,000		
1851	72,357		"

Paisley

1753	4,195		
1800	24,000		Groome
1801	24,324		"
1841	56,133	48,125 plus 8,008 in Johnstone and Kilbarchan	Gazetteer of World
1850	56,000		
1851	56,291	47,952 plus 8,339 in above suburbs	Groome; Hoffman; Lippincott, 1868

Plymouth

1500	c.2-3,000		Correspondence from Plymouth Public Library
1600	c.7,000		" " "
			" "
1700	c.8,000		" " "
			" "
1750	c.13,000	Including c. 4,000 in Devonport	" " "
			" "
1800	42,000		
1801	43,194	Including Devonport and Stonehouse	Ency. Brit., 1853
1841	80,058	36,527 plus 43,531 in Devonport and Stonehouse	" " "
1850	100,000		
1851	102,380	52,221 plus 50,159 in above suburbs	" " "

Portsmouth

1800	43,000		
1801	43,461	32,166 with Portsea, plus 11,295 in Gosport	Capper
1841	61,889	53,027 with Portsea, plus 8,862 in Gosport	Hoffmann
1850	77,000		
1851	79,510	72,096 with Portsea, plus 7,414 in Gosport	"

Preston

1801	14,300		Gazetteer of World
1841	50,073		M'Culloch
1850	70,000		
1851	72,136		Gazetteer of World

Sheffield

1615	2,152		Morse, II, p. 62
1736	14,105		Law, p. 93
1755	12,983		" "
1800	45,000		
1801	45,755		Ency. Brit., 1875
1841	118,166	110,891 plus 7,275 in Nether Hallam	Hoffmann
1850	141,000		
1851	144,207	135,310 plus 8,897 in Nether Hallam	Blackie (Suppl.)

Stockport

1801	14,830		Capper
1841	50,154		Hoffmann
1850	58,000		
1851	58,835		English Cyclopaedia

Stoke

1800	22,000		
1801	22,992	16,414 plus 6,578 in Burslem	Capper
1841	68,444	Including Burslem and Hanley	Hoffmann
1850	82,000		
1851	84,027	Including Burslem and Hanley	English Cyclopaedia

Sunderland

1801	12,412		Capper
1841	53,335		Hoffmann
1850	66,000		
1851	67,394		English Cyclopaedia

Winchester

1000	15,000	Prospering under good rule	
1066	20,000	2/3 the size of London	Compton, p. 94
1801	5,823		Capper

Wolverhampton

1801	12,566		Ency. Brit., 1853
1841	68,185		M'Culloch
1850	112,000		
1851	119,748		Ency. Brit., 1853

York

990		30,000, estimate (Looks too high)	Vivien
1000	12,000		
1066	12,000	1,890 burgesses; c. 9,000 total in burgess families (probably 1/3 more for non-burgesses)	Russell, 1948, p. 218
1377	10,000	7,248 over 14 years old	" p. 142
1801	16,145		Capper
1850	35,000		
1851	36,303		U.K. Census, 1851, report on religious worship

Bergen

1110-1299		Capital of Norway	Stagg, p. 38
c.1270	16,000	13 churches (times 1,250)	'' p. 64
1300	15,000		
1769	13,735		Büsching, "Magazin," 1774, p. 230
1801	18,080	With suburbs	'' '' '' ''
1845	24,279		Norge, III, p. 311
1850	26,000		
1865	31,800		'' '' ''

Copenhagen (København)

1100s		4 large parish churches	F. Schneider, p. 131
1300s	3-4,000		Bredsdorff, p. 41
1400s	8-10,000		'' ''
1443	4-5,000	Became capital of Denmark	Stat. Aarbog København, p. 1
1500	c.10,000		'' '' '' ''
1600	40,000		
1640	54,000	Including Fridiricia; calculated from births	Fussing, p. 23
1650		c. 30,000 (without Fredericia)	Stat. Aarbog København, p. 1
1699	62,000		Nordisk Familjebok
1700	62,000		
1728	76,000		Salmonsen
1750	79,000		
1769	82,086		Stat. Aarbog København, p. 1
1787	92,671		'' '' '' ''
1800	100,000		
1801	100,975		Ency. Brit., 1875
1850	135,641		Stat. Aarbog København, p. 1

Lejre

9th century		Capital of Denmark

Roskilde

1274	20,000	3 cloisters (cf. 1500)	Knudsen, p. 71
1300	22,000		
1400	31,000		
peak	33,000	27 total churches	Büsching, 1767, I, p. 141
''		70,000 (appears too high)	Meyer, 1839
1443	36,000	12 parish churches and 5 cloisters, while Copenhagen had 4 and 2	Bredsdorff, p. 41
1500	25,000	3 parish churches had closed	Knudsen, pp. 43-4
1800	2,000		Hassel, 1819, X, p. 76

Stockholm

1255		Founded	
1461	4-8,000	In 1,002 households	Ahnlund, pp. 296-8
1517	7,000	1,171 households, plus merchants, palace servants, garrison, nobles, and clergy	Elers, pp. 273, 275
1622-50		Rapid expansion depicted by maps	Gutkind, pp. 432-3
1663	40,000	14,953 in city alone	Nordisk Familjebok
1700	48,000		

1750	60,018		Stat. Årsbok Stockholms, p. 6
1800	75,517		"　　"　　　"　　"
1850	93,070		"　　"　　　"　　"

Visby

1200s		Main churches built	Ency. Brit., 1910
1300	<u>15,000</u>		
1361	<u>17,000</u>	13 churches (times 1,250)	Enci. Italiana
1361		56 hectares in area	Russell., 1958, p. 54
"		Destroyed	
1800	3,730		Nordisk Familjebok

Aachen (Aix-la-Chapelle)

768-814		Main capital of Charlemagne, but had only 1 church	Sullivan, p. 173
1100s		Walled area rose from 8 to 44 hectares	Plaitz, p. 201
1300	21,000	Walled area rose to 175 hectares (times 125; low density with new wall)	" "
1500	15-20,000		Deutsches Städtebuch, III, part 3, p. 33
1600	22,000	20,000-25,000	" " "
			" "
1656	25,000		" " "
			" "
1700	24,000		
1750	24,000		
1799	23,699		" " "
			" "
1800	23,000		
1849	56,190	50,533 plus 5,657 in Burtscheid	Ency. Brit., 1853
1850	56,000		
1852	55,702	48,688 plus 6,020 in Burtscheid	Hoffmann

Augsburg

c.800		Charlemagne built its 2nd parish church	Püschel, p. 169
1200	12,000	4 parishes	" "
1364	14,000	2,249 houses (times 6.3, cf. 1408)	Russell, 1958, p. 52
1373		Taxed barely less than Ulm	Kallsen, p. 608
1408	14,000	2,343 houses; 2,957 households (actually, taxpayers, or their equivalent, heads of households) times 5; this implies 6.3 persons per house	Russell, 1958, p. 52
1471	17,000	2,836 houses (times 6.3)	
1475	18,000		Enci. Italiana, "Augusta"
1498	19,000	3,046 homes (times 6.3)	Russell, 1958, p. 52
1500	20,000		
1550	55-60,000		Enci. Italiana, "Augusta"
1600	48,000		
1620	45,000		" " "
1645	21,018		" " "
1700	26,000		
1703	26,300		" " "
1750	31,000		
1792	36,000		" " "
1800	32,000		
1807	28,534		Morse, II, p. 307
1846	38,206		Hoffmann
1850	35,000		
1852	34,211		"

Barmen-Elberfeld (Wuppertal)

1817	19,171	In Barmen; probably not yet joined to Elberfeld	Hoffmann
1849		35,984 in Barmen	"
1850	75,000		
1851		39,944 in Elberfeld	"

Berlin

1602	8,000	Including garrison	Mulhall, p. 446
1698	22,400	Including garrison	Schmoller, p. 95

1700	24,000	Became royal place in 1701	
1709	56,600		Keyser, 1941, p. 375
1750	113,289		" " "
1800	172,132		" " "
1850	446,000	437,000 plus 9,357 in Charlottenburg	Hoffmann

Bremen

937-		An archbishopric	
1100s		Walled area rose from 12 to 49 hectares	Planitz, p. 201
c.1348		Plague killed 7,000	W. King, p. 429
1494	18,000	3,000 militia	Spiess, p. 24
1521	18,000	3,000 militia	" p. 26
1600	21,000		
1623	23,000		Schwarzwälder, p. 97
1700	22,000		
1744	22,000	4,550 adult males	Büsching, 1767, X, p. 2,599
1750	23,000		
c.1792	30,000		Keyser, 1941, p. 376
1800	31,000		
1836	36,000	54,581 in whole area (reduced 1/3; cf. 1842)	Gazetteer of World
1842	49,788	72,908 in whole area	" " "
1849	53,478		Hoffmann
1850	54,000		

Breslau (Wroclaw)

1242	12,000	4 parish churches	Maleczynski, map p. 64
1250		Wall enclosed 62 hectares	Planitz, p. 202
1300	14,000		
1325	15,000		Dlugoborski, p. 900
1327		Wall enclosed 133 ha.	Maleczynski, p. 83
1329	16,000		" p. 85
1348	21,866		Handwörterbuch, II, p. 675
1400	21,000		
1403	21,000		Schmoller, p. 95
"		2,510 burghers; 108 bakers	Bücher, p. 111
1470	21,000	18,500-21,000	Eulenburg in Maleczynski, p. 206
1500	21,000		
1505		30,000 (looks high)	Keyser, 1941, p. 196
1525	22,000		Burgemeister in Maleczynski, p. 206
1550	35,000	(Based on next item?)	Schmoller, p. 95
1579	34,200		Eulenburg in Maleczynski, p. 207
1599		3,942 died in epidemic	Maleczynski, p. 208n
1600	33,000		
1607-11	37,000	32,430 plus nobles etc.	" " ; Meyer 1874
1700	40,000		
1710	40,890		Ersch
1747	49,986		Dlugoburski, p. 738
1750	52,000		
1756	54,774		Ersch
1800	64,520		Keyser, 1941, p. 375
1849	110,702		Ency. Brit., 1853
1850	114,000		
1852	121,052		Hoffmann

Brunswick (Braunschweig)

861		Founded	
1181-95		Capital of Henry the Lion	
1200	21,000	7 parishes	Püschel, pp. 71, 77
1403	16,000	15-17,000	Keyser, 1941, p. 264
1700	17,000		Correspondence with Brunswick archives
1750	25,000		
1758	25,800	Including 3,000 garrison	" " " "
1783	27,063		Havemann, p. 663
1800	31,000		
1804	31,714		Morse, II, p. 300
1850	40,000		
1852	40,000	37,694 plus garrison	Ency. Brit., 1853

Cologne (Köln, Cöln)

800	15,000		
804	15,000	5 parishes	Püschel, p. 202
874	21,000	7 parishes	" "
1000	21,000		
1050	21,000	17 churches	Planitz, p. 63
1106-80		Walled area rose from 120 to 400 hectares	" pp. 200
1180	50,000	Area times 125; lower density with new wall	
1100s		Passed Mainz as first in Germany	Schmoller, p. 81
1200	50,000		
1200s	60,000	Probably too high an estimate	" "
1300	54,000	18 parishes	Püschel, p. 203
1333	57,000	19 parishes	" "
1359		1,500 militia	Meyer, 1839
1400	40,000		Schmoller, p. 79
1500	45,000		
c.1500		50,000, in 7,639 houses (his multiplier is probably too high)	Kallsen, p. 51
1574	37,000		Banck in Schmoller, p. 64n
1600	37,000		
1670	37,000		Correspondence from Cologne City Library
1700	39,000		
1750	44,000		Meyer, 1874
1754	44,512		
1800	41,000		
1801	41,685		Deutsches Städtebuch, III, part 3, p. 255
1850	95,082	90,085 plus 4,997 in Deutz (in 1849)	Meyer, 1874; Hoffmann

Danzig

1367	7,700		Simson, I, p. 78
1378	8,500		" " "
1430	20,000		" p. 165
1500	30,000		
1506	30,000		" p. 373
1600	49,000		
1601	49,000	Estimated from births	" II, p. 463
1700	50,000		
1705	50,400		Deutsches Städtebuch, I, p. 35

1745	47,600		″ ″ ″ ″
1750	47,000		
1800	41,072		″ ″ ″ ″
1849	63,917	Including garrison	Ency. Brit., 1853
1850	65,000		
1852	67,016	Including garrison	Hoffmann

Dresden

1489	4,800		Schmoller, p. 92
1603	14,793		Deutsches Städtebuch, III, p. 50
1699	21,298		″ ″ ″ ″
1700	22,000		″ ″ ″ ″
1727	46,472		″ ″ ″ ″
1750	60,000		
1755	63,209		″ ″ ″ ″
1800	61,000		
1801	61,794		″ ″ ″ ″
1849	94,902		Ency. Brit., 1853
1850	97,000		
1852	104,198		Enci. Italiana

Erfurt

805		Became Charlemagne's staple town for the Sorbs	Meyer, 1839
1167		127 hectares in area	Planitz, p. 201
1200	21,000	7 parishes	Püschel, p. 109
1300	30,000	10 parishes	″ pp. 113, 116-7
medieval		120 hectares in built-on area	Schünemann, p. 121
″		Peak: 32,000 at most	Schmoller, p. 168n
1400	24,000		
1498	18,680		Deutsches Städtebuch, II, p. 481
1620	19,014		Keyser, 1941, p. 375
1727	17,320		Schmoller, p. 288
1802	16,580		Deutsches Städtebuch, II, p. 481
1849	32,224		Hoffmann
1850	32,000		
1852	32,940		″

Frankfurt

840-876		Capital of Louis the German	Meyer, 1839
1200	3,000	Only 1 known parish church	Püschel, p. 122
1300	13,000	10% smaller than Soest	Rothert, p. 25
1311-50		Averaged 27 new burghers per year	″ ″
1351-1450		Averaged 40 new burghers per year	″ ″
1378	20,000	2,904 burghers over 12 (times 7; cf. Nuremberg, 1449)	Bücher, p. 111
1383		1,500 militia; area as in 1840 (128 ha.)	Meyer, 1874; Gerber in Voelcker, p. 17
1400	17,000		
1440		64 bakers (91 in 1387)	Bücher, p. 237
″	14,000	2,106 adult male burghers (times 7)	″ p. 199
1450		12,000 communicants	Nicholas V in Bücher, p. 198
1486		Taxed 5/6 as much as Strassburg	Schmoller, p. 80
1500	20,000		
1600	20,000		
1605	20,000		Deutsches Städtebuch, IV, p. 131

1700	35,000	Including Sachsenhausen for 1st time	Gerber in Voelcker, p. 17
1750	38,500		" " " "
1800	42,000		" " " "
1848		58,000 in city alone	Gutkind, "Cent. Europe," p. 270
1850	72,000		
1852	74,111	62,361 plus 6,100 in Bockenheim and Rödelheim, and 5,650 in garrison	Ency. Brit., Hoffmann

Hamburg

982-1020		Abandoned	Dathe, p. 5
1100s		18 hectares in walled area	Planitz, p. 201
1311	8,000	7,000 based on burghers (multiplier of 6 too low; assumes only 4 per burgher family and 1/3 total population as non-burghers), times 7/6	Laurent in Bücher, p. 28; cf. Mols, I, pp. 229, 260
1400	22,000		
1419	25,000	22,000 times 7/6, cf. 1311	Laurent in Bücher, p. 28
1451	20,000	2,958 burghers, times 7 (cf. Nuremberg)	" " " "
"		2,880 poor	Koppmann in Mols p. 230n
1487	22,000	3,264 poor, times 7 (cf. 1451)	" " " "
1500	22,000		
1538	23,000	3,360 poor, times 7 (cf. 1451)	" " " "
1594		19,000 based on new burghers, up from 12,000 in 1525 (these estimates are far too low; absolute number of burghers may have been frozen in 15th century; cf. 1451 and c. 1800)	Laurent in Bücher, p. 28
1600	40,000	Estimated from births; 6,600 in militia	Reincke, pp. 171, 176
1680	60,000	Including 10,260 in militia	" p. 173
1700	70,000		
1710	75,000	Estimated from births	" "
1750	90,000	Estimated from partial count in 1764	" p. 174
c.1800		3,000-4,000 burghers	Böhme, p. 871
1800	130,000		
1801	130,000	Including Altona	" p. 175n
1842		136,956 in city alone	Hoffmann
1850	193,000		
1852		148,754 plus Harburg (5,500 in c. 1850), Wandsbek (4,600 in 1850), and Altona (32,200 in 1845 and 53,039 in 1864)	" ; Deutsches Städtebuch, I, pp. 362, 453

Hannover

pre 1500	12-15,000		Hartmann, p. 117
1640	10,000		" p. 229
1670	7,000	1,318 burghers times 5.5 – the ratio that year at Göttingen	Havemann, II, pp. 440 471
1766	15,448		" p. 666
1796	18,000	16,500 plus 3 regiments	Hartmann, p. 754
1821	21,517	Including garrison	" p. 568n
1845	42,484	28,055 plus suburbs and garrison	Gazetteer of World
1848		34,874 in city alone	Hoffmann
1850	48,000		
1852	49,909	Including suburbs	Ency. Brit., 1853

Königsberg

1255		Founded	
1400	10-15,000		Keyser, 1939, p. 67
1500	8-10,000		Gause, I, p. 119
1550	14,000		" " p. 320
1700	32,000		
1723	39,475		Keyser, 1941, p. 375
1750	52,000		
1755	55,000		" " "
1798	49,900		Gause, II, p. 293
1800	53,000		
1802	56,410		Morse, II, p. 223
1850	76,122		Deutsches Städtebuch, I, p. 69

Leipzig

1506	8,556		Deutsches Städtebuch, II, p. 123
1617	15,136		" " " "
1700	21,696		" " " "
1748	29,760		" " " "
1750	30,000		
1753	32,384		" " " "
1797	31,847		" " " "
1800	32,000		
1811	35,230		" " " "
1849	62,374		" " " "
1850	63,000		
1852	66,682		English Cyclopaedia

Lübeck

1227	6,000	2 parish churches	Püschel, p. 17
1300	24,000		
1350	37,500		Laurent in Reisner, p. 38
1360	37,000		Schmoller, p. 94
1400	30,000	22,300 (times 1.35; cf. 1500-1503)	Handwörterbuch, II, p. 675
1500	32,000		
"		23,672	" " "
1503	32,000	5,322 houses (times 6; cf. Augsburg, Cologne)	Mols, II, p. 150
1548		Pestilence killed 12,227	Meyer, 1839
1600	31,000		
1642-61	31,000	Estimate based on 1,185 average annual births	Reisner, p. 54
1682-1700	23,000	Estimate based on 900 average annual births	Mols, III, p. 87
1700	23,000		
1720	19,978		Keyser, 1941, p. 375
1750	21,000		
1800	24,000		
1807	24,631		Deutsches Städtebuch, I, p. 419
1850	26,000		
1851	26,098		

Magdeburg

936-73		Otto I's main residence	
1300	15,000	5 parishes, 12 churches	Püschel, pp. 97, 100
1400	20,000		Enci. Italiana
1450	24,000		Schmoller, p. 94
"		Pestilence killed 8,000 (Schmoller may have just multiplied by 3)	Wolter, p. 86

1500	32,000		
1550		3,300 in militia	Meyer, 1839
"	40,000		Schmoller, p. 94
1600	37,000		
1631	36,000	Nearly all massacred	Enci. Italiana
1682	8,000		Schmoller, p. 94
1735	18,060		" "
1750	22,000		
1798	37,450		Meyer, 1874
1800	34,000		
1802	32,013		Morse, II, p. 299
1850	52,055		Deutsches Städtebuch, II, p. 595

Mainz

1000	30,000		
1074		Bigger than Cologne (contemporary opinion)	Schmoller, p. 81
1100s		Passed by Cologne	" "
1163		Lost its wall and its rights	
1200	25,000		
1200s	25,000		" "
1300	24,000		
1313	24,000	16,000 died	Deutsches Städtebuch, IV, p. 266
1463	7,000	1,468 families	" " " "
1700	20,000		
1730	22,000	Estimated from births	Dreyfus, p. 248
1740	25,000	Estimated from births	" "
1750	25,000		
1771	26,753	Estimated from births	Deutsches Städtebuch, IV, p. 266
1780	32,482	Including garrison	" " " "
1798	27,000	Including garrison	Smoller, p. 82, cf. Dreyfus, p. 243
1800	24,000		
1802	21,163		Schmoller, p. 82
1849	42,800	34,800 plus garrison (cf. 1852)	Hoffmann
1850	43,000		
1852	44,700	36,741 plus c. 8,000 in garrison	Ungewitter, I, p. 255

Munich

1500	13,000		Gutkind, "Cent. Europe," p. 339
1580	20,000		Enci. Italiana
1600	20,000		
1600-10	18-20,000		München Stat. Amt
1700	24,000		" " "
1722	29,097	Including suburbs	" " "
1750	30,000		
1771	31,000		" " "
1781	37,840	Including suburbs and garrison	" " "
1800	48,000		
1801	48,745		Schmoller, p. 95
1840	113,329	Including suburbs of Au, Geising, and Haidhausen	Bayerische Stat. Landesamt, p. 14
1850	125,000		

1852	127,385	Including suburbs of Au, Geising, and Haidhausen	

Nuremberg

1219	10,000	68 hectares in area	Planitz, p. 203
1363	13,000	11,746 plus clergy, Jews, and strangers	Bücher, pp. 105-111
1400	18,000		
1449	25,982	Including 5,817 temporary residents	Handwörterbuch, II, p. 675
"		3,753 burghers	Bücher, p. 34
1500	52,000		Celtes in Bücher, p. 10
1600	45,000		
1602	40,000	Slightly over, estimated from births	Schmoller, p. 88
1622	50,000	10,060 families	Mols, III, p. 175
1650	40,000		K. Weiss, p. 124
1700	35,000		
1750	30,000		" "
1800	25,000		
1806	25,000		Schmoller, p. 90
1846	50,460		Hoffmann
1850	50,000		
1852	49,841		"

Potsdam

1792	27,000		Keyser, p. 376
1800	27,000		
1816	20,254	(After wars)	Hoffmann
1849	31,394		"
1850	31,000		
1852	32,878		"

Ratisbon (Regensburg)

555-788		Capital of Bavaria	
1000	40,000	See 1750	
1050		1st in Germany	Otloh in Gutkind, "Cent. Europe," p. 349
1462		Pestilence killed 6,300	Waldendorff, p. 49
18th cent.	20-22,000		Schmoller, p. 87
1700	20,000		
1750		Half its medieval size	Püschel, p. 162
"	20,000		
1792	22,000		Keyser, 1941, p. 376
1800	23,000		
1802	23,000		Waldendorff, p. 587
1850	22,000		
1852	22,285		Hoffmann

Soest

1179-80		101 hectares in area	Planitz, p. 201
1200	15,000		
1300	15,000	10% larger than Frankfurt	Rothert, p. 25
1311-50		Averaged 30 new burghers per year	" "
1351-1450		Averaged 37 new burghers per year	" "
1400	18,000	Almost precisely equal to Frankfurt in number of persons in various professions	" "
"		6 parishes	Schünemann, p. 124

1420		25,000 (seems high)	Barthold in Schmoller, p. 77
1530	15,000		Schmoller, p. 78
1600	5,000		″ ″
1763	3,800		Ency. Brit., 1910
1806	5,400		Schmoller, p. 78

Spires (Speyer)

1125		"metropolis Germaniae"	Orderic in Bühler, p. 17
peak	30,000	Or more, based on area	Zeuss, p. 26
1200	30,000		
1220		Extramural suburbs already built	″ pp. 8-10
1237		Last medieval reichstag held there	Bühler, p. 22
1300	25,000		
1400	20,000		
1486	13,000	Taxed 1/2 as much as Strassburg	Schmoller, p. 80
1600s		Destroyed by French	″ ″
1801	3,703		″ ″

Stettin

12th cent.		Capital of Pomerania	
″ ″	5-9,000		Grabski, II, p. 404
c.1300		44 hectares in area	Planitz, p. 203
1300s	6,000		Grabski, II, p. 405
1400s	10,000		″ ″ ″
1600	12,200		Deutsches Städtebuch, I, p. 236
1709	10,900	Census	″ ″ ″ ″
1750	12,966		″ ″ ″ ″
1800	18,430		″ ″ ″ ″
1849	47,202	Including garrison	Hoffmann
1850	48,000		
1852	52,252	Including garrison	″

Stuttgart

1740-60	16,800		Schmoller, p. 288
1792	20,000		Keyser, 1941, p. 376
1800	21,000		
1808	22,680		Morse, II, p. 308
1849	47,837		Hoffmann
1850	48,000		
1852	50,003		″

Trier (Treves)

750	10,000	8 churches	Planitz, p. 39
800	15,000	Prosperity under Charlemagne	
882		City laid in ashes	″ ″
by 958	20,000	139 hectares in area	Deutsches Städtebuch, IV part 3, p. 423
1000	20,000		
c.1100-1252		Walls maintained and perhaps expanded	″ ″ ″
			″ ″
1200	25,000		
1730	7,778		Dreyfus, p. 243
1770	10,413		″ ″
1849	19,016		Hoffmann

Ulm

1400	20,000		
1427	20,000		Handwörterbuch, II, p. 675
1489	20,000		" " "
1500	17,000		Correspondence with Ulm city archive
1600	21,000		" " " " "
1650	13,000		" " " " "
1700s	10,000		Schmoller, p. 87
1750	15,000		" "
1795	13,000		" "
1850	20,000		
1855	21,076		Hoffmann

Worms

814-40		Often the residence of Emperor Louis	
1200	28,000	See 1500	
1250	60,000	Much too high; based on erroneous militia count and multiplier	Arnold in Boos, III, p. 41
"	25,000	4,200 in militia	" " " " "
1300	20,000		
1486	6-8,000	Tax 1/6 as much as Strassburg city-state	Schmoller, p. 80
1500		1/4 as big as in 1200	Illert, p. 49
1700	2,000		Schmoller, p. 80
1800	4,800		" "

Würzburg

1792	21,000		Keyser, 1941, p. 376
1800	22,000		
1818	26,465		Hoffmann
1840	26,814		"
1850	25,000		
1852	24,472		"

Brünn (Brno)

1466	15,000	Based on 12,000 communicants	List, p. 11
1666	9,000	443 houses (times 21, the multiplier in 1836)	" pp. 11-12
1754	14,972		" "
1800	22,000		
1804	23,367		Balbi, p. 200n
1842	42,000		Gazetteer of World
1850	51,000		
1857	58,809		Brockhaus, 1864

Graz

1598		328 houses	Popelka, I, p. 507
1708		334 houses	" " "
1800	28,000		
1810	29,576		Hassel, 1819, II, p. 231
1850	54,000		
1851	55,421		Ency. Brit., 1853

Maria Theresiopel (Szabadka, Subotica)

c.1770		Built up by Maria Theresa	Grande Ency.
1800	28,000		
c.1808	28,000		Morse, II, p. 324
1846	36,200		Ungewitter, I, p. 710
1850	34,000		
1851	33,918		" " "

Prague

by 929		Third church built	Guth, p. 195
1200	22,000	18 churches mentioned on a map	Helfert, pp. 9-11
1300	40,000		
1328		10,000 cavalry	Tomek, p. 600
1346	50,000		Vojtišek, p. 11
1349-1400		Capital of Holy Roman Empire	
c.1350		Walled area as in 1800s (c. 15 kilometers or 9.3 miles around; thus c. 1,400 ha.)	Guth, p. 24; Baedeker, 1896, p. 252
1378	95,000	76 churches (times 1,250)	Schürer, p. 88
"	100,000	Houses times 25, doubted by Heymann (but cf. 1605, 1624)	Heymann, p. 46
1400	95,000		
1400s		Down 1/4 as Germans fled	" "
1500	70,000		
c.1575	70,000		Vojtišek, p. 13
1576-1611		Again Imperial capital	
1600	100,000	See 1576, 1624	
1605		3,365 houses	Janáček, p. 292
1624	100,297		" p. 343
1628	43,523		" "
1700	48,000		
1703	48,427	Including garrison	Pelikanova, p. 33
1750	58,000		
1754	59,000		" p. 31
1800	77,403		" p. 33
1846	115,436		Blackie
1850	117,000		
1851	118,405		Ency. Brit., 1853

Triest

1719-1891		Imperial free port	Ency. Brit., 1910
1800	23,000		
1801	23,633		Morse, II, p. 325
1850	63,931		Brockhaus, 1864

Vienna (Wien)

1200	12,000	4 parish churches	Enci. Universal
1273-1330		Capital of the Holy Roman Empire	
1300	21,000	7 parish churches	" "
1394		10th parish church built	" "
1400	24,000		
1423	24,000	4,000 militia (times 6)	Kralik, p. 149
1440-1521		Capital of the Holy Roman Empire again	
c.1450		60,000 (too high)	Enci. Italiana
1500	45,000	With court etc. (cf. 1600-37, and Prague 1378-1575)	
1521-65		Capital of Germany, under emperor's brother	
1561		Area 7% less than Breslau	Markgraf, p. 27-8
1563		4,000 militia	Ortvay, IV, p. 405-6
1600	30,000		
1608	30,000	5,000 militia (times 6)	Kralik, p. 272
1611-1806		Again imperial capital	
1619		8,000 burghers, rejected by Weiss as exaggerated	Weiss, II, p. 95n
1637	60,000		Keyser, 1941, p. 375
1683	90,000		Hennings, p. 83
1700	105,000		
1710	113,800		Weiss, II, p. 95n
1750	169,000		
1754	175,460		" " p. 227
1800	231,079		" " "
1850	426,415		Stat. Jahrbuch Wien, p. 44

Wiener-Neustadt

1192	15,000	Founded with an area of 102 hectares	Planitz, p. 201
1200	15,000		
Middle Ages		No expansion	
1851	14,544		Ungewitter, II, p. 685

Budapest

1074		Ferry linked Buda and Pest	Acsay, p. 18
c.1250-1541		Capital	Kubinyi, p. 133
1255		Fortress completed	Acsay, p. 18
by 1300	15,000	3 parish churches plus 2 in suburbs	Kubinyi, pp. 138-9
Middle Ages		236 hectares combined for Buda and Pest	Russell, 1958, p. 100
1400	18,000		
1437	19,000	967 houses (times 20; cf. Pressburg, 1781)	Kubinyi, p. 154
c.1500		12,500-15,000 (probably too low)	" p. 155
"	20,000		
early 1500s	20,000	2,800 estimated burgesses (times 7; cf. Nuremberg), plus c. 500 in royal court)	" p. 156n
pre-1541		50-60,000 (probably exaggerated)	Lechner in Presisich, p. 9
1541-1686		Garrison of 10,000	Björkman, p. 67
1600	25,000		
1686	28-30,000		Preisich, p. 9
1690s	18,000	As the city lay in ruins	Kubinyi, p. 157m
1720	12,200		Révai Nagy Lexikona
1750	24,000		
1777	35,059		Preisich, p. 23
1799	54,179		Révai Nagy Lexikona
1800	54,000		
1810	60,259		" " "
1850	156,506		Preisich, p. 61

Debrecen

1770	23,546		Mátyás, p. 46
1787	28,873		Szücs, III, p. 880
1800	27,000		
1805	27,563		" " "
1839	48,840		" " "
1850	29,844	After war of 1848-49	" " "

Esztergom (Gran)

-c.1000		Hungary's first capital	
Middle Ages		Hungary's main commercial center	Ency. Brit., 1910
" "	18,000	6 parishes	Schünemann, p. 123
1200	18,000		
1850	11,454		Brockhaus, 1851, "Gran"

Pressburg (Pozsony, Bratislava)

1300s		12,000 (seems high)	Schünemann, p. 121, 128
1452	8,000	1,042 taxpayers	Lazistan, p. xiii
1526-1784		Hapsburg capital for Hungary	
1500s		3 (parish) churches	Ortvay, I, p. 243
1551		Raised 6 battalions (roughly 3,000 men)	" IV, p. 349
c.1665	15,000	5 (parish) churches	" II, p. 10
1700	18,000		
1750	24,000		
1773	26,486		Franz, p. 20
1781		1,300 houses	" p. 16
1787	28,740		" p. 20
1800	23,000		
1805	21,040		Hassel, 1819, II, p. 479
1850	42,238	Without garrison	Fiala, p. 269

Schemnitz (now Sélmeczbanya)

1800	22,000		
c.1808	22,241		Morse, II, p. 325
c.1850	20,000	8,500 in city alone	Ungewitter, I, p. 691

Szegedin (Szeged)

1522	7,000	From a register	Schünemann, p. 121, 128
1800	24,000		
1808	25,347		Morse, II, p. 324
1850	49,000		
1851	50,244		Ungewitter, I, p. 685

Székesfehérvár

c.1000-1318		Capital of Hungary	
-1526		Coronation and burial grounds for Hungarian kings	Boldizsar, p. 225
1572	11,660		Fitz, p. 24
c.1800	12,248		Morse, II, p. 326

Breslau, Danzig, Stettin, see under Germany

Halicz

1141-1259		Seat of a strong principality	
1745		1,592 taxpayers	Büsching, 1773, II, p. 459

Krakow (Cracow)

1136-1596		Capital of Poland	
1257		Depopulated but rose quickly from the ruins of the Tartar invasion	Saysse-Tobiczyk, p. 35
1300s		2nd to Breslau, but ahead of Danzig	" " p. 50
1400	18,000		
1400s		Including Kazimierz, did not reach 20,000	" " p. 42
1500	22,000		
c.1550		80,000 (probably exaggerated)	English Cyclopaedia
1600	26,000	Including 19,000 within walls	Dabrowski, 1965, p. 213
1700	30,000		" n.d., p. 205
1772	15,000		Arnolda, p. 229
1798	24,543	Including Kazimierz for 1st time	Dabrowski, 1965, p. 399
1800	25,000		
1802	27,278		" " "
1850	42,000	39,701 plus Podgorze (c. 2,000)	" " p. 259; Hoffmann

Lemberg (Lwow, Lvov)

1259		Founded to supplant Halicz as local capital	
c.1600	10,000	Or more, but less than 20,000	Gierowski, p. 16
1615		1,500 in militia	Rudnícki, p. 13
1700	20,000		
1750	25,000		
1765		6,000 Jews	Univ. Jewish Ency.
1772	30,000		Arnolda, p. 229
1795	38,749		Handwörterbuch, II, p. 676
1800	42,000		
1803	44,655		Ency. Edinensis
1849	75,000		Ency. Brit., 1853
1850	71,000		
1851	68,000		Arnolda, p. 232

Lublin

c.1550		40,000 or 70,000	Ency. Brit., 1875
c.1600	10,000	Or more, but less than 20,000	Gierowski, p. 16
1787	8,550		Dobrzanski, p. 213
c.1800	7,400		Morse, II, p. 326
1854	15,508		Ungewitter, II, p. 164

Polotsk

980-1100s		Seat of a lordship	
1500		100,000 (clearly an exaggeration), considered larger than Vilna	Jewish Ency.
1552	8,000		Kravchenko and Kamensky, p. 32
1600	20,000	15-20,000; at least 6 parish churches	" " " ", map p. 21
"		Pestilence killed 15,000 (probably exaggerated)	Ency. Brit., 1910
1800	4,300		Kravchenko and Kamensky, p. 82

Poznan (Posen)

968-1025		Capital of Poland	
1500	32,000		
1549		1,700 houses	Oehlschlaeger, p. 18-9
1500s	30,000		Larousse
1599		5,000 died of pestilence	C. Meyer, p. 171
c.1600		20,000 or more	Gierowski, p. 16
1600	30,000		
1653		1,600 houses	Lukaszewicz, p. 24-5
1797	12,376		Bergmann, p. 26
1803	15,992		Morse, II, p. 28
1849	47,963	Including garrison	Hoffmann
1850	46,000		
1852	44,039	Including garrison	''

Smolensk

c.1000		Small population	Sislov in Tikhomirov, p. 27
1127-60		Under Rostislav, it rivaled Kiev	Enci. Italiana
1200	40,000		
1200s	40,000		Ilenko, p. 80
''		400 hectares	Russell, 1958, p. 100
c.1230	23,900	Or somewhat later date	Golubovsky, p. 92
1300	25,000		
1400	25,000	Before the garrison	
1408		Taken by Lithuania	Ency. Brit., 1910
1482	50,000	Polish-Lithuanian garrison of 10,000 (doubtless from Troki; cf. Troki)	Ilenko, p. 26
1500	50,000		
1600	64,000		
1611	64,000	80,000 (probably exaggerated) in 8,000 houses (times 8; cf. Astrakhan, Kiev)	'' p. 49
''		70,000 killed	'' p. 46
1745	24,000	3,046 taxpayers (times 8; cf. Moscow)	Büsching, 1773, II, p. 46
1750	24,000		
1812	11,410		Ilenko, p. 80
1850	10,792		Hoffmann

Troki (Trakai)

-1323		Capital of Lithuania	
1400	50,000		
1414	50,000	Very large town; 10,000 cavalry stationed there (cf. Prague, 1328, 1346)	Lannoy, p. 40
1849	4,656		Hoffmann

Vilna

1323-1795		Capital of Lithuania, from 1386 linked to Poland	
1300s	20,000		Jurginis, p. 53
1399		Lost 14,000 citizens in a siege	Vivien
1500	25,000		
1503-22		3.4-mile wall built, enclosing slightly over half the area as of 1600	Correspondence with Vilna library
1533		Pestilence killed 25,000	Vivien
1500s	30,000		Jurginis, p. 54
1600	40,000		
1610		Fire destroyed 4,700 houses and 10 churches, followed by pestilence killing 1/3 the population	Polish Research Center, p. 5

1600s	45,000	35 churches, 1 synagogue	Lowmianska, p. 201
1700	40,000		
1709-10		22,862 died	Dobryansky, p. 83
1750	21,000		
1770	21,320		Jurginis, p. 186
1800	25,430		" p. 214
1850	55,916		" "

Warsaw

1379-1526		Capital of Mazovia Duchy	
1550	8-10,000	Rough guess	Enci. Italiana
1564	10,000		Pazyra, p. 275
late 1500s	20,000	Or more	Gierowski, p. 16
1596		Became capital of Poland	
1600	35,000		
1624	48,000		Pazyra, p. 276
1669	14,400	In 1,200 houses	" p. 277
1676	18,000		" "
1700	21,000		
1750	28,000		
1760	30,000		Ciborowski, p. 23
1792	120,000		" "
1800	75,000	63,563 plus clergy and military	Eisenbach and Grochulska, p. 116
1829	140,000		Arnolda, p. 235
1850	163,000		
1851	164,115		Gazetteer of World

Astrakhan (Itil, Atilia)

- 969		Capital of the Khazars until sacked	
c.1480-1521		Capital of a Mongol khanate	
1745	20,000	2,593 taxpayers (times 8; cf. Moscow, Pskov)	Büsching, 1773, II, p. 463
1750	20,000		
1767		2,541 houses	" 1784, IV, p. 48
1784	18,023		Bryce
1803	14,198		Bühler, p. 68
1849	44,798		Hoffmann
1850	44,000		
1860	44,587		Brockhaus, 1864

Bakhchiserai

c.1454-1783		Crim Tatar capital	Enci. Italiana, "Bachčisaraj"
1500	25,000		
1519		Main place built	Enci. Universal "Bachtchissarai"
1600	30,000	See 1784	
1700	24,000		
1700s	24,000	3,000 houses (times 8; cf. Astrakhan, Kiev)	Büsching, 1784, IV, p. 345
1736	16,000	2,000 houses (times 8)	Ency. of Islam, 1897, "Baghče Saray"
1784	5,776	1,566 houses (probably many vacant); 31 mosques, 2 churches, 2 synagogues (probably left over from peak)	" " " " " " "

Bolgary

922		Founded	Ency. of Islam, 1960, "Bulghar"
c. 950	30,000	10,000 men	Istakhri in Schünemann, p. 18
965		Sacked by Svyatoslav	Enci. Universal
1000	25,000		
1238		Destroyed	Ency. Brit., 1910
c.1300	50,000	In 13th and 14th centuries, 6 miles around	Ency. of Islam, 1960, "Bulghar"
c.1400		Destroyed again; supplanted by Kazan	Ency. Brit., 1910

Caffa (Kaffa, Theodosia, Feodosiya)

-1200s		Unmentioned since B.C. times	Ency. of Islam, 1897, "Kaffa"
1261-c.1382		Grew like a weed	R. López, p. 297, 357
1300	40,000		
1352		Wall built	" p. 301
1382		Longer wall built	" p. 357
1400	85,000		
c.1410	88,000	11,000 houses within outer wall (also 4,000 houses beyond, which could be rural)	Schiltberger, p. 49
1475	64,000	C. 70,000 (perhaps slightly high) in 8,000 houses (times 8; cf. Astrakhan, Kiev); sacked by Turks	Enci. Italiana; Ency. of Islam, 1897, "Kaffa"
1500	50,000		
1570-		In decline	Ency. of Islam, 1897, "Kaffa"
1600	40,000		
1671	32,000	4,000 houses (times 8)	Chardin, p. 34
1700	36,000		
c.1750	44,000	5,000-6,000 houses (times 8)	Büsching, 1767, III, p. 106
1783		Greater part of population deserted the city	Ency. Brit., 1910, "Theodosia"

1829	3,700		Ency. Slovar
1849	8,435		Hoffmann

Chernigov

907		Called 2nd to Kiev	Ency. Brit., 1910
1239		Wrecked by Mongols	
1849	6,011		Hoffmann, "Tschernigov"

Crim (Krim)

c.1300		Tatar capital of Crimea	Ency. of Islam, 1897
1712		Hardly a village	Wilson, p. 272

Kaluga

1745	27,000	Munitions center; 6,926 taxpayers (times 4; cf. Tula, another munitions center)	Büsching, 1773, II, p. 446
1750	27,000		
1800	23,000		
1811	23,000		German in Harris, p. 244
1846	32,345		English Cyclopaedia
1850	29,580		Hoffman

Kazan

1438-1552		Capital of a Mongol Khanate	
1552		1 mile long, with 10 gates	Ency. of Islam, 1897
"	15,000		Kalinin, p. 49
1646	10,000	1,272 households (times 8, cf. Kiev)	" p. 55
1700	23,000		
1745	37,000	4,722 taxpayers (times 8; cf. Moscow, Pskov)	Büsching, 1773, II, p. 461
1750	37,000		
1774		Massacre by Pugachev	
"	23,000	2,867 houses (times 8; cf. Astrakhan)	Ency. of Islam, 1897
1800	25,000		Kalinin, p. 87
1846	41,300		Brockhaus, 1853
1850	44,000		
1851	45,049		Ency. Brit, 1853, "Kasan"

Kiev

882-1157		Capital of Russia	
1000	45,000		
c.1010		400 churches; 8 market places	Thietmar of Merseburg in Tikhomirov, p. 50
1015	48,000	8,000 in militia	
1092		At least 7,000 died in epidemic	Tikhomirov, p. 147
1200	40,000	See Smolensk; larger than Novgorod	" "
1240		Destroyed by the Mongols	
1622	14,000	1,750 households (times 8; cf. 1766)	Kasymenko, p. 148
1727	15,000	1,914 households (times 8)	" p. 203
1750	23,000		
1766	28,877	In 3,596 households	" p. 206
1797	19,081		Ency. Slovar
1800	20,000		
1811	23,000		German in Harris, p. 244
1845	50,157		Tronko *et al*, p. 100
1850	52,000		
1856	55,590		" " p. 102

Kishinev

1813	13,000		English Cyclopaedia
1849	42,613		Ency. Brit., 1853, "Kischineff"
1850	46,000		
1862	91,532		Meyer, 1874

Kursk

1000s		In existence	Tikhomirov, p. 31
1800	23,000		
1811	23,000		German in Harris, p. 244
1849	30,469		Ungewitter, II, p. 134
1850	30,000		

Moscow

1147		In existence	Tikhomirov, p. 37
1328		Became capital of Russia	
1337	22,000	18 churches	Nazarevsky, p. 31
1343	35,000	28 churches	
1382		24,000 killed, rest carried away	" p. 47
1400	30,000		
1500	36,000		
c.1510	36,000	3,500 households in reign of Vasili III, 1505-1533 (times 8; cf. Kiev)	" p. 76
c.1550		Bigger than London; twice the size of Prague and Florence	Stevens, p. 16
1571	30,000	Reduced from alleged 200,000 by Crim Tartar invasion	Hürlimann, p. 27
1581	30,000	A decade after a sack and epidemic	Nazarevsky, p. 93
1600	80,000	Contemporary report	Bakhrushin, I, pp. 178-9
c.1650		Exaggerated estimate of 200,000 (implies city probably restored to its previous peak cize, c. 1570)	Bogoyavlensky in Voyce, p. 47
1700	130,000		
1701	131,000	16,358 households (times 8; cf. Kiev)	Nazarevsky, p. 205
1725	145,000	Roughly	Bakhrushin, II, pp. 62-3
1732	155,000	19,417 households (times 8)	Nazarevsky, p. 205
1745	166,000	20,849 taxpayers (times 8)	Büsching, 1773, II, p. 443
1750	161,000		
1770	152,790		Büsching, 1784, III, p. 443
1800	238,000		
1811	270,184		Bakhrushin, III, p. 31
1850	373,800		Ungewitter, II, p. 131

Nizhny-Novgorod (Gorki)

1221		Founded	Tikhomirov, p. 42
1619	5,000		Khramtsovsky, p. 86
1649	23,000	2,900 households (times 8; cf. Kiev, Moscow)	Archangelskaya, p. 21
1700	24,000		
1745	25,000	3,126 taxpayers (times 8; cf. Kiev, Moscow)	Büsching, 1773, II, p. 458
1750	25,000		
1800	23,000		
1834	21,687		Hoffmann
1849	30,710		Ungewitter, I, p. 315
1850	31,000		
1864	41,543		Brockhaus, 1864, "Nishnij-Nowgorod"

Novgorod

1000	<u>18,000</u>	Tikhomirov estimates 10-15,000, which seems a bit low	Tikhomirov, p. 146
c.1020	<u>18,000</u>	3,000 in militia (cf. 1471, 1400s)	" "
1200	<u>30,000</u>	Tikhomirov estimates 20-30,000	" "
1211		4,300 homes burned, but not all of the city	" "
1215		3-5,000 in militia	" "
1300	<u>40,000</u>	Still prospering	M. Thompson, p. xiv
1400	<u>50,000</u>	Trade expanding	
1471		10,000 in militia	Lessner, p. 252
1400s	60,000		Krasov in Pronshtein, p. 27
1500	<u>42,000</u>	Recovering from defeat in 1471	
1508	<u>42,000</u>	5,314 households (times 8; cf. Kiev, Moscow)	Pronshtein, p. 28
1546	43,000	5,477 households (times 8)	" p. 30
1500s	50,000		Krasov in Pronshtein, p. 27
1570		27,000 massacred; some survivors	S. Graham, p. 220
c.1800	7,126		Morse, II, p. 201

Odessa

1795	2,349		Vaenefa, p. 5
1803	7,000		Ungewitter, II, p. 173
1814	25,000		Vaenefa, p. 5
1850	71,392		Ungewitter, II, p. 173

Orel

1800	<u>25,000</u>		
1811	<u>25,000</u>		German in Harris, p. 244
1850	<u>25,000</u>		
1851	<u>25,630</u>		Hoffmann

Pskov

800s		Existence proven by excavations	Tikhomirov, p. 25
1100s	<u>9,000</u>	3 churches (parishes)	Tarakanova, p. 8
1300s		7 new dated religious buildings, 7 more in 1400s	Vasiliev, pp. 41-5
1400	<u>35,000</u>	Assuming even growth 1300-1500; cf. last item	
c.1500		60,000 (perhaps slightly high)	Ency. Brit., 1910
"	52,000	6,500 taxpayers (times 8; cf. Moscow)	Tarakanova, 1946, p. 33
1626	2,660		Tikhomirov (a), p. 15
1742	6,000	809 taxpayers (times 8)	Büsching, 1773, II, p. 449

Riga

1201-53		Capital of the Livonian Knights	
1253-1420		A free city or commune	
1400s	6-8,000		Enci. Italiana
1500s	10-15,000		" "
1710	14,000		" "
"		Pestilence killed 20,000	Meyer, 1839
1776	19,058		Matveeva, p. 63
1794	28,801		Lauks, p. 21
1800	<u>29,000</u>		
1804	30,219		" "
1850	61,543		Enci. Italiana

Saint Petersburg (Leningrad)

1703		Founded as capital
1750	138,000	Hoffmann, "Petersburg"
1765	153,300	Ency. Brit., 1969
1800	220,200	" " "
1848	473,437	English Cyclopaedia
1850	502,000	
1852	532,241	Hoffmann

Sarai (Serai)

1240-1480		Capital of the Golden Horde	Ency. Brit., 1910, XXIII, p. 893
" "		Two probable sites, both 8 miles long by two miles wide	Ency. of Islam, 1897
1300	100,000		
c.1330	117,000	13 large mosques (times 9,000; cf. Baghdad)	Ibn Battuta, p. 166
1395		Destroyed by Tamerlane	Ency. of Islam, 1897
1480		Permanently destroyed by Russians	" " " "

Saratov

1800	24,000	
1811	27,000	German in Harris, p. 244
1842	42,237	Ungewitter, II, p. 168
1847	52,000	Ency. Slovar
1850	59,000	
1851	61,610	Ency. Brit., 1853

Sevastopol

1841	41,155	Ungewitter, II, p. 171
1850	44,000	
1853	c.45,000	Brockhaus, 1851-55

Sudak (Soldaia)

1289		Sacked by Tatars	Enci. Universal
c.1300	30,000	Nearly equaled Caffa	Abulfeda in Canale, p. 434
peak		100 churches	Büsching, 1784, IV, p. 353
1400	30,000	Not growing like Caffa	R. López, pp. 297-357

Tula

1654	2,568		Novy Ency. Slovar
1705, 1714		Its gun factory (founded 1595) was greatly	Ency. Brit., 1910
1745		7,259 taxpayers	Büsching, 1773, II, p. 447
1750	30,000		
c.1768	30,000		" 1784, III, p. 359
1800	46,000		
1811	52,000		German in Harris, p. 244
1850	54,626		Hoffmann

Tver (Kalinin)

1300	27,000	Churches times 1,250 (cf. 1442)
1308		Fought Moscow, Novgorod, and the Mongols together
1400	20,000	After severe defeat in 1374
1442		22 churches (reflects peak c. 1300) Sakharov, p. 22

1486		Almost wholly burned by Muscovites	Ency. Brit., 1910
1570		90,000 massacred in its whole province	" " "
1745	26,000	3,262 taxpayers (times 8; cf. Moscow)	Büsching, 1773, II, p. 454
1750	25,000		
1811	18,000		German in Harris, p. 244
1849	14,142		Hoffmann

Vladimir

1157-1328		Capital of Russia	
1175	15,000	1,500 militia went off campaigning; remaining population beat off a 7-week siege	Tikhomirov, p. 148
1200	18,000		
1300	31,000		
once	31,000	25 churches	English Cyclopaedia
1849	13,405		Hoffmann

Voronezh

1742	25,000	3,183 taxpayers (times 8; cf. Moscow, Pskov)	Büsching, 1773, II, p. 448
1750	25,000		
1800	22,000		
1811	22,000		German in Harris, p. 244
1842	43,800		Brockhaus, 1851, "Woronesch"
1850	40,000		
1856	37,664		Ency. Brit., 1853-60

Yaroslavl

1071		In existence	Tikhomirov, p. 38
1783	18,996		Hoffmann, "Jaroslav"
1800	22,000		
1811	24,000		German in Harris, p. 244
1842	34,913		Hoffmann, "Jaroslav"
1850	35,000		

Bucharest

1458-76		Capital of Wallachia	
1500s		Grew throughout the century, while Tirgovishtea declined	Enci. Italiana, "Bucarest"
1532-1602		Capital of Wallachia again	
1600	60,000	Cf. 1640, 1798	
1640		12,000 houses (probably an out-of-date estimate)	Bacsisi in Enci. Italiana
1655-		Capital agian, except c. 1690-1698	
1700	50,000		Ency. of Islam, 1960
1738		30,000 killed by Turks	Enci. Italiana
1750	25,000		
1798	32,185	In 7,503 houses	Giurescu, p. 109
1800		20-60,000	Ency. of Islam, 1960
"	34,000		
1801		80,000 estimate (probably an exaggeration)	Batthyány in Giurescu, p. 266
1832	72,595		Giurescu, p. 266
1850	104,000		" "
1860	121,734		

Campulung

c.1290-c.1300		Capital of Wallachia	
c.1800	4,000		Hassel, 1819, X, pp. 810-11
c.1850	9,000		Murray, p. 147

Curtea de Arges

c.1300-1383		Capital of Wallachia	

Iasi (Jassy)

1565-		Capital of Moldavia	Jewish Ency.
1594		All Turks killed	" "
1650		Burned by Chmielnićki	Universal Jewish Ency.
1750	20,000		
1790	14,963	After 1/3 fled a pestilence	Hassel, 1819, X, p. 829
1800	20,000		
1819	27,500		" " " "
1850	50,000		Ency. Brit., 1853

Ismail

c.1570		Its importance began	Ency. of Islam, 1960
1774		Strongly fortified	" " " "
1790	35,000	All slain or removed	" " " "
1791		Again strongly fortified	" " " "
c.1800	30,000		Morse, II, p. 423
1849	26,243		Hoffmann
1850	26,000		

Suceava (Suczawa)

1371-1565		Capital of Moldavia	
1500	33,000	C. 300 ha. and 11 parishes (times 3,000) at peak	Romstorfer, map. p. 8
1600		Defended by 2,200 soldiers	" p. xliii

Tirgovishtea (Targoviste)

1383-1532		Usual capital of Wallachia	
1395		Sacked by Szeklers	Enci. Universal
1400	25,000		
1400s	40,000		Vivien
1500	50,000		
1500s	60,000	With 70 churches	Ency. Brit., 1910
"		Declined while Bucharest prospered	Enci. Italiana, "Bucarest"
1600	45,000		
1602-55		Capital of Wallachia again	
c.1650	60,000	During reign of 1633-1654; 12,000 houses (i.e., families)	Enci. Italiana, "Targoviste"; Ency. Brit., 1910 "Rumania"
c.1690-1698		Capital of Wallachia again	
c.1700	20,000	1/3 its peak population	Ency. Brit., 1910, "Rumania"
c.1800	5,000		Hassel, 1819, X, p. 809
c.1850	14,000		Murray, p. 148

Madara

681-893		2nd in Bulgaria	Angelov, p. 26

Ochrida (now Ohrid)

964-1014	40,000	Capital (Population: churches times 1,250)	
c.1600		37 churches (left over from peak)	Popovski, p. 11
c.1800	16,000		Morse, II, p. 424

Pliska (Aboba)

681-893		Capital of Bulgaria	
" "		23 square kilometers in area (230 ha.), unwalled	Angelov, p. 26
800	34,000	At 150 per hectare	
c. 814		10-mile rampart built	Runciman, p. 76

Plovdiv (Philippopolis)

970	20,000		Logio, p. 127
1000	20,000		
1205	20,000	1 of the 3 finest Byzantine cities	Villehardouin in Tivčev p. 154
1433	18,000	Slightly declined; smaller than Sofia (cf. Sofia)	La Brocquière, pp. 355-6
c.1500	30,000	29 Moslem, 6 non-Moslem places of worship (Moslem times 800, others times 1,000)	Ency. of Islam, 1960, article "Filibe"
1600	28,000		
1600s		23 Moslem, 7 non-Moslem places of worship	" " " " " "
1700	25,000		
1750	30,000		
1764	30,000	50,000 (too high), unwalled, nearly 4 miles around (c. 250 ha. 1/4 Adrianople's size)	Gorani, pp. 38, 42-3
c.1800	30,000		Hassel, 1819, X, p. 646
1850	35,000		Todière in Mikhov, IV, p. 449
1864	40,000	Census	Mikhov, III, p. 22

Preslav

821		Fortified	Enci. Italiana
893-967		Capital of Bulgaria	
" "	60,000	Wall 6 miles around (c. 580 ha., times 100)	Naidenov, map p. 225
1000	30,000	Capital off at Ochrida	Ency. Brit., 1910, "Bulgaria"

Rustchuk

1640	16,000	In 3,200 houses	Ency. of Islam, 1897, "Rusčuk"
c.1660	20,000	2,200 Turkish houses, 3 Christian quarters	" " " " "
1700	23,000		
1750	26,000		
c.1800	30,000	In 6,000 houses	Hassel, 1819, X, p. 642
1827	18-20,000		Ency. of Islam, 1897, "Rusčuk"
1850	23,000		
1856	24,000		" " " " "
1881	26,869		Mikhov, III, p. 81

Shumla

1700s		Enlarged	Ency. Brit., 1910
1750	20,000		

c.1800	24,000	In 5,000 houses	Mikhov, II, p. 110
1829		40,000 before war (looks high); 30,000 after	" " p. 64
1850	30,000		
1852	30,000		Todière in Mikhov, IV, p. 449

Silistria

1500s-1600s		3rd in Bulgaria	Ency. of Islam, 1960, "Bulgaria"
1595		Burned by Turks	Grande Ency.
1650		Main port at mouth of the Danube	Khalifa in Ency. Brit., 1910
1700	24,000	See 1500s-1600s, and Plovdiv, Rustchuk	
1750	22,000		
c.1800	20,000		Hassel, 1819, X, p. 637
1828	24,000	With garrison	Ency. Brit., 1910
1850	22,000		
1852	22,000		Todière in Mikhov, IV, p. 449

Sofia

809		Most citizens killed	Venedikov, p. 261
1365-c.1380		Capital of half Bulgaria, displacing Trnovo	Ency. of Islam, 1897, 1960 eds., "Bulgaria"
1382-1700s		Grew steadily	Ency. Brit., 1910
1400	20,000	See Plovdiv	
1500	22,000		
1500s	22,000	12 churches (times 1,250); 7,000 Turks, 300 Jews	Ivanov, pp. 40-1
1553		Became mostly Moslem	Ency. Brit., 1910
1600	30,000		
1600s	31,000	18,000 Turks, 2,000 Jews, 2,200 families of Bulgars	Ivanov, pp. 40-1
"	40,000		Monedzhikova, p. 71
1700	40,000		" "
1700s		8,000 Turks	Ivanov, p. 41
1764		Depopulated and desolate	Gorani, p. 42-3
c.1800	46,000		Morse, II, p. 423
1836	45,000	Before plague	Spencer in Mikhov, II, p. 359
1850		Less than 20,000	" " " ·· " "

Trnovo

1186-1393		Capital	
1200	35,000		
1218-41	48,000	16 parish churches at peak	Bochkareva, p. 221
1300	35,000		
c.1850	15,000		Murray, p. 143

Vidin

1794-1807		Expanded as Pasvanoglu's capital	Ency. Brit., 1910, "Bulgaria"
c.1800	25,000		Hassel, 1819, X, p. 644
1850	23,000		
1852	23,000		Todière in Mikhov, IV, p. 449

Belgrade (Beograd)

1403-27		Capital of Serbia	
1433	30,000	Garrison over 5,000	La Brocquière, p. 360
1456	30,000	5,000 militia including Czech and Polish volunteers	Zsolnay, p. 138
1500	30,000		
1500s		At least 9 churches or mosques	" map p. 148
"	50,000		Kostinski in Paunovic, p. 102
1600	55,000		
1632	60,000	In 8,000 households	Masarećki in Ency. of Islam, 1960
1660		98,000 (likely too high)	Evliya in Ency. of Islam, 1960
1700	50,000	Cf. 1717, 1721	
1717	80,000	Within walls, of which 30,000 were newly arrived soldiers	Trusler, VIII, p. 319
1721	45,000	6,020 households (times 7.5; cf. 1632)	Popović, 1950, p. 19
1735	45,000	6,000 households	" " "
1750	40,000		
c.1780	30,000		Beaufort in Mikhov, III, p. 29
c.1800	26,000		Engelman in Mikhov, IV, p. 94
1846	17,904		Paunović, p. 827

Nish (Nis)

c.1500	20,000	At peak under Turks	Ency. Jugoslavije
1521		War-base moved to Belgrade	Vučković, p. 10
1600s	18,000	3,000 homes	" "
1877	12,817		" p. 11

Prizren

1100s		Capital	
1600	22,000	(Stable in 17th century)	
1600s	22,000	12,000 hearths (probably in district; times 6 and times 40/106–cf. 1900)	Enci. Jugoslavije
1700	22,000		
1750	21,000		
c.1800	20,000	4,000 houses	Hassel, 1819, X, p. 698
1844	24,950		Enci. Jugoslavije
1850	28,000		
1859	32,000		Mikhov, IV, p. 9
c.1900	40,000	106,000 in district	Enci. Universal

Skoplje (Üsküb, now Skopje)

1165		1st monastery built	Hadri-Vasiljević, pp. 421-64
1336-92		Capital	Vivien
1300s		5 monasteries built	Hadri-Vasiljević, pp. 421-64
1400	22,000	Monasteries times 4,500 (cf. Cuzco)	
1436-1502		Its 6 finest mosques built	Ency. of Islam, 1897, "Üsküb"
c.1450	30,000	25 mosques, 8 churches (mosques times 800, cf. 1661; churches times 1,250	Enci. Jugoslavije
1500	50,000	Growth being mainly by 1502; cf. 1436	
1559		28,000 homes (surely exaggerated, or else a district figure)	Hadri-Vasiljević, p. 44
1600	55,000		
1661	60,000	10,060 houses	Evliya in Ency. of Islam, 1897, "Üskü▌
"		70 places of worship (nearly all mosques)	Evliya in Enci. Jugoslavije
1689		Wholly burned by Austrians	Ency. of Islam, 1897, "Üsküb"
1800	6,000		" " " " "
1840	15,000		Hadri-Vasijević, p. 58
1858	20,800		Hay in Sibinovic, p. 49
1859	27,000		Blount in Mikhov, IV, p. 4

Serajevo (Bosna-Serai, now Sarajevo)

1461		Became seat of a duke, but officially ranked as a small town	Ademović, p. 10
1500		No mosques yet	Ency. of Islam, 1897
1600	<u>45,000</u>	Mostly Christian; and 2 main mosques (times 9,000. For Christians, cf. ratio in 1895)	Ency. of Islam, 1897; Enci. Universal
1697		Completely devastated by Eugene; never recovered	Ademović, pp. 6, 11
c.1800	18,000		Hassel, 1819, X, p. 717
1850	<u>20,000</u>		
1879	21,377		Brockhaus, 1881
1895	41,543	40% Moslem	Enci. Universal

Athens

c.1140		Very populous	Edrisi in Tivčev, p. 155
1204-1458		Seat of a Latin kingdom	Ency. Brit., 1910
1300	25,000		
1370s	30,000	10,000 (probably Latins. Multiply by 3; cf. 1664)	Setton, p. 243, cf. p. 228
1400	35,000		
1456	50,000		American Cyclopaedia
1458		Conquered by Turkey	Ency. Brit., 1910
1500	40,000		
1578	36,000	12,000 (probably Latins. Multiply by 3; cf. 1664)	Setton, p. 244
1600	33,000		
1664	22,000	6-7,000 Latins, 1,000 Turks, c.25,000 Greeks (His figures do not check. The vague one, on Greeks, should be the wrong one)	Tavernier, I, p. 121
1676		7,000 (i.e., Latins only)	Setton, p. 244
1688-1689		Deserted	American Cyclopaedia
1769	9-10,000		Mikhov, IV, p. 337
c.1800	12,000		Morse, II, p. 424
1845	27,800		Ency. Brit., 1853
1850	26,000		
1853	30,590		Annuaire Stat. Grèce, p. 28

Candia (Irakleion)

827	15,000	Founding population	Lane-Poole, pp. 35-6
1300-1669	11,474	Sometime between these dates	Haudecourt in Noiret, p. xiii
1669		7,700 soldiers and 4,000 civilians fled	Bragadino, p. 233
c.1800	15,000		Hassel, 1817, X, p. 781
1850	18,910		Mikhov, IV, p. 3

Corinth

-1147		Flourished till sacked by Normans	Ency. Brit., 1910
1459		First Turkish capital of Morea	" " "
c.1850	15,000		Ungewitter, II, p. 214

Syracuse

-878		Capital of Sicily under the Byzantines	
1374	8,000	1,755 households	Beloch, 1929, I, p. 159
1548	·11,000	2,370 households	" " " "
1615	12,432		" " " "
1713	17,205		" " " "

Thessalonica (Salonica, Thessaloniki)

904	50,000	22,000 women and children enslaved	Tafrali, 1919, p. 55
926		Beat off siege by Simeon of Bulgaria	Enci. Italiana
1000	40,000		
1185	40,000	7,000 massacred (presumably men; some got away. 8,000 times 5)	Tafrali, 1919, p. 189
1200	30,000		
1300	50,000	See 1423, 1430	
1400	42,000	Declining	" p. 16
c.1423	40,000	Surely much less than a century earlier	" "
1430	7,000	Most had fled	" p. 16

1490s		20,000 Jews settled	Vacalopoulos, p. 78
1500	40,000	See 1490s, 1668	
1600	50,000		
1668		About half Jewish; 16 markets (like Adrianople when it had 50,000 population)	Evliya in Vacalopoulos, p. 83, 85
1700	40,000	In a commercial slump	Vacalopoulos, p. 94
1714	30,000	Plausible because of wars	Lucas in Mikhov, II, p. 125
1734	40,000		Mikhov, II, p. 125
1750	45,000		
c.1780	50,000		Beaufort in Mikhov, III, p. 29
c.1800	62,000		Morse, II, p. 423
c.1850	75,000		English Cyclopaedia

Yannina (Iannina)

c.1800	30,000		Morse, II, p. 423
1809	35,000	In 8,000 houses	Brougham, I, p. 60
1820	30,000	Plus soldiers; 16 mosques, 7 or 8 churches; pillaged by its pasha	Conder, 1827, pp. 355-6
pre-1821	36,000	In 6,000 houses	Ibrahim-Manzour in Mikhov, III, p. 227
c.1845	25,000		Hain in Mikhov, II, p. 123
1850	24,000		
1879	16,230		Vivien, "Ianina"

Nicosia

1192-1489		Capital of a kingdom	
1400	18,000		
1470	18,000	6 parish churches	Bustron, p. 498
1510-21	16,000		G. Hill, III, p. 875
1540	16,000	Or 21,000	" " "
1596		30,000 (probably too high)	Luke, IV, p. 31
c.1850	17,500		Hoffmann

Adrianople (Edirne)

812	10,000	All removed by Krum	Runciman, p. 65
1366-1453		De facto capital	
1400	28,000	1st main mosque begun (times 9,000. The 15 churches probably already there, built under Christian rule; cf. 1578; churches times 1,250)	Aslanapa, p. 2
1500	125,000	15 main mosques (times 7,500; cf. Constantinople, 1510) plus Christians (cf. 1578)	" pp. 2-122
1520s		22,000 (impossibly low, unless families were intended)	Lapidus, 1969, p. 264 citing Barkan
c.1578	183,000	15 churches (times 1,250); 22 main mosque (times 7,500 as at 1500	Ency. of Islam, 1897, "Edirne"; Aslanapa, pp. 1-211
1600	160,000		
1693	100,000	7-8 miles around	Gemelli, p. 60
c.1700	93,000	6,700 taxpayers (probably non-Moslems only, cf. Constantinople, 1690); 8 main mosques, 17 churches	Islam Ansiklopedisi, IV, p. 118
1750	96,000		
c.1800	100,000	In 16,000 houses	Hassel, 1819, X, p. 632
c.1850	85,000	Reduced from 130,000 since the late Russian war (1829)	Jochmus in Mikhov, IV, p. 159

Constantinople

447		Wall enclosed 1,200 hectares, of which c. 960 became built up	Stein in Russell, 1958, p. 66
700		800,000 estimate, based on consumption of bread (probably an exaggeration)	Andréadés, p. 80
800	300,000	In period of partial decline	
c.1000		250,000-350,000 (probably too low and may exclude suburbs)	Lot in Torres, p. 56n
"	450,000		
c.1050		Medieval peak; 500,000-1,000,000 according to most historians	Andréadés, p. 69
"	500,000	4,000 acres (c. 1,600 ha.), plus suburbs	Foord in Andréadés, p. 73
1057-1204		Period of decline and fall	Goodsell, p. 23
1200	200,000		
1204		Ruined by crusades	" "
1261	100,000		Baedeker, 1914, p. 142
1300	150,000	Prospered under Michael VIII, 1261-1282	
1340s	80,000	After plague	Pears in Goodsell, p. 23
1400	75,000		
1425	70,000	Estimated by authorities living there	Goodsell, p. 28
1453	40-50,000		Cusanus in A. Schneider, p. 237
1478		98,000 in city alone	Barkan in Jacoby, p. 103
"		15,824 houses in city alone	Mantran, p. 45
1500	200,000		
1510	250,000	198 places of worship, including 18 main mosques	A. Schneider, p. 241, map
1520-35	400,000	79,997 hearths	Mantran, p. 44
1552	660,000	110,000 houses (times 6; cf. 1478)	Jacoby, p. 103
c.1600	700,000		Braudel in Jacoby, p. 103
1690	700-800,000	With Scutari (probably closer to the lower figure); based on 62,000 non-Moslem taxpayers; non-Moslems were 42% of the total population	Mantran, p. 47
1700	700,000	Surely equal to Paris	Tournefort in Mantran, p. 45

1750	666,000		
1794	560,000	88,185 houses within wall (times 6), plus Scutari (30,000 in early 1800's)	A. Schneider, p. 242, n; Conder, p. 246n
1800	570,000		
1815	597,600	Including suburbs; estimated from consumption of bread	Hassel, 1819, X, p. 625
1830	700,000		Besse in Mikhov, III, p. 37n
1848	778,000	Estimated from mortality	" " " " p. 31
1850	785,000		
1885	873,565	Census	Grosvenor, I, p. 8

Gallipoli (Gelibolu)

1320-54		Chief Byzantine naval base	Ency. of Islam, 1960
1354-1453		Chief Turkish naval base	" " " "
1422		Very large	Lannoy, p. 160
1474	5,000	1,095 households	Ency. of Islam, 1960
1518	6,000	1,305 households	" " " "
1693	6,000		Gemelli, p. 58
c.1800	17,000		Hassel, 1819, X, p. 731
c.1850	12-17,000		Mikhov in Ency. of Islam, 1960

Albany

1800	5,389		U.S. Census, 1800
1850	<u>55,701</u>	50,756 plus 4,945 in Greenbush	" " 1850

Baltimore

1775	5,934		North, p. 11
1800	26,519		U.S. Census, 1800
1850	169,054		" " 1850

Boston

1700	6,700		North, p. 11
1750	20,000	With suburbs	Paullin, p. 42
1800	<u>35,248</u>	24,937 plus 10,311 in Cambridge, Charlestown, Dorchester, and Roxbury	U.S. Census, 1800
1850	<u>202,261</u>	136,881 plus 65,380 in Brookline, Cambridge, Charlestown, Chelsea, Dorchester, Newton, North Chelsea, Roxbury, Somerville, Waltham, and West Cambridge	" " 1850

Buffalo

1850	42,261		U.S. Census, 1850

Cahokia

c.1200-1500		150 mounds; 85 within a 1.5-mile radius	Moorehead, pp. 85, 106, 116

Charleston, S.C.

1800	18,844		U.S. Census, 1800
1850	42,985		" " 1850

Chillicothe

		Largest mound site in Ohio; "center of the highest culture of the moundbuilding people"	Miller, p. 62

Cincinnati

1810	2,540		U.S. Census, 1810
1850	<u>130,828</u>	115,435 plus 15,393 in Covington and Newport, Ky.	" " 1850

Etowah

c.1100-c.1500		Dates of occupation; large mound site in Georgia	Cane and Griffin, pp. 115-6; 1962, p. 190; Squier

Louisville

1800	359		U.S. Census, 1800
1850	<u>45,316</u>	43,194 plus 2,122 in Jeffersonville	" " 1850

Nanih Waiya

		Main shrine of the Choctaws, who till c. 1675 ruled the whole Southeast	Debo, p. 1

New Orleans

1803	10,000		Ency. Brit., 1910
1850	<u>132,035</u>	116,375 plus 15,660 in Carrolton and Lafayette	U.S. Census, 1850

New York

1703	4,436		North, p. 11
1749	13,296		" "
1800	63,735	60,437 plus 3,298 in Brooklyn	U.S. Census, 1800
1850	682,172	515,547 plus 166,625 in Brooklyn, Bushwick, Flatbush, Flushing, Hoboken, Jersey City, Newtown, West Farms, and Yonkers	" " 1850

Philadelphia

1700	4,400		North, p. 11
1753	14,563	With suburbs	" "
1800	68,200	41,220 plus 26,980 in Germantown, Southwark, Eastern Liberties, Northern Liberties, and part of Western Liberties	U.S. Census, 1800
1850	426,221	408,762 plus 17,459 in Camden, West Penn, and West Philadelphia	" " 1850

Pittsburgh

1800	1,565		" " 1800
1850	69,744	46,601 plus 23,143 in Allegheny and South Pittsburgh	" " 1850

Providence

1800	7,614		" " 1800
1850	49,193	41,513 plus 7,680 in North Providence	" " 1850

St. Louis

1810	5,667		" " 1810
1850	77,860		" " 1850

Troy

1800	4,926		" " 1800
1850	60,199	28,785 plus 31,414 in Brunswick, Cohoes, Watervliet, and West Troy	" " 1850

Washington

1800	8,144		" " 1800
1850	40,001		" " 1850

Montreal

1809	16,000	Morse, I, p. 60
1850	48,207	Brockhaus, 1851

Québec

1720	7,000	Le Moine, p. 422
1759	9,000	" " "
1800	12,000	Gazetteer of World
1844	35,673	New American Cyclopaedia
1850	40,000	
1852	42,052	Le Moine

Azcapotzalco

by 800		Important very early	Hardoy, pp. 111-2
1418-1431		Tepanec capital, dominating central México	
1571		1 monastery	López de V., p. 193

Calakmul

633-813		Peak; 15 pyramids	Palacios, 1937, pp. 19, 23
ever		5th Mayan city in importance	Morley, p. 318

Chakanputun (Chanpotón)

1500	20,000		
1528	20,000	8,000 houses (times 2.5; cf. Campeche)	Jakeman, p. 134

Chichén-Itzá

c.1000		A capital of Quetzalcoatl (Kukulcan)	Morley, pp. 85-7
c.1200		The Itzá clan departed	Hardoy, p. 275

Cholula

c.1000		A capital of Quetzalcoatl	Cortez in Clavigero, II, p. 49
1000s (?)	60,000	Fort spacious enough for 10,000 (presumably militia, times 6)	La Maza, p. 23
1500	36,000		
1519		Resembled Valladolid	Bernal Díaz, p. 153
"	36,000	Its militia massacred; either 6,000 (Gomara) or 3,000 (Díaz, whose figure seems low)	" " p. 154; La Maza, p. 35
1521		39 temples	La Maza, p. 7
1540		20,000 houses and as many in suburbs (clearly too high)	Cortez in Díaz, p. 154
"	30,000	15,000 adult males in its district (cf. 1581)	La Maza, p. 40
1571	24,000	11,786 adult males in district (cf. 1581)	López de V., p. 223
1581	18,000	9,000 adult males in district; 6 parishes (times 3,000)	La Maza, p. 40-1
1600	13,000		
1620	9,000	2 monasteries (times 4,500; cf. Cuzco, Quito)	" p. 44
1746	7,000	1,134 families	Villaseñor in La Maza, p. 47
1793	16,000		Humboldt, 1814, II, pp. 151, 155
c.1870	6,000		Vivien

Dzibalchaltun

pre-1000	50-75,000	Perhaps 1st in America	Andrews in Hardoy, p. 286

Guadalajara

1750	20,000		
1777	22,163		Páez B., p. 86
1792	24,249		" " p. 118

[a]With respect to Mayan cities, it is still not clear whether any ever got over 100,000 in size. In 1940, I corresponded with such authorities as Spinden, Means, and Martinez-Hernández, all of whom inclined to think so. More recently, Morely also falls in this category (cf. pp. 314-5 of his book listed in the bibliography). Ricketson, however, claims the centers were quite small, as do Willey and Hardoy. Ricketson's point is that rather few foundations of stone houses have been found. Yet in no country before our century have the common people been rich enough to have durable homes. Nevertheless this controversy must still be considered open.

1800	31,000		
1803	34,697		Páez B., p. 128
1850	63,000		Harper

Guanajuato

1554	6,000	In the Indian town	Camavitto, p. 236
1571	4,000	600 *vecinos* (adult male citizens)	López de V., p. 242
1700	16,000		F. Vargas, p. 48
1750	30,000		
1772-5		Silver production 2/3 as much as in 1800-3	Humboldt, 1811, III, p. 380
1793		32,098, without the mines	" 1824, p. 172
1800	66,000		
1803	71,600	41,000 plus 30,600 at the mines	" " "
c.1850	48,594		Harper

Mani

1500	22,000		
1528	22,000	45,000 (reduced by 1/2; cf. Mérida)	Jakeman, p. 134

Mayapán

c.1020-1194		Headed the League of Mayapán, of north Mayan cities; however Chichén-Itzá and Uxmal became the greatest cities of the empire	Morley, pp. 89, 91
1194-1441		Ruled North Yucatán	Morley, pp. 92-3
" "		Wall enclosed 420 hectares; ruins show 2,500 homes or home-groups, but there were also thatched huts (thatch leaves no trace, so a large population is possible)	Hardoy, p. 278; J. Graham
1400	25,000	Based on area and its successor, Mérida	

Mérida (Ticoh)

1528	25,000	50,000 (reduce by 1/2; cf. 1571, 1600)	Jakeman, p. 133
1571	5-10,000	1 monastery, 90-100 Spanish taxpayers	López de V., p. 250
by 1600		Yucatán had declined by 2/3	Jakeman, p. 130
1700	20,000		
1750	24,000		
1793	28,392		Humboldt, 1824, p. 72
1800	30,000		
c.1850	45,000		Hoffmann

Mexico City (Tenochtitlán till 1521)

1325		Founded	Clavigero, I, p. 85
1465		5,000 priests	Enci. Universal, "Moctezuma"
c.1495		200,000 from here and other lakeshore towns fled a flood	Dorantes in Camavitto, p. 92
1500	80,000		
1520	80,000		Bernal, p. 204
"		Equal to Seville and Córdova combined (they totaled 95,000), and its half called Tlatelolco twice size of Salamanca (19,000)	Cortez in Hardoy, p. 182 and in Clavigero, II, p. 435
"	70,000 plus	According to most observers; area 11.9 sq. mi. (3000 ha.)	"anonymous chronicler" in Cook Simpson, pp. 30, 32
"		62,000, based on a small sample—admittedly low because taken on the edge of town, where density was low	Hardoy, p. 184
"		Area only 750 ha., half swamp	" p. 116
1524	30,000	After destruction and rebuilding	Novo, p. 32n
1600	75,000		

1625		30-40,000 whites	Gage in Guthrie, p. 5n
1627-9		27,000 died, 100,000 fled in flood	Cobo, p. xxxiii
1629	90,000	15,000 *vecinos* (adult male citizens); 7,000 Spanish, 8,000 Indian	Hardoy & Aranovich in Sánchez-Albornoz & Moreno, p. 63; Enci. Universal
1646		30,000 houses	Calle in Guthrie, p. 5n
1698	100,000		Gemelli, p. 480
1700	100,000		
1750	110,000		
1772		112,463	Humboldt in Ency. Brit., 1970
1790	120,000	112,926, plus 2,392 clergy and 5-6,000 garrison	Humboldt, 1814, I, pp. 194-5
1800	128,000		
1802		Births 1/4 more than in Madrid	" " " p. 196n
1803		137,000 but including visitors	" " " p. 195
1850	170,000		Ency. Brit., 1853

Mitla

800s		Peak	Bernal, p. 50
1200s		Ruins cover 20 hectares and date from 13th century	Hardoy, p. 140; Ency. Americana
1484		Raided by Aztecs	Joyce, p. 25

Monte Albán

1 A.D.-900		Its golden age	Augur, p. 137
peak		100,000 (seems high)	" p. 182
c.1390-c.1420		Abandoned; thereafter a small village	" p. 205

Oaxaca (Zaachila till 1521)

1386-1521		Zapotec capital	Enci. Italiana, "Zapotecs" and "Oaxaca"
1486		Raided by Aztecs	
1571		350 Spanish adult males	López de V., p. 228
1629	10,000	2,000 (families; cf. Guatemala City)	Gage, p. 111
1750	20,000		
1792	24,400		Humboldt, 1827, p. 191
1800	25,000		
c.1840	33,000		Brockhaus, 1851
1850	33,000		

Pátzcuaro

c.1400-c.1450		Capital of a Tarascan branchline	Toussaint, p. 8
1571		2 monasteries	López de V., p. 241
1793	6,000		Humboldt, 1814, II, pp. 178-9

Piedras Negras

604-c.825		Seat of a dynasty	Proskouriakoff, 1960, pp. 455-60
761		Main building erected	Morley, p. 307

Puebla

1530		Founded	Gage, p. 50
1571	20,000	500 Spanish adult males, 500 Negro slaves, and 3,000 Indians (heads of families)	López de V., p. 209
1600	25,000	See 1634	

1629		2nd to Mexico City	Gage, p. 50
1634		Thousands settled there from Mexico City	" "
1636	50,000	10,000 (probably intended as heads of families)	" "
1678	69,800		Palacios, 1916, p. 667
1700	63,000		
1746	50,366		" " "
1750	53,000		
1771	71,366		" " "
1793	56,859		" " "
1800	65,000		
1802	67,800		Humboldt, 1814, I, p. 244
1848	71,631		Palacios, 1916, p. 667
1850	71,000		
1883	65,530		" " "

Querétaro

1792	17,005		Septien, p. 287
"		35,000 including Indians (who may have lived apart from the town)	Humboldt, 1814, I, p. 237
1800	24,000		
1803	27,000		Humboldt in Septien, p. 287
1850	43,000		
c.1860	48,000		Brockhaus, 1864

San Luis Potosí

1793	12,000		Humboldt, 1814, II, p. 235
1850	40,000		Harper

Tenochtitlán, see Mexico City

Texcoco (Tezcoco)

1298-		Capital of México from the start of Quinatzin's reign	Clavigero, I, p. 101
1400	70,000	Before Maxtla's war	
1427	60,000	10,000 provincial militia at the city	Boturini, p. 33-61
1427-70		Prospered	Prescott, I, p. 15
1470		Double its 1520 population	Ixtlilxochitl in Prescott, I, p. 180n
"	85,000	See 1521, 2nd item	
1500	60,000		
1521	42,000	30,000 houses (probably exaggerated like other estimates by Cortez)	Cortez in Clavigero, II, p. 428
"		With 3 suburbs, larger than Mexico City (Reflects peak, 1470)	Clavigero in Camavitto, p. 233
1571		1 monastery	López de V., p. 202
1636	2,000	400 families; cf. Guatemala City	Gage, p. 56

Ticoh, see Mérida

Tilantongo

692-c.1100		Mixtec capital	Coe, p. 149

Tlaxcala

c.1400		Founded in Uitziliuitl's time	Vázquez S., p. 32
1500	40,000		

1520	36,000	Sent 6,000 troops with Cortez (times 6)	Gibson, p. 22
''	42,000	30,000 in daily attendance at its market (to 60,000 at Tlatelolco within Mexico City. Hence 1/2 Mexico City's size)	R. Adams, p. 53
''		Larger than Granada or Segovia (comparison with Segovia looks valid)	"anonymous chronicler" in Clavigero, II, p. 429
1521		20,000 houses (probably exaggerated)	Cortez in Clavigero, II, p. 435
1530-85		Only 1 monastery till its province had 8 others	Gibson, 1952, p. 42-52
1538	33,000	Its province had 300,000 (times 1/9; cf. 1530)	'' '' p. 141
1560		Very sharp decline began	'' '' ''
1600	20,000		
1629	15,000	3,000 gathered to revolt (presumably most urban)	Vázquez S., p. 35
1793	3,357		Humboldt, 1820, p. 6

Tula

667		Founded	Clavigero, I, p. 85
667-1168		Toltec capital	Gallenkamp, p. 178
'' ''		Large site	Hardoy, p. 114

Tzintzuntzán

1300s-1522		Tarascan capital	Enci. Universal, "Michoacán"
1500	40,000		
1522	40,000	Estimated by first chroniclers	G. Foster, p. 22
1639	1,000		'' p. 25
—		Ruins extend 10 kilometers (c. 6 miles)	Enci. Italiana
1793	2,500		Humboldt, 1814, II, p. 179

Uxmal

| c.1000-1194 | | One of the 3 cities in the League of Maya-pán, considerably smaller than Chichén-Itzá | Morley, p. 331 |

Xochicalco

600-1100		First peak; a prominent city before and during the Toltec expansion	Hardoy, pp. 123-4
'' ''		At least 3 km. around	Hardoy, plate 15
c.1300		Probably abandoned	'' p. 132

Zaachila, see Oaxaca

Zacatecas

1567		1st monastery built	Salinas, p. 76
1571	4,000	300 Spanish adult males, 500 slaves (all times 5, as families)	López de V., p. 242
1576		2nd monastery built	Salinas, p. 77
1600	4,500		Bakewell, p. 265
1604		3rd monastery built	Salinas, p. 77
1610		4th monastery built	'' ''
1629		Smaller than Puebla; cf. Puebla	
1600s		Mining increased notably	Amador, p. 400
1700	30,000		
1702		5th monastery built	Salinas, p. 77
1732	40,000		'' p. 82
1736		7 monasteries	Arlegui, p. 43, 48

1750	50,000		
1750-85		Declined considerably	Amador, p. 580
1793	33,000		Humboldt, 1814, II, p. 141
1800	33,000		
c.1850	25,000		Ency. Brit., 1853

Cap François (now Cap Haitien)

1790	20,000		Edwards, p. 139
1791-1800		Sharply reduced by wars	

Copán

732-82		Main statues erected	Morley, pp. 279, 339
800s		Abandoned	″ p. 64
ever		2nd only to Tikal among Mayan cities	″ p. 318

Guatemala City (Iximché till 1524)

c.1475-1524		Cakchiquel capital	Brigham, pp. 259, 269
1500	24,000		
1524		Smaller than Utatlán	Juarros, pp. 86-7
1527	24,000	80 city blocks (times 300; cf. Cuzco)	Villacorta, map p. 448
1571		500 Spanish adult males	López de V., p. 286
1600	25,000		
1629	26,000	c.5,000 families, plus 200 more in an Indian suburb	Gage, p. 186
1686	30,000	6,000 *vecinos* (adult male citizens)	F. Fuentes, p. 151
1700	30,000		
1750	34,000		
pre-1773	34,000	Last pre-earthquake figure	Gazetteer of World
1773		Flattened by earthquake	
1795	24,434		Juarros, p. 82
1800	25,000		
1825	30,775		Gazetteer of World
1850	50,000		
1865	60,000		Ersch
1880	59,039		Grande Ency.

Havana (La Habana)

1600	7,000	Half of Cuba's 14-16,000	Guiteras, II, p. 90
1700	25,000		
1737	33,000	4,764 in militia (white foot-soldiers and cavalry only; cf. 1761)	Arrate, p. 70
1750	34,000		
1761	36,000	6,046 in militia, including cavalry and 882 blacks (times 6)	″ cf. p. 114
1791	51,307		Sánchez-Albornoz, p. 102
1800	60,000		
1810	106,000	96,304 plus clergy and 6,000 troops; rapid growth of La Salud and Guadalupe suburbs, 1802-10	Humboldt, 1826, I, pp. 16, 24, 26, 28
1841	196,994		Meyer, 1874
1850	199,000		
1863	203,676		″ ″

Kingston

1774	11,000		Long, II, p. 103
1788	26,478		Edwards, I, p. 261
1800	27,000		
1812?	29,000		Ency. Edinensis
1844	32,943		Ency. Brit., 1875
1850	33,000		
1871	34,314		Census of Jamaica, p. 3

Tikal

| 800 | 49,000 | | Haviland, p. 430 |
| 900 | | 95% abandoned | ″   p. 429 |

Utatlán (Gumarcaah)

-1524		Quiché capital for 8 reigns	"Popol Vuh," p. 213ff
1500	60,000		
1524		Largest in Guatemala; 5,000 schoolchildren	Juarros, pp. 86-7
″	60,000	12,000 in militia (times 5; low multiplier since fighting for its existence)	Brigham, p. 268
1539		Abandoned	"Popol Vuh," p. 217n

Arequipa

c.1425	5,000	Largest of 4 or 5 towns settled by Inca Mayta	Juan & Ulloa, II, p. 140
1574	13,000	400 Spanish adult males; 3 monasteries	López de V., p. 487
1582		Worst earthquake before 1858	Grande Ency.
1687		Partly destroyed by earthquake	Enci. Universal
1740	26,000	6 monasteries (cf. Cuzco, Quito)	Juan & Ulloa, II, p. 142
1750	26,000		
1785	30,000		Morse, I, p. 75
1800	26,000		
c.1810	24,000		Bonnycastle, II, p. 147
1850	21,000		
c.1855	21,700	(Higher figures refer to district)	Paz Soldán, 1861

Asunción

c. 1640	4,000		Rosenblatt, p. 230
1793	7,088		" p. 202
1850	44,000		
1857	48,000		Enci. Italiana

Bogotá (Teusquillo, Bacatá)

1538		Zipa Chibcha capital	Hardoy, p. 494
1569	12,000	Raised nearly 2,000 men for war (times 6)	Arciniegas, p. 247
1574		600 Spanish adult males	López de V., p. 360
1680	15,000	3,000 souls (i.e., families; cf. Guatemala City)	Samper, p. 88
1776	19,479		" p. 171
1800	21,464		Chambers Gaz.
1835	c.39,000		Colombia, govt., p. 10
1850	40,000		
1852	40,086	(not 1840 as in Samper)	" " "

Buenos Aires

1602	500		Martínez, p. 306
1664	4,000		" "
1750	13,840		Sánchez-Albornoz & Moreno p. 103
1778	24,205		Martínez, p. 306
1800	40,000		
1801	40,000		" "
1838	65,344		" "
1850	74,000		
1852	76,000		" "

Cajamarquilla

900		Already settled	Uhle in Means, p. 185
peak		50-60,000 in 10,000 houses (seems high)	Geisecke in Hardoy, p. 383
1400	40,000	Prior to rise of Chanchán in a rival state	
"	40,000	130 usual-size blocks (times 300; cf. Cuzco)	Hardoy, plate 56
c.1475		Fell to the Incas	Means, p. 258

Carácas

1607	3,000		Arellano, p. 35
1700	12,500		" p. 70

1759	18,986		Sánchez-Albornoz & Moreno, p. 102
1764	26,340	Church census	" " " "
1772	24,187		" " " "
1800	30,000		
1802	31,234		Arellano, p. 78
1850	43,000		Hoffmann

Chanchán

1400	50,000		
c.1430-c.1460		Its kingdom of Chimor expanded greatly	Rowe, p. 40
peak		Larger than Cajamarquilla	Hardoy, p. 382
"		68,000 at a minimum, but perhaps up to 100,000; 14 square kilometers	West, p. 84
"	75,000	Estimate of Alfred Kidder, II (conversation with one of the authors)	
1461		Fell to the Incas	Rowe, p. 42
1461-1533		Had sub-kings related to the Inca line	Brundage, p. 201
1500	40,000	Its real power gone	

Chavín

c. 800		Flourishing	Means, p. 141
c.1000		Fell	" p. 145
		Possibly not a city	Hardoy, p. 318

Chincha

900-1400		Seat of a kingdom	Means, p. 195
peak		Size of Pachacamac or Rimac	" "
"	25,000		

Chira

1400s		Capital of a densely populated valley conquered by the Incas	" pp. 179-81

Cochabamba

1750	20,000		
1788	22,305		Galdames, p. 99
1800	22,000		
1850	15,000		
1861	14,1700		Grande Ency.

Cuzco

c.1200-1532		Inca capital	Rowe in Brundage, p. 41; Brundage, p. 326
c.1470		15,000 settlers brought from Ecuador	Brundage, p. 142
1487-1526		King usually resided at Quito	Velasco, II, p. 160
1500	45,000		
1533		150 usual-size blocks	Hardoy, plate 62
"	40,000	3-4,000 houses, plus 19,000 additional people	Valverde in Hardoy, p. 443
1574		800 Spanish adult males, 5 monasteries	López de V., pp. 477-8
1600	30,000		
1615		2nd to Potosí in Spanish South America	Lizárraga, p. 77

1615	30,000	Had a cathedral, 5 monasteries, and 6 or 7 Indian parishes (parishes times 3,000, plus Spaniards)	Lizárraga, pp. 76-7
1700	35,000		
c.1740		Just about the size of Lima; 9 monasteries ("conventos")	Juan & Ulloa, 1758, I, p. 508; II, p. 134
1750	40,000		
c.1785	26,000	Probably after Tupac Amarú's revolt (1780-1781)	Morse, I, p. 750
1794	32,082		Haenke in H. Fuentes, p. 45
1800	34,000		
1826	46,123		Gazetteer of World
1850	41,152		Harper

Guayaquil

1734	15,500	12,000 white, 3,500 other	Enríquez, pp. 24, 35
1736	20,000		Juan & Ulloa, I, p. 178
1750	20,000		
c.1775	22,000		Enríquez, p. 62
1805	13,700	Census	" p. 109
1838	22,000		" p. 123
1850	26,000		

Huamanga (Guamanga, now Ayacucho)

c.1540		30,000 Indians in district; by 1578 much less	Olivas, pp. 355-8
1574	13,000	300 Spanish adult males, 3 monasteries (cf. Cuzco)	López de V., p. 475
1600	14,000	3 monasteries, 3 parishes	Olivas, pp. 327-36
1614		500 Spanish adult males	Ruiz, p. 76
1641	20,000	5 monasteries	" p. 54ff
1700	26,000		
1713	26,000	6 monasteries	" "
1740	26,000	6 monasteries	Juan & Ulloa, II, p. 127
1750	26,000		
1779		Mining in marked decline	Pozo, p. 21
1794	25,970		Olivas, pp. 327-36
1800	25,000		
1852	16,700		Ency. Brit., 1853, "Peru"

Huancavelica

c.1592	18,000	3,600 miners in the period 1588-95 (times 5)	Cobb, pp. 105-6
1600	20,000	Growing along with Potosí	" p. 23
c.1800	5,146	4 monasteries ("convents")	Whitaker, p. 12
1852	5,200		Ency. Brit., 1853, "Peru"

Huánuco

1500	25,000		
1532		Temple said to hold 30,000 (some of whom were probably non-urban)	Hardoy, p. 459
1574	13,000	3 monasteries	López de V., p. 473
1616		Large in area, but almost depopulated	Vásquez in Varallanos, p. 399
1784	7,000		H. Ruiz in Varallanos, p. 401

La Paz

1574	13,000	3 monasteries	López de V., p. 500
1675	12,600		Enci. Universal
1796	21,120		" "
1800	22,000		
1831	30,463		" "
1845	42,800		" "
1850	44,000		
1886	56,800		" "

Lima (Rimac till 1532)

1532		Temple smaller than Pachacamac's	Means, p. 186
1535	70		Paz Soldán, 1877, p. 522
1574		2,000 Spanish *vecinos*	López de V., p. 463
1599	14,262		Paz Sodán, 1877, p. 522
1700	37,259		" " " "
1746		Many killed by earthquake	Ency. Brit., 1910
1750	40,000		
1780	50,000		Paz Soldán, 1877, p. 522
1793	52,627		" " " "
1800	54,000		
1813	56,284		Gazetteer of World
1836	54,628		Paz Soldán, 1877, p. 522
1850	70,000	Population growth accelerating in 1850s	
1856	85,116		" " " "

Oruro

1595		Settled	
1700	72,000		Enci. Universal
1710	72,000		Mier, p. xxvii
1740		Decaying	" p. 5
1750	35,000		
1781	8,000	1,400 men (presumably workers)	" "
c.1800	15,000		Humboldt, 1826, VI, p. 366

Pachacamac

1500	25,000		
1533		Main Inca shrine, served by 30,000 (may include some non-urban)	Hardoy, pp. 383, 460

Potosí

1545		Founded	Ency. Brit., 1970
1574	120,000		Arzáns, I, p. 158
1598		16,000 houses	Martínez y Vela, p. 51
1600	148,000		
1611	160,000	76,000 Indians, 43,000 whites, 35,000 mixed, 6,000 blacks	Arzáns, I, p. 286
1626		4,000 *vecinos*, 80,000 Indians	Vázquez de Espinosa, p. 286
1700	95,000		
1719	82,000	Before pestilence; 60,000 after	Arzáns, III, pp. 82, 85
1720	56,000		" " p. 102
1750	39,000		
1779	22,622		Sánchez-Albornoz & Moreno, p. 103

1800	8,000		Averanga in correspondence from Hardoy
c.1830	9,000		Mitchell, p. 232
1850	23,000		
1854	25,600		Averanga in correspondence from Hardoy

Quito

c. 950		Founded	Velasco, II, p. 7
c.950-c.1370		Capital of Quito kingdom	" " pp. 7, 28
1487-1527		Fell to Perú, but became the favorite Inca residence	" " pp. 28, 32
1500	30,000		
1527		Fell to Spain	
1538	23,000	600 Spanish families and 20,000 Indians	Belalcazar in Velasco, II, p. 144
1574	15,000	400 Spanish adult males, 3 monasteries	López de V., p. 432
1600	18,000		
1645		Epidemic killed 11,000	Velasco, III, p. 79
1700	30,000		
1744	30,000	Nearly equaled Lima; built-up area c. 3/4 as large as Cuzco; 9 monasteries; 50-60,000 (clearly exaggerated, or includes tributary Indians)	Juan & Ulloa, I, pp. 262, 268, maps, I, p. 290, II, p. 28
1750	30,000		
1757		46-80,000, formerly 70,000 (probably includes rural tributary Indians)	Coletti in CEGAN, p. 90
1759		Epidemic killed 10,000	Velasco, III, p. 79
1765		Revolt of Indians and native-born whites was cruelly suppressed	CEGAN, p. 24
1779	24,919		" p. 90
1780	28,451		" "
1797		Flattened by earthquake; 40,000 killed in its district	Ency. Brit., 1875
1822	65,133	May be inflated by war refugees	CEGAN, p. 90
1850	36,000		
1857	36,075		" "

Riobamba

c.1350-1487		Capital of Quito: 60,000 (looks high)	Velasco, II, p. 160

Santiago

1657	4,918	In 516 houses	Barros, V, p. 315
1743		4,000 families, but probably includes ranching population; cf. 1802, 1810	Juan & Ulloa, II, p. 263
1778		24,318, but probably includes ranching population; cf. 1802, 1810	Barros, VI, p. 401n
1800	21,000		
1802	21,000	2,169 houses (times 10; cf. 1657), plus 809 ranches	" VII, p. 489n
1810		Slightly over 30,000 (roughly equals houses-plus-ranches in 1802 times 10)	" " p. 489
1830	48,000		Galdames, p. 244
c.1850	70,000		Enci. Italiana
1866	115,377		La Fuente, p. li

Tiahuanaco

c. 800	20,000	25,000 in whole valley, at a conservative estimate; 2.4 or 3 sq. km in area; 9,450 ft. around, oblong	Willey in Hardoy, p. 353; E. Lanning, p. 25; Means, p. 123

800		Its kingdom fell	E. Lanning, p. 130
c. 900		Its kingdom fell	Means, p. 170

Túmbez

c.900-c.1470		Had a strong kingdom	" p. 179

Valparaíso

1827	17,000		Poeppig in Wilhelmy, p. 2
1847	40,000		Lippincott, 1868
1850	<u>45,000</u>		
1854	52,413		Enci. Italiana

Vilcashuaman

		Extensive pre-Inca ruins	Means, pp. 109-0

Viñaque

		Important pre-Inca site	Cieza in Means, p. 120

Bahia (São Salvador, now Salvador)

1549	1,000		Dias, p. 80
1650	10,000		" "
"		2,500 in garrison	Southey, II, p. 659
c.1700		2,000 houses, 2-3 stories high, plus Indians, slaves, and garrison	Dampier in Southey, II, p. 660
"	24,000		
1706	25,000	21,601 with 4,296 hearths (probably excludes garrison)	Dias, p. 80
1750	53,000		
1757	58,000	36,323 plus 16,093 in suburbs and 5,250 in garrison (1759)	" " Caldas, pp. 222-5
1780	65,285	39,209 plus 20,076 in suburbs (probably omits garrison)	Accioli, III, p. 83; Azevedo, p. 165; Dias p. 64
1800	75,000	Including suburbs and garrison	
1805		45,600 in city alone	Azevedo, p. 71
1850	112,000		
1872	129,109		Dias (1960, p. 80)

Mariana

1699		Settled	Vivien
1735	42,000	26,982 slaves (times 11/7; cf. 1813)	Simonsen, p. 296
1743	40,000	25,495 slaves (times 11/7; cf. 1813)	" p. 297
1750	36,000		
1805	6-7,000		Mawe in Southey, III, p. 822
1813		Diocese of Mariana had 7 blacks and mulattoes for every 4 whites	Southey, III, pp. 819-20

Ouro Preto (Villa Rica)

1701		Founded	Ency. Brit., 1875
1735		20,863 slaves; cf. 1805	Simonsen, p. 296
1743		21,673 slaves; cf. 1805	" p. 297
peak	60,000		Enci. Italiana
1750	60,000		
1800	23,000		
1805	20,000	More whites than blacks	Mawe in Southey, III, p. 821
1818	8,500		Spix in Conde, 1830, p. 48

Pernambuco (Recife)

1635	10,000	7,000, plus Olinda (with 2,500 free families in 1630 but burned by Dutch 1631)	Boxer, 1957, p. 39; Southey, III, p. 772
1700	24,000		
1749	35,000	30,000 plus Olinda (cf. 1635, 1810)	Boxer, 1962, p. 168
1750	35,000		
1800	40,000		
1810		5,391 free families plus 1,100 more in Olinda	Southey, III, pp. 769n, 772
c.1817	45,000		Tollenare, p. 326
1842	102,130	Including 17,820 in Olinda	Fernandes G., p. 79
1850	106,000		
1872	116,671	Including Olinda	Statesman's Yearbook, 1877, p. 502

Rio de Janeiro

c.1650		2,500 plus slaves; 6,000 in garrison	Southey, II, p. 667
1700	20,000		
1710		12,000 whites	Rio Branco in Costa, p. 50
1749	29,000	24,397 communicants (plus 1/5 for non-communicants, presumably those under age 7)	Southey, III, p. 813
1750	29,000		
1799	43,376	Including suburbs	Brazil Relatorio, p. 35
1800	44,000	Before arrival of exiled king of Portugal	
1808	60,000		Simonsen, p. 328
1850	166,419		Brazil Relatorio, p. 35

Alexandria

730	<u>216,000</u>	216,000 males, estimated from tax (probably the total population)	Lane-Poole, p. 15n
800	200,000		
860	<u>100,000</u>	After several sieges	Hourani in Hamdan, p. 128
881		New wall enclosing half the area of Alexander's time	Lane-Poole, pp. 73, 90
928		Population removed; 200,000 died	Eutychius in Ency. Brit., 1853
1350		One of world's 5 leading ports	Ibn Battuta, p. 46
1365		Plundered by Cypriotes	Ency. of Islam, 1897, "Iskandariya"
1384		Half of Damietta's size	Frescobaldi, p. 43
1400	<u>40,000</u>		
1496		Nearly equal to Cologne	Harff, p. 93
1500	<u>35,000</u>		
1634		Almost nothing but a heap of ruins	Ency. of Islam, 1897, "Iskandariya"
1693	15,000		Gemelli, p. 12
1777	6,000		Savary in Leo Africanus, p. 907n
1798	4,000		E. M. Forster, p. 76
1828	12,528		Ency. of Islam, 1897, "Iskandariya"
1848	134,000		Hamdan, p. 133
1850	<u>138,000</u>		
1862	164,400		Ency. of Islam, 1897, "Iskandariya"

Asyut

medieval		60 or 75 churches	Ency. of Islam, 1960
1410-		It rose with the decline of Qus	
1850	28,000		
1876	28,000		'' '' '' ''

Cairo

969	<u>100,000</u>	At founding; perhaps doubled in 50 years	Clerget, I, pp. 124, 130
1000	<u>150,000</u>		
1046		20,000 shops, 15 mosques (surely main mosques)	Nasir-i-Khusraw, pp. 127, 147
1100		300,000 (Perhaps somewhat exaggerated)	Clerget, I, pp. 126, 238-239
1200	150-200,000		'' '' p. 239
''	200,000	Acceptable figure	Correspondence from Abu Lughod
1300	<u>400,000</u>		
1325	600,000	600,000 at peak (probably too high)	Clerget, I, p. 240
1348	500,000	At peak	Correspondence from Abu Lughod
1400	<u>450,000</u>		
c.1400		107 madrasas (colleges) and 108 main mosques, including those in Qarafa suburb	Maqrizi in Lapidus, 1961, p. 33
1500	450,000		
1550	430,000		Clerget, I, p. 241
1600	<u>400,000</u>		
1700	350,000		Correspondence from Abu Lughod
1750	<u>300,000</u>		
pre-1800	300,000	Census	Chabrol in correspondence from Abu Lughod
1800	263,000	Clerget estimated 245,000	U.S. Census, 1850, p. liii; Clerget, I, p. 241

1846	256,000	Rough census	Clerget, I, p. 241n
1848	254,000		Hamdan, p. 133
1850	260,000		
1872	349,883		Meyer, 1874, "Kairo"

Coptos (Qift, Quft)

| -1000 | | Main city in upper (southern) Egypt | Ency. of Islam, 1897 |
| c.1300 | | Devastated by then | Hamdan, p. 129 |

Damietta

c. 860		Walled	Savary, I, p. 309
early		3rd after Cairo and Alexandria for centuries	Ency. Brit., 1910
1193		Tinnis's population, reduced some by a siege, moved here	Hamdan, p. 128
1200	100,000		
1300	90,000		
1384		Twice Alexandria	Frescobaldi, p. 43
1400	80,000		
1500	70,000		
1517		Fell with Egypt to Turkey	
1534		Half ruined	Affagart, p. 210
1693		Ill-inhabited	Gemelli, p. 30
1750	23,000	A little town with c. 12 mosques; a miserable place	Hasselquist, pp. 110-1
1777	24,000		Savary, I, p. 316
1800	25,000		
c.1850	27,000		Ency. Brit., 1853
1872	29,383		Statesman's Yearbook, 1877

Fostat

| - 969 | | Forerunner of Cairo and successor to Memphis | |

Fuwa

1384		A large hamlet	Frescobaldi, p. 98
c.1515		Leo Africanus praised its shops	Vivien, "Fouah"
1530		2nd largest in Egypt, following decline of leading cities	Bélon in Hamdan, p. 133
1530-		Neglect by Turks led to its decline	Bélon in Hamdan (1964, p. 133)

Qus (Kus)

640-1000		Smaller than Coptos	Ency. of Islam, 1897
1000s		Passed Coptos as largest in upper Egypt	" " " "
1200		3rd in Egypt	Yaqut in Ency. of Islam
1300		2nd in Egypt	Abulfeda, II, p. 155
peak		6 *madrassas* or colleges	Ency. of Islam, 1897
1404		Plague killed 17,000; it then declined	" " " "

Tinnis

1000	83,000	Same ratio to Cairo as at 1193	
1049		2 chief mosques; 10,000 shops (Cairo had 20,000)	Nasir-i-Khusraw, pp. 110, 127
"		100 small mosques, 72 churches, 36 baths, 66 mills	Mohammed ibn Ahmed in Nasir-i-Khusraw, p. 110n
peak	125,000	83,000 adults subject to poll-tax	Suyuti in Hamdan, p. 128
1193	125,000	Remained populous to this date; besieged, and population fled to Damietta	Hamdan, p. 128

Axum (Aksum)

c.340-1270		Capital of Ethiopia	Budge, I, p. 123
c. 950		Burned	" " p. 213
c.1400	30,000	6 parts (cf. 1805)	
1434		A new convent built	Monneret, p. 56
c.1500	33,000	11 churches	" p. 50
1541		Destroyed	Budge, I, pp. 338, 405
1600s		150-200 houses	P. Páez in Monneret, p. 13
1770	3,000	600 houses	Bruce in Monneret, 1938
1805		Only part of 1 of its 6 quarters inhabited (If it was half-settled, past population would be 30,000)	Salt in Monneret, 1938
1838	1,500	350 houses	Sapeto in Monneret, 1938

Dongola (Pachoras, Mukarra)

500s-c.1500		Capital of Dongola	Ency. Brit., 1910
peak	30,000	Estimate from excavation	Michalowski, p. 68
1100s		Peak	Enci. Italiana
1200s		Kingdom split, Soba breaking away	" "
1200	30,000		
1517		10,000 families (probably out-of-date and likely too high)	Leo Africanus, p. 79
1698		Half-deserted	Poncet, p. 67

Emfras

1699		Smaller than Gondar, but better built	Poncet, p. 90

Gondar

1632-1855		Capital of Ethiopia	Budge, pp. 404, 492-4
1699		3-4 leagues (c. 10 miles) around, but houses only 1-story high; 100 churches	Poncet, pp. 80-1
c.1700	80,000		Parkhurst, p. 61
1750	70,000		
1770	65,000	Based on 10,000 houses	" " ; cf. Bruce in Ency. Brit., 1910
1830s	6,500		Rüppell in Parkhurst, p. 61
1855	14,000		Flad in Parkhurst, p. 61

Lalibala

c.1200		Churches carved out of solid rock by King Lalibala (died 1220)	Budge, I, pp. 164-5, 283
"		10 such churches	Columbia Lippincott Gaz.
late 1800s	3,000		Alamanni in Parkhurst, p. 68

Soba

900s		Mentioned	Enci. Universal
1200s-1505		Capital of Aloa	Chambers, 1967

Tegulat

c.1312		Capital of Ethiopia for awhile	Budge, I, p. 289
1528		Fortress destroyed by Moslems	Vivien
1600		Deserted	

Bonga

c.1575-1897	Capital	Grühl, p. 178
1897	Destroyed	Bieber, II, p. 171

Chonga

c.1450-c.1575	Capital	Grühl, p. 176

Maghreb
(Morocco, Algeria, Tunisia, and Libya)

Algiers

1500	20,000		
1515	20,000		Leo Africanus in Moll IV, p. 203
1600	75,000		
1612	80,000	60,000 in 12,000 houses (probably omits slaves; cf. 1634)	Haëdo in Ency. of Islam, 1897
1634 peak	100,000	In 15,000 houses (with 25,000 slaves) 22,000 militia	Dan in Ency. of Islam Cat, p. 314
1700	85,000	13,000 houses (cf. 1634); 107 mosques (Moll estimates population at 35-40,000)	Moll, IV, p. 195
c.1730		Larger than Tunis	Shaw, p. 565
1750	75,000		
1789	50,000	Probably too low	Ventre de Paradis in Ency. of Islam, 1897
1800	73,000		Boutin in Dureau, p. 151
1808	73,000		Soames, p. 180
1846	42,635		
1850	54,000		
1851	57,081		Harper

Azammur

1500	25,000		
1513	25,000	5,000 families	Leo Africanus, p. 47

Biskra

1200's		Became important	Brunschvig, I, p. 297
1350		One of the largest towns of the Maghreb	Ibn Khaldun in Brunschvig, I, p. 296
1402		Its local dynasty fell	Brunschvig, I, p. 213

Bougie

1067-1152 peak		Hammadid capital 21 quarters, 72 mosques	Ency. of Islam, 1960, "Bidjaya" " " " " "
"	60,000		Brunschvig, I, p. 384
"		24,000 hearths (obviously too high)	Leo Africanus in Gautier p. 351
-1500		2nd to Tlemcen in Algeria	Brunschvig, I, p. 377
1500	40,000		
1512	40,000	8,000 hearths	Leo Africanus in Brunschvig, I, p. 383
1674		500-600 hearths, plus 150 garrison	Arvieu in Gautier, p. 351
1833	2,000		Brunschvig, I, p. 384

Ceuta

1100-1300		Peak	Posac, p. 41
1415		1st in Mauretania	Leo Africanus in Mascarenhas, p. 96
"		5-10,000 Moors killed	Mascarenhas, pp. 77, 94
"		Portuguese garrison of 2,500 installed	" p. 100
1648		7 churches; in decline	" p. 13, cf pp 17-8

Constantine

1150		Ancient capital of Numidia; flourishing	Feÿ, p. 45
1350		Smaller than Bougie	Ibn Khaldun in Brunschvig, I, p. 388n

1500	40,000		
1515	40,000	8,000 hearths	Leo Africanus in Brunschvig, I, p. 388
1800	20,000		
1808	20,000		Boutin, p. 121
1850	28,000		
1851	28,711		Harper

Fez (Fès)

786	15,000	Founded (date is disputed) with 3,000 families	Leo Africanus, p. 418
800	20,000		
1000	75,000		
1067	90,000	300 mills (times 300; cf. 1513)	Bekri, p. 226
1199		467 inns (cf. 1513); 95 baths, 472 mills, 136 bakeries; 89,236 houses (perhaps a district figure)	Gautier, p. 56
1200	250,000		
1200s		More than 200,000	Martineau, p. 29
"	250,000	400 mills within the walls, 400 outside, cf. 1513	Reitemeyer, p. 150
1300	200,000	Declining from 1212 with Morocco's loss of Spain	
c.1400	150,000	1/3 size of Cairo	Qalqashandi, p. 22
1500	125,000		
1513	125,000	Almost 200 inns, at least 400 mills	Leo Africanus in Ency. of Islam, 1897, "Fas"
"		50 main mosques, 70 small ones	Leo Africanus, p. 55
1547-1729		No longer capital of Morocco	Ency. of Islam, 1960, "Fas"
1600	100,000		
1603-72		In decline, with frequent revolts	" " " " "
1672-1727		Held in order by Ismail, but almost nothing built here by him	" " " " "
1700	80,000		
1729		Became capital again	" " " " "
1729-57		Many emigrated in chaotic period	" " " " "
1757-90		Prospered	" " " " "
1799		Plague killed 60,000	Jackson, 1809, p. 272n
1800	60,000	See 1803	
1803		100,000 (hearsay, which is probably exaggerated), but double that number before the plague; mosques said to be 200	Badia, I. pp. 66, 68
c.1850	85,000	Others give it 35-40,000	Ungewitter, II, p. 509

Kairwan

670	10,000	Soldiers founded it (with families the population would soon be 50,000)	Cat, p. 139
670-920		Capital for most of North Africa	Ency. of Islam, 1897
800	80,000	See 1052	
876		Suburb of Rakkada founded with area 24,040 cubits (7.5 miles) around	Bekri, pp. 62-3
1000	65,000		
1052		Wall 22,000 cubits (c. 80 ha.; from peak c. 800); 48 baths, (cf. Damascus)	" pp. 57-60
1057		Sacked by Hilali Arabs; population removed	" p. 61n
1150		Still 3/4 ruined	Edrisi in Brunschvig, I, p. 359
1200s		Rallied	Brunschvig, I, p. 359
c.1730		2nd in Tunisia	Shaw, p. 585
c.1850	15,000		Hoffmann

Kalaa

1007-1090		Hammadid capital	Beylié, p. 1
1102		Still important	" p. 12
1114		1 Christian church	" p. 13
1152		18,000 killed, the rest scattered	Edrisi in Beylié, p. 14

Mahdia (Mahdiya)

916-9		Founded	Gautier, p. 328
921-45		Fatimid capital	" "
		Largest in Barbary (i.e., Maghreb)	Idhari in Ency. of Islam, 1897
1057-1148		Zirid capital	Ency. of Islam, 1897, "Zirids"
1850	4,000		Ganiage, p. 868n

Marrakesh (Morocco)

1070		Founded	Deverdun, I, p. 56
c.1125		100,000 houses during reign of Ali, 1106-1143 (unrealistic for urban area alone)	Leo Africanus, p. 42
1147		Wall 9 km (5.6 miles)	Deverdun, I, p. 142
"		70,000 killed; doubted by Deverdun	" " p. 160
1200		Probably smaller than Fez	" " p. 287
"	150,000		Torres in Deverdun, I, p. 299
"		647 hectares in area	Caillé, I, p. 70n
1269		Ceased to be capital; declined	Ency. of Islam, 1897
1300	100,000		
1350		Largely in ruins; bazaars inferior to Bagdad	Ibn Battuta, p. 316
1500	50,000		
1515		2/3 uninhabited	Leo Africanus, p. 43
1524-47		Independent capital of South Morocco, rising in importance	Ency. of Islam, 1897
1547-1664		Capital of Morocco	" " " "
1600	125,000	Essentially city of 1912 (1921 pop.: 149,000); 15-20,000 in garrison; population less than in 1200	Deverdun, p. 379, 417, 419, 453
c.1690	25,000		Dapper, p. 146
1700	25,000		
1750	30,000		
1757		Became co-capital with Fez	Ency. of Islam, 1897
1767		30,000; rejected by Deverdun as too low	Chénier in Deverdun, I, p. 597
1799		Plague killed 50,000	Jackson, 1809, p. 272n
1800	50,000	See Fez, 1799-1803	
1804		30,000; again too low	Badia in Deverdun, I, p. 597
1830	80-100,000		Irving in Deverdun, I, p. 597
1834	50,000		Gråberg in Deverdun, I, p. 597
1839	60,000		Balbi in Deverdun, I, p. 597
1850	50,000		
1864	40-50,000		Gatell in Ency. of Islam, 1897
1885	55,000	Considered especially reliable	Erckmann in Deverdun, I, p. 598

Meknes

c. 940		Founded	Larousse
1100	45,000	Probably larger than in the next centuries	Ency. of Islam, 1897
1182	45,000	5 main mosques (times 9,000)	" " " "
1200	40,000		
1276-1288		Capital of Morocco	" " " "

1500	35,000		
1512	35,000	6-8,000 hearths, in decline	Leo Africanus in Ency. of Islam 1897
1672		Had fallen into ruin	Windhus, p. 484
1672-1727		Capital, vigorously expanded; 130,000 soldiers barracked there	Ency. of Islam, 1897
1700	200,000		
1727-57		Sharp decline during civil war	" " " "
1757-90		Nearly restored	" " " "
1799	110,000		Jackson, p. 87
1800	110,000		
c.1850	56,000		Ungewitter, II, p. 520

Oran

645		In ruins	Feÿ, p. 35
955		Abandoned for some years	Bekri, p. 145
1500	36,000		
1509	36,000	6,000 houses	Feÿ, p. 51
"		4,000 killed, 8,000 enslaved, some escaped	" p. 71
1708	2,000		" p. 217
1770	5,138	2,317 citizens, 2,821 exiles	" p. 218
1832	3,800		Ency. Brit., 1910

Rabat, with Salé (Sallee)

1058		Salé's Zenata kingdom fell	Caillé, p. 41
c.1143		Rabat founded as a town	" p. 45
1197		Area 418 hectares, Rabat only	" p. 125
1212		Decline to a small agglomeration	" p. 78
c.1570	3-4,000	With 600 hearths, Rabat only	Marmol in Caillé, p. 183
c.1625		8,000 refugees from Spain formed the bulk of Salé's population	Caillé, p. 249
1627-41		Thriving as Morocco's pirate center	Brunot, p. 161
1799	43,000	25,000 in Rabat, 18,000 in Salé	Jackson, 1809, p. 87
1800	43,000		
1832		27,000 in Rabat alone	Gråberg in Caill,́ p. 347
1850	55,000		
1868	60,000		Beaumier in Caillé, p. 347 575

Rakkada, see Kairwan

Sijilmessa (Sidjilmasa)

771-958		Seat of a dynasty	Ency. of Islam, 1897
814		New wall with 14 gates	Bekri, p. 283
c.1010-1055		Seat of a dynasty again	Ency. of Islam, 1897
1274		Its population was enslaved	" " " "
1351		Still a beautiful town	Ibn Battuta, p. 317
1512		A ghost town	Leo Africanus, p. 64
		Its ruins are 5 mi. long	Ency. of Islam, 1897

Tagust

1500	40,000		
1513	40,000	8,000 families	Leo Africanus, p. 41
1600	30,000		
c.1690		In decline from 6,000 families	Dapper, p. 135

Tarudant

1100s		Flourishing from copper mines	Ency. Brit., 1910
1799	25,000	Considerably declined	Jackson, 1809, pp. 88, 103
1800	25,000		
c.1850	22,000		Ungewitter, II, p. 511

Taza

c. 800		Important town	Ency. of Islam, 1897
1500	25,000		
c.1515	25,000	5,000 households	Leo Africanus in Ency. of Islam, 1897
c.1850	12,000		Ungewitter, II, p. 510

Tedsi

1500	20,000		
1513	20,000	4,000 families	Leo Africanus, p. 41
c.1850	15,000		Ungewitter, II, p. 511

Tlemcen

1239-1554		Abd-el-Wadid capital	Ency. of Islam, 1897
1300s		According to Moslem authors 100,000	Bel, p. 14
peak		160 baths	Dapper, p. 161
''		At least 8 main mosques	Ency. of Islam,,1897, "Masdjid"
1400	70,000	Assuming 8 main mosques at peak	
1500	40,000	Declined as Tunis rose	
1520		6,000 houses	Dapper, p. 161
1500s		5 *madrasas* (colleges)	Marmol, II, p. 175
1670		Mostly destroyed for revolting	Shaw, p. 525
1720		4 miles around, but only 1/6 still occupied	'' ''
1859	19,067		Tombourel, p. 108

Tripoli

1000-1146		Had a kingdom	Enci. Italiana
1631-1702		Had a semi-free dynasty	Ency. Brit., 1910
1700	50,000	See 1800, 1855	
1714-1835		Had a free dynasty	'' '' ''
c.1750		60,000 migrated to Tunisia (probably from whole country)	Meyer, 1839
1784	14,000	Perhaps too low	Ency. of Islam, 1897
c.1800		4 miles around (thus, c. 250 ha.); in decline	Playfair, VI, p. 163
''	20,000	Not over 25,000	W. Adams, I, p. 361
1803	12-15,000	Just after plague	Badia, I, p. 234
1815	30,000	At most	Noah, p. 356
1840	25,000		Meyer, 1839 (-53)
1850	25,000		
1855		12 mosques, 6 main ones (left over from earlier peak)	Eyriès & Jacobs, p. 666

Tunis

799		Its rebel kingdom fell	Pellegrin, p. 90
1068		24,000 cubits (c. 7.5 miles) around; 15 baths (area probably too large; cf. 1300, when city was more important)	Bekri, pp. 80, 87
c.1100		City expanded	Brunschvig, I, p. 340
1228-1510		Hafsid capital	Ency. of Islam, 1897
1284-1318		Realm divided	'' ''' '' ''
1300	75,000	As big in area as in 1881, i.e., 265 ha. (times c. 300; much higher density in 1881)	Brunschvig, I, p. 340; Vivien
1361	49,000	7,000 houses (times 7, because of high density); low point	Brunschvig, I, p. 340; Ency. of Islam, 1897, "Hafsids"

1400	70,000		
c.1460	100,000	During reign of Othman, 1434-88	Brunschvig, I, p. 357
1462		Nearly equal to Damascus	Abd-al-Basit, p. 69
1465		200 mosques	Adorne, p. 185
1500	75,000	Declining	
1515	65,000	10,000 hearths (times 5), plus slaves, cf. 1535	Leo Africanus in Brunschvig, I, p. 356
1535		12,000 Christian slaves freed	Enci. Universal, "Túnez"
"		3,000 citizens revolted	Haider, p. 10
c.1570		20,000 houses, including suburbs (probably an exaggeration)	Marmol, II, p. 241
1700	70,000		
c.1730	72,000	12,000 houses (times 6); houses not as lofty as in Algiers	Shaw, pp. 565-6
1750	100,000	See Tripoli	
c.1800	120,000	100,000 or more; local estimate 150,000	Morse, II, p. 722
c.1850	90,000	Decaying under inept rule	Ency. Brit., 1910, "Tunisia"
1853		70,000 (Moslems only?)	Pellissier in Ganiage, p. 868n
1855		130,000 (seems high)	Eyriès & Jacobs, p. 658
1860	90,000	80-90,000	Ganiage, p. 868n
1867	100,000		Cubisol in Ganiage, p. 868n
1870	125,000		Maltzan in Ganiage, p. 868n
c.1895	153,000		Statesman's Yearbook, 1896

Awdaghost (Ghana)

- 971		Or later; seat of Berber empire, served by 20 black kings	Bekri, pp. 301
971-1054		Conquered by Ghana between these dates	Lugard, p. 93
-1054		Capital of Ghana	Cooley, pp. 6, 25
1055		Sacked by conquering Moslems	Lugard, p. 99
1067		1 main mosque, several smaller mosques	Bekri, p. 299

Ghana (possibly Walata)

1054-76		Capital of Ghana	Cooley, pp. 6, 29
1000s	30,000		Maquet, p. 204
1067		12 mosques plus 1 in the pagan part 6 miles away; all built up	Bekri, p. 328
1076		Some massacred in Moslem conquest	Ency. of Islam, 1897
1240		City leveled to the ground	" " " "

Segu

1660-1861		Capital of Bambara	Steele, p. 254
1670-1710		Dominated the upper Niger basin	Ency. of Islam, 1897
1710-54		Period of anarchy	" " " "
1796	30,000		Mungo Park, pp. 843, 876
1800	<u>30,000</u>		

Tademekka

1068		Better built than Ghana or Gao	Bekri, p. 339
1352		Importance mostly gone	Barth, IV, p. 591
c.1475		Destroyed	" " p. 593

Agades

c.1410		Founded 160 years before Marmol wrote (1571)	Marmol in Barth, I, p. 459
c.1475		Rose as Tademekka fell	Barth, IV, p. 593
1500	45,000		
1515	50,000	Or more at peak; 3 1/2 miles around with 70 mosques	" I, pp. 453, 473
"		Askia expelled its 5 tribes	" " p. 459
c.1790		Still prosperous to this time, after which most of its people emigrated	" " p. 474
1850	7,000		" " "

Alkalawa

1764		Founded as capital of Gober	" IV, pp. 526-7
c.1850		Gober still one of northern Nigeria's two main kingdoms, rivaling Sokoto	" " pp. 164-5

Gao (Kagho, Kukia, Gogo)

961		Already powerful	Barth, IV, p. 581
1150		Most celebrated city of Negroland	Edrisi in Ency. of Islam, 1897
1363		One of the largest Negro cities	Ibn Battuta, p. 334
1464-		Its country expanded rapidly	Lugard, ch. 19-24
1500	60,000		
1585	75,000	7,626 houses, plus grass huts	Hogben & Kirk-Greene, p. 67
1591		Fell to Morocco and sank to insignificance	Lugard, chapters 32-33

Gober

1353		In existence	Ibn Battuta, p. 336
1500	28,000		
c.1515		Almost 6,000 families	Leo Africanus, p. 828
1764		Capital moved to Alkalawa	Barth, IV, pp. 526-7

Ilade

1850		Capital of Nupé, whose king that year took Ilorin	Burton, p. 227

Ilorin

c.1820		Capital of Ilorin kingdom	Bowen, p. x
1850	65,000		
1856	70,000		Bowen in Bascom, p. 447
1858		Nearly 100,000 (probably too high)	Bowen, p. x

Kano (till 1410 usually pagan)

999		Kingdom founded	Trevallion, p. 4
1100s		12-mile wall completed	" p. 5
1200	40,000	Based on comparative wall lengths and peak population (1585)	
1500	50,000	Whole area prospered	
1585	65,000	A bit smaller than Gao	Hogben & Kirk-Greene, 1966, p. 67
1600	40,000	After wars and an 11-year famine	Lugard, pp. 303-4
1643-1807		Lost its commercial importance to Katsina	Barth, II, p. 117
1800	30,000		
1807-		Rose as Katsina declined	" " "
1820s	40,000	30-40,000 in 1824; 40-50,000 in 1826	Clapperton & Dixon, 1828, pp. 281-2, and 1829, p. 202
c.1850	40,000	30,000 at a minimum	Barth, II, p. 124

Katsina

c.1320-1643		First dynasty	Barth, pp. 76-77
c.1515		300 families	Leo Africanus, p. 829
1643-1807		Under Habe dynasty	Barth, II, pp. 77, 80
1600s, 1700s		Chief city of this part of Negroland	" " pp. 79-80
1740s		Peak; 13-14 miles around; Barth claims 100,000 but this seems high (cf. Kano's peak population and area)	" " pp. 78, 526-7
1750	75,000		
1807-		Declined rapidly	" " pp. 80-81
c.1850	7-8,000		" " p. 78

Kazargamu (Nkazargamu, Kasreggomo)

1472		Founded as capital by a strong king	Lugard, p. 273
1600	60,000	At approximate peak; cf. 1658 and Kuka	
peak		6 miles around (c. 580 ha.); Hogben's figure of 200,000 seems unreasonably high	Hogben & Kirk-Green, 1966, p. 313
1658		4 mosques each holding 12,000 (undoubtedly there were smaller mosques as well)	" " " " "
1670-	50,000	Declining	Urvoy, pp. 85-6
1808		Destroyed	Hogben & Kirk-Greene, 1966, p. 396

Kebbi (Birni-n-Kebbi)

1515-1806		Capital of Kebbi Kingdom	Enci. Universal

Kilwa

c. 975		Founded	Ency. Brit., 1910, "Zanzibar"
-1505		Capital of East African trading ports	" " " "
1505	4,000	But pehaps 10,000 (probably after conquest by Portuguese)	Randles, p. 975
"		300 mosques (looks high)	Ency. Brit., 1910, "Zanzibar"
1587		3,000 massacred	Freeman-Grenville in Oliver Mathew, pp. 138-9
c.1650	12,500	10 blocks (times 1,250; cf. Diu, India)	Faria, map p. 72

Kuka (Kukawa)

1812-93		Capital of Bornu; successor to Kazargamu	Ency. Brit., 1910
1840s	50-60,000	Usual population	Ency. of Islam, 1897
1850	50,000		

Mali (Melle)

1238		Founded	Ency. of Islam, 1897
c.1353		Its empire at its peak	Lugard, p. 117
1374-1513		Decline and fall	" p. 152
1400	50,000	See other capitals, such as Gao and Kazargamu	
1500	35,000		
c.1515	30,000	6,000 or more families	Leo Africanus, p. 823
1545		Sacked for a week	Ency. of Islam, 1897

Masenya

1500s-1871		Capital of Baghirmi	Ency of Islam, 1897, "Bagirmi"
1850	30,000		
1852	30,000	7 miles around (c. 800 ha.), 1/4 inhabited	Barth, III, p. 388; cf. p. 205

Masina (Macina)

c. 970		A kingdom	Bekri, pp. 301-2
1500		A provincial capital	Barth, IV, p. 421

Ngala (Ancalas?)

c.1150		Undoubtedly largest in Kawar (Urvoy however suggests Ancalas was Bilma)	Edrisi in Urvoy, p. 34
1300s		Its kingdom arose	Barth, III, p. 276
1850		In great decay	" " p. 270

Njimiye

c.1150		Very small	Edrisi in Urvoy, p. 33
-c.1386		Capital of Bornu	Ency. Brit., 1910, "Bornu"

Sennar

1504-1821		Capital of what is now Sudan	Ency. of Islam, 1897, "Fundj"
1699		100,000 (probably an exaggeration); 1.5 leagues (4.5 miles) around, with only 1-story houses (thus c. 325 ha.)	Poncet, p. 69
1700	30,000	Based on area	
1750	30,000	Kingdom remained strong till 1762	Ency. of Islam, 1897, "Fundj"
c.1850	7,000		Ungewitter, II, p. 485

Sokoto

1809		Walls built	Hogben & Kirk-Green, p. 389
1814-22		Capital of Sokoto kingdom	" " " pp. 390, 399
1824		Crowded	Clapperton in Barth, IV, p. 173
once		120,000 (seems high for the area)	Brockhaus, 1928
1850	33,000		Barth in English Cyclopaedia
"		Square area c. 5 miles around	Barth, IV, p. 182

Suramé (Birni-n-Kebbi)

1516		Capital of new-founded Kebbi kingdom, which soon ruled most of Northern Nigeria	Sadi, pp. 129, 269; Lugard, p. 196; Urvoy, p. 74
1808		Destroyed	Barth, IV, p. 213
c.1850		Thickly inhabited	" " p. 214

Timbuktu

1077		Founded	Enci. Universal "Tombouctou"
1325		Began to displace Walata as emporium for the South-Sahara	" " "
1400	20,000		
c.1500	25,000		Ventris de Paradis in Mauny, p. 497
1515		Temporarily de facto Songhai capital; garrison of 3,000 cavalry, plus infantry	Leo Africanus, pp. 824-5
by 1590		3 chief mosques	Minet, p. 3
1591		Fell to Morocco and began to decline	Lugard, p. 306
1600	25,000		
c.1800		C. 4 miles in circuit (thus, c. 250 ha.); Jackson claims 50,000 people plus slaves (surely too high)	Jackson, 1820, p. 10

1828	12,000	7 mosques	Caillié in Eyriès & Jacobs, p. 523
c.1850	13,000		Barth, IV, p. 482

Walata (Bíru, ancient Bakalatis)

-1469	Chief commercial center of western Negroland till Sonni Ali's time	Barth, IV, p. 421

Yakoba (Bauchi)

1809-		Capital of Bauchi	Ency. Brit., 1910
1850	40,000		
c.1900	50,000	Or more	Ency. Brit., 1910, "Nigeria"

Zagha

1153	Populous	Edrisi in Barth, IV, p. 585
"	Capital of Tekrur, ancient and important town	Barth, IV, p. 421

Zamfara (Zanfara)

1764	Capital of almost the most flourishing country of Negroland	Barth, IV, p. 120
"	Destroyed	" " p. 526

Zanzibar

1832-56		Capital of Oman (Muscat)	Ency. Brit, 1910
1850	60,000		
c.1870	60-80,000		Meyer, 1874

Zaria

c.1095		Founded	Hogben & Kirk-Greene, pp. 185-6
c.1550	40,000	Wall built nearly 10 miles around (c. 1,600 ha. times 25; cf. Katsina)	" " " p. 218
1600	50,000		
c.1600-c.1734		Capital of the dominant Hausa state	" " " pp. 217-219
1700	50,000		
1800	40,000		
1820s		Seemed larger than Kano's 40-50,000; advanced base for the Moslems against the pagans	Clapperton, 1829, pp. 201-2
"		On new site	Clapperton in Hogben & Kirk-Greene, p. 222
1846-53		Peak of its slave-raiding; king had 10,000 slaves	Hogben & Kirk-Greene, p. 223
1850	50,000		
1853-1937		In decline	" " " pp. 228-234
1900		60,000 estimate (probably too high)	Ency. Brit., 1910, "Nigeria"
1931	28,121		Webster Geographical Dictionary

Zyrmi

1764-c.1825	Capital of Zamfara	Barth, IV, pp. 120, 526
c.1850	Still well-inhabited	" " p. 121

Abeokuta

1830		Founded	Biobaku, pp. 17-8
			Freeman in Bascom, p. 447
1843	50,000		Townsend in Bascom,
			p. 447
1850	65,000		
1858	80,000		Bowen in Bascom, p. 447

Abomey

1600s-1892		Capital of Dahomey	Ency. Brit., 1910, "Dahomey"
1750	24,000		
c.1780	24,000		Norris, p. 92
1800	25,000		
1850	30,000	Prospering under Gezo	
1892		6 miles around (c. 600 ha.), but including fields and villages	Ency. Brit., 1910

Allada (Ardra)

1682		9 miles around; cf. its successor, Abomey, and Loanda	Barbot, p. 358
1700	25,000		
1724		Conquered by its offshoot kingdom Dahomey	Ency. Brit., 1910

Benin (Oedo)

c.1440-c.1473		Rose to importance	Egharevba, p. 14
late 1500s		Only it and Kano perhaps reached over the 75,000 of Gao	Mauny, p. 499
1600	65,000	See Kano	
1682		6 leagues (18 miles) around; many streets 2 miles long	Barbot, p. 358
1800	15,000		Mauny, p. 500

Bussa

600s		Founded, according to tradition	Hermon-Hodge, p. 118
by 1000		First and only capital of Borgu	" p. 117-189
c.1825	10-12,000		Clapperton, 1829, p. 143

Gbara

| c.1550-1806 | | Capital of Nupé | Hogben & Kirk-Greene, pp. 263-364 |
| 1500s | | 5,555 horses in royal stables | "   "   " p. 263 |

Ibadan

c.1829		A village, began rapid growth	Awe, p. 13
1850	55,000		
1853	60,000		Tucker in Bascom, p. 447
1856	70,000		Bowen in Bascom, p. 447
1857		Wall 10 miles around (c. 1,600 ha.)	Awe, p. 15

Ife

c.1200		Capital of Yorubaland	Hermon-Hodge, p. 116
c.1840		Briefly dominated most Yorubas	Awe, p. 14
1911	36,231	In decline	Bascom, p. 447

Ijaye

1820s		Founded; soon rivaled Ibadan in power	Awe, pp. 13, 18
1850	50,000		
1862	60,000		Ency. Brit., 1875, "Ibadan"
″		All fled in a civil war	S. Johnson, p. 352

Ijebu

| 1507 | | Very large town | Bascom, p. 448 |

Ikoso

| c.1300 | | Yoruba capital, with 10,000 stabled horses (surely for cavalry) | Burton, p. 187 |

Iseyin

-c.1850		Capital of a Yoruba state	″ 223
1853		70,000	Tucker in Bascom, p. 447
1856		20,000	Bowen in Bascom, p. 447

Krenik (Debabe Ngaya)

| c.1350-c.1600 | | The So capital sometime between these dates | Barth, III, p. 279; Ency. of Islam, 1897, "Bornu" |
| c.1600 | | Destroyed | Barth, III, p. 279 |

Kumasi

c.1663-1874		Capital of Ashanti	Ency. Brit., 1970
1800	40,000		
1816	40,000		W. Adams, I, p. 277
1825	20,000	Population reduced by war losses	Ency. Brit., 1910, "Kumasi" and "Ashanti"
1842		Half the size of Abeokuta	Freeman in Biobaku, p. 28
1850	25,000		

Nufi

| 1350 | | One of the largest Negro cities; it traded clear to the east coast | Ibn Battuta, pp. 112, 323 |

Ogbomosho

c.1650		Founded	Ency. Brit., 1970
1850	45,000		
1853	45,000		Tucker in Bascom, p. 447
1860	50,000		Campbell in Bascom, p. 447

Oshogbo

c.1600		Presumably founded by King Ajagbo	
1890		34-40,000 (probably too low)	Millson in Bascom, p. 447
1911	59,821		Bascom, p. 447

Ouagadougou (Wagadugu)

| c.1450-1898 | | A Mossi capital | Tauxier, p. 462 |
| c.1895 | 5,000 | | Vivien, suppl. |

Oyo

| c.1300-1838 | | Yoruba capital | S. Johnson, p. 49; Ency. Brit., 1970 |

1800	<u>85,000</u>		
1820s	<u>85,000</u>	c. 15 miles around (but higher density than Abeokuta which had a newer wall and ruled a much smaller territory)	Clapperton, 1829, p. 90
1839		Destroyed	Bowen, p. x
1856	20,000	On new site	Bowen in Bascom, p. 447

Puje

c.1650-1815		Capital of the Kwararafa or Jukun	Hogben & Kirk-Greene, p. 196
c.1820		Deserted	Meek, pp. 51-2

Su

1852		A large town, named for the So; in ruins (perhaps a former So capital, c. 1350-c.1600)	Barth, III, p. 278

Angoleme

1526-		Probably founded by Ngola, who who ruled by 1526 and till 1560	Plancquaert, p. 44; Barbot, p. 520
1564	<u>30,000</u>	5-6,000 huts	Gouveia in Randles, p. 972n
"		Perimeter of wall as great as that at Évora (Portugal)	" " "
			"

Chungo

c.1750		Capital of Lunda	Lacerda, p. 104

Dongo (Pungu n'Dongo)

1600		A great city, capital of Angola	Battel, pp. 322, 324
"	<u>30,000</u>	See its predecessor, Angoleme	
1671		Overrun by Portuguese	Childs, p. 272

Kasongo

1850		Perhaps 60,000 (probably too high)	S. Hinde in Ency. Brit., 1910, VI, p. 919

Loanda (Luanda)

1576		Founded as Portuguese capital of Angola	Ency. Brit., 1910
1641		6 churches	Jacques Barbot in Jean Barbot, p. 516
1667		3,000 whites and a multitude of slaves, including 12,000 serving the Jesuits and up to 3,000 per owner	Guatini & Carli, p. 157
1700	20,000		
c.1900	20,000		Enci. Universal

Loango

1600		Streets very wide and long	Battel, p. 329
c.1690		Nearly Rouen's size, but with much smaller houses (may have grown after Dongo fell, perhaps as new capital)	Dapper, p. 321
1700	<u>30,000</u>		
c.1750		Ceased to be important	Ency. Brit., 1910
1800's		10 miles around (left over from peak)	Harper

Mapungubwe

c. 700(?)		Large stone buildings resembling Zimbabwe's (hence, perhaps built c. 700)	Gordon-Brown, p. 637

Mengo Area (capital of Uganda)

-c.1890		Capital shifted each reign, but always within 10 miles of the same center	Southall & Gutkind, 1956, p. 1
1911	32,441	First census (of Kampala)	" " " " p. 6

São Salvador (earlier Congo)

c.1400-c.1570	Capital of Congo	Plancquaert, pp. 44, 52
1484	50,000 (appears too high)	Morse, II, p. 769
1491	100,000 (also appears too high; Randles's date 1591 should read 1491	Pigafetta in Randles, p. 972n
1548	3 churches	Duffy, p. 20
1568	Destroyed, but later resettled	" p. 21
1596	Declining fast	" p. 22
1690	Deserted, its 12 churches in ruins	" "

Zimbabwe

600s	Founded, according to two carbon-datings (distrusted by Summers), which fit very plausibly with known Arab history	Summers, p. 13
c.1100	Walled	" "
1868	Unpopulated when discovered by Europeans; ruins extend at least 2 miles by 1 1/4 miles	Ency. Brit., 1910; Hall, p. xv

Port Louis

1801	12,000	c. 4,000 whites, twice as many blacks	Bory, I, p. 163
1846	45,212		Mauritius, census commissioner, p. 6
1850	49,000		
1851	49,909		″ ″ ″ ″

Ani

763		Fortified	Brosset, p. 94
952-1045		Capital of Armenia	Ency. Britannica, 1971, "Armenia"
990-1020		Peak; 40 church cupolas have been found in the ruins	Ency. of Islam, 1897; Brosset, p. 136
1000	75,000		
1064		50,000 fled, rest were massacred	Brosset, pp. 124-5
1072		Repopulated by a Moslem lord	" p. 126
1208		12,000 slain	W. Allen, p. 108
1239		Ravaged by Charmagan	Brosset, p. 134
1319		Wholly destroyed by earthquake	" p. 136

Ankara (Angora)

1700	45,000		Tournefort, II, p. 349
1750	37,000		
c.1800	30,000		Playfair, V, p. 349
1850	40,000		Brockhaus, 1851
c.1880		27,825	Cuinet in Ency. of Islam, 1960

Bursa (Brusa)

1326-1453		Turkish capital, but only nominally after 1366	Ency. of Islam, 1897, "Brussa" and "Murad I"
1400		200,000 houses (obviously too high)	Schiltberger in Gabriel, p. 3
1432		Largest in Turkish hands	LaBrocquère, p. 331
1487	31,000	5,250 taxpayers (times 6, since taxpayers include Jews, but not unmarried youths, single women, slaves, garrison, staffs of dignitaries, and palace servants)	Gabriel, p. 3
1500	33,000		
1522	38,000	6,351 taxpayers (times 6)	" "
"		35,000 (which seems too low)	Barkan in Lapidus, 1967, p. 264
1573	77,000	12,852 taxpayers (times 6)	Gabriel, p. 3
1600	70,000		
1640		40,000 houses (surely too high)	Evliya in Gabriel, p. 3n
1675	55,000	40,000 Turks, 12,000 Jews, a few Christians	Spon in Gabriel, p. 3n
1700	60,000		
1701	60,000	12,000 families (10-12,000 of Turks, 1,200 others)	Tournefort, II, p. 355
1750	65,000		
1800	70,000		
1810		50,000 (probably excludes suburbs, cf. 1852, 1856)	Kinneir in Hassel, 1819, XIII, p. 125
1850	100,000		
1852		73,000 from a census	Murray, p. 182
1856	102,907	Including Kete, Jebeli, Atik, Trilia, and Siki	Mordtmann in Petermann, 1857, p. 89

Diyarbekir (Diarbekr, Amida)

1042		2,000 by 2,000 paces (c. 400 hectares)	Nasir-i-Khusraw, p. 26
1394		Destroyed by Tamerlane	
1664		20,000 Christians	Tavernier, I, p. 104
1700	40,000		
1750	40,000		Brockhaus, 1864
1800	38,000		
1810	38,000		Kinneir in Hassel, 1819, XIII, p. 306
1816		50,000 population (estimate); 25 mosques, only 10,000 Christians	Buckingham, I, pp. 377-78

1850	27,000		
1856	27,424		Mordtmann in Petermann, 1857, p. 91

Erzurum (Theodosiopolis, Erzerum)

1080-1201		Seat of a kingdom	Ency. of Islam, 1960
1201		140,000 slain, 100 churches destroyed	Chambers, 1870
1405		Not very populous	Clavijo, pp. 138-39
1700	24,000		Tournefort, II, p. 195
c.1800	80,000	100,000 (may include a large garrison; other estimates are even higher)	Hammer in Hassel, 1819, XIII, p. 244
1810		100,000; 2 churches; nearly 40 mosques, of which 4 were reckoned handsome (presumably main mosques)	Kinneir, p. 322
1829	80,000	In 16,378 houses	Smith in Gazetteer of World
c.1850	37,000		Murray (1854, p. 188)
1854	40,000	With 39 mosques and several Armenian churches	Chambers (1870)

Ganja (Elizavetpol, now Kirovabad)

c.951-c.1070		Had a local dynasty	Ency. of Islam, 1960
1138		130,000 killed by earthquake in and near the city, which was soon re-built in all its splendor (likely exaggerated)	'' '' '' 1897
1235		Burned by Mongols	'' '' '' ''
1860	13,169		'' '' '' ''

Kayseri (Caesarea Mazaca)

330-1064		1st in Asia Minor	Ency. Brit., 1910
1100	100,000	2nd under Seljuks (hence larger than Nishapur)	Ency. of Islam, 1897
1200s	100,000	(Vague estimate)	Rice, p. 111
1813	25,000		Kinneir in Ency. of Islam, 1960
1839	18,522		Ainsworth in Ency. of Islam, 1960
1858		8-10,000 houses (probably too high)	Barth in Ency. of Islam, 1960

Konia (now Konya)

1099-1302		Seljukid capital	Ency. Brit., 1970; Ency. of Islam, 1897, "Seldjuks"
1200	100,000		
1200s	100,000	(Vague estimate, but conceivable on historical grounds; its state dominated Asia Minor. Cf. 1810)	Rice, p. 11
1243		Declined with Seljuk defeat	Ency. Brit., 1910, "Seljuks"
c.1800		3 miles around, plus 2 suburbs	Playfair, V, p. 154
''	30,000		
1810	30,000	With 12 main mosques (probably left over from early peak; times 9,000 = 108,000)	Kinneir in Hassel, 1817, XIII, p. 198
c.1850	33,000		Murray, p. 209

Nicaea (now Iznik)

1200s		New wall built, 4,970 meters (c. 3 miles) long; the ancient Greek wall had been 2,893 meters	Schneider & Karnapp, pp. 1, 6
1204-1261		Byzantine capital	Ency. Brit., 1970

1332-1432		5 or 6 new mosques, plus 2 older churches	Firatli, pp. 12-18
1856	13,899		Mordtmann in Petermann, 1857, p. 89

Sivas

-1071		2nd in Asia Minor under Byzantine rule	Ency. Brit., 1910
c.1080-1174		Danishmandid capital	Ency. of Islam, 1897, "Danish-mandiya"
1200s		100,000 (vague estimate)	Rice, p. 111
1402	36,000	9,000 "virgins" carried off by Tamerlane (times 4; cf. Cambay)	Schiltberger, p. 20
c.1850	31,000	6,200 families	Murray, p. 208

Smyrna (now Izmir)

1097		10,000 massacred by Greeks	R. Chandler, p. 60
1200		In ruins; restored as a small town	" "
c.1335		Mostly in ruins	Ibn Battura, p. 134
1600	80,000	Turkey prospering in this period	
1631	90,000		Tavernier, p. 33
1700	135,000	27,000 (surely intended for families)	Tournefort, II, pp. 374-75
1750	130,000		
c.1800	125,000	120-130,000	Hassel, 1819, XIII, p. 154
1814	120,000	30,000 died of plague	Jowett in Mikhov, IV, p. 195
c.1850	150,000		Murray, p. 164

Tiflis

496-1802		Royal capital of Georgia	Ungewitter, II, p. 178
852		50,000 killed	Muir, p. 527
1200	80,000	Prospering during era of Queen Tamara	
1227	100,000	Perhaps slightly high	Meskhia, p. 64
1395		Destroyed by Tamerlane	" "
1500s		2,000 houses	" p. 93
1700	20,000		Tournefort, II, p. 237
"		2,800 houses	Meskhia, p. 141
1770s	24,000		" "
1795		All killed or enslaved	" "
1810	15,000		Kinneir, p. 344
1850	34,890		Meskhia, p. 141

Trebizond

1204-61		10,000 in militia	Fallmereyer, p. 304
1204-1461		Capital of a kingdom	
1300	60,000	Based on militia	
1694	20,000		Gemelli, p. 97
1700		Smaller than Erzurum	Tournefort, II, p. 195
c.1850	25-30,000		Murray, p. 200

Acre

1047		5,000 ells (c. 3 miles) around	Nasir-i-Khusraw, p. 49
1191	75,000	19 quarters, each with a church (thus, 19 parishes, plus infidels)	La Martinière, 1737
1200	75,000		
1291	60,000		Vivien
1291-1750		A heap of ruins; few dwellers	Ency. of Islam, 1960
c.1750-1804		Local capital	" " " "
1832		Destroyed by the Egyptians	" " " "

Aleppo

637	72,000	12,000 in militia	Baurain, p. 22
944-991		Capital of kingdom of Syria, except 967-76	" p. 33
962		All killed but 10,000 women and children	" p. 47
1046		Big as Balkh; very close-built (it would be more populous than Balkh, which was declining and therefore thinly built-up)	Nasir-i-Khusraw, p. 32
c.1170		5,000 Jews	Benjamin of Tudela, pp. 81-2
c.1250		38 markets	Ziadeh, p. 89
1260		Fierce Mongol sack	Sauvaget, p. 159
1299		Populace fled fearing the Mongols	" p. 160
c.1390	75,000	64 mosques (times 800, plus Jews and Christians)	Hafiz Abru in Rentz, p. 96
1400	75,000	But devastated by Tamerlane in October	Grousset, p. 527
1500	67,000		
1520	67,000	From taxes	Lapidus, 1967, p. 79
1530	57,000	From taxes	" " "
1600	61,000		
1679	66,000	13,360 hearths	Arvieux, p. xxv
1700	72,000		
"		15,000 Catholic Armenians	Baurain, p. 93
1737	84,000	14,000 houses	Otter, pp. 59, 91
1750	80,000		
1756		25,000 Greek Catholics	" p. 113
1780s		Probably does not exceed 100,000; not larger than Nantes or Marseilles	Volney, II, p. 152
c.1790	70,000		Taylor in Playfair, V, p. 209
1800	70,000		
1822		155,000 before the earthquake (probably too high), 50,000 after	Enci. Italiana
1840s	80,000		Bazili in Lapidus, 1969, p. 110
1850	95,000		
1856	99,383	Including Ravedan	Mordtmann in Petermann, 1857, p. 91

Anbar

750-762		Capital of the Caliphate	Ency. of Islam, 1897
927		Devastated by Qarmatians	" " " "
985		Small	" " " "
c.1170		3,000 Jews	Benjamin of Tudela, p. 94

Antioch

965		5,000 in militia (may exclude Christians)	Boucher, p. 215
1051		Garrison of 4,000	" p. 230
1097		360 churches (left over from the more populous past, c. 500 A.D.	Caplat, p. 72

1252		In deplorable condition	Rubruquis in Komroff, p. 207
1268		17,000 killed, 100,000 captured including 8,000 in castle	Boucher, p. 269
''		From this disaster it never recovered	Ency. Britannica, 1910
1432	1,800	300 houses	La Brocquière, p. 313
1780s		No more than a ruinous town	Volney, II, p. 154
1816	10,000	4th in Syria after Aleppo, Damascus, and Homs; 14 mosques	Buckingham, pp. 557-58
1856	21,396		Mordtmann in Petermann, 1857 p. 92

Bagdad (Baghdad)

765	480,000	Founded circular with a 2-mile radius (thus, c. 3,200 ha. in area, times 150; cf. 932)	Yaqubi in Le Strange, p. 18
800	700,000		
833		2,000,000 reputedly	Ency. Brit., 1910
''	900,000	43,750 by 1,366 meters, or 5,946 hectares (times 150; probably reflects 1st population peak in 833) in 892	Ency. of Islam, 1960
932		860 licensed doctors; thus, a minimum of 860,000 people	'' '' '' '' ; Hollingsworth, pp. 284-85
''		1,500,000; based on 1,500 baths (in 993) at the traditional 1 bath per 200 families	Ency. of Islam, 1960
''	1,100,000	53,750 by 1,366 meters, or 7,342 hectares (assuming density of 150 per ha.; cf. c. 1400 when the density was even higher)	'' '' '' ''
peak		240,000 houses	Cuinet, III, p. 93
956		Down 9/10 from 932	Tanukhi in Ency. of Islam, 1960
971		17,000 killed in a riot	Ency. of Islam, 1960
985		Larger than Cairo	Mukaddasi in Clerget, I, p. 133
1000	125,000	Cf. 956, 985, and Nishapur	
1171		40,000 Jews (probably an exaggeration)	Benjamin of Tudela in Ency. of Islam, 1960
1184		11 main mosques	Ibn Jubayr, pp. 234, 237
1200	100,000	Based on mosques (times 9,000; cf. 1258, 1350, and 1400)	
1258		Probably 100,000 killed, including refugees	Ency. of Islam, 1960
1282		2 main mosques	'' '' '' ''
1300	40,000	Based on mosques	
c.1350	100,000	11 main mosques	Ibn Battuta, p. 99
c.1400		Late medieval area was 562 hectares; Russell estimates 70,000 population	Russell, 1958, p. 130
''	90,000	Probably in decline after 1393 owing to Tamerlane's attacks	Ency. of Islam, 1897, "Persia"
1401		90,000 slain by Tamerlane	Meyer, 1874
1437		No mosque	Maqrizi in Ency. of Islam, 1960
1604		20-30,000 houses (either an exaggeration or many houses vacant)	Texeira in Ency. of Islam, 1960
1628		Hardly equal to Bristol	Herbert, p. 230
1638	30,000	All killed	Meyer, 1874
1652	14,000		Tavernier in Ency. of Islam, 1897
1773		60,000 died during epidemic	Meyer, 1874
1800	80,000		
1804	80,000		Olivier in Ency. of Islam, 1960
1809		45,000 (seems low)	Rousseau in Ency. of Islam, 1960
1831	110,000	Reduced to 30,000 by plague	Ency. Brit., 1875

1844	65,000		English Cyclopaedia
1850	62,000		
1853	60,000		Felix Jones in Ency. of Islam, 1960
1867	67,273	"Males" (likelier total)	Ency. of Islam, 1960
c.1870		9,000 houses	Meyer, 1874

Basra

671	200,000	80,000 warriors plus 120,000 others	Kremer, p. 310
700-850		200-800,000 range of estimates	Ency. of Islam, 1960
717		Garrison of Khorasan province consisted mainly of 40,000 soldiers from Basra	Kremer, p. 312
c. 975		3 miles across (thus, if c. 8 miles in circuit, it would be c. 1,000 ha. in area)	Mukaddasi in Hirth and Rockhill, p. 138
1000	50,000	Low density for declining population	
1051		Mostly ruined	Nasir-i-Khusraw, p. 236
c.1160		10,000 Jews	Benjamin of Tudela, p. 96
1525	10,000	2,000 families	Leo Africanus in Ency. of Islam, 1960
1691		80,000 died in epidemic	A. Hamilton, p. 55
1691-4		Deserted	" "
1700s	40-50,000		Islam Ansiklopedisi
1750		150,000 (probably an exaggeration)	Brockhaus, 1864
"	50,000		
1758	60-70,000	12 miles around (thus, enclosing c. 2,300 ha.; can reflect early peak)	Ives, p. 231
1800	60,000		
1810	60,000		Kinneir, p. 290
1838	12,000	After 2 epidemics	Brockhaus, 1864
1854	5,000		" "

Damascus

661-715		Capital of the Arab Caliphate	Ency. of Islam, 1897
705-715	250,000	45,000 got state annuities (times 5, since such annuities went only to those either capable of military service or holding a government job) plus slaves, plural wives, harem, etc.	Kremer, p. 148
1100s		57 public baths	Ziadeh, 1953, p. 90
"		241 mosques, 12 madrasas (colleges)	Ibn Asakir in Lapidus, 1969, p. 33
c.1170		3,000 Jews	Benjamin of Tudela, p. 80
c.1185		Saladin's main residence	Abdul-Hak, p. 61
1200	90,000	Based on public baths in 1100s and 1300s and population c. 1400	
1299		100,000 killed by Mongols	Ziadeh, 1964, p. 6
1300s		74 public baths	" 1953, p. 90
c.1400	100,000		Lapidus, 1967, p. 79
1401		All over 5 and not decrepit removed to Samarkand	Ibn Taghribirdi in Ziadeh, 1964, p. 13
1432	100,000	Larger than Aleppo	La Brocquière, pp. 294, 309
1500	70,000		
1520s	57,000		Lapidus, 1967, p. 79
1534		Same size as Rouen or Toulouse	Affagard, p. 218
1600	60,000		
1700	70,000		
1750	80,000		
1780s	80,000		Volney, I, p. 271
1800	90,000		
early 1800s	100,000		Hassel, 1817
c.1850	108,599	Census between 1848 and 1855	Porter, I, p. 139

Edessa (Urfa)

peak		9 miles around	Playfair, V, p. 215
638-		Declining	Ency. Brit., 1910
978		300 mosques (some probably left over from earlier times)	Ibn Hawqai in Ency. Brit., 1910
1098-1144		Crusaders' eastern bulwark	Ency. Brit., 1910
1393		Destroyed by Tamerlane	Playfair, V, p. 215
1796	20-24,000		Olivier in Ency. Brit., 1910
1800	20,000		
1810	20,000		Kinneir, p. 315
1850	33,000		
1873	40,000		Sachau in Ency. Brit., 1910

Hama

630		Unimportant	Ency. of Islam, 1897
c.1150		25,000 killed	Benjamin of Tudela, p. 81
c.1325		Briefly more important than Syrian Tripoli	Ency. of Islam, 1897
1800	50,000		
1807		Twice the size of Homs, hence 80-100,000 (probably an exaggeration since Badia gave Homs only 25-30,000)	Badia, II, pp. 288, 291
c.1850	44,000		Ency. Brit., 1853

Hasa (Lahsa, Ahsa, now Hofuf)

926		Founded	Ency. of Islam, 1897, "Ahsa"
926-1000s		Capital of the Qarmatians	Ency. Brit., 1910, "Arabia"
1000	150,000		
c.1045	150,000	20,000 bore arms; 30,000 Negro slaves	Nasir-i-Khusraw, pp. 225, 227

Jerusalem

c. 630	62,000		Margoliouth, p. 195
1000	60,000		
1047		20,000 men; main church held 8,000	Nasir-i-Khusraw, pp. 67, 108
1099	70,000	All slain	Margoliouth, p. 201
1243	20,000		Campbell, p. 165
"	7,000		Boudet, p. 245
1488	4,000		Jewish Ency.
1693		Under 20,000	Gemelli, p. 33
1780s	12-14,000		Volney, I, p. 304
1856	18,000		Jewish Ency.

Kufa

638		Founded	Kremer, p. 309
671	140,000		" p. 310
906-85		5 times sacked	Ency. of Islam, 1897
c. 980		Smaller than Basra	Ibn Hawqual, 1800, p. 65
1000	30,000	See Basra	
c.1160		7,000 Jews	Benjamin of Tudela, p. 93
1184		Over half deserted	Ibn Jubayr, p. 219
c.1350		In ruins	Ibn Battuta, p. 97

Mecca

630	70,000	Angels (presumably people) in God's house; reached full extent of area by this date	Wüstenfeld, IV, pp. 1, 57
peak	100,000		Badia, II, p. 103
800	100,000		
1050		7,000 males (probably adult), many having departed during a famine	Nasir-i-Khusraw, p. 188

1394-1400		Pilgrim caravan blocked by Tamerlane's wars	Gaury, p. 103
1500	60,000		
1503		4,000 sellers, 30,000 poor	Varthema, p. 39
1600	60,000		
1658		Size of Marseille	Thévenot, part 1, p. 155
1700	60,000		
1750	50,000	See 1807	
1783		Wahhabis began harassing the pilgrim caravans	Ency. Brit., 1910, "Arabia"
1807	16-18,000	2/3 of houses empty	Badia, II, p. 103
c.1850	45,000		Brockhaus, 1864

Medina

850		Inner wall built	Rutter, II, p. 209
c. 965		Ceased to be provincial capital	Gaury, p. 59
1157		Outer wall built, increasing built-up area by 1/3	Rutter, II, p. 209
1503		Small	Varthema in Hogarth, p. 67
1600	40,000		
1658		With suburbs, big as Marseille – but density low because of much open space	Thévenot, part 1, p. 156 Rutter, II, map p. 209
1700	45,000		
1853	16-18,000	1,300 houses, 5 mosques (surely main mosques, indicating previous pop. of c. 45,000)	Burton in Brockhaus, 1864, and in Ency. Brit., 1853
c.1900	48,000	Likely big as ever during railroad boom	Meyer, 1902; Rutter, I, p. 121

Mosul

927-1261		Seat of a kingdom, except 1095-1127	Ency. of Islam, 1897
c.1170		7,000 Jews	Benjamin of Tudela, p. 83
1184		3 main mosques, including one in a suburb	Ibn Jubayr, p. 244
1200	50,000	Based on mosques (times 9,000), plus Christians and Jews	
by 1300		4 main mosques	" " "
1300	55,000	See 1200	
1657		Nearly all ruined; garrison of 3,000	Tavernier, I, p. 71
1758		10-12,000 Christians	Ives, p. 322
1800	34,000		
1810	34,000	Nearly 35,000	Kinneir, p. 258
1850	45,000		
1873	50,000		Cernik, p. 4

Muscat

1347		Small	Ibn Battuta, p. 303
1650-		Capital of Oman	Ency. of Islam, 1897, "Maskat"
c.1800	12,000		Hassel, 1819, XIII, p. 474
c.1850	60,000		Ungewitter, II, p. 297

Samarra

836-92		Capital of the Caliphate	Muir, pp. 513, 544
" "		Garrison of 70,000	Ploetz, I, p. 399
" "	135,000	35 by 5 km, with considerable gaps (c. 2700 ha.; times 50)	J. M. Rogers in Hourani, pp. 123-24

Sanaa

c. 530-		Capital of Yemen	Ency. of Islam, 1897
1187		Mostly destroyed by hill Arabs	" " " "

1503	20,000	4,000 hearths	Varthema, p. 80
c.1590	12,500	2,500 families	P. Páez, p. 402
1850	40,000		
1856	40,000		Stern in Badger, p. 79n

Gundishapur

-900		Great and flourishing city; predecessor of Shushtar	Lockhart, 1960, pp. 147-48, 154
900s		Had fallen into decay	" " " " "

Hamadan

644-c.1150		Provincial capital	" " p. 97
968		1 square parasang (13.6 miles around; probably left over from antiquity)	Ibn Hawqal, 1822, pt. 3, p. 6
c.1160		30,000 Jews (probably exaggerated)	Benjamin of Tudela, p. 101
c.1200		Seljuk capital for 50 years	Iranian Army, p. 12
c.1335		2 leagues (6 miles) in diameter	Mustawfi in Lockhart, 1960, p. 98
1386		Destroyed, but quckly recovered	Lockhart, 1960, p. 98
1630		Sacked by Turks for 6 days, killing all the people	Sykes, p. 83
1736		More a heap of stones than a town	Emmanuel in Lockhart, 1960, p. 99
c.1800	40,000		Ker Porter in Lockhart, 1960, p. 99
1810	40,000		Kinneir, p. 127
1825	25,000		Alexander, p. 171
1860		70,000 (probably exaggerated)	Brugsch in Brockhaus, 1864
c.1890		15,000 (probably too low)	Curzon in Lockhart, 1960, p. 99

Hormuz (Ormuz)

c.1200		Displaced Siraf and Kish (Qais) as main lower Persian Gulf port	Ency. Brit., 1910
c.1300		New site, 6 miles around, triangular (c. 50 ha.)	" " "
1400	50,000	Ha. times 100. Cf. also Siraf	
1442		Unequaled as an entrepot	Abd-er-Razzak, p. 5
1622		Fell to Persia and declined	Ency. Brit., 1910
1665		Abandoned, except fort	Thévenot, II, p. 136

Isfahan

642-		Provincial capital	Lockhart, 1960, pp. 19-20
c. 903	30,000	Wall 1/2 parasang in diameter (3 miles around) plus the Jewish city 2 miles away	Ency. of Islam, 1897
935-76		Prospered under Rukn-ed-Dawla	" " " " p. 220
950		Wall built 21,000 paces (c. 12 miles) around (thus, c. 2,300 ha. in area)	Barbier, p. 41n
968		4th in Moslem East, just behind Rayy	Ibn Hawqal, 1800, p. 157
1000	92,000	Based on area times 40; cf. Nishapur c. 1000	
1033		40,000 died of famine	Ferishta, I, p. 61
1051-92		Seljuk capital	Lockhart, 1960, pp. 20-21
1052	130,000	Largest in Persia; 3.5 parasangs (c. 12 miles) around (cf. Merv)	Nasir-i-Khusraw in Lockhart, 1960, p. 20
c.1170		15,000 Jews	Benjamin of Tudela, p. 101
1200	70,000	No longer capital	
1300	70,000		
1387	70,000	All slain by Tamerlane	Vambéry, p. 184
1447		Population massacred	Ency. of Islam, 1897, "Djahan-Shah"
1500	40,000		
1598-1736		Capital	Lockhart, 1960, pp. 23, 37
1598	40,000		Lockhart in Toynbee, pp. 210, 219

1599	80,000		Lockhart in Toynbee, p. 220
1600	125,000		
1628	400-500,000		" " " p. 225
"		Toward 70,000 houses; 9 miles around	Herbert, p. 161
1673	600,000	24 miles around	Chardin in Ency. Brit., 1910; cf. Lockhart, 1960, p. 28
"		38,249 houses (29,469 within walls)	Chardin in Nweeya, p. 50
"		15,000 prostitutes	" " " p. 162
1700	600,000		
1720-1727		Devastated by Afghans; 9/10 population died	Lockhart, 1960, pp. 28-29
1750	60,000		
c.1797	50,000		Olivier in Hassel, 1819, XIII, p. 580
1800	50,000		
1811	60,000	Based on comparison with number of sheep slaughtered c. 1670	Morier, pp. 141-42
1850	60,000		Hytier in Bémont, p. 194
1869	76,000		Bémont
1882	73,654		Ency. Brit., 1910

Kashan

968		Small	Ibn Hawqal, 1822, pt. 3, p. 8
c.1050		Period of prosperity	Lockhart, 1960, p. 122
1628	20,000	4,000 families	Herbert, p. 223
1673	39,000	6,500 houses, 40 mosques	Chardin, p. 214
1700	40,000		
-1722		Prospered	Lockhart, 1960, p. 125
1775		Earthquake	Ency. of Islam, 1960
1800	15,000		" " " "
c.1850	30,000		Ungewitter, II, p. 303

Kerman

709		2nd to Sirjan in its province	Lockhart, 1960, p. 114
928		Became capital of province	" " "
1049-1187		Seat of a local dynasty	" " "
1222-1307		Capital of another state	Ency. Brit., 1910, "Seljuks"
c.1350		2 main mosques built	Ency. of Islam, 1897, "Kirman"
1600	40,000		
c.1640	45,000	10,000 Parsis; cf. 1794	Tavernier in Ency. of Islam, 1897
1700	60,000	After century of prosperity	Lockhart, 1960, pp. 116-17
1736-43		Famine	" " p. 117
c.1747		Parsi quarter destroyed	" " "
1750	50,000		
1794		12,000 Parsis	Khanikov in Ency. of Islam, 1897
"	55,000	35,000 massacred, 20,000 enslaved	Ency. Brit., 1910, XXI, p. 237
1820	20,000		Kinneir, p. 198
c.1850	30,000		Brockhaus, 1864
1865	30-40,000	1 by 3 miles; 32 baths, 28 caravanserais	English, p. 28
1878	41,170		Ency. of Islam, 1897

Kermanshah

pre 900		One of 4 great cities in province of Jibal, along with Hamadan, Isfahan, and Rayy	Lockhart, 1960, p. 103
c. 980		Densely populated	" " "
1220-		Declined	" " "
1340		A village	" " "
1500s		Regained its former size and prosperity	" " "
1798	8,000		Beauchamp in Bémont, p. 199

1813	<u>36,000</u>	60,000 in 12,000 houses, but only 4 mosques (presumably main mosques, times 9,000), 14 baths	Kinneir, p. 132
c.1850	30,000		Brockhaus, 1864

Maragheh

968		Barely smaller than Ardebil	Ibn Hawqal, 1800, p. 157
1256-1295		Capital of Persia	Lockhart, 1960, pp. 60-61
1810	15,000		Kinneir, p. 156
1869	15,000		Bémont, p. 69

Meshhed (Mashhad)

1404		Large town	Clavijo in Lockhart, 1960, p. 35
c.1510-		Capital of Khorasan	G. Forster, II, p. 122
1589-98		Massacre, then alien rule	Bémont, p. 151
1696		Large and populous	Lee in Lockhart, 1960, p. 37
1736-47		Capital of Persia	Lockhart, 1960, p. 37
1747	200-300,000	60,000 houses	Malcolm in Lockhart, 1938, p. 197
1750	<u>200,000</u>		
1796	18,000	3,000 houses	Bémont, p. 167
1800	<u>20,000</u>		
1807	24,000	4,000 houses	Trulhier in Bémont, p. 167
1810	50,000	12 quarters, 5 in ruins	Kinneir, pp. 175-76
1822	46,000	7,700 houses	Fraser in Bémont, p. 167
1832	40,000		Connolly in Bémont, p. 167
1850	<u>45,000</u>		
1860	<u>50,000</u>		Khanikov in Bémont, p. 167

Nishapur

300s-1153	<u>60,000</u>	Wall 15,000 paces (9 miles, enclosing c. 1,300 ha.)	Bosworth, p. 159
828-73		Tahirid capital	Ency. of Islam, 1897, "Tahirids"
968		It and Bagdad led in the Moslem east; 1 square parasang (i.e., c. 3,000 ha. in area)	Ibn Hawqal, 1800, p. 172
1000	<u>125,000</u>	See Bagdad; also quarters times 3,000	
c.1025		44 quarters; larger than Bagdad or Fostat, equal to Herat, Ghor, or Manichah	Abu Ali in Nasir-i-Khusraw, p. 279
1034	<u>120,000</u>	20,000 armed townsmen	Bosworth, p. 169
1052		1 square parasang	Nasir-i-Khusraw, p. 278
c.1150		Half Merv's size	Edrisi, p. 451
1153		Ravaged by Ghuzz	Ency. Brit., 1910
" -1208		Only the suburb occupied, smaller than the old site	Bosworth, p. 159
1200	<u>80,000</u>		
1208		Earthquake	Ency. Brit. 1910
"		New wall 6,900 paces around	Bosworth, p. 159
1220	<u>70,000</u>	Surpassed by Rayy in area but not in wealth	Yaqut, pp. 275-6
1221		Destroyed by Mongols	Ency. Brit., 1910
1269		Destroyed by Mongols	" " "
1280		Earthquake	" " "
1341		2nd in Khorasan	Ibn Battula, p. 175
1405		Wholly destroyed by earthquake	Lockhart, 1939, p. 43
1822	5,000		Fraser in Lockhart, 1960, p. 85
1869	8,000		Bémont, p. 69

Qazvin (Kazvin)

1548-98		Persian capital	Lockhart in Toynbee, p. 219
1600	150,000	See 1628, Tabriz, and 1810	
1628		2nd to Isfahan; 7 miles around (c. 800 ha. in area), with 20,000 families. Herbert's population estimate of 200,000 is too high for his family-count.	Herbert, pp. 210-11
1672		100,000 (looks high) in 12,000 houses; 6 miles around (c. 600 ha. in area)	Chardin, p. 196
1700	70,000	Based on houses and lower density for declining population	
1723		Beat off the Afghans	Ency. of Islam, 1897
1750	65,000		
1800	60,000		
1809	60,000		Gardanne in Hassel, 1819, XIII, p. 585
c.1810		Greater part in ruins, but still one of Persia's leading cities	Kinneir, p. 121
1811		2,000 yards larger than Tehran; 25,000 adult males (official estimate)	Morier, p. 203
1868	25,000		Thomson in Vivien

Qum (Kumm)

c. 720		New wall, but only a small town	Lockhart, 1960, p. 127
c. 867		Most inhabitants massacred	Ency. of Islam, 1897
1221		Thousands slaughtered by Mongols	Lockhart, 1960, p. 129
c.1335		Wall 10,000 paces (c. 6 miles) around, but much of town in ruins	Mustawfi; in Lockhart, 1960, p. 29
1474		20,000 houses (probably exaggerated)	Barbaro in Lockhart, 1960, p. 129
"		Small	Contarini in Lockhart, 1960, p. 129
1628		2,000 houses (perhaps too low)	Herbert in Lockhart, 1960, p. 130
1672	45,000	15,000 houses, half ruined (7,500 times 6)	Chardin, p. 202
1700	45,000		
1716		Reckoned among the chief towns of Persia	Bell in Lockhart, 1960, p. 130
1810		7 quarters; still ruined from Afghan sack of 1722	Kinneir, p. 116
1860	10,000		Brugsch in Vivien, "Koum"

Rayy

775-80		Peak	Barbier, p. 273n
968		3rd after Nishapur and Bagdad in the Moslem East	Ibn Hawqal, 1800, p. 157
1000	100,000	See Isfahan, 968-1000	
1200	80,000		
1220		Larger than Isfahan	Istakhri in Yaqut, p. 275
"		Several suburbs (more than 3), each with more than 10,000 population	Yaqut, p. 276
"		2/3 destroyed in religious riot	" p. 274
1221		Destroyed by Mongols	" "

Shiraz

693	25,000	Founded; 100 paces larger than Isfahan (cf. Isfahan; low density for new wall)	Ibn el-Balkhi, p. 316

967-83		Peak	Arberry, p. 39
c. 985		12,000-ell wall built (i.e., c. 9 miles around or c. 1,300 ha. in area)	" p. 43
1000	52,000	Based on area times 40; cf. Nishapur, c. 1000	
c.1100		Mostly in ruins	Ibn el-Balkhi, p. 316
c.1170		10,000 Jews	Benjamin of Tudela, p. 101
1300	50,000		
1340	51,000	17 quarters (times 3,000; cf. Acre, Málaga)	Arberry, p. 50
"		2nd to Damascus in Moslem east	Ibn Battuta, p. 92
1353-93		Mozaffarid capital	Ency. of Islam, 1897, "Muzaffarids"
1400	100,000		
c.1445		15 miles around (may be exaggerated)	Ulugh Beg in Herbert, p. 128
c.1470		20 miles around (probably exaggerated)	Barbarus in Herbert, pp. 128, 161
late 1400s	80,000		John of Perugia (misnamed Persia; d. 1510) in Herbert, p. 128
1500	60,000		
1515		Under 10,000 houses, though ruins extend 2 miles	Mandelslo in Nweeya, p. 50
1628		15 round mosques; 7 miles around	Herbert, p. 128
1694	20,000		Gemelli, p. 162
1744		14,000 died of plague	Lockhart, 1960, p. 47
1747-79		Capital of Persia	" " pp. 47-48
1809		12,000 houses (perhaps a peak figure c. 1775)	Morier, p. 110
1811	19,000	7,780 houses, scarcely 1/2 occupied	" p. 111
1825	30,000		Alexander, p. 125
1853	10,000	After earthquake killed 12,000	Gazetteer of World

Shushtar (Shuster)

c.870-c.1125		First mosque built	Ency. of Islam, 1897
c.1330		Large, beautiful, and prosperous	Ibn Battuta in Lockhart, 1960, p. 148
1500s		Seat of a local dynasty	Lockhart, 1960, p. 148
1632-67		Peak	
1722-29		Suffered greatly at the hands of Afghan, Turkish, and Russian invaders	" " p. 149
late 1700s		Provincial capital	" " "
c.1800	45,000		" " "
early 1800s		Capital of three provinces	" " "
1831-32		20,000 died in epidemics	" " "
1836	15,000		Ency. of Islam, 1897
1890	8,000		" " " "

Siraf

968		Size of Shiraz	Ibn Hawqal, 1822, pt. 1, p. 53
1000	50,000		
c.1200		Displaced by Hormuz	Ency. Brit., 1910, "Hormuz"

Sultaniya

1285		Founded	Lockhart, 1960, p. 12n
1313-36		Capital of Persia	" " p. 12
1336		Rapid decline	" " pp. 12-13

1405		Smaller than Tabriz, but greater trade	Clavijo, pp. 158-59
"		30,000 paces (c. 18 miles) around (c. 5,200 ha. in area, probably c. 1330)	Clavijo in Ency. of Islam, 1897

Tabriz

642		Small town then and long after	Lockhart, 1960, p. 10
c. 950		Small but walled	" " "
1041		40-50,000 died in an earthquake (looks too high for city alone)	" " p. 11
1046		Wall 5,600 paces (3.4 miles, or c. 175 ha. in area)	Nasir-i-Khusraw, p. 17
"		Capital of Azerbaijan province	Lockhart, 1960, p. 11
1100s		Smaller than Ardebil or Maragheh	" " "
1213		1st in Azerbaijan	Yaqut in Lockhart, 1960, p. 11
1295-1313		Capital of Persia	Lockhart, 1960, p. 11
c.1295		New wall 25,000 paces (c. 15 miles) around (thus, c. 3,600 ha. in area)	Ency. of Islam, 1897
1300	150,000	Based on area (times 40, cf. Nishapur, c. 1,000) and prosperity	
1300s		200,000 houses (clearly an exaggeration; perhaps intended for people)	Lamb, p. 294
c.1330		1st in world for trade	Odoric in Lamb, p. 294
1385-1405		Throve under Tamerlane	Lamb, p. 164
1400	200,000		
"		Larger than Samarkand, Damascus, or Bagdad	" p. 164n
1436-1548		Capital of West Persian kingdom, then of unified Persia	Ency. of Islam, 1897; Lockhart, 1960, pp. 13-14
1500	250,000		
1501	200-300,000		Lockhart, 1960, p. 13
1585-(1603)		Turkish garrison of 45,000	Ency. of Islam, 1897
1600	125,000	No longer capital and under alien rule	
1673	150,000	Chardin actually cites 550,000	Chardin, p. 184; Chardin in Lockhart, 1960, p. 14
"			
1694		15,000 houses, 250 mosques	Chardin, p. 153
		250,000 or less (probably out-of-date)	Gemelli, p. 112
1700	150,000		
1716		Large, but not near what it had been	Bell in Pinkerton, VII, p. 294
1721		Earthquake killed 80,000	Lockhart, 1960, p. 15
1737-38		Epidemic killed 47,000	" " "
1780		Earthquake	" " "
1800	30,000		
1806		50,000 at most	Jaubert in Lockhart, 1960, p. 15
1810	30,000		Kinneir, p. 151
1811		3.5 miles around (c. 200 ha. in area)	Morier, p. 225
1842	100-120,000		Berezin in Ency. of Islam, 1897
1850	125,000		
1871	165,000		Enci. Italiana

Tehran (Teheran)

1220		Survivors of Rayy's destruction settled here	Lockhart, 1960, p. 4
1224		A village	Ency. Brit., 1910
c.1340		Town of medium size	Mustawfi in Lockhart, 1960, p. 4
1553-54		Wall built 3 miles long (thus, c. 150 ha. in area)	Lockhart, 1960, p. 4
1628	25-30,000	Based on 3,000 houses	Herbert in Lockhart, 1960, pp. 4-5

1794-(now)		Capital	Ency. Brit., 1970
1796	15,000		Olivier in Ahrens, p. 37
1800	30,000		
1808	40-50,000		Gardanne in Ahrens, p. 37
1817	60-70,000		Ker Porter in Ahrens, p. 37
1850	80,000		
1860	80-120,000		Brugsch in Ahrens, p. 37
c.1860	85,000		Statesman's Yearbook, 1865, p. 693

Yezd (Yazd)

1119		Chief mosque built	Ency. Brit., 1910
c.1320		One of the 3 principal cities of the Persian empire (improbable)	Odoric in Lockhart, 1960, p. 108
1395	40,000	5-mile wall built (thus, c. 400 ha. in area)	Lockhart, 1939, pp. 61-62
1396		30,000 died of famine in siege; most houses had survivors	Aubin, p. 113
1813		24,000 houses (looks high)	Kinneir, p. 113
1846		7-8,000 died in epidemic	Lockhart, 1960, p. 110
1850	40,000		
1860s	40,000		Curzon in Lapidus, 1969, p. 110n

Note on cities of Persia and Turkestan at 1200

Samarkand lost 50 000 killed in 1220, only 30 000 being spared. Hence, its population had been 80 000. Also in Khorasan and vying for largest there were Merv and Nishapur. These then would have over 70 000. Indeed Nishapur had 125 000 back at 1000 according to two lines of evidence, but it had long since ceased to be provincial capital and would be declining as Merv rose. Hence under 125 000 and probably under 100 000—as Merv rose very fast as a Seljuk capital 1097-1153.

Nishapur was close to Rayy. In 1220 it had less wealth and less population than Rayy, but this was after its sack by the Ghuzz in 1153 and the earthquake of 1208. I estimate for Nishapur 100 000 in 1150, 80 000 in 1200, and 70 000 in 1220.

Rayy, smaller than Nishapur in 968, hence c. 100 000 then, was larger than Isfahan in 1220. Rayy was not a capital after c. 950 and might lose some population to growing Merv, 80 000 in 1200 would be plausible.

Isfahan had 92 000 in 1000 on the basis of its rank, its area, and the number (40 000) who died there in a famine in 1033. Its rank was fourth in the Moslem East, just behind Rayy, in 968. From 1051 to 1092 it was the capital of the Seljuk Empire. Thereafter it was not, as the court moved to Bagdad and then Merv. So it would drop back to 92 000 or less, perhaps by 1200 clear down to the 70 000 it had in 1387. In 1220 Rayy, just ahead of it, had as we have seen roughly 80 000.

All this material hangs together, with an upper level set around 100 000 by the former size of Nishapur, and a lower level of 70 000 set by the smallest of these cities, Isfahan.

Merv, capital of east Persia 1097-1118 and of the whole Seljuk Empire 1118-1153, was twice the size of Nishapur in 1150, i.e., 200 000, a very plausible figure for the capital of so strong an empire and comparable to other brief but strong Persian capitals: Tabriz 250 000, Meshhed 250 000. Its ruins covered over 15 sq. miles, or 4 000 ha., which is a sufficiently large (Isfahan with 36 sq. miles in 1673 had 600 000).

Aksu

c.1350		Capital of Sinkiang	Ency. Brit., 1910, "Turkestan"
1850	23,000	Including garrison of 3,000	Courcy, p. 129

Balasaghun (Balasaqun)

742-1141		Usual Uighur or Ilekkhanid capital (cf. Kashgar)	Ency. of Islam, 1960, "Ilek-Khans"
1200	47,000		
1210	47,000	Inhabitants killed as the city fell	Ency. of Islam, 1897

Bokhara (Bukhara)

874-999		Samanid capital, but never equaled Samarkand, the old capital, in size	" " " "
c. 975	100,000	Guess by the leading expert	Frye, p. 94
1000	100,000		
1265		Most beautiful in Persia	Marco Polo in Barthold, p. 9
1273		Destroyed by Mongols	Ency. of Islam, 1897
1320		30,000 men killed	Vámbéry, p. 130
1341		Mostly in ruin	Ibn Battuta, p. 172
1512-98		Uzbeg royal residence, more important than the official capital Samarkand	Ency. of Islam, 1897
1750s	60,000	Army 10,000 (cf. 1820)	Plath, p. 615
1800	70,000		
1820	70,000		Meyendorff in Ency. Brit., 1875
1850	70,000		
1897	68,000	Based on 11,420 houses	Sukhareva, p. 70

Gurganj

712-995		Capital of S. Khwarizm	Ency. of Islam, 1960
995-1210		Capital of Khwarizm	" " " ; Sykes, II, p. 79
1221		Destroyed by Mongols	Ency. of Islam, 1960

Kashgar

742-1141		Chief town of Sinkiang, but only occasionally capital, as 992-1032	Ency. of Islam, 1897, 1960 "Ilek-Khans" and 1897 "Bughra-Khan"
c.1350-c.1375		Capital of Sinkiang	Ency. Brit., 1910, "Turkestan"
1800	60,000		
1826	60,000	10,000 houses before rebellion of 1826-1827	Gazetteer of World
1800s	20-80,000	Estimates (even now there are no precise data)	Blackie
1847		20,000 families fled the region	Ency. Brit., 1910, XXVII, p. 425

Kokand (Khokand)

c.1700-1868		Capital of a khanate	Ency. of Islam, 1897
1807		Conquered Tashkent etc.	Ency. Brit., 1910, "Khokand"
c.1815	60,000		Hassel, 1817
1820 (?)		6,000 houses; equal to Bokhara	Meyendorff in Gazetteer of World
1850	60,000		
1881		35,000 (doubtful estimate)	Mikkelson in Vivien
1885	54,043		Brockhaus, 1892

Kulja (Ili)

1775-		Provincial capital	Timkovsky, pp. 436, 439
1821		Garrison of 3,800 and 2,000 government employees, plus their families, sent in new batches each year	" p. 436

1850	60,000		
1868	70,000	All massacred by rebels	Ency. Brit., 1910

Merv

700s		Arab base for taking the rest of Khorasan	" " "
- 821		Capital of Khorasan province	Frye, p. 30
985		1/3 in total ruin	Ency. of Islam, 1897
1097-1157		Sanjar's Seljuk capital	Ency. Brit., 1910, "Seljuks"
c.1150	200,000	Twice Nishapur's size; over 15 sq. miles	Edrisi, p. 451; Ency. Brit., 1910
1155		Wrecked by Ghuzz	Ency. Brit., 1910, "Seljuks"
1200	70,000		
1220		1st in Khorasan, as even a Nishapur man admitted (after Nishapur's earthquake 1208)	Yaqut, p. 526
1221		Most killed by Mongols	Ency. Brit., 1910
1341		Mostly in ruin	Ibn Battuta, p. 175
1794		Wholly destroyed by Bokhara	Ency. Brit., 1910

Otrar

900		In existence	Ency. of Islam, 1897
-c.1200		Capital of the Karakhitais	Ency. Brit., 1910, "Persia"
1218		Fell to Mongols	Ency. of Islam, 1897

Özkend

742-999		Karakhanid Western capital	Ency. of Islam, 1897, "Ilek-Khans"

Samarkand

- 712		Seat of a Turkish kingdom	Ency. of Islam, 1897
900s		Still rivaled Bokhara	" " " "
c. 980	80,000	Wall 2 parasangs (c. 7 miles around or c. 800 ha. in area)	Ibn Hawqal, 1800, p. 253
1000	80,000		
c.1170		50,000 Jews	Benjamin of Tudela, p. 101
1200	60,000		
1210-20		Capital of Khwarizm	Sykes, II, pp. 54, 79
1220		1st in Khorasan (however, cf. Merv)	Vámbéry, p. 131
"	80,000	50,000 killed by Mongols; 30,000 removed	Tolstova, I, p. 288
c.1340		One of the largest and most perfectly beautiful cities; mostly in ruins	Ibn Battuta, p. 174
c.1369-1405		Tamerlane's capital	Ency. of Islam, 1897
1400	100,000		
1405	150,000	After the mass enforced migration from Damascus (maybe half arrived)	Clavijo, p. 288
1700		Deserted, as reported by Chinese	Vivien
1834	8,000		Burnes in Vivien
c.1870	30,000		Fejenko in Vambery, xxxi

Tashkent

c.1800	25,000	5,000 houses (times 5, cf. 1868)	Playfair, V, p. 346
1850	65,000		
1868	76,053	15,500 houses	Azadaev, p. 24

Yarkand

c.1300		Capital of Sinkiang province	Ency. of Islam, 1897, "Kashghar"
1807		Became capital of Sinkiang again	Courcy, p. 130
1821	64,000	12,000 houses (times 5; cf. Tashkent), plus 4,500 in garrison	Timkovsky, p. 394
1850	70,000		

Balkh

- 671		Capital of Tokharistan	Ency. of Islam, 1897
968	30,000	1/2 by 1/2 parasang (c. 7 miles) around (c. 790 ha., times 40; cf. Nishapur)	Ibn Hawqal, 1822
c.1150	30,000	3 times the size of Bamian which had a main mosque, and 4 times Talecan which did not (thus, at 9,000 per main mosque, population would be 27-36,000)	Edrisi, pp. 475, 477
1220		All killed by Chingiz	Ency. Brit., 1910
1341		In ruins	Ibn Battuta, p. 175
c.1390		All killed by Tamerlane	Ency. Brit., 1910

Bust (Bost)

c.925-976		A free local capital	Bosworth, p. 37
976-1149		A secondary Ghaznavid capital	Ency. of Islam, 1960
1149	40,000	7 km by up to 2 km (c. 1,000 ha.), mostly unwalled (times 40; cf. Nishapur)	" " " "
"		Pillaged and burned	" " " "
c.1395		Pillaged and deserted	" " " "

Ghazni

961-1149		Ghaznavid capital	" " " 1897
c.1149		80,000 Jews (looks much too high)	Benjamin of Tudela, p. 101
1149		Entirely destroyed	Ency. of Islam, 1960, "Ghurids"
1173-1206		South Ghorid capital, ruling north India	" " " " "Ghazni"
1221		Sacked by Chingiz and declined	" " " " "
1809	9,000	1,500 houses	W. Hamilton

Ghor (Firuzkoh)

1148-1215		Ghorid main capital	Sykes, II, p. 48
1222		Destroyed by Mongols	Maricq, p. 55

Herat

c. 900		7,300 paces (c. 4.5 miles) around (thus, c. 325 ha. in area)	Razi in Barbier, p. 592n
1217		Largest city Yaqut had seen (he had perhaps not yet seen Nishapur nor Rayy; his huge population figure, 444,000, must refer to a district)	Yaqut, p. 592 & n
1222		All but 40 killed by Mongols	Ency. Brit, 1875
1245-1389		Seat of a kingdom	Imp. Gaz. India: Afghanistan, p. 79
c.1340		Wall 9,000 paces (c. 5.4 mi., or c. 475 ha. in area)	Mustawfi in Ibn Battuta, p. 175
1341		1st in Khorasan	Ibn Battuta, p. 175
1398		Destroyed by Tamerlane	Ency. Brit., 1910
1500	40,000		
1503	40,000	6-7,000 hearths	Varthema, p. 101
c.1510		Displaced by Meshhed as capital of Khorasan	G. Foster, II, p. 122
c.1740		Settled with Afghans	Ency. Brit., 1910
1800	45,000		
1809		100,000 (probably too high)	Christie in Vivien
1830	45,000		Conolly in Gazetteer of World
1833	60,000		Mohan Lal in Gazetteer of World
1837	70,000	Before siege; 6,000 after	Ency. Brit., 1875
1845	20-22,000		Ferrier in Badger, p. 101n

Kabul

-1021		Capital of a local kingdom	V. Smith, p. 328
1405-1526		Capital of a Timurid branch line	Ency. of Islam, 1897
1520s		Baber sometimes lived here	" " " "
-c.1730	20,000	Probable maximum	Balfour
1750	20,000		
1774-		Capital	Ency. Brit., 1853, "Cabul"
1782		1.5 miles around, not at all impressive (c. 50 ha. at most)	G. Forster, II, p. 69
1795-1842		Country divided and often at war	Ency. Brit., 1910
1800	80,000		
1809		100,000 (perhaps slightly high)	Elphinstone in Balbi
1836	60,000		Burnes in Gazetteer of World
1850	60,000		
1879	50,000		Roberts, II, p. 229

Kandahar (Qandahar)

1150		Began to be important	Ency. of Islam, 1897
1707-22		Ghilzai Afghan capital	" " " "Ghalzai"
1747-74		Capital of Afghanistan	Ency. of Islam, 1897; Ency. Brit., 1853, "Cabul"
1782		Larger than Herat	G. Forster, II, p. 120
1809		100,000 (probably exaggerated, but possible when capital)	Elphinstone in Imp. Gaz. India: Afghanistan, p. 72
c.1838		80,000 (probably out-of-date)	Hough in Imp. Gaz. India: Afghanistan, 1881, p. 72
1845	30,000		Ferrier in Imp. Gaz. India: Afghanistan, 1881, p. 72
c.1870		3.7 miles around; 182 mosques (left over from peak)	Ency. Brit., 1875

Agra

1500		A village	Imp. Gaz. India: United Provs., I, p. 393
1506-1618		Usual capital of N. India (cf. Lahore, Delhi, Gwalior)	Naqui, p. 17; Havell, pp. 13, 25; Hearn, pp. 215-16
1558		Founded on present site	Havell, p. 25
by 1575		Surpassed Delhi and Lahore	Naqui, p. 17
c.1585		Much larger than London	Fitch in Moreland, 1920, p. 13
c.1600	500,000		Jerónimo Xavier in Naqui, p. 81
1627-38		Again capital	
" "	660,000	660,000 plus foreigners (perhaps correct, but cf. next item)	Manrique in Naqui, p. 18
1638		Half its people moved to Delhi (c. 200,000 cf. Delhi, 1638)	Hodges, p. 118
c.1660		Larger than Delhi	Bernier in Moreland, p. 13
1712		In a deserted state	Naqui, p. 19
1800	60,000		
1813	60,000		Malcolm, II, p. 476
1846	76,570	66,003 plus 10,567 troops	Thornton
1850	108,000		
1852	125,262		Ungewitter, II, p. 335

Ahmedabad (Asawal till 1411)

1000s		3rd in Gujarat behind Anhilvada and Cambay	Mehta, p. 2
1297		Began to decline	" "
c.1400		In ruins	" "
1411		Present city founded as capital of Gujarat	" pp. 2, 5
1487	60,000	6-mile wall built (thus, c. 600 ha. in area, times 100)	Commissariat, I, pp. 96-97
1500	80,000	Period of prosperity; at least 3 suburbs	Mehta, pp. 4-5
1600	225,000		
1616	240,000	Very nearly the size of London (i.e., more or less)	Withington, p. 207
1638	266,000	7 leagues around, including suburbs (21 miles, thus enclosing c. 7,000 ha.; times 38; cf. 1800)	Mandelslo, p. 23
1699		In magnitude and wealth little inferior to the best towns in Europe	A. Hamilton, I, p. 86
c.1700		Peak	Mehta, p. 7
peak	400,000	360 wards (times 110; cf. 1750, 1866)	Commissariat, I, pp. 103-4
"		900,000 (surely too high)	Hunter
"	380,000	27 miles around (enclosing c. 10,000 ha.; times 38; cf. 1800)	Forbes in Conder, 1830s, IV, p. 155
1700	380,000		
1750	120,000	110 wards, including 18 deserted (92, times 1,000; cf. 1866)	Commissariat, I, pp. 103-4
1780	100,000		Forbes in Thornton
c.1800		12 miles around (enclosing c. 2,330 ha.)	Playfair, V, p. 453
1800	89,000		
1817	80,000		Mehta, pp. 7-8
1824	87,000		Gillion, p. 53
1846	94,390		" "
1850	96,000		
1851	97,048		Imp. Gaz. India: Bombay Pres. I, p. 255
1866		72 wards (likely from nadir in 1817)	Commissariat, I, p. 104
1872	116,873		Imp. Gaz. India: Bombay Pres. I, p. 255

Ahmednagar

1494		Founded	Ency. Brit., 1910
1494-1636		Capital of the Nizamshahis, except 1600-07 and c. 1621-1627	J. Campbell, XII, pp. 670, 707, 710
1496		Said to rival Cairo and Bagdad in splendor	Ferishta in J. Campbell, XVII, p. 707
1499		Wall slightly over 1 mile around (surely omitted sizeable suburbs)	J. Campbell, XVII, pp. 651, 707
1600	75,000	C. 15,000 garrison put to the sword (probably all who were able to bear arms)	Mahajan, 1965, pt. 2, p. 86
1817	17,000		Hunter
1850	26,012		"

Ajmer

c.1160-1193		Its king held Delhi	Imp. Gaz. India: Rajputana, p. 452
1193		Its people were massacred	" " " "
1500		Practically empty	Chaudhury, p. 50
1571		Wall built, 4,054 yards around (thus, c. 90 ha.)	Sarda, p. 35
1570-80		Akbar visited it almost yearly	Termizi, p. 12
1605-58		A Mogul royal residence	Imp. Gaz. India: Rajputana, p. 453
1608-11		Not large	Finch, p. 171
1654		Its lord sent 30,000 troops against Mewar (not all from the city)	Termizi, p. 23
1837	23,000		Thornton
1872	35,111		Imp. Gaz. India: Rajputana, p. 487

Allahabad (formerly Prayag)

1300-1575		Perhaps deserted	Puri, p. 88
1576		Present city founded	" "
c.1600		Residence of crown prince Jehangir	Imp. Gaz. India: United Provs., II, p. 81
1671		17,000 died in a flood	Marshall, p. 129n
1801	16,000	In ruins	Playfair, V, p. 423
1834	64,785		Thornton
1850	70,000		
1853	72,093		Ungewitter, II, p. 336

Amber

900s-1728		Capital of Jaipur	Imp. Gaz. India: Rajputana, p. 255
1614		Its lord ranked 1st in the Mogul army	" " " "
1901	4,956		"
			" " " "
			"

Amritsar

1581		Founded	Ency. Brit., 1878
1800	80,000		
1802		Became Sikh commercial capital	Imp. Gaz. India: Punjab, II, p. 53
1800s	80-90,000	Early in century	Thornton
1850	110,000		Datta, p. 114
1855	112,186		

Amroha

1847	72,677		A. Shakespear, p. 79n

Anhilvada

746-1298		Capital of Gujarat	Imp. Gaz. India: Bombay Pres., I, p. 192
996		Gujarat reached nearly its full limit	Commissariat, p. lvii
1000	100,000		
1094-1143		Peak of glory	" p. lxv
" "		84 markets; 12 coss or 15 miles around (thus, c. 3,600 ha. in area) at peak	Balfour
" "	135,000	Based on area (times 38; cf. its successor Ahmedabad)	
1143		In decline	Imp. Gaz. India: Bombay Pres., I, p. 192
1195		Sacked	Commissariat, p. lxxvi
1197	90,000	15,000 slain (presumably militia) and 20,000 captured (presumably women)	" "
1242-		Declining rapidly	Imp. Gaz. India: Bombay Pres., I, p. 192
1298		Sacked as its kingdom fell	Commissariat, p. 2
1298-1411		Local capital, under Delhi till 1407	" pp. lxxiv, 1

Arcot

1692-1801		Capital of Carnatic, free from c. 1715	Ency. Brit., 1910, "Carnatic"
1735		Small	Biervillas, p. 129
1850	53,000		
c.1853	53,474		Petermann, 1857, p. 349

Aurangabad

1610		Burned	Ency. of Islam, 1960, "Awranga-bad"
1653-1724		Capital of the Deccan	Imp. Gaz. India: Hyderabad, p. 208
1684		Aurangzeb briefly moved Delhi's population here, till c. 1690	" " " " "
"	200,000	At peak (cf. 1881)	Enci. Italiana
1687		Would decline fast as Mogul southern base shifted to Hyderabad	
1700	100,000		
1750	85,000		
1800	80,000		
1825	60,000	7 miles around (c. 800 ha. in area)	W. Hamilton
1850	45,000		
1881	30,219	1/5 inhabited	Imp. Gaz. India: Hyderabad, p. 208

Banda

1784		Fort built	Ency. Brit., 1910
c.1784-1802		Capital of Bundelkhand	" " "
" "		65 mosques, 174 temples	" " "

Bangalore

1537		Founded	Imp. Gaz. India: Mysore, p. 136
1687		12,000 weavers brought in	Josyer, p. 44
1759-99		2,000 by 750 yards (c. 3 miles around)	Venkatarayappa, p. 13
c.1760		Hyder Ali's palace built there	Imp. Gaz. India: Mysore, p. 176
1800	60,000		
1805	60,000		W. Hamilton
1809		Prospered as a British base	Venkatarayappa, p. 14

1850	<u>131,000</u>		
1852	134,628		Hunter

Bareilly

c.1575		Fort built	Ency. of Islam, 1960
1657-1774		Capital of Rohilkhand	" " " "
1800	65,000		
1822	65,796		W. Hamilton
1847	92,208		A. Shakespear, p. 90n
1850	<u>101,000</u>		
c.1853	111,332		Petermann, 1857, p. 349

Bari

1018-36		Capital of N. India (cf. Lahore for final date)	Biruni, p. 199

Baroda

1600s		1 sq. mile in area	Malkani, p. 3
1725		Outer wall built	Conder, 1830s, IV, p. 124
1764-(1948)		Capital of Baroda kingdom	Bombay Gaz.: Baroda, p. 531
1800	80,000		
1818	100,000		W. Hamilton
1838		140,000 (probably too high)	Thornton
1850	<u>106,000</u>		
1872	<u>106,000</u>	116,274 including c. 10,000 in villages later separated off	Bombay Gaz.: Baroda, p. 527

Bednur (Nagar)

1640-1763		Capital of Keladi	Imp. Gaz. India: Mysore, p. 252
" "		8 miles around	New International Ency.
c.1770		100,000 (looks high), then declined	Ungewitter, II, p. 364
1799	<u>10,000</u>	1,500 houses, plus huts	Ency. Brit., 1875
1871	<u>1,295</u>		Hunter

Belur

c.1101-1117		Hoysala capital	Cambridge History; V. Smith, p. 360
-1397		Main shrine of the Hoysalas and Vijayanagar	Heras, 1929, pp. 116-7

Benares (now Varanasi)

c. 630	<u>65,000</u>	3,000 Buddhist monks, 10,000 Hindu monks (times 5)	Hsüan Dsang, II, p. 44
1100s		Alternate N-Indian capital (with Kanauj)	Vaidya, III, p. 212
1192		1,000 temples destroyed (reflects peak c. 1150)	Tripathi, p. 330
1600	<u>50,000</u>		
1640s	<u>60,000</u>	More than 400 temples (times c. 120; cf. 1872), some mosques	Manrique in Naqui, p. 132
1750-c.1800		Capital of a small kingdom	Naqui, p. 127
1782		Largest Hindu-ruled city	Foster in Naqui, p. 111
1800	<u>179,000</u>		
1801	<u>179,000</u>	Estimated to have 29,935 houses (times 6), a few of them very large	Valentia, I, p. 461
c.1810	168,000	28,000 houses	W. Hamilton
1829	183,000	Estimated from taxes on salt, sugar, etc.	Thornton
1850	185,000		
1853	185,984		Brockhaus, 1864
1872	175,188	1,454 temples, 272 mosques	Lippincott Gaz.; Hunter

Bhagalpur (Boglipore)

1789-1822		Its district grew 24%	Martin, 1839, p. 288-89
1789-1872		Its district grew 283%	" " "
1800	28,000		
c.1810	30,000	5,000 houses	W. Hamilton
1850	55,000		
1872	69,678		Hunter

Bharatpur (Bhurtpore)

c.1733		Founded	Imp. Gaz. India: Rajputana, p. 336
1753		Its chief sacked Delhi	" " " " "
1800	75,000		
"		8 miles around	Lippincott Gaz., 1868, "Bhurtpore"
1850	69,000		
1881	66,163		Imp. Gaz. India: Rajputana, p. 336

Bhopal

1000s		Founded in time of raja Bhoja (1010-53)	Elliot in Ashfaq Ali, p. 8
1405-		Ruined and reduced to a village	" " " " "
c.1728-(1948)		Capital of Bhopal kingdom, except c. 1740-1754	Imp. Gaz. India: Central India pp. 242, 264
1850	55,000		
1881	55,402		" " " " " p. 265

Bidar

c.1250-		Important provincial capital	Imp. Gaz. India: Hyderabad, p. 290
1323		More important than Kalyan	Yazdani, p. 3
1422-92		Bahmanid capital; ruins 6 miles around (thus, c. 600 ha. in area)	Sherwani, p. 26; Vivien
1462-81	100,000	Peak (cf. Ujjain)	Ency. of Islam, 1960
1472		Largest in Moslem India	Nikitin in Oaten, p. 4
1492-1656		Capital of the Barids, a smaller kingdom	Imp. Gaz. India: Hyderabad, p. 291
1500	80,000		
1666		Garrison of 3,000	Thévenot, part 3, p. 7
1881	9,730		

Bihar

c.815-c.860		Capital of the strong Pala dynasty of Bengal	V. Smith, II, p. 344
1243-1540		Capital of Bihar district or province	" " pp. 344-5
1500	50,000		
c.1530-1539		Power base for Sher shah, who in 1539-45 ruled N. India	Martin, 1838, I, p. 32
peak	80,000	24 wards (cf. 1825) times 3,400 (cf. Talakad); also, it extended over 1 mile from old inner city (thus, radius c. 1.5 miles, enclosing c. 8,000 ha.; times 100)	
1600	50,000	Declining as new provincial capital Patna rose	
1700	40,000		
1742		Sacked and lost importance	Martin, 1838, I, p. 85
1800	30,000		Thornton
1825		24 wards, by then much interspersed with fields	Martin, 1838, I, pp. 84-5

1850	40,000		
1872	44,295		Brockhaus, 1881

Bijapur (Viziapur)

1489-1686		Adilshahi capital; buildings second only to Delhi in India	Ency. of Islam, 1960, "Bidjapur"
1565	60,000	6.2-mile wall built (thus, c. 600 ha. in area)	Cousens, pp. 9, 23
1600	200,000	Rapid growth after victory in 1565 over Vijayanagar	
1639	300,000	C. 5 leagues around (but cf. 1666; thus c. 3,000 ha. in area); garrison of 7,000	Mandelslo, pp. 72-3
peak		700 mosques and tombs	Cousens, p. 22
"		100,000 dwellings (probably exaggerated)	Chambers, 1870, "Bejapur"
1666		4-5 leagues (12-15 miles) around	Thévenot, pt. 3, p. 92
1688		150,000 died in epidemic	Ency. of Islam, 1960, "Bidjapur"
1852	11,000		Badger, p. 117n

Bombay

1661	10,000		Edwardes, I, p. 151
1698	10,000		Imp. Gaz. India: Bombay Pres., I, p. 224
1715	16,000		Edwardes, p. 152
1744	70,000		Niebuhr in Edwardes, p. 144
1750	77,000		
1759	88,000	1,195 European troops; 14,555 Indians able to bear arms (times 6)	Edwardes, XXVI, part 1, pp. 332-4
1764		60,000 (probably too low, unless war caused a temporary slump)	Edwardes, I, p. 155
1780	113,000	47,170 by census, but considered incomplete and raised to 113,726 by assigning 100,000 instead of 33,444 to the main district	" pp. 156-7
1800	174,000		
1815	221,000	Census	Zachariah, p. 10
1849	566,119		Edwardes, I, p. 162
1850	580,000		
1864	816,562		" " "

Broach

585-740		Capital of a Gujar dynasty	Imp. Gaz. India: Bombay Pres., I, p. 320
1031		Co-capital of S. Gujarat	" " " " " " "
1700	50,000	Its history stable 1685-1772	Ency. Brit., 1910
1750	50,000		
1777	50,000		Imp. Gaz. India: Bombay Pres., I, p. 318
1800	38,000		
1812	32,716		" " " " " " "
c.1850	31,332		Ungewitter, II, p. 368

Burdwan (Bardwan)

1695-(1948)		Seat of a kingdom	Ency. Brit., 1875
1789-1822		Its district gained 10%	Martin, 1839, pp. 288-9
1800	52,000		
1814	53,927	Based on houses times 4.5	Thornton
1850	40,000		
1872	32,321		Ency. Brit., 1878

Burhanpur

c.1400	48,000	Its country had 12,000 horseman, (presumably at the capital. Low multiplier for newly-settled city)	Thornton, "Candeish"
1400-1600		Farukid capital	Ency. of Islam, 1897
1500	75,000	Farukids' peak, though vassal to Gujarat	Thornton, "Candeish"
1561		All killed	Ency. of Islam, 1960
1600-35		Capital of the Deccan under the Moguls	C. Grant, p. 126
1610		Larger than London	Coverte in Oaten, p. 159
1626		Wall built, 12 coss around (15 miles, perhaps an exaggeration)	Pelsaert, p. 37 & n
1600s	130,000	Peak: 5 sq. miles as shown by extent of ruins (c. 1,300 ha. in area)	C. Grant, p. 126
1658		Very much ruined	Tavernier in Hunter
1685		Sacked by Marathas	Imp. Gaz. India: Central Provs., p. 289
1720-48		Often Nizam's capital	C. Grant, p. 128
1731	32,000	New wall enclosing only 1 1/4 sq. miles (c. 320 ha.)	Hunter
1780		Garrison 10,000	Hodges, p. 43
1800s		50,000 (looks high); formerly much more	Brockhaus, 1864
1866	34,137	In 8,000 houses	C. Grant, p. 129

Calcutta

1686		Founded	Balfour
1710	10-12,000		"
1750	110,000		
1752	117,000		Ency. Brit., 1910
1800	200,000		
1821	230,552	179,917 in city alone	Balfour; Hunter
1850	413,182		Ency. Brit., 1853

Calicut

600s		Grew from immigration of Moplahs	" " 1910
1344		One of the 5 great ports seen by Ibn Battuta	Ibn Battuta, p. 46
c.1400	50,000	20 or 30 mosques (c. 25, times 800, plus non-Moslems, who were 60% of the total in 1901)	Ma Huan in Menon, p. 185; Ency. of Islam, 1897
1442		8 miles around (but cf. 1503)	Conti, p. 20
1500		Main west-Indian port	Ency. Brit., 1910
"	60,000		
1503	60,000	6 miles around, unwalled (thus, c. 600 ha. in area)	Varthema, p. 136
1529-71		Blockaded by Portuguese, ruining its trade	Woodcock, pp. 148-9
1600	42,000		
1606	42,000	7,000 houses	Caerden in La Martinière, 1737
1720		City, "if it may be called one"	A. Hamilton, I, p. 105
1788		Inhabitants carried off	Ency. Brit., 1910
c.1820	30,000	5,000 houses	W. Hamilton
1850	40,000		
1871	48,338		Hunter

Cambay

915		Flourishing	Masudi in Cordier, II, p. 398n
1154		Flourishing	Edrisi in Cordier, II, p. 398n
1298	80,000	20,000 maidens taken in sack (assuming maidens equal 1/2 female population)	Commissariat, pp. 3-4

c. 1298		One of the 2 main oceanic ports	Sanudo in Cordier, II, p. 398n
1344		Very fine city	Ibn Battuta in Nilakanta, p. 229
1400	125,000		
1442	125,000	12 miles aronnd (probably less 1/4, cf. Calicut and Goa. Perhaps 1,250 ha. in area)	Conti, p. 20
1499		Rival Surat founded	Ency. Brit., 1910
1500	125,000	Held then by Gujarat, which was thriving	Commissariat, p. 207
1567		Still considerable trade	Cesar Frederick in Cordier, II, p. 398n
1594	72,000	12,000 fighting men raised there	Commissariat, II, p. 23
1600	70,000		
1626		Trade nearly ended	Pelsaert, p. 19
1699		Still busy, but not half inhabited	A. Hamilton, I, p. 86
1700	50,000		
1750	40,000		
1800s	37,000		Thornton
1872	33,709		Hunter

Cawnpore (now Kanpur)

1778		A village	Imp. Gaz. India: United Provs., II, p. 15
1848	108,796		A. Shakespear, p. 120n
1850	108,000		
1853	108,764	With cantonment	Ungewitter, II, p. 336

Chairadeo

1253-c.1390		Ahom capital	Gait, p. 78; L. Shakespeare, pp. 28-9

Champaner

1484-1535		Capital of Gujarat; very much smaller than Ahmedabad	Commissariat, pp. 197-8, 263
1611		Ruined	" p. 198
1812	1,000	200 inhabited houses	Conder, 1830s, IV, p. 129

Chanda

c.1100-1751		Gond capital; wall 5 1/2 miles enclosing c. 500 ha.)	Ency. Brit., 1910
1700	50,000		
1700s		Weakened by Maratha attacks	" " "
1797		Ravaged by a flood	Enci. Universal
1901	17,803		Ency. Brit., 1910

Chanderi

1030		First mentioned	Imp. Gaz. India: Central India p. 164
1500	70,000	Prior to rapid expansion	
1518		Peak of power, wholly dominating Mandu	Commissariat, I, p. 273
1500s	84,000	14,000 stone houses	Abu'l-Fazl in Conder, 1830s, IV, p. 216
c.1800		Decayed	Playfair, V, p. 456

Chandernagore

1676		Founded	Grande Enci.
c.1700		Small with a ruined appearance	Malleson, pp. 36-7
1740s		2,000 brick houses built	Catholic Ency.
1750	95,000		

1753	102,000		Catholic Ency., "Calcutta"
1800	45,000		
1812	41,377		Brockhaus, 1864
1836	31,235		Hoffmann
1861	28,512		Brockhaus, 1864

Chandragiri

1400s		Became storehouse for the royal treasure of Vijayanagar	Heras, p. 311
c.1592-(c.1652)		Capital of Vijayanagar	" p. 310
1871	4,235		Imp. Gaz. India: Madras, "Chandragiri"

Chapra (Chupra)

1800	43,000		
c.1820	43,000		Malcolm (a), p. 444
c.1850	40,000		Ungewitter, II, p. 334
1891	56,000		Ency. Brit., 1910

Chitor (Chittor)

734-1567		Capital of Mewar	Imp. Gaz. India: Rajputana, p. 132
1300	60,000		
1303	60,000	30,000 killed in one day (probably a general slaughter of males) after all women had performed suicide rites	Srivastava, pp. 120-1
1303-c.1345		Under Moslem rule from Delhi	Imp. Gaz. India: Rajputana, p. 110
1382-97		Its temples rebuilt	" " " " p. 111
1400	60,000		
1500	90,000		
1527		Peak	" " " " "
peak		Wall 12 miles long, but town is outside it	W. Hamilton, "Odeypoor"; India Tourism, rear map
1534		All killed	Imp. Gaz. India: Rajputana, p. 112
1567	96,000	40,000 inhabitants (surely male) plus 8,000 soldiers in the garrison (thus, 48,000 males) slain, rest taken prisoner (probably very few) after all women had again performed suicide rites	Srivastava, pp. 452-3
1666		100 temples; city almost ruined	Thévenot, Part 3, p. 70
1871	5,572		Hunter, "Chittur"

Chittagong (Satgaon, "Bengala" from 1575)

1500	50,000		
1540		Harbor silted and hard to reach	Marshall, p. 129n
1550	50,000	10,000 hearths	Ramusio in Rundall, p. cxvi
1600	50,000	Chief port of Bengal	Cortesão, p. 13
1666		Taken by Moguls	Stewart, p. 300
1872	20,304		Hunter

Chunar (Chandalgar)

c.730-1063		Apparently the usual Pala capital (cf. Bihar, Nadiya, Monghyr)	Martin, 1838, I, p. 28
1824	15,000		Heber in Conder, 1830s, III, p. 269
c.1850	11,058		Thornton

Cochin

1341		Founded	Imp. Gaz. India: Madras, II, p. 360
c.1440	<u>25,000</u>	5 miles around (probably c. 1/4 less, cf. Calicut and Goa; perhaps 200-250 ha. in area)	Conti, p. 19
1500	35,000		
1600	56,000		
early 1600s	<u>56,000</u>	15 churches (cf. Goa), 45 blocks of houses (times 1,250; cf. Diu)	Faria, I, map p. 58
c.1660		Taken by Dutch and reduced by 9/10	A. Hamilton, I, p. 183
1757		Smaller than Colombo	Ives, p. 193
1778-1806		Again flourishing	Ency. Brit., 1910
1800s	30,000		Brockhaus, 1864
1871	13,588		Hunter

Cuttack

953		Founded	Ency. Brit., 1910
989-1524		Capital of Orissa	W. W. Hunter *et al.*, II, pp. 234, 249
1135-96		Especially flourishing	Mahtab, I, p. 71; W.W. Hunter *et al.*, II, p. 236
1200	<u>150,000</u>	See 1708	
1300	<u>125,000</u>	Past peak, but stable	Mahtab
1674		2nd in Bengal, less than half Dacca's size, but prettier	Bowrey, p. 152
1708		Under 1/4 inhabited; garrison 5,500	A. Hamilton, I, p. 216
1800	40,000		
1822	40,000		W. Hamilton
1850	46,000		
1872	50,878		Vivien

Dacca (Jehangirnagar)

1608-1704		Capital of Bengal province, except 1639-1655	Emp. Gaz. India: Western Bengal p. 319
1627	<u>200,000</u>		Manrique, p. 45
once		250,000 (perhaps exaggerated)	Brockhaus, 1864, "Dakka"
1674		40 miles around	Bowrey, p. 150
1700	<u>200,000</u>		
1750	<u>135,000</u>	No longer capital	
1765		Much smaller than Murshidabad	Rennell in Sinha, p. 225
1789	<u>135,000</u>	See next item	
1789-1822		Its district declined 45%	Martin, 1839, pp. 288-9
1800	110,000		
1813	<u>85,000</u>	21,361 houses (times 4; cf. 1830)	Thornton
1830	66,989		Ency. Brit., 1875
"		16,279	Thornton
1838	68,000		Brockhaus, 1864, "Dakka"
c.1850	60,617		Thornton, "Bengal"
1860		4 by 1 1/4 miles (thus 10 1/2 miles around or c. 1,750 ha. in area), 180 mosques, 119 pagodas	Chambers, 1870
1867	51,536		Ency. Brit., 1875

Daulatabad (Deogiri till 1339)

1187		Founded	Imp. Gaz. India: Hyderabad, p. 210

1192-1318		Yadava capital	Imp. Gaz. India: Hyderbad, p. 210
" "		Old wall 2 3/4 miles around	Ency. Brit., 1910
1339-47		Capital of Hindustan	Imp. Gaz. India: Hyderabad, p. 210
c.1670		Of middling size	Thévenot, pt. 3, p. 76
1901	1,357		Imp. Gaz. India: Hyderabad, p. 210

Delhi

1052		Repeopled	Hearn, p. 73
"	10,000	2.5 miles around	Chandra, p. 13
1193	40,000	27 temples built in previous reign	" p. 14
1193-1803		Usual main Moslem capital of India	" pp. 15, 24
c.1200		Primarily a military headquarters	Mahajan, 1965, part 1, p. 76
1200	60,000	Growing as capital	
1211-36		Rose as Lahore declined; became a second Bagdad	" " " p. 81
c.1300	100,000	Equal of Bagdad, rival of Cairo and Constantinople	Barani in Mahajan, 1965, part I, p. 140
1327		Capital and entire population moved to Daulatabad; only partly repopulated when capital returned, same year, and only slowly regained its former prosperity	Srivastava, p. 151
"	40,000	5-mile wall built on new site (thus, c. 400 ha. in area)	Chandra, p. 20
1342		Partly deserted, but still largest in the Moslem east	Ibn Battuta in Mahajan, 1965, part 1, pp. 156, 158
1354	125,000	Unwalled new site; more than half a dozen main mosques (times 9; double to include Hindus)	Chandra, p. 29
1398		Sacked by Tamerlane; 100,000 killed	Martin, 1858, III, p. 143
1402		Derelict	P. Brown, II, p. 42
1500	100,000	Reviving under Lodi dynasty	
1530	130,000	New site, 9 miles around (thus, c. 1,300 ha. in area)	Chandra, p. 21
1540-(53)		Capital of India	Hambly, p. 39
1540	160,000	Entirely rebuilt, 3 miles long (c. 10 miles around, enclosing c. 1,600 ha.)	" p. 39 and map p. 12; Ency. Brit., 1910
1600		Almost deserted	Hearn, p. 165
1638		New site planned for 200,000	Chandra, p. 22; Hodges, p. 118
c.1660		About the size of Paris	Bernier, p. 282
1666	400,000	When king is there, but not 1/6 as many in his absence	Thévenot, part 3, p. 43
1700	500,000	Peak of Mogul expansion	Ency. Brit., 1910, "India"
1707-		Rapid decline	Chandra, p. 25
1739	180,000	2/3 the total or 120,000 killed by Nadir	Playfair, V, p. 409; Martin, 1858, III, p. 145
1750	100,000		
1800	125,000		
1803-57		Period of quiet prosperity	Ency. Brit., 1910
c.1820	150,000		Malcolm (a), p. 444
1836	151,000	130,672 plus suburbs	Martin, 1858, III, p. 292
1846	160,279	137,971 plus 22,302 in clearly urban suburbs	A. Shakespear, pp. 27-8, 33
1850	156,000		
1853	152,406	(Perhaps includes suburbs)	Ungewitter, II, p. 337

Dhar

c.900-1010		Nominal capital of Malwa	Imp. Gaz. India: Central India, p. 324
1010-1300		De facto capital, displacing Ujjain	" " " " " pp. 324-5
once	100,000	As it had 20,000 houses	Malcolm, II, p. 489
"	90,000	3 1/4 miles by 1/2, i.e., 7.5 miles around (enclosing c. 900 ha.; times 100)	Thornton
1300	90,000		
"		Kingdom fell to Delhi	Imp. Gaz. India: Central India, p. 325
1399-1408		Again capital of Malwa	" " " " " "
1820	20,000	3,000 houses; reviving	Conder, 1830s, IV, p. 229

Diu

1539		2,802 *bracas* (3.8 miles) around (thus, c. 250 ha. in area); a very recent city	Castro, II, pp. 154-5
1600	50,000		
early 1600s		40 blocks	Faria, I, map p. 322
peak	50,000		Imp. Gaz. India: Bombay Pres., II, p. 585
1670		Sacked by Muscat Arabs	A. Hamilton, I, p. 83
1700	30,000		
1720	40,000	Perhaps	" " "
1841	9,146		Hoffman, "Goa"
1852	10,765		Harper

Dorasamudra (Dwarasamudra, Halebid)

1133-1328		Hoysala capital except 1191-c.1200	Wilks, I, p. 13; Heras 1929, p. 66; L. Rice, p. 217
1300	40,000	Wall 4 miles; some temples outside	Narasimhachar, front map and pp. 2, 17
1352		Number 2 capital of Vijayanagar	Heras, 1929, p. 106

Ellora

c.740-814		Probable Rashtrakuta capital	Cousens in Altekar, p. 48
c.760-83		Finest temple built	Ency. Brit., 1910
800	90,000	Stone-built hectares times 200; cf. Majapahit	
c.1666		Ruined pagodas spread over an area 1 1/2-2 leagues around (c. 450 hectares)	Thévenot, part 3, p. 75

Farrukhabad

1714-1802		Semi-free capital	Ency. of Islam, 1897
1800	66,000		
1801	66,740	Based on 13,348 dwellings	W. Hamilton, "Furruckabad"
1811		14,999 dwellings	Malcolm, II, p. 492
1848	68,000	Including 12,000 in cantonment, 9,000 in suburbs	A. Shakespear, p. 105
1850	68,000		

Fatehpur Sikri

1569		Founded as Akbar's royal residence	Ency. Brit., 1910
"		Wall 6 miles around	Playfair, V, p. 416
c.1583		Larger than Agra; much larger than London	Fitch, pp. 17-8

1584		Much of the population shifted to Agra	Vivien
c.1610		In ruins, like a desert	Finch, pp. 149-50
1848	15,414		A. Shakespear, p. 123n
1853	20,864		Ungewitter, II, p. 336

Fyzabad (ancient Ayodhya, now Faizabad)

326-530		De facto Gupta capital	Dey, "Ayodhya"
" "		Twice the area of the city in 1870	Balfour, "Faizabad"
c.1610		In ruins	Finch, p. 176
1724-75		Capital of Oudh	Imp. Gaz. India: United Provs., II, p. 390
1750	90,000		
1775	90,000	See area c. 1870 (times 150)	
1775-1860		Population rapidly decreasing	American Cyclopaedia
1800	60,000		
1850	45,000		
c.1870		6 miles around (c. 600 ha. in area)	Balfour, "Faizabad"
1872	45,300	Including Ayodhya	Reclus, VIII, p. 381n

Gangaikondapuram (Jayakondacholapuram)

1012-1118		Chola capital	Imp. Gaz. India: Madras, II, p. 193
1118-1300s		Chola capital here or nearby	" " " " " "
1871	1,014		

Gargaon (Garhgaon)

c.1530-1699		Ahom capital	Imp. Gaz. India: Eastern Bengal and Assam, pp. 587-8
1600	40,000		
c.1615	40,000	Wall built, 3 kos in radius (12 miles around); density low, with scattered villages and fields (cf. Oyo and Gaur)	Gait, pp. 119, 149
1662	54,000	Royal guard 6-7,000. City sacked; victors found 9,100 muskets (times 6 for population), 7,828 spears. King fled with 5,000 men.	" p. 148; Bhattacharya, pp. 331-3

Gaur (Lakhnauti)

648-c.730		A capital of Bengal (perhaps along with Chunar	Thornton
c.1130-1199		Again capital of Bengal	"
" "		Many temples built	Dey, "Lakhshmanavati"
1203-82		Capital of Bengal under rule from Delhi	Hunter, "Nadiya"; Fergusson, II, pp. 254-5
1282-1338		Its governors hereditary and semi-free	Fergusson, II, pp. 254-5
1300	100,000	See 1514, its probable peak while a wholly free capital	
1338-52		Capital of free West Bengal	" " "
1442-1565		Capital of all Bengal	Abid-Ali, pp. 15-8
1500	200,000		
1514	200,000	40,000 hearths	Pires in Cortesão, pp. 10, 15
1500s	200,000		Barros in Moreland, p. 14, 1920
peak		13 sq. miles without suburbs, 22 or 30 with	Imp. Gaz. India: Eastern Bengal, p. 252
1537		Sacked and lost importance	Fergusson, p. 255
1575		Deserted	Imp. Gaz. India: Eastern Bengal, p. 251

1639		Last occupied by a prince	Ency. of Islam, 1897
1819	18,000	3,000 houses	W. Hamilton
1872	11,492		Hunter

Gawil

1348-1478		District capital	Ency. Brit., 1910, "Berar"
1478-1572		Capital of Berar kingdom	" " " "

Gaya

1800	32,000		
early 1800s	32,000	6,000 houses	Thornton
1840	43,451		"
1850	50,000		
1872	66,843		Balfour

Goa

1300	50,000		
1344	50,000	10,000 men (i.e., all able to bear arms) forceably converted	Ibn Battuta, p. 240
1400	50,000		
c.1440		8 miles around (but cf. 1600)	Conti, p. 19
1500		2nd to Calicut on W. Indian coast (i.e., below Cambay)	Ency. Brit., 1910
"	42,000		
1510	42,000	7,000 slain by Portuguese (i.e., militia, times 6)	La Martiniére, 1737
1600		6 miles around (thus, c. 600 ha. in area); 200,000 people (surely an exaggeration)	Cottineau, p. 17
c. "	63,000	17 churches (times 3,750, cf. Cochin); 3/4 Christian	Faria, I, map p. 142
1639		Had grown considerably under the Portuguese	Mandelslo, p. 82
1695	20,000		Gemelli, p. 203
1700	20,000	Almost 30,000 (perhaps too high)	Imp. Gaz. India: Bombay Pres., II, p. 589
1775	1,600		" " " " " " "
1876	14,134		Hunter

Golconda (Bagnagar)

1512-89		Capital of Golconda kingdom; fort 3 miles around	Imp. Gaz. India: Hyderabad, pp. 114-5
" "		Fort 5 miles around	Bowrey, p. 110
1655		A little smaller than Orléans	Tavernier, II, p. 61
1687		Fell to the Moguls	Ency. Brit., 1910

Gorakhpur

c.1400		Founded	Ency. Brit., 1910
c.1700		2nd main mosque built; no more before 1835	Martin, 1838, II, p. 348
c.1800	31,000	6 miles around (thus, 600 ha. in area)	Playfair, V, p. 430
1805	31,000	4,568 houses	Martin, 1838, II, p. 346
c.1835	42,000	6,121 houses, with estimated 7 3/4 per house	" " appendix, p. 9
1848	45,265		A. Shakespear, p. 140n
1850	48,000		
1853	54,529		Ungewitter, II, p. 337

Gulbarga

1347-1424		Bahmanid capital	Sherwani, p. 27
″ ″		Rival of Vijayanagar	Mahajan, part 1, pp. 242-7
1481		Destroyed by Kanchi	″ ″ p. 247
1490-1500		Capital of Dastur Dinar	Ency. of Islam, 1897
1881	22,384		Imp. Gaz. India: Hyderabad, p. 451

Gwalior (Lashkar)

773		Founded	Thornton
977-1128		Kachwaha capital	Imp. Gaz. India: Rajputana, (1881, p. 236)
1196		Again a capital	Imp. Gaz. India: Central India, p. 168
1210-32		Again a capital	″ ″ ″ ″ ″ ″
1398-1518		Again a capital	″ ″ ″ ″ ″ ″
1486-1517		Main palace built	″ ″ ″ ″ ″ p. 169
″ ″	90,000	Fort built large enough for 15,000 men	Martin, 1858, III, p. 140
1546-53		Frequent residence of king of N. India	Hearn, p. 216
1805-(1948)		Capital of the Sindhia Marathas	Conder, 1830s, IV, p. 211
c.1830	65,000	10-11,000 soldiers	″ ″ ″ p. 212
1850	74,000		
1881	88,066	On new site	Imp. Gaz. India: Central India, p. 166

Hugli (Hoogly)

1537		Prospered after arrival of Portuguese	Ency. Brit., 1910
1600	70,000		
1632	70,000	Nearly 50,000 fled, 10,000 slain, and 10,000 freed	Crawford, p. 8
1723		Still the port of Bengal	Das Gupta, p. 119
early 1800s	12,000		Petermann, 1857, p. 349
1872	34,761	Including Chinsura	Hunter

Hyderabad

1589		Founded	Imp. Gaz. India: Hyderabad, p. 115
1589-1687		Capital of Golconda; 6 miles around (thus c. 600 ha. in area)	″ ″ ″ ″ pp. 114-5
1600	80,000	Based on area; cf. 1875	
1655		20,000 prostitutes here and at Golconda	Tavernier, II, pp. 61, 65
c.1700	200,000	34,000 soldiers (times 6)	Wilks, I, p. 221
1724-(1948)		Nizam's capital	Imp. Gaz. India: Hyderabad, p. 115
1750	225,000		
1750-90		Nizam's lands reduced	Gribble, p. 125
1800	200,000		
c.1820	200,000		Malcolm (a), p. 444
c.1850	200,000		Ency. Brit., 1853
″		Country in disorder	″ ″ 1910, "Salar"
1853-83		Excellent administration	″ ″ ″ ″
c.1875	350,000	On 27 sq. km. (2,700 ha.)	Reclus, VIII, p. 505
1881	367,417		Imp. Gaz. India: Hyderabad, p. 114
1891	415,039		″ ″ ″ ″ ″

Hyderabad, Sind Province, see Mansura

Indore

c.1770-1818		District capital	Imp. Gaz. India: Central India, p. 227
1818-(1948)		Capital of the Holkar Marathas	" " " " " p. 203
early 1800s		Small	Malcolm, II, p. 496
c.1825		90,000 (may be too large)	Balbi
c.1850	60,000		Hoffmann
1871	92,330	With cantonment	Vivien

Jaipur (Jeypore)

1728		Founded as the Kachwaha capital; modeled on Ahmedabad	Imp. Gaz. India: Rajputana, p. 260
"	75,000	Wall nearly 7 miles around (enclosing c. 750 ha.)	India Tourism, rear map
1750	100,000	See 1825	
1798	72,000	12,000 soldiers (i.e., militia) plus 5,000 mercenaries	Imp. Gaz. India: Rajputana, p. 238
1800	72,000	In severe decline	" " " " "
1825	60,000	Most houses in decay	Heber in Conder, 1830s, IV, p. 62
1850	100,000		
1870	137,847		Hunter
1881	142,578		Imp. Gaz. India: Rajputana, p. 259

Jaunpur

1359		Founded	Imp. Gaz. India: United Provs., II, p. 160
1394-8		Capital of a province	" " " " " " "
1398-1479		Capital of a kingdom ruling most of the land previously held by Delhi	Ency. of Islam, 1960, "Djawn-pur"
"		The Shiraz of India	" " " " "
1479-1580		Capital of a province	" " " " "
1500	50,000	6 mosques left, rest pulled down c. 1496 (times 800, plus Hindus—cf. 1901)	" " " " "
1608		6-8 coss (10-12 miles) around	Finch, pp. 176-7
early 1800s	16,1777		Thornton
1853	27,160		Ungewitter, II, p. 337
1901		District 91% Hindu	Ency. Brit., 1910

Jayapuram

746-855		Capital of Kashmir	Ferguson, pp. 107-8; Kaul, p. 36

Jhansi

1850	60,000		
1856	60,000		Sleeman in Tahmankar, 1958, p. 19

Jodhpur

c.550-c.850		Seat of a kingdom	Ganguly, 1912, p. 15n
1459-(1948)		Again seat of a kingdom, ruled 1532-69 by Maldeo, "most powerful prince in Hindustan" (a considerable exaggeration)	Imp. Gaz. India: Rajputana, p. 174

1569		Became vassal to Moguls	Imp. Gaz. India: Rajputana, p. 175
1620-38		Its lord was Mogul governor for the Deccan	" " " " "
once	150,000		Brockhaus, "Dschodpur"
1750	150,000	Peak of power	Imp. Gaz. India: Rajputana, pp. 177-8
1780	129,150		Boileau in Thornton
c.1800 (?)	80,000	"Some years ago . . . now (1854) much less"	Thornton
c.1850	50,000		Brockhaus, "Dschodpur"
1881	63,329		Imp. Gaz. India: Rajputana, p. 196

Jullundur (Jalandhar)

c. 630		2 miles around	Hsüan Dsang in Imp. Gaz. India: Punjab, I, p. 421
pre 1846 (?)	40,000		Ungewitter, II, p. 347
1846		Cantonment founded (13,280 in 1901)	Imp. Gaz. India: Punjab, I, p. 422
1850	50,000		
1868	50,067		Hunter

Kalinjar

1182-1203		Chandel capital; 4 miles around, plus suburbs on the plain	Imp. Gaz. India: United Provs., II, pp. 47, 49, 62
1200	100,000		
1203		50,000 men enslaved when it fell	V. Smith, p. 340
1872	4,019		Hunter

Kalyan

c.1050-c.1189		Capital of the Chalukyas, till 1126 India's strongest kingdom	Imp. Gaz. India: Hyderabad, pp. 10-11, 291
c.1125		Praised as "the most beautiful city," by court poet. Hence rated above Kanauj, Cuttack, or Anhilvada	Vaidya, III, p. 260
1190-		Fell rapidly into decay	Burgess, p. 37
1323		Minor town	Yazdani, p. 3
1901	11,191		Imp. Gaz. India: Hyderabad, p. 291

Kamatapur

c.1300-1498		Cocch capital	Gait, pp. 43-4
1498	90,000	19 miles around (enclosing c. 5,700 ha., times 15.7; cf. Murshidabad)	Buchanan-Hamilton in L. Shakespear, p. 2
"		Sacked	Gait, p. 44

Kanauj

618-1168		Capital of N. India except briefly c. 800	Imp. Gaz. India: United Provs., I, p. 20; Moreland and Chatterjea, p. 113; Vaidya, III, p. 21
c. 630	100,000	Over 10,000 Buddhist monks; half population non-Buddhist, with 200 Hindu temples; 20 *li* by 4 or 5 in area (thus c. 1,000 hectares). Ruins confirm Hsüan's area. (Monks times 5)	Hsüan Dsang, I, pp. 206-7; Hunter
c. 800	80,000	Its country 2nd in India (cf. Ellora for population of leader)	Soliman in Major, p. xxvii
916		Its empire split up	Moreland and Chatterjee, p. 115

1000	60,000		
1018	60,000	10,000 men surrendered and converted to Islam	Mahajan, part 1, p. 42
"		Mostly reduced to ruins	Biruni, p. 199
1080-1155		Again dominated N. India	Vaidya, III, pp. 211-15
" "	92,000	84 wards in past (times 1,100; cf. Ahmedabad), presumably this time	Cunningham, p. 381
1194		Hindu men all slain (it had reverted to Hindu rule)	Mahajan, part 1, p. 63
c.1200		Moslems struck coins there	Ency. of Islam, 1897, "Farruk-habad"
1340		Its people massacred	Thornton, "Kunnoj"
1848	16,486		A. Shakespear, p. 105n

Kanchi (now Conjeeveram)

c. 630	100,000	More than 10,000 Buddhist monks; 80 non-Buddhist temples; 30 *li* (5 miles) around (population based on compari-son with Kanauj)	Hsüan Dsang, II, pp. 228-29
-1000s		Pallava capital	Imp. Gaz. India, Madras, I, p. 545
1000s-1310		Capital of a Chola branch line	" " " " " "
1310-c.1400		Seat of a local dynasty	Ency. Brit., 1910, "Carnatic"
1481		Sacked and destroyed	Subrahmanya, pp. 65-6
1500s		2 new temples built	Puri, p. 32
1871	35,396	In 6,447 houses	Hunter

Kanpur, see Cawnpore

Kasimbazar (adjacent to Murshidabad but under different rule)

1632-c.1700		The great emporium of Bengal (it would succeed Hugli)	Hunter
1700s		The silk mart of Bengal	Balfour
1829	3,538		Hunter

Kayal (Cail)

1292		Chief Pandyan emporium; great and noble city	Polo in Nilakanta, 1958, p. 214, in Imp. Gaz. India: Madras, II, p. 283
c.1850		Abandoned	Yule in Cordier, II, p. 373n

Khajuraho

950-99		Chandel capital	V. Smith, p. 340
950-1050		C. 30 temples built	Balfour: Imp. Gaz. India: Central India, p. 390
1000	100,000	Chandel peak, ruling to Benares; strongest country in India (cf. its successor Kalinjar)	Bose, pp. 39-50
by 1157		85 temples	Ency. Brit., 1971

Lahore

c. 630		Large; soon afterwards local capital moved to Sialkot	Hsüan Dsang in Imp. Gaz. India: Punjab, II, p. 31
1000		Capital of Punjab	Ency. Brit., 1910, "Mahmud of Ghazni"
1036-99		Ghaznavid capital east of the Indus	Imp. Gaz. India: Punjab, II, p. 31
1157-89		Capital of Ghaznavid empire	Stewart, pp. 24-5
1244		Population massacred by Mongols	Mahajan, pt. 1, p. 136
1266-		Western outpost for Delhi kingdom	Naqui, p. 14
1398		Destroyed by Tamerlane	Imp. Gaz. India: Punjab, II, p. 32

1422		Resettled	Imp. Gaz. India; Punjab, II, p. 32
1539		A mere village	Finch, p. 161
1555-6		Mogul capital	Thévenot, pt. 3, p. 60
1584-98		Mogul capital again	Imp. Gaz. India: Punjab, II, p. 33
1598	450,000	After 4/5 its years as capital	
c.1598		2nd to none in Europe	Montserrate in Moreland, p. 13
1600	350,000	Capital just moved away	
1615		Larger than Constantinople or Agra (but density low while not capital)	Coryat in Moreland, p. 13
"		Smaller than Agra	E. Terry, p. 65
1622-7	600,000	Again Mogul capital; 16 miles around including suburbs beyond the wall (thus c. 4,000 ha. in area, times 150; cf. 1660); area larger than in 1901	Imp. Gaz. India: Punjab, II, pp. 33-4
c.1660	200,00	Very lofty buildings unlike Delhi and Agra (suggests recent high density); most houses in ruinous state	Bernier, p. 384
1748-98		Sacked many times	Imp. Gaz. India: Punjab, II, p. 36
1798-1849		Sikh capital	" " " " " pp. 36-7
1800		Mere heap of ruins	" " " " " "
1850	94,000		
1855	94,143		

Lokigonda (now Lakkundi)

1191-c.1200		Hoysala capital	L. Rice, I, p. 217

Lucknow

c.1550		Began to rise	Imp. Gaz. India: United Provs., II, p. 302
1750	100,000		
1770	125,000	4 German miles around (13 miles, enclosing c. 2,700 ha.; cf. 1857)	Tieffenthaler in Conder, 1830s, IV, p. 296n
c.1800		7 miles around (probably excludes suburbs)	Playfair, V, p. 429
"	300,000		Hassel, 1819, XIV, p. 264
1850	300,000	Before loss of court	
1857		20 miles around (enclosing c. 6,500 ha.)	Imp. Gaz. India: United Provs., II, p. 307
1869	284,779		Hunter

Ludhiana

1850	47,000		
1855	47,191		Hunter

Madras

1640		Founded	Ency. Brit., 1910
c.1650	15,000	Estimate	Barlow, p. 18
1674		193 houses	Nayudu, p. 4
1750	55,000	8,700 houses, plus English in fort	" "
1800	125,000		
1823	160,000	In 26,786 houses	M'Culloch
1850	310,000		
1863	427,771		Statesman's Yearbook, 1877

Madurai

1170		Already Pandyan capital, became subject to Cholas	Logan

1310		Still Pandyan capital	Venkataramanyya, p. 46
c.1575-1739		Naik capital	Imp. Gaz. India: Madras, II, p. 215
c.1800	20,000	40,000 (high estimate)	W. Hamilton
1812	20,069		"
1850	41,601		Nelson, part 5, p. 156, part 2, p. 7

Maheshwar

1767-97		Holkar Maratha capital	Imp. Gaz. India: Central India, p. 231
c.1820	21,000	3,500 houses	Malcolm in Imp. Gaz. India: Central India, p. 231
c.1850	17,500		Petermann, 1857, p. 350 (under "Muhesur")

Mahoba

-1182		Capital of the Chandels (cf. Khajuraho, Kalinjar)	V. Smith, pp. 330, 335
1872	6,977		Hunter

Mandu

1408-1562		Capital of Malwa, replacing Dhar; with a wall covering an area of 25 miles	Ency. Brit., 1910, "Malwa"; Mahajan, pt. 1, p. 231
" "		Ruins 3 3/4 by 5 1/2 miles	Finch, p. 141n
1469	200,000	Peak (for size cf. 1628)	Yazdani, p. 19
"		15,000 women in harem	Mahajan, pt. 1, p. 231
1500	150,000		
1628	25,000	5 miles around; formerly 15 (thus, c. 3,600 ha., times 60; cf. Vijayanagar	Herbert, p. 80
1666		Of middling size	Thévenot, pt. 3, p. 69

Mansura (now Hyderabad, Pakistan)

c. 760		Founded by caliph Mansur (754-75)	Ibn Hawqal, 1822, p. 66
968		Twice Multan's size	" " " "
1768		Refounded as Hyderabad	Balfour
1810	14,000		Kinneir, p. 230
c.1850	24,000		Petermann, 1857, p. 349
1872	41,150		Hunter

Manyakheta (now Malkhed)

c.815-c.1050		Rashtrakuta and then Chalukya capital	Dey, "Manyakshetra" and "Kalyan"
c. 943		The great center of India	Masudi in Burgess, p. 32
972		Sacked	Altekar, pp. 124-5

Masulipatam

1612-(1948)		British-held, except briefly	Imp. Gaz. India: Madras, I, p. 325
1674		Without doubt first in trade on the Coromandel coast (E. India south of Bengal)	Bowrey, p. 61
c.1700		In decline (losing trade to Madras)	A. Hamilton, in Bowrey, p. 62n
1837	27,884		Thornton

Mau-Sahanya

- 831		Parihara capital	V. Smith, p. 335

Meerut

1399		Destroyed by Tamerlane	Conder, 1830s, IV, p. 3
1847	29,014		Imp. Gaz. India: United Provs., I, p. 325
1850	<u>55,000</u>		
1853	82,035		" " " " " " "

Mirzapur

c.1765		First mentioned	Imp. Gaz. India: United Provs., II, p. 157
1800	<u>50,000</u>		
1801	<u>50,000</u>		W. Hamilton
c.1820	69,000		Malcolm (a), p. 444
1850	<u>77,000</u>		
1853	79,526		Ungewitter, II, p. 336

Monghyr (Mudgagiri)

c.730-1063		A Pala capital, sometime between these dates	Paul, p. 129
1590-1600s		Base for Akbar's general in Bengal	Ency. Brit., 1910
1800	<u>30,000</u>		
1811	30,000	5 miles around, but with much open space	Buchanan in Hunter; Martin, 1838, II, p. 42
c.1850	40,000		Hoffmann
1869	53,981		Hunter

Moradabad

1625		Founded	"
1848	48,880		A. Shakespear, p. 79n
1850	<u>53,000</u>		
1852	57,414		Ungewitter, II, p. 339

Mukhalingam

-1135		Capital of a dynasty which was gradually taking Orissa	Mahtab, I, p. 71

Multan

800s-1005		Capital of a Hindu kingdom	Vivien
968		Half the size of Mansura	Ibn Hawqul, 1822, p. 66
1150		Same size as Seistan's port	Edrisi in Bémont, p. 32
1206-1528		A practically free capital	Imp. Gaz. India: Punjab, II, p. 241
c.1800		4.5 miles around (enclosing c. 325 ha.)	Elphinstone in "Asiatic Journal", p. 61
1818-49		Grew with new settlers	Ency. Brit., 1910
1850	<u>80,000</u>		
c.1854	80,966		Ungewitter, II, p. 346

Murshidabad

1704-72		Capital of Bengal	Ency. Brit., 1910
"		50 km. (30 miles) around	Vivien
1750	<u>200,000</u>		
1789	<u>207,000</u>	See next entry	
1789-1822		Its district declined from 1,020,572 to 762,690 (25%)	Martin, 1839, p. 288-9

1800	185,000		
1814	165,000	Based on 30,000 houses	W. Hamilton, "Moorshedabad"
1829	146,179		Hunter
1837	124,804		"
1850	96,000		
1872	46,182		"

Muttra (ancient Mathura, N. India)

c. 630		2,000 Buddhist monks and 5 Brahman temples; 20 *li* (3.3 miles) around (cf. Kanauj and Kanchi)	Hsüan Dsang, I, pp. 179-80
-1017		Sacked	G. Smith, p. 167
1850	65,000		
1853	65,749		Ungewitter, II, p. 335

Mysore

1799-1831		Local capital	Ency. Brit., 1910
1850	54,000		
1853	54,529		Hunter

Nadiya

1063-1203		Capital of Bengal	"
1872	8,863		

Nagpur

1739-1853		Bhonsla Maratha capital	Imp. Gaz. India: United Provs., pp. 337, 339
c.1800	80,000		Ency. Edinensis, IV, p. 231
c.1820	100,000		Malcolm (a), p. 444
1825	115,228		W. Hamilton
1850	111,000		
1854	111,231		Ungewitter, II, p. 343

Negapatam

1871	48,525		Imp. Gaz. India: Madras, II, p. 161

Pandua (Firozabad)

1100s		Probably capital of Bengal (but cf. Gaur, Chunar)	Abid-Ali, p. 17
1352-1442		Capital of Bengal	" "
" "		20 miles around	Stapelton in Abid-Ali, p. 15
1400	150,000	Based on area, compared with Gaur	
1800		Small	Playfair, V, p. 421

Patna (ancient Pataliputra)

c. 630		In ruins; 1,000 houses	Hsüan Dsang, II, p. 86
c. 811		King of Bengal ruled from here	Ghosh, p. 10
815		In ruins	V. Smith, p. 344
1000s		Destroyed	Chaudhury, p. 114
c.1500		Insignificant town	Naqui, p. 91
1574-1765		Capital of Bihar province	Martin, 1838, I, p. 32; Naqui, p. 91
early 1600s		Rose rapidly	Naqui, p. 104
1634		Wall built 4.5 miles around, but whole area including gardens and marshes was 18 mi. around	Hunter

1641		200,000 (seems slightly high)	Manrique in Naqui, p. 104
1670-1	170,000	20,000 died of famine, 150,000 left the city	Marshall, pp. 149-50
1673		103,000 died of famine in and near the city	'' ''
1700	170,000		
1750	200,000		
1780s		Crowded, whereas in 1600's it had been spacious	Naqui, p. 133
''		Bankipur and Dinapur already suburbs	Hodges, p. 46
c.1800		5 miles by 2 (thus, c. 3,100 ha. in area)	Playfair, V, p. 433
''	235,000		
1811	245,000	40,944 urban houses, and 11,000 rural ones; 6 people per house	Martin, 1838, I, p. 38 and appendix, p. 1
1822	265,705		'' 1839, p. 239
c.1830		45,867 houses (i.e., 6 per house) plus 3,236 houses in Dinapur	'' 1838, I, pp. 38, 45
1837	284,132	(May include Dinapur?)	Blackie
1850	263,000		
1871	230,000	158,900 plus Dinapur (42,085 in town and cantonment) and Sonpur and Hajipur (together 30,285 in 1901)	Statesman's Yearbook, 1877; Vivien; Imp. Gaz. India: Bengal, II, p. 466

Penukonda

c.1354		Fortified	Heras, 1927, p. 237
1370s		Residence of Vijayanagar's crown prince	Imp. Gaz. India: Madras, I, I, p. 494
1400	75,000		
1442	90,000	10 miles around (probably 1/4 less; cf. Calicut, Goa; thus, c. 900 ha. in area)	Conti, p. 7
1500	90,000		
1567-92		Capital of Vijayanagar	Heras, 1937, pp. 235, 303-4; Imp. Gaz. India: Madras, I, p. 493
1652		Fell to Moslems	Imp. Gaz. India: Madras, I, p. 493
1901	6,806		'' '' '' '' '' ''

Peshawar (ancient Pushkalavati)

ancient		Capital of Gandhara	Dey
c.1000		15,000 Hindus killed	Mahajan, pt. 1, p. 39
1750-		An alternate Afghan royal residence	Ency. Brit., 1910
c.1800	80,000		Hassel, 1817
1809		100,000 (possibly an exaggeration); big as Bokhara; 5 miles around	Elphinstone in Hassel, 1819, XIII, p. 753, and in Thornton
1850	53,000		
1853	53,295		Brockhaus, 1864; "Peschawar"

Pondichéry

1683		Founded	Ency. Brit., 1910
1700	35,000		
1706	40,000	40,000 natives were grouped around the rising and prosperous town; capital of French India, but few Frenchmen	Malleson, p. 22
1750	65,000		
1756		50,000 (perhaps too low)	Playfair, V, p. 513
1761	70,000		Brockhaus, 1864
1802	25,000		Ency. Edinensis, IV, p. 245
1856	34,000	119,755 in its territory; cf. 1885	Ency. Brit., 1853 (-60)
1885	41,860	145,204 in its territory	Vivien

Poona

1604-62		Local lordship	Imp. Gaz. India: Bombay Pres., I, p. 522
1700	25,000	See 1703, 1755, 1760's	
1703		6 city wards	Gadgil, pt. 1, p. 14
1750-1817		Main Maratha capital	J. Campbell, XIX, p. 577; Imp. Gaz. India: Bombay Pres., I, p. 488
1755		3 city wards added	Gadgil, pt. 1, p. 14
early 1760s	40,000		" pt. 2, p. 11
1780	150,000	Rough estimate	" pt. 1, p. 19
1796-1803		Considerable decline with political unrest	" pt. 1, pp. 19-20
c.1800	100,000		" pt. 2, p. 12
1818	110,000		Elphinstone in Gadgil, pt. 2, p. 12
1822	81,402		Gadgil, pt. II, p. 12
1838	75,170		Thornton
1850	73,000		
1851	73,209		Gadgil, pt. 1, p. 20

Quilon

660		Mentioned	Yule in Cordier, II, p. 377n
851		Traded with Arabia and China	" " " " "
1102-1503		Local capital	Woodcock, p. 90
c.1300		Peak in the 13th and 14th centuries	Imp. Gaz. India: Madras, II, p. 435
"	100,000		
peak	100,000		Herbert, p. 339
1344		One of the world's 5 busiest ports	Ibn Battuta, p. 46
1400	90,000		
c.1440		12 miles around (probably less; cf. Calicut and Goa)	Conti, p. 17
1500	75,000		
c.1503		Very great city; after that its decline must have been very rapid	Varthema in Cordier, II, p. 377n
1600s		Had sunk into utter insignificance	Yule in Cordier, II, p. 377n
early 1800s	20,000		Petermann, 1857, p. 350
1875	14,366		Hunter

Raigarh

1662-90		Maratha capital	Imp. Gaz. India: Bombay Pres., II, pp. 141-2

Rajmahal

1592-1608		Capital of Bengal	Imp. Gaz. India: Bengal, II, p. 240
1600	100,000		
1639-55		Capital of Bengal	" " " " " "
1800	25-30,000	Said to have 20,000 houses (house-count should reflect peak in 1600s)	Buchanan in Imp. Gaz. India: Bengal, II, p. 240; Martin, 1838, II, p. 79
1901	2,047		Imp. Gaz. India: Bengal, II, p. 240

Ramavati

c.730-c.1130		A Pala capital, sometime between these dates (likely a name for either Bihar, Chunar, Gaur, Monghyr, or Nadiya)	Paul, I, p. 129

Rampur

1719-(1948)		Capital of Rohilkhand
once	100,000	
c.1850	80,000	
1872	68,301	

Imp. Gaz. India: United Provs., II, p. 451
Ency. Edinensis, IV, p. 215
Hoffmann
Balfour

Rangpur

1699-1786		Ahom capital
1794		20 miles around
c.1800	20,000	Almost
1872	14,845	

Imp. Gaz. India: Eastern Bengal and Assam, p. 588
Welsh in Shakespear, p. 55
Ency. Edinensis, IV, p. 203
Hunter

Satara

1699-1750		Maratha capital, except 1700-8
1872	25,603	

J. Campbell, XIX, pp. 291, 57b
Brockhaus, 1881, p. 560

Seringapatam

1454-1609		Capital of Mysore province
1609-1799		Capital of Mysore country
1750	60,000	
1754		Army 10,000
1774		12,000 families brought from Sira
1799	150,000	As it fell to British
1800	31,895	
1820	10,000	
1871	10,594	

Bowring, p. 54
    ''   ; Imp. Gaz. India: Mysore, p. 198

Wilks, I, p. 328
Imp. Gaz. India: Mysore, p. 165
Playfair, V, p. 496
W. Hamilton
    ''
Hunter

Shahjahanpur

1647		Founded
1800	50,000	
early 1800s	50,000	
1847	62,785	
1850	62,000	

Imp. Gaz. India: United Provs., I, p. 561

W. Hamilton
A. Shakespear, p. 93n

Sira

1638		Founded
1687-c.1720		Mogul capital for South Carnatic
1750		50,000 houses (clearly an exaggeration)
''	60,000	See 1774
1774		12,000 families moved to Seringapatam (perhaps the whole population)
1800		3,000 houses
1871	4,231	

Imp. Gaz. India: Mysore, p. 175
    ''   ''   ''   ''   ''
    ''   ''   ''   ''   p. 176

    ''   ''   ''   ''   p. 165

Ency. Edinensis, IV, p. 241
Hunter

Somnath

1000	54,000	
1025		50,000 slain in general slaughter
''		Of the defenders, 5,000 were slain, 4,000 got away
1169		Last and most elaborate restoration of its temple
early 1800s	5,000	

Srivastava, p. 17
Forbes, I, p. 77

Commissariat, p. lxi

Petermann, 1857, p. 350

Sonargaon

1338-52		Capital of East Bengal

Ferguson, II, p. 254

Srinagar

c. 630		12 by 4 *li* (2 by 2/3 miles) in area (thus, c. 450 ha.)	Hsüan Dsang, I, p. 148
1028-(now)		Capital of Kashmir	Imp. Gaz. India: Kashmir, p. 16
1605-58		Greatly favored by Mogul emperors	″ ″ ″ ″ p. 25
c.1660		No wall, but at least 2 1/2 leagues (7 1/2 miles) around (c. 900 ha. in area)	Bernier, pp. 397-8
1700	150,000	Based partly on area; cf. 1782, Cf. also 1809.	
1735-41		20,000 houses burned (whole city?)	Kaul, p. 65
1739-41		15,000 houses burned	″ ″
1750	100,000		
1756-1819		Under Afghan rule	Ency. Brit., 1910, "Kashmir"
1782		3 by 2 miles at most (c. 8 miles around); many 2 or 3-storey houses; oppressed by Afghans with 5-fold increase in taxes	G. Forster, II, p. 9-10
c.1800		8 mi. around (seems same area as in 1660)	Playfair, V, pp. 399-400
″	125,000		
1809	125,000	150-200,000 (less 1/4; cf. Elphinstone's probable over-estimate on Kabul)	Elphinstone in Blackie, "Serinugur"
c.1820	100,000		Malcolm (a), p. 444
1823		Population much diminished	Moorcroft, II, p. 123
1845	40,000	After wars, etc.	Hügel in Blackie, "Serinugur"
1850	55,000		
1871	127,400		Imp. Gaz. India: "Kashmir"

Surat

1499		Founded	Ency. Brit., 1910
1514		Important seaport	Varthema in Ency. Brit., 1910
1600	75,000	Rising steadily	Ency. Brit., 1910
1626	90,000	Main Mogul port, c. 2 Dutch miles (7-8 miles) around (c. 900 ha.)	Pelsaert, pp. 38-9
″		3rd city in Gujarat, after Ahmedabad and Cambay (perhaps in prestige)	Herbert, p. 43
1666		Many houses outside the wall	Thévenot, part 3, p. 15
1700	200,000		
1705	200,000	New wall 5 miles around (population probably includes some outside the wall, and Rander across the river)	A. Hamilton, I, pp. 88-9
1750	165,000	Including Rander; declining with rise of Bombay	
1800	130,000		
1808	125,000	28,871 houses in Surat (times 4; cf. 1816, 1818), plus Rander	W. Hamilton
1816	134,487	Including 10,081 in Rander	Imp. Gaz. India: Bombay Pres., I, p. 345; Martin, 1839, appendix, p. 114
1818		31,439 houses in Surat alone	W. Hamilton
1838		133,544 in Surat alone	Thornton
1850	99,000		
1851	99,000	89,505 plus 10,000 in Rander (c. 1870)	Imp. Gaz. India: Bombay Pres., I, p. 345; Reclus, VIII, p. 479n

Tamralipti

300s-1100s		Port of Bengal	Dey
c. 630	45,000	Capital of Bengal; 1,000 Buddhist monks and 50 Deva temples; c. 10 *li* (c. 2 miles) around (Monks times 5; temples times 800. Cf. Kanauj and Kanchi)	Hsüan Dsang, II, p. 200

Tanda

1565-95		Capital of Bengal	Abid-Ali, p. 18
1819		Scarcely a trace	W. Hamilton

Tanjore

c.1000		Chola capital	V. Smith, p. 376
1678-1855		Again a capital	Brockhaus, 1864
1850	52,000	Pre-census estimates range from 35,000 to 80,000	Ungewitter, II, p. 356; Harper
1871	52,175		Imp. Gaz. India: Madras,,II, pp. 134-5

Tatta (Thatta)

c.1100-1592		Usual capital of Sind	Imp. Gaz. India: Bombay., II, p. 249
1600	50,000	See 1810	
once		100,000 (likely exaggerated)	Ungewitter, II, p. 369
1666		Chief town of Sind	Thévenot, part 3, p. 53
1696-9		80,000 died in epidemic (may refer to district)	A. Hamilton, I, p. 75
d 1810	18,000	4 miles around (reflects peak: c. 330 ha., with possible high multiplier of 150 for a long-established seaport)	Kinneir, p. 231
c.1850	10,000		Ungewitter, II, p. 369

Thana

c.1000-c.1300		Capital of a small kingdom	Yule, pp. 395, 396n
1502		Many mosques, but trade small	Barbosa in Yule, p. 396n
1538		60 small mosques	Castro, II, p. 55
c.1580		5,000 weavers; ruins of a large city	Botero in Yule, p. 396n
c.1853	14,000		Ungewitter, II, p. 366
1872	14,299		Hunter

Thaneswar

-c.610		Capital of N. India	Dey, "Kanyakubja"
634		C. 20 li (c. 3 miles) around	Hsüan Dsang, I, p. 183
1011		200,000 (looks exaggerated)	Ungewitter, II, p. 344
1014		Sacked by Mahmud and lay desolate for centuries	Imp. Gaz. India: Madras, II, p. 203
c.1853	12,103		Petermann, 1857, p. 350

Tiruvannamalai (Unnamalepattana)

1328-1346		Hoysala capital	Heras, 1929, p. 66

Trichinopoly

-1500s		Its suburb Uraiyur was a lord's seat	Imp. Gaz. India: Madras, II, p. 203
c.1600-1740		Seat of a kingdom	Vivien, "Tritchinopoli"
1800	80,000		
1820	80,000		W. Hamilton
c.1850		35,000 with garrison (seems unduly low)	Ungewitter, II, p. 357
1850	76,000		
1871	76,530		Imp. Gaz. India: Madras, II, p. 202

Trivandrum

1875	57,611		Hunter

Udaipur

1571-(1948)		Capital of Mewar, succeeding Chitor	Imp. Gaz. India: Rajputana, p. 143
" "		Wall 4 miles around	India Tourism, rear map
1600	72,000		
1611	72,000	Standing army 12,000	Finch, p. 170
1613-c.1670		Vassal to Moguls	Vivien
c.1670-1736		Again wholly free	" ; Imp. Gaz. India: Rajputana, pp. 113-4
peak		100,000 (seems high)	Blackie
1799		Standing army 12,000 (out-of-date information?)	G. Thomas, p. 202
1818		3,000 houses	Thornton, "Oodeypoor"
1825		5 miles around	Heber in Conder, 1830's, IV, p. 98
c.1850	18,000		Ungewitter
1881	38,215		Vivien, "Oudeipour"

Ujjain

- 900		De facto capital of Malwa	Imp. Gaz. India: Central India, p. 190
-c.1010		De jure capital of Malwa	" " " " " "
-1309		Again capital of Malwa	Ency. Brit., 1875, "Malwa"
1613		One of the 5 Mogul provincial capitals	Hawkins, p. 100
c.1750-1805		Sindhia Maratha capital	Imp. Gaz. India: Central India, p. 191; Conder, 1830's, IV, p. 211
c.1800	100,000		Hassel, 1817; "Oojain"
"		6 miles around (thus, c. 600 ha. in area); mostly well-settled	Playfair, V, p. 461
c.1850		84 temples, 4 mosques	Ungewitter, II, p. 249
1881	32,932		Ency. Brit., 1910

Vatapi (now Badami)

c.550-c.750		Chalukya capital	Ency. Brit., 1910, "Chalukyas"
1901	4,482		Imp. Gaz. India: Bombay Pres., II, p. 43

Vellore

1638	95,000	Nearly 20,000 houses in Bisantagan, i.e., Vijayanagar's new capital, which had been a mere village	Mandelslo, p. 49; Heras, 1927, p. 313
1652		Fell to Moslems	Imp. Gaz. India: Madras, I, p. 493
c.1850	51,408		Blackie, suppl.
1872	38,022		Hunter

Vengi

615-1070		Eastern Chalukya capital	Ency. Brit., 1910, "Chalukyas"
996		Overrun by the Cholas	V. Smith, p. 391

Vijayanagar

1346-1565		Capital of S. India	Heras, 1929, pp. 110-1; Sewell, p. 196
1356-1568		Greatly expanded, and walled	Heras, 1929, pp. 58-9
1379-1404		A new section built	" " p. 47
1400	350,000		

1443	450,000	1st in the world; 90,000 males able to bear arms; 60 miles around (probably less; cf. Calicut and Goa)	Conti, pp. 5-6
"		7 fortified walls, one within the other; 2 parasangs (c. 7 miles) in diameter (thus, c. 22 miles around—however, cf. 1880); its density would be low as outer 3 walls enclosed fields and gardens as well as houses	Abd-er-Razzaq in Mahajan, part 1, p. 265
1500	500,000	Its empire still expanding	
1565		Defended by 80,000 men	Caesar Frederick in J. Harris, I, p. 276
"		Wholly looted, partly burned, but by no means destroyed	Heras, 1927, pp. 225-8
1567		Still large	Caesar Frederick in Badger, p. 126n
1589		Larger than Rome; 100,000 houses (probably refers to peak)	P. Páez in Sewell, p. 290
1600		A small village	Heras, 1927, p. 240
1628		4 miles around	Herbert, p. 346
c.1880		Known ruins cover 24 sq. km (2,400 ha.)	Reclus, VIII, p. 504

Vikrampura, Bengal

-c.1175		Capital of the Chandra, Varman, and Sena dynasties	Paul, pp. 104-5, 129

Warangal

1067-1323		Kakatiya capital	Wilks, I, p. 13; Heras, 1929; pp. 62ff
" "		Fort 12,546 yards around (7.1 miles, enclosing c. 800 ha.)	H. Khusrau, p. xxii
1300	100,000	Based partly on area	
1323		50,000 males slew the women and children to spare them from capture, then fought on against the Moslems till slain (This account was told of Vijayanagar's fore-runner Annegondi, but as Heras pointed out, the tale of Vijayanagar's founding was closely related to the fall of Warangal. So big a population seems impossible for Annegondi but suitable for Warangal)	Heras, 1929, pp. 36-7
1300s-1422		Capital of a lordship	Imp. Gaz. India: Hyderabad, pp. 163-4
1400	42,000		
1422	42,000	7,000 slain as it fell (times 6, as militia)	Ferishta(a), p. 102

Bhatgaon

880		12,000 houses at foundation	Lévi, II, p. 63
1700s		12,000 houses	" " p. 65
1905	30-40,000	Actual urban population	" " "

Katmandu

724		Founded with 18,000 houses	" p. 52
1480-1769		Nepal split into 3 kingdoms, reducing Katmandu's importance	Landon, pp. 39, 63-4
c.1800		Estimates of 20,000 and 50,000 people, 5,000 houses (in this instance surely urban)	Buchanan-Hamilton and Kirkpatrick in Hassel, 1819, IX, p. 351
"	25,000	Based on houses	
1905	40,000	Actual urban population; 1 sq. miles	Lévi, II, p. 55

Patan

700s		Important	Reclus, VIII, p. 182
1768		1st in Nepal	Lévi II, p. 62
1803	24,000		W. Hamilton, "Lalita Patan"
1920		104,928 in its whole area	Landon, p. 257

[a]Nepalese data, unless otherwise specified, include nonurban areas (Lévi, II, p. 62). In 1920 the districts of Bhatgaon and Katmandu had 93,176 and 108,805, respectively (Landon, p. 257), whereas in 1905 the actual urban population of these places was estimated by Lévi to be 30-40,000 and 40,000 respectively.

Polonnaruwa

769-1235		Capital	Tennent, I, pp. 400, 414
c.1000		Kingdom in anarchy	" " p. 402
1065		4-mile wall built (enclosing c. 260 ha.)	Mitton, p. 179
1153-96		Peak; area reached 112 sq. miles (some rural)	Raven-Hart, p. 72; Paranavitana, pp. 4-5
1200		Built-up area in stone c. 2 x 1 miles (enclosing c. 600 ha. Likely thatched huts beyond)	Tennent, II, map p. 585 and text, p. 587
1200	140,000	From stone-built area, compared to Majapahit	
1215		Largely destroyed	Raven-Hart, p. 78

Amarapura

1783-1857		Capital, except 1823-1837	Harvey, p. 367
1785		20,000 settlers brought from Arakan	" p. 268
peak		200,000 (perhaps slightly high)	Sangermano in Harvey, p. 265n
1800	175,000		Cox in Fortia, III, p. 455
1810	170,000		Ency. Brit., 1853, "Ummera-poora"
1819		Wholly destroyed by fire	" " " "
1827		30,000 (probably within wall)	Hamilton in Fortia, III, p. 455
1835	90,000	26,670 within wall	Hunter
1839		Mostly destroyed by earthquake	Ency. Brit., 1853, "Ummera-poora"
1891	11,004		Imp. Gaz. India: Burma, III, p. 89

Arakan (now Mrauk-U)

c.900-994		Capital of Arakan kingdom	Spearman, II, p. 7
1433-1785		" " " "	Harvey, p. 371
c.1440		Very large	Conti, p. 10
1599		Got 3,000 households from Pegu and profited immensely from its sack of that city	Harvey, p. 183
1600	125,000		
1631	160,000	Peak; ruins 14 miles around	Manrique, pp. 217, 218n
1690-1785		Kingdom in anarchy	Brockhaus, 1864
1700	100,000		
1785		20,000 taken to Amarapura	Harvey, p. 268
c.1800	16,000		Hamilton in Fortia, III, p. 482n
1825		18,000 stone houses (clearly left over from peak)	Vivien
1835	8-10,000		Thornton, "Arracan"
1877	2,068		Hunter

Ava

1364-1526		Capital	Balfour
c.1440		15 miles around (probably lower; cf. Calicut, Goa)	Conti, p. 11
once		8-10 miles around	New International Ency.
1601-1837		Again capital, except 1752-66 and 1783-1823	Balfour; Imp. Gaz. India: Burma, p. 202
1755	8,000		Hunter
1783		Wholly abandoned to provide people for Amarapura	Sangermano, p. 68; Symes, p. 571
1795		About 4 miles around	Symes, p. 570
1800		Not above 1,000 families	Pennant, p. 7
1826	50,000		Crawford in Harvey, p. 264n

Chittagong—see under India

Martaban

1269-1323	Capital of Pegu kingdom	Spearman, II, p. 356
1500s	Equaled Pegu in commerce	Scott, p. 91
1540	40,000 houses and 2,000 temples destroyed and 60,000 slain, but report seems ex-agerrated	Spearman, II, p. 356
1661	3,000 killed for desertion; 6,000 remaining ousted the Burmese, burned the city, and fled to Siam	Harvey, pp. 197-8

Pagan

742-1280		Capital	Imp. Gaz. India: Burma, I, pp. 292, 417
c.1050		30,000 brought from Thaton	Harvey, p. 28
1200		Peak	Imp. Gaz. India: Burma, I, p. 290
"		16 square miles in area at peak; 800 temples	Harvey, p. 70; Beylié, p. 253
"	180,000	Area = Mandalay's in 1901	Ency. Brit., 1910
c.1300		Abandoned	Syme, p. 570

Pegu

700s-1000s		Capital of kingdom	Imp. Gaz. India: Burma, I, pp. 274-5
1280-1534		Talaing capital	" " " " " " ; Spearman, II, p. 356
1400	60,000		
c.1440	60,000	12 miles around (probably 1/4 less; cf. Calicut and Goa. 1,300 ha., times 44 as at Pagan)	Conti, p. 15
1534-81		Capital of all Burma	Imp. Gaz. India: Burma, I, pp. 274-5
1596	150,000	But only 30,000 survived the Portuguese sack	Pennant, p. 3
1599		Sacked by Arakan; 3,000 households removed	Harvey, p. 183
1600		Nearly deserted	" "
1613-34		Capital of Burma	" pp. 191, 193
1740-57		Capital of a coastal dynasty	Imp. Gaz. India: Burma, I, pp. 274-5
1757		Inhabitants all removed; houses all destroyed	Symes, p. 562
1790		Resettled	" "
1878	4,337		Hunter,

Toungoo

614-c.975		Capital of a small kingdom	Sangermano, pp. 57-8
1299-1510		Seat of a lordship	Imp. Gaz. India: Burma, I, p. 375
1510-34		Seat of a kingdom	" " " " " pp. 275, 375
1596-1612		Seat of a local kingdom	" " " " " p. 375
1872	10,732		" " " " " p. 389

Ayutia (Dvaravati, Hong Sano, Ayudhaya)

469-c.650		Capital of a kingdom	W. Graham, p. 29
c.1189-1350		Again capital of a kingdom	" "
1350-1767		Capital of Siam, except 1463-1488	Wood, p. 250
1500	150,000		
1545	150,000	Assuming 1/3 of city burned when 10,050 houses did, with 5 per house	" p. 104
1569		All but 10,000 removed	" "
1600	100,000		
1636	120,000	Wall 2 leagues (6 miles) around the island city, plus mainland suburbs equal to the city (thus, c. 1,200 ha. in area, assuming 100 per ha.)	Mandelslo, p. 98
1700	150,000		
1720	160,000	10 miles around (thus, c. 1,600 ha. in area, times 100); 50,000 monks	A. Hamilton, II, pp. 86, 88
1750	150,000		
1767		30-200,000, some from nearby towns	V. Thompson, p. 27; J. Bowring, II, p. 347
"		Destroyed	Wood, p. 250
1855	30,000	20-40,000	Bowring, I, p. 15-6

Bangkok

1685-1766		A provincial capital	Chaumont, p. 40; Turpin, p. 298
1767-(now)		Capital of Siam, at suburban Dhonburi till 1782, then at Bangkok itself	Ency. Brit., 1910
1800	40,000		
1809	48,000	8,000 paraded at a coronation	Chula, p. 119
1822	50,000		Crawfurd in Skinner, p. 81
1828	77,300	Corrected by Skinner for an obvious extra decimal	Tomlinson in Skinner, p. 81
1849	160,154	5,457 died of cholera	Malloch in Skinner, p. 81; Waugh, p. 74-5
1850	160,000		

Chiengmai

1296	25,000	Founded; 2,000 by 1,600 meters (320 ha. low density for new wall)	Wells, p. 12
1345-1662		Capital of a kingdom of N. Siam	Jumsai, p. 52; Wood, p. 193
c.1590		Very great town; well-peopled	Finch, p. 38
1776-96		Abandoned	Wood, pp. 266 and 274
1850	50,000		
1854	50,000		Paillegoix, I, p. 45

Chiengrai

1268-1345		Capital of a kingdom, from 1281 ruling all of N. Siam	Jumsai, pp. 42, 50

Haripunjai (now Lampun)

654-1281		Capital of a kingdom of N. Siam	Jumsai, pp. 49-50

Sukotai

-1238		Capital of Cambodia's northern province	Wood, p. 51
1238-1350		Capital of Siam	" pp. 51, 59
" "		Wall 3,400 *brasses* (3 1/2-4 miles)	Madrolle, 1926, p. 284

(Cambodia, Champa, Annam, Laos)

Angkor

889-1431		Capital of Cambodia	Coedès, p. 3
1177		Sacked by Champa	Briggs, p. 207
1177-		Feverish period of building activity	" p. 210
c.1200		Peak	Coedès, pp. 84-107
"		Exceeded any in Europe; wall 13.2 km (8.3 miles around or c. 1,100 ha. in area)	Briggs, p. 219
"	150,000	Based on area and presence of numerous construction workers	
1300		Still renowned for its wealth	" p. 250
"	125,000		
1357		90,000 removed by Siamese	Madrolle, 1926, p. 103
1400	50,000		
1404		40,000 removed by Siamese	" " "
1433		Abandoned	" " "

Hanoi

767		Founded	Bouinais, II, p. 523
c.950-1558		Capital of Annam kingdom, except 1408-26	Mesny, pp. 35, 63-9, 88; Bouinais, 1885, p. 685
1010	25,000	4.7-km. wall built	Madrolle, 1907, part 3, p. 5
1665		Equal to a middle-sized Italian city	Marini in Silvestre, p. 27
c.1700	40,000		Bissachère in Silvestre, p. 27
"		20,000 houses (perhaps an exaggeration)	Dampier in Silvestre, p. 27
1821		Twice Bangkok's size (seems slightly high)	Finlayson, p. 312
1850	75,000		
1884-1885		Declined probably 1/3	Ency. Brit., 1875-1889, XXIII, p. 440
1891	51,000		Vivien, suppl.

Hué

1558-1884		Capital of Annam	Bouinais, II, p. 685
1774-1801		Held by rebels	Vivien
1793		Garrison of 30,000	Macartney, p. 146
c.1800		C. 5 leagues (15 miles) around, but unwalled	Fortia, III, p. 106
c.1850	60,000		Blackie
1894	50,325		Vivien, suppl.

Indrapura, Cambodia

598	Became capital of a fief	Briggs, p. 45
c. 802	Briefly capital of Cambodia	" p. 33

Indrapura, Champa

c. 700	Capital of Champa	Briggs, p. 67
875-(c.1100's)	Capital of Champa; cf. Vijaya	" p. 90

Lovek (Lawek)

1468-1593	Usual capital of Cambodia	Leclère, pp. 233-6, 288
1593	90,000, the whole province's population, taken away captive	" p. 288

Luang Prabang

-1325-c.1550		Capital of Laos	V. Thompson, p. 363
1500	50,000	Cf. 1870	
1700-1893		Capital of part of Laos	" "
1867	15,000		Garnier, p. 296
c.1870	20,000	Large enough for 50,000	Vivien

Oudong (Udong)

1594-1866		Capital of Cambodia	Ency. Brit., 1910, "Cambodia"
1854	12,000		Paillegoix, I, p. 30
c.1890	16,000	In ruin	Vivien

Pnompenh (Phnom Penh, with h's silent)

1389-1431		Capital of Cambodia	Leclère, pp. 218-21
1866-		Again capital	Vivien
c.1885	30-35,000		" suppl.

Saigon

-1859		Capital of Champa's southern provinces	Ency. Brit., 1910
1774		20,000 slain in a civil war	Barrow, 1806, p. 250
1778		Its big suburb, Cholon, founded	Bouinais, I, p. 299
1850	50,000		
1859	50,000		Brockhaus, 1864
1881-3	53,273	Including 39,925 in Cholon	Bouinais, I, pp. 296, 300

Vijaya (Binhdinh)

1069		2,560 families; 3rd in Champa	Maspèro, p. 26
by 1144-c.1300		Capital of Champa	Briggs, pp. 192, 241
1190, 1194		Overrun by Cambodia	" pp. 215-16
1283		Overrun by Mongols	" p. 241

Virapura

(c.1300)-1471		Capital of Champa; cf. Vijaya	Maspèro, p. 25

Achin

c.1514-1874		Seat of a sultanate	Ency. of Islam, 1897
c.1575		6 times greater than in 1621	Beulieu in J. Harris, p. 253
			J. Harris, I, p. 255
c.1603		New king brought 22,000 from other places trying to repopulate it, but in 1621 only 1,500 of these remained	
1699-1874		Its kingdom rapidly decayed	Ency. Brit., 1875
peak	45,000	7-8,000 houses	Wilson, p. 129
1700	45,000		
1750	45,000		
1800	40,000		
1800s	36,000		Blackie

Bantam

1600	50,000	Capital of a strong kingdom	Ency. Brit., 1910
1630	50,000	1st in Java (hence larger than Surabaja); nearly 2 miles long (if 5.5 mi. around, enclosing c. 500 ha.)	Herbert, p. 364
1683		Conquered by Dutch	Ency. Brit., 1910

Batavia (till 1619 Jakarta, now Djakarta)

1619		Settled by Dutch	Ency. Brit., 1910
1700	52,550	Including suburbs	Raffles, II, appendix ii
1750	94,875	" "	" " appendix iii
1793	127,418	" "	" " "
1800	92,000		
1804	72,830	" "	" " "
1844	60,850		Brockhaus, 1864
1850	71,000		
1879	121,547		" 1892

Brunei

1225	10,000		Chau Ju-kua, p. 155
1521		25,000 families (probably exaggerated)	Pigafetta, p. 189
1578		40,000 houses (perhaps a district figure)	Enci. Universal, "Borneo"
c.1600		2,000 houses	Mandelslo, p. 124
1750	40,000		
1770	40,000		Blundell, p. 76
1800	30,000		
1851	14,000		" p. 68

Demak

1477-1577		Main Javanese capital	Raffles, II, pp. 136, 230

Gresik (Grisée)

c. 750		Capital of Java	Briggs, p. 65
1523	30,000	(Probably in decline after the fall of Majapahit, 1486)	Urdaneta in Meilnik-Roelofsz, p. 270
1600		Important port	Ency. Brit., 1910, XV, p. 290
1601		1,000 houses	Noort in Meilnik-Roelofsz, p. 270
pre-1800		Forerunner of Surabaja	Thorn, p. 303
1812	17,555	In the "division" (probably the town)	Raffles, II, p. 274
1815		Small town	W. Hamilton

Jogjakarta (Jokjarkarta)

1753-		Capital of part of Java	Raffles, II, p. 230
1800	90,000		
1812		A bit less than Surakarta	" , p. 63n
1850	55,000		
1858	50,000		Kloeden, p. 589
1880	44,999		Brockhaus, 1881, "Dschokjo-karta"

Kertasura

1677-1749	Capital of a sultanate, forerunner of Jogjakarta	Raffles, II, p. 230

Majapahit

c. 550		3-4 *li* (1/2-2/3 miles) around	Stutterheim, p. 7
1292-1486		Capital of Indonesia	Krom, pp. 354, 449
1300	40,000		
1365		Royal compound much smaller than 18th-century Surakarta's or Jogjakarta's	Pigeaud, IV, p. 14
"		Stone ruins c. 4 miles around (c. 250 ha.)	Stutterheim, map p. 124
1400	50,000	Presumably larger than its port Gresik; and cf. 1365	

Mataram

1614-77		Capital of Java's strongest kingdom	Raffles, II, p. 230
1667		15,000 slain as it was overrun	" " pp. 164-5

Pajajaran

c.1160-1292	Capital of Java (dates converted from Saka—era dates given by Raffles)	Raffles, II, pp. 94, 98; Krom, p. 354

Pajang

1577-1614	Capital of Mataram kingdom	Raffles, II, p. 230

Palembang

c.670-c.750		Capital of Srivijaya (Sumatra and part of Java)	Nilakanta, 1949, pp. 34, 52
c. 800		Perhaps again capital	Briggs, p. 68
1820	25,000		W. Hamilton
1849	40,000		Pahud, p. 5
1850	40,000		
1858	40,000		Kloeden, p. 575

Pasar Gede

c.1568-1618	Capital of Mataram kingdom	Raffles, II, pp. 142, 230

Prambanan (Brambanan)

778	A temple built	Briggs, p. 65
978-1080	Capital of Java (dates converted from Saka—era dates given by Raffles)	Raffles, II, p. 80

Semarang

1812	20,000	Raffles, II, p. 63n
1845	50,000	Blackie
1850	40,000	
1858	30,000	Kloeden, p. 588
1882	65,000	Brockhaus, 1881-7

Surabaja (Soerabaya)

1590		A hamlet	Meilink-Roelofsz, p. 269
1600		Seat of a kingdom	" p. "
"	50,000	To 60,000 (perhaps slightly high)	" p. 270
1812	24,574		Raffles, II, p. 277
1849	60-70,000		Hageman cites in "Dud Soerabaia" p. 3
1850	60,000		
1858	130,000	(Perhaps too high)	Kloeden, p. 588
1882	121,047		Brockhaus, 1881-7

Surakarta (Soerakarta)

1749-		Capital of a sultanate	Raffles, II, pp. 230-1
1800	105,000		
1812	105,000	Estimate	" " p. 63n
1845	100,000		Blackie
1850	100,000		
1880	124,041		Brockhaus, 1881

Malacca

1252		Founded	Larousse
-1511		Seat of a kingdom	Ency. Brit., 1910
1509		4,000 foreign merchants	Pires in Wheatley, p. 312
"		Only 1 chief mosque	Pires in Bastin and Winks, p. 35
1511		100,000 (probably too high)	Ljungstedt, p. 123
early 1600s		4 churches, 13 blocks	Faria, I, map p. 148
1641	20,000	Before the Dutch siege, 2,706 after	Bastin, Winks, p. 111
1678	4,884		" " "
1822		22,000 in the territory	W. Hamilton

Manila

1571		2,000 townsmen opposed the invading Spaniards	Census of Philippines, I, p. 418
1591	30,640	Including two suburbs	" " " " p. 421
1600	30,000		
1604		1,200 Spanish houses; wall 1 league (3 miles) around	Morga, pp. 311, 314
1639		15,000 Chinese	Mandeslo, p. 35
1697	30,000	3,000 (adult male) souls, and 3,000 in a Chinese suburb; 15 additional suburbs (rural ones; cf. 1870)	Gemelli, pp. 400-1
1700	30,000	Trade as much as c. 1600	Dermigny, I, p. 100
1750	50,000		
1762	54,000	Comprised of 40,000 Malays, 10,000 Chinese, 3,000 Spaniards, and 900 soldiers	J. Wright, p. 3
1800	77,000		
1814	85,000		Ortiz, p. 73
1850	114,000		
c. "		140,000 (must include rural districts; cf. next item)	Blackie
1870	129,582	Including 6 suburbs within the commune and 5 outside it	Vivien

Metalanim (Nan Matol)

| c.1180-c.1430 | Occupied, at least for ceremonial fires, as shown by carbon-14 dates | A. Long, p. 253 |
| "   " | 11 square miles | J. Brown, pp. 100, 103, 107 |

Sydney

1846	38,358	Harper
1850	48,000	
1851	51,000	Daniel, I, p. 863

Kyongju

668-919		Capital	Longford, pp. 84, 87
c.1430	18,000	1,553 households; 5,898 adult males	Se-jong, p. 101
1597		Sacked	Longford, p. 188

Pyongyang

668		20,000 removed by Chinese; Chinese garrison of 20,000 placed here	Hulbert, I, pp. 113-4
1894	80,000	Fell to 15,000 in war	Terry, p. 755

Seoul (Hanyang)

1360-(now)		Capital, except 1384-1388	Osgood, pp. 193-4
1390s		9.5 mile wall built (enclosing c. 1,450 ha.); 200,000 worked on it	" p. 194; Longford, p. 126
1400	100,000		
c.1430	103,328	In 17,015 households	Pek, p. 82
1500	150,000	After a century of prosperity for Korea	Osgood, pp. 195-6
1593		Almost a desert	Hulbert, II, p. 16
1700	170,000	Korea's population c. 1/10 less than in 1800	Osgood, p. 203n
1750	183,000	Korea's population c. 1/30 less than in 1800	" "
1793	190,027		Petermann, 1872, p. 87
1800	190,000		
1850	194,000		
1881	199,127		Brockhaus, 1892, "Korea"

Songdo (now Kaesong)

918-1360		Capital, except 1232-1270	Osgood, pp. 16, 188, 193
c.1430	24,000	4,819 households; 8,372 adult males	Se-jong, p. 6
c.1900	60,000		Ency. Brit., 1910, "Korea"

China[a]

Amoy

1350		Probably not yet founded	Crow, p. 231
1647-80		Capital for Koxinga and his successor	American Cyclopaedia
1624-1730		Open to Dutch commerce	Enci. Italiana
1832		144,893 (in unspecified area)	Hsia Men Chih, V, p. 3
1850	85,000		
1862		De facto reopened to foreign trade	Enci. Italiana
c.1870		185,000 with suburbs (probably some rural)	Williams, I, p. 136
1879	88,000		Reclus, VII, p. 488n
c.1900		9 miles around (thus, c. 1,300 ha. in area)	Ency. Brit., 1910

Anking

1290		Provincial capital	Cordier, p. 157
c.1900		Estimates of 40,000 and 70,000	Richard, p. 150; Crow, p. 119

Canton

742		221,500 in 13 *hsiens* comprising a *chung*	24 Histories, XXI, pp. 16, 102
795-		Foreign vessels deserted it for some years	Berncastle, II, p. 111
877	120,000?	120,000 aliens killed, also all Chinese	Renaudot, pp. 51-2
1000	100,000		
1067	120,000	6-mile wall built (c. 900 ha., times 100, plus 1/4 for houseboats; cf. 1836)	Ljungstedt, p. 226; Crow
906-1279	206,694	In 49,726 households in the *fu* sometime during Sung period; later household counts of 64,796 and 78,465 under the Sung may be inflated by war refugees	Kwangchow Fu, XXVI
1200	200,000		
1279-		Commerce stopped a few years	Berncastle, II, p. 113
1300	300,000	As trade throve	
1325	330,000	Equal to 3 Venices	Odoric in Yule, p. 105n
1400	300,000	After war of 1355-68	
1418-33		3 Chinese voyages to Africa; i.e., trade open	"T'oung Pao," 1915
by 1500	250,000	Foreign trade forbidden	Bowring, I, p. 75
1517		Opened to Portuguese trade	Ency. Brit., 1910
1600	350,000		
c.1648	385,649	In the *fu*	Kwangtung Tung Chih, II, p. 1,755
1650		100,000 men slain	Berncastle (1850, II, p. 117)
c.1665	224,216	In the *fu* in the period 1662-72	Kwangtung Tung Chih (1934, II, p. 1,755)
1700	300,000		
c. "		Got monopoly on foreign trade	Phipps, p. 2
1720		900,000 estimated from food supply (a poor method, as much food was in transit)	A. Hamilton, II, p. 128

[a] Early Chinese data on population are deficient in many respects, and urban data *per se* are frequently lacking altogether. Population figures, as reported in local gazetteers, usually refer to a *hsien*, a county-like administrative unit, or to a *fu*, a grouping of *hsiens* into a larger administrative unit. Some *hsiens*, however, may coincide with the urban area, and in certain cases a city may be comprised of two or more *hsiens*. The *fu* unit is never purely urban, but the capital of a *fu*, especially if it is also a provincial or higher capital, is commonly called *fu* even though it is actually a city. In general, the Chinese data must be regarded with caution, and each urban case must be considered on its own merits.

1700-50		Tea-trade increased 5-fold	Phipps, p. 100
1750	500,000		
1700-1800		Tea-trade increased 25-fold	" p. 100
c.1800	800,0000		
1805		1,000,000 estimate	Richenet in Fortia, III, p. 36n
1830s		1,236,000, very rough estimate; wall 6 miles long, but as many lived outside as inside (c. 1,165 ha.)	Ljungstedt, pp. 234-5
1836		84,000 dwelling boats	Phipps, p. 133n
1838	800-900,000	Chinese say over 1 million; 40,000 prostitutes	Dobel in Fortia, III, p. 36n
1850	800,000	After Shanghai opened	
1895	560,000	Also 30,000 transients	Madrolle, 1916, p. 31

Changan, see Sian

Changchow (Lungchi)

1502		95,011 in its *hsien*	Lungchi Hsien Chii, p. 55
1612		63,689 in its *hsien*	" " " "
c.1644		26,514 in its *hsien*	" " " "
1800s		In decline	Columbia Lippincott Gaz.
1948	62,399		" " "

Changchun

c.1900	80,000		New Int. Ency., XIV, p. 775

Changsha

c. 750		192,657 in its *chung* (like a *fu*)	24 Histories, XIX, p. 14,692
769-906		Capital of Hunan province	Madrolle, 1916, p. 69
1600	50,000		
1637	50,000	New wall 9 km (5.5 miles) around (thus, c. 500 ha. in area)	" " " ; Enci. Universal
c.1650	7,242	In its *hsien* (perhaps after a sack)	Hunan Tung Chih, XXII, p. 14
c.1900	230,000		Crow, p. 129

Chaochow (now Chaohsien)

c.1725		Of recent growth	Du Halde, p. 168
1794	50,000	10,000 families; 1/2 as large as Canton	Guignes, I, p. 273
1800	50,000		
c.1870		6 km (3.7 miles) around	Vivien, "Tchao-tcheou"
c.1925		250,000 (perhaps an exaggeration)	Cressey, 1934, p. 344

Chengtu

c. 750	81,000	16,256 households in its *hsien* in 742-755	24 Histories, XIX, p. 14,703
800	88,000		
881-6	100,000	8-mile wall built (thus, c. 1,000 ha. in area)	T. Carter, p. 67
1290		215,888 in its *lu* (perhaps 1/2 in the city; cf. Kingtehchen, Sian)	25 Histories: New Yüan
1300	110,000	Very prosperous epoch	
c.1370	65,000	130,953 in its *fu* (perhaps 1/2 in city; cf. 1600)	Szechwan Tung Chih, LVII, p. 1
1400	88,000		
1393-1491		Szechwan grew 70%	Enci. Italiana, "Cina"
1500	112,000		
1491-1578		Szechwan grew 19%	" " "

1600	130,000	Still within wall of 881	
1646		600,000 slain (in *fu*, or maybe all Szechwan)	Martini (1665, p. 302)
1728		50,934 families in its *fu*, comprising 16 *hsiens*	Szechwan Tung Chih (1815, LVIII, p. 1)
c.1725		Not yet wholly recovered	DuHalde (1741, p. 233)
1796		386,397 in its *hsien* (new administrative area with new dynasty)	Szechwan Tung Chih (1815, LVIII, p. 1)
c.1800	110,000	Present wall built 9 miles around (thus, c. 1,300 ha. in area; cf. 1887)	Crow (1915, p. 138); Viven (1879-1895) "Tching-tou"
1850	240,000		
1887	350,000	Census; urban area 25 kilometers (16 miles) around (thus, c. 4,000 ha. in area)	Vivien (1879-1895) "Tching-tou"

Chinkiang

by 900	30,000	Wall built 26 *li* (4.3 miles) long (thus, c. 300 ha. in area)	Clennell, p. 256
1300	42,000		
1331	42,000	69,325 in 15,758 families (probably in its *fu*; cf. 1644)	" "
1600	39,000		
c.1640	39,811		Kiangnan Tung Chih, X, p. 21
c.1644	44,256	In its *hsien*; 71,910 in its *fu*	" " " " "
1688		Only a league around, but considerable commerce	DuHalde, I, p. 83
1700	68,000		
1735	84,000	138,176 in its *fu* (cf. 1644)	Kiangnan Tung Chih, X, p. 21
1750	90,000		
1800	106,000		
1850	130,000		
c.1860		Wall 4 miles around, but suburbs extended 1/2 mile	Mayers, pp. 421
c.1870	130-150,000		Brockhaus, 1881, "Kiangsu"

Chüanchow (Chinchiang, now Tsinkiang)

800s		Began trading abroad	Hirth & Rockhill, p. 17
1292		One of the world's two main ports	Polo, p. 237n
1300	100,000		
1325	100,000	Twice the size of Bologna	Odoric in Yule, p. 108
1340		Perhaps the world's chief port (he had not yet seen Hangchow)	Ibn Battuta, p. 287
1600	56,000		
1608	56,159	In Chinchiang *hsien*	Chuanchow Fu Chih, II, p. 18
1645		Its people massacred	Martini, p. 297
1700	43,000		
1750	44,000		
1761	43,727	In Chinchiang *hsien*	Chüanchow Fu Chih, i II, p. 5
1850s		Wiped out by Taipings	Collier's Ency.

Chungking

1600	36,000		Vivien, "Tchoungking"
1758	16,504		Pa Hsien Chih, I, p. 449
1761		5-mile wall built	Crow, p. 137
1796		218,079 in its *hsien*	Pa Hsien Chih, I, p. 449
c.1850	200,000		Sarel in Petermann, 1861, p. 420
c.1870	250,000		Brockhaus, 1881

Fatshan (Nanhai)

Year	Population	Notes	Source
1600	50,000	Growing with nearby Canton	
c.1667	59,044	In 1662-1672	Kwangtung Tung Chih, II, p. 1,755
1695		2 miles along each riverbank	Gemelli, p. 282
1700	90,000		
c.1725		3 leagues (9 miles) around (thus, c. 1,300 ha. in area)	Duhalde, p. 240
1750	130,000	Based on area	
c.1800	175,000	200,000 (possibly slightly exaggerated; cf. 1846)	Guignes in Balbi
1846	175,000	1/4-1/3 size of Canton (without latter's houseboats)	anon. in "Chinese Repository," 1846, p. 62
1850	175,000		
1931	163,314		Cressey, 1955, p. 219

Fuchow (Hokchiu)

Year	Population	Notes	Source
742		75,876 in 10 *hsiens*	24 Histories, XXI, p. 16,094
1283		Succeeded Chüanchow as provincial capital	
1300	50,000	Based on area (cf. 1368)	
1368		6.5 mile wall built (thus, c. 700 ha. in area)	Enci. Italiana; New Int. Ency.
1381	81,164	In Min and Houkuan *hsiens* (equal to walled area)	Fuchow Fu Chih, I, p. 200
1400	81,000		
1500	83,000		
1512	83,904	In Min and Houkuan *hsiens*	" " " " "
c.1573	76,530	In Min and Houkuan *hsiens*	" " " " "
1600	76,000		
c.1660	54,730	In Min and Houkuan *hsiens* (after a war)	" " " " p. 195
1751		83,411 in the same two *hsiens* (may exclude some suburbs)	" " " " "
1832		Perhaps big as Ningpo	Gutzlaff, pp. 196-200
1846		About double Ningpo's size (but cf. 1832); 20,000 in a suburb	G. Smith, pp. 206, 208
1850	250,000		
1853		De facto opened to European trade	Ency. Brit., 1910
1867-73		Naval arsenal built	Enci. Italiana
1874	250,000	Wall 5 miles around, but 3-mile area from walls to river wholly built up; others lived on the river (thus, urban area probably c. 12 miles around or c. 2,300 ha. in area, times 110; cf. 1368-1381	Ency. Brit., 1878
1931	322,725		Cressey, 1934, p. 344

Hangchow

Year	Population	Notes	Source
591	60,000	First wall made, 36 *li* (6 miles; thus c. 600 ha. in area)	Crow, p. 94
893	220,000	New wall, 70 *li* (11 2/3 miles; thus c. 2,200 ha. in area)	" "
1132-1276		Capital	G. Moule, pp. 4-5
c.1170	145,808		Balazs, p. 233n
1200	255,000		
1201	260,000	52,000 houses burned (probably whole city; cf. similar loss in 1208; houses here perhaps mean households or dwellings)	" "
1208		58,092 dwellings burned	" "

c.1250	320,489		Balazs, p. 233n
1273	432,046		" "
1300	432,000		
1325		Big enough to hold 12 cities such as Venice or Padua	Odoric in Yule, p. 115
1340		1st in world	Pegolotti, p. 289
1350	432,000	1st in world; 72,000 militia (times 6)	Ibn Battuta, pp. 287, 293
1360		12-mile wall built during prolonged war (would enclose c. 2,300 ha.)	Cloud, p. 6
1400	325,000		
c.1440	360,000	15-mile wall built (thus, c. 3,600 ha. in area; Conti claims a 30-mile wall, but cf. Peking)	Conti, p. 15
1500	375,000	Prior to Japanese raids on Chinese coast	
1577	350,000	Perhaps 70,000 houses (times 5; cf. 1201)	González de M., p. 59
1600	350,000	Before Manchu conquest (cf. Soochow)	
c.1657	281,851	In the *fu*	Chekiang Tung Chih, II, pp. 1,364-5
1681	292,420	In the *fu*	" " " " "
1700	292,000		
1731	322,300	In the *fu*	" " " " "
1750	350,000		
1793		A bit smaller than Peking	Macartney in González de. M., p. 173
1795	500,000	60 *li* or 6 leagues (18 miles) around (thus, c. 5,000 ha. in area); houses only 1-story high	Braam, II, p. 212
1800	500,000		
1850	700,000		
c.1850	700,000		Blackie
1862		600,000 or 4/5 the population killed	Cloud, p. 8

Hsinking (now Changchun)

1450		Manchu power rising	Griffis, p. 83
-1621		Manchu capital before Mukden	Crow, p. 156

Hsüchow (Süchow)

c.1400	60,000	6-mile wall built (thus, c. 600 ha. in area)	Madrolle, 1912, p. 435
c.1644		73,961 in its *hsien*	Chiangnan Tung Chih, X, p. 30
1850	60,000		
c.1880	60,000		Lippincott, 1898, "Hoo-chou"

Hwaian

1688		Larger than Yangchow	Boures *et al.* in DuHalde, I, p. 85
1700	65,000	See Yangchow	
1922	180,000	Estimate	Cressey, 1934, p. 300

Hweining

1151		Kin western capital	Mailla, VIII, p. 551; Yule, p. cxvii

Jehol (now Chengteh)

1703-1820		Favorite royal residence	Crow, p. 172

1703-1820		6 miles around (c. 600 ha. in area)	Ency. Brit., 1910
1782	41,496	In the *fu*	Chengte Fu Chih, III, p. 729
1800	68,000		
1827	110,171	In the *fu*	" " " " "
1850	70,000		
1866	40,000		Williamson in Reclus, VII, p. 221n

Kaifeng (Bienliang, Pienliang)

781		Built as provincial capital, of nearly 3 sq. miles (c. 750 ha.)	Eberhard, p. 48
800	75,000	Based on area	
907-60		Capital of part of China	Gov't of Japan, IV, p. 87
955		16.6 sq. miles (c. 4,300 ha.) in area	Eberhard, p. 48
960-1127		Capital of China	Crow, p. 145; Favier, p. 25
1000	400,000	Based on area and China's stability 1000-1102	Mailla, VIII
1102	442,000	In the *fu* (16 *hsiens*)	24 Histories, XXVI, p. 19,992
1126	420,000	70,000 soldiers (times 6)	Mailla, VIII, p. 447
1200	150,000		
1215-27		Kin capital	Ency. Brit., 1797, "China"
1232	240,000	40,000 (or 30,000) militia	" " " Harlez, p. 263
"		900,000 (90,000?) died	Mailla, IX, p. 170
"		Taken without massacre	Lamb, 1927, p. 190
1642		200,000 or 300,000 (i.e., whole *fu*; cf. 1659) drowned in flood to break a siege	Mailla, X, p. 477; Grosier, p. 56
1659		261,395 in the *fu* (surely few urban; cf. 1766-1800)	Honan Tung Chih, II, p. 10
1700	60,000		
1750	78,000		
1751		366,065 in the *fu*	" " " " "
1766		366,704 in the *fu*	" " " " "
c.1800	80,000		Oberländer in Ersch
1850	95,000		
c.1870			Vivien

Kalgan

| 1850 | 70,000 | | |
| 1872 | 70,000 | | Przevalsky in Chambers, 1888 |

Kanchow, Kiangsi Province

c.1725		Size of Roan (probably referring to Roanne, a place then under 20,000)	Du Halde, p. 160
1750	50,000		
c.1900	100,000		Enci. Universal

Karakorum

1234-68		Mongol capital	Ency. Brit., 1910
1240s		500 wagonloads of provisions daily (Vienna had 723 in 1548)	Lamb, 1927, p. 191
1268		Completely wiped out	Ency. Brit., 1910

Kingtehchen

1004		Royal porcelain works founded	Williams, II, p. 23
-1368		Only small production	Hirth, p. 42
c.1725		500 pottery kilns; 1.5 km (4.5 miles) long	Du Halde, p. 154
1750	100,000		
1782	125,000	250,290 in Fowliang (times 1/2; cf. 1948)	"Kiangsi", XXXIV, pp. 28-9
1800	138,000		
1802	140,000	281,477 in Fowliang	" " "
1850	143,000		
1851	143,000	286,874 in Fowliang	" " "
c.1900	100-200,000	160 furnaces (kilns)	Crow, p. 124
1948	86,744	164,175 in Fowliang district	Columbia Lippincott Gaz.

Kiukiang

500's		Wall built	Enci. Italiana
1400	40,000		
1412	40,000	Wall extended; 5 miles in all (thus, c. 400 ha. in area)	" " ; New Int. Ency.
1794		Only 1/10 the walled area built upon	Braam, I, p. 101
1850	50,000	5-6 miles around (thus, c. 500 ha. in area)	Mayers, p. 430
1853		Wholly destroyed by Taipings	Ency. Brit., 1910
1874	35,000		Hippisley in Vivien

Kuku Khoto (Kweisui)

1583		Mongol khan Altan's residence	Baddeley, p. lxxvii
c.1870		200,000 (probably exaggerated)	Vivien
1948	110,142		Columbia Lippincott Gaz.

Kweilin

1050		Wall built; restored 1356	Enci. Italiana
c.1900	80,000		Couling

Kweiyang

c.1900	100,000		Richard, p. 188

Lanchow

c. 750	14,226	In 742-755	24 Histories, XIX, p. 14,697
1750	130,000		
1772-1830		*Hsien* population grew 17%	Chung Hsui Kao Lan Hsien Chih, II, pp. 605-8
1800	150,000		
1830-87		*Hsien* population grew 3%	" " " " " " " "
1850	170,000		
c.1870		4 km around (seem low)	Brockhaus, 1881
"		40,000 houses (seems high)	Vivien, "Lan-tcheou"
c.1900	175,000		Ency. Brit., 1910

Lhasa

c.1700	80,000		Balbi, p. 269
1750	65,000		
1800	50,000		

c.1800	50,000		Blackie
1850	42,000		
1854	42,000	Census	Ency. Brit., 1910

Liaoyang

644		20,000 in garrison	Gilbert, "Leao-tong"
928-1116		Khitan capital; 30 *li* around	" "
1000	100,000		
1116	100,000	40,640 families, i.e., c. 200,000 people, in prefecture (c. half in city; cf. Kingteh-chen, Sian) as Khitans yielded it to Kins: both dynasties used this same figure	"' "
1116-1210		Kin co-capital, till 1151 the main one	Gilbert; Ency. Brit., 1910 "China"; Mailla, VIII, p. 551
1288	13,231		Gilbert
1620s		Garrison of 30,000 slain	Martini, p. 262
1850	80,000		
c.1866	80,000		Williamson in Vivien

Loyang (Honan)

c. 528	550,000	109,000 households	Ho, p. 66
618-907		Secondary Chinese capital	" p. 55
880		Sacked by a rebel	Yule, p. cvii
1000			
c.1104		233,280 in its *fu* in 1102-6	24 Histories, XXVII, p. 19,996
1161	50,000	Refounded with 10,000 Kin soldiers (most would already have families)	Harlez, p. 94
1200	60,000		
1659		76,983 in Honan *fu* (16 *hsiens*)	Honan Tung Chih, II, p. 1
1691		108,722 in Honan *fu* (16 *hsiens*)	" " " " "
1711		127,579 in Honan *fu* (16 *hsiens*)	" " " " "
1751		98,633 in Honan *fu* (16 *hsiens*)	Hsu Honan Tung Chih, I. huko section 3, pp. 1-5
1766		99,004 in Honan *fu* (16 *hsiens*)	" " " " " " " " " "
c.1900	30,000		Enci. Italiana

Macao

1583		900 Portuguese (men)	Ljungstedt, p. 27
1635	35,000	900 Portuguese, 5-6,000 Chinese workers of all sorts	Semmedo, p. 170
1697		In decline since end of trade with Japan, 1624	Gemelli, p. 412
c.1700	75,000	19,500 under Portuguese rule (cf. 1834)	Ljungstedt, p. 27
1750	60,000		
1800	45,000		
1821		4,800 under Portuguese	" "
1834	35,000	5,093 Portuguese	" pp. 31-208
1850	44,000		
1878	59,950		Vivien

Mukden (Fengtien, now Shenyang)

c.1331	25,000	5,813 households in its *fu* in 1330-2	24 Histories, XXXIV, p. 27,351
1621-1858		Capital of Manchuria	Vivien, "Moukden"
1631	50,000	New wall; 32 *li*, 48 paces (5 1/2 miles; enclosing c. 490 ha.)	Chien Lung, pp. 50-1, 202

1644		80,000 warriors moved to Peking	Adachi, p. 38
1725		437,870 in its *shih* (*shih* is now "urban area," but this figure doesn't fit the wall)	Shen Chen Hui Lan, Fengtien, p. 45
1850	180,000		
1866	180,000		Williamson in Vivien, "Moukden"
c.1870		Wall 18 km (11 miles), plus a 3-km quadrangle (total enclosing c. 2,500 ha.)	Vivien, "Moukden"

Nanchang

962-975		Capital of a local kingdom	Wegener, p. 113
1649	45,000	Over 40,000 old and young slain for revolt	Wegener, p. 114, from Nieufoff
1800		Large tracts unbuilt; houses very old	Barrow, 1804, p. 593
c.1870	90-160,000		Brockhaus, 1881, "Kiangsi"
1900		3 sq. mi. (c. 800 ha.); resembled Changsha	Wegener, p. 114, from Clennell

Nanking

1102	75,000	157,440 in its *fu*, of 6 *hsiens*. (The 4 rural *hsiens* should roughly equal the urban 2; cf. 1391-4)	24 Histories, XXVI, p. 19,994
1127-32		Capital	Mailla, VIII, pp. 455, 503
c.1100s	180,000	32,357 households in 1 (Shang Yao) *hsien* during Sung period	Shou Tu Chih, I, p. 497
1200	180,000		
c.1300	300,000	132,787 in 22,705 houses in Shang Yao *hsien*; 29,277 houses in its other *hsien*	" " " " "
1368-1409		Again capital	Favier, p. 25
1368		Wall built 22 miles around	Crow, pp. 112-3
1391	473,200	In 2 *hsiens*; 60,00 homes	Shou Tu Chih, I, p. 497
1394		1,193,620 in its *lu* (8 *hsiens*; cf. 1391: each rural *hsien* averaged 1/4 as large as the urban population)	24 Histories, XXXVII, p. 29,335
1400	473,000		
1492	282,000	711,300 in its *lu* (cf. 1391, 1394)	" " " "
1500	285,000		
1579	313,000	790,513 in its *lu* (cf. 1391, 1394)	" " " "
1592	317,000	45,307 households (times 7. Lower multiplier than in 1391 because court had moved away)	Shou Tu Chih, I, p. 498
1600	317,000		
1700	300,000	After Manchu massacre of males, 1658	Brunem, II, p. 111
c.1725	320,000	1/3 desolate, 2/3 well inhabited (cf. 1391)	Du Halde, p. 134
1750	285,000		
c.1800	220,000	400,000 (seems out-of-date)	Ency. Brit., 1853
1816	200,000	Only a corner of former city; most empty	Davis, I, p. 364; II, p. 1
c.1850	200,000		

Nanning

1850	40,000		
c.1870	40,000	2 km square (c. 5 miles around and c. 400 ha. in area)	Colquhoun in Vivien

Ninghsia (Yuwei, Yingchuan)

c.1000-1227		Tangut capital	Columbia Lippincott Gaz.
1123		Tangut army 30,000 (not all necessarily at capital)	Harlez, p. 42

1700	90,000		
1724	90,000	Including 40,000 garrison	Favier, p. 178
1750	90,000	After more than 50 years of relative calm as China's northwestern frontier post	Mailla, XI, pp. 280, 548-75
c.1925	85,000		Cressey, 1943, p. 196

Ningpo

713		Founded	Ency. Brit., 1970
c.1371		Became one of China's 3 officially open ports	Chen, p. 224
c.1685	71,000	214,710 in its *hsien* in 1671-1701 (times 1/3; cf. 1948)	Ningpo Fu Chih, II, p. 597
1700	88,000		
1750	144,000		
1800	200,000		
1843	250,800		Vivien
1850	230,000		
1872	160,000		Reclus, VII, p. 472n
1948	210,327	617,657 in county	Columbia Lippincott Gaz.

Paoting

1402	25,000	Wall built, 4 miles around (c. 250 ha. in area enclosed)	Crow, p. 178
1866		120-150,000 (probably an exaggeration)	Williamson in Vivien
c.1900	60,000		Crow, p. 178

Peking

- 935		Area 2/3 that of 936	Hubrecht, map p. 8
936	60,000	36-*li* (6-mile) wall built (thus, c. 600 ha. in area)	Sirén, p. 17
936-1115		Southern capital of the Khitans	Lin, p. 62
1000	80,000		
1151	130,000	54-*li* (9-mile) wall built (thus, c. 1,300 ha. in area)	Sirén, pp. 17-8
1151-1215		Main capital of the Kins	Yule, p. cxvii
1200	150,000		
1264-1937		Capital of China, except 1368-1409	Lin, p. 62; Favier, p. 25
1264-8		New city built adjacent to old one, 48 *li* around, nearly doubling the Kin city (thus, total 15 miles around, enclosing c. 3,600 ha.)	Favier, pp. 20-1; Polo, II, ch. 7
1265	160,369	In its *lu*	24 Histories, XXXIV, p. 27,331
1270	401,350	In its *lu*	" " "
1300	401,000	Under 432,000; cf. Hangchow	
1368		Wall shortened 5 *li* (c. 1 mile) to 14 miles (thus, c. 3,200 ha. in area)	Sirén, pp. 37, 41-2
1400	320,000	While not capital (based on area)	
c.1440		Wall 30 miles around (an obvious error as wall was unchanged from 1368)	Conti, p. 14
1492	669,033	In 11 *hsiens* of 24 in its *fu* (probably the urban area)	24 Histories, XXXViI, p. 29,325
1500	672,000		
1553		48-*li* addition to wall proposed, to take in suburbs; never completed	Sirén, pp. 107-8
1579	706,861	In 11 *hsiens*	24 Histories, XXXVII, p. 29,325
1600	706,000		

1644		80,000 Manchu warriors moved in from Mukden	Adachi, p. 38
1650		100,000 slain as Manchus retook city after siege	Favier, p. 143
c.1725		Garrison 100,000 cavalry (resident: cf. 1644), partly Chinese; plus suburbs	Du Halde, pp. 112, 124
c.1750	900,000	700,000 within walls, plus 12 suburbs up to 3/4 league long (at 1 sq. mile each, 3,000 ha. Use low density, c. 70 per ha., because newly settled)	de l'Isle, p. 9-10
"		Beyond comparison with European cities	La Martinière, 1768
c.1793		About 1/3 larger than London, not counting the Chinese city, which was 9 sq. miles but partly empty and partly farmed	Macartney, pp. 326, 330
c.1800		1,500,000 (perhaps slightly high)	Playfair, V, p. 666
"	1,100,000		
1821	1,300,000		Timkovsky, p. 23
1845	1,648,000		Zakharov in Petermann, 1872, p. 86
1850	1,648,000	Before the Taiping revolt	
1861	1,310,000	Mostly from rounded figures; includes garrison of 110,000	Blackie, suppl.

Shanghai

1264		Became a town	Lanning & Couling, p. 258
c.1554	25,000	3 3/4-mile wall built	" " " ; anon, in "Chinese Repository," 1847, p. 78
1586		70,623 with Nanhui. Montalto, perhaps erroneously, regarded these as rural tributaries	Tung-chih Shanghai Hsien Chih, III, p. 8; Montalto p. xxvii
c.1632		81,000 with Nanhui	Tung-chih Shanghai Hsien Chih, III, p. 8
1683		86,725 with Nanhui	" " " " " "
1700	45,000		
1726		93,294 with Nanhui, regarded by Montalto as rural, not urban	" " " " " ", Montalto p. xxvii
c.1730	48,209	In Shanghai alone, after Nanhui became a separate town	Tung-chih Shanghai Hasien Chih, III, p. 8
1750	60,000		
1800	100,000	See 1847, 1850	
1831		Principal city for native commerce	Gutzlaff, p. 83
1843		Opened to foreign trade	Murphey, p. 15
"	270,000	(Perhaps slightly exaggerated)	Fortune, p. 55
1850	250,000	115-135,000 in two foreign settlements, plus the original Chinese city	Ency. Brit., 1853

Shaohing

c.1850		270,000 (probably a district figure)	Blackie, suppl.
1948	92,533		Columbia Lippincott Gaz.

Shasi

900		Flourishing	Enci. Italiana

Year	Population	Description	Source
1877		Lost trade as Ichang was opened to foreigners; closed to foreign trade till 1895	Ency. Brit., 1910
c.1900	80,000		" " "

Sian (Changan)

Year	Population	Description	Source
583-906		Capital	Wright in Toynbee, p. 144; Enci. Italiana
" "		Greatest walled city ever built by man	Ho, p. 53
" "		30 square miles (c. 8,000 ha.) in area	Hiraoka in Ho, p. 53
c. 700	1,000,000	Within the walls	Reischauer and Fairbank, X, p. 186
751-		Steady decline, yet till past 850 by far the greatest city in Asia	Wright in Toynbee, p. 149
800	800,000		
1000	300,000	China stable 1000-1102	
1102	300,000	537,288 (some probably non-urban; cf. 1312 and 1370)	24 Histories, XXVI, p. 20,007
1200	150,000	After fall to the Kins, 1141	Mailla, VIII, p. 543
1300	150,000	See 1312, 1744	
1312		271,399 in its *lu*, which included 4 towns as well as farmers	24 Histories, XXXIV, p. 27,363
1370	150,000	Present wall built, 9.8 miles (thus, c. 1,500 ha. in area)	Enci. Italiana; Ency. Brit., 1970
1400	150,000		
1500	150,000	Inland China stable 1368-1640	Ency. Brit., 1910
1600	150,000	Before the sack	
1643		People spared by Manchus, but city sacked 3 days	Mailla, X, p. 482
c.1665	147,109	In 1 *hsien* (probably nearly all urban)	Sian, China, I, pp. 615-6
1700	167,000		
1744		Its province's 12 cities had a total of 59,383 taxpayers (hence, c. 300,000 total people)	Büsching, "Magazin," 1768, p. 581
1750	195,000		
1800	224,000		
1812	231,530	In its *hsien*	Hsu Hsiu . . . ., XVIII, p. 3
1823	259,100	In its *hsien*	" " " "
1850	275,000		
c.1870		10 sq. km (1,000 ha.) of suburbs	Vivien, "Si-ngan"
c.1925	200,000		Cressey, 1934, p. 196

Siangtan

Year	Population	Description	Source
c.1870		Wall 5 km along the river, but trade centered in suburbs; larger than Changsha	Reclus, VII, p. 443
c.1900		3 x 2 miles	Ency. Brit., 1910
1943	82,589		Columbia Lippincott Gaz.

Siangyang

Year	Population	Description	Source
1134		A strong place	Mailla, VIII, p. 509
1268-71		Besieged and taken by Mongols, but continued to be a "very great city"	Polo, pp. 158-9, 167n
" "		Wall 5 km (c. 3 miles) around	Vivien
" "		Fancheng, the cross-river suburb, already existed	Ency. Brit., 1910, "Kublai"

c.1860		140,000 including 100,000 in Fancheng (probably too high)	Michaelis in Vivien
c.1930	83,000	17,966 plus c. 65,000 in Fancheng	Columbia Lippincott Gaz.

Soochow

c. 750	75,000	31,361 households in 742-55 in its *hsien* (less 40%, then times 5; cf. 1371); 632,655 in *fu* (4 times as much as *hsien*)	Soochow Fu Chih, I, p. 346
800	75,000		
1000	87,000		
1080	94,000	379,487 in its *fu* (times 1/3; c. 1948)	" " " " "
1102	112,000	448,310 in its *fu*	" " " " "
1184	77,000	298,405 in its *fu*	" " " " "
1200	90,000		
1290	160,000	Wall 10 miles around (thus, c. 1,600 ha. in area)	Ency. Brit., 1910
1300	160,000		
1371	150,000	245,112 in 60,335 households within its *hsien* (less 40% to be consistent with walled area; cf. 1376, 1662)	Soochow Fu Chih, I, p. 347
1376	170,000	285,247 in its *hsien* (cf. 1371)	" " " " "
1400	175,000		
1500	200,000		
1522	200,000	339,042 in its *hsien* (cf. 1371)	" " " " p. 348
1600	175,000	See 1522, 1643	
1632		65,610 in its *hsien*—with massive evasion	" " " " "
1643	170,000	631,060 in its *fu*, which had 16% more in 1538	" " " " "
1657	145,000	538,888 in its *fu*	" " " " "
1662	170,000	New 12-mile wall (thus, c. 2,300 ha. in area, times 75—low multiplier for new wall of war-torn city)	Crow, p. 105
1700	245,000		
1711	265,000	438,830 in its *hsien* (cf. 1371)	Soochow Fu Chih, I, p. 349
1735	275,000	463,846 in its *hsien* (cf. 1371)	" " " " "
1750	302,000		
1800	392,000		
1810	410,000	1,170,833 in the *fu* (in the wider sense; times .35; cf. 1948)	" " " " p. 350
1830	505,000	1,441,753 in the *fu* (times .35; cf. 1948)	" " " " "
1850	550,000		
1863		100,000 able-bodied men (perhaps an army) among the 200,000 submitting to Chinese troops	Cheng, p. 126
c.1880	200-300,000	After sack by Taipings	Brockhaus, 1892
1948	381,288	1,088,085 in county	Columbia Lippincott Gaz.

Süchow, see Hsüchow

Taichow

1161		10,000 soldiers raised there	Harlez, p. 97
1644		Slew 12,000 besiegers	Mailla, X, p. 485

Taitong

1200	42,000		
1211	42,000	7,000 soldiers	Harlez, p. 209 & n

Taiwan (now Tainan)

1650		Founded by Dutch	Columbia Lippincott Gaz.
c.1725	40,000	Nearly 1 league long (cf. Kingtehchen)	Du Halde, p. 175
1750	45,000		
c.1800	50,000	Garrison of 10,000	Pennent, p. 150
1850	60,000		
1858		Opened to foreign trade	Vivien, "Formose"
c.1870	70,000		" "

Taiyüan

700s		Sometimes a royal residence	Yule, p. xcvii
900s		Sometimes local capital	Madrolle, 1912, p. 187
			Enci. Italiana;
			New Ency.
c.1383	53,719	In 1368-98	Taiyüan Hsien Chih, II, p. 8
1400	51,000		
c.1414	50,228		" " " " "
c.1476	51,652		" " " " "
1500	61,000		
c.1544	79,068	In 1522-66	" " " " "
1600	80,000		
c.1624	81,200	In 1621-7	" " " " "
1647	75,000	15,000 men slain	Mailla, X, p. 485
c.1650	27,339	In 1644-61	Taiyüan Hsien Chih, II, p. 8
c.1690	31,735	In 1662-1722	" " " " "
c.1730	34,761	In 1723-35	" " " " "
c.1770		C. 3 leagues (9 miles) around, but much in decline	Grosier, pp. 63-4
1800	40,000		
1850	45,000		
1890	50,000	Includes unoccupied spaces	Vivien

Taku

1850	40,000		
1865	40-60,000	1 league (3 miles) long	Schliemann, p. 9

Tali

621		3,700 households	24 Histories, XXI, p. 16,099
c.750-1253		Capital of Nanchao kingdom	Rocher, pp. 116-7
1200	100,000		
peak	100,000	20,000 households in its *fu*	24 Histories, XXI, p. 16,099
1377		12-*li* (c. 4 miles) wall built	Madrolle, 1916, p. 255
1850	50,000		
1873	50,000	Half killed	Vivien

Tientsiku

1865		100,000 (probably an exaggeration)	Schliemann, p. 10; cf. Columbia Lippincott Gaz.

Tientsin

1368		Founded as a garrison town	Gov't of Japan, IV, p. 21

1404		3-mile sq.-shaped wall built (thus 145 ha. in area)	Gov't of Japan, IV, p. 21
1655		Reckoned the greatest trading town of China and one of its 3 chief ports	Nieuhoff in Pinkerton, VII, p. 258
1700	92,000		
c.1730	92,369	In its *fu* before 1734 (High density, 650 per ha., because of the barracks)	Tientsin Fu Chih, VI, p. 2,360
1734	64,912	In its *fu*	" " " " "
1750	80,000		
1793		700,000 (clearly too high) and appeared as long as London	Macartney, p. 277
1850	200,000	Cf. 1870	
1860		300,000 with much evasion (probably includes rural)	Rasmussen, p. 8
1865		400,000, rather over 1/2 within the 3-mile wall (making a density of 1,400 per ha., which is impossible, as the houses were only 2 stories high)	Mayers, p. 472
1870	250,000	Urban area 6 miles around	Rasmussen, map p. 45
c.1890	569,445	In its *hsien* in 1875-1908	Chi Fu Tung Chih, III, p. 3,918
1900	700,000	Urban area 15 miles around but irregular, enclosing 5 times the area in 1870 (Density decreasing, as barracks no longer dominant)	Rasmussen, map p. 212

Tsinan

300		12-*li* (2 mile) wall built	Crow, p. 201
1300s		Capital of Shantung province	Columbia Lippincott Gaz.
c.1660	52,120	In Licheng *hsien*	Shantung Tung Chih, II, p. 2,571
1700	55,000		
1850	70,000		
c.1855	70,000	New wall, 12 km (c. 7 1/2 miles) long, enclosing 1/4 swampy ground useless for building (thus, c. 700 inhabitable ha. in area)	Crow, p. 201; Vivien
c.1900	100,000		Ency. Brit., 1910, "Chinan"

Urumchi

1763		Enlarged to a small city of 10.8 sq. km (1,080 ha.)	Wiens, p. 450
once		150,000 (probably exaggerated)	Behm and Wagner in Vivien, "Ouroumtsi"
c.1865		Destroyed; its people massacred	Vivien, "Ouroumtsi"
1879	10-30,000	Largely in ruins	Regel in Vivien, "Ouroumtsi"

Wanhsien

c.1769		137,878 in its *hsien*	Szechwan Tung Chih, LVIII, p. 13
c.1900	140,000		Richard, p. 115

Wenchow

c. 300		Founded	Ency. Brit., 1910
900s		4-mile wall built (thus, c. 250 ha. in area)	" " "
1500s		One of 5 leading Chinese seaports	Hirth, p. 68-9
1876		Opened to foreign trade	Ency. Brit., 1910
c.1900	80,000		" " "

Wuchang (now part of Wuhan)

c. 750	84,563	In the *chow* (city), 742-55	24 Histories, XIX, p. 14,691
800	84,000		
c.1370		4-km (2.5 mile) wall built at Hanyang suburb (thus c. 100 ha. in area)	Madrolle, 1912, p. 385; Enci. Italiana, "Han-k'ou," map
1371		10-km (6.2 miles) wall restored at Wuchang (thus, c. 625 ha. in area)	Enci. Italiana
1400	72,000	Based on areas	
1700	150,000	With Hanyang	
1723		142,565 in Wuchang *fu*	Hupeh Tung Chih, XXVIII, p. 6
1750	165,000	With Hanyang	
1862		Adjacent Hankow, largely of modern growth, opened to foreign trade	Chambers, 1967
c.1900	450,000	250,000 in Hankow, 120,000 in Wuchang, and 80,000 in Hanyang	Madrolle, 1912, pp. 383, 385
1908		244,892 in Hankow *ting* (urban area)	Hupeh Tung Chih, XXVIII, p. 13

Xanadu (Shangtu)

1264-c.1350		Summer resort of emperors	Yule, p. 134n

Yangchow

800	100,000		
838	100,000	40 *li* (6 2/3 miles) around; 20,000 soldiers	Ennin, p. 38
1102-6	107,579	In the *hsien*	Chiangnan Tung Chih, X, p. 26
1200	100,000		
1600	75,000		
c.1644	58,138	In the *fu* (in this case may coincide wtih *hsien*)	" " " " "
1655		At least 5 miles around, plus one large suburb which was mostly destroyed c. 1644 but was being rapidly rebuilt	Nieuhoff in Pinkerton, VII, p. 250
1700	60,000		
c.1770		2 leagues (6 miles) around (clearly same as in 838)	Grosier, p. 27
c.1900		60,000 or 100,000	Richard, pp. 163, 530
"		Wall 3-4 miles around (new wall?)	Ency. Brit., 1910

Yünnanfu (now Kunming)

1276-(now)		Capital of Yünnan	Madrolle, 1916, p. 220
"		Wall 6.5 miles (thus, c. 700 ha. in area)	Ency. Brit., 1910
c.1694	38,946	(After war of 1674-8)	Yünnanfu Chih, p. 159
1700	39,000		
1850	50,000		
c.1873	50,000		Garnier in Vivien

Hakata

Once	50,000	(Presumably c.1500)	Yazaki, p. 131
1873	22,000		Reclus, VII, p. 814n

Hiraizumi

1095		Founded Fujiwara to rival Kyoto	Sansom, I, p. 254
1189		Conquered; its importance ended	" " p. 328

Hiroshima

1591		Castle built, and the town began to grow	Correspondence with Hiroshima University Library
1677	51,000	31,205 plus c. 20,000 samurais	" " "
			" "
1700	53,000		
1715	56,349		Correspondence with Nagoya City Library
1746	53,000	33,191 plus c. 20,000 samurais	Correspondence with Hiroshima University Library
1750	51,000		
1764	47,000	27,989 plus c. 20,000 samurais	" " "
			" "
1799	49,000	29,211 plus c. 20,000 samurais	" " "
			" "
1800	49,000		
1804	49,748		Correspondence with Nagoya City Library
1822	48,660		" " "
			" "
1850	63,000		
1873	75,000		Reclus, VII, p. 814n

Hyogo (now Kobe)

1160-1183		De facto capital	Sansom, I, pp. 268, 304
1182		42,000 died in a few months	" pp. 286, 293
1750	22,000		
1770	22,146		Sekiyama, ch. 5
1800	20,853		" "
1850	21,861		" "

Kagoshima

1684	49,096		Correspondence with Kagoshima Perfecture Library
1764	59,727		Yazaki, p. 134
1800	66,000		
1826	72,350		Yazaki, p. 130
1863		Almost wholly burned by British	Lippincott, 1898, p. 28
1882	54,316		Statesman's Yearbook, 1885

Kamakura

1185-1333		De facto capital; base for a large court army from the start	Sansom, II, pp. 299-301, 327-8, 467
1200	175,000		
peak	200,000		Terry, p. 29
1300	200,000		
1333		Burned	Sansom, II, p. 467
1336		Revived as secondary capital, but never really recovered	Mutsu, p. 25

1454		Much damaged by siege	Mutsu, p. 26
1526		Mostly burned, and many people left	" "
1603		Lost its last importance as Tokyo became capital	" "

Kanazawa

1600	50,000		
1664	55,106		Sekiyama, ch. 5
1697	58,636		" "
1700	67,000		
1710	64,987		" "
1721	67,302		Correspondence from Kanazawa library
1750	78,000		
1800	97,000		
1850	116,000		" " " "

Kyoto (Miyako)

794-1868		De jure capital	Sansom, I, pp. 93-100; III, p. 241
794		400,000 (probably exaggerated)	Usui in Ponsonby-Fane, p. 13
"		11.8 miles around and oblong (thus, c. 2,000 ha. in area); modeled on city plan of Changan	Cole, pp. 9-10
"		1,126 blocks	" p. 55
800	200,000		
818		500,000 at peak (probably exaggerated)	Usui in Ponsonby-Fane, p. 13
peak	250,000	Area times 125, the density of Changan	
825		Western half of city already in decline	Ponsonby-Fane, p. 24
c. 925		Eastern half of city began extending beyond the wall	" p. 25
967		Past its peak of prosperity but notable temples continued to be built	" p. 26
1000	200,000		
1177		Several tens of thousands of houses burned (hence, 100,000 absolute minimum)	" p. 39
1180-1333		Court removed	" pp. 117, 162
1185		Great earthquake	" p. 114
1200s		3/4 of Western part of city had disappeared	" p. 123
1333		Almost entirely rebuilt	Cole, p. 11
1400	200,000		
1480		82,000 died	" p. 14
1500	40,000	Or less	" p. 55
1551	108,000	18,000 houses	Xavier in Cole, p. 4
1571	360,000	60,000 houses	Vilela in Cole, p. 54
1600	350,000	After a period of turmoil and departure of de facto capital	
1624	410,000		Cole, p. 55
1632	410,098		Sekiyama, ch. 5
1696	350,986		" "
1700	350,000		
1716	350,367		" "
1750	362,000		
1798	379,274		" "
1800	377,000		
1804	374,687		" "

1846	337,842		Sekiyama, ch. 5
1850	323,000		
1852	316,784		" "

Matsmaye

1594-c.1860		Capital of Hokkaido	Rosny, p. 78
c.1850	50,000	(May actually refer to earlier date)	Gazetteer of World
1850	65,000		
1864	65,000		Rosny, p. 79

Nagasaki

1616	24,693		Sekiyama, ch. 5
1696	64,523		" "
1700	59,000		
1715	41,553		" "
1750	37,000		
1789	31,893		" "
1800	30,000		
1838	27,166		" "
1850	27,000		
1853	27,343		" "

Nagoya

1568-76		Nobunaga's capital	Wald, p. 46
1600	65,000	With samurais (cf. 1870)	
1610		1st city plan based on 50,000	Nagoya city, p. 4
1694		55,665 townsfolk	Sekiyama, ch. 5
1700	69,000	With samurais	
1721		42,136	" "
1750	96,000	72,583 (plus samurais)	Correspondence from Nagoya municipal library
1800	97,000	With samurais	
1840		75,779 townsfolk	" " "
1850	100,000	With samurais	" " "
1865		73,963 townsfolk	Sekiyama, ch. 5
1870		c. 30,000 samurais	Yazaki, p. 134
1873	130,000		Reclus, VII, p. 814n

Nara

710-784		Capital	Sansom, I, pp. 82, 99
" "		11.5 miles around (thus, c. 2,000 ha. in area)	Reischauer & Fairbank, I, p. 480
" "	200,000		Yazaki, p. i
1568		Taxed 1/20 as much as Sakai	Wald, p. 32
1877	22,746		Lippincott, 1898, p. 27

Osaka (including Sakai)

645-654		Capital	Japan Biog, Ency.
1200s-1500s		Sakai was probably the richest city in Japan	Wald, pp. 7, 48
1568		Sakai taxed 4 times as much as Osaka	" p. 32
1580	30-60,000	In Osaka alone, and growing; 6,000 houses	" pp. 23-4
1583-98		Hideyoshi's capital	" pp. 45, 66
1590-		Sakai was built in to Osaka	" p. 56
1600	400,000		
1623	360,000	Estimate of 280,000 without Sakai	" p. 57

1665	338,128	268,760 plus 69,368 in Sakai	Correspondence from Osaka library; Sekiyama, ch. 5
1675		63,706 in Sakai	Sekiyama, ch. 5
1679		287,891 in Osaka alone	Correspondence from Osaka library
1689		330,244 in Osaka alone, but increase from 1679 mainly from taking in an area being converted from waste to farming	" " " "
1699		364,154 in Osaka alone	" " " "
1700	<u>370,000</u>	Including Sakai, but minus c. 50,000 rural (cf. 1689)	" " " "
1709		381,626 in Osaka alone	" " " "
1731		52,446 in Sakai	Yazaki, p. 256
1749		404,146 in Osaka alone	" p. 137
1750	<u>403,000</u>	Including Sakai, but minus c. 50,000 rural (cf. 1689)	
1800	<u>373,000</u>	" " " " "	
1801		376,117 in Osaka alone	" p. 255
1848		40,977 in Sakai	" p. 256
1850	<u>300,000</u>	Including Sakai, but minus c. 50,000 rural (cf. 1689)	
1854		317,436 in Osaka alone	" p. 255

Sendai

1661	58,000		" p. 143
1764	67,000		" p. 134
1873	52,000		Reclus, VII, p. 814n

Tokushima

1873	48,900		Reclus, VII, p. 814n

Tokyo (Yedo, Edo)

1456-		Lord's capital	Nouët, p. 6
1590s		80,000 warriors were settled here	Ency. Brit., 1970, "Tokugawa"
1598-		De facto capital of Japan	" " " "
1600	350,000	70,000 warriors times 5 (low multiplier because of very new settlement)	
1605		Feudal escort of 70,000	Nouët, p. 39
1636		100,000 houses; 30 miles around	Caron, pp. 20, 22
1700	<u>500,000</u>		
1721	501,394		Sekiyama, ch. 5
1750	509,708		" "
1798	492,449		" "
1800	<u>492,000</u>		
1804	492,053		" "
1844	559,497		" "
1850	<u>567,000</u>		
1854	573,619		" "

Wakayama

1882	57,247		Statesman's Yearbook, 1885

Yamaguchi

1500s		Capital of Choshu fief	New Int. Ency.

Yoshino

1336-92		Capital of S. Japan	Ency. Brit., 1910, "Japan"

	1360 B.C.		1200 B.C.		650 B.C.
	Thebes	100	Memphis		Nineveh	120
	Memphis		Thebes		Loyang	117
	Babylon		Babylon		Yenhsiatu	
	Chengchow	40	Anyang		Memphis	
	Khattushas	40	Erech	50	Chicheng	
	Nineveh		Susa		Babylon	
	Ecbatana		Hastinapura		Changan	
	Mycenae	30	Khattushas	40	Ecbatana	
	Amarna	30	Nineveh		Kausambi	
10	Knossos	30	Mycenae	30	Marib	60
	Susa		Chengchow		Napata	
	Cordova		Ayodhya		Ayodhya	
	Erech		Athens	25	Miletus	50
	Athens	25	Duras		Sais	
	Hazor		Loyang		Hsüeh	
	Argos		Tanis		Jerusalem	
	Washshukani		Argos		Van	
	Hsia		Tamralipti		Calah	40
	Jerusalem		Seville		Anyang	
20	Mohenjo-daro	20	Troy		Camelot	

430 B.C.

	Babylon	Persia	250 000
	Ecbatana	Persia	200
	Athens	Attica	155
	Sravasti	India	150
	Champa	India	150
	Loyang	China	145
	Yenhsiatu	China	
	Rajagriha	India	
	Syracuse	Syracuse	125
10	Memphis	Egypt	100
	Rome	Rome	100
	Soochow	China	100
	Chicheng	China	
	Carthage	Carthage	
	Persepolis	Persia	
	Lintzu	China	
	Changan	China	
	Corinth	Corinth	70
	Lucheng	China	
20	Susa	Persia	
	Kausambi	India	
	Dantapura	India	
	Peking	China	
	Sardis	Persia	
25	Patna	India	

Marib	50
Benares	50
Jerusalem	49
Anuradhapura	
Wuchang	
Meroé	
Vaisali	45
Ayodhya	
Sparta	40
Argos	40
Tarentum	40
Agrigentum	40
Megalopolis	40
Sidon	40
Damascus	
Changsha	
Capua	
Suvarnagiri	
Erech	
Ujjain	
Hsüeh	
Tyre	35
Thebes, Greece	35
Cyrene	35
Corcyra	35

200 B.C.

	City	Country	Population
	Patna	India	350 000
	Alexandria	Egypt	300
	Seleucia	Syria	300
	Changan	China	
	Loyang	China	
	Carthage	Carthage	150
	Rome	Rome	150
	Lintzu	China	
	Antioch	Rome	120
10	Jerusalem	Syria	120
	Syracuse	Rome	
	Yenying	China	
	Kavery	Cholas	
	Anuradhapura	Ceylon	100
	Memphis	Egypt	
	Ujjain	India	
	Rajagriha	India	
	Yenhsiatu	China	
	Vaisali	India	
20	Pergamum	Pergamum	
	Balkh	Bactria	75
	Ayodhya	India	
	Ecbatana	Medea	
	Soochow	China	
25	Lucheng	China	

Babylon	
Taxila	
Kolhapur	
Broach	
Benares	
Sravasti	
Champa	
Tosali	
Changsha	
Nanking	
Rayy	
Marib	
Rhodes	42
Hsüeh	
Srinagar	
Damascus	
Pyongyang	
Sardis	
London	35
Jullundur	
Trichinopoly	
Capua	
Meroé	
Ephesus	

100 A.D.

	City	Empire/Region	Population
	Rome	Rome	650 000
	Loyang	China	
	Alexandria	Rome	400
	Seleucia	Persia	300
	Changan	China	
	Ephesus	Rome	200
	Antioch	Rome	150
	Kavery	Cholas	
	Anuradhapura	Ceylon	130
10	Apamea	Rome	125
	Pergamum	Rome	120
	Broach	Kushans	
	Paithan	Andhras	
	Cádiz	Rome	100
	Corinth	Rome	100
	Sardis	Rome	100
	Soochow	China	
	Memphis	Rome	
	Carthage	Rome	90
20	Edessa	Rome	
	Patna	Kushans	
	Madurai	Pandyas	
	Ecbatana	Persia	
	Nanking	China	
25	Patala	Kushans	

Syracuse		Cordova	
Smyrna		Damascus	
Taxila	75	Caesarea	
Hangchow		Ujjain	
Kolhapur		Volubilis	
Pyongyang		Merv	
Wuchang		Taiyüan	
Lintzu		Peshawar	
Ayodhya		Tsinan	
Kyongju		Stakhr	
Rayy		Milan	40
Benares		Autun	40
Babylon		London	40
Tosali			
Cranganore			
Yenhsiatu			
Sravasti			
Kashiwara			
Canton			
Marib			
Kanchi			
Teotihuacán	45		
Balkh			
Srinagar			

361

	Constantinople	Rome	350 000
	Loyang	China	
	Rome	Rome	250
	Patna	Guptas	
	Ctesiphon	Persia	200
	Alexandria	Rome	200
	Changan	China	
	Carthage	Rome	
	Antioch	Rome	150
10	Ayodhya	Guptas	140
	Broach	Kshatrapas	
	Memphis	Rome	
	Ephesus	Rome	
	Teotihuacán	México	90
	Milan	Rome	
	Madurai	Pandyas	
	Soochow	China	
	Nanking	China	
	Edessa	Rome	
20	Anuradhapura	Ceylon	
	Ujjain	Kshatrapas	
	Tamralipti	Guptas	
	Prome	Burma	
	Corinth	Rome	
25	Pergamum	Rome	

Smyrna			Pyongyang		
Kanchow			Chengtu		
Kinchow			Capua		
Kalgan			Kavery		
Cordova			Caesarea		
Dvin			Nishapur		60 000
Peshawar			Trier		60
Kyongju			Jerusalem		60
Thessalonica		42 000	Rayy		
Isfahan			Aquileia		
Puyo			Arles		
Namhan			Kanchi		
Mecca			Kolkai		
London			Seville		
			Taxila		
			Wuchang		
			Stakhr		
			Canton		
			Indrapura		
			Gundishapur		
			Kolhapur		
			Srinagar		
			Axum		
			Marib		
			50 Syracuse		

622

Constantinople	Byzantium	500 000
Changan	China	
Loyang	China	400
Ctesiphon	Persia	
Alexandria	Persia	200
Teotihuacán	México	125
Kanauj	N. India	100
Kanchi	Pallavas	100
Vatapi	Chalukyas	
10 Memphis	Persia	
Soochow	China	
Anuradhapura	Ceylon	
Thaneswar	N. India	
Antioch	Persia	
Edessa	Persia	
Ecbatana	Persia	
Prome	Burma	
Nanking	China	
20 Ayodhya	N. India	
Aleppo	Persia	72
Isanapura	Cambodia	70
Mecca	Arabia	70
Malakuta	S. India	70
25 Chengtu	China	

Rayy		Canton	
Pagan		Theodosiopolis	
Benares	65	Coptos	
Pyongyang		Kermanshah	
Caesarea		Yangchow	
Wuchang		Tamralipti	45
Nishapur	60	Tenasserim	
Hangchow	60	Gauhati	
Kolkai		Asuka	
Dvaravati		Axum	
Smyrna		Gundishapur	
Ujjain		Changsha	
Ye		Taiyan	
Indrapura		Kolhapur	
Kyongju		Kalyan the elder	
Merv		Lhasa	
Srinagar		Seville	40
Osaka		Kausambi	40
Madurai		Valabhi	40
Rome	50	Stakhr	40
Pingcheng		Peking	40
Jerusalem		Kamarupa	40
Medina		Pundravardhana	40
Gwalior			

800

Changan	China	800 000
Bagdad	Arabia	700
Constantinople	Byzantium	300
Loyang	China	
Kyoto	Japan	200
Alexandria	Arabia	200
Hangchow	China	
Cordova	Spain	160
Basra	Arabia	
10 Damascus	Arabia	
Lhasa	Tibet	
Fostat	Arabia	100
Mecca	Arabia	100
Yangchow	China	100
Rayy	Arabia	
Ellora	Rashtrakutas	90
Edessa	Arabia	
Chengtu	China	88
Chunar	Bengal	
20 Wuchang	China	84
Kanauj	N. India	80
Kairwan	Arabia	80
Canton	China	
Kanchi	Pallavas	
25 Anhilvada	Gujarat	

Nanking			Merv	
Kufa			Benares	
Vengi			Monte Albán	
Soochow	75 000		Tula	
Kaifeng	75		Qum	
Thaneswar			Zimbabwe	
Kyongju			Aleppo	
Nara			Rome	50 000
Hamadan			Tikal	49
Palembang			Indrapura, Champa	
Tanjore			Indrapura, Cambodia	
Cambay			Dzibalchaltún	
Chüanchow			Pagan	
Nanchang			Jayapuram	
Mansura			Vatapi	
Jerusalem			Osaka	
Caesarea			Sivas	
Copán			Antioch	
Samarkand			Siraf	
Tali			Anbar	
Ayodhya			Balasaghun	
Tamralipti			Nishapur	
Patna			Pyongyang	
Mau-Sahanya			Tsinan	
50 Kashgar			Gundishapur	

900

	Bagdad	Arabia	900 000
	Changan	China	750
	Constantinople	Byzantium	300
	Kyoto	Japan	225
	Hangchow	China	220
	Alexandria	Egypt	200
	Cordova	Spain	200
	Manyakheta	Rashtrakutas	
	Loyang	China	
10	Fostat	Egypt	125
	Damascus	Egypt	
	Kairwan	Tunisia	100
	Chengtu	China	100
	Rayy	Tabaristan	100
	Yangchow	China	100
	Samarkand	Samanids	
	Nishapur	Samanids	
	Chunar	Bengal	
	Angkor	Cambodia	
20	Anhilvada	Gujarat	
	Soochow	China	81
	Kanauj	N. India	80
	Kaifeng	China	
	Kufa	Arabia	
25	Kyongju	Korea	

Vengi		Quilon	
Lhasa		Kashgar	
Basra		Aleppo	
Tanjore		Kanchi	
Nanking		Broach	
Mecca		Thaneswar	
Edessa		Ujjain	
Tali		Hamadan	
Monghyr		Nara	
Caesarea		Pyongyang	
Benares		Chitor	
Bihar		Sivas	
Wuchang		Ani	
Nanchang		Balasaghun	
Chüanchang		Seville	42 000
Mansura		Zimbabwe	
Canton		Merv	
Tamralipti		Ayodhya	
Bokhara		Preslav	40
Jerusalem		Peking	40
Cambay		Fez	40
Ellora		Mérida	40
Samarra		Rome	40
Siraf	50 000		
50 Thessalonica	50		

1000

	Cordova	Spain	450 000
	Constantinople	Byzantium	450
	Kaifeng	China	400
	Sian	China	300
	Kyoto	Japan	200
	Cairo	Egypt	150
	Hasa	Qarmatians	150
	Hangchow	China	
	Angkor	Cambodia	
10	Bagdad	Persia	125
	Nishapur	Uighurs	125
	Chengtu	China	
	Khajuraho	Chandels	100
	Anhilvada	Gujarat	100
	Bokhara	Uighurs	100
	Liaoyang	Khitans	100
	Canton	China	100
	Rayy	Persia	100
	Tanjore	Cholas	
	Songdo	Korea	
20	Isfahan	Persia	92
	Seville	Spain	90
	Chunar	Bengal	
	Soochow	China	87
25	Ninghsia	Tangut	

	Loyang			Benares	
	Yangchow			Quilon	
	Tinnis	83 000		Tamralipti	
	Edessa			Binhdinh	
	Vengi			Mansura	
	Samarkand	80		Somnath	54
	Peking	80		Shiraz	52
	Manyakheta			Lhasa	
	Nanking			Pyongyang	
	Aleppo			Siraf	50
	Fez	75		Basra	50
	Ani	75		Kanchi	
	Palermo	75		Thaneswar	
	Nanchang			Tula	
	Tali			Kiev	45
	Chüanchow			Venice	45
	Hamadan			Mecca	
	Wuchang			Monghyr	
	Vengi			Sivas	
	Caesarea			Ujjain	
	Kairwan	65		Kayal	
	Kashgar			Thessalonica	40
	Cambay			Ratisbon	40
	Damascus			Ochrida	40
	Kanauj	60			
50	Jerusalem	60			

1100

	City	Country	Population
	Kaifeng	China	442 000
	Constantinople	Byzantium	350
	Sian	China	300
	Cairo	Egypt	200
	Kyoto	Japan	200
	Marrakesh	Morocco	150
	Bagdad	Seljuks	150
	Hangchow	China	150
	Canton	China	140
10	Kalyan	Chalukyas	125
	Angkor	Cambodia	125
	Anhilvada	Gujarat	125
	Fez	Morocco	125
	Seville	Morocco	125
	Tinnis	Egypt	125
	Soochow	China	110
	Isfahan	Seljuks	110
	Yangchow	China	107
	Kayseri	Seljukids	100
20	Pagan	Burma	100
	Liaoyang	Khitans	100
	Nishapur	Seljuks	100
	Chengtu	China	
	Kanauj	N. India	90
25	Palermo	Sicily	90

	City			City	
	Ninghsia			Quilon	
	Gangaikondapuram			Virapura	
	Ghazni			Kashgar	
	Songdo			Balasaghun	55 000
	Rayy	85 000		Venice	55
	Loyang			Tanjore	
	Tali			Gaur	
	Nadiya			Tula	
	Peking	80		Merv	
	Lahore			Mecca	
	Chüanchow			Kiev	50
	Nanking	75		Bougie	50
	Benares			Salerno	50
	Chunar			Polonnaruwa	50
	Samarkand	70		Basra	50
	Cambay			Siraf	50
	Wuchang			Chitor	
	Khajuraho			Mukhalingam	
	Edessa			Nanchang	
	Cuttack			Hasa	
	Dhar			Sivas	
	Cordova	60		Bokhara	
	Granada	60		Milan	45
	Cholula	60		Pyongyang	
50	Damascus			Mahdia	

1150

	City	Region	Population
	Constantinople	Byzantium	300 000
	Merv	Seljuks	200
	Nanking	China	180
	Cairo	Egypt	175
	Kaifeng	Kins	175
	Canton	China	170
	Fez	Morocco	160
	Kalyan	Chalukyas	150
	Marrakesh	Morocco	150
10	Pagan	Burma	150
	Sian	Kins	150
	Kyoto	Japan	150
	Hangchow	China	145
	Anhilvada	Gujarat	135
	Peking	Kins	130
	Palermo	Sicily	125
	Angkor	Cambodia	125
	Bagdad	Seljuks	125
	Seville	Morocco	125
20	Cuttack	Orissa	125
	Tinnis	Egypt	125
	Liaoyang	Kins	100
	Yangchow	China	100
	Kayseri	Seljukids	100
25	Nishapur	Seljuks	100

City	Pop.	City	Pop.
Songdo		Cordova	60 000
Kanauj	92 000	Granada	60
Soochow	91	Peking	
Hiraizumi		Ghor	
Ninghsia		Nadiya	
Benares		Damascus	
Chengtu		Tanjore	
Tali		Herat	
Gaur		Sivas	
Rayy	80	Virapura	
Konia	75	Tula	
Isfahan	75	Bokhara	
Polonnaruwa	75	Cholula	
Quilon		Chitor	
Gangaikondapuram		Mecca	
Chüanchow		Pyongyang	
Cambay		Mosul	50
Dhar		Milan	50
Wuchang		Kiev	50
Lahore		Acre	50
Paris	65	Tiflis	50
Mahoba		Basra	50
Bougie	60	Balasaghun	50
Samarkand	60	Gurganj	
50 Venice	60	Nanchang	

1200

	Hangchow	China	255 000
	Fez	Morocco	250
	Cairo	Egypt	200
	Constantinople	Byzantium	200
	Canton	China	200
	Pagan	Burma	180
	Nanking	China	180
	Kamakura	Japan	175
	Angkor	Cambodia	150
10	Palermo	Sicily	150
	Marrakesh	Morocco	150
	Seville	Morocco	150
	Cuttack	Orissa	150
	Peking	Kins	150
	Sian	Kins	150
	Kaifeng	Kins	150
	Polonnaruwa	Ceylon	140
	Paris	France	110
	Bagdad	Seljuks	100
20	Tali	Nanchao	100
	Konia	Seljukids	100
	Damietta	Egypt	100
	Yangchow	China	100
	Kalinjar	Chandels	100
25	Chengtu	China	

	Ghazni			Otrar	
	Damascus	90 000		Kayseri	
	Soochow	90		Liaoyang	60 000
	Ninghsia			Delhi	60
	Rabat			Milan	60
	Kyoto			Loyang	60
	Songdo			Samarkand	60
	Alexandria			Cordova	60
	Nadiya			Granada	60
	Nishapur	80		Lahore	
	Rayy	80		Herat	
	Tiflis	80		Bokhara	
	Chüanchow			Chitor	
	Gaur			Aleppo	
	Cambay			Tanjore	
	Quilon			Cholula	
	Acre	75		Kalyan	
	Gurganj			Cologne	50
	Ghor			Mosul	50
	Gangaikondapuram			Basra	
	Wuchang			Warangal	
	Venice	70		Balasaghun	47
	Isfahan	70		Pyongyang	
	Merv			Ife	
50	Dhar			Ninghsia	
				Bindinh	

1250

	City	Country	Population
	Hangchow	China	320 000
	Cairo	Egypt	300
	Canton	China	250
	Nanking	China	250
	Fez	Morocco	200
	Kamakura	Japan	200
	Pagan	Burma	180
	Sian	Mongols	175
	Paris	France	160
10	Peking	Mongols	160
	Constantinople	Latin Kingdom	150
	Marrakesh	Morocco	150
	Kaifeng	Mongols	150
	Cuttack	Orissa	135
	Angkor	Cambodia	125
	Soochow	China	125
	Bagdad	Seljuks	100
	Konia	Seljukids	100
	Tali	Nanchao	100
20	Damietta	Egypt	95
	Chengtu	China	
	Venice	Venice	90
	Seville	Castile	90
	Granada	Granada	90
25	Quilon	Travancore	90

City	Pop.	City	Pop.
Yangchow		Alexandria	
Gaur		Marseille	60 000
Kyoto		Trebizond	60
Chüanchow		Chitor	60
Dhar	80 000	Mecca	
Cambay	80	Aleppo	
Milan	80	Kashgar	
Delhi	80	Loyang	
Anhilvada		Bologna	55
Tiflis	75	Mosul	55
Damascus	75	Kayseri	
Acre	75	Cologne	52
Warangal	75	Shiraz	
Palermo	75	Karakorum	50
Tunis	70	Trnovo	50
Genoa	70	Pisa	50
Isfahan	70	Cholula	
Bokhara		Virapura	
Gangaikondapuram		Tlemcen	
Wuchang		Qus	
Calicut		Siangyang	
Njimiye		Cholula	
Nicaea		Sijilmessa	
Songdo		Hormuz	45
50 Rabat		Goa	

1300

	City	Country	Population
	Hangchow	China	432 000
	Peking	China	401
	Cairo	Egypt	400
	Canton	China	300
	Nanking	China	300
	Paris	France	228
	Fez	Morocco	200
	Kamakura	Japan	200
	Soochow	China	160
10	Sian	China	150
	Granada	Granada	150
	Constantinople	Byzantium	150
	Tabriz	Persia	150
	Angkor	Cambodia	125
	Cuttack	Orissa	125
	Venice	Venice	110
	Chengtu	China	110
	Milan	Milan	100
	Genoa	Genoa	100
20	Delhi	N. India	100
	Sarai	Golden Horde	100
	Gaur	N. India	100
	Chüanchow	China	100
	Marrakesh	Morocco	100
25	Quilon	Travancore	100

Warangal	100 000	Mosul	55 000
Kaifeng		Cologne	54
Yangchow		Siangyang	
Damietta	90	Aksu	
Seville	90	Shiraz	50
Dhar	90	Rouen	50
Songdo		Bruges	50
Tali		Goa	50
Tunis	75	Fuchow	50
Wuchang		Bologna	50
Isfahan	70	Thessalonica	50
Maragheh		Hormuz	50
Hamadan		Kyoto	
Njimiye		Meknes	
Tlemcen		Alexandria	
Mecca		Sonargaon	
Florence	60	Sukotai	
Chitor	60	Benares	
Trebizond	60	Loyang	
Konia		Pyongyang	
Gangaikondapuram		Hsüchow	
Qus		Oyo	
Anhilvada		Cholula	
Virapura		Valencia	44
50 Calicut		Kano	
		Kingtehchen	

1350

	City	Country	Population
	Cairo	Egypt	450 000
	Hangchow	China	432
	Peking	China	400
	Canton	China	330
	Nanking	China	300
	Paris	France	200
	Fez	Morocco	175
	Sian	China	150
	Tabriz	Persia	150
10	Granada	Granada	150
	Kyoto	Japan	150
	Soochow	China	150
	Delhi	N. India	125
	Sarai	Golden Horde	120
	Cambay	N. India	100
	Chüanchow	China	100
	Damascus	Egypt	100
	Quilon	S. India	100
	Sultaniya	Persia	100
20	Pandua	Bengal	100
	Vijayanagar	S. India	
	Kaifeng	China	
	Angkor	Cambodia	90
	Bagdad	Jelairids	90
25	Cuttack	Orissa	

	City	Pop.		City	Pop.
	Gaur			Anhilvada	
	Damietta	85 000		Qus	
	Yangchow			Ghent	57 000
	Constantinople	80		Tunis	56
	Seville	80		Virapura	
	Venice	75		Sukotai	
	Tali			Bursa	
	Songdo			Yoshino	
	Sonargaon			Aksu	
	Daulatabad			Njimiye	
	Texcoco	70		Ikoso	
	Genoa	70		Shiraz	50
	Milan	70		Prague	50
	Marrakesh	70		Calicut	50
	Isfahan	70		Rouen	50
	Aleppo	70		Cologne	50
	Wuchang			Majapahit	50
	Chengtu	65		Goa	50
	Fuchow	65		Mosul	50
	Mecca			Hormuz	50
	Mali	60		Taiyüan	50
	Trebizond	60		Valencia	48
	Caffa	60		Hsüchow	
	Bruges	60		Toledo	45
50	Tlemcen			Meknes	45

1400

	Nanking	China	473 000
	Cairo	Egypt	450
	Vijayanagar	S. India	350
	Hangchow	China	325
	Peking	China	320
	Canton	China	300
	Paris	France	275
	Tabriz	Persia	200
	Kyoto	Japan	200
10	Soochow	China	175
	Pandua	Bengal	150
	Fez	Morocco	150
	Sian	China	150
	Cambay	N. India	125
	Milan	Milan	125
	Bruges	France	125
	Venice	Venice	110
	Genoa	Genoa	100
	Granada	Granada	100
20	Samarkand	Timurids	100
	Seoul	Korea	100
	Shiraz	Timurids	100
	Damascus	Egypt	100
	Prague	Germany	95
25	Bursa	Turkey	

Bagdad	90 000	Kamakura		
Quilon	90	Jaunpur		
Chengtu	88	Benares		
Chüanchow		Florence	61 000	
Kaifeng		Marrakesh		
Caffa	85	Hsüchow	60	
Gaur		Chitor	60	
Gulbarga		Pegu	60	
Fuchow	81	Yoshino		
Damietta	80	Ava		
Yangchow		Bokhara		
Cuttack		Lisbon	55	
Constantinople	75	Anhilvada		
Aleppo	75	Mecca		
Penukonda	75	Taiyüan	51	
Ayutia		Metalanim		
Wuchang	72	Mali	50	
Texcoco	70	Novgorod	50	
Ghent	70	Majapahit	50	
Tlemcen	70	Troki	50	
Rouen	70	Angkor	50	
Tunis	70	Hormuz	50	
Seville	70	Calicut	50	
Kamatapur		Goa	50	
Ningpo		Trebizond		

1450

	City	Country	Population
	Peking	China	600 000
	Vijayanagar	S. India	455
	Cairo	Egypt	450
	Hangchow	China	360
	Nanking	China	350
	Canton	China	300
	Tabriz	Persia	200
	Soochow	China	200
	Mandu	Malwa	200
10	Granada	Granada	165
	Sian	China	150
	Kyoto	Japan	150
	Gaur	Bengal	150
	Seoul	Korea	125
	Fez	Morocco	125
	Paris	France	125
	Cambay	Gujarat	125
	Ayutia	Siam	125
	Milan	Milan	110
20	Jaunpur	Jaunpur	100
	Samarkand	Timurids	100
	Genoa	Genoa	100
	Venice	Venice	100
	Tunis	Hafsids	100
25	Chengtu	China	100

Bruges	95 000		Caffa	70 000
Pandua			Ahmedabad	
Penukonda	90		Kingtehchen	
Adrianople	85		Ningpo	
Damascus	85		Lisbon	66
Ava	85		Seville	65
Fuchow	82		Burhanpur	65
Chüanchow			Kaifeng	
Shiraz	80		Mecca	60
Quilon	80		Tlemcen	60
Kamatapur	80		Damietta	60
Bidar	80		Marrakesh	60
Wuchang			Novgorod	60
Yangchow			Rouen	60
Texcoco	75		Lyon	60
London	75		Pegu	60
Aleppo	75		Hsüchow	60
Chitor	75		Herat	
Ghent	75		Pyongyang	
Naples	75		Bokhara	
Bursa			Calicut	55
Cuttack			Tientsin	
Chanchán	70		Florence	53
Tenochtitlán	70		Oyo	
50 Prague	70		Troki	50

1500

	City	Country	Population
	Peking	China	672 000
	Vijayanagar	S. India	500
	Cairo	Egypt	450
	Hangchow	China	375
	Nanking	China	285
	Canton	China	250
	Tabriz	Persia	250
	Paris	France	225
	Constantinople	Turkey	200
10	Gaur	Bengal	200
	Soochow	China	200
	Sian	China	150
	Seoul	Korea	150
	Mandu	Malwa	150
	Ayutia	Siam	150
	Fez	Morocco	125
	Adrianople	Turkey	125
	Naples	Naples	125
	Cambay	Gujarat	125
20	Venice	Venice	115
	Chengtu	China	112
	Milan	France	104
	Delhi	N. India	100
	Kaifeng	China	
25	Chitor	Mewar	90

City	Pop.		City	Pop.
Penukonda	90 000		Bokhara	
Bruges	90		Aleppo	67 000
Gwalior	90		Ningpo	
Fuchow	83		Chüanchow	
Wuchang			Kingtehchen	
Bidar	80		Genoa	62
Ahmedabad	80		Brescia	61
Tenochtitlán	80		Taiyüan	61
Lyon	80		Hsüchow	
Ghent	80		Calicut	60
Ava			Gao	60
Samarkand			Tours	60
Yangchow			Shiraz	60
Rouen	75		Mecca	60
Tunis	75		Texcoco	60
Quilon	75		Utatlán	60
Burhanpur			Pyongyang	
Sakai			Tientsin	
Prague	70		Chiengmai	
Florence	70		Srinagar	
Lisbon	70		Bologna	55
Granada	70		Hanoi	
Damascus	70		Nuremberg	52
Chanderi	70		Pskov	52
Cuttack			Oyo	

1550

	City	Country	Population
	Peking	China	690 000
	Constantinople	Turkey	660
	Vijayanagar	S. India	500
	Cairo	Turkey	430
	Hangchow	China	375
	Canton	China	300
	Nanking	China	300
	Paris	France	260
	Naples	Spain	245
10	Tabriz	Persia	200
	Ahmedabad	Gujarat	175
	Venice	Venice	171
	Soochow	China	160
	Delhi	N. India	160
	Adrianople	Turkey	160
	Seoul	Korea	150
	Ayutia	Siam	150
	Gaur	N. India	150
	Sian	China	150
20	Pegu	Burma	125
	Chengtu	China	120
	Kyoto	Japan	108
	Lyon	France	108
	Moscow	Russia	100
25	Mandu	Malwa	100

	City	Pop.		City	Pop.
	Fez	100 000		Valencia	68 000
	Qazvin	100		Tientsin	
	Cambay	100		Golconda	
	Kaifeng			Smyrna	
	Wuchang			Arakan	
	Gwalior	90		Palermo	65
	Penukonda	90		Genoa	65
	Jodhpur			Marrakesh	
	Sakai			Kingtehchen	
	Granada	85		Yangchow	
	Seville	85		Valladolid	61
	Milan	85		Bijapur	60
	Lisbon	85		Algiers	60
	Bihar	80		Toledo	60
	Taiyüan	79		Bruges	60
	Fuchow	79		Ghent	60
	Bokhara			Damascus	60
	London	76		Goa	60
	Antwerp	76		Mexico City	60
	Gao	75		Tours	60
	Rouen	75		Kano	60
	Agra			Tunis	60
	Prague	70		Florence	59
	Chitor	70		Augsburg	58
50	Burhanpur	70		Samarkand	

1600

	City	Country	Population
	Peking	China	706 000
	Constantinople	Turkey	700
	Agra	Moguls	500
	Cairo	Turkey	400
	Osaka	Japan	400
	Canton	China	350
	Yedo	Japan	350
	Kyoto	Japan	350
	Hangchow	China	350
10	Lahore	Moguls	350
	Nanking	China	317
	Naples	Spain	275
	Paris	France	250
	Ahmedabad	Moguls	225
	Bijapur	Bijapur	200
	London	England	187
	Soochow	China	175
	Adrianople	Turkey	160
	Venice	Venice	151
20	Sian	China	150
	Qazvin	Persia	150
	Potosí	Spain	148
	Seville	Spain	144
	Chengtu	China	130
25	Marrakesh	Morocco	125

Arakan	125 000	Chandragiri	
Isfahan	125	Fuchow	76 000
Milan	119	Mexico City	75
Lisbon	110	Algiers	75
Granada	110	Ahmednagar	75
Rome	109	Surat	75
Palermo	105	Yangchow	75
Prague	100	Patna	
Ayutia	100	Burhanpur	
Fez	100	Golconda	
Tabriz	100	Udaipur	72
Rajmahal	100	Srinagar	
Wuchang		Ujjain	
Kaifeng		Bursa	70
Bokhara		Genoa	70
Lyon	90	Hugli	70
Valencia	86	Cambay	70
Jodhpur		Rouen	68
Tientsin		Kingtehchen	
Toledo	80	Tours	65
Smyrna	80	Florence	65
Moscow	80	Nagoya	65
Hyderabad	80	Benin	65
Taiyuüan	79	Barcelona	64
50 Madrid	79	Smolensk	64

1650

	Constantinople	Turkey	700 000
	Peking	China	600
	Isfahan	Persia	500
	Yedo	Japan	500
	Agra	Moguls	500
	Paris	France	455
	London	England	410
	Delhi	Moguls	400
	Kyoto	Japan	390
10	Canton	China	385
	Cairo	Turkey	350
	Osaka	Japan	346
	Nanking	China	300
	Naples	Spain	300
	Bijapur	Bijapur	300
	Hangchow	Chian	281
	Ahmedabad	Moguls	275
	Lahore	Moguls	250
	Lisbon	Portugal	170
20	Patna	Moguls	150
	Surat	Moguls	150
	Tabriz	Persia	150
	Sian	China	147
	Arakan	Arakan	145
25	Soochow	China	145

Venice	134		Bokhara	
Adrianople	132		Seville	80
Potosí	130		Granada	80
Palermo	128		Tatta	80
Ayutia	125		Danzig	77
Srinagar	125		Amoy	
Rome	124		Golconda	
Wuchang			Marrakesh	75
Amsterdam	110		Nagoya	72
Lyon	110		Chandragiri	
Milan	105		Ujjain	
Smyrna	102		Rouen	70
Seoul			Mukden	70
Moscow	100		Oyo	
Rajmahal	100		Genoa	67
Algiers	100		Florence	66
Qazvin	100		Ningpo	
Madrid	100		Kasimbazar	
Dacca	100		Vienna	65
Jodhpur			Damascus	65
Vellore	95		Aleppo	64
Fez			Barcelona	64
Hyderabad	90		Madurai	
Mexico City	90		Ajmer	
50 Tientsin			Kazargamu	60

1700

	Constantinople	Turkey	700 000
	Peking	China	
	Isfahan	Persia	600
	London	Britain	550
	Paris	France	530
	Yedo	Japan	500
	Delhi	Moguls	500
	Ahmedabad	Moguls	380
	Osaka	Japan	370
10	Kyoto	Japan	350
	Cairo	Turkey	350
	Canton	China	300
	Nanking	China	300
	Hangchow	China	292
	Soochow	China	245
	Naples	Spain	207
	Meknes	Morocco	200
	Dacca	Moguls	200
	Surat	Moguls	200
20	Hyderabad	Moguls	200
	Lisbon	Portugal	188
	Amsterdam	Holland	172
	Patna	Moguls	170
	Seoul	Korea	170
25	Sian	China	167

Ayutia	150	Marseille	88
Tabriz	150	Algiers	85
Wuchang	150	Agra	
Srinagar	150	Kingtehchen	
Rome	149	Fez	
Venice	143	Seville	80
Mukden		Lhasa	80
Smyrna	135	Dublin	80
Moscow	130	Gondar	80
Milan	124	Benares	
Palermo	113	Chengtu	
Madrid	110	Amoy	
Vienna	105	Bijapur	
Mexico City	100	Macao	75
Arakan	100	Barcelona	73
Aurangabad	100	Oruro	72
Jodhpur		Aleppo	72
Lahore		Lyon	71
Potosí	95	Oyo	
Adrianople	93	Damascus	70
Tientsin	92	Brussels	70
Fatshan	90	Hamburg	70
Ninghsia	90	Qazvin	70
Fuchow		Tunis	70
Ningpo	88	Granada	70

1750

	Peking	China	900 000
	London	Britain	676
	Constantinople	Turkey	666
	Paris	France	560
	Yedo	Japan	509
	Canton	China	500
	Osaka	Japan	375
	Kyoto	Japan	362
	Hangchow	China	350
10	Naples	Naples	324
	Soochow	China	302
	Cairo	Turkey	300
	Nanking	China	285
	Hyderabad	Hyderabad	225
	Amsterdam	Holland	219
	Lisbon	Portugal	213
	Patna	Moguls	250
	Meshhed	Persia	200
	Murshidabad	Moguls	200
20	Sian	China	195
	Seoul	Korea	183
	Vienna	Austria	169
	Surat	Marathas	165
	Wuchang	China	165
25	Moscow	Russia	161

Venice	158	Jaipur	100
Rome	157	Srinagar	100
Mukden		Chengtu	
Ayutia	150	Adrianople	96
Jodhpur	150	Nagoya	96
Ningpo	144	Chandernagore	95
St. Petersburg	138	Batavia	94
Dacca	135	Ninghsia	90
Fatshan	130	Chinkiang	90
Lanchow	130	Hamburg	90
Smyrna	130	Fyzabad	90
Dublin	125	Marseille	88
Palermo	124	Rouen	88
Madrid	123	Aurangabad	85
Milan	123	Benares	
Ahmedabad	120	Oyo	
Kingtehchen	120	Changsha	
Lyon	115	Tientsin	80
Berlin	113	Copenhagen	79
Mexico City	110	Kanazawa	78
Calcutta	110	Kaifeng	78
Fuchow		Bombay	77
Tunis	100	Amoy	
Delhi	100	Katsina	75
Lucknow	100	Algiers	75
		Damascus	75

1800

	Peking	China	1 100 000
	London	Britain	861
	Canton	China	800
	Constantinople	Turkey	570
	Paris	France	547
	Hangchow	China	500
	Yedo	Japan	492
	Naples	Naples	430
	Soochow	China	392
10	Osaka	Japan	380
	Kyoto	Japan	377
	Lucknow	Oudh	300
	Cairo	French	263
	Moscow	Russia	238
	Lisbon	Portugal	237
	Patna	British	235
	Vienna	Austria	231
	Sian	China	224
	Nanking	China	220
20	St. Petersburg	Russia	220
	Amsterdam	Batavian Rep.	201
	Ningpo	China	200
	Calcutta	British	200
	Hyderabad	Hyderabad	200
25	Seoul	Korea	190

Wuchang		Srinagar	125
Murshidabad	185	Barcelona	120
Mukden		Tunis	120
Benares	179	Chengtu	110
Amarapura	175	Dacca	110
Fatshan	175	Meknes	110
Bombay	175	Lyon	110
Berlin	172	Marseille	109
Madrid	169	Chinkiang	106
Dublin	165	Surakarta	105
Fuchow		Nanchang	
Tientsin		Copenhagen	100
Rome	153	Poona	100
Lanchow	150	Ujjain	100
Venice	146	Adrianople	100
Palermo	146	Shanghai	100
Kingtehchen	138	Nagoya	97
Chungking		Kanazawa	97
Milan	134	Bordeaux	97
Hamburg	130	Seville	96
Surat	130	Batavia	92
Mexico City	128	Jogjakarta	90
Delhi	125	Damascus	90
Madras	125	Genoa	90
Smyrna	125	Ahmedabad	89
		Cádiz	87

1800

Changsha		Hanoi		Urumchi	
Oyo	85	Salonica	62	Tali	
Rouen	85	Sendai	62	Yünnanfu	
Glasgow	85	Dresden	61	Kalgan	
Valencia	82	Banda		Sofia	46
Edinburgh	82	Siangtan		Tula	46
Manchester	81	Siangyang		Shasi	
Amoy		Kandahar		Chüanchow	
Erzurum	80	Fez	60	Paoting	
Bagdad	80	Havana	60	Kiukiang	
Kabul	80	Agra	60	Chandernagore	45
Peshawar	80	Basra	60	Sheffield	45
Nagpur	80	Qazvin	60	Padua	45
Baroda	80	Bangalore	60	200 Herat	45
Amritsar	80	Fyzabad	60	Shushtar	45
Jodhpur	80	Lhasa	60	Saigon	
Kaifeng	80	Kashgar	60	Macao	45
Trichinopoly	80	Rotterdam	60	Rio de Janeiro	44
Florence	79	Kweilin		Murcia	44
Prague	77	Muttra		Changchow	
Manila	77	Pyongyang		Changchun	
Liverpool	76	Liaoyang		Portsmouth	43
Ningshia		Shaohing		Rabat	43
Wanhsien		Kanchow		Chapra	43
Stockholm	75	Lille	55	Wakayama	
Warsaw	75	Verona	55	Plymouth	42
Bahia	75	Zaragoza	55	Frankfurt	42
Jaipur	75	Buda-Pest	54	Lemberg	42
Bharatpur	75	Ghent	54	Danzig	41
Algiers	73	Lima	54	Cologne	41
Birmingham	72	Arcot		the Hague	41
Nantes	72	Antwerp	53	Kokand	
Hué		Königsberg	53	Sanaa	
Rampur		Leeds	52	Gwalior	
Hwaian		Leghorn	52	Vellore	
Yangchow		Burdwan	52	Matsmaye	
Aleppo	70	Maheshwar		Kuku Khoto	
Bursa	70	Katsina		Kazargamu	
Bokhara	70	Hsüchow		Kweiyang	
Granada	70	Toulouse	50	Loyang	
Aurangabad	70	Isfahan	50	Ife	
Jehol	68	Marrakesh	50	Yezd	
Philadelphia	68	Hama	50	Bangkok	40
Oporto	67	Meshhed	50	Tabriz	40
Bristol	66	Mirzapur	50	Amiens	40
Brussels	66	Shahjahanpur	50	Liège	40
Farrukhabad	66	Chaochow	50	Taiyüan	40
Turin	66	Kagoshima		Pernambuco	40
Bologna	66	Strasbourg	49	Buenos Aires	40
Guanajuato	66	Hiroshima	49	Gondar	40
Kagoshima	66	Málaga	49	Zaria	40
Tsinan		Tanjore		Kumasi	40
Bareilly	65	Mysore		Cuttack	40
Puebla	65	Catania	48	Hamadan	40
Breslau	64	Munich	48	Achin	40
Cork	63	Taiwan		Nimes	39
New York	63			Brescia	38
				Diyarbekir	38

Broach	38	Gorakhpur	31	Écija	28
Metz	37	300 Kastamuni		Pusan	28
Cambay	37	Malatya		Bhagalpur	28
Kirin	37	Hsinking		Tarsus	
Orléans	36	Kolhapur		Zamfara	
Newcastle	36	Multan		Debrecen	27
Norwich	36	Mysore		Bergamo	27
Messina	36	Taipei		Brest	27
Fukuoka		Ogbomosho		Kingston	27
Afyon-Karahissar		Mengo		Jaén	27
Kulja		Wenchow		Potsdam	27
Aydin		Nanning		Masulipatam	27
Changteh		Wusih		Rewarri	
Weihsien		Ichang		Pilibit	
Raikot		Anking		Aberdeen	26
Iseyin		Taku		Geneva	26
Ghazipur		Segu	30	Baltimore	26
Saharanpur		Dariya	30	Bitlis	26
Negapatam		Limerick	30	Arequipa	26
Kanchi	35	Tokat	30	Maria Theresiopel	26
Boston	35	Caen	30	Rennes	26
Valetta	35	Yannina	30	Belgrade	26
Cordova	35	Plovdiv	30	Barfrush	
Akita	35	Ferrara	30	Bonga	
Tokushima		Valladolid	30	Mirta	
Vizagapatam		Besançon	30	Satara	
Jullundur		Rustchuk	30	Ellichpur	
Moradabad		Carácas	30	Kingchow	
Bhopal		Mérida	30	Kingyang	
Dabhoi		Nagasaki	30	Luang Prabang	
Cuzco	34	Tehran	30	Namdinh	
Bucharest	34	Ankara	30	Haidzuong	
Magdeburg	34	Konia	30	Jiddah	
Mosul	34	Kars	30	Iznik	
Burhanpur	33	Dinajpur	30	Sining	
Zacatecas	33	Monghyr	30	Fowchow	
Montpellier	33	Porbandar	30	Hengchow	
Parma	33	Bihar	30	Hwaian	
Xérez	33	Cochin	30	Dundee	25
Cartagena	33	Rangoon	30	Krakow	25
Angers	32	Prome	30	Versailles	25
Utrecht	32	Brunei	30	Vilna	25
Augsburg	32	Ismail	30	Nuremberg	25
Leipzig	32	Mandvi	30	Kazan	25
Kutahia	32	Mangalore	30	Vidin	25
Gaya	32	Dera Ghazi Khan	30	Orel	25
Okayama	32	Riga	29	Shumla	25
Mecca		Palma	29	Katmandu	25
Yarkand		Hodeida		Guatemala City	25
Sivas	31	Kanchow, Kansuh		Oaxaca	25
Seringapatam	31	Tinnevelly		Huamanga	25
Bath	31	Gbara		Cochabamba	25
Alessandria	31	Wuchow		Damietta	25
Bremen	31	Hull	28	Kano	25
Brunswick	31	Graz	28	Tarudant	25
Leiden	31	Vicenza	28	Abomey	25
Bruges	31	Piacenza	28	Asyut	25
		Nottingham	28	Fukui	25

Rajmahal	25	Purnea	22
Tashkent	25	Würzburg	22
Trebizond	25	La Paz	22
Homs	25	Makassar	
Pondichéry	25	Kawkaban	
Khoi	25	Nara	
Kayseri	25	Gulbarga	
Aivali	25	Ajmer	
Palembang	25	Kochi	
Tinghai	25	Hathras	
Nizampatam		Bogotá	21
Lakhon		Santiago, Chile	21
Kweichow		Kumamoto	21
Szegedin	24	Stuttgart	21
Clermont	24	Sistova	21
Mainz	24	Avignon	21
Lübeck	24	Haarlem	21
Paisley	24	Tournai	21
Troyes	24	Dunkerque	21
Saratov	24	Cremona	21
Groningen	24	Dijon	21
Pavia	24	Toulon	21
Patan, Nepal	24	Asti	21
Surabaja	24	Kebbi	
Etawah		Ede	
Aligarh		Puje	
Nganshun		Tientsiku	
Sungkiang		Bahawalpur	
Tsinchow		Hofuf	
Hsuchow, Szechwan		Meerut	
Tsochow		Kurnaul	
Sialkot		Bellary	
Panipat		Guntur	
Salerno	23	Rajamundry	
Nizhny-Novgord	23	Puri	20
Kaluga	23	Gaur	20
Aachen	23	Limoges	20
Grenoble	23	Kiev	20
Valenciennes	23	Reims	20
Pressburg	23	St. Omer	20
Triest	23	Chatham	20
Ratisbon	23	Dieppe	20
Kursk	23	Prizren	20
Ouro Preto	23	Mondovi	20
Tüngnai		Silistria	20
Cooch Behar		Iasi	20
Ambala		Constantine	20
Calpi		Tripoli, Africa	20
Acre		Shiraz	20
Mengtze		Medina	20
Stoke	22	Edessa	20
Brünn	22	Bhuj	20
Tours	22	Kelat	20
Yaroslav	22	Nujufabad	20
Mantua	22	Quilon	20
Belfast	22	Rangpur	20
Voronezh	22	Madurai	20
Schemnitz	22		

1825

	Peking	China	1 350 000
	London	Britain	1 335
	Canton	China	900
	Paris	France	855
	Constantinople	Turkey	675
	Hangchow	China	600
	Yedo	Japan	530
	Soochow	China	480
	Kyoto	Japan	350
10	Naples	Naples	350
	Osaka	Japan	340
	St. Petersburg	Russia	324
	Bombay	British	300
	Lucknow	Oudh	300
	Vienna	Austria	288
	Patna	British	269
	Moscow	Russia	262
	Cairo	Egypt	260
	Sian	China	259
20	Lisbon	Portugal	249
	Ningpo	China	230
	Calcutta	British	230
	Fuchow	China	225
	Berlin	Prussia	222
25	Nanking	China	200

	Wuchang			Lyon	141
	Hyderabad	200		Philadelphia	138
	Amsterdam	196		Rome	138
	Dublin	194		Surat	138
	Seoul	192		Smyrna	135
	Mukden	180		Hamburg	130
	Madrid	178		Adrianople	125
	Mexico City	176		Nanchang	
	Benares	176		Warsaw	124
	Chungking			Birmingham	122
	Chengtu	175		Havana	121
	Tientsin	175		Barcelona	120
	Fatshan	175		Marseille	119
	Glasgow	173		Chinkiang	118
	Madras	172		Nagpur	115
	Liverpool	170		Shanghai	115
	New York	170		Bagdad	110
	Milan	168		Poona	110
	Palermo	168		Turin	109
	Lanchow	160		Amritsar	109
	Manchester	155		Copenhagen	108
	Delhi	150		Jehol	107
	Edinburgh	145		Tunis	105
	Murshidabad	145		Kanazawa	103
50	Kingtehchen	144		Leeds	102

1850

	London	Britain	2 320 000
	Peking	China	1 648
	Paris	France	1 314
	Canton	China	800
	Constantinople	Turkey	785
	Hangchow	China	700
	New York	U.S.	682
	Bombay	British	575
	Yedo	Japan	567
10	Soochow	China	550
	St. Petersburg	Russia	502
	Berlin	Prussia	446
	Vienna	Austria	426
	Philadelphia	U.S.	426
	Liverpool	Britain	422
	Naples	Naples	416
	Calcutta	British	413
	Manchester	British	412
	Moscow	Russia	373
20	Glasgow	British	346
	Kyoto	Japan	323
	Madras	British	310
	Osaka	Japan	300
	Nanking	China	300
25	Lucknow	British	300

	Birmingham	294	Benares	185
	Sian	275	Leeds	184
	Dublin	263	Palermo	182
	Madrid	263	Mukden	180
	Patna	263	Fatshan	175
	Lisbon	257	Mexico City	170
	Cairo	256	Rome	170
	Lyon	254	Lanchow	170
	Fuchow	250	Baltimore	169
	Shanghai	250	Barcelona	167
	Chengtu	240	Rio de Janeiro	166
	Wuchang		Warsaw	163
	Ningpo	230	Bangkok	160
	Amsterdam	225	Budapest	156
	Brussels	208	Delhi	156
	Boston	202	Smyrna	150
	Hyderabad	200	Bristol	150
	Tientsin	200	Kingtehchen	144
	Chungking	200	Sheffield	143
	Havana	199	Bordeaux	142
	Edinburgh	194	Venice	141
	Seoul	194	Turin	138
	Hamburg	193	Alexandria	138
	Marseille	193	Copenhagen	135
50	Milan	193	New Orleans	132

1875

	London	Britain	4 241 000
	Paris	France	2 250
	New York	U.S.	1 900
	Peking	China	1 310
	Berlin	Germany	1 045
	Vienna	Austria	1 001
	Canton	China	944
	Philadelphia	U.S.	791
	Tokyo	Japan	780
10	St. Petersburg	Russia	764
	Bombay	Brit. India	718
	Calcutta	Brit. India	680
	Liverpool	Britain	650
	Glasgow	Britain	635
	Moscow	Russia	600
	Constantinople	Turkey	600
	Manchester	Britain	590
	Birmingham	Britain	480
	Boston	U.S.	450
20	Naples	Italy	450
	Madrid	Spain	407
	Chicago	U.S.	405
	Shanghai	British	400
	Madras	Brit. India	400
25	Cairo	Egypt	355

Hyderabad	350		Ningpo	250
Hamburg	348		Fuchow	250
St. Louis	338		Mexico City	250
Lyon	331		Chungking	250
Brussels	327		Soochow	250
Budapest	325		Copenhagen	241
Tientsin	325		Lisbon	240
Osaka	320		Barcelona	240
Marseille	316		Breslau	239
Warsaw	311		Kyoto	238
Chengtu	310		Havana	230
Dublin	310		Bordeaux	225
Bangkok	300		Patna	225
Wuchang	300		Melbourne	222
Baltimore	299		Palermo	219
Leeds	296		Turin	216
Sheffield	292		Buenos Aires	216
Amsterdam	289		San Francisco	214
Cincinnati	280		Alexandria	212
Milan	277		New Orleans	210
Lucknow	276		Leipzig	209
Rio de Janeiro	274		Bristol	200
Edinburgh	274		Mandalay	200
Rome	252		Munich	198
50 Sian	250		Dresden	197

1900

London	Britain	6 480 000
New York	U.S.	4 242
Paris	France	3 330
Berlin	Germany	2 424
Chicago	U.S.	1 717
Vienna	Austria	1 662
Tokyo	Japan	1 497
St. Petersburg	Russia	1 439
Philadelphia	U.S.	1 418
10 Manchester	Britain	1 255
Birmingham	Britain	1 248
Moscow	Russia	1 120
Peking	China	1 100
Calcutta	British India	1 085
Boston	U.S.	1 075
Glasgow	Britian	1 072
Liverpool	Britain	940
Osaka	Japan	931
Constantinople	Turkey	900
20 Hamburg	Germany	895
Shanghai	British	837
Buenos Aires	Argentina	806
Budapest	Hungary	792
Bombay	British India	780
25 Ruhr	Germany	766

Rio de Janeiro	750	San Francisco	439	Sian	300
Warsaw	724	Cologne	437	Kiev	300
Tientsin	700	Leeds	436	Barmen-Elberfeld	298
Canton	670	Breslau	422	Detroit	297
Newcastle	615	Fuchow	420	Liège	295
St. Louis	614	Cincinnati	417	Riga	294
Pittsburgh	604	Sheffield	403	Bordeaux	292
Cairo	595	Edinburgh	386	New Orleans	291
Naples	563	Cleveland	385	Santiago	290
Brussels	561	Prague	384	Lille	289
Barcelona	552	Dublin	382	Hannover	286
Bangkok	540	Rotterdam	368	Milwaukee	285
Madrid	539	Rhondda	367	100 Bucharest	282
Leipzig	532	Minneapolis	366	Tsinan	280
Amsterdam	510	Lisbon	363	Tehran	280
Baltimore	508	Kyoto	362	Washington	278
Madras	505	Antwerp	361	Nanking	270
Soochow	500	Buffalo	354	Genoa	269
Munich	499	75 Gleiwitz	353	Montevideo	268
Milan	491	Lodz	351	Roubaix	267
Lyon	487	Hangchow	350	Lucknow	265
Rome	487	Turin	347	Nuremberg	261
Marseille	486	Mexico City	344	Ningpo	260
Melbourne	485	Belfast	339	Nagoya	260
50 Sydney	478	Frankfurt	338	Kobe	250
Chengtu	475	Chungking	325	Mukden	250
Copenhagen	462	Montreal	325	Providence	248
Hankow	450	Bristol	320	Yokohama	245
Odessa	449	Alexandria	314	Havana	243
Hyderabad	445	Bradford	303	Palermo	242
Dresden	440	Stockholm	300	Nottingham	237

Hull	236	Chinkiang	168	Nagasaki	130
Louisville	236	Bolton	166	Surat	128
the Hague	236	Damascus	165	Brunswick	128
Taiyüan	230	Vilna	162	Blackburn	126
Changsha	230	Rochester	162	Nagpur	126
Magdeburg	229	Bangalore	161	Kishinev	125
Rangoon	229	Dundee	160	Columbus	125
Christiania	227	Jaipur	160	Changchow	125
Stuttgart	224	Amritsar	159	Kabul	125
Kansas City	215	Lemberg	159	Lima	122
Düsseldorf	213	Tashkent	159	Scinagar	122
Valencia	213	Adelaide	159	Astrakhan	121
Portsmouth	212	Brighton	158	Hiroshima	121
Benares	211	Halle	156	Preston	120
Florence	210	Tunis	156	Marrakesh	120
Stettin	210	Pernambuco	155	Beirut	118
Leicester	207	Poona	154	Worcester, U.S.	118
Delhi	207	Omaha	154	Brisbane	118
Chemnitz	206	Colombo	152	Meerut	118
São Paulo	205	Bologna	151	Troy	117
Stoke	205	Nantes	151	Kiel	117
Toronto	205	Zürich	150	Amoy	117
Mannheim	203	Aberdeen	150	Posen	117
Smyrna	201	Kaifeng	150	Batavia	115
Lahore	201	Tsining	150	Karachi	114
Nanchang	200	Toulouse	149	Charleroi	114
Wusih	200	Seville	148	Cádiz	113
Fatshan	200	Cape Town	148	New Haven	113
Chaochow	200	Surabaja	146	Shasi	113
Tabriz	200	Rouen	145	Derby	112
Ghent	198	Bagdad	145	Geneva	112
Cawnpore	197	Valparaíso	145	Rosario	112
Kharkov	197	Scranton	144	Murcia	111
Seoul	195	Sunderland	144	Norwich	110
Patna	194	Kazan	143	Rochester, Eng.	110
Singapore	193	Saratov	143	Anking	110
Hong Kong	192	Dortmund	142	Bogotá	110
Manila	190	Rostov	142	Tula	109
Bahia	190	Danzig	140	Wilkes-Barre	109
Königsberg	189	Ibadan	140	Surakarta	109
Agra	186	Algiers	140	Basel	109
Mainz-Wiesbaden	185	Salonica	140	Krefeld	109
Mandalay	184	Wanhsien	140	Reims	108
Bremen	182	St. Étienne	138	Krakow	108
Ahmedabad	181	Catania	138	Syracuse, U.S.	108
Athens	181	Graz	138	Los Angeles	107
Changteh	180	Brünn	137	Cassel	106
Plymouth	179	Wuhu	137	Paterson	105
Baku	179	Ekaterinoslav	135	Baroda	105
Lanchow	175	Aachen	135	Fall River	104
Oporto	175	le Havre	135	Halifax, Eng.	104
Saigon	175	Denver	133	Madurai	104
Johannesburg	173	Triest	132	Utrecht	104
Strassburg	172	Toledo, U.S.	131	Nice	103
Allahabad	172	Göteborg	130	Brest	103
Venice	171	Bareilly	130	Trichinopoly	103
Cardiff	169	Málaga	130		
Indianapolis	169				

Szeged	102	Rochdale	82	Vitebsk	73
St. Joseph	102	Angers	82	Ottawa	73
Augsburg	102	Padua	82	Darmstadt	72
Southampton	102	Szabadka	82	Jogjakarta	72
Memphis, U. S.	102	Lübeck	82	Bergen	72
Albany	101	Carácas	82	Kayseri	72
Toulon	101	Chefoo	82	Davenport	71
Guadalajara	101	Adrianople	81	Dijon	71
Yangchow	100	Görlitz	80	Alessandria	71
Kingtehchen	100	Nashville	80	Gaya	71
300 Kuku Khoto	100	Hakodate	80	Lawrence	71
Kweiyang	100	Zhitomir	80	Reading, England	71
Cartagena	99	Seattle	80	Bridgeport	70
Zaragoza	99	Nimes	80	Brescia	70
Samara	99	Mirzapur	80	Salem, India	70
Leghorn	98	Isfahan	80	Orel	70
Karlsruhe	97	Hanchung	80	Ogbomosho	70
Helsingfors	97	Paoting	80	Liaoyang	70
Burnley	96	Pohchow	80	Meshhed	70
Peshawar	95	Wenchow	80	Kerman	70
Huddersfield	95	Hanoi	80	Yarkand	70
Nikolayev	95	Reading, U.S.	78	Dunkerque	70
Lowell	94	Ambala	78	Ekaterinodar	69
Minsk	94	Rampur	78	Lorca	69
Swansea	91	Iasi	78	Aligarh	69
Nizhny-Novgorod	91	Bari	77	Belgrade	69
Lashkar	90	Kuala Lumpur	77	Mysore	68
Amiens	90	Shahjahanpur	76	Valladolid	68
Dacca	90	Wilmington	76	Grenoble	68
Portland, Oregon	90	Plauen	76	Coventry	68
Sendai	90	Brusa	76	Farukhabad	68
Kanazawa	90	Bhopal	76	Pilsen	68
Shaohing	90	Tinnevelly	76	Shimonoseki	68
Shihlung	90	York	76	Fukuoka	68
Atlanta	90	Cork	76	Hyderabad, Sind	68
Middlesbrough	89	Québec	76	Sofia	67
Jubbulpore	89	Yaroslavl	76	Czernowitz	67
Hartford	89	Montpellier, France	75	Groningwen	67
Mülhausen	89	Granada	75	Jullundur	67
Semarang	89	Calicut	75	Orléans	67
Springfield, Mass.	88	Saarbrücken	75	Greenock	67
Oran	87	Würzburg	75	Okayama	67
Ferrara	87	Fyzabad	75	Imphal	67
Grand Rapids	87	Bhagalpur	75	Libau	67
Multan	87	Debrecen	75	Darbhanga	66
Kokand	86	Serampur	75	Reval	66
Indore	86	Kiating	75	Elizavetgrad	66
Rawalpindi	86	Bokhara	75	New Bedford	66
Northampton, Eng.	85	Pará	75	Newport, England	66
Dayton	85	Guatemala City	74	Orenburg	65
Richmond	85	Moradabad	74	Saharanpur	65
Erfurt	85	Lucca	74	Pozsony	65
Voronezh	84	Rennes	74	Otaru	65
Limoges	84	400 Verona	74	Wakayama	65
Duluth	84	Ajmer	73	Kremenchug	65
Hartlepool	83	Kovno	73	Bialystok	65
Bilbao	83	Trenton	73	Hastings	65
St. Helens	83	Dvinsk	73	Haarlem	65
		Kherson	73		

Spandau	65		Calais	59		Newcastle, Australia	54
Kashgar	65		San Salvador	59		Santander	54
Tsingkiangpo	65		Trapani	59		Leiden	54
Wuchow	65		Kumbakonam	59		Savannah	54
Auckland	65		Evansville	59		Fürth	54
Kerbela	65		Poltava	59		Port-of-Spain	54
Namangan	65		La Plata	58		Ekaterinburg	54
Penza	65		Taganrog	58		Tananarive	54
Wheeling	65		Kursk	58		Patiala	53
Modena	64		Linz	58		Navanagar	53
Ivanovo-Voznesensk	64		Reggio, Emilia	58		Cagliari	53
Tours	64		Metz	58		Czestochowa	53
Gorakhpur	64		Braila	58		Salt Lake City	53
Palma	63		Bellary	58		Tver	53
Sholapur	63		Cordova	58		San Antonio	53
Münster	63		Samarkand	58		Jamnagar	53
Tomsk	63		Remscheid	58		Troyes	53
Jérez	63		Charleston	58		Foggia	53
Warrington	63		Mönchen-Gladbach	58		Rotherham	53
León, México	63		Berdichev	58	600	Bruges	53
le Mans	63		Bury	57		Omsk	53
Bielefeld	63		Kecskemét	57		Temesvár	53
Galatz	62		Trivandrum	57		Constantine	52
Zwickau	62		Moulmein	57		Clermont	52
Tokushima	62		Sevastopol	57		Bikaner	52
Monterrey	62		Coatbridge	57		Erie	52
Des Moines	62		Sialkot	57		Port Louis	52
Grimsby	62		Tanjore	57		Elbing	52
Ludwigshafen	61		Dewsbury	57		Béziers	52
Frankfurt-on-Oder	61		Arnhem	57		Coimbatore	52
Freiburg	61		Smolensk	57		Hamilton, Canada	52
Perugia	61		Negapatam	57		Bromberg	52
Pisa	61		Lublin	57		Asunción	52
Taihoku	61		Manchester, U.S.	56		Cuddalore	51
500 Zagreb	61		Barrow	56		Norfolk	51
San Luis Potosí	61		Ancona	56		Osnabrück	51
Mosul	61		Bhavnagar	56		Kolhapur	51
Kronstadt	60		Mecheln	56		Cuttack	51
Newchwang	60		Durban	56		Aarhus	51
Hódmezö-Vásárhely	60		Tanta	56		Waterbury	51
Malmö	60		Portland, Maine	56		Novocherkask	51
Kumamoto	60		Utica	56		Great Yarmouth	51
Simferopol	60		Arad	56		Dunedin	51
Jodhpur	60		Alwar	56		Guayaquil	51
Wigan	60		Peoria	56		Stockton	51
Hubli	60		Christchurch	55		Dessau	50
Muttra	60		Niigata	55		Bonn	50
Siangyang	60		Kagoshima	55		St.-Quentin	50
Huchow	60		Jhansi	55		Kaluga	50
Sining	60		Besançon	55		Nagyvárad	50
Swatow	60		Birmingham, U.S.	55		Harrisburg	50
Kure	60		Oshogbo	55		Alicante	50
Mecca	60		Yazd	55		Quito	50
Rabat	60		Jerusalem	55		Bath	50
Abeokuta	60		Omdurman	55		Barfrush	50
Porto Alegre	60		Liegnitz	54		Shiraz	50
Zaria	60		Rostock	54		Meknes	50
Potsdam	59		La Paz	54			

Port-au-Prince	50	700 Perm	45	Ploesti	42
Chüanchow	50	Craiova	45	Dallas	42
Fowchow	50	Regensburg	45	Broach	42
Hengchow	50	Bihar	45	Sambhal	42
Yakoba	50	Solingen	45	Caen	42
Chiengmai	50	Halifax, Canada	45	Eastbourne	42
Hwaian	50	Novara	45	Dorpat	42
Nganshun	50	Fort Wayne	45	Lorient	42
Sungkiang	50	Medellín	45	Saginaw	42
Tsinchow	50	Tucumán	45	Iquique	42
Córdoba, Arg.	49	Maracaibo	45	Hathras	42
Burton	49	Ichang	45	Etawah	42
Salem, U.S.	49	Tainan	45	Little Rock	42
Boulogne	49	Shizuoka	45	Asyut	41
Ferozepore	49	León, Nicaragua	45	Saugor	42
Verviers	49	Adana	45	Paraná	42
Kolozsvár	49	Laoag	45	Ahmednagar	42
Ufa	49	Youngstown	44	Bamberg	41
Brandenburg	49	Vicenza	44	Hué	41
Tambov	49	Houston	44	Kozlov	41
Irkutsk	49	Sapporo	44	Tilburg	41
Sasebo	49	Ryazan	44	Guanajuato	41
Oxford	49	Las Palmas	44	Winnipeg	41
Flensburg	48	Reggio, Calabria	44	Keighley	41
Shikarpur	48	Port Said	44	Kostroma	41
Cheltenham	48	Arezzo	44	Norrköping	41
Ludhiana	48	Swindon	44	Tripoli, Libya	40
Kaiserslautern	48	Simbirsk	44	Dover	40
Oviedo	48	Serajevo	44	Lipa	40
Lincoln, England	48	Nimeguen	44	Worms	40
Lintsing	48	Konia	44	Kofu	40
Wellington	48	Pécs	43	Mobile	40
Medina	48	Coruña	43	Wakefield	40
Santa Ana	48	Darlington	43	Ostend	40
Pondichéry	47	Blackpool	43	St. John	40
Bergamo	47	Mangalore	43	Barnsley	40
Mogilev	47	Brest-Litovsk	43	Valletta	40
Gijón	47	Palghat	43	Vizagapatam	40
Gloucester, Eng.	47	Forli	43	Lincoln, U.S.	40
Kokanada	47	Vellore	43	Heidelberg	40
Chapra	47	Mérida, México	43	Brockton	40
Exeter	47	Trier	43	Ife	40
Concepción	46	Pfozheim	43	Kano	40
Puri	46	Caltanissetta	43	800 Ede	40
Avignon	46	Grodno	43	London, Canada	40
Fukui	46	Miskolc	43	Anking	40
Bourges	46	Santiago, Cuba	43	Hsingi	40
Kingston	46	Sivas	43	Hsuchow, Kiangsi	40
Przemysl	46	Ballarat	43	Kweichow	40
Worcester, Eng.	46	Ulm	42	Nanning	40
Bournemouth	46	Hildesheim	42	Pyongyang	40
Udaipur	46	Marghelan	42	Muscat	40
Muzaffarpur	46	Plovdiv	42	Zanzibar	40
Bharatpur	45	Louvain	42	Hamadan	40
Conjeeveram	45	Jaunpur	42	Qazvin	40
Arrah	45	Akron	42	Urumchi	40
Holyoke	45	Cherbourg	42	Ghazipur	40
Gera	45	Salerno	42	Zacatecas	39
Hsüchow	45	Pnom-Penh	42	Poitiers	39

Mansura	39	Talca	39	Patras	38
Binghampton	39	Altoona	38	Santa Cruz	38
Lancaster, Eng.	39	Topeka	38	Sassari	38
Amroha	39	Fiume	38	Springfield, Ohio	38
Tonk	39	Erzurum	38	Åbo	38
Ujjain	39	Como	38	Cambridge	38
Masulipatam	39	Dordrecht	38	Trondhjem	38
Yamagata	39	Bitlis	38	Vladivostok	38
Budweis	39	Schwerin	38	Urga	38
Cottbus	39	Budaun	38	Monghyr	37
Honolulu	39	Elets	38	Udine	37
Kampti	39	Nafa	38		

1925

	New York	U.S.	7 774 000
	London	Britain	7 742
	Tokyo	Japan	5 300
	Paris	France	4 800
	Berlin	Germany	4 013
	Chicago	U.S.	3 564
	Ruhr	Germany	3 400
	Buenos Aires	Argentina	2 410
	Osaka	Japan	2 219
10	Philadelphia	U.S.	2 085
	Vienna	Austria	1 862
	Boston	U.S.	1 773
	Moscow	Russia	1 764
	Manchester	Britain	1 725
	Birmingham	Britain	1 700
	Shanghai	British	1 500
	Leningrad	Russia	1 430
	Glasgow	Britain	1 396
	Detroit	U.S.	1 394
20	Calcutta	Brit. India	1 390
	Hamburg	Germany	1 369
	Budapest	Hungary	1 318
	Peking	China	1 266
	Rio de Janeiro	Brazil	1 240
25	Liverpool	Britain	1 235

Bombay	1 170		Tientsin	800	Leipzig	679
Los Angeles	1 147		Canton	798	Minneapolis	675
Sydney	1 039		Madrid	791	Katowice	675
Warsaw	1 002		Mexico City	772	Lyon	653
Hankow	1 000		Baltimore	679	Kobe	644
Cairo	1 000		Nagoya	768	Rotterdam	623
Cleveland	990		Rome	758	Dresden	619
San Francisco	935	50	Hong Kong	750	Marseille	612
St. Louis	930		Newcastle	750	Chungking	608
Milan	917		Prague	745	Madras	575
Melbourne	912		São Paulo	740	Breslau	573
Naples	852		Copenhagen	731	Cincinnati	568
Bangkok	827		Montréal	728	Lisbon	567
Pittsburgh	823		Amsterdam	718	Toronto	565
Constantinople	817		Cologne	698	Frankfurt	563
Barcelona	803		Munich	680	75 Buffalo	558
Brussels	801		Kyoto	679		

	Havana	550		Riga	337	Poona	232
	Bucharest	550		Rosario	335	Göteborg	230
	Athens	542		Chemnitz	331	Cawnpore	230
	Milwaukee	541		Saigon	429	Lwow	230
	Alexandria	540		Liège	327	Surabaja	230
	Johannesburg	538		Bordeaux	324	Bologna	227
	Changsha	538		Bradford	323	Venice	226
	Sheffield	534		Fuchow	322	Porto Alegre	226
	Cincinnati	531		Dortmund	320	Danzig	226
	Genoa	525		Rochester	311	Lima	225
	Lodz	522		Tashkent	310	Cape Town	222
	Kansas City	521		Pernambuco	309	Algiers	222
	Santiago	521		Bahia	306	Taiyüan	220
	Turin	520		Adelaide	303	Zürich	213
	Lille	504		Amoy	300	200 Kiel	216
	Chengtu	500		Nanchang	300	Amritsar	212
	Singapore	485		Seoul	297	Seville	212
	Rhondda	485		Rostov	295	Poznan	212
	Düsseldorf	477		Bremen	294	Helsinki	211
	Hangchow	475		Ahmedabad	293	Thessalonica	210
	Leeds	470		Magdeburg	292	Plymouth	209
	Antwerp	466		Batavia	290	Strasbourg	208
	Nuremberg	466		Ningpo	284	Agra	207
	Kiev	462		Portsmouth	283	Wenchow	202
100	Washington	463		Portland	280	Benares	201
	Edinburgh	444		Königsberg	279	Dairen	201
	Stockholm	442		Tiflis	274	Sofia	201
	Montevideo	429		Denver	272	Ostrava	200
	Hyderabad	429		Stoke	272		
	New Orleans	429		Bangalore	271		
	Hannover	422		Columbus	268		
	Palermo	419		Toledo, U.S.	266		
	Dublin	418		Nottingham	265		
	Baku	416		Colombo	264		
	Belfast	415		Brisbane	263		
	Yokohama	405		Catania	263		
	Providence	402		Valencia	262		
	Odessa	400		Scranton	261		
	Soochow	400		Mainz-Wiesbaden	260		
	the Hague	398		Pará	257		
	Nanking	395		Lucknow	257		
	Kharkov	388		Birmingham, U.S.	257		
	Bristol	387		Oporto	256		
	Tsinan	377		Oslo	255		
	Rangoon	376		Stettin	253		
	Delhi	375		Lanchow	250		
	Mukden	360		Atlanta	245		
	Lahore	355		Omaha	243		
	Barmen-Elberfeld	354		Trieste	242		
	Tehran	350		Brno	240		
	Mannheim	348		Karachi	240		
	Louisville	343		Cardiff	238		
	Stuttgart	341		Leicester	236		
	Seattle	340		Akron	233		
	Indianapolis	339		Kaifeng	233		

1950

	New York	U.S.	12 300 000
	London	Britain	8 860
	Tokyo	Japan	7 547
	Paris	France	5 900
	Shanghai	China	5 406
	Moscow	Russia	5 100
	Buenos Aires	Argentina	5 000
	Chicago	U.S.	4 906
	Ruhr	Germany	4 900
10	Calcutta	India	4 800
	Los Angeles	U.S.	3 900
	Berlin	Germany	3 707
	Osaka	Japan	3 480
	Mexico City	México	3 190
	Cairo	Egypt	2 950
	Philadelphia	U.S.	2 894
	Rio de Janeiro	Brazil	2 866
	Detroit	U.S.	2 784
	Leningrad	Russia	2 700
20	Bombay	India	2 680
	Manchester	Britain	2 382
	São Paulo	Brazil	2 227
	Boston	U.S.	2 212
	Birmingham	Britain	2 196
25	Hong Kong	British	2 100

	Peking	2 031		Liverpool	1 260
	San Francisco	1 941		Santiago	1 250
	Tientsin	1 795		Montréal	1 242
	Vienna	1 755		Naples	1 210
	Rome	1 665		Wuhan	1 200
	Sydney	1 635		Leeds	1 164
	Hamburg	1 580		Baltimore	1 159
	Mukden	1 551		Copenhagen	1 150
	Seoul	1 550		Athens	1 140
	Pittsburgh	1 530		Kyoto	1 101
	Madrid	1 527		Bucharest	1 100
	Budapest	1 500		Alexandria	1 100
	Canton	1 496		Chungking	1 100
	Barcelona	1 425		Havana	1 090
	Johannesburg	1 425		Dairen	1 054
	Djakarta	1 400		Hyderabad	1 035
	Manila	1 400		Nagoya	1 030
	Milan	1 400		Nanking	1 020
	St. Louis	1 394		Saigon	1 000
	Cleveland	1 372		Istanbul	1 000
	Madras	1 356		Tehran	989
	Melbourne	1 350		Bangkok	985
	Glasgow	1 320		Minneapolis	980
	Delhi	1 306		Katowice	977
50	Washington	1 285	75	Brussels	964

Karachi	950	Tiflis	585	San Diego	413
Amsterdam	940	Düsseldorf	570	San Antonio	408
Prague	938	Cape Town	565	Tunis	405
Lima	923	Sian	559	Zürich	405
Stockholm	889	Pernambuco	550	Pyongyang	400
Lisbon	885	Taiyüan	550	Rochester	400
Munich	870	Bogotá	543	Fuchow	400
Baku	840	Dallas	536	Changsha	396
Newcastle	830	Valencia	534	Memphis, U.S.	395
Milwaukee	820	Tsinan	532	Fukuoka	392
Lahore	815	Edinburgh	531	Ibadan	390
Cincinnati	808	Hangchow	517	Bahia	389
Rotterdam	803	Stuttgart	515	San Juan	385
Warsaw	803	Dortmund	507	Norfolk	385
Kiev	800	Kazan	505	Florence	384
Tsingtao	800	Atlanta	504	Göteborg	383
Surabaya	800	Indianapolis	502	Vancouver	383
Montevideo	797	Kunming	500	Seville	383
Buffalo	794	Rostov	500	Soochow	381
Changchun	788	Stalino (Donetsk)	500	Guadalajara	377
Gorki	775	Lanchow	500	Córdoba, Arg.	375
Ahmedabad	758	Bagdad	500	Porto Alegre	375
Toronto	754	Pusan	498	Charleroi	375
Harbin	750	Palermo	497	Bordeaux	370
Shimonoseki	750	Denver	492	Voronezh	370
Singapore	740	Bremen	490	Helsinki	367
Kharkov	730	Portland, Ore.	486	Akron	365
Sheffield	730	Chelyabinsk	485	Agra	364
Bangalore	725	Lucknow	481	Wuppertal	363
Turin	725	Nuremberg	479	Aleppo	362
Tashkent	700	Saratov	475	Toledo, U.S.	361
Bandung	700	Rosario	475	Dacca	360
Chengtu	698	Belfast	475	Oporto	355
Houston	694	Riga	475	Venice	354
Carácas	693	Durban	470	Madurai	352
Cologne	692	Hannover	469	Krakow	347
Kansas City	689	Louisville	465	Bologna	346
Frankfurt	680	Providence	464	Benares	345
Genoa	676	Poona	460	Stoke	345
Lodz	675	Miami	458	Springfield	344
Kanpur	670	Taipei	450	Dayton	343
Lille	670	Chengchow	450	Poznán	342
New Orleans	656	Dnepropetrovsk	450	Sendai	341
Kuibyshev	650	Liège	450	Hsüchow	339
Lyon	650	Belgrade	445	Belo Horizonte	338
Casablanca	647	Brisbane	440	Damascus	335
Leipzig	645	Bristol	440	Wiesbaden	335
the Hague	638	Molotov (Perm)	440	Léopoldville	334
Dresden	635	Sofia	437	Monterrey	333
Marseille	625	Birmingham, U.S.	435	Zaporozhye	330
Seattle	619	Oslo	434	Surakarta	330
Antwerp	610	Nottingham	434	Taegu	328
Sverdlovsk	610	Nagpur	432	Yaroslavl	328
Novosibirsk	605	Algiers	430	Allahabad	328
Rangoon	600	Columbus	430	Semarang	325
Colombo	600	Omsk	430	Zagreb	325
Odessa	600	Mannheim	421	Addis Ababa	325
Dublin	595	Adelaide	420	Auckland	323

Tel Aviv	321	Hartford	265	Strasbourg	230
La Paz	321	Winnipeg	265	Meerut	229
Amritsar	320	Medellín	264	Tainan	229
Bilbao	320	Zaragoza	264	Kagoshima	229
Erivan	315	Syracuse, U.S.	264	Hakodate	228
Sapporo	313	Sholapur	261	Ghent	228
Fort Worth	313	Krivoi Rog	260	Plymouth	228
Omaha	308	Lens	260	Tallinn	225
Brighton	305	Honolulu	258	Rouen	225
Cardiff	304	Ottawa	258	Nantes	225
Indore	304	Guayaquil	258	Penang	225
Tula	304	Hiroshima	258	Allentown	225
Perth, Australia	302	Richmond	257	Izhevsk	225
Middlesbrough	302	Nashville	257	Brno	225
Stalingrad		Cali	256	Marrakesh	224
Minsk	300	Khabarovsk	255	Graz	224
Lvov (Lemberg)	300	Vilna	255	Braunschweig	223
Wusih	300	Palembang	255	Sunderland	223
Catania	299	Pará	254	Halle	222
Hull	299	Kiel	254	Salt Lake City	221
Valparaíso	298	El Paso	253	Grand Rapids	220
Youngstown	297	Jabalpur	252	Nice	220
La Plata	295	Coventry	252	Niigata	220
Portsmouth	291	Kanazawa	252	Barnaul	220
Albany	290	Archangel	252	Kalinin (Tver)	220
Makassar	290	Trichinopoly	251	Surat	218
Irkutsk	288	Oklahoma City	250	Málaga	218
Jaipur	286	Malang	250	Rabat	217
Ankara	286	Antung	250	Thessalonica	217
Leicester	285	Lagos	247	Québec	216
Stalinsk	285	Basel	246	Voroshilovgrad	215
Guatemala City	284	Nizhny-Tagil	245	Kabul	215
Kaifeng	280	Ufa	245	Swatow	214
Alma-Ata	280	New Haven	244	Hanoi	214
Pretoria	280	Homs	244	Tucumán	214
Patna	280	Srinagar	243	Haarlem	214
Chittagong	280	Jacksonville	242	Worcester, U.S.	213
Barranquilla	280	Nagasaki	241	Jamshedpur	212
Wroclaw	279	Mysore	240	Augsburg	212
Inchon	278	Krasnodar	240	Himeji	212
Kure	276	Vladivostok	240	Gifu	211
Kaohsiung	275	Jogjakarta	240	Puebla	211
Krasnoyarsk	275	Kweiyang	239	Meshhed	210
Ivanova	275	Bournemouth	238	Khartoum	210
Utrecht	274	Gwalior	238	Ningpo	210
Tabriz	274	Shizuoka	238	Ostrava	210
Wilkes-Barre	273	Scranton	237	Southampton	210
Bari	271	Bridgeport	237	Phoenix	210
Oran	270	Lübeck	237	Saarbrücken	209
Gorlovka	270	Magdeburg	236	Quito	209
Karaganda	270	Hyderabad, Pak.	235	Grozny	208
Astrakhan	270	Maracaibo	235	Chkalov (Orenburg)	208
Pnom-Penh	270	Zhdanov (Mariupol)	235	Baroda	208
Trieste	270	Toulouse	235	Port Said	208
Medan	270	Fushun	233	Taichung	207
Santa Fé, Arg.	270	Izmir	231	Wuchow	206
Kumamoto	267	Rawalpindi	231	Murcia	206
Nanchang	266	Magnitogorsk	230	Sacramento	206

Prokopievsk	205	Isfahan	204	Mönchen-Gladbach	203
Asunción	205	Wellington	204	Penza	203
Tulsa	205	Beirut	203	Kemerovo	202
Fortaleza	205	Wuhu	203	Bonn	201

1968

	Tokyo	Japan	20 500
	New York	U.S.	16 900
	London	Britain	11 025
	Osaka	Japan	10 900
	Moscow	Russia	9 150
	Paris	France	8 850
	Buenos Aires	Argentina	8 600
	Los Angeles	U.S.	8 455
	Calcutta	India	7 900
10	Shanghai	China	7 800
	Chicago	U.S.	7 435
	Mexico City	México	7 200
	São Paulo	Brazil	6 600
	Rio de Janeiro	Brazil	6 100
	Cairo	Egypt	5 900
	Bombay	India	5 650
	Ruhr	Germany	5 150
	Philadelphia	U.S.	5 025
	Peking	China	4 750
20	Detroit	U.S.	4 625
	Leningrad	Russia	4 350
	Seoul	South Korea	4 175
	San Francisco	U.S.	4 150
	Djakarta	Indonesia	3 750
25	Delhi	India	3 750

	Boston	3 575	Budapest	2 350
	Hong Kong	3 500	Hamburg	2 335
	Tientsin	3 500	Istanbul	2 325
	Milan	3 365	Melbourne	2 300
	Tehran	3 250	Toronto	2 275
	Manila	3 200	St. Louis	2 255
	Mukden	3 000	Saigon	2 250
	Madrid	2 980	Canton	2 250
	Nagoya	2 925	Cleveland	2 250
	Wuhan (Hankow)	2 900	Bogotá	2 200
	Manchester, Br.	2 890	Carácas	2 150
	Rome	2 810	Harbin	2 100
	Santiago	2 725	Athens	2 100
	Bangkok	2 700	Alexandria	2 075
	Washington	2 695	Brussels	2 070
	Birmingham, Br.	2 665	Katowice	2 025
	Chungking	2 600	Vienna	2 020
	Sydney	2 600	Taipei	2 000
	Lima	2 550	Singapore	1 980
	Johannesburg	2 550	Pittsburgh	1 920
	Montreal	2 540	Bagdad	1 900
	West Berlin	2 500	Donetsk	1 875
	Barcelona	2 475	Naples	1 875
	Karachi	2 400	Glasgow	1 860
50	Madras	2 350	75 Amsterdam	1 805

Data from Richard Forstall's table for Rand McNally & Co.
However, Berlin is considered divided, and some spellings differ.

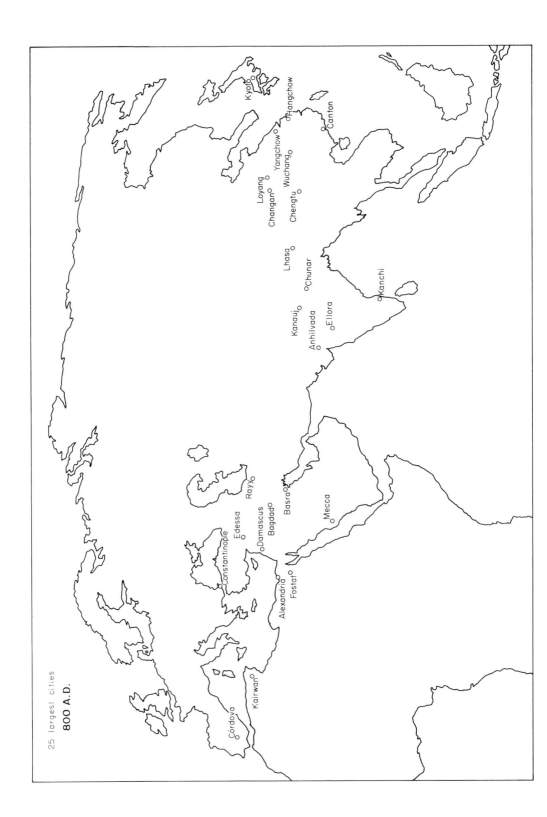

25 largest cities
800 A.D.

Kyoto

Loyang
Changan
Yangchow
Wuchang
Chengtu
Hangchow
Canton

Lhasa
Chunar
Kanchi

Kanauj
Ellora
Anhilvada

Rayy
Basra
Edessa
Damascus
Bagdad
Mecca
Constantinople

Alexandria
Fostat

Kairwan

Córdova

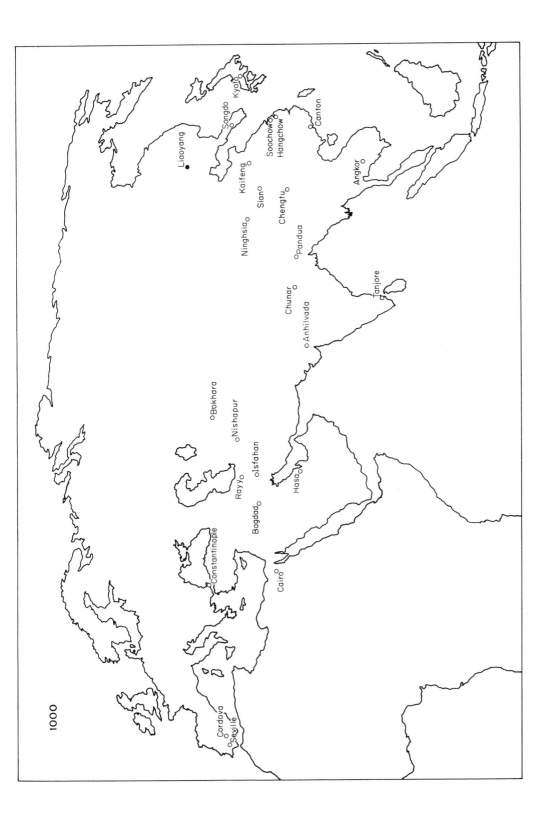

1000

Kyoto
Songdo
Liaoyang
Kaifeng
Ninghsia
Sian
Soochow
Hangchow
Chengtu
Canton
Pandua
Angkor
Chunar
Tanjore
Anhilvada
Bokhara
Nishapur
Rayy
Isfahan
Haso
Bagdad
Constantinople
Cairo
Cordova
Seville

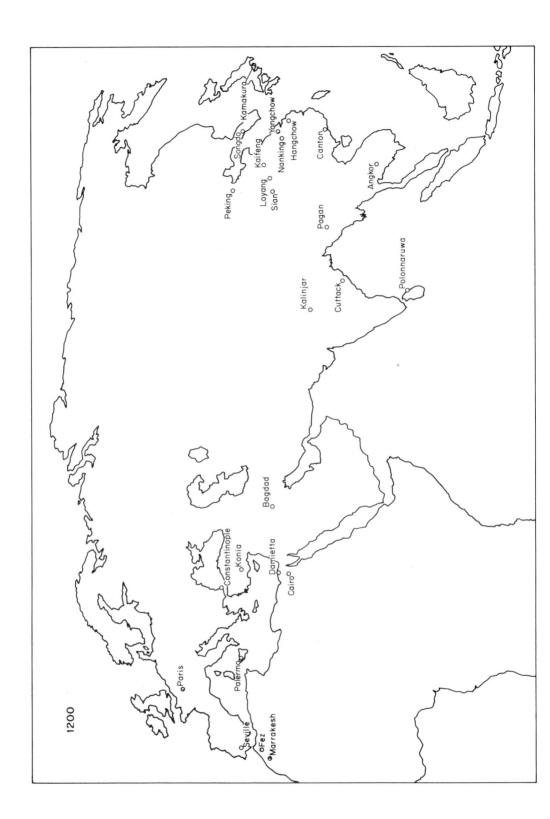

1200

Paris

Seville
Fez
Marrakesh

Palermo

Constantinople
Konia
Damietta
Cairo

Bagdad

Peking
Songdo
Kamakura
Kaifeng
Loyang
Sian
Nankingo
Hangchow
Yangchow
Canton
Angkor

Pagan

Polonnaruwa

Kalinjar
Cuttack

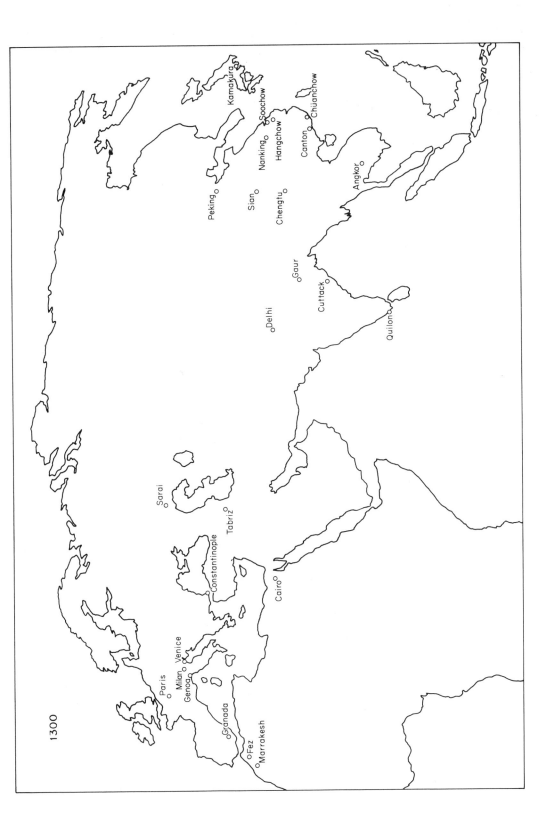

1300

Kamakura
Soochow
Chüanchow
Peking
Nanking
Hangchow
Canton
Sian
Chengtu
Angkor
Gaur
Cuttack
Delhi
Quilon
Sarai
Tabriz
Constantinople
Cairo
Paris
Milan
Venice
Genoa
Granada
Fez
Marrakesh

345

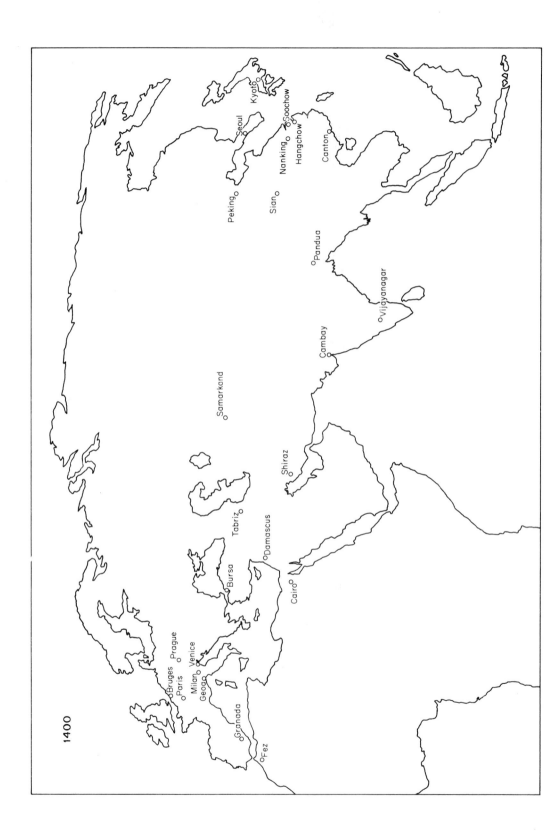

1400

Bruges
Prague
Paris
Milan Venice
Genoa
Granada
Fez

Cairo
Damascus
Bursa
Tabriz
Shiraz
Samarkand

Cambay
Vijayanagar
Pandua

Peking
Sian
Seoul
Kyoto
Nanking
Soochow
Hangchow
Canton

346

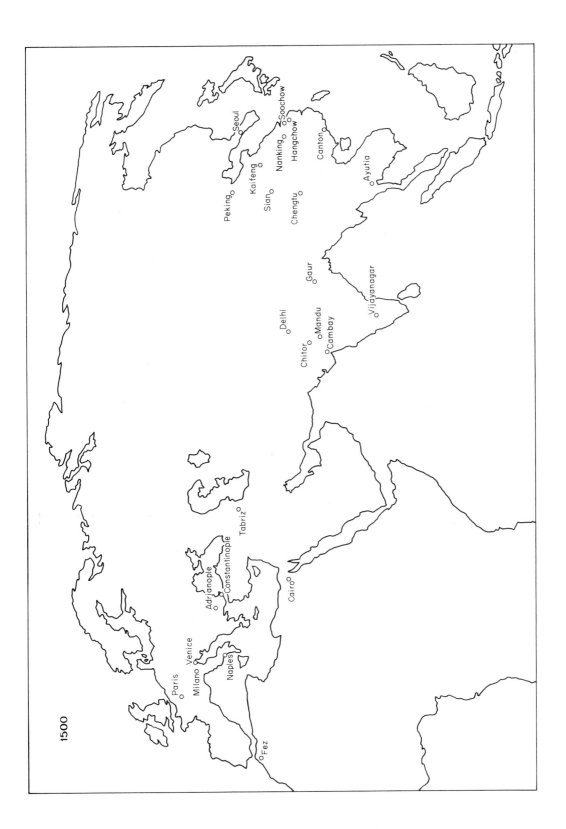

1500

Paris
Milano
Venice
Naples
Fez
Adrianople
Constantinople
Tabriz
Cairo
Peking
Kaifeng
Sian
Seoul
Nanking
Soochow
Hangchow
Canton
Chengtu
Ayutia
Gaur
Vijayanagar
Delhi
Chitor
Mandu
Cambay

1600

Yedo
Osaka
Kyoto
Soochow
Nanking Hangchow
Peking Canton
Sian Chengtu

Lahore
Agra
Ahmedabad Bijapur

Qazvin

Adrianople
Constantinople

Cairo

Venice
Naples

London
Paris

Seville
Marrakesh

← Potosí

348

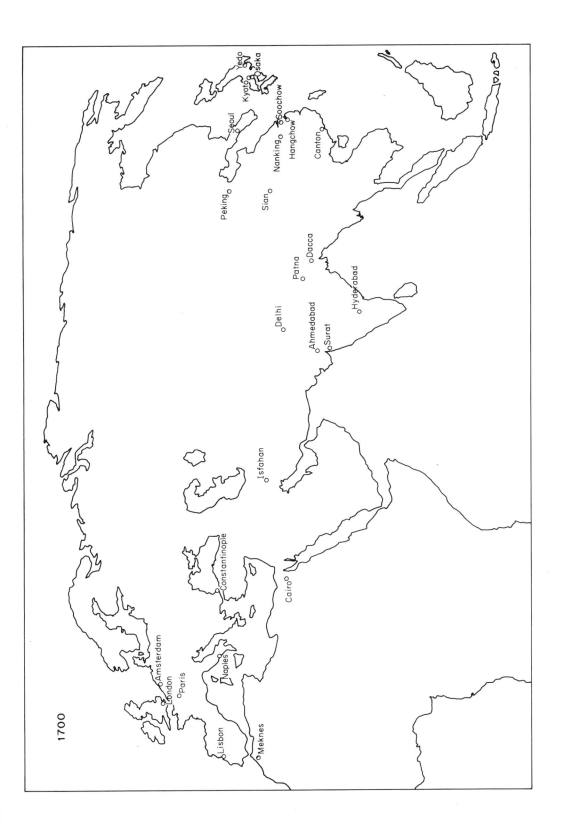

1700

Yedo
Osaka
Kyoto
Seoul
Soochow
Nanking
Hangchow
Canton
Peking
Sian
Patna
Dacca
Delhi
Hyderabad
Ahmedabad
Surat
Isfahan
Constantinople
Cairo
Amsterdam
London
Paris
Naples
Lisbon
Meknes

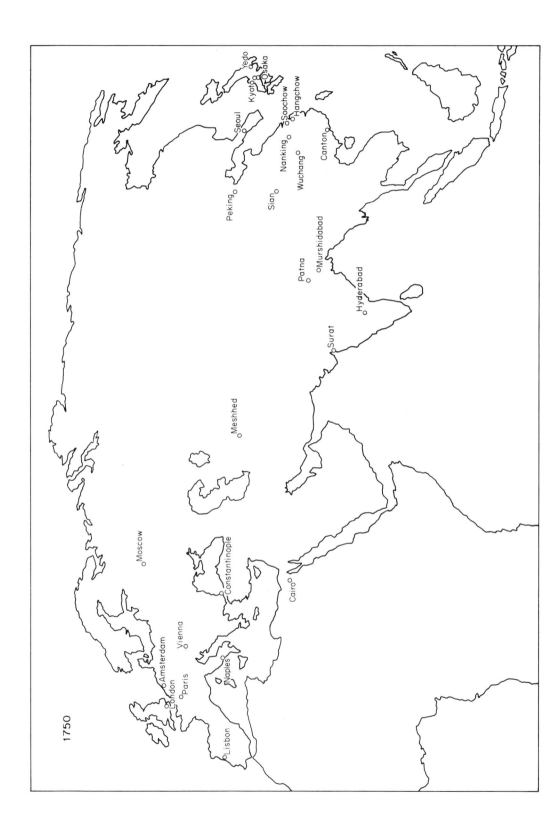

1750

Yedo
Osaka
Kyoto
Soochow
Hangchow
Seoul
Nanking
Wuchang
Canton
Peking
Sian
Murshidabad
Patna
Hyderabad
Surat
Meshhed
Moscow
Constantinople
Cairo
Vienna
Amsterdam
Naples
London
Paris
Lisbon

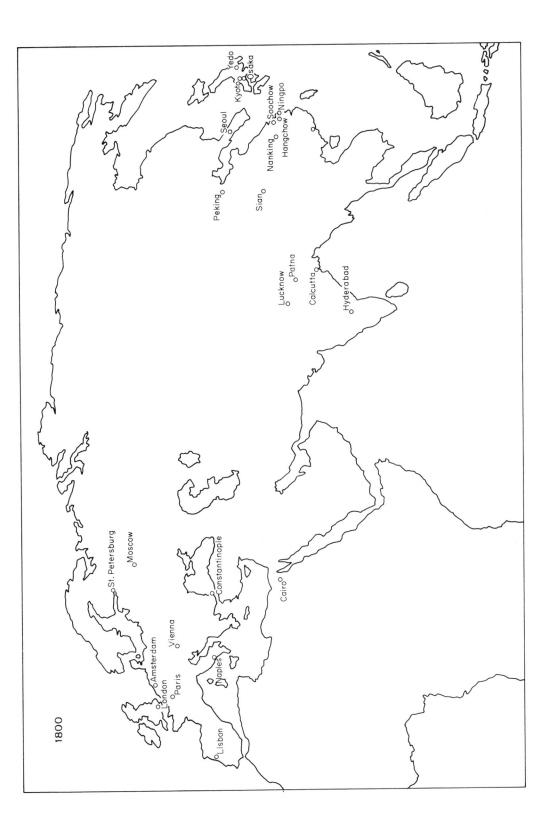

1800

Yedo
Kyoto Osaka
Seoul
Soochow
Nanking Ningpo
Hangchow
Peking
Sian

Lucknow
Patna
Calcutta
Hyderabad

St. Petersburg
Moscow

Constantinople

Cairo

Vienna
Amsterdam
London Paris
Naples

Lisbon

1850

New York
Philadelphia

Glasgow
Liverpool Manchester
Birmingham London
Paris

St. Petersburg
Moscow

Berlin

Naples

Constantinople

Peking

Kyoto Yedo
Osaka
Soochow
Hangchow
Canton

Lucknow
Calcutta
Madras
Bombay

352

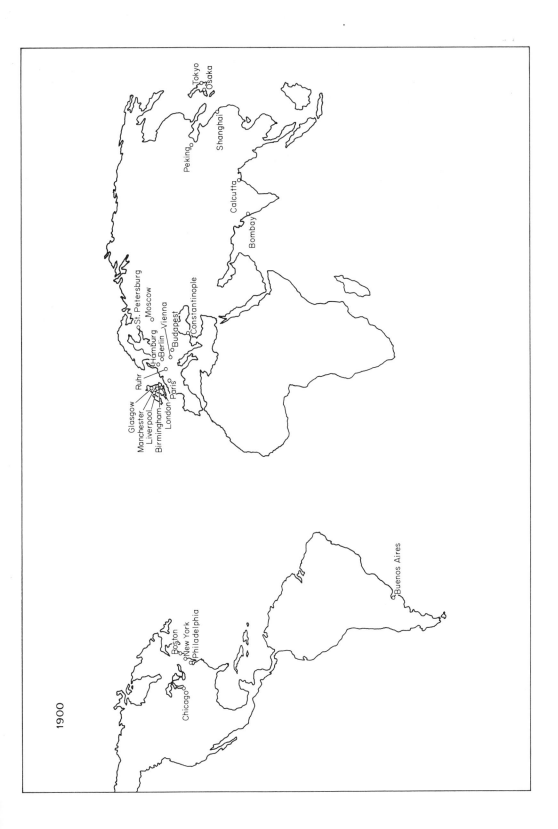

1900

Chicago
Boston
New York
Philadelphia

Buenos Aires

Glasgow
Manchester
Liverpool
Birmingham
London
Paris
Ruhr
Hamburg
Berlin
Budapest
Vienna
St. Petersburg
Moscow
Constantinople

Bombay
Calcutta

Peking
Shanghai
Tokyo
Osaka

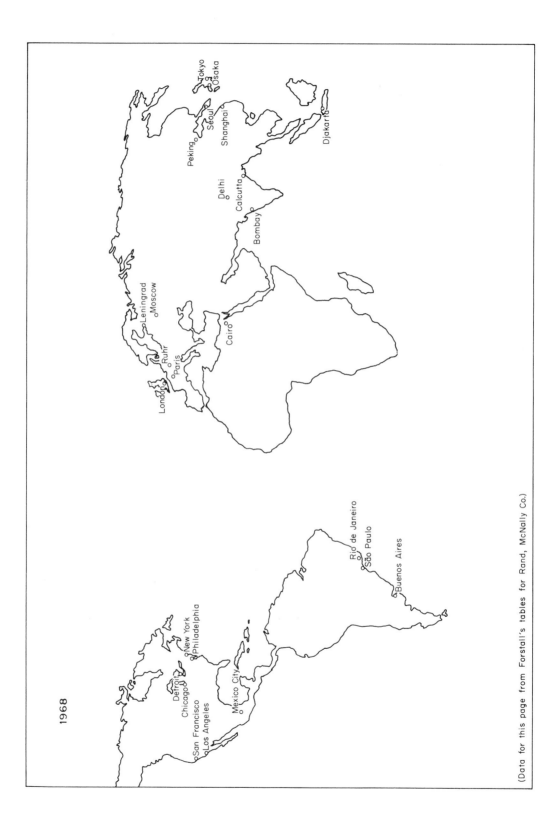

1968

Rio de Janeiro
São Paulo
Buenos Aires

Detroit
Chicago
San Francisco
Los Angeles
New York
Philadelphia
Mexico City

Leningrad
Moscow
Ruhr
Paris
London
Cairo
Delhi
Calcutta
Bombay
Peking
Seoul
Shanghai
Tokyo
Osaka
Djakarta

(Data for this page from Forstall's tables for Rand, McNally Co.)

354

Chinese indented 3 spaces to right; Moslem 1 space

	Hangchow	432 000		Sukotai	
	Peking	401		Shiraz	50 000
Cairo		400		Rouen	50
	Canton	300		Bruges	50
	Nanking	300		Goa	50
Paris		228		Fuchow	50
Fez		200		Bologna	50
Kamakura		200		Thessalonica	50
	Soochow	160		Hormuz	50
10	Sian	150		Meknes	
Granada		150		Benares	
Constantinople		150		Loyang	
Tabriz		150		Pyongyang	
Angkor		125		Hsüchow	
Cuttack		125	Oyo		
Venice		110	Alexandria		
	Chengtu	110	Cholula		
Milan		100	Valencia		44
Genoa		100	Kano		
Delhi		100		Kingtehchen	
Sarai		100	Toledo		42
Gaur		100		Chinkiang	42
	Chüanchow	100	Ghent		42
Marrakesh		100	Sakai		
25 Quilon		100		Yezd	
Warangal		100	Thana		
	Kaifeng		Kayal		
	Yangchow			Sonargaon	
Damietta		90		Nanchang	
Seville		90		Ninghsia	
Dhar		90		Ningpo	
	Songdo			Rabat	
Kyoto				Mali	
	Tali		Cahokia		
Tunis		75	London		40
	Wuchang		Majapahit		40
Isfahan		70	Marseille		40
Maragheh			Palermo		40
Hamadan			Prague		40
Njimiye			Novgorod		40
Tlemcen			Bagdad		40
Mecca			Caffa		40
Florence		60	98 Dorasamudra		40
Chitor		60	Cordova		40
Trebizond		60			
Konia					
Gangaikondapuram					
Qus					
50 Anhilvada					
Virapura					
Calicut					
	Mosul	55			
Cologne		54			
	Siangyang				
Aksu					

Cities of the World, 1400
Chinese indented 3 spaces to right; Moslem 1 space

	Nanking	473 000		Florence	61
	Cairo	450		Hsüchow	
	Vijayanagar	350		Marrakesh	
	Hangchow	325		Chitor	60
	Peking	320		Pegu	60
	Canton	300		Kanchi	
	Paris	275		Yoshino	
	Tabriz	200		Ava	
	Kyoto	200		Bokhara	
10	Soochow	175		Lisbon	55
	Pandua	150		Anhilvada	
	Fez	150		Mecca	
	Sian	150		Taiyüan	51
	Cambay	125		Metalanim	
	Milan	125		Mali	50
	Bruges	125		Novgorod	50
	Venice	110		Majapahit	50
	Genoa	100		Troki	50
	Granada	100		Angkor	50
	Samarkand	100		Hormuz	50
	Seoul	100		Calicut	50
	Shiraz	100		Goa	50
	Damascus	100		Trebizond	
	Prague	95		Cholula	
25	Bursa			Valencia	48
	Bagdad	90		Burhanpur	48
	Quilon	90		Ninghsia	
	Chengtu	88		Tsinan	
	Chüanchow			Oyo	
	Kaifeng			Sonargaon	
	Caffa	85		Daulatabad	
	Gaur			Dhar	
	Gulbarga			London	45
	Fuchow	81		Toledo	45
	Damietta	80		Bihar	
	Yangchow			Changchow	
	Cuttack			Konia	
	Constantinople	75		Bologna	43
	Aleppo	75		Qus	
	Penukonda	75		Sultaniya	
	Ayutia			Salonica	42
	Wuchang	72		Warangal	42
	Texcoco	70		Loyang	
	Ghent	70		Meknes	
	Tlemcen	70	100	Thana	
	Rouen	70			
	Tunis	70			
	Seville	70			
50	Kamatapur				
	Ningpo				
	Kamakura				
	Jaunpur				
	Kingtehchen				
	Songdo				
	Benares				

Chinese indented 3 spaces to right; Moslem 1 space

	Peking	672 000		Brescia	61
	Vijayanagar	500		Taiyüan	61
	Cairo	450		Hsüchow	
	Hangchow	375		Calicut	60
	Nanking	285		Gao	60
	Canton	250		Tours	60
	Tabriz	250		Shiraz	60
	Paris	225		Mecca	60
	Constantinople	200		Texcoco	60
10	Gaur	200		Utatlán	60
	Soochow	200		Pyongyang	
	Sian	150		Tientsin	
	Seoul	150		Chiengmai	
	Mandu	150		Srinagar	
	Ayutia	150		Bologna	55
	Fez	125		Hanoi	
	Adrianople	125		Nuremberg	52
	Naples	125		Pskov	52
	Cambay	125		Oyo	
	Venice	115		Kamatapur	
	Chengtu	112		Caffa	50
	Milan	104		London	50
	Delhi	100		Valencia	50
	Kaifeng			Seville	50
25	Chitor	90		Smolensk	50
	Penukonda	90		Kano	50
	Bruges	90		Marrakesh	50
	Gwalior	90		Luang Prabang	50
	Ningpo			Bihar	50
	Fuchow	83		Jaunpur	50
	Wuchang			Chittagong	50
	Bidar	80		Brunei	50
	Ahmedabad	80		Üsküb	50
	Tenochtitlán	80		Hakata	50
	Lyon	80		Palermo	48
	Ghent	80		Valladolid	48
	Ava			Toledo	47
	Samarkand			Arakan	
	Yangchow			Demak	
	Rouen	75		Benares	
	Tunis	75		Kazargamu	
	Quilon	75		Changchow	
	Burhanpur	75		Cuzco	45
	Sakai		100	Cologne	45
	Prague	70		Marseille	45
	Florence	70		Vienna	45
	Lisbon	70		Agades	45
	Granada	70			
	Damascus	70			
50	Chanderi	70			
	Cuttack				
	Bokhara				
	Aleppo	67			
	Chüanchow				
	Kingtehchen				
	Genoa	62			

Cities of the World, 1600

Chinese indented 3 spaces to right; Moslem 1 space

	Peking	706 000	Surat	75 000
	Constantinople	700	Yangchow	75
	Agra	500	Patna	
	Cairo	400	Burhanpur	
	Osaka	400	Golconda	
	Canton	350	Udaipur	72
	Yedo	350	Srinagar	
	Kyoto	350	Bursa	
	Hangchow	350	Genoa	70
10	Lahore	350	Hugli	70
	Nanking	317	Cambay	70
	Naples	275	Rouen	68
	Paris	250	Kingtehchen	
	Ahmedabad	225	Tours	65
	Bijapur	200	Florence	65
	London	187	Nagoya	65
	Soochow	175	Benin	65
	Adrianople	160	Barcelona	64
	Venice	151	Smolensk	64
	Sian	150	Goa	63
	Qazvin	150	Bologna	62
	Potosí	148	Aleppo	61
	Seville	144	Messina	61
	Chengtu	130	Kazargamu	60
25	Marrakesh	125	Damascus	60
	Arakan	125	Bucharest	60
	Isfahan	125	Mecca	60
	Milan	119	Benares	60
	Lisbon	110	Ningpo	
	Granada	110	Oyo	
	Rome	109	Samarkand	
	Palermo	105	Hué	
	Prague	100	Hsüchow	
	Ayutia	100	Valladolid	56
	Fez	100	Chüanchow	56
	Tabriz	100	Gwalior	
	Wuchang		Tunis	
	Kaifeng		Antwerp	55
	Bokhara		Brussels	55
	Lyon	90	Marseille	55
	Valencia	86	Belgrade	55
	Jodhpur		Üsküb	55
	Tientsin		100 Verona	54
	Toledo	80		
	Smyrna	80		
	Moscow	80		
	Hyderabad	80		
	Taiyüan	79		
50	Madrid	79		
	Rajmahal			
	Chandragiri			
	Seoul			
	Fuchow	76		
	Mexico City	75		
	Algiers	75		
	Ahmednagar	75		

Cities of the World, 1700
Chinese indented 3 spaces to right; Moslem 1 space

	Constantinople	700 000
	Peking	
	Isfahan	600
	London	550
	Paris	530
	Yedo	500
	Delhi	500
	Ahmedabad	380
	Osaka	370
10	Kyoto	350
	Cairo	350
	Canton	300
	Nanking	300
	Hangchow	292
	Soochow	245
	Naples	207
	Meknes	200
	Dacca	200
	Surat	200
	Hyderabad	200
	Lisbon	188
	Amsterdam	172
	Patna	170
	Seoul	170
25	Sian	167
	Ayutia	150
	Tabriz	150
	Wuchang	150
	Srinagar	150
	Rome	149
	Venice	143
	Mukden	
	Smyrna	135
	Moscow	130
	Milan	124
	Palermo	113
	Madrid	110
	Vienna	105
	Mexico City	100
	Arakan	100
	Aurangabad	100
	Jodhpur	
	Lahore	
	Potosí	95
	Adrianople	93
	Tientsin	92
	Fatshan	90
	Ninghsia	90
	Fuchow	
50	Ningpo	88
	Marseille	88
	Algiers	85

	Agra	
	Kingtehchen	
	Fez	
	Seville	80
	Lhasa	80
	Dublin	80
	Gondar	80
	Benares	
	Chengtu	
	Amoy	
	Bijapur	
	Macao	75
	Barcelona	73
	Oruro	72
	Aleppo	72
	Lyon	71
	Oyo	
	Damascus	70
	Brussels	70
	Hamburg	70
	Qazvin	70
	Tunis	70
	Granada	70
	Florence	69
	Nagoya	69
	Bokhara	
	Hanoi	
	Chinkiang	68
	Rouen	68
	Antwerp	67
	Genoa	67
	Kanazawa	67
	Kasimbazar	
	Kuku Khoto	
	Hwaian	65
	Ava	
	Hué	
	Bologna	63
	Puebla	63
	Leiden	62
	Copenhagen	62
	Siangyang	
	Sendai	61
	Bursa	60
	Mecca	60
	Yangchow	60
	Kaifeng	60
100	Kerman	60
	Nagasaki	59

Cities of the World, 1750

Chinese indented 3 spaces to right; Japanese 4 spaces

	City	Pop.
	Peking	900
	London	676
	Constantinople	666
	Paris	560
	Yedo	509
	Canton	500
	Osaka	375
	Kyoto	362
	Hangchow	350
10	Naples	324
	Soochow	302
	Cairo	300
	Nanking	285
	Hyderabad	225
	Amsterdam	219
	Lisbon	213
	Patna	200
	Meshhed	200
	Murshidabad	200
	Sian	195
	Seoul	183
	Vienna	169
	Surat	165
	Wuchang	165
25	Moscow	161
	Venice	158
	Rome	157
	Mukden	
	Ayutia	150
	Jodhpur	150
	Ningpo	144
	St. Petersburg	138
	Dacca	135
	Fatshan	130
	Lanchow	130
	Smyrna	130
	Dublin	125
	Palermo	124
	Madrid	123
	Milan	123
	Ahmedabad	120
	Kingtehchen	120
	Lyon	115
	Berlin	113
	Mexico City	110
	Calcutta	110
	Fuchow	
	Tunis	100
	Delhi	100
50	Lucknow	100
	Jaipur	100
	Srinagar	100
	Chengtu	
	Adrianople	96
	Nagoya	
	Chandernagore	95
	Batavia	94
	Ninghsia	90
	Chinkiang	90

	City	Pop.
	Hamburg	90
	Fyzabad	90
	Marseille	88
	Rouen	88
	Aurangabad	85
	Benares	
	Oyo	
	Tientsin	80
	Copenhagen	79
	Kanazawa	78
	Kaifeng	78
	Bombay	77
	Amoy	
	Katsina	75
	Algiers	75
	Damascus	75
	Hué	
	Florence	74
	Rampur	
	Agra	
	Yangchow	
	Hwaian	
	Genoa	72
	Gondar	70
	Aleppo	70
	Granada	70
	Barcelona	70
	Meknes	
	Kuku Khoto	
	Seville	68
	Bagdad	
	Fez	
	Sendai	66
	Bologna	66
	Changsha	
	Nanchang	
	Lhasa	65
	Bursa	65
	Qazvin	65
	Bordeaux	64
100	Hsüchow	
	Siangtan	
	Siangyang	
	Hanoi	
	Ava	
	Seringapatam	60
	Macao	60
	Shanghai	60
	Valencia	60
	Isfahan	60
	Stockholm	60
	Dresden	60
	Sira	60
	Ouro Preto	60
	Cádiz	60
	Turin	60
	Bokhara	60
	Tsinan	
	Prague	58

British at left; Chinese indented 3 spaces to right

	London	2 320 000		Barcelona	167
	Peking	1 648		Rio de Janeiro	166
	Paris	1 314		Warsaw	163
	Canton	800		Bangkok	160
	Constantinople	785		Budapest	156
	Hangchow	700		Smyrna	150
	New York	682		Bristol	150
	Bombay	575		Delhi	146
	Yedo	567		Kingtehchen	144
10	Soochow	550		Sheffield	143
	St. Petersburg	502		Bordeaux	142
	Berlin	446		Venice	141
	Vienna	426		Turin	138
	Philadelphia	426		Alexandria	138
	Liverpool	422		Copenhagen	135
	Naples	416		New Orleans	132
	Calcutta	413		Bangalore	131
	Manchester	412		Cincinnati	130
	Kyoto	377		Chinkiang	130
	Moscow	373		Changsha	
	Glasgow	346		Nanchang	
	Madras	310		Tabriz	125
	Lucknow	300		Breslau	120
	Birmingham	294		Prague	117
25	Sian	275		Kanazawa	116
	Dublin	263		Manila	114
	Madrid	263		Bahia	112
	Patna	263		Rotterdam	112
	Lisbon	257		Wolverhampton	112
	Cairo	256		Newcastle	111
	Lyon	254		Nagpur	111
	Fuchow	250		Amritsar	111
	Shanghai	250		Valencia	110
	Chengtu	240		Cawnpore	108
	Wuchang			Damascus	108
	Ningpo	230		Agra	108
	Amsterdam	225		Florence	107
	Brussels	208		Seville	106
	Boston	202		Pernambuco	106
	Hyderabad	200		Baroda	106
	Nanking	200		Bucharest	105
	Tientsin	200		Rouen	104
	Chungking	200		Genoa	103
	Havana	199	100	Bareilly	101
	Edinburgh	194		Ava	
	Seoul	194		Siangtan	
	Hamburg	193		Bursa	100
	Marseille	193		Surakarta	100
	Milan	193		Plymouth	100
	Benares	185		Bradford	100
50	Leeds	184		Jaipur	100
	Palermo	182		Nagoya	100
	Mukden	180			
	Fatshan	175			
	Mexico City	170			
	Rome	170			
	Lanchow	170			
	Baltimore	169			

THE LARGEST CITY IN THE WORLD

In 1933, aged 18, I scrawled on the back of an old envelope the names of cities which might, at one time, have been largest in the world. Now after 40 years I can put together another list, still tentative in the nature of the case but this time with at least some claim to completeness.

There were towns, including several thousand people, in western Asia from 6,000 B.C. But the first place that could properly be called a city was probably Abydos near Thebes in Egypt, with perhaps 20,000 people about 3500 B.C. It is the earliest surely known capital of Egypt, the first country to leave traditions, the country where culture began.

The best location for a city in the ancient world was almost surely that of Memphis-Cairo, which has always been a great city under one name or another. Memphis, founded by the pharaoh Menes probably about 3100 B.C., stood right at the head of the Nile delta, where the river leaves its firm banks and spreads out over the alluvial plain in many streamlets that flow by shifting courses to the Mediterranean. The firm riverbanks made a solid and flood-proof foundation for the city. The location 100 miles from the open sea gave security from overseas attack, while large deserts to east and to west afforded nearly perfect protection by land. Add to this that the Nile provided abundant water and each year a new supply of fertile soil for the farmland near the river, and one can see how great were Memphis's natural advantages. There was, moreover, a warm climate and no inconvenience of rain, which almost never falls on Egypt. It should be no surprise that civilization started there. By 3000 B.C., Memphis may have had 40 000 people.

In the 22nd century B.C. the Babylonians under Sargon and Naramsin were strong while Egypt was weak. Their capital was Akkad, which about 2240 likely edged ahead of Memphis in size. By 2100 the Babylonian capital had shifted to Lagash, whose kings contacted north Egypt and used Egyptian materials in their temples. Lagash might be the world's new largest city. Its population has been estimated by Diakonoff at 100,000.

In 2059 B.C. king Gudea of Lagash fell, overthrown by an invasion from Persia, while a dynasty from upper Egypt overran northern Egypt from its up-river base at Thebes. This dynasty promptly, however, in 1991 B.C., moved the capital down-river again to Memphis, which once more became the world's greatest city. Just about this time Memphis had 10,000 priests and so may have had a total population of 100,000.

Babylonia again took the lead, this time at Babylon city, when the competent line at Memphis rather abruptly ended in 1778 B.C. Legend gives credit to Baal and his daughter-in-law Semiramis for raising Babylon to greatness and dominating Egypt, and both Egyptian and Babylonians archaeology corroborate the legend. In any case, from about 1770 B.C. Babylon would be the new largest city. Under Hammurabi, of another dynasty, it continued to be the outstanding capital, though no longer ruling over Egypt.

Babylon was sacked by the Hittite prince Murshil in 1595 B.C., and world primacy among cities probably passed over to Avaris in Egypt, which was then under Hyksos rule.

A native Egyptian line based at Thebes ousted the Hyksos in 1580 and soon rivaled the glories of earlier Egyptian dynasties. Among its rulers were the conqueror Thutmose III and the inspiring idealist Ikhnaton. Egypt's *de facto* capital seems however to have returned to Memphis which, except when displaced by Thebes c. 1400-c. 1350 B.C., could have been the largest city for nearly a thousand years.

From Nineveh in 668 B.C. the Assyrians marched in to capture Egypt from a Nubian dynasty. Nineveh's population was 120,000—as we know from the Bible and can confirm from measurements of its area.

Nineveh's preeminence was short-lived. In 612 it was sacked in an onslaught by two or three foes, the one with the biggest city being Babylon. Judging from the number of its temples, Babylon soon reached new splendor under Nebuchadnezzar, with about 200,000 people.

Babylon fell to king Cyrus of Persia but must have stayed larger than the Persian capitals, which were poorly situated for trade or administration.

The next top-ranking city would be in India, where Sravasti, the main place in 479 B.C., had

57,000 families. A few of these may have been rural. Sravasti was soon surpassed by Rajagriha, the huge capital of all north India.

Then from c. 440 B.C. Babylon can have led again awhile.

Alexander the Great founded a new capital in Egypt at Alexandria, and it speedily surpassed all other cities, becoming the world's largest almost within his short lifetime, about 320 B.C. Under a Greek dynasty founded by his general Ptolemy, it continued to grow for a century, closely pressed by Seleucia, a capital founded in Mesopotamia by another of Alexander's generals, Seleucus. Both Alexandria and Seleucia surpassed 300,000.

Even so, both can have been excelled from 300 to 220 and 206-c. 190 B.C. by Patna in India, a city 21 miles around.

China must have led 220-206 B.C. with Hsienyang, near Changan, which was founded with 120,000 families. Changan itself likely led about 190 B.C. China rivaled the Roman Empire. Each had 60,000,000 in total population.

Meanwhile, Seleucia may have briefly stood first just after Antiochus IV overran part of Egypt in 170 B.C.

Rome concentrated her power and wealth the most completely in one city, so that from about 1 A.D. Rome City was the world's largest. It had 486,000 people in 57 B.C. Aurelian's wall, made 271-280 A.D., enclosed 3,263 acres (1,305 hectares), mostly thickly inhabited. At 500 per ha., it had about 650,000 people. At its ancient peak, a century earlier, it can have had 800,000.

In 330 Constantine moved the Roman capital from Rome to Constantinople. By 350 this new capital took the lead, while Rome's population quickly declined.

The next world leader could have been Patna, still called Pataliputra, where the Gupta dynasty was then ruling over about half of India, especially the valley of the Ganges. Patna's supremacy this time would be rather short, about 410-450.

Constantinople, after a temporary decline as Germanic tribes overran the Roman Empire around 410, regained much of the lost provinces. Saved repeatedly from capture by its strong walls, and helped in trade by its admir-

able location, it rose to great prosperity. It can have led all cities from 450 to 650, with a population of around 500,000.

Changan was again capital of China under the Tang dynasty, 618-907. Its huge area indicates a peak population probably over 1,000,000. It would easily pass Constantinople, which was declining as it lost its southern provinces to the Arabs. Even the sack of Changan by the Tibetans in 763 would not likely cost that city its world lead.

Already Bagdad was rising as capital of the Moslems, by then under mainly Persian leadership. Built in 763-6, Bagdad was pretty surely the world's largest city from 775 to 935, with over 1,000,000 part of the way.

From c. 935 Cordova and Constantinople probably vied for the lead with about 450,000 each. Changan, no longer Chinese capital, would be not far behind. Cordova was disastrously sacked in 1013. Constantinople declined with the Byzantine defeat by the Turks at Manzikert in 1071 and the resulting loss of Asia Minor.

Kaifeng, capital of most of China from 960, would be largest in the world by 1102, when it had 442,000.

Morocco in the 12th century enjoyed a surprising degree of prosperity. It ruled north Africa as far as Tunis and also the southern half of Spain. Its culture was for once original and as broadminded as that of Bagdad in its palmiest days, with thinkers such as Ibn Tufail, Avempace, and Averroes. Soon after a change of capitals in China, Fez in Morocco with about 250,000 people may just possibly have been world's largest city from c. 1160 to c. 1180.

Polonnaruwa during its brief moment of glory around 1180-1200 had an immense area and just possibly might have been unequaled by any other city.

The high claims sometimes made for Angkor fall down on the basis of its area, for the city wall built right at its peak, 1177, precludes a population much above 150,000.

Hangchow was certainly the next leader. According to Marco Polo it had several millions. That figure refers to a large district rather than to the strictly urban area. Hangchow's urban population in the year 1273 was 432,000. Polo and other visitors called it the busiest port in the world. It and Peking were the metropolises of a Mongol empire that stretched across Asia and well into Europe, the greatest continuous land empire the world has ever seen.

Cairo should be the next top-ranking city, even before China was divided during the "Long War" of liberation from the Mongols in 1355-68. Cairo reached its medieval peak around 1325 with a population of about 500,000. It was capital for the Mamelukes, who ruled not only Egypt but also Syria, as had the ancient pharaohs.

Already by 1400 the new world leader must have been in China, where the new Ming dynasty was thriving. The Chinese capital was Nanking till 1409 and thereafter Peking. Peking passed Nanking in population at 450,000 right around 1420. Both these cities fell considerably at the time of their conquest by the Manchus, which for Peking was 1644.

About 1635, Agra, the usual early capital of Mogul India, with 660,000, may have passed the declining Peking to take the world lead, till it ceased to be capital in 1638.

Constantinople, thriving under the far-flung Ottoman Turkish empire, reached about 700,000, more than under Justinian. From 1637 it can have been the largest city.

Delhi in India came to be considered the world's biggest city for awhile under the Mogul emperor Aurangzeb. This can have been correct. Harem life had corrupted the Turkish court at Constantinople, and Peking in China would not yet be fully recovered up to its former size. About 1670 to 1684 Delhi can have stood first.

In 1684 the emperor Aurangzeb moved Delhi's people en masse to his new capital in south-central India, named for himself as Aurangabad. Some people would remain behind, and the new location, not on a major river nor on a major trade-route, was not propitious for a large city, and in fact the emperor soon gave it up and moved back. Sixteen eighty-four can be taken as the end of India's times of having the top-most city, for when Aurangzeb did return to Delhi, his empire was already decaying as a result of his own prolonged aggressive wars.

Paris in 1684 was known to be still a bit larger than London. Henry IV's policy of toleration for both Protestants and Catholics had made France alert-minded, and competent government continued after him as Richelieu, Mazarin, and Colbert made it the greatest nation in Europe. It may have been Paris that took over as largest city as Delhi abdicated in 1684. But the very next year, 1685, Louis XIV expelled the Huguenots, or French Protestants. Several hundred thousand went into exile, mainly from the cities. Paris fell at one swoop behind London. Her time in first place, if it happened at all, lasted just 1 year.

Nor was it yet London's time to excel.

Constantinople would resume her lead.

Then Peking, prospering steadily under the long-ruling emperor Kang-hsi (1661-1722), should be largest from 1700 until about 1825. Its exact population then is not known, but in 1845 it had 1,648,000 according to the Russian ambassador, while another Chinese city, Canton, in 1847 was reported at 1,236,000.

After 1800, London began growing rapidly again. The industrial revolution, which had started in England, and the gain of new big colonies that replaced the lost American ones, gave the British capital a dynamic expansion. A democratic base from 1784 onward, growing broader with the passing years, also helped the health and strength of the British body politic. After passing Peking around 1825, London went on to become the world's first urban area to top 2,000,000 as it recorded 2,235,344 in the census of 1841. By 1900 it had 6,000,000.

New York had bases in commerce, democracy, and an industrial hinterland much like London's. But the hinterland was bigger; it had a whole new continent to be developed. It passed London around 1925 at about 8,000,000.

Tokyo, an island capital like London, pulled a surprise by passing New York at 15,000,000 about 1965, in the very peak of American dominance in world affairs. Another Japanese urban area, Osaka, is just now in 1970 passing London, giving Japan two of the world's three largest cities. So well have the Japanese been able to apply European-American techniques in building a thriving up-to-date economy.

T. C.

Top 6 Cities in Each Continent
(Population in Thousands)

AFRICA

Rank	800	1000	1200	1300	1400
1	Alexandria 200	Cairo 150	Fez 250	Cairo 400	Cairo 450
2	Fostat 100	Tinnis 125	Cairo 200	Fez 200	Fez 150
3	Kairwan 80	Fez 75	Marrakesh 200	Marrakesh 100	Damietta 80
4	Zimbabwe	Kairwan 50	Damietta 100	Damietta 90	Tlemcen 70
5	Axum	Zimbabwe	Rabat	Tunis 75	Tunis 70
6	Dongola	Coptos	Alexandria	Njimiye	Marrakesh

ASIA

Rank	800	1000	1200	1300	1400
1	Changan 800	Kaifeng 400	Hangchow 255	Hangchow 432	Nanking 473
2	Bagdad 700	Sian 300	Canton 200	Peking 401	Vijayanagar 350
3	Loyang 200	Kyoto 200	Pagan 180	Canton 325	Hangchow 325
4	Kyoto 140	Hasa 150	Nanking 180	Nanking 200	Peking 320
5	Hangchow	Hangchow	Kamakura 175	Kamakura 200	Canton 300
6	Kanauj	Angkor	Angkor 150	Soochow 160	Tabriz 200

EUROPE

Rank	800	1000	1200	1300	1400
1	Constantinople 300	Cordova 450	Constantinople 200	Paris 228	Paris 275
2	Cordova 160	Constantinople 400	Seville 150	Granada 150	Milan 125
3	Rome 50	Seville 90	Cordova 150	Constantinople 150	Bruges 125
4	Pliska 34	Palermo 75	Paris 110	Venice 110	Venice 110
5	Toledo	Kiev 45	Palermo 100	Milan 100	Genoa 100
6	Seville	Venice 45	Venice 70	Genoa 100	Granada 100

NORTH AMERICA

Rank	800	1000	1200	1300	1400
1	Copán	Tula 49	?	Cholula	Texcoco 70
2	Monte Albán	Chichén-Itzá		Mayapán	Cholula 25
3	Tikal	Cholula			Mayapán
4	Tula	Uxmal			Tzintzuntzán
5	Dzibalchaltun	Tilantongo			Utatlán
6	Piedras Negras				

SOUTH AMERICA

Rank	800	1000	1200	1300	1400
1	?	Tiahuanaco 20	?	Quito	Chanchán 40
2				Riobamba	Cajamarquilla 40
3				Cuzco	Riobamba
4				Cajamarquilla	Chincha 25
5				Chincha	Cuzco
6					Quito

Top 6 Cities in Each Continent

AFRICA

1500	1600	1700	1800	1850
Cairo	Cairo 450	Cairo 400	Cairo 263	Cairo 256
Fez	Marrakesh 125	Meknes 125	Tunis 120	Alexandria 138
Tunis	Fez 75	Algiers 100	Meknes 110	Tunis 80
Gao	Algiers 60	Fez 75	Oyo 85	Fez 85
Oyo	Benin	Gondar 65	Algiers 73	Abeokuta 65
Kano	Kazargamu 50	Tunis 60	Fez 60	Ilorin 65

ASIA

1500	1600	1700	1800	1850
Peking	Peking 672	Peking 706	Peking 1 250	Peking 1 648
Vijayanagar	Agra 500	Isfahan 500	Canton 800	Canton 800
Hangchow	Osaka 375	Yedo 400	Hangchow 500	Hangchow 700
Nanking	Canton 285	Delhi 385	Yedo 492	Bombay 575
Canton	Yedo 250	Ahmedabad 350	Soochow 392	Yedo 567
Tabriz	Kyoto 250	Osaka 350	Osaka 380	Soochow 550

EUROPE

1500	1600	1700	1800	1850
Paris 225	Constantinople 700	Constantinople 700	London 861	London 2 340
Constantinople 200	Naples 275	London 550	Constantinople 570	Paris 1 314
Naples 125	Paris 250	Paris 530	Paris 547	Constantinople 785
Venice 115	London 187	Naples 207	Naples 430	St. Petersburg 502
Milan 104	Adrianople 160	Lisbon 188	Moscow 238	Berlin 446
Granada 100	Venice 151	Amsterdam 172	Lisbon 237	Vienna 426

NORTH AMERICA

1500	1600	1700	1800	1850
Tenochtitlán 80	Mexico City 75	Mexico City 100	Mexico City 128	New York 682
Texcoco 60	Puebla 25	Puebla 63	Philadelphia 68	Philadelphia 426
Utatlán 60	Guatemala City 25	Zacatecas 30	Guanajuato 66	Boston 202
Tzintzuntzán 40	Zacatecas 20	Guatemala City 30	Puebla 65	Havana 199
Tlaxcala 40	Tlaxcala 20	Havana 25	New York 63	Mexico City 170
Cholula 36	Tayasal 15	Mérida 20	Havana 60	Baltimore 169

SOUTH AMERICA

1500	1600	1700	1800	1850
Cuzco 45	Potosí 148	Potosí 85	Bahia 75	Rio de Janeiro 166
Chanchán 40	Cuzco 30	Oruro 72	Lima 54	Bahia 130
Quito 30	Huancavelica 20	Lima 37	Rio de Janeiro 44	Pernambuco 100
Huánuco 25	Quito 18	Cuzco 35	Pernambuco 40	Buenos Aires 74
Pachacamac 25	Lima 14	Quito 30	Buenos Aires 40	Santiago 70
Cajamarquilla	La Paz 13	Huamanga 25	Cuzco 34	Lima 70

Top 12 Cities, with Suburbs
(Population in Thousands)

1360 B.C.
Thebes	100
Memphis	
Babylon	
Chengchow	40
Khattushas	40
Nineveh	
Ecbatana	30
Mycenae	30
Amarna	30
Knossos	
Susa	
Cordova	

650 B.C.
Nineveh	100
Loyang	
Yenhsiatu	
Memphis	40
Chichen	40
Babylon	
Changan	
Ecbatana	30
Kausambi	30
Marib	30
Napata	
Ayodhya	

430 B.C.
Babylon	120
Ecbatana	117
Athens	
Sravasti	
Champa	
Loyang	
Yenhsiatu	
Rajagriha	
Syracuse	
Memphis	
Rome	60
Soochow	

100 A.D.
Rome	650
Loyang	400
Alexandria	300
Seleucia	200
Changan	150
Ephesus	130
Antioch	125
Kavery	120
Anuradhapura	
Apamea	
Pergamum	
Broach	

361
Constantinople	350
Loyang	
Rome	250
Patna	
Ctesiphon	200
Alexandria	200
Changan	
Carthage	
Antioch	140
Ayodhya	
Broach	
Memphis	

622
Constantinople	500
Changan	400
Loyang	200
Ctesiphon	
Alexandria	125
Teotihuacán	
Kanauj	100
Kanchi	100
Vatapi	
Antioch	
Memphis	
Soochow	

900
Bagdad	500
Changan	400
Constantinople	200
Kyoto	
Hangchow	
Alexandria	125
Cordova	100
Manyakheta	100
Loyang	
Fostat (Memphis)	
Damascus	
Kairwan	

1200
Hangchow	900
Fez	750
Cairo (Memphis)	300
Constantinople	225
Canton	220
Pagan	200
Nanking	200
Kamakura	200
Angkor	
Marrakesh	125
Seville	
Cordova	100

1500
Peking	672
Vijayanagar	500
Cairo	450
Hangchow	375
Nanking	285
Canton	250
Tabriz	250
Paris	225
Constantinople	200
Gaur	200
Soochow	200
Sian (Changan)	150

1700
Constantinople	700
Peking	600
Isfahan	550
London	530
Paris	500
Yedo	500
Delhi	500
Ahmedabad	380
Osaka	370
Kyoto	350
Cairo	350
Canton	300

1800
Peking	1 100
London	861
Canton	800
Constantinople	570
Paris	547
Hangchow	500
Yedo	492
Naples	430
Soochow	392
Kyoto	377
Osaka	373
Lucknow	300

1850
London	2 320
Peking	1 648
Paris	1 314
Canton	800
Constantinople	785
Hangchow	700
New York	682
Bombay	575
Yedo	567
Soochow	550
St. Petersburg	502
Berlin	446

1900
London	6 480
New York	4 242
Paris	3 330
Berlin	2 424
Chicago	1 717
Vienna	1 662
Tokyo (Yedo)	1 497
St. Petersburg	1 439
Philadelphia	1 418
Manchester	1 255
Birmingham	1 248
Moscow	1 120

1925
New York	7 774
London	7 742
Tokyo	5 300
Paris	4 800
Berlin	4 013
Chicago	3 564
Ruhr	3 400
Buenos Aires	2 410
Osaka	2 219
Philadelphia	2 085
Vienna	1 862
Boston	1 773

1968
Tokyo	20 500
New York	16 900
London	11 025
Osaka	10 900
Moscow	9 150
Paris	8 850
Buenos Aires	8 600
Los Angeles	8 455
Calcutta	7 900
Shanghai	7 800
Chicago	7 435
Mexico City	7 200

Top 7 Cities
(Population in Thousands)

1360 B.C.		650 B.C.		430 B.C.		200 B.C.		100 A.D.	
Thebes	100	Nineveh	120	Babylon	250	Patna	350	Rome	650
Memphis		Loyang	117	Ecbatana	200	Alexandria	300	Loyang	400
Babylon		Yenhsiatu		Athens	155	Seleucia	300	Alexandria	300
Chengchow	40	Memphis		Sravasti	150	Changan		Seleucia	
Khattushas	40	Chicheng		Champa	150	Loyang	150	Changan	200
Nineveh		Babylon		Loyang	145	Carthage	150	Ephesus	150
Ecbatana		Changan		Yenhsiatu		Rome		Antioch	150

361		622		800		900		1000	
Constantinople	350	Constantinople	500	Changan	800	Bagdad	900	Cordova	450
Loyang	250	Changan	400	Bagdad	700	Changan	750	Constantinople	450
Rome	200	Loyang	200	Constantinople	300	Constantinople	300	Kaifeng	400
Patna	200	Ctesiphon	125	Loyang	200	Kyoto	225	Sian (Changan)	300
Ctesiphon		Alexandria	100	Kyoto	200	Hangchow	220	Kyoto	200
Alexandria		Teotihuacán		Alexandria	200	Alexandria	200	Cairo	150
Changan		Kanauj		Hangchow		Cordova	200	Hasa	150

1100		1150		1200		1300		1350	
Kaifeng	442	Constantinople	450	Hangchow	300	Hangchow	255	Cairo	450
Constantinople	350	Merv	200	Fez	200	Peking	250	Hangchow	432
Sian	300	Nanking	300	Constantinople	180	Cairo	200	Peking	400
Cairo	200	Cairo	200	Canton	175	Canton	200	Canton	330
Kyoto	200	Kaifeng	200	Pagan	170	Nanking	200	Nanking	300
Marrakesh	150	Canton	150	Nanking	160	Paris	180	Paris	200
Bagdad	150	Fez	150			Fez	180	Fez	175

1400		1500		1600		1650		1700	
Nanking	473	Peking	672	Peking	706	Constantinople	700	Constantinople	700
Cairo	450	Vijayanagar	500	Constantinople	700	Peking	600	Peking	650
Vijayanagar	350	Cairo	450	Agra	500	Isfahan	500	Isfahan	600
Hangchow	325	Hangchow	375	Cairo	400	Yedo	500	London	550
Peking	320	Nanking	285	Osaka	400	Agra	500	Paris	530
Canton	300	Canton	250	Canton	350	Paris	455	Yedo	500
Paris	275	Tabriz	250	Yedo	350	London	410	Delhi	500

1750	
Peking	900
London	676
Constantinople	666
Paris	560
Yedo	509
Canton	500
Osaka	403

1800	
Peking	1 100
London	861
Canton	800
Constantinople	570
Paris	547
Hangchow	500
Yedo	403

1850	
London	2 320
Peking	1 648
Paris	1 314
Canton	800
Constantinople	785
Hangchow	700
New York	682

1875	
London	4 241
Paris	2 250
New York	1 900
Peking	1 310
Berlin	1 045
Vienna	1 001
Canton	944

1900	
London	6 480
New York	4 242
Paris	3 330
Berlin	2 424
Chicago	1 717
Vienna	1 662
Tokyo	1 497

1925	
New York	7 774
London	7 742
Tokyo (Yedo)	5 300
Paris	4 800
Berlin	4 013
Chicago	3 564
Buenos Aires	2 410

1950	
New York	12 300
London	8 860
Tokyo	7 547
Paris	5 900
Shanghai	5 407
Moscow	5 100
Buenos Aires	5 000

1970	
Tokyo	21 000
New York	17 252
Osaka	11 250
London	10 925
Moscow	9 800
Buenos Aires	9 500
Paris	8 875

Top 20 Cities
(Population in Thousands)

1360 B.C.

Thebes	100
Memphis	
Babylon	
Chengchow	40
Khattushas	40
Nineveh	
Ecbatana	30
Mycenae	30
Amarna	30
Knossos	
Susa	
Cordova	
Erech	
Athens	25
Hazor	
Argos	
Washshukani	
Hsia	
Jerusalem	
Mohenjo-daro	20

650 B.C.

Nineveh	120
Loyang	117
Yenhsiatu	
Memphis	
Chicheng	
Babylon	
Changan	
Ecbatana	
Kausambi	
Marib	60
Napata	
Ayodhya	
Miletus	
Sais	50
Peking	
Jerusalem	
Van	
Calah	
Anyang	
Camelot	

100 A.D.

Rome	650
Loyang	
Alexandria	400
Seleucia	300
Changan	
Ephesus	200
Antioch	150
Kavery	
Anuradhapura	130
Apamea	125
Pergamum	120
Broach	
Paithan	
Cádiz	100
Corinth	100
Sardis	100
Soochow	
Memphis	40
Carthage	
Edessa	

900

Bagdad	900
Changan	750
Constantinople	300
Kyoto	225
Hangchow	220
Alexandria	200
Cordova	200
Manyakheta	
Loyang	125
Fostat	
Damascus	
Kairwan	
Chengtu	100
Rayy	
Yangchow	100
Samarkand	100
Nishapur	
Chunar	
Angkor	90
Anhilvada	

1200

Hangchow	255
Fez	250
Cairo	200
Constantinople	200
Canton	200
Pagan	180
Nanking	180
Kamakura	175
Angkor	150
Palermo	150
Marrakesh	150
Seville	150
Cuttack	150
Peking	150
Sian	150
Kaifeng	150
Polonnaruwa	140
Paris	110
Bagdad	100
Chengtu	100
Tali	100

1500

Peking	672
Vijayanagar	500
Cairo	450
Hangchow	375
Nanking	285
Canton	250
Tabriz	250
Paris	225
Constantinople	200
Gaur	200
Soochow	200
Sian	150
Seoul	150
Mandu	150
Ayutia	150
Fez	125
Adrianople	125
Naples	125
Cambay	125
Venice	125

1650

Constantinople	700
Peking	600
Isfahan	500
Yedo	500
Agra	500
Delhi	400
London	400
Kyoto	390
Canton	385
Cairo	350
Osaka	346
Nanking	300
Naples	300
Bijapur	300
Hangchow	300
Ahmedabad	281
Lahore	275
Lisbon	250
Patna	170

1800

Peking	1 100
London	861
Canton	800
Constantinople	570
Paris	547
Hangchow	500
Yedo	492
Naples	430
Soochow	392
Kyoto	377
Osaka	373
Lucknow	300
Cairo	263
Moscow	238
Lisbon	237
Patna	235
Vienna	231
Sian	224
St. Petersburg	220
Nanking	220

1900

London	6 480
New York	4 242
Paris	3 330
Berlin	2 424
Chicago	1 711
Vienna	1 662
Tokyo	1 497
St. Petersburg	1 439
Philadelphia	1 418
Manchester	1 255
Birmingham	1 248
Moscow	1 120
Peking	1 100
Calcutta	1 085
Boston	1 075
Glasgow	1 072
Liverpool	940
Osaka	931
Constantinople	900
Hamburg	895

1968

Tokyo	20 500
New York	16 900
London	11 025
Osaka	10 900
Moscow	9 150
Paris	8 850
Buenos Aires	8 600
Los Angeles	8 455
Calcutta	7 900
Shanghai	7 800
Chicago	7 435
Mexico City	7 200
São Paulo	6 600
Rio de Janeiro	6 100
Cairo	5 900
Bombay	5 650
Ruhr	5 025
Philadelphia	4 750
Peking	4 625
Detroit	4 625

Top 15 Cities

(Population in Thousands)

1650

City	Population
Constantinople	700
Peking	600
Isfahan	500
Yedo	500
Agra	500
Paris	455
London	410
Delhi	400
Kyoto	390
Canton	385
Cairo	350
Osaka	346
Nanking	300
Naples	300
Bijapur	300

1700

City	Population
Constantinople	700
Peking	650
Isfahan	600
London	550
Paris	530
Yedo	500
Delhi	500
Ahmedabad	380
Osaka	370
Kyoto	350
Cairo	350
Canton	300
Nanking	300
Hangchow	300
Soochow	300

1750

City	Population
Peking	900
London	676
Constantinople	666
Paris	560
Yedo	509
Canton	500
Osaka	403
Kyoto	362
Hangchow	350
Nanking	325
Naples	324
Soochow	302
Cairo	300
Hyderabad	292
Amsterdam	245

1800

City	Population
Peking	1 100
London	861
Canton	800
Constantinople	570
Paris	547
Hangchow	500
Yedo	492
Naples	430
Soochow	392
Kyoto	377
Osaka	373
Lucknow	300
Cairo	263
Moscow	238
Lisbon	237

1850

City	Population
London	2 320
Peking	1 648
Paris	1 314
Canton	800
Constantinople	785
Hangchow	700
New York	682
Bombay	575
Yedo	567
Soochow	550
St. Petersburg	502
Berlin	446
Vienna	426
Philadelphia	426
Liverpool	422

1875

City	Population
London	4 241
Paris	2 250
New York	1 900
Peking	1 310
Berlin	1 045
Vienna	1 001
Canton	944
Philadelphia	791
Tokyo (Yedo)	780
St. Petersburg	764
Bombay	718
Calcutta	680
Liverpool	650
Glasgow	635
Moscow	600

1900

City	Population
London	6 480
New York	4 242
Paris	3 330
Berlin	2 424
Chicago	1 717
Vienna	1 662
Tokyo	1 497
St. Petersburg	1 439
Philadelphia	1 418
Manchester	1 255
Birmingham	1 248
Moscow	1 120
Peking	1 100
Calcutta	1 085
Boston	1 075

1925

City	Population
New York	7 774
London	7 742
Tokyo	5 300
Paris	4 800
Berlin	4 013
Chicago	3 564
Buenos Aires	2 410
Osaka	2 219
Ruhr	2 180
Philadelphia	2 085
Vienna	1 862
Boston	1 773
Moscow	1 764
Manchester	1 725
Birmingham	1 700

1950

City	Population
New York	12 300
London	8 860
Tokyo	7 547
Paris	5 900
Shanghai	5 406
Moscow	5 100
Chicago	4 906
Ruhr	4 900
Calcutta	4 800
Buenos Aires	4 600
Los Angeles	3 900
Berlin	3 707
Osaka	3 480
Mexico City	3 190
Cairo	2 950

1968

City	Population
Tokyo	20 500
New York	16 900
London	11 025
Osaka	10 900
Moscow	9 150
Paris	8 850
Buenos Aires	8 600
Los Angeles	8 455
Calcutta	7 900
Shanghai	7 800
Chicago	7 435
Mexico City	7 200
São Paulo	6 600
Rio de Janeiro	6 100
Cairo	5 900

Top 40 Cities

Top 40 Cities

(Population in Thousands)

1650	(000s)	1750	(000s)	1825	(000s)	1900	(000s)	1968	(000s)
Constantinople	700	Peking	900	Peking	1 350	London	6 480	Tokyo	20 500
Peking	600	London	676	London	1 335	New York	4 242	New York	16 900
Isfahan	500	Constantinople	666	Canton	900	Paris	3 330	London	11 025
Yedo (Tokyo)	500	Paris	560	Paris	855	Berlin	2 424	Osaka	10 900
Agra	500	Yedo	509	Constantinople	675	Chicago	1 717	Moscow	9 150
Paris	455	Canton	500	Hangchow	600	Vienna	1 662	Paris	8 850
London	410	Osaka	403	Yedo	530	Tokyo	1 497	Buenos Aires	8 600
Delhi	400	Kyoto	362	Soochow	480	St. Petersburg	1 439	Los Angeles	8 455
Kyoto	390	Hangchow	350	Kyoto	350	Philadelphia	1 418	Calcutta	7 900
Canton	385	Nanking	325	Naples	350	Manchester	1 255	Shanghai	7 800
Cairo	350	Naples	324	Osaka	340	Birmingham	1 248	Chicago	7 435
Osaka	346	Soochow	302	St. Petersburg	324	Moscow	1 120	Mexico City	7 200
Nanking	300	Cairo	300	Bombay	300	Peking	1 100	São Paulo	5 600
Naples	300	Hyderabad	300	Lucknow	300	Calcutta	1 085	Rio de Janeiro	6 100
Bijapur	300	Amsterdam	225	Vienna	288	Boston	1 075	Cairo	5 900
Hangchow	281	Lisbon	219	Patna	269	Glasgow	1 072	Bombay	5 650
Ahmedabad	275	Patna	213	Moscow	262	Liverpool	940	Ruhr	5 150
Lahore	250	Meshhed	200	Cairo	260	Osaka	931	Philadelphia	5 025
Lisbon	170	Murshidabad	200	Sian	259	Constantinople	900	Peking	4 750
Patna	150	Sian	195	Lisbon	249	Hamburg	895	Detroit	4 625
Surat	150	Seoul	183	Ningpo	230	Shanghai	837	Leningrad	4 350
Tabriz	150	Vienna	169	Calcutta	230	Buenos Aires	806	Seoul	4 175
Sian	147	Surat	165	Fuchow	225	Budapest	792	San Francisco	4 150
Arakan	145	Wuchang	165	Berlin	222	Bombay	780	Djakarta	3 750
Soochow	145	Moscow	161	Wuchang	200	Ruhr	766	Delhi	3 750
Venice	134	Venice	158	Nanking	200	Rio de Janeiro	735	Boston	3 575
Adrianople	132	Rome	157	Hyderabad	196	Warsaw	724	Hong Kong	3 500
Potosí	130	Mukden	150	Amsterdam	194	Tientsin	700	Tientsin	3 500
Palermo	128	Ayutia	150	Dublin	192	Canton	670	Milan	3 500
Ayutia	125	Jodhpur	150	Seoul	180	Newcastle	615	Tehran	3 365
Srinagar	125	Ningpo	144	Mukden	178	St. Louis	614	Manila	3 250
Rome	124	St. Petersburg	138	Madrid	176	Pittsburgh	603	Mukden	3 200
Wuchang	110	Fatshan	130	Mexico City	176	Cairo	595	Madrid	3 000
Amsterdam	110	Lanchow	130	Benares	175	Naples	563	Nagoya	2 980
Lyon	105	Smyrna	130	Chungking	175	Brussels	561	Wuhan	2 925
Milan	102	Dacca	125	Chengtu	175	Barcelona	552	Manchester	2 900
Smyrna	100	Dublin	125	Tientsin	173	Bangkok	540	Rome	2 890
Seoul	100	Palermo	124	Fatshan	172	Madrid	539	Santiago	2 810
Moscow	100	Madrid	123	Glasgow	123	Leipzig	532	Bangkok	2 725
Rajmahal	100	Milan	123	Madras	123	Amsterdam	510	Washington	2 700

(Population in Thousands)

1825		1850		1875		1900	
Peking	1 350	London	2 320	London	4 241	London	6 480
London	1 335	Peking	1 648	Paris	2 250	New York	4 242
Canton	900	Paris	1 314	New York	1 900	Paris	3 330
Paris	855	Canton	800	Peking	1 310	Berlin	2 424
Constantinople	675	Constantinople	785	Berlin	1 045	Chicago	1 717
Hangchow	600	Hangchow	700	Vienna	1 001	Vienna	1 662
Yedo (Tokyo)	530	New York	682	Canton	944	Tokyo	1 497
Soochow	392	Bombay	575	Philadelphia	791	St. Petersburg	1 439
Kyoto	350	Yedo	567	Tokyo	780	Philadelphia	1 418
Naples	350	Soochow	550	St. Petersburg	764	Manchester	1 255
Osaka	340	St. Petersburg	502	Bombay	718	Birmingham	1 248
St. Petersburg	324	Berlin	446	Calcutta	680	Moscow	1 120
Bombay	300	Vienna	426	Liverpool	650	Peking	1 100
Lucknow	300	Philadelphia	426	Glasgow	635	Calcutta	1 085
Vienna	288	Liverpool	422	Moscow	600	Boston	1 075
Patna	269	Naples	416	Constantinople	600	Glasgow	1 072
Moscow	262	Calcutta	413	Manchester	590	Liverpool	940
Cairo	260	Manchester	412	Birmingham	480	Osaka	931
Sian	259	Moscow	373	Boston	450	Constantinople	900
Lisbon	249	Glasgow	346	Naples	450	Hamburg	895
Ningpo	230	Kyoto	323	Madrid	407	Shanghai	837
Calcutta	230	Madras	310	Chicago	405	Buenos Aires	806
Fuchow	225	Osaka	300	Shanghai	400	Budapest	792
Berlin	222	Nanking	300	Madras	400	Bombay	780
Wuchang		Lucknow	300	Cairo	355	Ruhr	766
Nanking	200	Birmingham	294	Hyderabad	350	Rio de Janeiro	735
Hyderabad	200	Sian	275	Hamburg	348	Warsaw	724
Amsterdam	196	Dublin	263	St. Louis	338	Tientsin	700
Dublin	194	Madrid	263	Lyon	331	Canton	670
Seoul	192	Patna	263	Brussels	327	Newcastle	615
Mukden	180	Lisbon	257	Budapest	325	St. Louis	614
Madrid	178	Cairo	256	Tientsin	325	Pittsburgh	603
Mexico City	176	Lyon	254	Osaka	320	Cairo	595
Benares	176	Shanghai	250	Marseille	316	Naples	563
Chungking		Chengtu	240	Warsaw	311	Brussels	561
Chengtu	175	Wuchang		Chengtu	310	Barcelona	552
Tientsin	175	Ningpo	230	Dublin	310	Bangkok	540
Fatshan	175	Amsterdam	225	Bangkok	300	Madrid	539
Glasgow	173	Brussels	208	Wuchang	200	Leipzig	532
Madras	172	Boston	202	Baltimore	299	Amsterdam	510
Liverpool	170	Hyderabad	200	Leeds	296	Baltimore	508
New York	170	Tientsin	200	Sheffield	292	Madras	505
Milan	168	Mukden	200	Amsterdam	289	Soochow	500
Palermo	168	Fuchow	200	Cincinnati	280	Munich	499
Lanchow	160	Chungking	200	Milan	277	Milan	491
Manchester		Havana	199	Lucknow	276	Lyon	487
Edinburgh	145	Edinburgh	194	Rio de Janeiro	274	Rome	487
Murshidabad	145	Seoul	194	Edinburgh	274	Marseille	486
Delhi	144	Hamburg	193	Rome	252	Melbourne	485
Kingtehchen	144	Marseille	193	Sian	250	Sydney	478
Lyon	141	Milan	193	Ningpo	250	Lille	475
Philadelphia	138	Benares	185	Fuchow	250	Chengtu	475
Rome	138	Leeds	184	Mexico City	250	Copenhagen	462
Surat	138	Palermo	182	Chungking	250	Hankow	450
Smyrna	135	Mukden	180	Soochow	250	Odessa	449
Hamburg	130	Fatshan	175	Copenhagen	241	Hyderabad	445
Adrianople	125	Mexico City	170	Lisbon	240	Dresden	440
Warsaw	124	Rome	170	Barcelona	240	San Francisco	439
Birmingham	122	Lanchow	170	Breslau	239	Cologne	437
Havana	121	Baltimore	169	Kyoto	238	Leeds	423

(Population in Thousands)

622		900		1150		1400	
Constantinople	500	Bagdad	900	Constantinople	300	Nanking	473
Changan		Changan	750	Merv	200	Cairo	450
Loyang	400	Constantinople	300	Nanking	180	Vijayanagar	350
Ctesiphon		Cordova	250	Cairo	175	Hangchow	325
Alexandria	200	Kyoto	225	Kaifeng	175	Peking	320
Teotihuacán	125	Hangchow	220	Canton	170	Canton	300
Kanauj	100	Alexandria	200	Fez	160	Paris	275
Kanchi	100	Manyakheta		Kalyan	150	Tabriz	200
Vatapi		Loyang		Marrakesh	150	Kyoto	200
Memphis		Fostat	125	Pagan	150	Soochow	175
Soochow		Damascus		Sian	150	Pandua	150
Anuradhapura		Kairwan	100	Kyoto	150	Fez	150
Thaneswar		Chengtu	100	Hangchow	145	Sian	150
Antioch		Rayy	100	Anhilvada	135	Cambay	125
Edessa		Yangchow	100	Peking	130	Milan	125
Ecbatana		Samarkand		Palermo	125	Bruges	125
Prome		Nishapur		Angkor	125	Venice	110
Broach		Chunar		Bagdad	125	Genoa	100
Nanking		Angkor		Seville	125	Granada	100
Ayodhya		Anhilvada		Cuttack	125	Samarkand	100
Aleppo	72	Soochow	81	Tinnis	125	Seoul	100
Isanapura	70	Kanauj	80	Liaoyang	100	Shiraz	100
Mecca	70	Kaifeng		Yangchow	100	Damascus	100
Malakuta	70	Kufa		Kayseri	100	Prague	95
Chengtu		Kyongju		Songdo		Bursa	
Rayy		Vengi		Hiraizumi		Bagdad	90
Pagan		Lhasa		Kanauj	92	Quilon	90
Benares	65	Basra		Soochow	91	Chengtu	88
Pyongyang		Tanjore		Ninghsia		Chüanchow	
Caesarea		Nanking		Benares		Kaifeng	

1600		1700		1800		1900	
Peking	706	Constantinople	700	Peking	1 100	London	6 480
Constantinople	700	Peking		London	861	New York	4 242
Agra	500	Isfahan	600	Canton	800	Paris	3 330
Cairo	400	London	550	Constantinople	570	Berlin	2 424
Osaka	400	Paris	530	Paris	547	Chicago	1 717
Canton	350	Yedo	500	Hangchow	500	Vienna	1 662
Yedo	350	Delhi	500	Yedo	492	Tokyo (Yedo)	1 497
Kyoto	350	Ahmedabad	380	Naples	430	St. Petersburg	1 439
Hangchow	350	Osaka	370	Soochow	392	Philadelphia	1 418
Lahore	350	Kyoto	350	Kyoto	377	Manchester	1 255
Nanking	317	Cairo	300	Osaka	373	Birmingham	1 248
Naples	275	Canton	300	Nanking	350	Moscow	1 220
Paris	250	Nanking	300	Lucknow	300	Peking	1 100
Ahmedabad	225	Hangchow	292	Cairo	263	Calcutta	1 085
Bijapur	200	Soochow	245	Moscow	238	Boston	1 075
London	187	Naples	207	Lisbon	237	Glasgow	1 072
Soochow	175	Meknes	200	Patna	235	Liverpool	940
Adrianople	160	Dacca	200	Vienna	231	Osaka	931
Venice	151	Surat	200	Sian	224	Constantinople	900
Sian	150	Lisbon	188	St. Petersburg	220	Hamburg	895
Qazvin	150	Amsterdam	172	Amsterdam	201	Shanghai	837
Potosí	148	Patna	170	Ningpo	200	Buenos Aires	806
Seville	144	Seoul	170	Calcutta	200	Budapest	792
Chengtu	130	Sian	167	Hyderabad	200	Bombay	780
Marrakesh	125	Ayutia	150	Seoul	190	Ruhr	766
Arakan	125	Tabriz	150	Wuchang		Rio de Janeiro	735
Isfahan	125	Aurangabad	150	Murshidabad	185	Warsaw	724
Milan	119	Wuchang	150	Mukden		Tientsin	700
Lisbon	110	Srinagar	150	Benares	179	Canton	670
Granada	110	Rome	149	Amarapura	175	Newcastle	615

Cities of Europe
(Population in Thousands)

900	1000	1100	1200	1300 (pop / pop)
Constantinople 350	Cordova 350	Constantinople 450	Constantinople 300	Paris 250 / 228
Cordova 200	Constantinople 200	Seville 450	Palermo 125	Granada 150 / 150
Thessalonica 50	Seville 50	Palermo 90	Seville 90	Constantinople 150 / 150
Seville 42	Palermo 42	Cordova 75	Paris 60	Venice 110 / 110
Preslav 40	Kiev 40	Granada 45	Venice 60	Milan 70 / 100
Mérida 40	Venice 40	Venice 45	Milan 55	Genoa 60 / 100
Rome 40	Thessalonica 40	Kiev 40	Cordova 50	Sarai 60 / 100
Itil 36	Ratisbon 36	Salerno 40	Granada 50	Seville 60 / 90
Borbastro	Ochrida 35	Milan 40	Cologne 45	Florence 50 / 60
Palermo 35	Amalfi 35	Thessalonica 35	London 40	Cologne 40 / 54
Venice 35	Rome 35	Spires 35	Kiev 35	Rouen 40 / 50
Almería	Almería	London 35	Rouen 35	Bruges 40 / 50
Toledo 25	Cartagena 25	Rouen 33	Smolensk 35	Bolgary 40 / 50
Ratisbon	Toledo	Rome 31	León 35	Thessalonica 40 / 50
Lejre	Pavia	Almería 30	Toledo 35	Valencia 35 / 44
Pavia 22	Mainz 22	Paris 30	Bologna 30	Toledo 35 / 42
Corinth	Naples	Ratisbon 30	Rome 30	Ghent 35 / 42
Cartagena	Milan	Mainz 30	Trnovo 30	London 35 / 40
Naples	Preslav	Pavia 30	Verona 30	Marseille 33 / 40
Milan 20	London 20	León 25	Spires 30	Palermo 30 / 40
Kiev 20	Bolgary 20	Verona 25	Messina 30	Prague 30 / 40
Plovdiv 20	Elvira 20	Naples 22	Genoa 30	Novgorod 30 / 40
Candia 20	Cologne 20	Toledo 21	Pisa 27	Caffa 30 / 40
London 20	Paris 20	Palma 20	Novgorod 27	Cordova 30 / 40
	Palma 20	Angers 20	Thessalonica 27	Bologna 30 / 39
	Plovdiv 20	Amalfi 20	Palma 25	Padua 30 / 38
	Rouen 20	Orléans 20	Angers 25	Cremona 30 / 36
	Verona 20	Cologne 20	Naples 25	Orléans 30 / 36
	Trier 20	Arles 20	Orléans 25	Ferrara 27 / 36
		Novgorod 20	Ferrara 25	Verona 27

Cities of Europe—southern offset

(Population in Thousands)

1400		1500		1600		1700	
Paris	275	Paris	225	Constantinople	700	Constantinople	700
Milan	125	Constantinople	200	Naples	275	London	550
Bruges	125	Adrianople	125	Paris	250	Paris	530
Venice	110	Naples	125	London	187	Naples	207
Genoa	100	Venice	115	Adrianople	160	Lisbon	188
Granada	100	Milan	104	Venice	151	Amsterdam	172
Prague	95	Bruges	90	Seville	144	Rome	149
Caffa	85	Lyon	80	Milan	119	Venice	143
Constantinople	75	Ghent	80	Granada	110	Moscow	130
Ghent	70	Rouen	75	Lisbon	110	Milan	124
Rouen	70	Prague	70	Rome	109	Palermo	113
Seville	70	Florence	70	Palermo	105	Madrid	110
Florence	61	Lisbon	70	Prague	100	Vienna	105
Lisbon	55	Granada	70	Lyon	90	Marseille	88
Novgorod	50	Genoa	62	Valencia	86	Seville	80
Troki	50	Brescia	61	Toledo	80	Dublin	80
Valencia	48	Tours	60	Moscow	80	Barcelona	73
London	45	Bologna	55	Madrid	79	Lyon	71
Toledo	45	Nuremberg	52	Genoa	70	Brussels	70
Bologna	43	Pskov	52	Rouen	70	Hamburg	70
Salonica	42	London	50	Tours	65	Granada	70
Cologne	40	Seville	50	Florence	65	Florence	69
Naples	40	Smolensk	50	Smolensk	64	Rouen	68
Ferrara	40	Caffa	50	Bologna	62	Antwerp	67
Cordova	40	Tirgovishtea	50	Messina	61	Genoa	67
Barcelona	37	Üskub	50	Bucharest	60	Bologna	63
Málaga	35	Valencia	50	Valladolid	56	Leiden	62
Pskov	35	Valladolid	48	Antwerp	55	Copenhagen	62
Verona	35	Palermo	48	Brussels	55	Lille	55
Cremona	35	Toledo	47	Marseille	55	Belgrade	50

Cities of Americas—South offset

(Population in Thousands)

1400		1500		1600		1700	
Tezcoco	70	Tenochtitlán	80	Potosí	148	Mexico City	100
Chanchán	40	Tezcoco	60	Mexico City	75	Potosí	95
Cajamarquilla	40	Utatlán	60	Cuzco	30	Oruro	72
Cholula		Cuzco	45	Puebla	25	Puebla	63
Riobamba		Tzintzuntzán	40	Guatemala	25	Lima	37
Mayapán	25	Tlaxcala	40	Huancavelica	20	Cuzco	35
Chincha	25	Chanchán	40	Tlaxcala	20	Zacatecas	30
Tzintzuntzán		Cholula	36	Quito	18	Quito	30
Utatlán		Quito	30	Tayasal	15	Guatemala	30
Cuzco		Ticoh (Mérida)	25	Lima	14	Havana	25

Cities of Europe

(Population in Thousands)

1800		1861		1900		1950	
London	861	London	2 803	London	6 480	London	8 860
Constantinople	570	Paris	1 800	Paris	3 330	Paris	5 900
Paris	547	Constantinople	800	Berlin	2 424	Moscow	5 100
Naples	430	Vienna	670	Vienna	1 662	Berlin	3 707
Moscow	238	Berlin	582	St. Petersburg	1 439	Ruhr	2 937
Lisbon	237	St. Petersburg	565	Manchester	1 255	Leningrad	2 900
Vienna	231	Liverpool	505	Birmingham	1 248	Birmingham	2 196
St. Petersburg	220	Moscow	500	Moscow	1 120	Manchester	1 908
Amsterdam	201	Manchester	488	Glasgow	1 072	Vienna	1 795
Berlin	172	Naples	447	Liverpool	940	Rome	1 665
Madrid	169	Glasgow	429	Constantinople	900	Madrid	1 602
Dublin	165	Birmingham	400	Hamburg	895	Hamburg	1 580
Rome	153	Dublin	313	Budapest	792	Barcelona	1 535
Venice	146	Madrid	303	Ruhr	766	Glasgow	1 320
Palermo	146	Lyon	293	Warsaw	724	Milan	1 289
Milan	134	Brussels	283	Naples	563	Athens	1 270
Hamburg	130	Lisbon	280	Brussels	561	Liverpool	1 260
Barcelona	120	Hamburg	250	Barcelona	552	Naples	1 200
Lyon	110	Amsterdam	247	Madrid	539	Bucharest	1 200
Marseille	109	Sheffield	242	Leipzig	532	Copenhagen	1 150
Copenhagen	100	Marseille	232	Amsterdam	510	Budapest	1 080
Adrianople	100	Leeds	222	Munich	499	Prague	1 000
Bordeaux	97	Milan	220	Milan	491	Istanbul	1 000
Seville	96	Buda-Pesth	210	Lyon	487	Katowice	977
Genoa	90	Edinburgh	209	Copenhagen	462	Brussels	964
Cádiz	87	Bordeaux	198	Odessa	449	Amsterdam	941
Rouen	85	Rome	194	Dresden	440	Stockholm	876
Glasgow	85	Barcelona	193	Cologne	437	Newcastle	860
Edinburgh	82	Turin	185	Leeds	436	Munich	844
Manchester	81	Warsaw	163	Breslau	422	Lisbon	832

Cities of Americas

(Population in Thousands)

1800		1861		1900		1950	
Mexico City	128	New York	1 220	New York	4 242	New York	12 300
Bahia	75	Philadelphia	590	Chicago	1 717	Buenos Aires	5 000
Philadelphia	68	Boston	318	Philadelphia	1 418	Chicago	4 906
Guanajuato	65	Baltimore	217	Boston	1 075	Los Angeles	3 900
Puebla	65	Mexico City	215	Buenos Aires	806	Philadelphia	2 894
New York	63	Rio de Janeiro	208	Rio de Janeiro	750	Detroit	2 784
Havana	60	Havana	203	St. Louis	614	Mexico City	2 550
Lima	54	Cincinnati	200	Pittsburgh	603	Rio de Janeiro	2 510
Rio de Janeiro	44	New Orleans	183	Baltimore	508	São Paulo	2 445
Pernambuco	40	St. Louis	176	San Francisco	439	Boston	2 212

Cities of Australia

(Population in Thousands)

1800		1861		1900		1950	
				Melbourne	491	Sydney	1 550
				Sydney	476	Melbourne	1 335

1575

	City	Country	Population
	Peking	China	706 000
	Constantinople	Turkey	680
	Cairo	Turkey	415
	Kyoto	Japan	360
	Hangchow	China	350
	Canton	China	325
	Nanking	China	312
	Paris	France	240
	Naples	Spain	240
10	Pegu	Burma	175
	Ahmedabad	Moguls	170
	Soochow	China	170
	Adrianople	Turkey	160
	Venice	Venice	157
	Tabriz	Persia	150
	Fatehpur Sikri	Moguls	150
	Sian	China	150
	Seville	Spain	125
	Seoul	Korea	125
20	Chengtu	China	125
	Potosí	Spain	120
	London	England	112
	Antwerp	Spain	110
	Milan	Spain	109
25	Penukonda	S. India	100

	City	Pop.		City	Pop.
	Agra	100 000		Valencia	72 000
	Marrakesh	100		Mexico City	70
	Bijapur	100		Prague	70
	Qazvin	100		Algiers	70
	Fez	100		Palermo	70
	Arakan	100		Rouen	70
	Bokhara			Smyrna	70
	Delhi			Yangchow	
	Sakai			Genoa	67
	Lisbon	90		Tunis	
	Nagoya			Vijayanagar	
	Kaifeng			Kano	65
	Wuchang			Bologna	65
	Cambay	85		Gwalior	
	Lyon	80		Kingtehchen	
	Taiyüan	79		Srinagar	
	Jodhpur			Lahore	
	Bursa	76		Surat	
	Fuchow	76		Valladolid	60
	Gao	75		Damascus	60
	Toledo	75		Bihar	60
	Granada	75		Ahmednagar	60
	Rome	75		Tours	60
	Tientsin			Florence	59
50	Golconda			Aleppo	59

Cities 20-40 000 in Americas and Africa, 1850

Americas		Africa	
Newark	38 000	Shaki	
Rochester	36	Oshogbo	
Quito	36	Sokoto	33 000
León, México		Ede	
San Francisco	34	Dikwa	30
Maranhão	34	Constantine	28
Montevideo	33	Asyut	28
Lowell	33	Damietta	27
Oaxaca	33	Cape Town	26
Kingston	33	Iwo	
Pará	32	Bonga	
Colima	31	Segu	
Aguascalientes	31	Tripoli	25
San Salvador	30	Rabbah	25
Chicago	29	Suramé	
St. John's	27	Iseyin	
Richmond	27	Wurno	
Toronto	27	Ofa	
Salem	26	Tarudant	22
Guayaquil	26	Esneh	22
Durango	26	Ilushi	
Zacatecas	25	Oyo	20
Quezaltenango	25	Zagazig	20
Morelia	25	Tanta	20
Georgetown	25	Khartoum	20
Santiago, Cuba	24	Masenya	20
Potosí	23		
Córdoba, Argentina	22		
Syracuse	22		
Arequipa	21		
Port-au-Prince	21		
Medellín	21		
Detroit	21		
St. John	21		
Portland, Maine	20		
Mobile	20		
New Haven	20		
St. Pierre	20		
Cuenca	20		
Valencia, Venezuela	20		
Milwaukee	20		

Åbo, also called Turku, in W. Finland
Agrigentum, midpoint of Sicily's Southern coast
Aivali, port in W Asia Minor facing Lesbos
Amarna, 250 miles beeline up the Nile
Anking, 400 miles W of Hangchow
Anuradhapura, north-central Ceylon
Anyang, a bit north of Kaifeng
Apamea, in Northern Syria, SE of Antioch
Aquileia, very near Venice
Arad, 100 miles N of Belgrade
Argos, 60 miles SW of Athens
Arrah, quite near Patna
Assur, 50 miles S of Mosul
Autun, 90 miles N of Lyon
Ávila, 50 miles NW of Toledo
Babylon, on Euphrates 50 miles S of Bagdad
Barfrush, 90 miles SE of Tehran, near the Caspian
Barnsley, 15 miles N of Sheffield
Belur, 100 miles W of Bangalore
Bhatgaon, 8 miles from Katmandu
Bhuj, 30 miles N of Mandu
Bikaner, 2/5 the way from Delhi to Karachi
Bitlis, 110 miles SSE of Erzurum
Blackburn, 25 miles NNW of Manchester
Bromberg, 200 miles ENE of Berlin
Brünn, now Brno, in mid-Czechoslovakia
Budaun, 28 miles SW of Bareilly
Burton, 127 miles NW of London
Bury, 10 miles NW of Manchester
Bust, S-central Afghanistan, where the Helmand joins the Arghendab
Calpi, 51 miles S of Cawnpore
Camelot, now Colchester, 50 miles NE of London
Capua, just N of Naples
Carthage, where Africa approaches Sicily
Chairadeo, 350 miles NE of Dacca
Champa, 60 miles E of Patna, 4 miles W of Bhagalpur
Champaner, 75 miles E of Ahmedabad
Chanda, 80 miles SSE of Nagpur
Chaochow, now Chaohsien, a bit E of Canton
Chapra, 25 miles up the Ganges WNW of Patna
Chatham, 34 miles E of London
Cheltenham, 35 miles NE of Bristol
Chicheng, in Shantung
Coatbridge, 8 miles E of Glasgow
Coimbatore, 1/3 the way from Calicut to Tanjore
Corcyra, now Corfu, on Corfu island W of Greece
Cranganore, port 125 miles N of India's southern tip, on the west coast
Ctesiphon, 25 miles S of Bagdad
Cyrene, at the N bulge of Libya, slightly inland
Dabhoi, 20 miles SE of Baroda
Dantapura, capital of Kalinga–modern Andhra state, SW of Calcutta
Dariya, 450 miles NE of Mecca, very near Riyadh
Darlington, 15 miles W of Middlesbrough
Dewsbury, 8 miles SW of Leeds
Dinajpur, 41 miles SW of Rangpur
Dorpat, now Tartu, 175 miles WSW of St. Petersburg
Duras, on the mid-Euphrates
Eastbourne, 61 miles SSE of London, on the sea
Ecbatana, now Hamadan

Ekaterinburg, now Sverdlovsk, W Siberia near the Urals
Elbing, port 50 miles SE of Danzig
Elets, 122 miles SE of Orel
Elizavetgrad, now Kirovograd
Ephesus, mid-west-coastal Asia Minor
Erech, on lower Euphrates 150miles S of Bagdad
Etawah, on the Jumna 200 miles above Allahabad
Ferozepore, near Jullundur
Fowchow, now Fouling, 50 miles ENE of Chungking
Gawil, 100 miles NW of Nagpur
Ghazipur, 44 miles E of Benares
Gouda, 12 miles E of Rotterdam
Haidzuong, 30 miles ESE of Hanoi
Hanchung, 125 miles SW of Sian
Harappa, 100 miles SW of Lahore
Hastinapura, probably quite near Delhi
Hathras, 29 miles N of Agra
Hazor, 50 miles SW of Damascus
Hengchow, 300 miles NNW of Canton
Heracleopolis, 80 miles S of Cairo
Hiraizumi, 280 miles N of Tokyo
Hodeida, port 125 miles up the Arabian Western coast
Hofuf, about halfway up the Arabian side of the Persian Gulf, near the base of Qatar peninsula, about 50
    miles inland
Hsingi, 125 miles W of Canton
Hsuchow, 110 miles S of Chengtu
Hsüeh, NE China
Huchow, a bit S of lake Taihu
Imphal, 250 miles ENE of Dacca
Isanapura, 80 miles E of Angkor
Ismail, at head of the Danube's delta
Jhansi, 130 miles SW of Cawnpore
Jiddah, port of Mecca
Kadesh, 60 miles N of Damascus
Kalyan the elder, a bit NE of Bombay
Kamarapura, E of Rangpur
Kamptu, 10 miles NE of Nagpur
Kanchow, Kansuh, 250 miles NW of Lanchow
Karakorum, 250 miles S of lake Baikal
Kashiwara, 7 miles E of Osaka
Kastamuni, 300 miles E of Constantinople
Kausambi, now Kosam, 28 miles WSW of Allahabad
Kavery, at mouth of the Kavery river
Kawkaban, a short way NW of Sanaa
Keighley, 17 miles WNW of Leeds
Kelat (Kalat), 85 miles SW of Quetta
Kerbela, 60 miles SW of Bagdad
Khattushas, 75 miles NW of Ankara
Khoi, 77 miles NW of Tabriz, on site of Artaxata
Kiating, 75 miles S of Chengtu
Kingchow, 155 miles W of Hankow, just above Shasi
Kingyang, 115 miles NNW of Sian
Kirin, 450 miles N of Seoul
Knossos, middle of Crete's northern coast
Kofu, 60 miles W of Tokyo
Kolkai, now Tinnevelly
Kolozsvár, 248 miles ESE of Budapest
Kozlov, 45 miles WNW of Tambov
Kumbakonam, 20 miles NE of Tanjore

Kweichow, halfway from Chengtu to Hankow
Kweiyang, 500 miles WNW of Canton
Lakhon, on the mid-Menam in Siam's Laotian province
Lakkundi, 340 miles SE of Bombay
Lashkar, formerly and now again called Gwalior
Libau, now Liepaja, 110 miles W of Riga
Liegnitz, 40 miles NW of Breslau
Limerick, at mouth of the Shannon
Lintsing, 60 miles W of Tsinan
Lintzu, by modern Weifang, 250 miles S of Peking
Lipa, 90 miles SE of Manila
Lovek, location unknown
Lucheng, SE Shansi
Mahoba, 200 miles S of Cawnpore
Malakuta, S India, not certainly identified (perhaps Kavery city?)
Mandvi, port 182 miles SE of Karachi
Mangalore, seaport NW of Bangalore
Marghelan, 150 miles E of Tashkent
Maria Theresiopel, now Subotica, 100 miles NNW of Belgrade
Marib, 200 miles N of Aden, SW Arabia
Masulipatam, port 400 miles E of Hyderabad
Mataram, NE Java near Cheribon
Mecheln, midway from Brussels to Antwerp
Megalopolis, mid-Peloponnesus
Memphis, Egypt, 100 miles up the Nile
Mengtze, in SE Yünnan
Meroé (not modern Merowe), 150 miles NNE of Khartoum
Miletus, 60 miles S of Smyrna
Mirta, 76 miles NE of Jodhpur
Mohenjo-daro, 250 miles beeline up the Indus
Mondovi, equidistant from Turin, Nice, and Genoa
Muzaffarpur, a bit N of Patna
Mycenae, 15 miles S of Corinth
Nafa, on Okinawa near the southern tip
Nagyvárad, 153 miles SE of Budapest
Napata, modern Merowe, 200 miles NNW of Khartoum
Nevanagar, 160 miles W of Ahmedabad
Negapatam, 300 miles S of Madras
Newchwang, port 100 miles SW of Mukden
Nganshun, 40 miles SW of Kweiyang
Nineveh, E opposite Mosul
Nippur, 75 miles SW of Babylon
Nizampatam, port 35 miles S of Masulipatam
Nujufabad, 20 miles NW of Isfahan
Ockaseer, 5 miles S of Broach
Otrar, 82 miles NE of Chimkent in central Asia
Oudong, 200 miles NNW of Pnompenh
Özkend, in Sinkiang
Paithan, on upper Godavari, 200 miles E of Bombay
Palghat, 70 miles SE of Calicut
Panipat, 100 miles NW of Delhi
Pasar Gede, NE Java
Patala, probably modern Tatta, 125 miles up the Indus
Pergamum, 50 miles N of Smyrna, a bit inland
Pilibit, 30 miles NW of Bareilly
Pohchow, in NW Andhra
Pundravardhana, near Rangpur
Purnea, 12 miles N of Gaur
Rajagriha, a few miles S of Patna

Ramavati, in Bengal, site probably unknown.
Remscheid, 6 miles S of Barmen (part of present-day Wuppertal)
Reval, now Tallinn, 150 miles N of Riga
Rewarri or Rewari, 45 miles S of Delhi
Rhodes, on Rhodes island off SW Turkey
Rotherham, 5 miles N of Sheffield
Roubaix, now a suburb of Lille
Rustchuk, on Danube 40 miles S of Bucharest
Ryazan, 124 miles SE of Moscow
Sais, 50 miles up the main western branch of the Nile delta
Samarra, on Tigris 50 miles above Bagdad
Sambhal, 22 miles SW of Moradabad
Santa Ana, 50 miles NW of San Salvador
Sardis, 50 miles inland from Smyrna
Saugor, 90 miles NW of Jubbulpore
Schemnitz, 152 miles N of Budapest
Seleucia, W opposite Ctesiphon
Serampur, 15 miles N of Calcutta
Shasi, on the Yangtze 150 miles W of Hankow
Shihlung, 50 miles E of Canton
Sidon, a port of Damascus
Simbirsk, now Ulyanovsk, 100 miles S of Kazan
Sining, 100 miles NW of Lanchow
Sistova, on the Danube 40 miles W of Rustchuk
Sparta, inland SE Peloponnesus
Sravasti, 250 miles NW of Patna
Stakhr, on site of Persepolis
Sungkiang, a short way W of Shanghai
Susa, 300 miles SE of Bagdad
Suvarnagiri, perhaps modern Maski in W Mysore
Swindon, 77 miles W of London
Taku, on coast SE of Tientsin
Tanda, site uncertain, in Maldob district, Bhagalpur division, Bengal
Tanis, in the lower E part of the Nile delta
Tarentum, inside the heel of Italy's boot
Taxila, 400 miles SE of Bombay
Teotihuacán, 30 miles W of Mexico City
Thebes, Egypt, 400 miles beeline up the Nile
Tientsiku, a bit E of Tientsin
Tinghai, on the E point east of Hangchow, facing Chusan island
Tinnevelly, inland, 40 miles from India's southern tip
Tiruvannamalai, near Tanjore
Tosali, near mouth of the Mahanadi, 200 miles SW of Calcutta
Tournai, 15 miles E of Lille
Tsingchow, in SE Shantung
Tsining, 125 miles N of Nanking
Tsingkiangpo, 10 miles N of Hwaian, 120 miles N of Nanking
Tsaochow, SW Shantung
Tüngnai, 5 miles NW of Pusan
Tyre, port 100 miles N of Jerusalem
Ur, on Euphrates 80 miles above its junction with the Tigris
Urga, 500 miles S of lake Baikal and a bit E of Karakorum
Urumchi, now Tihua, 1,000 miles S of lake Baikal
Vaisali, 50 miles N of Patna
Valabhi, near the eastern edge of Gujarat peninsula
Van, on E of lake Van, 250 miles SSW of Tiflis
Vikrampura, near Dacca

Vizagapatam, port, 484 miles NE of Madras
Volubilis, near Fez
Washshukkani, probably on or near the mid-Euphrates
Weihsien, now Weifang, 30 miles NW of Tsingtao
Wuhu, 50 miles up the Yangtze from Nanking
Wusih, on Yangtze 200 miles W of Shanghai
Xanadu, ruins beside modern Dolonnor in E Mongolia
Yakoba, halfway from lade Chad to the Niger's mouth
Yannina, 150 miles SE of Thessalonica
Ye, in N part of Honan province
Yenhsiatu, a bit N of Peking
Yenying, 100 miles NW of Hankow
Yoshino, 22 miles S of Nara
Yünnanfu, now Kunming, 350 miles NW of Hanoi

"Aarbog for Kobenhavn," see Copenhagen, city of.

Abd-al-Basit, chapter in Brunschvig (ed.) (1936).

Abd-er-Razzaq, chapter in Major (1857).

Abdul-Hak, Selim, "Aspects of Ancient Damascus" (no date).

Abid-Ali, "Memoirs of Gaur and Pandua." Bengal Secretariat Book Depot, Calcutta, 1931.

Abulfeda, I., "Géographie." Paris, 1848-88.

Abu Lughod, J., by correspondence.

Académie Nationale de Reims, "Travaux."

Accioli, I., and Amaral, B., "Memorias Históricas e Políticas da Provincia da Bahia," State Press, Bahia, 1919-40.

Acsay, L., "Save the Splendor of Budapest." Amer. Hungarian Library and Historical Soc., New York, 1965.

Adachi, K., "Manchuria." McBride, New York, 1925.

Adams, R., "The Evolution of Urban Society." Aldine, Chicago, 1966.

Adams, W., "Flowers of Modern Voyages and Travels." London, 1820.

Ademović, F., "Sarajevo." Sarajevo, 1965 ("Zadrugar").

Adorne, A., chapter in Brunschvig (ed.) (1936).

Affagart, G., "Relation de Terre Sainte." Lecoffre, Paris, 1902.

Ahnlund, N., "Stockholms Historie före Gustav Vasa." Norstedt, Stockholm, 1953.

Aigrefeuille, C., "Histoire de Montpellier." Montpellier, 1876-83.

Aillard, L., "Chroniques du Vieux Nimes." Nimes, 1923.

Ainsworth, W., "A Personal Narrative of the Euphrates Expedition." London, 1888.

Alden, D., "Royal Government in Colonial Brazil." Univ. of California Press, Berkeley, 1968.

Alexander, J., "Travels from India to England." London, 1827.

Ali, A., "Bhopal, Past and Present." Lyall Book Depot, Bhopal, 1969.

Allan, F., "De Stad Utrecht." Amsterdam, 1856.

Allen, A. M., "A History of Verona." Putnam, New York, 1910.

Allen, W. E. D., "A History of the Georgian People." Paul, Trench, Trubner, London, 1932.

Alsop, J., "From the Silent Earth." Harper, New York, 1964.

Altekar, A., "The Rashtrakutas and Their Times." Oriental Book Agency, Poona, 1934.

Amador, E., "Bosquejo Histórico de Zacatecas." Zacatecas, 1892.

Amari, M., "Storia dei Musulmani di Sicilia," Florence, 1868.

American Cyclopaedia, New York, 1873-76.

Ammann, H., chapter in "Studien zu den Anfängen der europäischer Städtewesens." 1955.

Amsterdam, city of, "Statistisch Jaarbuch der Gemeente Amsterdam 1938-9." Amsterdam, 1941.

Anderson, A., "A Narrative of the British Embassy to China." London, 1795.

Andréadés, A., *Métron*, I, no. 2 (1920).

Andrews, E. W., "Dzibalchaltun." Tulane, New Orleans, 1961.

Angelov, chapter in "Medieval Bulgarian Culture." Foreign Languages Press, Sofia, 1964.

"Annales de Démographie Historique."

"Annuaire Statistique de la Grèce." See Greece, government of.

"Annuario Statistico de Roma." See Roma, city of.

Arberry, A., "Shiraz." Univ. of Oklahoma Press, Norman, Oklahoma, 1960.

Archangelskaya, "Nizhny-Novgorod v XVII Veke," n.d.

"Archives de la Gironde."

Arciniegas, G., "The Knight of El Dorado." Viking, New York, 1942.

Arellano Moreno, A., "Carácas," Comisión Nacional de Cuatricentenario, Carácas, 1966.

Arlegui, J., "Crónica de la Provincia de San Francisco de Zacatecas." Mexico City, 1851.

Arnold, S., "Polska w Rozwoju Dziejowym." Panstwowe Zaklady Wydawn, Warsaw, 1966.

Arnould, M., "Les Dénombrements de Foyers dans le Comté de Hainaut (XIVe-XVIe Siècle)." Palais des Académies, Brussels, 1956.

Arrate, J. M. F. de, Llave del Nuevo Mundo, *in* "Los Tres Primeros Historiadores de la Isla de Cuba." (Cowley, ed.). Cuba, 1876-7.

Arvieux, L. d', "Mémoires." Paris, 1717.

Arzans, B., "Historia de la Villa Imperial de Potosí." Brown Univ. Press, Providence, 1965.

Aslanapa, O., "Edirne Osmanli devri Abedeleri." Ücler Basimevi, Istanbul, 1949.

Asso, I. de, "Historia de la Economía Política de Aragón." Zaragoza, 1798.

Aubin, J., *in* "Studia Islamica." 1963.

Augur, H. "Zapotec." Doubleday, Garden City, New York, 1954.

Averanga, A., "Algunos Aspectos de la Población de Bolivia" (no date).

Awe, B., "The City of Ibadan" (P. Lloyd, ed.). Cambridge Univ. Press, London and New York, 1967.

Azadaev, P., "Tashkent." Russian National Acad., Tashkent, 1959.

Azevedo, T. de *et al.,* "Povoamento da Cidade do Salvador." National Press, São Paulo, 1955.

Baddeley, J. (ed.), "Russia, Mongolia, China . . . to 1676." Macmillan, New York, 1919.

Badger, G., "Travels of Ludovico di Varthema." London, 1863.

Badia, D., "Travels of Ali Bey." London, 1816.

Baedeker, K., co., "Belgium and Holland." 1901.

      "   "Die Rheinlände." 1881.

      "   "Konstantinopel." 1914.

      "   "Österreich-Ungarn." 1896.

Bakewell, Peter, "Silver Mining and Society in . . . Zacatecas 1546-1700," University Press, Cambridge, 1971.

Bakhrushin, S. *et al.,* "Istoriya Moskvii." Russian National Academy, Moscow, 1952.

Balazs, E., "Les Villes Chinoises," *Rec. Soc. Jean Bodin* **6**, 225-40, Brussels, 1954

Balbi, A., "Abrégée de Géographie," Paris, 1833.

      "   "Essai Statistique sur le Royaume de Portugal." Paris, 1822.

Balfour, E., "Cyclopaedia of India." London, 1885.

Ballesteros, A., "Sevilla en el Siglo XIII." Madrid, 1913.

Baratier, É., "Histoire de la Provence." Privat, Toulouse, 1969.

Barbier, C., edition of Yaqut. Paris, 1861.

Barbot, J., chapter in A. Churchill, V (1774-6).

Barlow, G., "The Story of Madras." Oxford Univ. Press, London and New York, 1921.

Barros Arana, D., "Historia General de Chile." Editorial Nascimento, Santiago, 1930-7.

Barrow, J., "Travels in China." London, 1804.

      "   "A Voyage to Cochinchina." London, 1806.

Barth, H., "Travels and Discoveries in North and Central Africa." London, 1857-8.

Barthold, V., "Herat unter Husein Baiqara." Brockhaus, Leipzig, 1938.

Bascom, W., chapter in *Amer. J. Sociol.* (March 1955).

Basham, A., "The Wonder That Was India." Sidgwick and Jackson, London, 1967.

Bastin, J., and Winks, R., "Malaysia: Selected Historical Readings." Oxford Univ. Press, London and New York, 1966.

Batra, H., "The Relations of Jaipur State with the East India Company." Chand, Delhi, 1958.

Battel, A., chapter in Pinkerton, XVI (1808-14).

Baurain, P., "Alep." Librairie Castoun, Aleppo, 1930.

Bégin, É., "Metz depuis Dix-Huit Siecles," Paris & Metz, 1945.

Begley, J., "The Diocese of Limerick in the Sixteenth and Seventeenth Centuries." Browne and Nolan, Dublin, 1927.

Bekri, Abdullah el-, "Descripcion de l'Afrique Septentrionale." Jourdan, Algiers, 1913.

Bel, A., "Tlemcen." Thiriat, Paris, n. d.

Beloch, J., "Bevölkerungsgeschichte Italiens." De Gruyter, Berlin, 1937-61.

" "Die Bevölkerung der griechisch-römischen Welt." Leipzig, 1886.

Belotti, B., "Storia di Bergamo e dei Bergamaschi." Ceschina, Milan, 1940.

Bémont, F., "Les Villes de l'Iran." Private, Paris, 1969.

Benjamin of Tudela, "Viajes." Sanz Calleja, Madrid, 1918.

Bennassar, B. "Valladolid au Siécle d'Or." Mouton, Paris, 1967.

Bergmann, E. von, "Zur Geschichte der Entwicklung deutscher, polnischer und jüdischer Bevölkerung in der Provinz Posen." Tübingen, 1883.

Bernal, I., "Ancient Mexico in Color." McGraw-Hill, New York, 1968.

Bernard, M., "La Municipalité de Brest de 1750 à 1790." Champion, Paris, 1915.

Berncastle, "A Voyage to China." London, 1850.

Bernier, F., "Travels in the Mogul Empire 1656-1668." Oxford Univ. Press, London and New York, 1914.

Beyer, G., "The Urban Explosion in Latin America." Cornell Univ. Press, Ithaca, New York, 1967.

Beylie, L., "La Kalaa des Beni-Hammad." Leroux, Paris, 1909.

Bhattacharya, S. N., "A History of Mughal North-East Frontier Policy." Chuckervertty, Chatterjea, Calcutta, 1929.

Bible.

Bieber, F., "Kaffa." Aschendorff, Münster, 1920-23.

Biervillas, I. de, "Voyage." Paris, 1736.

Bingham, W., "Factors Contributing to the Foundation of the Tang Dynasty." Univ. of California Press, Berkeley, California, 1934.

Biobaku, S., "The Egba and Their Neighbors." Oxford Univ. Press (Clarendon), London and New York, 1957.

Biraben, J., in "Journal des Savants." Paris, 1964.

Biruni, M. al-, "Alberuni's India." Chand, Delhi, 1964.

Bittel, K., "Grundzüge der Vor- und Frühgeschichte Kleinasiens." Wasmuth, Tübingen, 1945.

" "Hattusha." Oxford Univ. Press, London and New York, 1970.

Bivar, A., and Shinnie, P., J. Afr. History (1962).

Björkman, W., "Ofen zur Türkenzeit." Friederischsen, Hamburg, 1920.

Blackie, W., "The Imperial Gazetteer." Glasgow and London, 1860.

Blanchard, R., "Le Flandre." Colin, Paris, 1906.

Bleiberg, G., "Diccionario Geográfico de España." Ediciones Prensa Gráfica, Madrid, 1961.

Blockmans, F., chapter in "Antwerpen in de XVIIIde Eeuw." 1952.

Blok, P., "Geschiedenis eenen Hollandsche Stad." The Hague, 1882-84.

" "History of the People of the Netherlands." New York, 1898-1912.

Blondel, L., "Histoire de Genève." Geneva, 1951.

Blundell, P., "A City of Many Waters." Arrowsmith, London, 1923.

Bofarull, P. de, "Censo de Cataluña Ordenado en Tiempo del Rey Don Pedro el Ceremonioso." Barcelona, 1856.

Böhme, H., "Frankfurt und Hamburg." Europäische Verlaganstalt, Frankfurt, 1968.

Boix, V., "Historia de la Ciudad de Valencia." Valencia, 1845.

Bojpai, K. D., "The Geographical Encyclopaedia of Ancient and Medieval India." India Acad., Varanasi, 1967.

Bolato, A., "Monografiá de Guayaquil." 1887.

Boldizar, I. (ed.), "Hungary." Hastings House, New York, 1969.

Bonnycastle, R., "Account of the Dominions of Spain in the Western Hemisphere." London, 1818.

Boos, H., "Geschichte der rheinischen Städtekultur." Berlin, 1897-1901.

Bory de St.-Vincent, J. B. G. M., "Voyage dans les Quatre Principales Iles des Mers d'Afrique." Paris, 1804.

Bose, N. "History of the Candellas of Jejakabhukti." Mukhopadhyay, Calcutta, 1956.

Bosque, J., "Geografiá Urbana de Granada." Zaragoza, 1962.

Bosworth, C., "The Ghaznavids." Edinburgh Univ. Press, Edinburgh, 1963.

Boturini, L., "Tezcoco en Los Tiempos de Sus Ultimos Reyes." Mexico City, 1826.

Boucher, E., "A Short History of Antioch." Oxford Univ. Press (Clarendon), London and New York, 1921.

Boudet, J. (ed.), "Jerusalem, a History." Putnam, New York, 1967.

Bouinais, A., and Paulus, A., "L'Indo-Chine Française Contemporaine." Paris, 1885.

Boulainvilliers, H., "État de la France." London, 1752.

Bourdigné, J. de, in "L'Anjou Historique." 1908.

Boussinesq, G., "Histoire de la Ville de Reims," Matot-Braine, Reims, 1933.

Boutin, V., "Reconnaissance des Villes." Paris, 1927.

Bowen, T. J., Grammar and Dictionary of the Yoruba Language with Introductory Description of the Country and People of Yoruba, in "Smithsonian Contributions to Knowledge." X, Washington, D.C., 1858.

Bowrey, T., "A Geographical Account of Countries Round the Bay of Bengal, 1669 to 1679." Hakluyt Soc., Cambridge, 1905.

Bowring, J., "The Kingdom and People of Siam." London, 1856-57.

Boxer, C., "The Dutch in Brazil." Oxford Univ. Press (Clarendon), London and New York, 1957.

Braam, A. van, "An Authentic Account of the Embassy of the Dutch East-India Company to the Court of the Emperor of China." London, 1798.

Bragadino, M. A., "Histoire des Républiques Maritimes Italiennes." Payot, Paris, 1955.

Brand, J., "The History and Antiquities of the Town and County of Newcastle upon Tyne." London, 1789.

Brazil, Government of, "Annuaire Statistique du Brésil 1908-12," I. Rio de Janeiro, 1916.

           "   "Relatorio, 1922," Rio de Janeiro, 1923.

Bredsdorff, P., in "Kobenhaven For og Nu" (Svend Aekjaer et al.), I, Hassing, Copenhagen, 1949.

Briggs, L., "The Ancient Khmer Kingdom." Amer. Philos. Soc., Philadelphia, 1951.

Brigham, W., "Guatemala, Land of the Quetzal." New York, 1887.

Brockhaus, F., co., "Conversations-Lexikon." Leipzig, 1864-68.

Brosse, J. (ed.), "Dictionnaire des Églises de France." Lafont, Paris, 1966.

Brosset, M., "Les Ruines d'Ani." St. Petersburg, 1860.

Brougham, H., "Journey through Albania." London, 1858.

Brown, H. G., and Harris, P. J., "Bristol, England." Burleigh, Bristol, 1964.

Brown, J. M., "People and Problems of the Pacific." Sears, New York, 1927.

Brugmans, H., "Opkomst en Bloei van Amsterdam." Meulenhoff, Amsterdam, 1911.

Brugmans, H., and Peters C., "Oud-Nederlandsche Steden." Sijthoff, Leiden, 1909-11.

Brundage, B., "Empire of the Inca." Univ. of Oklahoma Press, Norman, 1963.

Brunot, L., *in* "Ecole Supérieur de Langue Arabe." 1920.

Brunschvig, R., "La Berberie Orientale sous les Hafsides." Adrien-Maisonneuve, Paris, 1940-47.

     "   (ed.), "Deux Récits de Voyage Inédits en Afrique du Nord au XVe Siécle." Larose, Paris, 1936.

Bruzen, A., "Le Grand Dictionnaire Géographique," Paris, 1737 and 1768 editions.

Bryce, J., "A Cyclopaedia of Geography." London and Glasgow, 1856.

Bücher, K., "Die Bevölkerung von Frankfurt am Main im XIV und XV Jahrhundert." Tübingen, 1886.

Buckingham, J. S., "Travels among the Arab Tribes East of Syria and Palestine." London, 1825.

Budapest, city of, "Statistisches Jahrbuch der Haupt-und Residenzstadt Budapest, 1895-1896." Budapest, 1898.

Budge, E. A. W., "A History of Ethiopia." Methuen, London, 1928.

Bueno, C., *in* "Colección de Historiadores de Chile." 1876ff. Santiago, Chile.

Bühler, F., "Kochuiushchik i Osiedlozhivushchie v Astrakhanskoi." St. Petersburg, 1846.

Bulgaria, Kingdom, "Annuaire Statistique du Royaume de Bulgarie, 1909." Sofia, 1910.

Burgess, J., "Archaeological Survey of Western India: Bidar and Aurangabad Districts." London, 1878.

Burigny, J., "Histoire Générale de Sicile," The Hague, 1745.

Burney, H., *J. Asiatic Soc.* (1835), Calcutta.

Burton, R., "Abeokuta and the Cameroons Mountains." London, 1863.

Büsching, A., "Grosse Erdbeschreibung." Troppau, 1784.

     "   "Magazin." Hamburg and Halle, 1772-93.

     "   "Neue Erdbeschreibung." Hamburg, 1767-71.

Busquet, R., "Histoire de Marseille." Laffont, Paris, 1945.

Bustron, F., "Chronique de l'Ile de Chypre." Paris, 1886.

Butler, W. F. T., "The Lombard Communes." Unwin, London, 1906.

Buzonnière, L. de, "Histoire Architecturale de la Ville d'Orléans." Paris, 1849.

Caillé, J., "La Ville de Rabat jusqu'au Protectorat Français." Vanoest, Paris, 1949.

Caldas, J., "Noticias Geral de Toda Este Capitania de Bahia." Tip. Beneditina, Salvador, 1951.

Camavitto, D., "La Decadenza delle Popolazioni Messicane al Tiempo della Conquista." Rome, 1935.

Campbell, G. A., "The Knights Templars." Duckworth, London, 1937.

Campbell, J. H., "Gazetteer of the Bombay Presidency." Bombay, 1877-1904.

Canale, M., "Nuova Istoria della Repubblica di Genova." Florence, 1858.

Cantu, I., "Bergamo." Milan, 1861.

Caplat, J., "Histoire de Blois." Blois, 1959.

Capper, B., "A Topographical Dictionary of the United Kingdom." London, 1808.

Caron, F., and Schouten, J., "A True Description of the Mighty Kingdom of Japan and Siam." Argonaut Press, London, 1935.

Carter, A. C., "The Kingdom of Siam." Putnam, New York, 1904.

Carter, T. F., "The Invention of Printing in China." Ronald Press, New York, 1955.

Castro, J. de, "Roteiros." Colonial Agency, Lisbon, 1939-40.

Castro de Posada, E., "El Pasado Aborigén." Editorial Stilcograf, Buenos Aires, 1955.

Cat, E., "Petite Histoire de l'Algérie." Algiers, 1889.

"Catholic Encyclopedia." Appleton, New York, 1907-14.

Cavanilles, A. J., "Observaciones sobre . . . la Reina de Valencia." Valencia, 1797.

Cavitelli, Lodovico, "Cremonenses Annales," 2nd ed. Forni, Bologna, 1968.

CEGAN (organization), "Libro de . . . Quito." Quito, 1950-51.

"Censo de España, 1797." Madrid.

"Censo de la Población de España, 1857." Madrid.

"Censo de la Población de España . . . 1877." Madrid.

Census of Canada, see "First Report."

"Census of Jamaica, 1943." Kingston, 1943.

"Census of the Philippine Islands." Washington, D.C., 1904.

Cernik, J., in "Petermanns Mittheilungen." 1876.

Chalmel, J., "Histoire de Touraine." Paris, 1828.

Chambers, R. and W., co., "Concise Gazetteer of the World." London, 1907.

        "   "Chambers's Cyclopaedia," 1870-71; 1888-92." Edinburgh, 1967.

Chandler, R., "Travels in Asia Minor." Oxford, 1775.

Chandra, J. P., "Delhi." Delhi, 1969.

"Changchow Fu Chih." China, 1877.

Chardin, J., "Voyage en Perse." Amsterdam, 1711.

Chart, D., "The Story of Dublin." Dent, London, 1907.

Chau Ju-kua, see Hirth and Rockhill (1911).

Chaudhury, B. N., "Buddhist Centers in India." Sanskrit College Calcutta, 1969.

Chaumont, A. E., "Relation de l'Ambassade de Mr. le Chevalier de Chaumont à la Cour du Roy de Siam." Paris, 1687.

"Chekiang Tung Chih." Shanghai, 1934.

Chen Cheung, chapter in Drake (1967).

Cheng, J. C., "Chinese Sources for the Taiping Rebellion, 1850-1864." Hong Kong, 1963.

"Chengte Fu Chih." Taiwan, 1968.

"Chi Fu Tung Chih." Shanghai, 1934.

"Chiangnan Tung Chih." China, 1737.

Childs, G., in "Journal of African History." Cambridge, England, 1960.

"Chilin Tung Chih." China, 1891.

"Chinan Fu Chih." Taipei, 1968.

"Chinese Repository."

"Chüanchow Fu Chih." China, 1870.

Chula Chakrabongse, "Lords of Life." Redman, London, 1967.

"Chung Hsui Kao Lan Hsien Chih." Taipei, 1967.

Church, R., "Economic and Social Change in a Midland Town." Cass, London, 1966.

Churchill, A., "A Collection of Voyages and Travels." London, 1744-6.

Ciborowski, A., "Warszawa." Wstep Napisal Karol Malcuzynski, Warsaw, 1964.

Clapperton, H., "Journal of a Second Expedition into the Interior of Africa." Philadelphia, 1829.

Clapperton, H., and Dixon, D., "Narrative of Travels and Discoveries in Northern and Central Africa." London, 1828.

Claude, D., "Topographie und Verfassung des Städte Bourges und Poitiers bis in das ll Jahrhundert." Matthiesen, Lübeck, 1960.

Clavigero, F. J., "The History of Mexico." London, 1807.

Clavijo, R. G. de, "Embassy to Tamerlane." Routledge, London, 1928.

Clennell, W., *in* "New China Review." Shanghai, 1922.

Clerget, M., "Le Caire." Schindler, Cairo, 1934.

Cloud, Frederick, "Hangchow." Presbyterian Mission Press, Shanghai, 1906.

Cobb, Gwendolin, "Potosí and Huancavelica . . . 1545 to 1640." Univ. of California Press, Berkeley, 1947.

Cobo, B., *in* "Biblioteca de Autores Españoles." Atlas, Madrid, 1956.

Coe, M., "Mexico." Praeger, New York, 1962.

Coedès, G., "Angkor." Oxford Univ. Press, London and New York, 1963.

Cole, W., "Kyoto in the Momoyama Period." Univ. of Oklahoma Press, Norman, 1967.

Collier, Jeremy, "Historical, Geographical . . . Dictionary," London, 1688.

"Collier's Encyclopedia." Crowell-Collier, New York, 1968.

Colombia, Government of, "Estadística Jeneral de la Nueva Granada." Bogotá, 1852.

"Columbia Lippincott Gazetteer." Columbia Univ. Press, New York, 1952.

Commissariat, M. S., "History of Gujarat." Longmans, Green, New York, 1938-57.

Compton, P., "Harold the King." London, 1961.

Conder, J., "Brazil." London, 1830.

             "   "India." London, 1830's.

             "   "Turkey." London, 1827.

Conti, N. di, chapter in Major (1857).

Cook, S. and Simpson, L., *in* "Ibero-Americana." Vol. 31 (1948, but volumes are not in chronological sequence).

Cooley, W., "The Negroland of the Arabs." London, 1841.

Copenhagen, city, "Aarbog for Kobenhavn, 1942." Copenhagen, 1942.

Coppolani, J., "Toulouse au XXe Siècle." Privat, Toulouse, 1963.

Cordier, H., "The Book of Ser Marco Polo." Murray, London, 1903.

Corridore, F., "La Popolazione dello Stato Romano 1656-1901." Loescher, Rome, 1906.

Cortesão, A., "A Cidade de Bangala." Sociedad de Geografia, Lisbon, 1944.

Coryat, T., "Coryat's Crudities." London, 1776.

Costa, N., "Historia da Cidade do Rio de Janeiro." Livraria Jacintho, Rio de Janeiro, 1935.

Cottineau, D., "History of Goa," Madrid, 1831.

Couling, S., "Encyclopedia Sinica." Kelly and Walsh, Shanghai, 1917.

Courcy, "L'Empire du Milieu." Paris, 1867.

Cousens, H., "Bijapur and Its Architectural Remains." Bombay, 1916.

Cowan, S., "The Ancient Capital of Scotland." Pott, New York, 1904.

Crane, H., and Griffin, J., *in* "Radiocarbon." 1961-62.

Crawford, D. G., "A Brief History of the Hughli District." Bengal Secretariat Press, Calcutta, 1902.

Cressey, G., "China's Geographical Foundations." McGraw-Hill, New York, 1934.

             "   "Land of the 500 Million." McGraw-Hill, New York, 1955.

Crouvezier, G., "La Vie d'une Cité—Reims," Nouvelles Editions Latines, Paris, 1970.

Crow, C., "Handbook for China." Kelly and Walsh, San Francisco, 1915.

Crozet, R., "Histoire d'Orléanais." Boivin, Paris, 1936.

Cuinet, V., "La Turquie d'Asie." Paris, 1890-95.

Cunningham, A., "The Ancient Geography of India." London, 1871.

Cuvelier, J., "Formation de la Ville de Louvain." Palais des Académies Brussels, 1935.

             "   "Les Dénombrements de Foyer en Brabant (XIV-XVI Siècles)." Kiessling, Brussels, 1912.

Dabrowski, J., "Krakow." Wydawn. Literackie, Krakow, 1957.
      ″   "Krakow." Arkady, Warsaw, 1965.

Dainville, F. de, *in* "Population." Paris, 1958.

Dameto (anon.), "The Ancient and Modern History of the Balearic Islands." London, 1716.

Daniel, H., "Handbuch der Geographie." Leipzig, 1866-8.

Dapper, O., "Description de l'Afrique." Amsterdam, 1686.

Dardel, P., "Commerce, Industrie et Navigation à Rouen et au Havre au XVIIIe Siècle." Société Libre d'Émulation de la Seine-Maritime, Rouen, 1966.

Das Gupta, Y. N., "Bengal in the Sixteenth Century." Calcutta, 1914.

Dathe, M., "An Essay on the History of Hamburgh." London, 1766.

Datta, V. N., "Amritsar, Past and Present." Municipal Committee, Amritsar, 1967.

Davies, H. R., "Yünnan." Cambridge Univ. Press, London and New York, 1909.

Davis, John K., "The Chinese." London, 1840.

Debo, A., "The Rise and Fall of the Choctaw Republic." Univ. of Oklahoma Press, Norman, 1961.

Debrozy, C., and Bachelet, Th., "Dictionnaire Générale de Biographie et d'Histoire." Paris, 1888.

Decaux, A., "La Belle Historie de Versailles." Berger-Levrault, Paris, 1962.

Delarue, G., "Nouveaux Essais Historiques sur la Ville de Caen." Caen, 1842.

de l'Isle, "Description de la Ville de Péking." Paris, 1765.

Delumeau, J., manuscript.

Demey, J., *in* "Revue Belgique de Philologie et d'Histoire." 1950.

Dermigny, L., "La Chine et l'Orient: le Commerce à Canton au XVIII Siècle." S.E.V.P.E.N., Paris, 1964.

Desmarquets, J. A. S., "Mémoires Chronologiques pour Servir à l'Histoire de Dieppe." Paris, 1785.

Desportes, *in* "Moyen Age." (1966).

"Deutsches Städtebuch," see Keyser (1939).

Deverdun, Gaston, "Marrakech des Origines à 1912." Editions Techniques Nord-Africaines, Rabat, 1912.

Dey, N. L., "The Geographical Dictionary of Ancient and Medieval India." Luzac, London, 1927.

Deyon, Pierre, "Amiens au 17e Siècle." Mouton, Paris, 1967.

Dias da Silva Carvalho, A., *in* "Citade do Salvador." Coleção Estudios Baianos, Salvador, 1960.

Díaz, B., "The True History of the Conquest of Mexico." Harrap, London, 1928.

"Diccionario Enciclopédico Hispano Americano." Barcelona, 1887-99.

Dickinson, R., "The West European City." Routledge and Paul, London, 1951.

Diehl, C., "Palerme et Syracuse." Laurens, Paris 1907.

Diodorus, "The Library of History."

Dlugoborski, W., Gierowski, J., and Maleczynski, K., "Dzieje Wroclaw do roku 1807." Panstwowe Wydawn. Naukowe, Warsaw, 1958.

Dobrzanski, F., "Staraya i Novaya Vilnia." Vilna, 1904.

Dollinger-Leonard, Y., *in* "Studien zu den Anfängen der europäischen Städtewesens." 1955-6.

Downey, G., "Antioch in the Time of Theodosius the Great." Univ. of Oklahoma Press, Norman, 1962.

      ″   "A History of Antioch." Princeton Univ. Press, Princeton, New Jersey, 1961.

Dozy, R., "Spanish Islam." Chatto and Windus, London, 1913.

Drake, F. S. (ed.), *Symp. Historical, Archaeolog. Linguist. Stud.* London and Hong Kong (1967).

Dreyfus, F. A., *in* "Revue d'Histoire et Société." 1956.

Duby, G., and Mandrou, R., "Histoire de la Civilization Française." Colin, Paris, 1958.

Duclos, A., "Bruges." Bruges, 1918.

Duffy, J., "Portuguese Africa." Harvard Univ. Press, Cambridge, Mass., 1959.

Dugast-Matifeux, C., "Nantes Ancien." Nantes, 1879.

Du Halde, J. B., "The General History of China." London, 1741.

Dulaure, J., "Histoire de Paris." Paris, 1846.

Durant, W., "The Age of Faith." Simon and Schuster, New York, 1950.

Dureau de la Malle, "Province de Constantine." Paris, 1837.

Eberhard, W., "Settlement and Social Change in Asia." Hong Kong Univ. Press, Hong Kong, 1967.

Edrisi (Idrisi), M., "Géographie." Paris, 1836.

Edwardes, S., "The Gazetteer of Bombay City and Island." Times Press, Bombay, 1909-10.

Edwards, B., "An Historical Survey of the Island of Santo Domingo." London, 1801.
  " "The History, Civil and Commercial, of the British Colonies in the West Indies." London, 1794.

Egharevba, J., "A Short History of Benin." Ibadan Univ., Ibadan, 1960.

Ehingen, J. von, "Diary." Oxford Univ. Press, London and New York, 1929.

Eisenbach, A., and Brochulska, B., Population en Pologne (Fin XIIIe au Début XIXe Siècle), *in* "Annales de Démographie Historique." Paris, 1965.

Elers, J., "Stockholm." Stockholm, 1800-1.

Elphinstone, M., "An Account of the Kingdom of Cabul." London, 1815.

"Enciclopedia Italiana." Treccani, Rome, 1929-37.

"Enciclopedia Universal Ilustrada Europeo-Americana." Barcelona, 1908-30.

"Enciklopedija Jugoslavije." Zagreb, 1955.

"Encyclopaedia Britannica." Edinburgh, 1853-60.

"Encyclopaedia Britannica." Boston, 1875-80.

"Encyclopaedia Britannica." Chicago, 1970.

"Encyclopaedia Edinensis." Edinburgh, 1827.

"Encyclopaedia of Islam." Leiden, 1897-1924; 1960-

"Encyclopaedia Slovar." St. Petersburg, 1890-1907.

Encyclopedia Americana." Americana, New York, 1969.

Engelmann, E., "Zur städtischen Volksbewegung in Sudfrankreich." Akademie-Verlag, Berlin, 1959.

English, P., "City and Village in Iran." Univ. of Wisconsin Press, Madison, 1966. 1966.

"English Cyclopedia." London, 1856-8.

Ennin, "Diary." Ronald Press, New York, 1955.

Enríquez B., E., "Guayaquil a traves de los Siglos." Gráf. Nacionales, Quito, 1946.

Ersch, J., and Gruber, "Allgemeine Encyclopädie." Leipzig, 1827.

Ewig, E., *in* "Rheinische Fünfjahresblatt." 1952.

Eyriès, J. B., and Jacobs, A., "Voyage en Asie et en Afrique." Paris, 1855.

Fabre, A., "Histoire de Marseille." Paris, 1829.
  " "Histoire de Provence." Marseille, 1833-53.

Fallmereyer, J., "Geschichte des Kaisertums von Trapezunt." Olms, Hildesheim, 1964.

Fancourt, C., "The History of Yucatán." London, 1954.

Faria e Sousa, M., "Imperio de la China." Lisbon, 1731.

″   "Portuguese Asia." 1695.

Favier, A., "Péking." Desclée, De Brouwer, Lille, 1902.

Fei-shi, "Guide to Peking and Its Environs." Tientsin, 1909.

Ferguson, J. R., "Kashmir." Centaur, London, 1961.

Fergusson, J., "History of Indian and Eastern Architecture." Murray, London, 1910.

Ferishta, M., "The Rise of the Mohammedan Power in India." Editions Indian, Calcutta, 1966.

″   "History of Dekkan." Shrewsbury, 1794.

Fernandes Gama, J. B., "Memorias Históricas da Provincia de Pernambuco." Pernambuco, 1844.

Février, P., "La Développement Urbaine en Provence." Boccard, Paris, 1964.

Feÿ, H., "Histoire d'Oran." Oran, 1858.

Fiala, A. (ed.), "Slovanská Bratislava." Ustredny Narodny Vybor, Bratislava, 1948.

Finch, W., chapter in Foster (1968).

Fitton, M., "Málaga," Allen & Unwin, London, 1971.

Finlayson, G., "The Mission to Siam and Hué." London, 1826.

Firatli, N., "Guide to Iznik." Istanbul Matbaasi, Istanbul, 1961.

"First Report—Census of the Canadas for 1851-2," Québec, 1853.

Fitch, Ralph, chapter in Moreland (1953).

Fitz, J., "Székesfehérvár." Müszaki Könyvkiadó, 1966.

Fohlen, C., (ed.), "Histoire de Besançon." Nouvelle Librairie de France, Paris, 1964-5.

Foligno, C., "The Story of Padua." Dent, London, 1910.

Forbes, A., "Ras Mala." Oxford Univ. Press, London and New York, 1924.

Ford, F., "Strasbourg in Transition." Harvard Univ. Press, Cambridge, Mass., 1958.

Forstall, R., by correspondence.

Forster, E. M., "Alexandria." Smith, Gloucester, 1938.

Forster, G., "A Journey from Bengal to England." London, 1798.

Fortia, "Description de la Chine." Paris, 1840.

Fortune, R., "Wanderings in China." Leipzig, 1854.

Foster, G. M., "Tzintzuntzán." Little, Brown, Boston, 1967.

Foster, W., "Early Travels in India, 1583-1619." Chand, Delhi, 1968.

França, J. A., "Lisbõa Pombalina." Livros Horizonte, Lisbon, 1965.

Franco, J., "Testimonio de Guadalajara." 1942.

Franz, A. R., "Pressburg." Verlag Grenze und Ausland, Stuttgart, 1935.

Frescobaldi, L., "Visit to the Holy Places." Jerusalem, 1948.

Fris, V., "Histoire de Gand." Ghent, 1913.

Froissart, J., "Chronicles." Nutt, London, 1901.

Frye, R., "Bukhara." Univ. of Oklahoma Press, Norman, 1965.

"Fuchow Fu Chih." Taipei, 1967.

Fuentes, F., "Recordación Florida." Guatemala City, 1922.

Fuentes, H., "El Cuzco y Sus Ruinas." Lima, 1905.

Fuentes, M., "Biblioteca Peruana de Historia." 1861-4.

Fussing, H., "Bybefolkning 1600-1660." Aarhus, 1967.

Gabriel, A., "Une Capitale Turque, Brousse." Boccard, Paris, 1958.

Gadgil, D. R., "Poona: a Socio-Economic Survey." Poona (private), 1945-52.

Gage, T., "Travels in the New World." Univ. of Oklahoma Press, Norman, 1958.

Gait, E., "A History of Assam." Thacker, Spink, Calcutta, 1926.

Galdames, L., "History of Chile." Univ. of North Carolina Press, Chapel Hill, North Carolina, 1941.

Gallenkamp, C., "Maya." McKay, New York, 1959.

Ganguly, D. C., "History of the Paramara Dynasty." Dacca Univ., Dacca, 1933.

Ganguly, M., "Orissa." Bangiya Sahitya Parishad, Calcutta, 1912.

Ganshof, F., "Études sur la Développement des Villes entre Loire et Rhin au Moyen Age." Presses Univ. de France, Paris, 1943.

García Pastor, J., by correspondence.

Garibay, A., "Diccionario Porrúa." Porrúa, Mexico City, 1964.

Garnier, F., "Voyage d'Exploration en Indo-Chine." Paris, 1885.

Gaudenzio, L., "Padova attraverso i Secoli." Draghi, Padua, 1960.

Gaury, G. de, "Rulers of Mecca." Harrap, London, 1951.

Gause, F., "Die Geschichte der Stadt Köningsberg." Böhlau, Cologne, 1968.

Gautier, E., "Le Passé de l'Afrique du Nord." Payot, Paris, 1952.

"Gazetteer of the Bombay Presidency." Bombay, 1885.

Gazetteer of the World," anonymous. Edinburgh, 1850-6.

Gemelli, G. F., "A Voyage around the World." London, 1724.

Géraud, H., "Paris sous Philippe-le-Bel." Paris, 1837.

Gerber, chapter in Voelcker (1932).

German, K., "Statisticheskiia Issledovanum." 1819.

Ghosh, M., "The Pataliputra." Patna Law Press, Patna, 1919.

Gibert, L., "Dictionnaire Historique et Géographique de la Mandchourie." Société des Missions-Étrangèrs, Nazareth and Hong Kong, 1934.

Gibson, C., "Tlaxcala in the 16th Century." Stanford Univ. Press, Stanford, California, 1952.

Gierowski, J., "Historia Polski 1492-1864." Panstwowe Wydawn. Naukowe, Warsaw, 1967.

Giles, H., "A Chinese Biographical Dictionary." London, 1898.

Gillion, K., "Ahmedabad." Univ. of California Press, Berkeley, 1968.

Giraudet, E., "Histoire de la Ville de Tours." Tours, 1873.

Giurescu, C., "Istoria Bucurestilor." Editura pentru Literatura, Bucharest, 1966.

Golubovsky, P., "Istoriya Smolenskoi zemli do Nachala XV Veka." Kiev, 1895.

Gomme, A., "The Population of Athens in the Fifth and Fourth Centuries B.C.." Blackwell, Oxford, 1933.

Góngora, A. de, "Materiales para la Historia de Jérez." El Guadalete, Jérez, 1901.

González, T., "Censo de Población de . . . Castilla en el Siglo XVI." Madrid, 1829.

González de Mendoza, J., "The History of the Great and Mighty Kingdom of China." London, 1853-4.

Gonzáles Llubera, I., "Viajes de Benjamín de Tudela." Madrid, 1918.

González Suárez, F., "Historia Eclesiástica del Ecuador." Quito, 1881.

Gorani, G., "Corte e Paese." Mondadori, Milan, 1938.

Gordon-Brown, A., "Southern Africa, Year Book & Guide." 1963.

Gower, R., "Joan of Arc." London, 1893.

Grabski, W., "300 Miast Wrocila do Polski." Pax, Warsaw, 1960.

Graham, J., Course lecture at Univ. of California, Berkeley, 1968.

Graham, S., "Ivan the Terrible." Yale Univ. Press, New Haven, Connecticut, 1933.

Graham, W. A., "Siam." Moring, Chicago, 1913.

"Grande Enciclopedia Portuguesa." Lisbon, 1935-60.

"Grande Encyclopédie." Paris, 1886-1902.

Grant, C., "The Gazetteer of the Central Provinces of India." Nagpur, 1870.

Grant, J., "Cassel's Old and New Edinburgh." Edinburgh, 1881-3.

Greece, government of, "Annuaire Statistique de la Grèce, 1930." Athens, 1932.

Gribble, J., "A History of the Deccan." Luzac, London, 1896-1924.

Griffis, W., "Corea, the Hermit Kingdom." Harper, New York, 1905.

Griffith, F., in "Journal of Egyptian Archaeology." 1924.

Groome, F., "Ordnance Gazetteer of Scotland." Jack, Edinburgh, 1901.

Grose, J., "A Voyage to the East-Indies." London, 1772.

Grosier, abbé, "Description Générale de la Chine." Paris, 1785.

"Grosse Brockhaus." Leipzig, 1928-35.

Grosvenor, E., "Constantinople." Boston, 1895.

Grousset, R., "L'Empire des Steppes." Payot, Paris, 1939.

Grühl, M., "The Citadel of Ethiopia." Cape, London, 1932.

Guatini, M. A., and Carli, D., in Pinkerton, XVI (1808-14).

Guépin, A., "Histoire de Nantes." Nantes, 1839.

Guignes, J. de, "Voyages à Péking, Manilla, et l'Ile de France." Paris, 1808.

Guilbert, A., "Histoire des Villes de France." Paris, 1844-9.

Guillén Robles, F., "Málaga Musulmana." Oliver, Málaga, 1957.

Guilloux, F., "Précis d'Histoire de Nantes." Nantes, 1922.

Guiteras, A., "Historia de Cuba." 1927-8.

Guth, K., chapter in Vojtisek et al. (1960), "Prague." Prague, 1935.

Guthrie, C., "Riots in Seventeenth Century Mexico City." Univ. of California Press, Berkeley, 1937.

Gutkind, E., "Urban Development in Scandinavia." Free Press of Glencoe, New York, 1964.

Gutzlaff, C., "The Journal of Two Voyages along the Coast of China." New York, 1833.

Guys, H., "Voyage en Syrie." Paris, 1855.

Hadri-Vasiljević, "Skoplje i Njegova Okolina." Belgrade, 1930.

Hagen, V. von, "Sonnenkönigreiche." Munich, 1962.

Haider, A., "Histoire Abrégée de Tunis." Paris, 1857.

Hakuwonsa Co., "Korea." Korea, 1960.

Hall, R. H., "Great Zimbabwe." London, 1905.

Hambly, G., "Cities of Mughul India." Elek, London, 1968.

Hamdan, G., in "Geography." 1964.

Hamilton, A., "A New Account of the East Indies." Argonaut, London, 1930.

Hamilton, W., "East Indian Gazetteer." London, 1828.

"Handbuch der Weltgeschichte." 1954-6 Olten (Walter)

"Handwörterbuch der Staatswissenschaften." Fischer, Jena, 1923-8.

Häpke, R., "Brugges Entwicklung zum mittelalterlichen Weltmarkt." Curtius, Berlin, 1908.

Hardoy, J., "Ciudades Precolumbianos." Ediciones Infinito, Buenos Aires, 1964.

Harff, A. von, "Pilgrimage." Hakluyt Soc., London, 1946.

Harlez, C. de. (translator), "Histoire de l'Empire de Kin." Louvain, 1887.

Harper's Statistical Gazetteer of the World. New York (1855).

Harris, C., "Cities of the Soviet Union." Rand McNally, Chicago, 1970.

Harris, J., "Collection of Voyages and Travels." London, 1705.

Harsin, P., "Études Critiques sur l'Histoire de la Principauté de Liège 1477-1795." Sciences and Lettres, Liège, 1955.

Hartmann, R., "Geschichte der Residenzstadt Hannover." Hannover, 1880.

Harvey, G. E., "History of Burma from the Earliest Times to 1824." London, 1925.

Hassel, G., "Geographisches-statistisches Handwörterbuch." Weimar, 1817.
    ″   (with collaborators), "Vollständiges Handwörterbuch der neuesten Erdbeschreibung." Weimar, 1819-25.

Hasselquist, F., "Voyages and Travels in the Levant." London, 1766,

Haulleville, P., "Histoire des Communes Lombardes." 1857-8.

Havell, E., "A Handbook to Agra." Longmans, Green, New York, 1912.

Havemann, W., "Geschichte der Lande Braunschweig un Lüneburg." Göttingen, 1857.

Haviland, W., *in* "American Antiquity." 1969.

Hawkins, chapter in Foster (1967).

Hayavadana Rao, C., "History of Mysore." Government Press, Bangalore, 1948.

Hazewinkel, H. C., "Geschiedenis van Rotterdam." Joost van den Vondel, Amsterdam, 1904-2.

Hazlitt, W. C., "The Venetian Republic." Black, London, 1900.

Hearn, G., "The Seven Cities of Delhi." Thacker, Spink, London, 1928.

Heers, J., "Gènes au XVe Siècle." S.E.V.P.E.N., Paris, 1961.

Heins, M., "La Belgique et Ses Grandes Villes au XIX Siècle." Ghent, 1897.

Helfert, J., "Drei Stadtpläne und eine Stadtansicht von alten Prag." Prague, 1893.

Hélin, É., "Le Paysage Urbain de Liège avant la Révolution Industrielle." Commission Communale de l'Histoire, Liège, 1963.

Henne, A., and Wauters, A., "Histoire de la Ville de Bruxelles." Brussels, 1845.

Hennings, F., "Das Barocke Wien." Herold, Munich, 1965.

Heras, H., "Beginnings of Vijayanagar History." Indian Historical Res. Soc., Bombay, 1929.
    ″   "The Aravidu Dynasty in Vijayanagar." Paul, Madras, 1927.

Herbert, T., "Some Years of Travel in Africa and Asia." London, 1677.

Hermon-Hodge, H., "Gazetteer of Ilorin Province." Allen and Unwin, London, 1929.

Hessel, A., "Geschichte der Stadt Bologna von 1116 bis 1280," Eberling, Berlin, 1910.

Heymann, F., "John Zizka and the Hussite Revolution." Princeton Univ. Press, Princeton, New Jersey, 1955.

Higounet, C., "Histoire de Bordeaux." Bordeaux, 1962-9.

Hill, G., "Cyprus." Cambridge Univ. Press, London and New York, 1948.

Hill, J., "Medieval Lincoln." Cambridge Univ. Press, London and New York, 1948.

Hirth, F., "Ancient Chinese Porcelain." Leipzig, 1888.
    ″   and Rockhill, W., "Chau Ju-kua." Paragon, New York, 1911.

Ho, Ping-ti, *in* "Harvard Journal of Asiatic Studies." Harvard Univ. Press, Cambridge, Mass., 1966.

Hocquard, G., "Metz." Hachette, Paris, 1961.

Hodges, W., "Travels in India." London, 1783.

Hoffmann, W., "Encyclopädie der Erd-, Völker-, und Staatskunde." Leipzig, 1864-9.

Hogarth, D., "The Penetration of Arabia." Stokes, New York, 1904.

Hogben, S., and Kirk-Greene, A., "The Emirates of Northern Nigeria." Oxford Univ. Press, London and New York, 1966.

Hollingsworth, T., "Historical Demography." Hodder and Stoughton, London, 1969.

Homer, "Iliad." Macmillan, New York, 1935.

"Honan Tung Chih." China, 1914.

Honjo, E., "History of Japanese Population." Tokyo, 1967.
    ″   by correspondence.

Hourani, A., and Stern, S. (eds.), "The Islamic City." Oxford Univ. Press (Clarendon), London and New York, 1970.

Howe, A., "Guadalajara." Guadalajara, 1955 (private).

Howell, R., "Newcastle upon Tyne and the Puritan Revolution." Oxford Univ. Press (Clarendon), London and New York, 1967.

Howlett, J., "An Examination of Dr. Price's Essay on the Population of England and Wales." Kelley, New York, 1968.

"Hsia Men Chih." China, 1839.

Hsu, Cho-yun, "Ancient China in Transition." Stanford Univ. Press, Stanford, California, 1935.

"Hsu Honan Tung Chih." China, 1914.

"Hsu Hsiu Shensi Shen Tun Chih Hao." China, 1934.

Hsüan Dsang (or Hsüan Tsang), "Buddhist Records of the Western World." Paul, Trench, Trübner, London, 1906.

Hubrecht, A., "Grandeur et Suprematie de Péking." Imprimerie des Lazaristes, Peking, 1928.

Hughes, W., "The Treasury of Geography." London, 1860.

Hulbert, H., "History of Korea." 2nd ed., Hillary House, New York, 1962.

Humboldt, A. von, "Essai Politique sur la Nouvelle Espagne." Paris, 1811.
      "   "Essai Politique sur l'Ile de Cuba." Paris, 1826.
      "   "Idea Estadistica de Nueva España." 1823.
      "   "Población de Nueva España." Mexico City, 1820.
      "   "Political Essay on the Kingdom of New Spain." London, 1814.
      "   "Selections." London, 1824.
      "   "Voyage to the Equinoctial Regions of the New Continent." London, 1826.

"Hunan Tung Chih." China, 1885.

Hunter, W., "Imperial Gazetteer of India." London, 1881.

Hunter, W. W. et al., "A History of Orissa." Gupta, Calcutta, 1956.

"Hupeh Tung Chih." China, 1885.

Hürliman, M., "Moscow and Leningrad." Thames and Hudson, London, 1958.

Hymans, H. S., "Bruges and Ypres." Laurens, Paris, 1907.

Ibn el-Balkhi, in "Journal of the Royal Asiatic Society." 1912.

Ibn Battuta, M., "Travels in Asia and Africa." Routledge, London, 1929.

Ibn Hawqal, M., "Iracae Persicae Descriptio." Leiden, 1822.

Ibn Jubayr, M., "Travels." Cape, London, 1952.

Ilenko, A., "Smolensk." St. Petersburg, 1894.

Illert, F. M., "Worms in wechselnden Spiel der Jahrtausende." Norberg, Worms, 1958.

Illiers, L., "Histoire d'Orléans," Houzé, Orléans, 1954.

"Imperial Gazetteer of India." 1st ed.—see Hunter (1881).
      "   2nd ed. Superintendent of Government Printing, Oxford, 1907-1909.

India Tourism Develop. Corp., "Jaipur, Udaipur, Chittorgarh." Delhi, 1967.

Iranian Army, "A Guide to Hamadan." 1963.

Irving, W., "The Conquest of Granada." Dutton, New York, 1910.

"Islam Ansiklopedisi." Milli Egitim Basimevi, Istanbul, 1949.

Istoja, A., in "Ferrara" magazine, no. 2 (1957).

Ivanov, I., et al., "Iubeleina Kniga na Grad Sofia." Komitet za Istoria na Sofia, Sofia, 1928.

Ives, E., "A Voyage from England to India." London, 1773.

Jacoby, D., *in* "Byzantion." XXXI (1961).

Jackson, J., "An Account of the Empire of Morocco." London, 1809.
      "   "An Account of Timbuctoo and Houssa." London, 1820.

Jadart, H., *in Travaux Acad. Nat. Reims* **71** (1881-2).

Jaimes, J., "La Villa Imperial de Potosí." Rosso, Buenos Aires, 1903.

Jakeman, M. W., "The Maya States of Yucatán, 1441-1541." Univ. of California Press, Berkeley, 1938.

Janaĉek, chapter in Vojtisek *et al.,* "Praha" (1960).

Japan, Government of, "Official Guide to Eastern Asia."

Jehangir, "Memoirs of Jahangir." Delhi, 1968.

"Jewish Encyclopedia." Funk and Wagnalls, New York, 1901-6.

Johnson, C. R., "Constantinople Today." Macmillan, New York, 1922.

Johnson, S., "History of the Yorubas." Bookshops, Nigeria, Boston and New York, 1921.

Josyer, G. R., "History of Mysore." Mysore (private).

Joubert, A., "Étude sur les Misères de l'Anjou aux XVe et XVIe Siècles." Angers, 1886.

Joyce, T., "Mexican Archaeology." Warner, London, 1914.

Juan, J., and Ulloa, A., "A Voyage to South America." London, 1758.

Juarros, D., "A Statistical and Commercial History of the Kingdom of Guatemala." London, 1823.

"Jüdisches Lexikon." Jüdischer Verlag, Berlin, 1927-30.

Jullian, C., cited in Vivier and Millet (1943).

Jumsai, M., "History of Laos." Chalermnit, Bangkok, 1967.

Jürgens, O., "Spanische Städte." Friederichsen, Hamburg, 1926.

Jurginis, J., "Vilnius miesto Istoriya." Mintes, Vilna, 1968.

Kahlenberg, F., *Beitr. Geschichte Stadt Mainz* **19** (1963).

Kahrstedt, *in* "Handwörterbuch der Staatswissenschaften." Jena, 1923-8.

Kalinin, N., "Kazan." Tatknigoizdat, Kazan, 1955.

Kallsen, O., "Gründung und Entwicklung der deutschen Städte in Mittelalter." Halle, 1891.

Kanitz, F., "La Bulgarie Danubienne et le Balkan." Paris, 1882.

Kasymenko, O., (ed.), "Istorija Kieva." Akademii Nauk, Kiev, 1960-4.

Kaul, G. L., "A Six Millenium Review of Kashmir." Chronicle Publ. House, Srinagar, 1969.

Kees, H., "Ancient Egypt." Chicago Univ. Press, Chicago, 1961.

Keyser, E., "Bevölkerungsgeschichte Deutschlands." Hirzl, Leipzig, 1941. Keyser in text refers to this book.
      "   "Deutsche Städtebuch." Kohlhammer, Stuttgart, 1939-62.

Khramtsovsky, N., "Kratki Ocherk Istorii i Opisanie Nizhny-Novgorod." Nizhny-Novgorod, 1857.

Khusraw, H., "The Campaigns of Ala'u'd-din Khilji." Madras, 1931.

"Kiangsi." China, 1881.

Kidder, A. II, in conversation.

King, G., "Natural . . . Condition of England." London, 1696.

King, W., "Chronicles of Three Free Cities." Dent, London, and Dutton, New York, 1914.

Kinneir, J. M., "Geographical Memoir of the Persian Empire." London, 1813.

Kloeden, G. von, "Handbuch der Länder- und Staatskunde." Berlin, 1873-7.

Knudsen, J., "Roskilde," Gad, Copenhagen, 1971.

Komroff, M., "Contemporaries of Marco Polo." Boni and Liveright, New York, 1928.

Kralik, R., and Schlitter, H., "Wien." Holzhausen, Vienna, 1912.

Kravchenko, I., and Kamensky, N., "Polotsk." Nauk VSSR, Minsk, 1962.

Kremer, A. von, "The Orient under the Caliphs." Univ. of Calcutta, Calcutta, 1920.

Krom, N., "Hindoe-Javaansche Geschiedenis." Nijhoff, The Hague, 1931.

Kubinyi, A., in "Nouvelle Études Historiques." Budapest, 1965.

Kunze, H., "Erfurt." Deutscher Kunstverlag, Berlin, 1928.

Kurth G., "La Cité de Liège au Moyen Age." Dewit, Brussels, 1910.

    "   "Notger de Liège." Picard, Paris, 1905.

"Kwangchow Fu." Canton, 1879.

"Kwangtung Tung Chih." Shanghai, 1934.

Laborde, A., "A View of Spain." London, 1809.

La Brocquière, Bertrandin de, chapter in Wright (1848).

Lacerda, F., "The Lands of Cazembe." London, 1873.

la Fuente, D., "Primer Censo de la República Argentina." Buenos Aires, 1872.

Lafuente, M., "Historia de Granada." Madrid, 1852.

Lal, K. S., "History of the Khaljis." Indian Press, Allahabad, 1950.

La Maza, F. de, "La Ciudad de Cholula y Sus Iglesias." Imprenta Univ., Mexico City, 1959.

Lamb, H., "Genghis Khan." McBride, New York, 1927.

    "   "Tamerlane." McBride, New York, 1928.

La Mène, M., "La Ville de Nantes au XVe Siècle." Rennes, 1959, mimeographed.

Landon, P., "Nepal." Constable, London, 1928.

Lane-Poole, S., "A History of Egypt in the Middle Ages." Scribner, New York, 1901.

Lanning, E., "Peru before the Incas." Prentice-Hall, Englewood Cliffs, New Jersey, 1967.

Lanning, G., and Couling, S., "The History of Shanghai." Kelly and Walsh, Shanghai, 1921.

Lannoy, G. de, "Oeuvres." Louvain, 1878.

Lapidus, I., "Middle Eastern Cities." Univ. of California Press, Berkeley, 1969.

    "   "Muslim Cities in the Late Middle Ages." Harvard Univ.Press, Cambridge, Mass., 1967.

Larousse, P., "Grand Dictionnaire Universel." Paris, 1866-76.

Lascaris, M., "Salonique à la Fin du XVIIIe Siècle." Flamma, Athens, 1939.

Latimer, J., "The Annals of Bristol in the Eighteenth Century." Frome and London, 1893.

    "   "The Annals of Bristol in the Seventeenth Century." Wm. George's Sons, Bristol, 1900.

Lauks, A. (ed.), "Riga i Rizhskoe Vzmore." Latgosizdat, Riga, 1954.

Lautensack, H., in "Berichte und Mittheilungen des Altertums-Verein zu Wien." 1856.

Law, C., in Population Studies, March 1969.

Lazistan, E., "Bratislava." Osveta, Martin, 1956.

Leblond, M. (Ary), "Madagascar." Plon, Paris, 1934.

Leclerc, F., "Clermont." Clermont, 1962.

Leclère, A., "Histoire de Cambodge." Geuthner, Paris, 1914.

Leewen, S. van, "Korte Besgryvning van Leyden." Leiden, 1672.

le Long, N., "Histoire du Diocèse de Laon." Chalons, 1783.

Lemaitre, E., "Laon-Guide." Laon, 1896.

Le Moine, J., "Quebec, Past and Present." Quebec, 1876.

Lenthéric, C., "The Riviera, Ancient and Modern." London, 1895.

Leo Africanus, "Description of Africa." Hakluyt ed. 1896.

Lesage, G., "Marseille Angevine." Boccard, Paris, 1950.

Lessner, E., "Cradle of Conquerors." Doubleday, Garden City, New York, 1955.

Lestocquoy, J., "Aux Origines de la Bourgeoisie: les Villes de Flandres et d'Italie." Presses Univ. de France, Paris, 1922.

Le Strange, G., "Baghdad during the Abbasid Caliphate." Oxford Univ. Press (Clarendon), London and New York, 1900.

Letts, M., "Bruges and Its Past." Berry, London, 1926.

Levasseur, E., "La Population Française." Paris, 1889-92.

Leveel, P., "Histoire de la Touraine." Presses Univ. de France, Paris, 1956.

Levene, R., "Historia de la Provincia de Buenos Aires." Impresiones Oficiales, La Plata, 1940-41.

Lévi, S., "Le Népal." Paris, 1905-8.

Lévi-Provençal, É., "L'Espagne Musulmane au Xe Siècle." Larose, Paris, 1932.
           ″   "Histoire de l'Espagne Musulmane," Maisonneuve, Paris, 1953.

Lewis, S., "A Topographical Dictionary of Ireland." London, 1837.

Leyden, F., "Die Städte der flämischen Landes." Engelhorn, Stuttgart, 1924.

Lin Yu-tang, "Pékin, Cité Impériale." Michel, Paris, 1961.

Lippincott's Pronouncing Gazetteer, Philadelphia, 1868, 1880, 1898.

List, R., "Brünn." Sankt Pöltner Zeitung-Verlag, Sankt Pölten, 1942.

Livi, L., "Prime Linee par una Storia Demografica di Rodi." Sansoni, Florence, 1944.

Livy, T., "History."

Lizárraga, R. de, in "Cusco." Lima, 1945.

Ljungstedt, A., "An Historical Sketch of the Portuguese Settlements in China." Boston, 1836.

Lockhart, L., "Famous Cities of Iran." Pearce, Brantford, 1939.
        ″   "Nadir Shah." Luzac, London, 1938.
        ″   "Persian Cities." Luzac, London, 1960.

Logan, W., "Malabar." Government Press, Madras, 1951.

Logio, G., "Bulgaria Past and Present." Sherratt and Hughes, Manchester, 1936.

Lonati, G., "Stato Totalitario della Fine del Secolo XIV." Toscolano, 1936, in "Ateneo de Brescia," 1935 supplement.

Long, A., in "Radiocarbon." 1965.

Long, E., "The History of Jamaica." London, 1774.

Longford, J., "The Story of Korea." Scribner, New York, 1911.

López, R., "Storia delle Colonie Genovesi." Zanichelli, Bologna, 1938.

López de Velasco, J., "Geografía y Descripción Universal de las Indias." Madrid, 1894.

López Mata, T., "La Ciudad y Castilla de Burgos." Burgos.

Loridan, J., "Valenciennes au XVIII Siécle." Reboux, Roubaix, 1913.

Lot, F., "Recherches sur la Population et la Superficie des Cités." Champion, Paris, 1945.

Louvet, J., in "Revue de l'Anjou." Angers, 1854-6.

Louville, C., "Mémoires." Paris, 1818.

Lowmianska, M., in "Bibljoteczka Wilenska." no. 3, Vilna, 1929.

Luchaire, A., "Les Communes Françaises." Paris, 1890.

Lugard, F., "A Tropical Dependency . . . Nigeria." Nisbet, London, 1905.

Lukaszewicz, J., "Historisch-statistisches Bild der Stadt Posen." Posen, 1878.

Luke, H., "Cyprus under the Turks." Oxford Univ. Press, London and New York, 1921.

"Lungchi Hsien Chih." Taiwan, 1967.

Lybyer, A., "The Government of the Ottoman Empire in the Time of Suleiman the Magnificent." Harvard Univ. Press, Cambridge, Mass., 1913.

Macartney, G., "A Complete View of the Chinese Empire." London, 1798.

MacBride, *in* "A Citade de Évora." March 1943.

M'Culloch, John, "A Dictionary . . . of Commerce." Philadelphia, 1852.

Madoz, P., "Diccionario Geográfico, Estadístico y Histórico de España y Sus Posesiones de Ultramar." Madrid, 1848-50.

Madrolle, C., "Chine du Sud, Java, Japon." Hachette, Paris, 1916.
        "   "Indochine du Sud." Hachette, Paris, 1926.
        "   "Northern China, Korea." Hachette, Paris, 1912.

Mahajan, V., "Ancient India." Chand, Delhi, 1968.
        "   "The Muslim Rule in India." Chand, Delhi, 1965.

Mahalingam, T. V., "Kancipuram in Early South Indian History." Asia Publ. House, New York, 1969.

Mailla, J. de, "Histoire Générale de la Chine." Paris, 177-85.

Major, R., "India in the Fifteenth Century." London, 1857.

Malcolm, J., "A Memoir of Central India." London, 1823.
        "   (a), *in* "Asiatic Journal." 1823.

Maleczynski, chapters in Dlugoborski *et al.* (1958).

Malkani, H., "A Socio-economic Survey of Baroda City." Planning Commission of India, and Maharaja Sayajirao Univ., Baroda, 1958.

Malleson, G., "Dupleix." Oxford, 1890.

Mandelslo, J. A. de, "Voyage and Travels." London, 1669.

Manrique, S., "Travels." Hakluyt Soc., Oxford, 1927.

Mantran, R., "Istanbul dans la Seconde Moitié du XVIII Siècle." Maisonneuve, Paris, 1962.

Maqqari, A., "The Breath of Perfume from the Branch of Green Andalusia." London, 1840.

Maquet, J., "Afrique: les Civilizations Noires." Horizons de France, Paris, 1962.

Margoliouth, D., "Cairo, Jerusalem, and Damascus." Chatto and Windus, London, 1907.

Mari, E., and Savonuzzi, G., "Sviluppo Urbanistico di Ferrara attraverso i Tempi." Florence, 1952.

Maricq, André, "Le Minaret de Djam." Klincksieck, Paris, 1959.

Marini, G. F. de, "Historia et Relatione del Tunchino e del Giappone." Rome, 1665.

Markgraf, Hermann, "Geschichte Breslaus." Breslau, 1888.

Markham, Clements, "The Conquest of New Granada." Smith, Elder, London, 1912.

Marmol, L. de, "Descripción General de Africa." Granada, 1573-9.

Marquant, R., "La Vie Économique à Lille sous Philippe le Bon." Champion, Paris, 1940.

Marshall, J., "John Marshall in India." Oxford Univ. Press, London and New York, 1927.

Martin, (R.), M., "Statistics of the Colonies of the British Empire." London, 1839.
        "   "The History, Antiquities, Topography, and Statistics of Eastern India." London, 1838.
        "   "The Indian Empire Illustrated." London, 1858-61.

Martineau, G. (ed.), "Nagel's Morocco: Travel Guide." Paris, 1953.

Martínez, A., chapter *in* "Censo General . . . de Buenos Aires." III, Buenos Aires, 1910.

Martínez y Vela, B., "Anales de la Villa Imperial de Potosí." Artística, La Paz, 1939.

Mascarenhas, J. de, "Historia de la Ciudad de Ceuta." Acad. das Sci., Lisbon, 1918.

Maspéro, G., "La Royaume de Champa." Paris, 1928.

Masson, A., *in* "Annales de la Faculté des Lettres d'Aix." 1955.

Matute, J., "Anales Eclesiásticos y Seculares de . . . Sevilla." Seville, 1887.

Matveeva, E. (ed.), "Riga." Liesma, Riga, 1967.

Mátyás, B. (ed.), "A Hatszézéves Debrecen." Komoróczy György, Debrecen, 1961.

Maucomble, J. F., "Histoire Abrégée de la Ville de Nimes." Amsterdam, 1767.

Mauny, R., "Tableau Géographique de l'Ouest Africain au Moyen Age." IFAN, Dakar, 1961.

Mauritius, census commissioner, "Census of Mauritius, 1871." Port Louis, 1871.

Maxwell, C., "Dublin under the Georges." Routledge, London, 1936.

Mayers, W., "The Treaty Ports of China and Japan." London, 1867.

Mazza, A., "Historiarum Epitome de Rebus Salernitanis." Naples, 1681.

Means, P. A., "Ancient Civilizations of the Andes." Scribner, New York and London, 1931.

Meek, C., "A Sudanese Kingdom." Paul, Trench, Trübner, London, 1931.

Mehta, K., "Ahmedabad." Ahmedabad, 1958.

Meilink-Roelofsz, M., "Asian Trade and European Influence in the Indonesian Archipelago between 1500 and about 1630." The Hague, 1692.

Méry, L., "Histoire Analitique et Chronologique des Actes et des Délibérations du Corps et du Conseil de Marseille depuis le Xe Siècle." Marseille, 1841-73.

Meskhia, S., "Goroda i Gorodskoi stroi Feodalni Grusii." Ied-vo Tiblisskogo, Tiflis, 1959.

Mesny chapter in Moule *et al.* (1854-89).

Messance, "Nouvelles Récherches sur la Population de la France." Lyon, 1788.

Methold, W., chapter in Moreland (1920).

Meyer, C., "Geschichte des Landes Posen." Posen, 1881.

Meyer, J., "Neues Konversations-Lexicon." Leipzig, 1839-53; 1874-8.

Michalowski, K., *in* Time, September 5, 1969.

Middlebrook, S., "Newcastle." S. R. Publ., 1968.

Mier, Adolfo, "Noticias y Proceso de . . . Oruro." Oruro, 1909.

Mikhov, N., "Bibliographie de la Turquie, de la Bulgarie et de la Macédoine." Sofia, 1908.

Miller, William E., quoted in "Chillicothe.' (1941) (WPA project).

Millon, René, *in* Science, December 1970.

Miñano, S., "Diccionario Geográfico-estadístico de España y Portugal." Madrid, 1826-9.

Miner, H., "The Primitive City of Timbuctoo." Doubleday, Garden City, New York, 1965.

Mitchell, S., "A General View of the World." Philadelphia, 1842.

Mitton, Geraldine, "The Lost Cities of Ceylon." Murray, London, 1916.

Molina, G., "Notizie Storiche Profane della Città d'Asti." Asti, 1774-6.

Moll, H., "Atlas Geographicus." 1711-4.

Mols, R., "Introduction á la Démographie Historique des Villes d'Europe du XIV au XVIIe Siècle." Duculot, Gembloux, 1954-6.

Monedzhikova, A., "Sofia pres Vekovete." Fakel, Sofia, 1946.

Monneret, U., "Aksum." Pontificum Institutum Biblicum, Rome, 1938.

Montalto de Jesus, C. A., "Historic Shanghai." Shanghai Mercury, Shanghai, 1909.

Montaner y Simon, see "Diccionario Enciclopedico Hispano Americano."

Moorcroft, W., "Travels in the Himalayan Provinces of Hindustan and Panjab; in Ladakh and Kashmir." Murray, London, 1841.

Moorehead, W., "The Cahokia Mounds." Univ. of Illinois Press, Urbana, Illinois, 1929.

Moreland, W., "Relations of Golconda in the Early Seventeenth Century." Hakluyt Soc., London, 1931.

       "   "India at the Death of Akbar." Macmillan, New York, 1920.

       "   and Chatterjee, "A Short History of India." Longmans, Green, London, 1953.

Morga, A. de, "The Philippine Islands." Hakluyt Soc., London, 1868.

Morier, J., "Morier's Second Journey through Persia." London, 1818.

Morley, S., "The Ancient Maya." Oxford Univ. Press, London and New York, 1946.

Morse, J., "The American Universal Geography." Boston, 1812.

Moscardo, L., "Historia di Verona," Verona, 1668.

Moule, G., et al.,"Miscellaneous Papers on Chinese Affairs." Hong Kong etc., 1854-89.

Muir, W., "The Caliphate." London, 1898.

Mulhall, M., "Dictionary of Statistics." London, 1892.

Munich, statistical dept. (München Stat. Amt), "München Landeshauptstadt Bayerns." 1958.

Münzer, H., "Viaje por España y Portugal, 1494-1495." Colección Almenara, Madrid, 1951.

Murphey, R., "Shanghai: Key to Modern China." Harvard Univ. Press, Cambridge, Mass., 1953.

Murray, J., co., "A Handbook for Travellers in Turkey." London, 1854.

Mutsu, Iso, "Kamakura." Times Publ., Tokyo, 1930.

Nadal Oller, J., "La Población Española, Siglos XVI a XX." Ediciones Ariel, Barcelona, 1966.

Nagoya city, "City Planning for the City of Nagoya." 1962.

Naidenov, N. (ed.), "Bulgaria, 1000 Godini 927-1927." Ministerstvoto na Narodnoto Prosvishchenne, Sofia, 1930.

"Nanchang." Taipei, 1970."Nanhai Tung Chih." China, 1910.

Naqui, H. K., "Urban Centers and Industries in Upper India 1556-1803." Asia Publ. House, Bombay and New York, 1968.

Narasimhacher, L., "A Guide to Halebid," Government Press, Mysore, 1950.

Nasir-i-Khusraw, "Sefer Nameh." Paris, 1881.

Nayudu, "Old Madras." Madras, 1965.

Nazarevsky, V., "Histoire de Moscou." Payot, Paris, 1932.

Nelson, J. H., "The Madura Country." Madras, 1868.

Neumann, K. F., "Ostasiatische Geschichte (1840-1860)." Leipzig, 1861.

"New American Cyclopaedia." New York, 1858-63.

"New International Encyclopaedia." Dodd, Mead, New York, 1930.

Nieuwenhuis, G. M., "De Stad aan Het Spaarn in Seven Eeuwen." Uitgeversmaatschappij Holland, Amsterdam, 1946.

Nieuwenhuis, G., "Nieuwenhuis' Woordenboek." Leiden, 1866.

Nigam, N., "Delhi in 1857." Chand, Delhi, 1957.

Nikitin, chapter in Oaten (1909).

Nilakanta S. K., "A History of South India." Oxford Univ. Press (Indian Branch), Madras, London and New York, 1958.

Nilakanta, S. K., (ed.), "Foreign Notices of South India from Megasthenes to Ma Huan." Univ. of Madras, Madras, 1939.
　　　"   "History of Sri Vijaya." Univ. of Madras, Madras, 1949.
　　　"   "The Pandyan Kingdom." Luzac, London, 1929.

"Ningpo Fu Chih." Taipei, 1957.

Noah, S., "Travels in England, France, Spain, and the Barbary." London, 1819.

Noiret, H. (ed.), "Documents Inédits pour Servir à l'Histoire Vénitienne en Créte de 1380 à 1485." Paris, 1892.

"Nordisk Familjebok." Stockholm, 1923.

"Norge." Cappelen, Oslo, 1963.

Norris, Robert, "Memoirs of the Reign of Bossa Ahádee, King of Dahomey." London, 1789.

North, S., and helpers, "A Century of Population Growth." Genealogical Publ. Co., Baltimore, Maryland, 1967.

Nouët, N., "Histoire de Tokyo." Presses Univ. de France, Paris, 1961.

Novo, S., "México." Ediciones Destino, Barcelona, 1968.

"Novy Encyclopedia Slovar." St. Petersburg, 1904-16.

Nowell, C. (ed.), "Magellan's Voyage around the World." Northwestern Univ., Evanston, 1962.

Nweeya, S. K., "Persia." Urmia, 1913 (private).

Oaten, E., "Travellers in India during the 15th, 16th, and 17th Centuries." Paul, Trench, Trübner, London, 1909.

O'Brien, G., "The Economic History of Ireland in the Eighteenth Century." Maunsell, Dublin and London, 1918.

Oderico, G. L., "Lettere . . . con le Memoria Storiche di Caffa." Rome (no date).

Oehlschlaeger, E., "Posen." Posen, 1866.

Ogée, J., "Dictionnaire Historique et Géographique de la Provence de Bretagne." Rennes, 1853.

Okey, T., "The Story of Avignon." Dutton, New York, 1911.

Olearius, A., "Voyages and Travels." London, 1669.

Olivas Escudero, F., "Apuntes para la Historia de Huamanga o Ayacucho." Impresa Diocesana, Ayacucho, 1924.

Oliver, R., and Mathew, G. (eds.), "History of East Africa." Oxford Univ. Press (Clarendon), London and New York, 1963.

Orlers, J., "Beschrijvinghe der Stadt Leyden." Leiden, 1641.

Ortiz Armengol, P., "Intramuros de Manila." Ediciones de Cultura Hispánica, Madrid, 1958.

Ortvay, Theodor, "Geschichte der Stadt Pressburg." Pressburg, 1892.

Osgood, C., "The Koreans and Their Culture." Ronald Press, New York, 1951.

O'Sullivan, W., "The Economic History of Cork City." Cork Univ., Cork, 1937.

Otter, J., "Voyage en Turquie et en Perse." Paris, 1748.

Oudenhoven, J. van, "Beschrijvinghe van Dordrecht." Haarlem, 1670.

"Oud Soerabaia," city publication, Surabaja, 1931.

"Pa Hsien Chih." Taiwan, 1967.

Páez, P., "Historia de Etiopia." Livraria Civilizacão, Oporto, 1945.

Páez, Brotchie, L., "Guadalajara, Jalisco, México." Guadalajara, 1951.

Pahud, C. (ed.), "Kolonial Verslag, 1849." no. 47, The Hague.

Paillard, C., "Histoire des Troubles Réligieux de Valenciennes." Paris, 1874-6.

Paillegoix, "Description de Royaume Thai ou Siam." Paris, 1854.

Palacios, E., "La Misteriosa Ciudad de Calakmul." Secretaria de Educacion Públ., Mexico City, 1937.

       "   *in* "Memorias y Revista de la Sociedad 'Antonio Alzate'." 1916.

Paranavitana, S., "Guide to Polonnaruwa." Colombo, 1950.

Park, M., in Pinkerton, XVI (1808-1814).

Parkhurst, C., *in* Ethiopian Observor, IX, no. 1.

Paul, P. L., "The History of Early Bengal." Indian Res. Inst., Calcutta, 1940.

Paullin, C., "Atlas of the Historical Geography of the United States." Carnegie Inst. and Amer. Geog. Soc., Washington and New York, 1932.

Paunović, M., "Beograd." Svetozar Marković, Belgrade, 1968.

Paz Soldán, M., "Diccionario Geográfico-estadístico del Perú." Lima, 1877.

       "   "Geografía del Perú." Lima, 1877.

Pazyra, S., "Studia z Dziejów Miast na Mazoszu." Inst. Popierania Polskiej Tworczosci, Lwow, 1939.

Pegolotti, F. B., chapter in Yule (1866).

Pek, Nam-shan, "Seoul Tae Kwan." Seoul, 1955.

Pelham, C., "The World." London, 1808.

Pelikanova, *in* "Praszky Sbornik Historićky." 1967.

Pellegrin, A., "Histoire de la Tunisie." Peyronnet, Paris, 1938.

Pelsaert, F., "Jahangir's India." Heffer, Cambridge, England, 1925.

Pennant, T., "The View of India extra Gangem, China, and Japan." London, 1800.

"Penny Cyclopaedia." London, 1833-43.

Pépin, E., "Histoire de Touraine." Boivin, Paris, 1935.

Pereira de Sousa, F., "O Terremoto de 1 de Nov. de 1755 em Portugal." Lisbon, 1919.

Perpiña Grau, Ramón, "Historia de la Economía Española." Bosch, Barcelona, 1943-7.

Pesch, Heinz, "Bürger und Bürgerrecht in Köln." Marburg, 1908.

"Petermann's Geographische Mittheilungen." 1865ff. Gotha, 1857.

Phipps, J., "A Practical Treatise on the China and Eastern Trade." London, 1836.

Pigeaud, Th., "Java in the 14th Century." Nijhoff, The Hague, 1963.

Pinkerton, J., "A General Collection . . . of Voyages and Travels." London, 1808-14.

Plancquaert, M., "Les Jagas et les Bayaka du Kwango." Inst. Roy. Colonial Belge, Brussels, 1932.

Planitz, H., "Die deutsche Stadt im Mittelalter." Böhlau, Graz, 1954.

Plath, J. H., "Die Völker der Mandschurey." Göttingen, 1831.

Platter, F., "Beloved Son, Felix." Muller, London, 1961.

Plato, "Critias."

Playfair, J., "A System of Geography." London, 1808-14.

Pliny, C., "Natural History." Heinemann, London, 1938-63.

Ploetz co., "Bevölkerung-Ploetz." Würzburg, 1955-6.

Poëte, M., "L'Enfance de Paris." Colin, Paris, 1908.

Polish Res. Center, "The Story of Wilno." London, 1942.

Polo, M., "The Book of Ser Marco Polo." Scribner, New York, 1903.

Poncet, C., in Pinkerton, XV (1808-14).

Ponsonby-Fane, R., "Kyoto." Ponsonby Memorial Soc., Kyoto, 1956.

Popelka, F., "Geschichte der Stadt Graz." Verlag Styria, Graz, 1959-60.

"Popol Vuh." Univ. of Oklahoma Press, Norman, 1950.

Popović, Dusan J., "Srbije i Beograd." Kultura, Belgrade, 1950.

Popovski, J., "Ohrid," Izdavac, Skopje, 1967.

Porter, J., "Five Years in Damascus." London, 1855.

Posac, M., C., "Estudios Arqueológico de Ceuta." Inst. Nacional de Enseñanza Media, Ceuta, 1962.

Pozo, M., "Historia de Huamanga." Tipografia de la República, Ayacucho, 1924.

Preisich, G., "Budapest Városépétésének Törtenete." Müszaki Könyvkiadó, Budapest, 1960.

Prentout, H., "La Prise de Caen en 1340." Delesques, Caen, 1904.

Prescott, W. H., "Conquest of Mexico," Philadelphia, Pennsylvania, 1868.

Pronshtein, A., "Veliki Novgorod e XVI Veke." Kharkov Univ., Kharkov, 1957.

Proskouriakoff, T., *in* "American Antiquity." 1960.

Puri, Baij Nath, "Cities of Ancient India." Meenakski Prakashan, Meerut, 1966.

Püschel, A., "Das Anwachsen der deutschen Städte in der Zeit der mittelalterlichen Kolonialbewegung." Curtius, Berlin, 1910.

Qalqashandi, Ahmed el-, "Marruecos a Comienzos del Sieglo XV." Editora Marroqui, Tetuán, 1952.

Raffles, S., "History of Java." Oxford Univ. Press, London and New York, 1965.

Rambert, G., "Histoire du Commerce de Marseille." Plon, Paris, 1949.

Ramírez de Arellano, T., "Paseos por Córdoba," Cordova, 1873-7.

Randles, W., "L'Ancien Royaume du Congo des Origines à la Fin du XIXe Siècle." Mouton, Paris, 1968.

Rangeard, *in* "L'Anjou Historique." 1905.

Rasmussen, O., "Tientsin." Tientsin Press, Tientsin, 1925.

Raven-Hart, R., "Ceylon: History in Stone." Associated Newspapers of Ceylon, Colombo, 1964.

Rebello da Costa, A., "Descripcaõ . . . do Porto." Oporto, 1789.

Reclus, É., "Nouvelle Géographie Universelle." Paris, 1876-94.

Reincke, H., "Forschungen und Skizzen zur hamburgischer Geschichte." Bremen, 1951.

Reischauer, E., and Fairbank, J., "East Asia: the Great Tradition." Houghton, Boston, 1965.

Reisner, Wilhelm, "Die Einwohnerzahl . . . Lübecks." Halle, 1902.

Reitemeyer, E., "Die Städtegründungen der Araber im Islam." Straub, Munich, 1912.

Renouard, Yves, "Les Villes d'Italie de la Fin du Xe Siècle au Début du XIVe Siècle." Centre de Documentation Univ., Paris, 1961-5.

Rentz, G., "The Mameluke Empire at the Close of the 14th Century." Univ. of California Press, Berkeley, 1937.

"Révai Nagy Lexikona." Révai, 1911-35.

Rice, T., "The Seljuks in Asia Minor." Thames and Hudson, London, 1961.

Richard, L., "Comprehensive Geography of the Chinese Empire." T'usewei Press, Shanghai, 1908.

Ricketson, O., "Uaxactun." Carnegie Inst., Washington, D.C., 1937.

Riera y Sans, P. "Diccionario Geográfico, Histórico, Biográfico, Postal, Municipal, Militar, Maritimo y Eclesiastico de España." Barcelona, 1881-7.

Roberts, F. E., "Forty-One Years in India." London, 1897.

Rocher, É., *in* "T'oung Pao." 1899.

Roland, B., "Speyer," Peters, Bad Honnef, 1961.

Rome, city of, "Annuario Statistico della Citta di Roma, 1951." Rome, 1954.

Romstorfer, K., "Cetatea Suceava." Inst. de Arte Grafica "Carol Göbl," Bucharest, 1913.

Rosenblatt, A., "La Población Indígena y el Mestizaje en América." Editorial Nova, Buenos Aires, 1954.

Rosny, L. de, "Études Asiatiques." Paris, 1864.

Rothert, H., "Das älteste Bürgerbuch der Stadt Soest." Aschendorff, Münster, 1958.

Roupnel, Gaston, "La Ville et la Campagne au XVIIIe Siècle." Leroux, Paris, 1922.

Rowe, J., *Acta Americana* (January 1948).

Roy, S., *in* "La Ville." Brussels, 1954.

Royal Commission on the Ancient and Historical Monuments, "An Inventory on the Ancient and Historical Monuments of the City of Edinburgh." Edinburgh, 1951.

Rudnićki, J., "Lwow, Karta z Dziejów Polski." Polish Res. Center, Glasgow, 1943.

Ruiz Fowler, J., "Monografia Histórica-geográfica del Departamento de Ayacucho." Torres Aguirre, Lima, 1924.

Runciman, S., "The History of the First Bulgarian Empire." Bell and Sons, London, 1930.

Rundall, T., "Narratives of Voyages towards the Northwest." London, 1849.

Russell, J., *in Trans. Amer. Philolog. Soc.* (1958).
    "   *in* "Annales du Midi." Toulouse, 1962.
    "   "British Medieval Population." Univ. of New Mexico Press, Albuquerque, 1948.
    "   *in Demography* **III** no. 2 (1966).
Rutter, E., "The Holy Cities of Arabia." Putnam, London, 1928.
Sadi, Abderrahman es-, "Tarikh es-Soudan." Paris, 1898-1900.
Saint-Léger, "Histoire de Lille." 1942.
Sakharov, A., "Goroda Severo-Vostchnoi Rusi XIV-XV Vekov." Gos. Uchebno-pedagog. Ied-vo, Moscow, 1959.
Salinas, G., "Testimonias de Zacatecas." Mexico City, 1946.
"Salmonsens Konversationslexikon." Schultz, Copenhagen, 1915-30.
Samper Ortega, D., "Bogotá, 1538.1938," Bogotá, 1938 (lithographed).
Sánchez-Albornoz, N., and Moreno, L., "La Población de América Latina." Paidós, Buenos Aires, 1968.
Sander, P., "Geschichte des deutschen Städtewesens." Schroeder, Bonn, 1922.
Sangermano, "A Description of the Burmese Empire." 5th ed., Gupta, London, 1966.
Sansom, G., "A History of Japan." Stanford, Palo Alto, 1958-63.
Sarda, H. B., "Ajmer." Scottish Mission Industries, Ajmer, 1911.
Sauvaget, J., "Alep." Geuthner, Paris, 1941.
Savary, C., "Lettres sur l'Égypte," Paris, 1801.
Saysse-Tobiczek, K., "Cracow." Polonia, Warsaw, 1961.
Scalabrini, G., "Memorie Istoriche delle Chiese di Ferrara." Ferrara, 1773.
Schiltberger, J., "Bondage and Travels." London, 1879.
Schliemann, H., "La Chine et le Japon." Paris, 1867.
Schmoller, G. von, "Deutsches Städtewesen in älterer Zeit." Bonner Staatswissenschaftliche Untersuchungen, Bonn and Leipzig, 1922.
Schneider, A., *in* "Akademie der Wissenschaften in Göttingen, philologisch-historisch Klasse." 1949.
    "   and Karnapp, W., "Die Stadtmauer von Iznik." Archáologisches Inst., Berlin, 1938.
Schneider, F., "Danish Grammar . . . to Which Are Added, a Short Historical Description of Copenhagen." Copenhagen, 1803.
Schneider, J., "La Ville de Metz aux XIII et XIVe Siècles." Nancy, 1950.
Schouten, J., and Caron, F., "A True Description of the Mighty Kingdoms of Japan and Siam." Argonaut, London, 1935.
Schraa, P., *in* "Amstelodanum." Amsterdam, 1954.
Schünemann, K., "Die Entstehung des Städtewesens in Südeuropa." Priebatsch, Breslau, 1929.
Schürer, O., "Prag." Callwey, Munich, 1940.
Schwarzwälder, H., "Reise in Bremens Vergangenheit." Schünemann, Bremen, 1966.
Scott, J. G., "Burma from the Earliest Times to the Present Day." Unwin, London, 1924.
Scott-Moncrieff, G., "Edinburgh." Batsford, London, 1965.
Se-jong, "Se-jong Sillokjiriji." Seoul, 1938.
Sekiyama, Naotoro, "Kinsei Nihon no Jinko Kozo." Tokyo, 1969.
Semmedo, A., "The History of China." London, 1655.
Septien, J., "Memoria Estadística del Estado de Querétaro." Querétaro, 1875.
Setton, K. "Catalan Domination of Athens 1311-1388." Medieval Academy of America, Cambridge, United States, 1948.

Sewell, R., "A Forgotten Empire (Vijayanagar)." Sonnenschein, London, 1900.

Shakespear, A., "Memoir on the Statistics of the North Western Provinces of the Bengal Presidency." Calcutta, 1848.

Shakespear, L., "History of Upper Assam, Upper Burmah, and North-Eastern Frontier." Macmillan, New York, 1914.

"Shantung Tung Chih." Shanghai, 1934.

Shaw, Thomas, in Pinkerton, XV (1808-14).

"Shen Chen Hui Lan, Fengtien." Japan, 1727.

"Shen Chin Tung Chih." China, 1852.

Sherwani, H., "The Bahmani Kingdom." National Information, Bombay, 1947.

"Shou Tu Chih." Taiwan, 1966.

"Sian." Taiwan, 1970.

Sibinović, M., "Vardar." Zavod za Vodostopanstvo na C P Macedonia, Skopje, 1968.

Silvestre, J., "L'Empire d'Annam et le Peuple Annamite." Paris, 1889.

Simioni, A., "Storia di Padova." Randi, Padua, 1968.

Simonet, F., "Descripción del Reino de Granada," Granada, 1872.

Simonsen, R., "Historia Económica do Brasil 1500-1820." Companhia Editora Nacional, São Paulo, 1937.

Simson, P., "Geschichte der Stadt Danzig." Scientia, Aalen, 1967.

Sirén, O., "The Walls and Gates of Peking." John Lane, London, 1924.

Skinner, G. W., "Chinese Society in Thailand." Cornell Univ. Press, Ithaca, New York, 1957.

Smeaton, W. O., "The Story of Edinburgh." Dent, London, 1905.

Smet, J. de, "Brugge in Het Begin van de XIIe Eeuw." A. van Poelvoorde, Bruges, 1941.

Smith, C., "The Ancient and Present State of the County of Cork." Cork, 1893-4.

Smith, D., "Medieval Sicily," Viking, New York, 1968.

Smith, G., in "Chinese Repository." 1846.

        "   "The Geography of British India." London, 1882.

Smith, V., "History of India." Vol. 2, Oxford Univ. Press, London and New York, 1906.

Soames, J., "The Coast of Barbary." Cape, London, 1938.

"Soochow Fu Chih." Taipei, 1970.

Sossaj, L., "Modena." Modena, 1841.

Southall, A., and Gutkind, P.. in "East African Studies." Nairobi, 1956.

Southey, R., "History of Brazil." London, 1817-22.

Spearman, H. (anon.), "The British Burma Gazetteer." Rangoon, 1879.

Spies, W., "Geschichte der Stadt Bremen in Nachmittelalter." Waisenhaus, Brunswick, 1966.

Spies, W. (a), "Braunschweig in Nachmittelalter." Waisenhaus, Brunswick, 1966.

Squier, E. G., "Pamphlets."

Srivastava, A., "History of India, 1000-1707." Agarwala, Agra, 1964.

Stagg, F. N., "West Norway and Its Fiords." Allen and Unwin, London, 1954.

"Statesman's Yearbook," 1864ff. London.

"Stat. Jahrbuch der Stadt Wien." See Vienna, city of (1909).

"Stat. Årsbok för Stockholms Stad 1960," Stockholm, 1961.

Steele, R. W., in "Essays on African Population" (K. M. Barbour and R. Prothero, eds.), Praeger, New York, 1961.

Stephens, E. (ed.), "Guide to the City of Moscow." Cooperative Publ. Soc., Moscow, 1937.

Stewart, C., "The History of Bengal." London, 1813.

Steyert, A., "Nouvelle Histoire de Lyon." Lyon, 1895-9.

Strabo, "Geography." Heinemann, London, 1917-32.

Stratton, M., "Bruges." Batsford, London, 1914.

Stutterheim, W., "De Kraton van Majapahit." Koninklijk Inst. voor de Tael-, Land-, en Volkenkunde van Nederlandsch-Indië, The Hague, 1948.

Subrahmanya Aiyar, "Historical Sketch of Ancient Dekhan." Madras, 1917.

Sukhareva, O., "K Istorii Gorodov Bukharskogo." Akad. Nauk Uzbekskoi SSR, Tashkent, 1958.

Sullivan, R. E., "Aix-la-Chapelle in the Age of Charlemagne." Univ. of Oklahoma Press, Norman, 1963.

Summers, R., *in J. Afr. Hist.* (1961).

Swinburne, H., "Travels through Spain in the Years 1775 and 1776." London, 1787.

Sykes, P., "A History of Persia." Macmillan, New York, 1915.

Syme, M., chapter in Pelham (1808).

"Szechwan Tung Chih." China, 1815.

Szücz, István, "Szabad Királyi Debrecen város Történelme." Debrecen, 1870-1.

Tafrali, O., "Thessalonique au Quatrième Siècle." Geuthner, Paris, 1913.

Tahmankar, D. V., "The Rani of Jhansi." MacGibbon and Kee, London, 1958.

"Taiyüan Hsien Chih." China, 1826.

Takekoshi, Y., "The Economic Aspects of the History of the Civilization of Japan." London, 1930.

Tarakanova, S., "Dvernii Pskov." Akad. Nauk SSSR, Moscow, 1946.

Tasis i Marca, R., "Barcelona: Imatge i Historia d'une Ciutat." Dalmau, Barcelona, 1961.

Tauxier, L., "Le Noir du Soudan." Larose, Paris, 1912.

Tavernier, J., "The Six Voyages." London, 1678.

Tennent, E., "Ceylon." London, 1860.

Termizi, S., "Ajmer through Inscriptions: 532-1852 A.D.." Delhi, 1968.

Terry, E., "A Voyage to East-India." London, 1777.

Terry, T. P., "Terry's Guide to the Japanese Empire." Houghton, Boston, 1930.

Thévenot, J. de, "The Travels of Monsieur de Thévenot into the Levant." London, 1687.

Thomas, G., "Military Memoirs." Calcutta, 1805.

Thompson, M. W., "Novgorod the Great." Evelyn, Adams, and Mackay, London, 1962.

Thompson, V., "French Indo-China." Allen and Unwin, London, 1937.

Thorn, W., "Memoir of the Conquest of Java." London, 1815.

Thornton, E., "A Gazetteer of India." London, 1854.

Thubron, C., "Mirror to Damascus." Heinemann, London, 1967.

"Tientsin Fu Chih," Taipei, 1968.

Tikhomirov, M., "The Towns of Ancient Rus." Foreign Languages Publ. House, Moscow, 1959.

″ "Pskovskoe Vosstanie 1650 Goda." Akad. Nauk SSSR, Leningrad, 1935.

Tilley, A. (ed.), "Medieval France." Cambridge Univ. Press, London and New York, 1922.

Timkovsky, G., "Travels of the Russian Mission through Mongolia to China." London, 1827.

Tivčev, P., *in* "Byzantinobulgarica." 1962.

Tollenare, L., "Notas Dominicais Tomadas durante uma Viagem en Portugal e no Brasil." Livreria Progresso, Salvador, 1956.

Tolstova, S. P. *et al.*, "Istoriya Uzbekskoy SSR." Akad. Nauk Uzbekskogo SSR, Tashkent, 1955.

Tombourel, "Annuaire Administrative et Commerciale de l'Algérie." 1859.

Tomek, W., "Geschichte der Stadt Prag." Prague, 1856.

Torres Balbas, L., chapter in "Resumen Histórico del Urbanismo en España." Inst. dè Estudios de Administración Local, Madrid, 1954.
               "   *in* "Studia Islamica." 1955.

Tournefort, J. de, "A Voyage to the Levant." London, 1718.

Toussaint, M., "Pátzcuaro." Imprenta Univ., Mexico City, 1942.

Townsend, J., "A Journey through Spain." London, 1792.

Toynbee, A. (ed.), "Cities of Destiny." Thames and Hudson, London, 1967.

Trasselli, C., "I Privilegi di Messina e di Trapani," Segesta, Palermo, 1949.

Treccani, G., (ed.), "Storia di Brescia," Morcelliana, Brescia, 1961.

Trevellion, B., "Metropolitan Kano." Oxford Univ. Press (Clarendon), London and New York, 1963.

Tripathi, R. S., "History of Kanauj." Banarsidass, Delhi, 1969.

Tronko, P. *et al.*, "Kiev." Akad. Nauk URSR, Kiev, 1968.

Trusler, J., "The Habitable World." London, 1788-93.

"Tung-chih Shanghai Hsien Chih." China, 1863.

Turpin, "Histoire Civile et Naturelle du Royaume de Siam." Paris, 1771.

"24 Histories." Taiwan, 1968.

"25 Histories." Peking, 1934.

Ulloa, see with Juan (1758).

Ungewitter, F., "Neueste Erdbeschreibung und Staatenkunde." Dresden, 1858-9.

U.K. census, London, 1851.

U.S. census, 1800, 1810, 1850; see U.S. government.

U.S. Government, "Aggregate Amount of Persons within the United States in the Year 1810." Washington, D.C., 1811.
            "   "Second Census of the United States, 1800." Washington, D.C., 1801.
            "   "The Seventh Census of the United States: 1850." Washington, D.C., 1853.

"Universal Jewish Encyclopedia." New York, 1939-43.

Urvoy, Y., "Histoire de l'Empire du Bornou." Larose, Paris, 1949.

Usher, A. P., "The Early History of Deposit Banking in Mediterranean Europe." Harvard Univ. Press, Cambridge, Mass., 1943.

Uylenbroek, P., "Iracae Persicae Descriptio." Leiden, 1822.

Uztariz, G. de, "The Theory and Practice of Commerce and Maritime Affairs." London, 1751.

Vacalopoulos, A., "A History of Thessaloniki." Thessaloniki Press, Thessalonica, 1963.

Vaenefa, D. I., co., "Odessa." Odessa, 1900.

Vaidya, C. V., "History of Medieval Hindu India." Oriental Book-supplying Agency, Poona, 1921-6.

Valentia, G., "Voyages and Travels." London, 1809.

Vámbéry, A., "History of Bokhara." London, 1873.

Van de Woude, A., and Mentink, G., *in* "Population." Paris, 1966.

Vanselow, O. F., "Zur Geschichte der pommerschen Städte unter der Regierung Friedrich Wilhelm I." Herrcke and Lebeling, Stettin, 1903.

Varrallanos, J., "Historia de Huánuco." López, Buenos Aires, 1959.

Vargas, F., "Proceso Histórico de la Metropoli Guanajuatense." Imprenta Aldina, Mexico City, 1941.

Vargas, J. de, "Descripciones de las Islas Pithiusas a Baleares." Madrid, 1787.

Varthema, L. di, "Travels." London, 1863.

Vasiliev, I., "Istoryko-statisticheskii Ukazetel Goroda Pskova." Pskov, 1889.

Vasselle, F., by correspondence.

Vázquez de Espinoza, A., "Compendio de las Indias Occidentales." Smithsonian Inst., Washington, D.C., 1948.

Velasco, J. de, "Historia del Reino de Quito." El Comercio, Quito, 1946.

Vázquez Santa Ana, H., "Apuntes Geográfico e Histórico del Estado de Tlaxcala." State Government Press, Tlaxcala, 1927.

Venkataramanyya, N., "The Early Muslim Expansion in Southern India." Univ. of Madras Press, Madras, 1942.

Venkatarayappa, K., "Bangalore." Univ. of Bombay, Bombay, 1957.

Venedikov, in "Byzantinobulgarica." Sofia, 1962.

Verbruggen, J., "Het Gemeentelegen van Brugge van 1338 tot 1340." Palais des Acad., Brussels, 1962.

Vercauteren, F., "Études sur les Civitates de la Belgique Seconde." Acad. Roy. de Belgique, Brussels, 1934.

Verniers, L., "Un Millénnaire d'Histoire de Bruxelles." Brussels, 1965.

Vicens Vives, J., "An Economic History of Spain." Princeton Univ. Press, Princeton, New Jersey, 1969.

Vienna, city of, "Statistisches Jahrbuch der Stadt Wien, 1909." Vienna, 1911.

Vilar, P., "La Catalogne dans l'Espagne Moderne." S.E.V.P.E.N., Paris, 1962.

Villacorte Calderón, J. A., "Prehistoria e Historia Antiqua de Guatemala." Guatemala City, 1938.

Vivien de St. -Martin, L., "Nouveau Dictionnaire de Géographie Universelle." Paris, 1879-95.

Vivier, R., and Millet, E., "Promenades dans Tours." Arrault, Tours, 1943.

Voelcker, H., "Die Stadt Goethes." Blazek and Bergmann, Frankfurt, 1932.

Vojtišek, V. et al., "Praha." Sportovni a Turistické Nakladatelatví, Prague, 1960.

Volney, C., "Travels through Syria and Egypt." London, 1787.

Voyce, A., "Moscow and the Roots of Russian Culture." Univ. of Oklahoma Press, Norman, 1964.

Vuckovič, Ivan, "Niš." Turistička Stampa, Belgrade, 1966.

Waern, C., "Medieval Sicily." Duckworth, London, 1910.

Wald, R., "The Development of Osaka during the Sixteenth Century." Univ. of California Press, Berkeley, 1943.

Waldendorff, H. von, "Regensburg." Regensburg, 1896.

Walsh, J. H. T., "A History of Murshidabad Distric.," London, 1902.

Warner, R., "History and Antiquities of Bath." Bath, 1801.

Watkeys, F., "Old Edinburgh." Page, Boston, 1908.

Waugh, A., "Bangkok." Allen, London, 1970.

"Webster's Geographical Dictionary." Merriam, Springfield, 1949.

Wegener, Georg, "Im innersten China." Scherl, Berlin, 1920.

Weiss, K., "Geschichte der Stadt Wien." Vienna, 1882-3.

       "   "Geschichte der Stadt Nürnberg." Koch, Nuremberg, 1928.

Welford, R. et al., "History of Newcastle and Gateshead." London, 1884-7.

Wells, M., "Guide to Chiang Mai." Kramol Tiranasar, Bangkok, 1962.

Werveke, H. van, "Bruges and Anvers." Librarie Encyclopédique, Brussels, 1944.

       "   "Gand." La Renaissance du Livre, Brussels, 1946.

West, M., in American Antiquity (January 1970).

Wheatley, P., "The Golden Khersonese." Univ. of Malaya, Kuala Lumpur, 1961.

Whitaker, A., "The Huancavelica Mercury Mine." Harvard Univ. Press, Cambridge, Mass., 1941.

Wiens, H., *in Ann. Ass. Amer. Geographers* (December 1963).

Wijffels, M., *in* "Belgisch Tijdschrift voor Philologie en Geschiedenis." 1958.

Wilhelmy, H., "Südamerika im Spiegel seiner Städte." De Gruyter, Hamburg, 1952.

Wilks, M., "History of Mysore." London, 1810-7.

Willett, *H. Historical Soc. Nigeria* (December 1960).

Willey, G., *in* "Collier's Encyclopedia."

Williams, S. W., "The Middle Kingdom." Allen New York, 1914.

Wilson, H., "Geography," London, 1738.

Windhus, J., in Pinkerton, XV (1808-1814).

Wolff, P., "Commerce et Marchands de Toulouse." Plon, Paris, 1954.

Wolter, F., "Geschichte der Stadt Magdeburg." Faber, Magdeburg, 1901.

Wood, W. A. R., "A History of Siam." Siam Barnakich, Bangkok, 1933.

Woodcock, G., "Kerala." London, 1967.

Wright, J. (ed.), "Annual Register." London, 1763.

Wright, T. (ed.), "Early Travels in Palestine." London, 1848.

Wüstenfeld, F., "Die Chroniken der Stadt Mekka." Leipzig, 1857-61.

Ximenes Paton, B., "Historia de la Antiqua, y Continuada, Nobleza de la Ciudad de Jaén." Jaén, 1628.

Yaqut, "Diccionario Géographique, Historique et Litéraire de la Perse." Paris, 1861.

Yazaki, T., "Social Change and the City in Japan," Japan Publ. Trading Co. Tokyo, 1968.

Yazdani, G., "Bidar, Its History and Monuments." Oxford Univ. Press, London and New York, 1947.

Yule, H., "Cathay and the Way Thither." London, 1866.

     "   "Marco Polo." Re-edited by Cordier (1903).

"Yünnanfu Chih." Taipei, 1967.

Zachariah, K. C., "Migrants in Greater Bombay." Asia Publ. House, Bombay, 1968.

Zeller, G., "La Réunion de Metz à la France (1552-1648)." Oxford Univ. Press, London and New York, 1926.

Zeuss, "Die freie Reichstadt Speyer," Spires, 1843.

Ziadeh, N., "Damascus under the Mamelukes." Univ. of Oklahoma Press, Norman, 1964.

     "   "Urban Life in Syria." American Press, Beirut, 1953.

Zocca, M., "Sommario di Storia Urbanistica delle Citta Italiana dalle Origini al 1861." Liguori, Naples, 1961.

Zsolnay, V. von, "Vereinigungsversuche Südosteuropas im XV Jahrhundert." Selke, Frankfurt, 1967.

Index